TEACHER'S EDITION

Auténtico

A

Go Online to practice

PearsonSchool.com/Autentico

AUDIO VIDEO WRITING SPEAK/RECORD MAPA GLOBAL AUTÉNTICO FLASHCARDS ETEXT 2.0 GAMES

Peggy Palo Boyles
OKLAHOMA CITY, OK

Myriam Met
EDGEWATER, MD

Richard S. Sayers
LONGMONT, CO

Pearson

Boston, Massachusetts   Chandler, Arizona
Glenview, Illinois   New York, New York

Front cover: Margarita Island, Venezuela

Pearson, 330 Hudson Street, New York, NY 10013.

ISBN-13:   978-0-328-93445-4
ISBN-10:   0-328-93445-3

TEACHER'S EDITION

A

Auténtico

Go **Online** to practice

PearsonSchool.com/Autentico

PEARSON
realize™

AUDIO   VIDEO   WRITING   SPEAK/RECORD   MAPA GLOBAL   AUTÉNTICO   FLASHCARDS   ETEXT 2.0   GAMES

Professional Development Handbook

Table of Contents

» Go online at www.PearsonSchool.com/Autentico.
Each *tema* is supported wtih video, audio, activities,
games, and more.

PEARSON
realize™

ACTFL World Readiness Standards

ACTFL's World-Readiness Standards (the 5 C's) encompasses five goal areas for language learning and instruction: Communication, Cultures, Connections, Comparisons, and Communities. Within Communication, ACTFL identifies three modes of communication: Interpersonal, Interpretive, and Presentational. The emphasis of these revised Standards is for learners to use the target language to explore the products, practices, and perspectives of the target culture, make connections with other disciplines, compare the language and culture of Spanish-speaking countries with their own, and explore opportunities to use their Spanish language skills in their own community. *Auténtico* provides users with culturally authentic resources for students to view, listen to, or read to better meet these standards. As students gain skills and confidence in the target language, they are encouraged to apply their learning beyond the classroom and become active participants in the global community.

GOAL AREAS	STANDARDS		
COMMUNICATION Communicate effectively in more than one language in order to function in a variety of situations and for multiple purposes	**Interpersonal Communication** Learners interact and negotiate meaning in spoken, signed, or written conversations to share information, reactions, feelings, and opinions.	**Interpretive Communication** Learners understand, interpret, and analyze what is heard, read, or viewed on a variety of topics.	**Presentational Communication:** Learners present information, concepts, and ideas to inform, explain, persuade, and narrate on a variety of topics using appropriate media and adapting to various audiences of listeners, readers, or viewers.
CULTURES Interact with cultural competence and understanding	**Relating Cultural Practices to Perspectives** Learners use the language to investigate, explain, and reflect on the relationship between the practices and perspectives of the cultures studied		**Relating Cultural Products to Perspectives** Learners use the language to investigate, explain, and reflect on the relationship between the products and perspectives of the cultures studied
CONNECTIONS Connect with other disciplines and acquire information and diverse perspectives in order to use the language to function in academic and career-related situations	**Making Connections** Learners build, reinforce, and expand their knowledge of other disciplines while using the language to develop critical thinking and to solve problems creatively		**Acquiring Information and Diverse Perspectives** Learners access and evaluate information and diverse perspectives that are available through the language and its cultures
COMPARISONS Develop insight into the nature of language and culture in order to interact with cultural competence	**Language Comparisons** Learners use the language to investigate, explain, and reflect on the nature of language through comparisons of the language studied and their own.		**Cultural Comparisons** Learners use the language to investigate, explain, and reflect on the concept of culture through comparisons of the cultures studied and their own.
COMMUNITIES Communicate and interact with cultural competence in order to participate in multilingual communities at home and around the world	**School and Global Communities** Learners use the language both within and beyond the classroom to interact and collaborate in their community and the globalized world		**Lifelong Learning** Learners set goals and reflect on their progress in using languages for enjoyment, enrichment, and advancement.

Proficiency

Attention to communication and proficiency is consistently emphasized in guidelines and standards developed by the American Council on the Teaching of Foreign Languages (ACTFL), such as the ACTFL World-Readiness Standards, the ACTFL Proficiency Guidelines 2012, and the ACTFL Performance Descriptors for Language Learners. Expectations regarding the functional use of language and the level of proficiency students are expected to achieve are clearly stated within the NCSSFL-ACTFL Global Can-Do Benchmarks.

The Can-Do Benchmarks reflect a change in measuring proficiency, a way to guide curriculum development, and a shift in classroom emphasis onto the learner. The Can-Do Statements provide assessment guidelines for both the instructor and the learner. Written in a checklist style, these statements express what the learner "can do," and they place a shared responsibility for learning and assessment onto both instructor and student. Using these benchmarks with your students helps them to become more independent learners and gives them the skills for life-long learning.

What are the Can-Do Statements?

The Can-Do Statements incorporate a context and purpose for second language learning in a checklist format. The result of a collaboration between the NCSSFL[1], developers of LinguaFolio®, a learner-directed portfolio assessment instrument, and ACTFL, the Can-Do Statements provide specific language tasks within proficiency guidelines broken down into five levels of language ability, from the beginning of language instruction through advanced language study and use. The three base levels of Novice, Intermediate and Advanced are further broken down into Low, Mid, and High levels.

To use *Auténtico* with the Can-Do Statements, refer to the following level alignment. The level of your class or curriculum may vary from these suggestions:

Auténtico, Level 1, A/B: Novice Low/Mid to Novice High

Auténtico, Level 2: Novice High/Intermediate Low to Intermediate Mid

Auténtico, Level 3: Intermediate Low/Intermediate Mid to Intermediate High

Auténtico and the Can-Do Statements

The three Modes of Communication—Interpersonal, Interpretive, and Presentational—are at the core of the Can-Do Statements and also form the foundation of learning and practice within *Auténtico*. The Can-Do statements provide the framework and contexts for language use in a learner's everyday life. The same contexts can be found throughout the themes of *Auténtico*.

How to use *Auténtico* with the Can-Do Statements

As an instructor, you may wish to use the NCSSFL-ACTFL Can-Do Statements to set goals for your students and to guide their assessment. Ask students to be responsible for their own personal lists of Can-Do's, which they can monitor and refer to throughout the year.

Auténtico provides you and your students a series of tools and resources to help you create additional individual goals that fit into your curriculum benchmarks or students' learning plans. These tools include chapter and section objectives, end-of chapter personal self-assessments, and rubrics.

Use the Chapter Objectives to set personal goals. These objectives are highlighted on the first page of each chapter, and are easily aligned to the three Modes of Communication:

> *Interpretive:* Listen and read ...
>
> *Presentational:* Talk and write about ...
>
> *Interpersonal:* Exchange information ...

Objectives also appear at the beginning of each section in the chapter. These objectives are the steps and contexts that support the overarching chapter goals.

On the first page of each chapter, the section "You will demonstrate what you know and can do" directs students to the end of the chapter, *Preparación para el examen,* where self-assessment tasks relate back to the Chapter Objectives. These tasks are written and labeled so that students can directly assess what they "can do" as they progress through the chapter, and where they need to go in the chapter if they need more practice.

The following pages show the Global Can-Do Benchmarks for each proficiency mode and the main Can-Do indicators that correspond to Auténtico, Levels 1, A/B. The benchmarks are aligned with pages in *Auténtico* that support these proficiencies and indicators. This is not meant to be a complete correlation, but rather a guide for you as you plan your lessons.

[1]National Council of State Supervisors for Languages

NCSSFL-ACTFL Global Can-Do Benchmarks

Performance Indicators for Language Learners

AUTÉNTICO supports the Global Can-Do Benchmarks across all levels. Use this chart to track where the global benchmarks and progress indicators are addressed throughout the Student and Teacher Edition for this level of the program. This is not meant to be a complete correlation, but rather a guide for you as you plan your lessons.

Interpersonal Communication

Novice Mid	
I can communicate on very familiar topics using a variety of words and phrases that I have practiced and memorized.	
I can greet and leave people in a polite way.	**SE/TE:** pp. 2–5, 97
I can introduce myself and others.	**SE/TE:** pp. 2–5, 13, 97
I can answer a variety of simple questions.	**SE/TE:** pp. 31, 37, 178, 184, 186, 229, 382
I can make some simple statements in a conversation.	**SE/TE:** pp. 178, 181, 186, 204, 382
I can ask some simple questions.	**SE/TE:** pp. 178, 184, 186, 191, 229, 280, 413
I can communicate basic information about myself and people I know.	**SE/TE:** pp. 3, 56, 57, 229
I can communicate basic information about my everyday life.	**SE/TE:** pp. 16, 19, 134, 176, 204, 334

Novice High	
I can communicate and exchange information about familiar topics using phrases and simple sentences, sometimes supported by memorized language. I can usually handle short social interactions in everyday situations by asking and answering simple questions.	
I can exchange some personal information.	**SE/TE:** pp. 87, 227, 229, 258
I can exchange information using texts, graphs, or pictures.	**SE/TE:** pp. 21, 105, 204, 233, 304
I can ask for and give simple directions.	**SE/TE:** pp. 105, 111, 302, 304, 351
I can make plans with others.	**SE/TE:** pp. 203, 204, 215, 351
I can interact with others in everyday situations.	**SE/TE:** pp. 254, 339, 352

Presentational Speaking

Novice Mid

I can present information about myself and some other very familiar topics using a variety of words, phrases, and memorized expressions.	
I can present information about myself and others using words and phrases.	**SE/TE:** pp. 57, 63, 71, 269
I can express my likes and dislikes using words, phrases, and memorized expressions.	**SE/TE:** pp. 43, 47, 161, 202
I can present information about familiar items in my immediate environment.	**SE/TE:** pp. 80, 106, 283, 291
I can talk about my daily activities using words, phrases, and memorized expressions.	**SE/TE:** pp. 80, 88, 205, 195, 413
I can present simple information about something I learned using words, phrases, and memorized expressions.	**SE/TE:** pp. 208, 290, 291, 362, 407

Novice High

I can present basic information on familiar topics using language I have practiced using phrases and simple sentences.	
I can present information about my life using phrases and simple sentences.	**SE/TE:** pp. 88, 227, 195
I can tell about a familiar experience or event using phrases and simple sentences.	**SE/TE:** pp. 93, 178, 195
I can present basic information about a familiar person, place, or thing using phrases and simple sentences.	**SE/TE:** pp. 231, 382, 443, 471
I can present information about others using phrases and simple sentences.	**SE/TE:** pp. 51, 206, 237, 241
I can give basic instructions on how to make or do something using phrases and simple sentences.	**SE/TE:** pp. 140, 161, 306
I can present basic information about things I have learned using phrases and simple sentences.	**SE/TE:** pp. 109, 314, 363, 393, 406

Presentational Writing

Novice Mid

I can write lists and memorized phrases on familiar topics.	
I can fill out a simple form with some basic personal information.	**SE/TE:** pp. 3, 7 8, 13, 15, 71, 78, 97, 343, 471
I can write about myself using learned phrases and memorized expressions.	**SE/TE:** pp. 67, 71, 78, 229
I can list my daily activities and write lists that help me in my day-to-day life.	**SE/TE:** pp. 67, 87, 181, 169, 195

Presentational Writing, *continued*

I can write notes about something I have learned using lists, phrases, and memorized expressions.	**SE/TE:** pp. 15, 55, 128, 203
Novice High	
I can write short messages and notes on familiar topics related to everyday life.	
I can write information about my daily life, in a letter, blog, discussion board, or an email message.	**SE/TE:** pp. 47, 67, 117, 245
I can write short notes using phrases and simple sentences.	**SE/TE:** pp. 59, 133, 215
I can write about a familiar experience or event using practiced material.	**SE/TE:** pp. 97, 219, 265, 423
I can write basic information about things I have learned.	**SE/TE:** pp. xxxi-b, 122-b, 202, 423, 419
I can ask for information in writing.	**TE:** pp. 214, 404, 413

Interpretive Listening

Novice Mid	
I can recognize some familiar words and phrases when I hear them spoken.	
I can understand a few courtesy phrases.	**SE/TE:** pp. 3, 5, 23
I can recognize and sometimes understand basic information in words and phrases that I have memorized.	**SE/TE:** pp. 8, 19, 23
I can recognize and sometimes understand words and phrases that I have learned for specific purposes.	**SE/TE:** pp. 9, 128, 158
Novice High	
I can often understand words, phrases, and simple sentences related to everyday life. I can recognize pieces of information and sometimes understand the main topic of what is being said.	
I can sometimes understand simple questions or statements on familiar topics.	**SE/TE:** pp. 51, 62, 71, 184, 206, 223, 245, 252
I can understand simple information when presented with pictures and graphs.	**SE/TE:** pp. 18, 19, 235, 252
I can sometimes understand the main topics of conversations that I overhear.	**SE/TE:** pp. 84, 206, 219, 269, 325, 326, 343, 468–469

Interpretive Reading

Novice Mid	
I can recognize some letters or characters. I can understand some learned or memorized words and phrases when I read.	
I can recognize words, phrases, and characters with the help of visuals.	**SE/TE:** pp. 155, 162–163, 223, 230, 307, 385
I can recognize words, phrases, and characters when I associate them with things I already know.	**SE/TE:** pp. 35, 97, 166–167, 202, 255

Novice High	
I can understand familiar words, phrases, and sentences within short and simple texts related to everyday life. I can sometimes understand the main idea of what I have read.	
I can usually understand short simple messages on familiar topics.	**SE/TE:** pp. 91, 166–167, 185, 186, 255
I can sometimes understand short, simple descriptions with the help of pictures or graphs.	**SE/TE:** pp. 91, 162–163, 310, 311, 338
I can sometimes understand the main idea of published materials.	**SE/TE:** pp. 187, 211, 235, 381
I can understand simple everyday notices in public places on topics that are familiar to me.	**SE/TE:** pp. 91, 188–189, 383, 404

Authentic Materials

Using Authentic Materials in the Spanish Classroom
Focusing on the Interpretive Mode of Communication

The ACTFL World-Readiness Standards

1.2 Interpretive **Communication**

Learners understand, interpret, and analyze what is heard, read, or viewed on a variety of topics.

When language learners first interact with native speakers they may feel intimidated by the speed of the language or the amount of unfamiliar vocabulary. Frequent and regular exposure to authentic materials in the classroom, however, can build students' skills and give them the confidence to take their language learning beyond the classroom. Each chapter of *Auténtico* features opportunities for students to view, read, and listen to authentic materials that were created by native speakers of Spanish for native speakers of Spanish. As students become accustomed to interpreting these materials, they develop the skills necessary to use their Spanish in the real world.

Choose the right material

It can be difficult to choose level-appropriate authentic content for students in the earliest stages of language learning. While students at the beginning levels will not understand everything, encountering some familiar vocabulary will help them access the content and increase their confidence in their ability to understand native speakers. Choosing video, audio, and texts that are thematically related to what students are already learning will offer a sense of familiarity and provide students with a connection to the material.

Prepare students

Preparing students before watching an authentic video, listening to audio, or reading authentic content is essential to success.

- **Activate background knowledge** Ask questions to uncover what students already know about the topic in the authentic material. This will help students connect their prior knowledge to the new content.

- **Provide context** Before watching the video, give students an overview of the type of content that they will be viewing. Talk about cultural elements that would be commonly understood by a native speaker viewing the material but that may be unfamiliar to language learners.

- **Introduce key vocabulary** Pre-teach vocabulary that is key to understanding the content.

Tailor the viewing or listening task

One of the most important aspects of using authentic material with language learners is to make sure that the task is level appropriate so students can succeed. Tasks will vary according to the type of authentic resource. Tasks that are appropriate for early learners include:

ALL GENRES

- **Write down cognates** Ask students to write down any cognates that they encounter.

- **Focus on main ideas and key details** Provide students with graphic organizers to help them identify main ideas. Do a Concept Map or Webbing activity with the class to identify the main concepts and related details. Or have students do a Scavenger Hunt, in which students watch or listen for key ideas or cultural details.

- **Predict** Ask students to predict what they might see, hear, or read based on the type of reading or the general topic.

- **Discuss cultural context** Have students focus on cultural elements or the cultural context of the resource. Discuss with them cultural details that were unexpected or impressed them in some way.

- **Create individual vocabulary lists** Ask each student to make a list of five words they heard or saw that they didn't know and want to learn, have students compare lists. Teach students how to look up words they may not know how to spell.

VIDEO

- **Assign group work** As students become more comfortable with authentic materials, let them work as a group to dissect a video, discuss with their partners, then present what they learned to the class.

- **Turn off the sound** Show the video first without audio and have students focus on the visuals, ask them to write words they think they might hear, then put a checkmark next to any they hear when you play the video with sound.

AUDIO

- **Give students control** have students listen to the audio alone on a computer where they can pause and rewind as many times as they like.

READING

- **Focus on common features of the reading genre** Ask students to guess the meaning of new vocabulary by considering what type of information is expected. When reading a web page, for example, students can reasonably guess that the *Buscar* button next to the search box means "search" because they are familiar with navigating web pages.

After viewing or listening

Take the time after working with authentic materials, either as a class or as homework, to reflect on the content.

- **Consider cultural perspectives** Ask students to consider the relationship between the products and practices in the authentic material and the perspectives of the culture of the intended audience.

- **Personalize understanding** Give students the opportunity to think critically about the content and to personalize their understanding.

- **Provide a self-assessment rubric** Create a simple rubric for students to assess their understanding of a resource.

Assign varying points for criteria such as: Can I identify the main idea? Can I understand supporting details? Can I infer meaning of new words from the context? Can I identify cultural products or practices, and the related cultural perspectives?

Revisit the content

Throughout the course of the school year, have students watch previously viewed videos or listen to an audio selection from an earlier chapter. Assign students a new task for their second encounter with the same content. Ask students to discuss or write about how their understanding of the content changed over time.

Authentic Resources in AUTÉNTICO

Auténtico **feature in the Student Edition** *Auténtico pages* in the Student Edition feature strategies that build students' language skills and increase their confidence by watching, listening to, and reading carefully-curated authentic resources. ▼

Authentic Resources Folder on **Realize** In the the digital course on Realize, you'll find a carefully curated library of authentic resources that match the themes and content in *Auténtico.* ▼

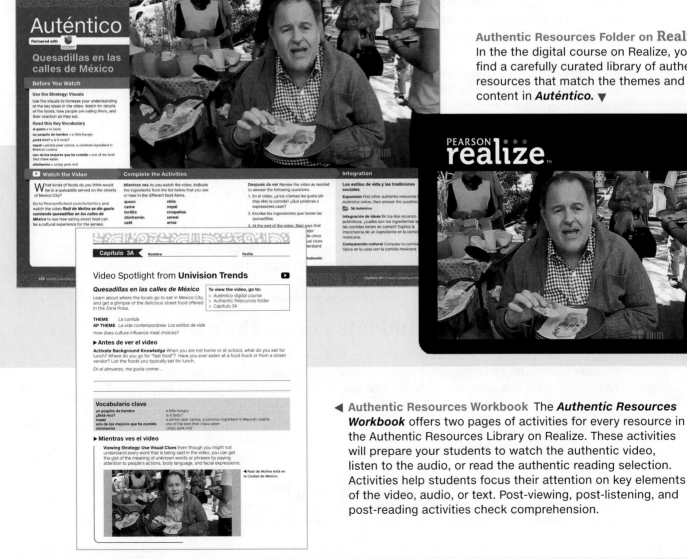

◀ **Authentic Resources Workbook** The *Authentic Resources Workbook* offers two pages of activities for every resource in the Authentic Resources Library on Realize. These activities will prepare your students to watch the authentic video, listen to the audio, or read the authentic reading selection. Activities help students focus their attention on key elements of the video, audio, or text. Post-viewing, post-listening, and post-reading activities check comprehension.

The goal of most Spanish teachers is to get students speaking Spanish in the classroom so that students will develop the language proficiency and cultural understanding necessary to use the language beyond the classroom. This is a challenging goal to meet, especially in the earliest stages of language learning. Here are some strategies to help you and your students spend as much of your instructional time as possible speaking Spanish.

Use English Strategically

- At the beginning of the year, set an expectation as to when English will be allowed in the classroom. As students develop their vocabulary and improve their fluency, reset expectations. Students can be expected to rely less on English in Levels 2 and 3 than they do at the beginning of Level 1.

- Present the Lesson Objectives and the standards that will be taught in the lesson in English so students have a clear idea of the expectations. Also review lesson objectives/standards at end of each class to make sure goals were met.

- In the first chapters of *Auténtico* Level 1, the direction lines are in English to allow students to focus their attention on the task. As students acquire a basic vocabulary, direction lines begin to shift to Spanish. By the time students begin Level 2, all direction lines for activities are in Spanish. Similarly, you may wish to use English to set the task in the first few weeks of school, but steadily move toward more instruction in Spanish.

- If a student is confused or frustrated and struggling to complete an activity that was explained in Spanish, using English may decrease frustration and help the student be more receptive to doing the task in Spanish.

- Consider when using English is more effective for the instructional goal, for example, when learning about concepts that go beyond the language level of the class, such as discussing cultural products, practices, and perspectives. Encourage students to use the Spanish language they know to describe a piece or art or a type of food, but allow English discussion for higher level concepts.

Use strategies that help students access the content

- Focus on the chapter communicative objectives and the key phrases in the chapter vocabulary that support those objectives. For example: A Chapter 1A objective is: Talk and write about what you and others like to do. The key phrases from Chapter 1A vocabulary to meet that goal are:

    ¿Qué te gusta hacer?

    ¿A mí (no) me gusta....?

    ¿Y a tí?

- These key phrases are used to present the vocabulary lexically in each chapter, and are repeated in the *Vocabulario en uso* activities. They help guide students in communicating in Spanish right from the start of each chapter.

- Use gestures and body language to help communication.
- Speak slowly and simplify.
- Read the models aloud with students or show the *Videomodelos.*
- Use the video and audio program for listening exercises so students become accustomed to hearing and understanding different Spanish speakers.
- Repeat key phrases.
- Restate things in different ways.
- Provide visual support for your instruction.
- Use simple familiar phrases when possible.
- Use cognates.
- Encourage personalization and student use of language.
- Check often for understanding.
- Use the *Exploración del lenguaje* feature in Levels 1 and 2 to have students compare Spanish with their own language in order to increase understanding. These boxes highlight strategies to decode language and build vocabulary.

Provide students with the support they need to keep classroom conversation in Spanish

- Start the year with the *Para empezar* chapter. Pay special attention to the classroom phrases on page 6.
- Write key phrases or sentence frames that link to the objectives on the board.
- Post word walls and language ladders to help students with reminders of language they can use to negotiate meaning with each other.
- Write sentence starters on the board for challenging activities.
- Use the Differentiated Instruction suggestions in the Teacher's Edition to tailor activities to students' learning needs so students can complete tasks at their proficiency level.
- Create word walls with the *Expresiones útiles para conversar* in the back of the Student Edition so that students can refer to these expressions during conversations.
- Use frequent comprehension checks.

- Teach key words for comprehension checks – *¿Comprenden? ¿Verdad? ¿Están de acuerdo?*
- Model ways students can ask for clarification or help.

Assign tasks that require English as homework

- Assign vocabulary and grammar presentations and receptive practice activities as homework so that class time is free for communicative activities.
- Assign the *Exploración del lenguaje* reading as homework and then do the *Try it out!* activity in Spanish in class.
- Have students read the culture notes or watch the *Videocultura* at home and write their thoughts about the products, practices, and perspectives they learned about.
- Assign the *Perspectivas* cultural reading and reflection as homework. Have students preview the activity and look up words in Spanish to answer the questions.
- Have students read the *Presentación oral* assignment the night before they do the work together in class. Provide language ladders on the wall or on the whiteboard to provide students with the language they need to negotiate who is playing each role and other discussions around the task.
- Assign the *Conexiones* reading as homework and use visuals in class to check student comprehension.

Use technology to provide additional support

- Assign the grammar explanations in the textbook or online course as homework. Ask students to read the explanations then watch the *GramActiva* videos, the Animated Verbs, or the Grammar Tutorial Videos. When students come to class, you can briefly review the grammar in Spanish or have students work immediately on the communicative grammar activities.
- Use the Interactive Whiteboard activities to present the *Vocabulario en contexto.*
- Encourage students to use the online flashcards and games at home for vocabulary practice.
- Have students read the culture notes or watch the *Videocultura* at home and write their thoughts about the products, practices, and perspectives they learned about.

Integrating 21st Century Skills in the Spanish Classroom

Spanish teachers recognize the need for students to interact effectively with the many Spanish speakers in the United States and across the globe. Today's world languages curriculum and instruction are based upon the 5Cs (Communication, Cultures, Connections, Comparisons, and Communities) with the goal of building communicative proficiency and cultural understanding. World languages learners are 21st Century Learners. However, as today's students enter into an increasingly global economy, it is important that they have a diverse range of skills to succeed. The Partnership for 21st Century Skills, a national organization that advocates for 21st century readiness for every student, has developed a Framework for 21st Century Learning. This document fuses the traditional 3Rs with what they call the 4Cs:

- Critical thinking and problem solving
- Communication
- Collaboration
- Creativity and innovation

World Languages 21st Century Skills Map

The American Council on the Teaching of Foreign Languages (ACTFL) has worked with the Partnership for 21st Century Skills to create a 21st Century Skills Map that describes the integration of World Languages and 21st Century Skills. This map provides concrete examples of how 21st Century Skills can be integrated into all world language classrooms.

By combining the 5Cs of the ACTFL World-Readiness Standards for Learning Languages with the 4Cs from the Partnership for 21st Century Skills, world languages teachers now have a unique opportunity. As schools, districts, and states expand assessment and instruction to focus on 21st Century Skills, we can further prepare students for their future. The 4Cs can be seamlessly integrated on a daily basis within the world languages classroom.

Auténtico and the 21st Century World Languages Classroom

Teachers using *Auténtico* will easily be able to integrate 21st Century Skills into daily instruction due to the series' pedagogical framework, the alignment of assessment and instruction, and the integration of print and digital resources. In *Auténtico*:

- Each chapter is built around thematic instruction based upon real-world tasks and authentic sources.
- Instruction is learner-centered; students take responsibility for the learning and creation of new content.
- Technology is integrated with instruction and assessment to support and enhance learning.
- Instruction and assessment are differentiated to meet the needs of individual learners.
- Assessment is focused on what students can do with the language; students know what they will be asked to do and how they will be assessed.
- Instruction and assessment of culture focuses on the relationship between the products, practices, and perspectives of the target culture as well as comparisons between cultures.
- Students explore opportunities to use the language outside of the classroom.

Auténtico and the 4 Cs

Auténtico provides a wide range of resources, activities, and assessments that support the 4Cs. At the beginning of each Tema in the Teacher's Edition for Levels 1–3, the "b" page contains a chart with recommended activities and assessments in each chapter that build the skills outlined on the 21st Century Skills Map for World Languages.

For further information about the Partnership for 21st Century Skills, please visit their Web site: www.p21.org.

AUTÉNTICO prepares your students for success on the College Board's AP Spanish Language and Culture Examination.

Each chapter of the Student Edition features academically challenging Integration activities that require students to integrate ideas from multiple authentic sources. ▼

Differentiation suggestions and Pre-AP Integration ideas are included throughout the Teacher's Edition. ▼

Differentiated Instruction

Challenge/Pre-AP®

Ask students to think of three brand names of food or drink items. Have them say only the brand name, and call on a volunteer to explain what it is. The student who responds should continue the game by saying another brand name and calling on another volunteer to describe it.

Special Needs

For *Actividad* 4, pair visually-impaired students with other students who will say the Spanish names of the items pictured. Then have the visually impaired students say whether or not the item is appropriate for *desayuno*, *almuerzo*, or *los dos*.

Pre-AP® Integration

- **Learning Objective:** Interpersonal Writing
- **Activity:** As a warm-up activity for five days, have students list what they have eaten for breakfast or lunch. At the end of the week, have them write a short email to a nutritionist asking for tips to improve their eating habits–or indicating how well they follow healthy eating guidelines.
- **Pre-AP® Resource Materials:** Comprehensive guide to Pre-AP® writing skill development

Differentiated Assessment

Core Assessment
- Assessment Program: Examen del capítulo 3A
- Technology: Audio Cap. 3A
- ExamView: Chapter Test, Test Banks A and B

Challenge/Pre-AP®
- ExamView: Pre-AP® Test Bank
- Pre-AP® Resource Materials

Extra Support
- Alternate Assessment Program: Examen del capítulo 3A
- Technology: Audio Cap. 3A

Heritage Speakers
- Assessment Program: *Para hispanohablantes:* Examen del capítulo 3A
- ExamView: Heritage Learner Test Bank

▲ Assessment options allow you to customize tests for your Pre-AP students.

Additional Pre-AP Resources on **Realize** ▶ feature thematic planning charts, teaching tips, a focus on pre-AP activities per chapter, and additional practice.

Scope and Sequence

AUTÉNTICO 1

AUTÉNTICO offers a completely articulated Scope and Sequence across all levels. The recursive themes allow for the recycling, review, and reteaching of vocabulary and grammar.

TEMA	CAPÍTULO	
Para empezar	• En la escuela: greetings; introductions; leave-takings; numbers; time; body parts • En la clase: classroom, dates, asking for help • El tiempo: weather, seasons	
1 Mis amigos y yo	**1A ¿Qué te gusta hacer?** **VOCABULARY:** activities and expressions for saying what you like and don't like to do **GRAMMAR:** infinitives; making negative statements	**1B Y tú, ¿cómo eres?** **VOCABULARY:** adjectives and vocabulary to ask about and describe someone's personality **GRAMMAR:** adjectives; definite and indefinite articles; word order
2 La escuela	**2A Tu día en la escuela** **VOCABULARY:** classroom items and furniture; parts of the classroom; prepositions of location **GRAMMAR:** subject pronouns; the present tense of -ar verbs	**2B Tu sala de clases** **VOCABULARY:** classroom items and furniture; parts of the classroom; prepositions of location **GRAMMAR:** the verb *estar;* plurals of nouns and articles
3 La comida	**3A ¿Desayuno o almuerzo?** **VOCABULARY:** foods; beverages; adverbs of frequency; expressions to show surprise **GRAMMAR:** present tense of -er and -ir verbs; *me gusta(n), me encanta(n)*	**3B Para mantener la salud** **VOCABULARY:** food; beverages; expressions to discuss health; expressions to discuss preferences, agreement, disagreement, and quantity; adjectives to describe food **GRAMMAR:** the plural of adjectives; the verb *ser*
4 Los pasatiempos	**4A ¿Adónde vas?** **VOCABULARY:** leisure activities; places; expressions to tell where and with whom you go; expressions to talk about when things are done **GRAMMAR:** the verb *ir;* interrogative words	**4B ¿Quieres ir conmigo?** **VOCABULARY:** leisure activities; feelings; expressions for extending, accepting, and declining invitations; expressions to tell when something happens **GRAMMAR:** *ir + a* + infinitive; the verb *jugar*
5 Fiesta en familia	**5A Una fiesta de cumpleaños** **VOCABULARY:** family and parties **GRAMMAR:** the verb *tener;* possessive adjectives	**5B ¡Vamos a un restaurante!** **VOCABULARY:** describing people and ordering a meal **GRAMMAR:** the verb *venir;* the verbs *ser* and *estar*
6 La casa	**6A En mi dormitorio** **VOCABULARY:** bedroom items; electronic equipment; colors; adjectives to describe things **GRAMMAR:** comparisons and superlatives; stem-changing verbs: *poder* and *dormir*	**6B ¿Cómo es tu casa?** **VOCABULARY:** rooms in a house and household chores **GRAMMAR:** affirmative *tú* commands; the present progressive tense
7 De compras	**7A ¿Cuánto cuesta?** **VOCABULARY:** clothing; shopping; numbers 200–1,000 **GRAMMAR:** stem-changing verbs: *pensar, querer,* and *preferir;* demonstrative adjectives	**7B ¡Qué regalo!** **VOCABULARY:** places to shop; gifts; accessories; buying and selling **GRAMMAR:** preterite of -ar, -car, and -gar verbs; direct object pronouns *lo, la, los, las*
8 Experiencias	**8A De vacaciones** **VOCABULARY:** vacation places; activities; modes of transportation **GRAMMAR:** preterite of -er and -ir verbs; preterite of *ir;* the personal *a*	**8B Ayudando en la comunidad** **VOCABULARY:** recycling and volunteer work; places in a community **GRAMMAR:** the verb *decir;* indirect object pronouns; preterite of *hacer* and *dar*
9 Medios de comunicación	**9A El cine y la televisión** **VOCABULARY:** television shows; movie genres; giving opinions **GRAMMAR:** *acabar de* + infinitive; gustar and similar verbs	**9B La tecnología** **VOCABULARY:** computers; communication; computer-related activities **GRAMMAR:** the verbs *pedir* and *servir; saber* and *conocer*

AUTÉNTICO A covers the same content as the *Para empezar* section and *Temas 1–4*.

TEMA	CAPÍTULO
Para empezar	• En la escuela: greetings; introductions; leave-takings; numbers; time; body parts • En la clase: classroom, dates, asking for help • El tiempo: weather, seasons

TEMA	CAPÍTULO	
1 **Mis amigos y yo**	**1A ¿Qué te gusta hacer?** **VOCABULARY:** activities and expressions for saying what you like and don't like to do **GRAMMAR:** infinitives; making negative statements	**1B Y tú, ¿cómo eres?** **VOCABULARY:** adjectives and vocabulary to ask about and describe someone's personality **GRAMMAR:** adjectives; definite and indefinite articles; word order
2 **La escuela**	**2A Tu día en la escuela** **VOCABULARY:** classroom items and furniture; parts of the classroom; prepositions of location **GRAMMAR:** subject pronouns; the present tense of *-ar* verbs	**2B Tu sala de clases** **VOCABULARY:** classroom items and furniture; parts of the classroom; prepositions of location **GRAMMAR:** the verb *estar;* plurals of nouns and articles
3 **La comida**	**3A ¿Desayuno o almuerzo?** **VOCABULARY:** foods; beverages; adverbs of frequency; expressions to show surprise **GRAMMAR:** present tense of *-er* and *-ir* verbs; *me gusta(n), me encanta(n)*	**3B Para mantener la salud** **VOCABULARY:** food; beverages; expressions to discuss health; expressions to discuss preferences, agreement, disagreement, and quantity; adjectives to describe food **GRAMMAR:** the plural of adjectives; the verb *ser*
4 **Los pasatiempos**	**4A ¿Adónde vas?** **VOCABULARY:** leisure activities; places; expressions to tell where and with whom you go; expressions to talk about when things are done **GRAMMAR:** the verb *ir;* interrogative words	**4B ¿Quieres ir conmigo?** **VOCABULARY:** leisure activities; feelings; expressions for extending, accepting, and declining invitations; expressions to tell when something happens **GRAMMAR:** *ir + a +* infinitive; the verb *jugar*

AUTÉNTICO B provides a review section called *Para empezar* and continues with *Temas 5–9*.

TEMA	CAPÍTULO	
5 **Fiesta en familia**	**5A Una fiesta de cumpleaños** **VOCABULARY:** family and parties **GRAMMAR:** the verb *tener;* possessive adjectives	**5B ¡Vamos a un restaurante!** **VOCABULARY:** describing people and ordering a meal **GRAMMAR:** the verb *venir;* the verbs *ser* and *estar*
6 **La casa**	**6A En mi dormitorio** **VOCABULARY:** bedroom items; electronic equipment; colors; adjectives to describe things **GRAMMAR:** comparisons and superlatives; stem-changing verbs: *poder* and *dormir*	**6B ¿Cómo es tu casa?** **VOCABULARY:** rooms in a house and household chores **GRAMMAR:** affirmative *tú* commands; the present progressive tense
7 **De compras**	**7A ¿Cuánto cuesta?** **VOCABULARY:** clothing; shopping; numbers 200–1,000 **GRAMMAR:** stem-changing verbs: *pensar, querer,* and *preferir;* demonstrative adjectives	**7B ¡Qué regalo!** **VOCABULARY:** places to shop; gifts; accessories; buying and selling **GRAMMAR:** preterite of *-ar, -car,* and *-gar* verbs; direct object pronouns *lo, la, los, las*
8 **Experiencias**	**8A De vacaciones** **VOCABULARY:** vacation places; activities; modes of transportation **GRAMMAR:** preterite of *-er* and *-ir* verbs; preterite of *ir;* the personal *a*	**8B Ayudando en la comunidad** **VOCABULARY:** recycling and volunteer work; places in a community **GRAMMAR:** the verb *decir;* indirect object pronouns; preterite of *hacer* and *dar*
9 **Medios de comunicación**	**9A El cine y la televisión** **VOCABULARY:** television shows; movie genres; giving opinions **GRAMMAR:** *acabar de +* infinitive; gustar and similar verbs	**9B La tecnología** **VOCABULARY:** computers; communication; computer-related activities **GRAMMAR:** the verbs *pedir* and *servir; saber* and *conocer*

AUTÉNTICO 2

Auténtico 2 uses a recursive Scope and Sequence that revisits the themes from *Auténtico A, B,* or *1.* This natural recycling allows for important review and reteaching. In addition, students expand their vocabulary, grammar, and cultural understanding as they revisit each theme in greater depth.

TEMA	CAPÍTULO	
Para empezar	**A. ¿Cómo eres tú?** *Repaso:* describing people; asking for information; nationalities; adjective agreement; the verb *ser* **B. ¿Qué haces?** t*Repaso:* leisure activities; seasons of the year; regular *-ar, -er,* and *-ir* verbs	
1 **Tu día escolar**	**1A ¿Qué haces en la escuela?** **VOCABULARY:** classroom items, activities, and rules **GRAMMAR:** *(Repaso)* stem-changing verbs; affirmative and negative words	**1B ¿Qué haces después de las clases?** **VOCABULARY:** extracurricular activities **GRAMMAR:** making comparisons; *(Repaso)* the verbs *saber* and *conocer; hace* + time expressions
2 **Un evento especial**	**2A ¿Cómo te preparas?** **VOCABULARY:** daily routines, getting ready for an event **GRAMMAR:** reflexive verbs; *(Repaso)* the verbs *ser* and *estar;* possessive adjectives *mío, tuyo, suyo*	**2B ¿Qué ropa compraste?** **VOCABULARY:** shopping vocabulary, prices, money **GRAMMAR:** *(Repaso)* the preterite of regular verbs; demonstrative adjectives
3 **Tú y tu comunidad**	**3A ¿Qué hiciste ayer?** **VOCABULARY:** running errands; locations in a downtown; items purchased **GRAMMAR:** *(Repaso)* direct object pronouns; the irregular preterite of the verbs *ir, ser, hacer, tener, estar, poder*	**3B ¿Cómo se va . . . ?** **VOCABULARY:** places in a city or town; driving terms; modes of transportation **GRAMMAR:** *(Repaso)* direct object pronouns: *me, te, nos;* irregular affirmative *tú* commands; *(Repaso)* present progressive: irregular forms
4 **Recuerdos del pasado**	**4A Cuando éramos niños** **VOCABULARY:** toys; play terms; describing children **GRAMMAR:** the imperfect tense: regular verbs and irregular verbs; *(Repaso)* indirect object pronouns	**4B Celebrando los días festivos** **VOCABULARY:** expressions describing etiquette; holiday and family celebrations **GRAMMAR:** the imperfect tense: describing a situation; reciprocal actions
5 **En las noticias**	**5A Un acto heroico** **VOCABULARY:** natural disasters; emergencies; rescues; heroes **GRAMMAR:** the imperfect tense: other uses; the preterite of the verbs *oír, leer, creer,* and *destruir*	**5B Un accidente** **VOCABULARY:** parts of the body; accidents; events in the emergency room **GRAMMAR:** the irregular preterites: *venir, poner; decir, traer;* the imperfect progressive and preterite
6 **La televisión y el cine**	**6A ¿Viste el partido en la televisión?** **VOCABULARY:** watching television programs; sporting events **GRAMMAR:** the preterite of *-ir* stem-changing verbs; other reflexive verbs	**6B ¿Qué película has visto?** **VOCABULARY:** movies; making a movie **GRAMMAR:** verbs that use indirect objects; the present perfect
7 **Buen provecho**	**7A ¿Cómo se hace la paella?** **VOCABULARY:** cooking expressions; food; appliances; following a recipe; giving directions in a kitchen **GRAMMAR:** negative *tú* commands; the impersonal *se*	**7B ¿Te gusta comer al aire libre?** **VOCABULARY:** camping and cookouts; food **GRAMMAR:** *Usted* and *ustedes* commands; uses of *por*
8 **Cómo ser un buen turista**	**8A Un viaje en avión** **VOCABULARY:** visiting an airport; planning a trip; traveling safely **GRAMMAR:** the present subjunctive; irregular verbs in the subjunctive	**8B Quiero que disfrutes de tu viaje** **VOCABULARY:** staying in a hotel; appropriate tourist behaviors; traveling in a foreign city **GRAMMAR:** the present subjunctive with impersonal expressions; the present subjunctive of stem-changing verbs
9 **¿Cómo será el futuro?**	**9A ¿Qué profesión tendrás?** **VOCABULARY:** professions; making plans for the future; earning a living **GRAMMAR:** the future tense; the future tense of irregular verbs	**9B ¿Qué haremos para mejorar el mundo?** **VOCABULARY:** environment; environmental issues and solutions **GRAMMAR:** the future tense: other irregular verbs; the present subjunctive with expressions of doubt

AUTÉNTICO 3

Auténtico 3 offers ten thought-provoking thematic chapters that integrate rich vocabulary groups and a thorough presentation of grammar. Chapter activities combine communication, culture, and cross-curricular content with authentic literature and poetry.

CAPÍTULO	Each thematic chapter is divided into two sections. Each of these sections (1 and 2) present and practice vocabulary and grammar.	
Para empezar	**1. Tu vida diaria** *Repaso:* daily routines; school life; leisure activities; present tense verbs; reflective verbs	
	2. Días especiales *Repaso:* weekend activities; celebrations; special events; verbs like *gustar*: possessive adjectives	
	1	**2**
1 **Un día inolvidable**	**VOCABULARY:** hiking objects, activities, and perils; weather **GRAMMAR:** *(Repaso)* preterite verbs with the spelling change *i–y*; *(Repaso)* preterite of irregular verbs; *(Repaso)* preterite of verbs with the spelling change *e–i* and *o–u*	**VOCABULARY:** getting ready for an athletic or academic competition; emotional responses to competition; awards and ceremonies **GRAMMAR:** *(Repaso)* the imperfect; uses of the imperfect
2 **¿Cómo te expresas?**	**VOCABULARY:** describing art and sculpture; tools for painting; describing what influences art **GRAMMAR:** *(Repaso)* the preterite vs. the imperfect; *estar* + participle	**VOCABULARY:** musical instruments; describing dance; describing drama **GRAMMAR:** *(Repaso) ser* and *estar;* verbs with special meanings in the preterite vs. the imperfect
3 **¿Qué haces para estar en forma?**	**VOCABULARY:** nutrition; illnesses and pains; medicine; habits for good health **GRAMMAR:** *(Repaso)* affirmative *tú* commands; *(Repaso)* affirmative and negative commands with *Ud.* and *Uds.*	**VOCABULARY:** exercises; getting and staying in shape; health advice **GRAMMAR:** *(Repaso)* the subjunctive: regular verbs; *(Repaso)* the subjunctive: irregular verbs; *(Repaso)* the subjunctive with stem changing *-ar* and *-er* verbs
4 **¿Cómo te llevas con los demás?**	**VOCABULARY:** personality traits; interpersonal behavior; friendship **GRAMMAR:** *(Repaso)* the subjunctive with verbs of emotion; *(Repaso)* the uses of *por* and *para*	**VOCABULARY:** expressing and resolving interpersonal problems; interpersonal relationships **GRAMMAR:** commands with *nosotros;* possessive pronouns
5 **Trabajo y comunidad**	**VOCABULARY:** after-school work; describing a job **GRAMMAR:** *(Repaso)* the present perfect; *(Repaso)* the past perfect	**VOCABULARY:** volunteer activities; the benefits and importance of volunteer work **GRAMMAR:** the present perfect subjunctive; demonstrative adjectives and pronouns
6 **¿Qué nos traerá en el futuro?**	**VOCABULARY:** jobs and professions; qualities of a good employee **GRAMMAR:** *(Repaso)* the future; *(Repaso)* the future of probability	**VOCABULARY:** technology; inventions; jobs in the future **GRAMMAR:** the future perfect; *(Repaso)* the use of direct and indirect object pronouns
7 **¿Mito o realidad?**	**VOCABULARY:** archaeological terms and activities; describing archaeological sites **GRAMMAR:** the present and past subjunctive in expressions of doubt	**VOCABULARY:** myths and legends; ancient beliefs; pre-Columbian scientific discoveries **GRAMMAR:** the subjunctive in adverbial clauses
8 **Encuentro entre culturas**	**VOCABULARY:** architecture and history of Spain **GRAMMAR:** the conditional	**VOCABULARY:** Spain in the Americas; the encounter between Cortés and the Aztecs; family heritage **GRAMMAR:** the past subjunctive; the past subjunctive with *si* clauses
9 **Cuidemos nuestro planeta**	**VOCABULARY:** caring for the environment **GRAMMAR:** present subjunctive with conjunctions (*mientras, tan pronto como,* etc.); relative pronouns *que, quien, lo que*	**VOCABULARY:** environmental issues; endangered animals **GRAMMAR:** present subjunctive with other conjunctions (*a menos que, sin que, para que,* etc.)
10 **¿Cuáles son tus derechos y responsabilidades?**	**VOCABULARY:** rights and responsibilties **GRAMMAR:** the passive voice: *ser* + past participle; the present vs. the past subjunctive	**VOCABULARY:** government; the role of government; individual rights **GRAMMAR:** the past perfect subjunctive; the conditional perfect

Program Components for Students

AUTÉNTICO The digital course puts the complete student edition, workbooks, audio, video, songs, flashcards, games, and more right at your students' fingertips.

PEARSON realize™

The digital course on Realize!
The program's digital course on Realize puts engaging standards-aligned content, embedded assessments, instant data, and flexible tools at your fingertips.

📖 **ETEXT 2.0**
The complete interactive textbook online with audio and video files

📁 **AUTÉNTICO**
A folder of curated authentic resources that relate to each theme

🔊 **AUDIO**
Audio files for Student Edition, Leveled Vocabulary and Grammar Workbook, and *Canciones de hip hop*

▶ **VIDEO**
Videocultura Cultural overview of each theme

Videohistoria Vocabulary video to help present the new vocabulary

GramActiva Grammar explanations to help present the new grammar

Grammar Tutorials Clear explanations of grammar with comparisons to English

Animated Verbs Animations that highlight verb conjugations

📚 **WORKBOOKS**
Available in print and as part of the digital course on Realize

Leveled Vocabulary and Grammar Workbook
Part 1
 Guided Workbook
 Vocabulary clip art and study sheets
 Step-by-step grammar activities
 Simplified reading, speaking, and writing activities
Part 2
 Core Workbook
 Focused practice for vocabulary and grammar
 End-of-chapter Crossword Puzzle and Organizer

Authentic Resources Workbook
Strategies to help students access the authentic materials
Key vocabulary lists for each resource
Pre- and post-viewing, reading, and listening activities

Literacy Skills Workbook
Standards-based skills practice
Two to three thematically linked readings per *Tema*

Also available as part of the digital course on **Realize:**
Flashcards, Communication Activities, Test Preparation, *Para hispanohablantes,* Grammar Study Guide, Games, Mapa global interactivo, Animated Grammar

Program Components for Teachers

A wide variety of planning, teaching, and assessment options for **AUTÉNTICO** are available in the print Teacher Edition and online at PearsonSchool.com/Autentico.

PLAN

Digital Teacher's Edition

Authentic Resources Lesson Plans

PDF Files of Student Resources

Pre-AP® Resource Materials

Para hispanohablantes Printable PDF Worksheets and Answer Key

Communicative Pair Activities

Project-based Learning for each *Tema* (Levels 1 and 2) or *Capítulo* (Level 3)

Situation Cards

School-to-Home Letters

Input Scripts

Vocabulary Clip Art

Audio and Video Scripts

Answer Keys for Workbooks and *Mapa global interactivo*

Editable Rubrics

PRESENT

Activities and Tools for Interactive Whiteboards for use with or without a SMART™ Interactive Whiteboard

Interactive practice activities for vocabulary and grammar

Teaching suggestions, extensions, and answers

Vocabulary images and clip art

Animated Verbs

Videohistoria Vocabulary presentation videos

GramActiva Engaging grammar explanation videos (Levels 1 and 2)

Videomodelo Videos that model speaking tasks

Videocultura Theme-based culture videos (Levels 1 and 2)

¡Pura vida! Videonovela (Level 3)

Videodocumentario (Level 3)

Student Edition audio

ASSESS

Pruebas for Vocabulary Recognition (auto-graded)

Pruebas with remediation for Vocabulary Production and Grammar (auto-graded)

Examen del capítulo (auto- and teacher-graded)

Speak and Record Speaking Tasks: *Presentación oral, Examen del capítulo,* Integrated Performance Assessments

Alternate Assessment Program

Assessment Program for Heritage Speakers

Four editable test banks per chapter: two for core assessment, one for heritage speakers, one for Pre-AP® learners

Zip file of project and assessment rubrics

Assessment audio

Getting Started with the Student Edition

Students get started in **AUTÉNTICO A** with these colorful reference and introductory sections:

Mapas ▶

Colorful atlas pages support geography skills. Students can explore more online with

🌐 Mapa global interactivo

Digital Course on Realize

AUTÉNTICO includes lots of online resources to help you learn Spanish! You'll find these resources highlighted with technology icons on the pages of your print or online Student Edition.

PEARSON
realize ···

The digital course on Realize!
The program's digital course on Realize puts the Student Edition, workbooks, video, audio, flashcards, games, and more at your fingertips.

Look for these icons in your *Auténtico* textbook or digital course.

🔊 AUDIO
Audio to learn and practice vocabulary and pronunciation, and increase your listening skills

▶ VIDEO
Videocultura Cultural overviews of each theme
Videohistoria Vocabulary videos with an entertaining storyline to practice listening to new words in an authentic context
GramActiva Grammar explanations that present new concepts with humorous examples
Grammar Tutorials Clear explanations of grammar with comparisons to English
Animated Verbs Animations that highlight verb conjugations

✏ WRITING
Practice activities with writing

🎤 SPEAK/RECORD
Speak-and-record tool for speaking activities, you can save your recording

🌐 MAPA GLOBAL INTERACTIVO
Links to interactive maps for virtual exploration of the Spanish-speaking world. You can download .kmz files from PearsonSchool.com/Autentico and link to sites using Google Earth™ or other geographic information systems.

📁 AUTÉNTICO
Collection of authentic video, audio, and text resources organized by theme

🔖 FLASHCARDS
Practice for the new vocabulary

📖 ETEXT 2.0
Complete textbook online

▦ GAMES
Interactive, fun practice and review games such as concentration, crosswords, word search and more

📄 PDF
Video scripts, readings

📓 WORKBOOK
Core and Guided practice activities

vi Digital Course on Realize

The Digital Course ▲

Students get a complete overview of the online resources available on the digital course on Realize.

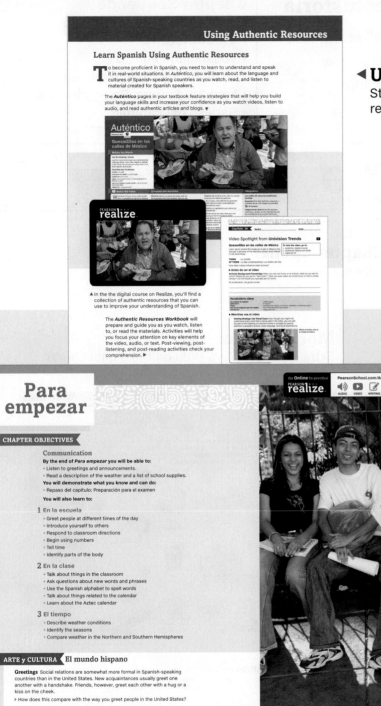

◀ Using Authentic Resources

Students are introduced to the types of authentic resources that they will learn from in *Auténtico.*

Para empezar ▲

This introductory section gets students started in Spanish. Topics include greetings, classroom items and commands, the calendar and dates, and weather expressions.

Chapter Organization

Vocabulario en contexto and Videohistoria

This four-page section gives students a "first look" at the new vocabulary and grammar and focuses on the interpretive mode of communication through comprehensible input that integrates visuals and text with audio and video.

Chapter Sequence
- Vocabulario en contexto
- Videohistoria
- Vocabulario en uso
- Gramática y vocabulario en uso
- Lectura, Cultura, Presentaciones, Auténtico
- Repaso del capítulo

Go Online to practice — PEARSON realize™ — PearsonSchool.com/Autentico

AUDIO   VIDEO   WRITING   SPEAK/RECORD   MAPA GLOBAL   AUTÉNTICO   FLASHCARDS   ETEXT 2.0   GAMES

◄ Chapter opener
Capítulo 3A

More Practice
Extra practice is available on the digital course on Realize or in the print workbooks. ▼

Visualized Vocabulary ▶
New words are presented visually and in context.

Language Input ▲
Input continues with visuals accompanied by narrative. All new vocabulary words and grammar are highlighted in blue.

Listening Comprehension ▲
Short interpretive listening activities check comprehension.

Reading and Language Input

The input of new vocabulary and grammar continues with an example of an interpersonal exchange in spoken or written conversation, followed by a short activity to check comprehension. ▼

María y Carlos mandan mensajes para hablar de las bebidas y comidas. María es de México pero está en San Antonio.

mensajes 06:07 AM

María — ¿Cuál es tu almuerzo favorito?

Carlos — Me encantan los sándwiches. ☺

María — A mí me encantan las tortas.

Carlos — No comprendo. ❓ ¿Qué es una torta?

María — En México, una torta es un sándwich, pero el pan es especial.

Carlos — ¿Hay tortas de salchicha?

María — Por supuesto. Las tortas de huevo con salchicha son deliciosas. También me gusta comer ensalada de verduras, de frutas o de huevos.

Carlos — ¿Ensalada de huevos? ¡Qué asco! ☹ No me gusta nada.

María — ¿Qué bebes con los sándwiches? ¿Te gustan los jugos?

Carlos — Más o menos. ☺

María — Me encantan las aguas frescas. Es como jugo pero con menos fruta. Mañana, yo comparto mi bebida y tú compartes tu sándwich.

3

El almuerzo favorito

ESCRIBIR Lee las frases. Escribe C (cierto) si la frase es correcta o F (falso) si la frase es incorrecta.

1. A María le encantan las tortas.
2. En México, una torta es un taco.
3. A Carlos le encantan los jugos.
4. Las aguas frescas tienen fruta.

126 ciento veintiséis • Tema 3 • La comida

Strategies

Pre-viewing and viewing strategies and activities help students access the content in the Videohistoria. Post-viewing activities check comprehension and encourage students to consider the cultural products, practices, and perspectives in the video. ▼

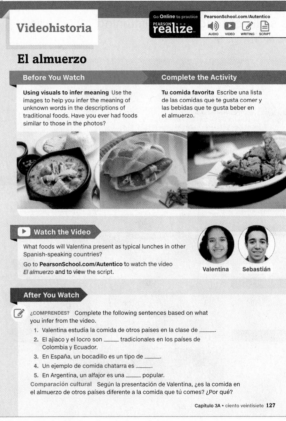

Videohistoria

Go **Online** to practice PearsonSchool.com/Autentico

PEARSON **realize**™

AUDIO VIDEO WRITING SCRIPT

El almuerzo

Before You Watch

Using visuals to infer meaning Use the images to help you infer the meaning of unknown words in the descriptions of traditional foods. Have you ever had foods similar to those in the photos?

Complete the Activity

Tu comida favorita Escribe una lista de las comidas que te gusta comer y las bebidas que te gusta beber en el almuerzo.

▶ Watch the Video

What foods will Valentina present as typical lunches in other Spanish-speaking countries?

Go to **PearsonSchool.com/Autentico** to watch the video *El almuerzo* and to view the script.

Valentina Sebastián

After You Watch

¿COMPRENDES? Complete the following sentences based on what you infer from the video.

1. Valentina estudia la comida de otros países en la clase de _____.
2. El ajiaco y el locro son _____ tradicionales en los países de Colombia y Ecuador.
3. En España, un bocadillo es un tipo de _____.
4. Un ejemplo de comida chatarra es _____.
5. En Argentina, un alfajor es una _____ popular.

Comparación cultural Según la presentación de Valentina, ¿es la comida en el almuerzo de otros países diferente a la comida que tú comes? ¿Por qué?

Capítulo 3A • ciento veintisiete **127**

▶ Videos and Language Input ▲

Students continue to develop their interpretive listening skills with the Videohistoria. Characters from Spanish-speaking families around the United States interact with each other, their local friends and family, and relatives throughout the Spanish-speaking world. The characters participate in video calls and share authentic content with each other online.

Chapter Organization

Vocabulario en uso and Gramática

Students begin to actively use the chapter's new vocabulary and grammar.

Chapter Sequence
- Vocabulario en contexto
- Videohistoria
- **Vocabulario en uso**
- **Gramática y vocabulario en uso**
- Lectura, Cultura, Presentaciones, Auténtico
- Repaso del capítulo

▶ **Modelo** Students can view videos that model the conversation.

🎤 **PAIRED STUDENTS** can record their conversations online!

Focused Practice

Students start with activities that focus on the interpretive skills of reading and listening and some basic writing. ▼

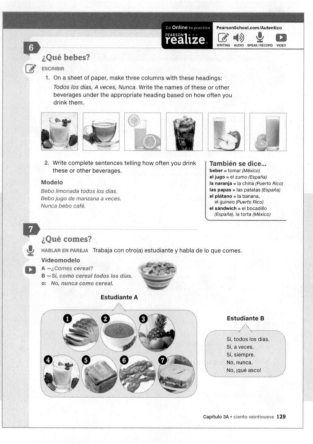

Interpersonal Practice ▲

Students transition to paired practice activities that focus on the new vocabulary in the interpersonal mode of communication.

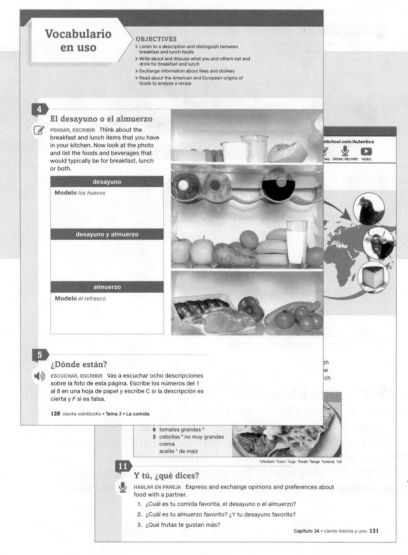

◀ Personal Responses

The sequence of exercises culminates with personalized speaking and writing activities.

Grammar Integrated with Communication

The complete grammar presentation features clear explanations helping students to acquire accuracy of expression. ▼

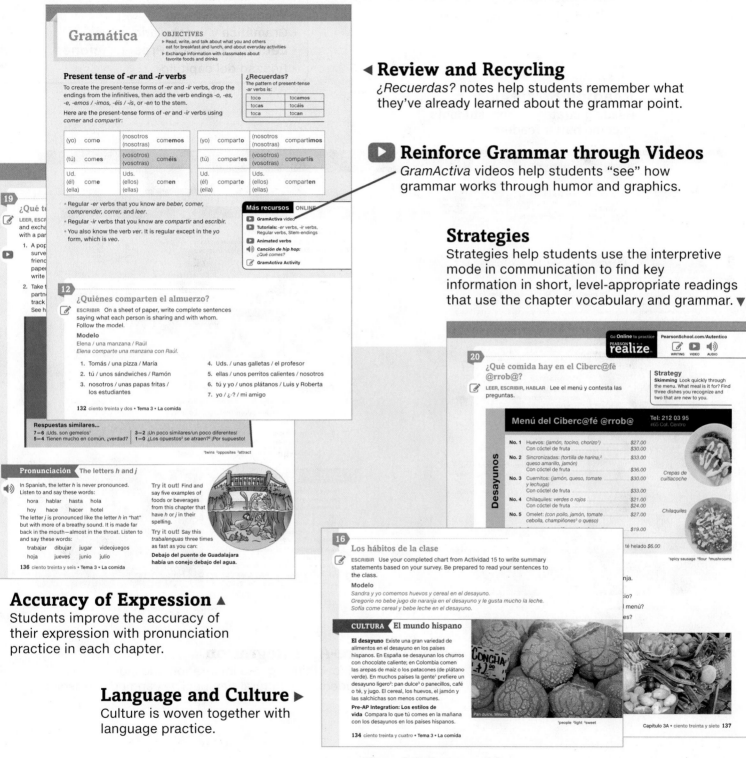

◄ Review and Recycling

¿Recuerdas? notes help students remember what they've already learned about the grammar point.

▶ Reinforce Grammar through Videos

GramActiva videos help students "see" how grammar works through humor and graphics.

Strategies

Strategies help students use the interpretive mode in communication to find key information in short, level-appropriate readings that use the chapter vocabulary and grammar. ▼

Accuracy of Expression ▲

Students improve the accuracy of their expression with pronunciation practice in each chapter.

Language and Culture ▶

Culture is woven together with language practice.

▲ Pre-AP Integration

Integration activities accompany the culture notes. These level-appropriate activities encourage students to think critically and to compare the culture being studied to their own.

Chapter Organization

Lectura

Students apply their language skills in the interpretive mode with culturally authentic readings.

Chapter Sequence
- Vocabulario en contexto
- Videohistoria
- Vocabulario en uso
- Gramática y vocabulario en uso
- **Lectura, Cultura, Presentaciones, Auténtico**
- Repaso del capítulo

Reading Strategies
Reading strategies help students become better readers. ▼

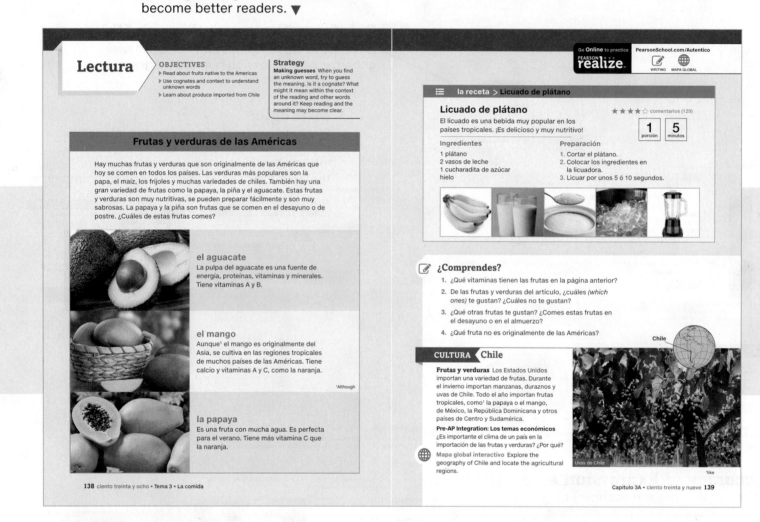

Lectura

OBJECTIVES
▸ Read about fruits native to the Americas
▸ Use cognates and context to understand unknown words
▸ Learn about produce imported from Chile

Strategy
Making guesses When you find an unknown word, try to guess the meaning. Is it a cognate? What might it mean within the context of the reading and other words around it? Keep reading and the meaning may become clear.

Frutas y verduras de las Américas

Hay muchas frutas y verduras que son originalmente de las Américas que hoy se comen en todos los países. Las verduras más populares son la papa, el maíz, los frijoles y muchas variedades de chiles. También hay una gran variedad de frutas como la papaya, la piña y el aguacate. Estas frutas y verduras son muy nutritivas, se pueden preparar fácilmente y son muy sabrosas. La papaya y la piña son frutas que se comen en el desayuno o de postre. ¿Cuáles de estas frutas comes?

el aguacate
La pulpa del aguacate es una fuente de energía, proteínas, vitaminas y minerales. Tiene vitaminas A y B.

el mango
Aunque¹ el mango es originalmente del Asia, se cultiva en las regiones tropicales de muchos países de las Américas. Tiene calcio y vitaminas A y C, como la naranja.

¹Although

la papaya
Es una fruta con mucha agua. Es perfecta para el verano. Tiene más vitamina C que la naranja.

138 ciento treinta y ocho • Tema 3 • La comida

Go **Online** to practice   PearsonSchool.com/Autentico
PEARSON **realize**   WRITING   MAPA GLOBAL

☰ **la receta** ᐳ Licuado de plátano

Licuado de plátano   ★ ★ ★ ★ ☆ comentarios (129)
El licuado es una bebida muy popular en los países tropicales. ¡Es delicioso y muy nutritivo!

| **1** porción | **5** minutos |

Ingredientes
1 plátano
2 vasos de leche
1 cucharadita de azúcar
hielo

Preparación
1. Cortar el plátano.
2. Colocar los ingredientes en la licuadora.
3. Licuar por unos 5 ó 10 segundos.

🖉 **¿Comprendes?**
1. ¿Qué vitaminas tienen las frutas en la página anterior?
2. De las frutas y verduras del artículo, ¿cuáles (which ones) te gustan? ¿Cuáles no te gustan?
3. ¿Qué otras frutas te gustan? ¿Comes estas frutas en el desayuno o en el almuerzo?
4. ¿Qué fruta no es originalmente de las Américas?

CULTURA ᐳ Chile

Chile

Frutas y verduras Los Estados Unidos importan una variedad de frutas. Durante el invierno importan manzanas, duraznos y uvas de Chile. Todo el año importan frutas tropicales, como¹ la papaya o el mango, de México, la República Dominicana y otros países de Centro y Sudamérica.

Pre-AP Integration: Los temas económicos ¿Es importante el clima de un país en la importación de las frutas y verduras? ¿Por qué?

🌐 **Mapa global interactivo** Explore the geography of Chile and locate the agricultural regions.

Uvas de Chile

¹like

Capítulo 3A • ciento treinta y nueve **139**

Real-world Readings ▲
Students are able to connect to the cultural richness and diversity in the Spanish-speaking world.

Pre-AP Integration ▲
Critical thinking and integration questions focus students on cultural perspectives and comparisons.

La cultura en vivo
Churros y chocolate

Empezar el día con churros y chocolate es una tradición muy española y también de otros países de habla hispana. Hay restaurantes o cafés que se llaman churrerías y se especializan en los churros o puedes comprar los churros en puestos de la calle.

Los churros son pastas *(pastries)* que se fríen *(are fried)* en aceite *(oil)*. Lo típico es comer los churros con chocolate caliente, una bebida rica y espesa *(thick)*. Puedes tomar esta comida deliciosa en el desayuno o una merienda *(snack)*. Pero cuidado... no debes comer muchos porque tienen grasa.

Comparación cultural ¿Qué combinaciones de comida o bebida les gustan a ti y a tus amigos? ¿Comen algo parecido *(like)* a los churros y chocolate?

Online Cultural Reading

Go to PearsonSchool.com/Autentico
ONLINE to read and understand a website with information about meals on a day trip.

Strategy: Use background knowledge to identify cultural differences. Notice information in a website that differs from your own experience.

Aplicación: Find the section about food on the web site and identify cultural practices related to food and mealtimes. Identify the meals and foods for purchase and compare the times of each meal to times you eat and foods you typically have.

Churros

1 cup water	1/2 cup unsalted butter (= 1 stick)
1/4 teaspoon salt	1 cup all-purpose flour
4 large eggs	oil for deep frying
1 cup sugar	

In a heavy saucepan, bring water, butter, and salt to a full boil. Remove from heat. Add the flour all at once, stirring briskly. Stir until the mixture pulls away from the side of the pan and forms a ball. Put the mixture in a bowl. With an electric mixer on medium speed, add one egg at a time. After adding the last egg, beat the mixture for one more minute.

With adult supervision, heat 2–3 inches of oil to 375° F in a deep, heavy pan. Fit a pastry bag or cookie press with a 1/2 inch star tip. Pipe out 6 inch-long tubes of dough into the oil. *Be extremely cautious adding dough to the oil, because the oil may spatter and burn you!* Fry, turning a few times, for 3–5 minutes or until golden brown. Place the sugar on a plate. Drain the *churros* well on paper towels and then roll them in the sugar.

Churros y chocolate

Chocolate caliente

To make hot chocolate in Mexico, cacao beans are ground to a powder. Cinnamon, powdered almonds, and sugar are then added, and hot milk is poured in. The mixture is whipped with a wooden whisk called *un molinillo* or *un batidor*. You can find Mexican-style chocolate for making *chocolate caliente* in many supermarkets.

Chocolate caliente

140 ciento cuarenta • Tema 3 • La comida

◀ Hands-on Culture
La cultura en vivo offers a fun, hands-on experience with a wide range of cultural products and practices.

Perspectivas del mundo hispano
¿Qué haces para mantener la salud?

Have you ever eaten chicken soup when you have a cold? How about putting aloe on a sunburn? In many countries, including those in the Spanish-speaking world, traditional remedies consisting of medicinal herbs have been used for centuries to treat common medical problems. In Mexico, a mint known as *yerbabuena* may be made into tea and given to someone with a stomachache. Remedies such as these may not be prescribed by licensed physicians, but people have confidence in them because they have been passed down through the generations.

Researchers study traditional herbal remedies to find modern-day medical solutions. In the Amazon rainforest in South America, an amazing abundance of plant life may hold the key to treating a wide variety of common ailments and diseases. Drug companies are looking for cures found in these plants and herbs that could be reproduced in today's modern drugs.

Increasingly, medicinal herbs are accepted not only as the basis for pharmaceutical drugs, but also for their own inherent healing qualities. In many countries, including the United States, herbal remedies are sometimes used in combination with conventional health care.

Analizar In many Spanish-speaking cultures, herbal remedies have been accepted for centuries. Do you think that medicinal herbs can provide relief and cures? Why or why not?

Comparación cultural What special foods or drinks do you like to have when you don't feel well? Answer the following questions, then write a statement explaining what, if any, foods or drinks help you when you feel sick.

Modelo
Cuando estoy enfermo *(sick)* prefiero comer sopa de pollo.

1. Cuando estoy enfermo, prefiero comer _____.
2. Cuando estoy enfermo, me gusta beber _____.
3. Cuando me duele el estómago, (no) me gusta _____.
4. Cuando me duele la cabeza, prefiero _____.

Online Cultural Reading

Go to Auténtico ONLINE to read and understand a website with menus from the Spanish-speaking world.

En un mercado de Guanajuato, México

164 ciento sesenta y cuatro • Tema 3 • La comida

Cultural Perspectives ▶
Perspectivas del mundo hispano provides a thought-provoking overview of a product or practice (and its related perspectives) from the Spanish-speaking world.

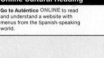

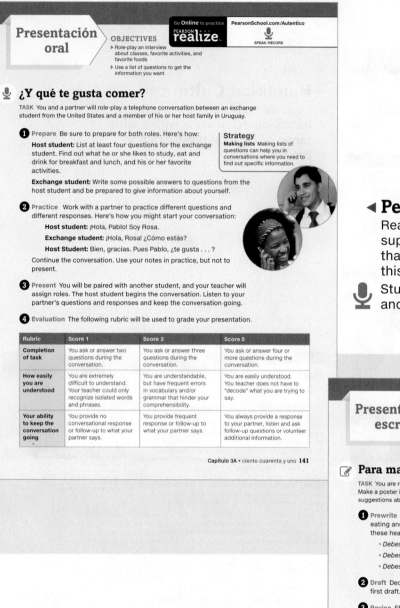

Presentación oral

OBJECTIVES
- Role-play an interview about classes, favorite activities, and favorite foods
- Use a list of questions to get the information you want

Go Online to practice
PEARSON **realize.**
PearsonSchool.com/Autentico
SPEAK/RECORD

🎤 ¿Y qué te gusta comer?

TASK You and a partner will role-play a telephone conversation between an exchange student from the United States and a member of his or her host family in Uruguay.

① Prepare Be sure to prepare for both roles. Here's how:

Host student: List at least four questions for the exchange student. Find out what he or she likes to study, eat and drink for breakfast and lunch, and his or her favorite activities.

Exchange student: Write some possible answers to questions from the host student and be prepared to give information about yourself.

Strategy
Making lists Making lists of questions can help you in conversations where you need to find out specific information.

② Practice Work with a partner to practice different questions and different responses. Here's how you might start your conversation:

Host student: ¡Hola, Pablo! Soy Rosa.

Exchange student: ¡Hola, Rosa! ¿Cómo estás?

Host Student: Bien, gracias. Pues Pablo, ¿te gusta . . . ?

Continue the conversation. Use your notes in practice, but not to present.

③ Present You will be paired with another student, and your teacher will assign roles. The host student begins the conversation. Listen to your partner's questions and responses and keep the conversation going.

④ Evaluation The following rubric will be used to grade your presentation.

Rubric	Score 1	Score 3	Score 5
Completion of task	You ask or answer two questions during the conversation.	You ask or answer three questions during the conversation.	You ask or answer four or more questions during the conversation.
How easily you are understood	You are extremely difficult to understand. Your teacher could only recognize isolated words and phrases.	You are understandable, but have frequent errors in vocabulary and/or grammar that hinder your comprehensibility.	You are easily understood. You teacher does not have to "decode" what you are trying to say.
Your ability to keep the conversation going	You provide no conversational response or follow-up to what your partner says.	You provide frequent response or follow-up to what your partner says.	You always provide a response to your partner, listen and ask follow-up questions or volunteer additional information.

Capítulo 3A • ciento cuarenta y uno **141**

Chapter Sequence
- Vocabulario en contexto
- Videohistoria
- Vocabulario en uso
- Gramática y vocabulario en uso
- **Lectura, Cultura, Presentaciones, Auténtico**
- Repaso del capítulo

◀ Performance-based Speaking Tasks

Real-life interpersonal speaking tasks are supported by strategies and a step-by-step process that helps all students to be successful. A rubric for this task appears at the bottom of the page.

🎤 Students can record their speaking using Speak and Record on **Realize.**

Performance-based Writing Tasks ▶

Students become better writers with real-life tasks that are supported with the writing process and focused strategies. As with the speaking tasks, a rubric has been specially written for each *Presentación escrita*.

✎ Students can submit writing tasks on **Realize** for easy teacher grading!

Presentación escrita

OBJECTIVES
- Create a poster promoting healthy choices
- Gather information from a number of sources

Go Online to practice
PEARSON **realize.**
PearsonSchool.com/Autentico
AUDIO

✎ Para mantener la salud

TASK You are researching good eating and exercise habits for your health class. Make a poster in Spanish in which you state your opinion with five supporting suggestions about how to lead a healthier life.

① Prewrite Ask people at school and home about good eating and exercise habits for teens. List their ideas under these headings to organize your information.

- Debes comer . . .
- Debes beber . . .
- Debes . . . para mantener la salud
- No debes beber mucho(a) . . .
- No debes comer mucho(a) . . .

Strategy
Gathering information Use information and opinions from a variety of sources to help you support your presentation on a topic.

② Draft Decide how to present the information logically as you write your first draft. Use visuals for clarity and give your poster a title.

③ Revise Share your draft with a partner. Your partner should check the following:

- Have you communicated your opinion and supporting statements well?
- Do the visuals convey meaning? Is the poster attractive?
- Are the vocabulary and grammar correct?

Rewrite your poster making any necessary changes.

④ Publish Make a final copy for posting in the nurse's office, a community center, your classroom, or your portfolio.

⑤ Evaluation The following rubric will be used to grade your presentation.

Rubric	Score 1	Score 3	Score 5
Completion of task	You included at least three opinions about how to follow a healthy lifestyle.	You included at least four opinions about how to follow a healthy lifestyle.	You included five or more opinions about how to follow a healthy lifestyle.
Accuracy of vocabulary and grammar	You had very little variation of vocabulary use with many grammar errors.	You had limited usage of vocabulary and some grammar errors.	You had extended use of a variety of vocabulary with very few grammar errors.
Effective use of visuals	You included only three visuals that clearly connect to information.	You included only four visuals that clearly connect to information.	You included five visuals that clearly connect to information.

Capítulo 3B • ciento sesenta y cinco **165**

Auténtico

Students use the interpretive mode of communication to comprehend culturally authentic video, audio, and readings.

Partnered with *Univision*

Students watch, listen to, and read content that was created by native speakers for native speakers. ▼

Auténtico

Partnered with **univision**

Quesadillas en las calles de México

Before You Watch

Use the Strategy: Visuals
Use the visuals to increase your understanding of the key ideas in the video. Watch for details of the foods, how people are eating them, and their reaction as they eat.

Read this Key Vocabulary
al gusto = to taste
un poquito de hambre = a little hungry
¿está rico? = Is it tasty?
nopal = prickly pear cactus, a common ingredient in Mexican cuisine
uno de los mejores que he comido = one of the best that I have eaten
chicharrón = crispy pork rind

▶ Watch the Video

What kinds of foods do you think would be in a *quesadilla* served on the streets of Mexico City?

Go to PearsonSchool.com/Autentico and watch the video *Raúl de Molina se dio gusto comiendo quesadillas en las calles de México* to see how eating street food can be a cultural experience for the senses.

Complete the Activities

Mientras ves As you watch the video, indicate the ingredients from the list below that you see or hear in the different food items.

queso   chile
carne   nopal
tortilla   croquetas
chicharrón   cereal
café   arroz

Integration

Los estilos de vida y las tradiciones sociales

Expansión Find other authentic resources in *Auténtico* online, then answer the question.

📁 3A Auténtico

Integración de ideas En los dos recursos auténticos, ¿cuáles son los ingredientes que las comidas tienen en común? Explica la importancia de un ingrediente en la comida mexicana.

Comparación cultural Compara la comida típica en tu casa con la comida mexicana.

Después de ver Review the video as needed to answer the following questions.

1. En el video, ¿a los clientes les gusta (*do they like*) la comida? ¿Qué palabras o expresiones usan?

2. Escribe los ingredientes que tienen las quesadillas.

3. At the end of the video, Raúl says that eating at this food stand is "mejor que comer en un restaurante de cinco estrellas". What words and visual clues from the video help you to understand what he means?

📖 **For more activities, go to the *Authentic Resources Workbook*.**

142 ciento cuarenta y dos • Tema 3 • La comida   Capítulo 3A • ciento cuarenta y tres 143

Authentic Resources Workbook ▲

The digital course on Realize features a library of authentic materials. Students use the accompanying **Authentic Resources Workbook** (in print or on Realize) to guide them through the content with tasks that are appropriate for their level of proficiency.

Integration ▲

Students respond to open-ended questions that require them to integrate their thoughts on a variety of authentic materials. Additional authentic resources for each chapter are available on **Realize.**

Chapter Organization

Repaso del capítulo

These two pages provide complete review and preparation for the chapter test.

Chapter Sequence
- Vocabulario en contexto
- Videohistoria
- Vocabulario en uso
- Gramática y vocabulario en uso
- Lectura, Cultura, Presentaciones, Auténtico
- **Repaso del capítulo**

Vocabulary List

Chapter vocabulary is listed as language functions and with English translations. ▼

Additional Review

Flashcards, Tutorials, *GramActiva* Videos, Animated Verbs, and *Canciones de hip hop* for this chapter are available online. ▼

Repaso del capítulo

OBJECTIVES
▶ Review the vocabulary and grammar
▶ Demonstrate you can perform the tasks on p. 145

🔊 Vocabulario

to talk about breakfast

en el desayuno	for breakfast
el cereal	cereal
el desayuno	breakfast
los huevos	eggs
el pan	bread
el pan tostado	toast
el plátano	banana
la salchicha	sausage
el tocino	bacon
el yogur	yogurt

to talk about lunch

en el almuerzo	for lunch
la ensalada	salad
la ensalada de frutas	fruit salad
las fresas	strawberries
la galleta	cookie
la hamburguesa	hamburger
el jamón	ham
la manzana	apple
la naranja	orange
las papas fritas	French fries
el perrito caliente	hot dog
la pizza	pizza
el queso	cheese
el sándwich de jamón y queso	ham and cheese sandwich
la sopa de verduras	vegetable soup

to talk about beverages

el agua f.	water
el café	coffee
el jugo de manzana	apple juice
el jugo de naranja	orange juice
la leche	milk
la limonada	lemonade
el refresco	soft drink
el té	tea
el té helado	iced tea

to talk about eating and drinking

beber	to drink
comer	to eat
la comida	food, meal
compartir	to share

to indicate how often

nunca	never
siempre	always
todos los días	every day

to say that you like / love something

Me / te encanta(n) ___.	I / you love (___).
Me / te gusta(n) ___.	I / you like (___).

other useful words

comprender	to understand
con	with
¿Cuál?	Which? What?
más o menos	more or less
por supuesto	of course
¡Qué asco!	How awful!
sin	without
¿Verdad?	Right?

Gramática

present tense of *-er* verbs

como	comemos
comes	coméis
come	comen

present tense of *-ir* verbs

comparto	compartimos
compartes	compartís
comparte	comparten

For *Vocabulario adicional*, see pp. 472–473.

Más recursos PearsonSchool.com/Autentico

🎮 Games	🃏 Flashcards	✏️ Instant check
▶️ Tutorials	▶️ *GramActiva* videos	▶️ Animated verbs

Preparación para el examen

What you need to be able to do for the exam...	Here are practice tasks similar to those you will find on the exam...	For review go to your print or digital textbook...
Interpretive		
🔊 **1 ESCUCHAR** I can understand descriptions of what people eat and drink for lunch.	Listen as three students describe what they typically eat and drink for lunch. Which is most like the kind of lunch you eat? Did they mention anything you could not buy in your school cafeteria?	pp. 124–127 *Vocabulario en contexto* p. 125 Actividades 1–2 p. 128 Actividad 5
Interpersonal		
2 HABLAR I can tell someone what I typically eat for breakfast and ask them the same.	Your Spanish club is meeting for breakfast before school next week. Find out what other people in your class typically eat for breakfast. After you tell at least two people what you eat for breakfast, ask what they like to eat. Does everyone eat the same kind of breakfast or do you all like to eat different things?	p. 129 Actividad 7 p. 130 Actividad 8 p. 131 Actividad 11 p. 133 Actividad 13 p. 134 Actividades 15–16 p. 141 *Presentación oral*
Interpretive		
3 LEER I can read and understand words on a menu.	You are trying to help a child order from the lunch menu below, but he is very difficult to please. He doesn't like anything white. And he refuses to eat anything that grows on trees. Which items from the menu do you think he would refuse to eat or drink? **Almuerzo** hamburguesa plátanos pizza manzana ensalada leche	pp. 124–127 *Vocabulario en contexto* p. 131 Actividad 10 p. 137 Actividad 20 pp. 138–139 *Lectura*
Presentational		
4 ESCRIBIR I can write a list of the foods that I like and dislike.	Your Spanish club is sponsoring a "Super Spanish Saturday." Your teacher wants to know what foods the class likes and dislikes so that the club can buy what most people like. Write the headings *Me gusta(n)* and *No me gusta(n)* in two columns. List at least four items that you like to eat and drink for breakfast and four items for lunch. Then list what you don't like to eat and drink for these same meals.	p. 128 Actividad 4 p. 129 Actividad 6 p. 131 Actividad 11 p. 134 Actividad 16 p. 135 Actividad 18 p. 137 Actividad 20
Culture		
5 COMPARAR I can understand some cultural differences regarding snacks.	Think about popular food combinations in the United States, such as a cup of coffee and a doughnut. What is a similar combination that is popular in many Spanish-speaking countries, and where are you able to buy it?	p. 140 *La cultura en vivo*

Grammar Summary ▲

Chapter grammar is conveniently summarized.

Complete Test Preparation ▲

This spread prepares students for the proficiency and culture sections of the chapter test. Students are told how they will be tested, what the task might be like, and how to review.

Additional Thematic Vocabulary

Useful lists provide additional thematic vocabulary. ▼

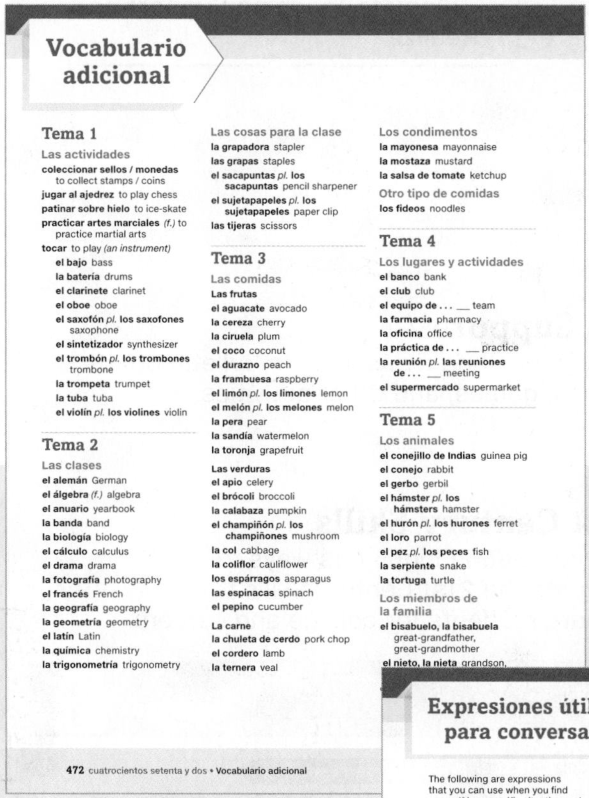

Vocabulario adicional

Tema 1

Las actividades

coleccionar sellos / monedas to collect stamps / coins
jugar al ajedrez to play chess
patinar sobre hielo to ice-skate
practicar artes marciales *(f.)* to practice martial arts
tocar to play *(an instrument)*
el bajo bass
la batería drums
el clarinete clarinet
el oboe oboe
el saxofón *pl.* **los saxofones** saxophone
el sintetizador synthesizer
el trombón *pl.* **los trombones** trombone
la trompeta trumpet
la tuba tuba
el violín *pl.* **los violines** violin

Tema 2

Las clases

el alemán German
el álgebra *(f.)* algebra
el anuario yearbook
la banda band
la biología biology
el cálculo calculus
el drama drama
la fotografía photography
el francés French
la geografía geography
la geometría geometry
el latín Latin
la química chemistry
la trigonometría trigonometry

Las cosas para la clase

la grapadora stapler
las grapas staples
el sacapuntas *pl.* **los sacapuntas** pencil sharpener
el sujetapapeles *pl.* **los sujetapapeles** paper clip
las tijeras scissors

Tema 3

Las comidas

Las frutas
el aguacate avocado
la cereza cherry
la ciruela plum
el coco coconut
el durazno peach
la frambuesa raspberry
el limón *pl.* **los limones** lemon
el melón *pl.* **los melones** melon
la pera pear
la sandía watermelon
la toronja grapefruit

Las verduras
el apio celery
el brócoli broccoli
la calabaza pumpkin
el champiñón *pl.* **los champiñones** mushroom
la col cabbage
la coliflor cauliflower
los espárragos asparagus
las espinacas spinach
el pepino cucumber

La carne
la chuleta de cerdo pork chop
el cordero lamb
la ternera veal

Los condimentos

la mayonesa mayonnaise
la mostaza mustard
la salsa de tomate ketchup

Otro tipo de comidas

los fideos noodles

Tema 4

Los lugares y actividades

el banco bank
el club club
el equipo de ... ___ team
la farmacia pharmacy
la oficina office
la práctica de ... ___ practice
la reunión *pl.* **las reuniones de ...** ___ meeting
el supermercado supermarket

Tema 5

Los animales

el conejillo de Indias guinea pig
el conejo rabbit
el gerbo gerbil
el hámster *pl.* **los hámsters** hamster
el hurón *pl.* **los hurones** ferret
el loro parrot
el pez *pl.* **los peces** fish
la serpiente snake
la tortuga turtle

Los miembros de la familia

el bisabuelo, la bisabuela great-grandfather, great-grandmother
el nieto, la nieta grandson,

472 cuatrocientos setenta y dos • Vocabulario adicional

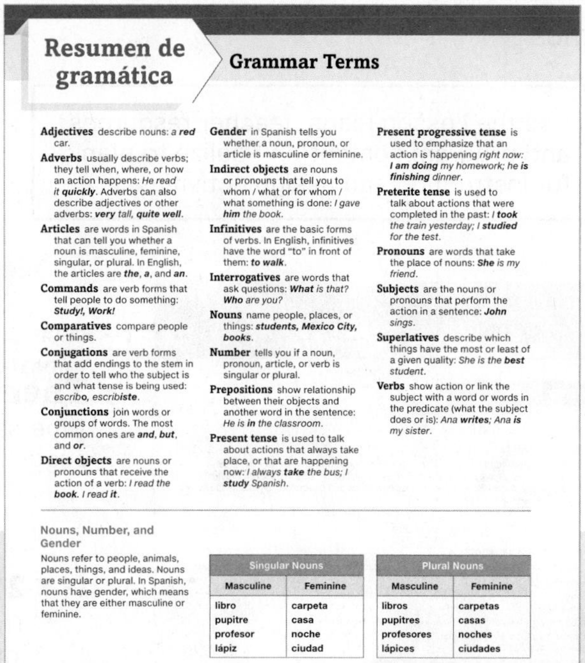

Resumen de gramática

Grammar Terms

Adjectives describe nouns: *a **red** car.*

Adverbs usually describe verbs; they tell when, where, or how an action happens: *He read it **quickly**.* Adverbs can also describe adjectives or other adverbs: ***very** tall, **quite** well.*

Articles are words in Spanish that can tell you whether a noun is masculine, feminine, singular, or plural. In English, the articles are ***the**, **a**,* and ***an***.

Commands are verb forms that tell people to do something: ***Study!, Work!***

Comparatives compare people or things.

Conjugations are verb forms that add endings to the stem in order to tell who the subject is and what tense is being used: *escribo, escribiste*.

Conjunctions join words or groups of words. The most common ones are ***and**, **but**,* and ***or***.

Direct objects are nouns or pronouns that receive the action of a verb: *I read **the book**. I read **it**.*

Gender in Spanish tells you whether a noun, pronoun, or article is masculine or feminine.

Indirect objects are nouns or pronouns that tell you to whom / what or for whom / what something is done: *I gave **him** the book.*

Infinitives are the basic forms of verbs. In English, infinitives have the word "to" in front of them: ***to walk***.

Interrogatives are words that ask questions: ***What** is that? **Who** are you?*

Nouns name people, places, or things: ***students, Mexico City, books***.

Number tells you if a noun, pronoun, article, or verb is singular or plural.

Prepositions show relationship between their objects and another word in the sentence: *He is **in** the classroom.*

Present tense is used to talk about actions that always take place, or that are happening now: *I always **take** the bus; I **study** Spanish.*

Present progressive tense is used to emphasize that an action is happening *right now: **I am doing** my homework; he **is finishing** dinner.*

Preterite tense is used to talk about actions that were completed in the past: *I **took** the train yesterday; I **studied** for the test.*

Pronouns are words that take the place of nouns: ***She** is my friend.*

Subjects are the nouns or pronouns that perform the action in a sentence: ***John** sings.*

Superlatives describe which things have the most or least of a given quality: *She is the **best** student.*

Verbs show action or link the subject with a word or words in the predicate (what the subject does or is): *Ana **writes**; Ana **is** my sister.*

Nouns, Number, and Gender

Nouns refer to people, animals, places, things, and ideas. Nouns are singular or plural. In Spanish, nouns have gender, which means that they are either masculine or feminine.

Singular Nouns	
Masculine	**Feminine**
libro	carpeta
pupitre	casa
profesor	noche
lápiz	ciudad

Plural Nouns	
Masculine	**Feminine**
libros	carpetas
pupitres	casas
profesores	noches
lápices	ciudades

Grammar Summary and Charts

◀ This quick reference guide helps students build a strong grammar foundation.

Expresiones útiles para conversar

The following are expressions that you can use when you find yourself in a specific situation and need help to begin, continue, or end a conversation.

Greeting Someone

Buenos días. Good morning.
Buenas tardes. Good afternoon.
Buenas noches. Good evening. Good night.

Making Introductions

Me llamo ... My name is ...
Soy ... I'm ...
¿Cómo te llamas? What's your name?
Éste es mi amigo *m*. ... This is my friend ...
Ésta es mi amiga *f*. ... This is my friend ...
Se llama ... His / Her name is ...
¡Mucho gusto! It's a pleasure!
Encantado, -a. Delighted.
Igualmente. Likewise.

Asking How Someone Is

¿Cómo estás? How are you?
¿Cómo andas? How's it going?
¿Cómo te sientes? How do you feel?
¿Qué tal? How's it going?
Estoy bien, gracias. I'm fine, thank you.
Muy bien. ¿Y tú? Very well. And you?
Regular. Okay. Alright.
Más o menos. More or less.
(Muy) mal. (Very) bad.
¡Horrible! Awful!
¡Excelente! Great!

Talking on the Phone

Aló. Hello.
Diga. Hello.
Bueno. Hello.
¿Quién habla? Who's calling?
Habla ... It's [name of person calling].
¿Está ..., por favor? Is ... there, please?
¿De parte de quién? Who is calling?
¿Puedo dejar un recado? May I leave a message?
Un momento. Just a moment.
Llamo más tarde. I'll call later.
¿Cómo? No le oigo. What? I can't hear you.

Making Plans

¿Adónde vas? Where are you going?
Voy a ... I'm going to ...
¿Estás listo, -a? Are you ready?
Tengo prisa. I'm in a hurry.
¡Date prisa! Hurry up!
Sí, ahora voy. OK, I'm coming.
Todavía necesito ... I still need ...
¿Te gustaría ...? Would you like to ...?
Sí, me gustaría ... Yes, I'd like to ...
¡Claro que sí (no)! Of course (not)!
¿Quieres ...? Do you want to ...?
Quiero ... I want to ...
¿Qué quieres hacer hoy? What do you want to do today?
¿Qué haces después de las clases? What do you do after school (class)?
¿Qué estás haciendo? What are you doing?
Te invito. It's my treat.
¿Qué tal si ...? What about ...?
Primero ... First ...
Después ... Later ...
Luego ... Then ...

Making an Excuse

Estoy ocupado, -a. I'm busy.
Lo siento, pero no puedo. I'm sorry, but I can't.
¡Qué lástima! What a shame!
Ya tengo planes. I already have plans.
Tal vez otro día. Maybe another day.

Being Polite

Con mucho gusto. With great pleasure.
De nada. You're welcome.
Disculpe. Excuse me.
Lo siento. I'm sorry.
Muchísimas gracias. Thank you very much.
Te (Se) lo agradezco mucho. I appreciate it a lot.
Muy amable. That's very kind of you.
Perdón. Pardon me.
¿Puede Ud. repetirlo? Can you repeat that?
¿Puede Ud. hablar más despacio? Can you speak more slowly?

Keeping a Conversation Going

¿De veras? Really?
¿Verdad? Isn't that so? Right?
¿En serio? Seriously?
¡No lo puedo creer! I don't believe it!
¡No me digas! You don't say!
Y entonces, ¿qué? And then what?
¿Qué hiciste? What did you do?
¿Qué dijiste? What did you say?
¿Crees que ...? Do you think that ...?
Me parece bien. It seems alright.
Perfecto. Perfect.
¡Qué buena idea! What a good idea!
¡Cómo no! Of course!
De acuerdo. Agreed.
Está bien. It's all right.

Giving a Description When You Don't Know the Name of Someone or Something

Se usa para ... It's used to / for ...
Es la palabra que significa ... It's the word that means ...
Es la persona que ... It's the person who ...

Ending a Conversation

Bueno, tengo que irme. Well, I have to go.
Chao. (Chau.) Bye.
Hasta pronto. See you soon.
Hasta mañana. See you tomorrow.

Expresiones útiles para conversar • cuatrocientos ochenta y tres 483

Expressions for Communication ▶

This handy list can help students become better communicators.

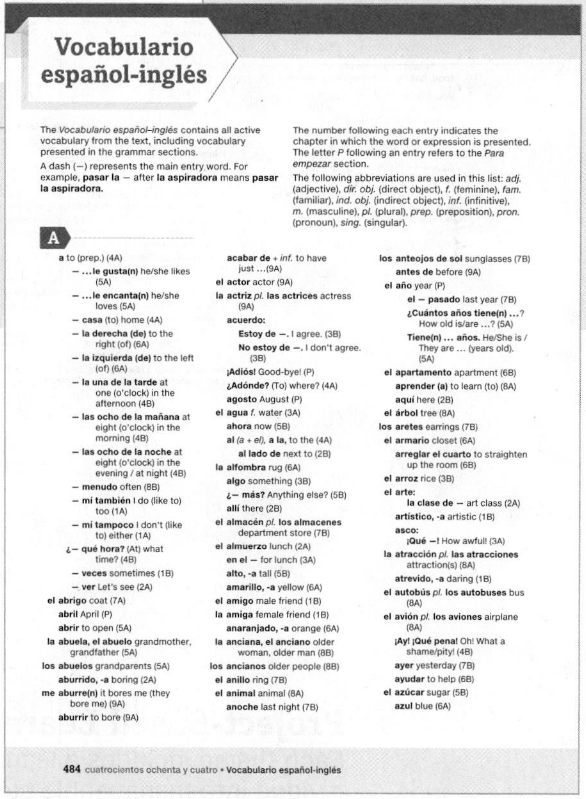

Vocabulario español-inglés

The *Vocabulario español-inglés* contains all active vocabulary from the text, including vocabulary presented in the grammar sections.

A dash (—) represents the main entry word. For example, **pasar la —** after **la aspiradora** means **pasar la aspiradora.**

The number following each entry indicates the chapter in which the word or expression is presented. The letter *P* following an entry refers to the *Para empezar* section.

The following abbreviations are used in this list: *adj.* (adjective), *dir. obj.* (direct object), *f.* (feminine), *fam.* (familiar), *ind. obj.* (indirect object), *inf.* (infinitive), *m.* (masculine), *pl.* (plural), *prep.* (preposition), *pron.* (pronoun), *sing.* (singular).

A

a to (prep.) (4A)
— ...le gusta(n) he/she likes (5A)
— ...le encanta(n) he/she loves (5A)
— casa (to) home (4A)
— la derecha (de) to the right (of) (6A)
— la izquierda (de) to the left (of) (6A)
— la una de la tarde at one (o'clock) in the afternoon (4B)
— las ocho de la mañana at eight (o'clock) in the morning (4B)
— las ocho de la noche at eight (o'clock) in the evening / at night (4B)
— menudo often (8B)
— mí también I do (like to) too (1A)
— mí tampoco I don't (like to) either (1A)
¿— qué hora? (At) what time? (4B)
— veces sometimes (1B)
— ver Let's see (2A)
el abrigo coat (7A)
abril April (P)
abrir to open (5A)
la abuela, el abuelo grandmother, grandfather (5A)
los abuelos grandparents (5A)
aburrido, -a boring (2A)
me aburre(n) it bores me (they bore me) (9A)
aburrir to bore (9A)
acabar de + *inf.* to have just ... (9A)
el actor actor (9A)
la actriz *pl.* **las actrices** actress (9A)
acuerdo:
Estoy de —. I agree. (3B)
No estoy de —. I don't agree. (3B)
¡Adiós! Good-bye! (P)
¿Adónde? (To) where? (4A)
agosto August (P)
el agua *f.* water (3A)
ahora now (5B)
al *(a + el)*, **a la,** to the (4A)
al lado de next to (2B)
la alfombra rug (6A)
algo something (3B)
¿— más? Anything else? (5B)
allí there (2B)
el almacén *pl.* **los almacenes** department store (7B)
el almuerzo lunch (2A)
en el — for lunch (3A)
alto, -a tall (5B)
amarillo, -a yellow (6A)
el amigo male friend (1B)
la amiga female friend (1B)
anaranjado, -a orange (6A)
la anciana, el anciano older woman, older man (8B)
los ancianos older people (8B)
el anillo ring (7B)
el animal animal (8A)
anoche last night (7B)
los anteojos de sol sunglasses (7B)
antes de before (9A)
el año year (P)
el — pasado last year (7B)
¿Cuántos años tiene(n) ...? How old is/are ...? (5A)
Tiene(n) ... años. He/She is / They are ... (years old). (5A)
el apartamento apartment (6B)
aprender (a) to learn (to) (8A)
aquí here (2B)
el árbol tree (8A)
los aretes earrings (7B)
el armario closet (6A)
arreglar el cuarto to straighten up the room (6B)
el arroz rice (3B)
el arte:
la clase de — art class (2A)
artístico, -a artistic (1B)
asco:
¡Qué —! How awful! (3A)
la atracción *pl.* **las atracciones** attraction(s) (8A)
atrevido, -a daring (1B)
el autobús *pl.* **los autobuses** bus (8A)
el avión *pl.* **los aviones** airplane (8A)
¡Ay! ¡Qué pena! Oh! What a shame/pity! (4B)
ayer yesterday (7B)
ayudar to help (6B)
el azúcar sugar (5B)
azul blue (6A)

484 cuatrocientos ochenta y cuatro • Vocabulario español-inglés

End Glossaries ▲

Helpful Spanish-English and English-Spanish glossaries are located at the end of the book

Students can listen to pronunciation on **Realize.**

Using the Teacher's Edition

Teaching the Theme

The Teacher's Edition provides complete planning support for teaching the themes.

Go Online to practice
PEARSON realize™

Use the Lesson Plans, teacher resources, and program content on Realize to plan for instruction and assign activities.

- **Teaching the Theme**
- **Planning for Instruction**
- **Alignment with the ACTFL World-Readiness Standards**
- **Complete Teaching Support on Realize**

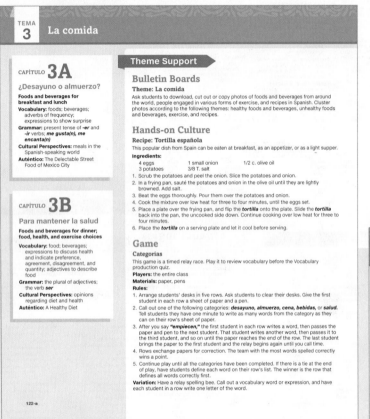

◀ Theme Support
Time-saving teaching ideas include bulletin board suggestions, games, and other activities.

▼ 21st Century Skills
This correlation highlights ways to integrate the 21st Century Skills to prepare students for college and careers.

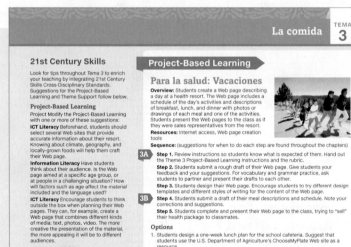

Project-Based Learning ▶
Each theme includes a learning project divided into manageable steps. The rubric is at the bottom of the page as well as on **Realize.**

Planning for Instruction

The Teacher's Edition provides four pages of planning support interleaved at the beginning of each chapter.

▼ Chapter Overview

This section gives a quick overview of each chapter.

3A ¿Desayuno o almuerzo?

AT A GLANCE

Objectives
- Listen to and read descriptions of meals and menus
- Talk and write about foods you and others like and dislike
- Exchange information about food preferences
- Identify cultural practices viewed in an authentic video about food
- Trace the history of some foods originally native to the Americas and Europe

Vocabulary
- Foods and beverages for breakfast and lunch
- Expressions of frequency

Grammar
- Present tense of -er and -ir verbs
- *Me gustan, me encantan*

Culture
- Bartolomé Murillo, p. 123
- Fruits and vegetables from the Americas, p. 131
- Typical breakfasts in Spanish-speaking countries, p. 134
- Fruits imported from Chile, p. 139
- Popular snacks in Spanish-speaking countries, p. 140.

Recycle
- Present tense of -ar verbs
- Expressions of agreement and disagreement

Authentic Resources
- Video about the rich variety of street foods in Mexico City pp. 142–143

Chapter Resources 3A

RESOURCES		FOR THE STUDENT	DIGITAL	PRINT	FOR THE TEACHER	DIGITAL	PRINT
Vocabulario en uso pp. 128–131							
Present & Practice		Student Edition, pp. 128–131	•	•	Interactive Whiteboard Vocabulary Activities	•	
		Instant Check	•		Teacher's Edition, pp. 128–131		•
		Communication Activities	•		Teacher's Resource Materials		
		Para hispanohablantes	•		Communicative Pair Activities		•
		Communicative Pair Activities	•		Technology: Audio	•	
					Videomodelos	•	
Assess and Remediate					Prueba 3A-2 with Remediation	•	
					Prueba 3A-2: Assessment Program, pp. 69–70	•	•
					Assessment Program para hispanohablantes, pp. 69–70	•	
Gramática pp. 132–137							
Present & Practice		Student Edition, pp. 132–137	•	•	Interactive Whiteboard Grammar Activities	•	
		Instant Check	•		Teacher's Edition, pp. 132–137		•
		Animated Verbs	•		Teacher's Resource Materials		
		Tutorial Video: Grammar	•		Communicative Pair Activities		•
		Canción de hip hop	•		Technology: Audio	•	
		Guided WB, pp. 93–96	•	•	Videomodelos	•	
		Core WB, pp. 53–55	•	•	Video Program: GramActiva	•	
		Communication Activities	•				
		Para hispanohablantes	•				
		Communicative Pair Activities	•				
Assess and Remediate					Pruebas 3A-3 and 3A-4 with Remediation	•	
					Pruebas 3A-3, 3A-4: Assessment Program, pp. 71, 72	•	•
					Assessment Program para hispanohablantes, pp. 71, 72	•	
Aplicación pp. 138–139							
Apply							

RESOURCES		FOR THE STUDENT	DIGITAL	PRINT	FOR THE TEACHER	DIGITAL	PRINT
Plan					Teacher's Edition, pp. 122a–122f	•	•
					Teacher's Resource Materials		
					Pre-AP® Resource Materials		•
					Lesson Plans, pp. 122-e, 122-f		•
					Mapa global interactivo	•	
Introducción pp. 122–123							
Present		Student Edition, pp. 122–123	•	•	Teacher's Edition, pp. 122–123	•	•
		DK Reference Atlas	•		Teacher's Resource Materials		•
		Videocultura	•		Mapa global interactivo	•	
		Para hispanohablantes	•				
Vocabulario en contexto pp. 124–127							
Present & Practice		Student Edition, pp. 124–127	•	•	Teacher's Edition, pp. 124–127	•	•
		Audio	•		Teacher's Resources		
		Videohistoria	•		Vocabulary Clip Art	•	
		Flashcards	•		Technology: Audio	•	
		Instant Check	•		Video Program: Videohistoria	•	
		Guided WB, pp. 83–92	•	•			
		Core WB, pp. 49–52	•	•			
		Communication Activities	•				
		Para hispanohablantes	•				
Assess and Remediate					Prueba 3A-1: Assessment Program, pp. 67–68	•	•
					Assessment Program para hispanohablantes, pp. 67–68	•	

122-c

Program Resources ▲

This section shows all the program resources available for this chapter. All resources are conveniently referenced at point of use in the chapter.

Lesson Plans ▶

Lesson Plans are provided for instruction on a 50-minute or alternate schedule. Lesson plans are also available on **Realize**.

3A Lesson Plans

Lesson Plans 3A

ALTERNATE LESSON PLAN (90 MINUTES)

DAY	Warm-up / Assess	Preview / Present / Practice / Communicate	Wrap-up / Homework Options
1	Warm-up (10 min.)	Chapter Opener (5 min.) • Video Activities 1, 2, 3	Wrap-up and Homework Options (5 min.)

LESSON PLAN

DAY	Warm-up / Assess	Preview / Present / Practice / Communicate		Wrap-up / Homework Options
1	Warm-up (10 min.) • Return Examen del capítulo 2B	Chapter Opener (5 min.) • Objectives • Arte y cultura	Vocabulario en contexto (30 min.) • Presentation: Vocabulario en contexto • Actividades 1, 2	Wrap-up and Homework Options (5 min.) • Core Practice 3A-1, 3A-2
2	Warm-up (5 min.) • Homework check	Vocabulario en contexto (40 min.) • Presentation: Videohistoria El almuerzo • View: Videohistoria	• Video Activities 1, 2, 3, 4 • Actividad 3	Wrap-up and Homework Options (5 min.) • Core Practice 6, 9, 10, 11 • Prueba 3A-1: Vocabulary recognition
3	Warm-up (10 min.) • Actividad 4 • Homework check • Formative Assessment (10 min.) • Prueba 3A-1: Vocabulary recognition	Vocabulario en uso (25 min.) • Interactive Whiteboard Vocabulary Activities • Actividades 5, 7, 8 • Exploración del lenguaje • Audio Activities 5, 6		Wrap-up and Homework Options (5 min.) • Actividades 6, 9, 10, 11 • Prueba 3A-2 with Remediation: Vocabulary production
4	Warm-up (15 min.) • Writing Activity 10 • Communicative Pair Activity • Homework check • Formative Assessment (10 min.) • Prueba 3A-2 with Remediation: Vocabulary production	Gramática y vocabulario en uso (20 min.) • Presentation: Present tense of -er and -ir verbs • View: GramActiva video • Interactive Whiteboard Grammar Activities • Actividades 12, 13 • Audio Activity 7		Wrap-up and Homework Options (5 min.) • Core Practice 3A-5
5	Warm-up (10 min.) • Writing Activity 11 • Homework check	Gramática y vocabulario en uso (35 min.) • Actividades 14, 15, 16 • Cultura • Communicative Pair Activity		Wrap-up and Homework Options (5 min.) • Prueba 3A-3 with Remediation: Present tense of -er and -ir verbs
6	Warm-up (5 min.) • Review of -er and -ir verbs • Formative Assessment (10 min.) • Prueba 3A-3 with Remediation: Present tense of -er and -ir verbs	Gramática y vocabulario en uso (30 min.) • Presentation: Me gustan, me encantan • View: GramActiva video • Interactive Whiteboard Grammar Activities	• Actividades 17, 18, 19 • Audio Activities 8, 9	Wrap-up and Homework Options (5 min.) • Core Practice 3A-6, 3A-7 • Actividad 20 • Prueba 3A-4 with Remediation: Me gustan, me encantan
7	Warm-up (15 min.) • Writing Activities 12, 13 • Homework check • Formative Assessment (10 min.) • Prueba 3A-4 with Remediation: Me gustan, me encantan	Gramática y vocabulario en uso (10 min.) • Pronunciación • El español en la comunidad • Aplicación (10 min.) • Lectura • ¿Comprendes?		Wrap-up and Homework Options (5 min.) • La cultura en vivo: Make recipe • Lectura
8	Warm-up (5 min.) • Cultura	Aplicación (40 min.) • La cultura en vivo: Finish • Auténtico • Presentación oral: Step 1	• Situation Cards • Communicative Pair Activities	Wrap-up and Homework Options (5 min.) • Presentación oral: Step 2 • Preparación para el examen 3, 4, 5
9	Warm-up (5 min.) • Homework check	Aplicación (30 min.) • Presentación oral: Step 3	Repaso del capítulo (10 min.) • Vocabulario y gramática • Preparación para el examen 1, 2	Wrap-up and Homework Options (5 min.) • Core Practice 3A-8, 3A-9 • Instant Check • Auténtico • Examen del capítulo 3A
10	Warm-up (10 min.) • Homework check • Answer questions • Summative Assessment (40 min.) • Examen del capítulo 3A			

122-e

122-f

Using the Teacher's Edition

Alignment with the ACTFL World-Readiness Standards

AUTÉNTICO provides complete coverage of the ACTFL World-Readiness Standards for Learning Languages

- Teaching the Theme
- Planning for Instruction
- **Alignment with the ACTFL World-Readiness Standards**
- Complete Teaching Support on Realize

▼ ACTFL World-Readiness Standards

A complete correlation of chapter activities to the standards is provided at the beginning of each chapter.

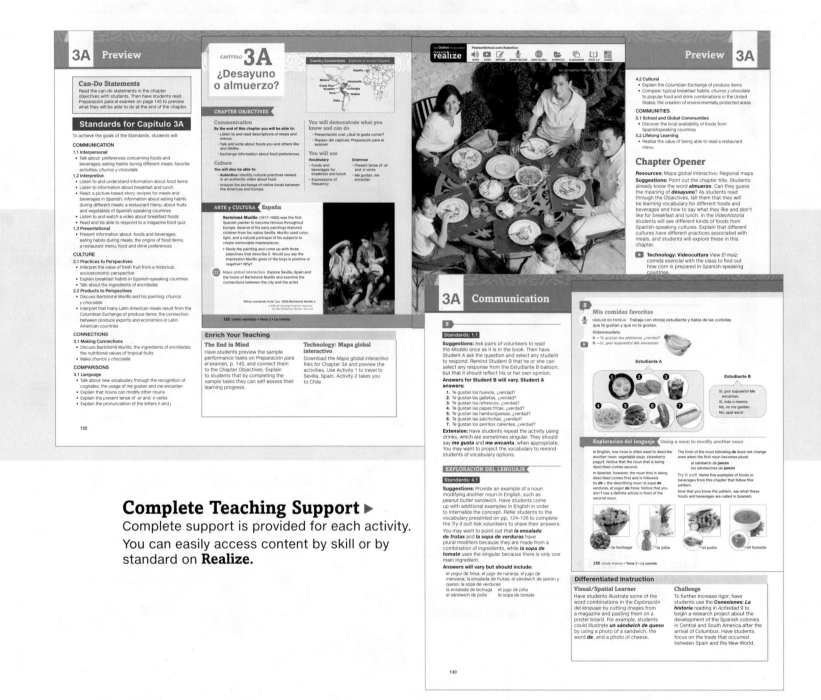

Complete Teaching Support ▶

Complete support is provided for each activity. You can easily access content by skill or by standard on **Realize**.

Complete Teaching Support

AUTÉNTICO provides teachers with complete instructional support in both print and technology formats.

Chapter Objectives ▶

Each chapter provides a well-organized structure, clear student outcomes and a variety of activities that develop all language skills.

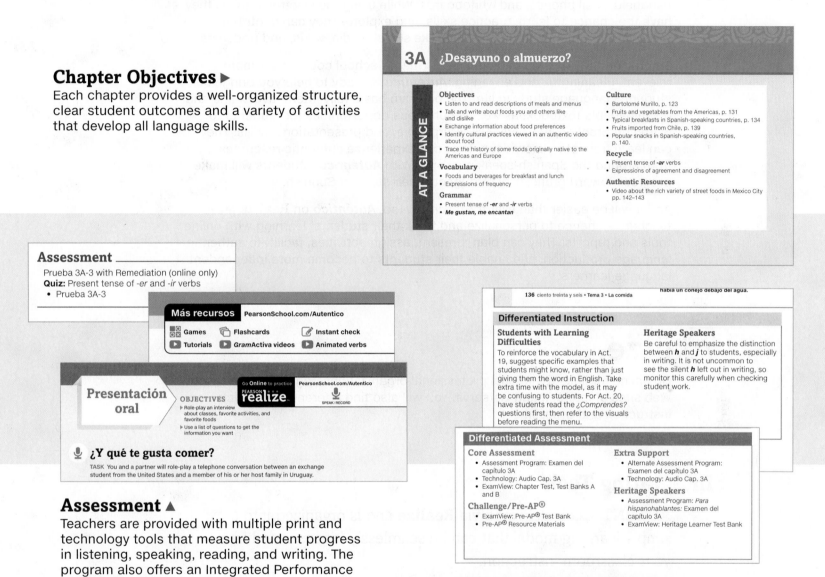

3A ¿Desayuno o almuerzo?

AT A GLANCE

Objectives
- Listen to and read descriptions of meals and menus
- Talk and write about foods you and others like and dislike
- Exchange information about food preferences
- Identify cultural practices viewed in an authentic video about food
- Trace the history of some foods originally native to the Americas and Europe

Vocabulary
- Foods and beverages for breakfast and lunch
- Expressions of frequency

Grammar
- Present tense of -er and -ir verbs
- Me gustan, me encantan

Culture
- Bartolomé Murillo, p. 123
- Fruits and vegetables from the Americas, p. 131
- Typical breakfasts in Spanish-speaking countries, p. 134
- Fruits imported from Chile, p. 139
- Popular snacks in Spanish-speaking countries, p. 140.

Recycle
- Present tense of -ar verbs
- Expressions of agreement and disagreement

Authentic Resources
- Video about the rich variety of street foods in Mexico City pp. 142–143

Assessment

Prueba 3A-3 with Remediation (online only)
Quiz: Present tense of -er and -ir verbs
- Prueba 3A-3

Más recursos PearsonSchool.com/Autentico

- Games
- Flashcards
- Instant check
- Tutorials
- GramActiva videos
- Animated verbs

Presentación oral

Go Online to practice
PEARSON **realize.**
PearsonSchool.com/Autentico
SPEAK/RECORD

OBJECTIVES
▶ Role-play an interview about classes, favorite activities, and favorite foods
▶ Use a list of questions to get the information you want

¿Y qué te gusta comer?

TASK You and a partner will role-play a telephone conversation between an exchange student from the United States and a member of his or her host family in Uruguay.

136 ciento treinta y seis • Tema 3 • La comida

había un conejo debajo del agua.

Differentiated Instruction

Students with Learning Difficulties
To reinforce the vocabulary in Act. 19, suggest specific examples that students might know, rather than just giving them the word in English. Take extra time with the model, as it may be confusing to students. For Act. 20, have students read the ¿Comprendes? questions first, then refer to the visuals before reading the menu.

Heritage Speakers
Be careful to emphasize the distinction between **h** and **j** to students, especially in writing. It is not uncommon to see the silent **h** left out in writing, so monitor this carefully when checking student work.

Differentiated Assessment

Core Assessment
- Assessment Program: Examen del capítulo 3A
- Technology: Audio Cap. 3A
- ExamView: Chapter Test, Test Banks A and B

Challenge/Pre-AP®
- ExamView: Pre-AP® Test Bank
- Pre-AP® Resource Materials

Extra Support
- Alternate Assessment Program: Examen del capítulo 3A
- Technology: Audio Cap. 3A

Heritage Speakers
- Assessment Program: Para hispanohablantes: Examen del capítulo 3A
- ExamView: Heritage Learner Test Bank

Assessment ▲

Teachers are provided with multiple print and technology tools that measure student progress in listening, speaking, reading, and writing. The program also offers an Integrated Performance Assesssment for each chapter.

Differentiated Instruction ▲

Auténtico provides teaching suggestions to help all students learn Spanish. Each level also provides differentiated assessment.

Instructional Planning and Support

Auténtico provides complete planning and teaching support. The Teacher's Edition and the teacher resources on Realize provide time-saving teaching tools to help you teach all your students.

From wireless communication tools to the virtual world, technology has changed the lives of today's students. Access to technology in schools and society is integrated into their lives, and their world has expanded through laptops, handhelds, cell phones, and whiteboards. While using the electronic tools, they have the chance to learn, practice skills, and explore. They can contribute to the online community through outlets like social media, wikis, and podcasts.

Embracing the changes to digital media makes school coursework more relevant, meaningful, and engaging. *Auténtico* is ready to help you bring your students' language study to life. The program has a fully interactive online and downloadable textbook, as well as numerous opportunities for students to learn and practice interpersonal, interpretive, and presentational skills. They can learn from storyline videos. They can experience authentic resources from around the Spanish-speaking world. With *Auténtico*, students will make progress toward proficiency throughout their study of Spanish.

And it will be easier than ever for teachers, too. *Auténtico* on **Realize** gives teachers a chance to personalize and track their students' learning with online tools and reports. They can plan, present, assign activities, facilitate authentic language production, and enable their students to become more independent language learners.

PEARSON
realize.™

Go online for links to national professional organizations, regional conferences, Web sites of interest, and Listservs. You will also find references to articles on instruction and assessment.

Integrating Tech

AUTÉNTICO is delivered via **Realize** and is organized into a simple learning model that can be seamlessly incorporated into your classroom instruction.

Present

Everything you need to teach key concepts to your students in the classroom, or at home, including offline access to your eText.

Selected Examples

Videohistoria Brand new videos to engage your students

Interactive Whiteboard Presentations Engage students in new grammar points and vocabulary

Practice and Communicate

Let your students practice what they've learned, with activities you assign for classroom or at-home work.

eText activities, all activities in the SE can be done online
Speak-and-Record tasks
Grammar tutorials for preview, learning, or review
GramActiva **activities,** to reinforce instruction

More Practice

Additional practice resources are here to help reinforce the concepts of each chapter.
Vocabulary App, a fun way for students to practice chapter vocabulary
Videomodelos, for students to watch and re-watch vocabulary in context
Culture Reading Activity, support for engaging *Lectura* in the student book and etext

Assess

Test your students' knowledge as they progress through a chapter with auto-corrected quizzes and assigned remediation activities. At the end of each chapter, assess your students' ability to show what they've learned with communicative, gradable tests.

Lesson quizzes with remediation, so you and your students can check understanding
Chapter Tests and Cumulative Tests, for summative assessment
Situation Cards, for students to demonstrate authentic use of new vocabulary and grammar skills
Integrated Performance Assessment, alternative assessment in authentic contexts
ExamView® Assessment Suite, editable banks of test items

More Resources

Do your students need more help or different help? Each chapter includes a *Más Recursos* folder with many differentiated resources to help your struggling students.

Leveled Vocabulary and Grammar Workbook: Guided Practice, for more practice designed to help students at all levels of proficiency; in print and online
Para hispanohablantes, support for your heritage speakers

Looking for authentic Spanish resources?

Each chapter includes an *Auténtico* folder with videos, audio recordings, and articles from our partners Univision, NBC Learn, EFE News, and the Inter-American Development Bank.

Assessment

Topics Covered

- Assessing Student Progress
- Purposes of Assessment
- Forms of Assessment
- **AUTÉNTICO** and the standards
- Integrating Technology with Assessment on **Realize**
- Assessment Resources in **AUTÉNTICO**

An assessment program in a second language classroom should be based on the premise that the main purpose of learning a language is to communicate in a meaningful and culturally appropriate way. As you begin to teach a unit of instruction, you might want to start by asking a few key questions: What do I expect my students to learn? What do I want them to be able to do? How can I assess what I am looking for in student performance?

Assessing Student Progress

The role of assessment in the world languages classroom is to provide both the teacher and students with a measure of progress toward achieving predetermined outcomes. It is an integral and ongoing part of the learning process. Here are key factors to consider as you develop curriculum that aligns assessment with instruction:

- Focus assessment on what students can do in the language (not just what they know).
- Performance tasks should be based upon real-world, authentic activities.
- Consider the principles of backward design to align assessment with instruction: determine outcomes, decide upon the evidence of transfer (performance tasks), and then create the learning activities.
- Give students multiple opportunities to show what they can do with the language that take into consideration cultures, learning styles, languages, and individual abilities.
- Use rubrics to evaluate performance tasks. This tool measures specific criteria against a defined scale. Provide the rubric to students in advance of the performance task.
- Provide students with anchors, or representative samples, of the performance task so that they can better understand the desired outcomes.
- Utilize both formative and summative assessments to provide ongoing feedback to students.
- Provide opportunities for students to self-evaluate and reflect upon their learning and progress.
- Provide an opportunity for students to create a portfolio of representative work. This could be in a physical or online location. With a portfolio, students can see progress throughout the year. If your school allows, you might save students' portfolios across the years of language study as well.

Purposes of Assessment

The following chart outlines the various purposes for assessment:

Purposes of Assessment	
Entry-level assessment	• Analyzes students' ability to communicate as a basis for placing students at an appropriate level in an established world languages program
Formative assessment	• Provides real-time feedback during the instructional process • Can take many different forms in the classroom • Helps the teacher and student determine the next steps to further learning • Takes place prior to the summative assessment
Summative assessment	• Documents and evaluates students' learning or success at a point in time such as the end of a unit, chapter, or course of study

Forms of Assessment

Achievement tests determine what students know by evaluating them on specific, previously learned material, such as the names of items of clothing or the conjugation of *-ar* verbs. Students are tested on discrete bits of information. Achievement tests are used to measure the incremental steps involved in learning a second language—for example, to cover what was taught in a specific chapter. Achievement may be quizzed or tested with some frequency as proof of regular progress for both student and teacher.

Performance-based assessment measures what students can do with this knowledge and how well they can perform in the language. These tests do not involve testing specific items; rather they are performance-based, checking how well students integrate what they have learned. Their characteristic open-endedness permits students to use what they know to receive or communicate a message, since the emphasis is on communication needs. Performance-based assessment addresses this question: How well and at what level can the student use the language to receive and express meaningful communication?

▼ Performance-based presentational speaking task in *Auténtico 1 Capítulo 3A*

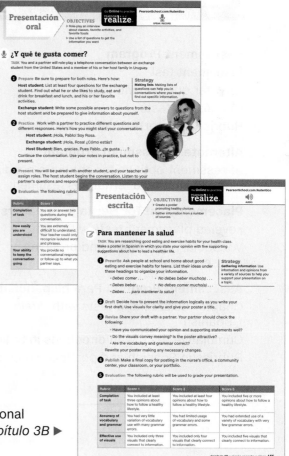

Performance-based presentational writing task in *Auténtico 1 Capítulo 3B* ▶

Assessment

Assess Standards and Demonstrate Understanding

Auténtico is fully aligned to the ACTFL World-Readiness Standards for Learning Languages. The standards are organized around five goal areas: Communication, Culture, Connections, Comparisons, and Communities. The three modes of communication (Interpersonal, Interpretive, and Presentational), encompass a number of skills, including reading, writing, speaking, and listening. These skills are best practiced through authentic situations and through working with materials from a variety of authentic sources.

Auténtico has been carefully written to provide activities that develop and assess communication at levels appropriate to the students' proficiency. The last page in each chapter of Levels 1–3, called *Preparación para el examen,* provides an overview of the chapter outcomes and performance tasks organized around the interpretive, interpersonal, and presentational modes of communication. Numerous online activities on **Realize** provide opportunities for formative and summative assessment of all three modes of communication.

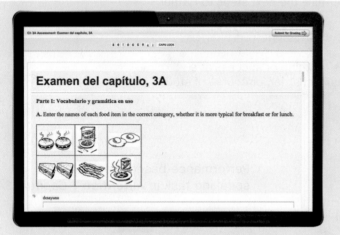

PEARSON realize™

Assessment Resources on Realize

Auténtico offers a wide range of assessment resources for teachers and students on **Realize.** Or create your own test using the **Exam***View*® Test Bank CD-ROM.

Assessment Program
Placement test
Chapter quizzes and tests
Cumulative tests
Rubrics and portfolio support

Alternate Assessment Program
Assessment options for students needing extra help and alternate assessment

Placement Test for Heritage Speakers
Leveled placement tests with audio
Vocabulary, grammar, and proficiency assessment

Assessment Program Para hispanohablantes
Chapter quizzes and tests with direction in Spanish
Cumulative tests with directions in Spanish
Rubrics in Spanish and portfolio support

🎤 SPEAK / RECORD
Use the Speak and Record feature on Realize to evaluate your students' interpersonal and presentation skills.

🎮 GAMES
Who says learning can't be fun? Each chapter of *Auténtico* offers a variety of games on Realize that help students monitor their learning.

📱 INTERACTIVE WHITEBOARD
Get your students talking using the *¡Cuéntame!* and *Encuesta* Interactive Whiteboard Activities.

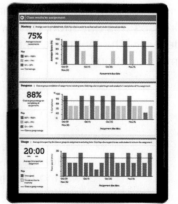

◀ **Mastery Reports**
Grading and reporting data is available for individual students and classroom instruction. Real-time data helps provide remediation and ensures student mastery and understanding of the standards.

Assessment Resources in AUTÉNTICO

Assessment Resources	Self-Evaluation	Formative	Summative: Achievement	Summative: Performance
Student Edition				
Actividades (various)		✖		✖
Presentación oral				✖
Presentación escrita				✖
Preparación para el examen				✖
Print and Digital Resources				
Literacy Skills Workbook Two to three thematically linked readings per *Tema*				✖
Examview® Computer Test Generator Test Banks			✖	
PEARSON realize™				
Placement Tests				✖
Actividades with Speak and Record	✖	✖		✖
Presentación oral				✖
Communicative Pair Activities		✖		
Instant Checks	✖	✖		
Situation Cards				✖
Interactive Whiteboard Activities		✖		✖
Chapter Quizzes	✖	✖		
Practice Tests				✖
Chapter Tests with Speak and Record			✖	✖
Integrated Performance Assessments with Speak and Record				✖
Cumulative Tests			✖	✖
Rubrics				✖
Chapter Checklist and Self-Assessment worksheet	✖			
Pre-AP® Activities				✖
Mobile Apps				
Auténtico eText		✖		✖
Vocabulary App	✖	✖		

Differentiated Instruction

Topics Covered

- Success in Teaching All Students
- Effective Instructional Strategies
- Teaching Today's Students
- Teaching Spanish to Students with Learning Disabilities
- Accommodating Instruction
- Accommodations for Students with Special Needs
- Accommodation in **AUTÉNTICO**
- Heritage Speakers

  Teaching Heritage Speakers

  Teaching Heritage Speakers with *Para hispanohablantes*

  Teaching Heritage Speakers with **AUTÉNTICO A**
- Teaching All Students: Summary

All students are capable of and can benefit from learning a second language. However, today's students bring into the classroom a wide range of needs, interests, motivations, home languages, and literacy levels. This diversity presents heightened challenges to both curriculum and instruction. It should be clearly acknowledged that individual needs of some students require additional specialized support. However, the goal of a comprehensive program remains the provision of teaching all students to develop proficiency in Spanish. All students should have access to a communicative and culturally rich program in addition to whatever specialized intervention may be required. *Auténtico* has been developed especially to meet the diverse needs of students in Spanish classrooms.

Success in Teaching All Students

All students are able to access learning when teachers provide curriculum and instruction in ways that allow all learners in the classroom to participate and achieve the instructional and behavioral goals of general education, as well as those of the core curriculum. Success is achieved in classrooms that consistently and systematically integrate instructional strategies that are responsive to the needs of all learners with a special focus on students that need extra help—students with learning difficulties, heritage speakers, and students who are eligible for and receiving special education services.

Effective Instructional Strategies

Here are general strategies that deliver effective instruction for all learners in the Spanish classroom.

- **Clarify the objectives for a chapter.** Students need to understand the outcomes for which they will be assessed.

- **Provide "thinking time" before students have to talk.** You may want to ask a question and then count to 10 before expecting a response. If a student is struggling, state that you want him/her to think about it, and indicate that you'll be back for the response in a minute. Move on to another student, and then return to the student for his/her response.

- **Write all assignments on the board.** Assignments given both verbally and visually are clearer to all students.

- **Use visuals throughout the lesson.** Present vocabulary visually. Use charts to present grammar. Use video that provides visual support (such as vocabulary words highlighted on the screen) and grammar videos that visualize grammar patterns. Use graphic organizers whenever possible. Connect communicative tasks to photos, art, and realia.

- **Assist in time management.** When requiring students to complete projects or long-term assignments, provide a calendar that breaks down requirements by due dates. Many students experience significant difficulties in self-managing the time needed to complete complex projects.

- **Build in opportunities for reteaching and practicing vocabulary words and grammar.** Students need many opportunities to learn new concepts and need to practice in a variety of formats.

- **Build vocabulary skills by teaching the patterns of language.** Teach the meaning of prefixes, suffixes, and the role of cognates. Point out connections between English, Spanish, and Latin.

- **Work with students based on their strengths rather than their weaknesses.** Allow students to experience success by using their strengths while working on areas of weakness.

- **Consider alternative means for demonstrating understanding.** Think beyond the common modes of reading and writing. Students could present information orally, create a poster or visual representation of work, record their ideas on an audio file, or act out their understanding.

- **Have students begin all work in class.** Prior to class dismissal, check to ensure that each student has a good start and understands what is expected.

- **Assign work on Realize or create a class Web page.** Homework assignments could be posted and easily accessed by parents and students outside of school hours.

Teaching Today's Students

The strategies presented on these pages provide an overview of instructional strategies that are effective with all learners. Today's students need instruction that enables them to see how learning is relevant, that helps them organize their time and learning, that provides focus on what is important (either within instructional materials or with classroom activities), that provides multiple opportunities to learn utilizing different modalities, and that assures students know what is expected of them whether in the classroom or for homework.

> " All students are **capable** of and can **benefit** from learning a second language. "

Differentiated Instruction

Teaching Spanish to Students with Learning Disabilities

There are many reasons why students may experience difficulties in learning a second language. In general, these difficulties may be characterized by the inability to spell or read well, problems with auditory discrimination and in understanding auditory input, and difficulty with abstract thinking. Research by Ganchow and Sparks (1991) indicates that difficulties with one's first language are a major factor in foreign language learning difficulties.

It is not always evident which students will experience difficulties with learning a second language. Many times these students are bright and outgoing. They may have experienced reading or spelling problems in elementary school, but they have learned to compensate over time. Ask students what problems they may have experienced with their first language, especially in the areas of reading and dictation.

Accommodating Instruction

Students with learning disabilities can develop a level of proficiency in a second language with some modifications to instruction and testing. These learners benefit from a highly structured approach that teaches new content in context and in incremental amounts. Teach, practice, and assess using multi-sensory strategies. Many students benefit when instruction combines seeing, hearing, saying, and writing. For example, a teacher would first show a visual of a word and say it aloud. This is followed by using the new word in context. The teacher then writes the word on the board. Students would say the word aloud with the teacher. They then write it down and say it aloud again. In subsequent days, many students benefit from frequent reviews of learned auditory materials.

Accommodations for Students with Special Needs

Here are suggestions for instruction for students with special needs. For additional support, see the *Auténtico* Alternate Assessment Program.

Hearing impairments

- Help students comprehend oral information or instructions. Provide written directions/materials and/or visual cues to support what is presented orally. Face the students when speaking, repeat as needed, and speak clearly. Seat these students in the front of the classroom. Provide outlines of lectures or oral presentations. Have another student take notes and make copies of notes available to all students. Use the audio and video scripts on **Realize.** Turn the close-caption feature on.

- Allow students to refer to their textbooks or to other written materials during oral presentations.

- Limit background noises that may distract students. Avoid seating these students where they may hear extraneous noise.

- Change listening activities and assessments to reading/writing activities. In activities that require aural/oral skills, let students demonstrate skills through alternative responses such as writing.

- Provide access to the audio and video materials on **Realize.** The eText provides pronunciation support, access to all Student Edition listening activities, and access to the vocabulary and grammar videos.

Visual perception problems

- Help students access information provided visually. Allow for preferred seating in the front of the class, including providing space for a guide dog, if necessary. Avoid seating students where they will be distracted by extraneous auditory or visual stimuli. Give students additional time to review visual input prior to an oral or written task. Highlight important information by providing key words, visuals, and simple outlines.

- Provide support for accessing printed information. Make sure the print is easy to read. The readings should be designed to maximize readability: easy-to-read font, layout, and design. Teach reading strategies that highlight the visual aspects of a selection: text organization, use of visuals, titles and headers, and the use of color. Provide copies of reading selections with additional support: underline key words/sentences/concepts or magnify the text in duplication.

- Teach, practice, and assess using multi-sensory strategies.

ADHD/ADD

- Provide additional support that enables students to focus. Present information in small "chunks." This includes new content, short instructions or directions, and shorter assignments, or break assignments into steps. Limit extraneous auditory and visual stimulation. Provide visual and written support for aural instructions or input. Repeat and explain (again) as needed. Provide outlines of oral presentations. Support readings with strategies similar to those for students with visual perception problems. Use graphic organizers.

- Verify that students "got it." Check that students are looking at you (eye contact) when providing oral instructions. Ask students to repeat what you just told them. Move closer to students to increase attention. Provide preferential seating that allows you to monitor students' focus and attention. Allow extra wait time when students are responding.

- Provide a variety of different learning activities that reach different learning styles. This will also allow for frequent changes of activities within a class. Provide for hands-on activities, vocabulary clip art, and grammar manipulatives.

- Use technology to provide interactive learning. These students will benefit from using the online resources on **Realize.**

- Be predictable. Establish a daily routine for managing the classroom and be consistent. Avoid surprises with these students.

- Help students organize themselves and their learning. Ask students to maintain notebooks that are organized by dividers. Provide study guides, summary sheets, and organizers for daily or weekly assignments.

Accommodation in *Auténtico*

Auténtico A provides a wide range of support for accommodating instruction.

STUDENT EDITION

Clean design and layout of pages

Visualized presentation of vocabulary

Step-by-step scaffolding of activities

Online vocabulary and grammar tutorials and extra practice available on **Realize**

TEACHER'S EDITION

Differentiated Instruction article

Differentiated Instruction suggestions

LEVELED VOCABULARY AND GRAMMAR WORKBOOK: GUIDED PRACTICE

Vocabulary clip art to create flashcards

Focused vocabulary practice

Simplified grammar instruction

Answer Key in Teacher's Resource Materials on **Realize**

ALTERNATE ASSESSMENT PROGRAM ON **REALIZE** AND TESTNAV

Additional suggestions for accommodating assessment for students needing extra help

Differentiated Instruction

Heritage Speakers

Teaching Heritage Speakers

A diverse background Those who have a home language other than English bring a wider range of language abilities to the classroom. These abilities range from minimal functioning in the language to complete fluency and literacy. It is important for teachers to assess the language skills of the different heritage speakers in the classroom. This diversity includes:

- Students who are able to understand the spoken language, but are unable to respond in the language beyond single-word answers.

- Students who are able to understand the language and communicate at a minimal level. These students may be able to read some items, but because of their limited vocabulary, they may not comprehend much information. They may write what they are able to sound out, but errors are evident.

- Students who can speak the language fluently but who have little to no experience with the language in its written form.

- Students who have come to the United States from non-English-speaking countries. They can understand and speak the language fluently; however, their reading and writing skills may be limited due to lack of a formal education in their country of origin.

- Fluent bilingual students who can understand, speak, read, and write another language very well and have possibly received formal instruction in that language in the United States or in another country.

Program goals Heritage speakers bring rich home language experiences to the classroom that can serve as a foundation for learning. Because of their language background, these students have the potential to be bilingual, biliterate, and bicultural. Heritage speakers need to be exposed to a program that can improve and maintain the home language. Students need to study the grammar and focus on vocabulary development. Emphasis should be placed on building reading and writing skills. It is important that students develop a sensitivity to when standard and non-standard language should be employed and comfortably adjust their language accordingly. In addition, students should be exposed to the diverse cultures within the Spanish-speaking community while developing a sense of pride in their own heritage. Heritage speakers need to reach a high level of proficiency and accuracy that will ensure success at the advanced level of language study and testing. These students should also be ready to transition into a focused study of Spanish in specific professional areas.

Focus on individual needs Due to their diverse backgrounds, heritage speakers differ greatly in language skills and may need individualized instruction. In many of today's classrooms, teachers encounter classes that contain a mixture of beginning-level students and heritage speakers. These groups need different materials, different instructional approaches, and different objectives. Here are several strategies that may be helpful for heritage speakers:

- Build upon their background knowledge. Develop instructional units around themes and topics that relate to their life experiences. Encourage students to use these experiences as the foundation for building language skills through vocabulary development, reading, and writing.

- Help students connect aural with written language. If students don't understand a word in a reading, have them read it aloud or ask a friend or teacher to read it aloud. Often they can recognize the word once they hear it. Allow for opportunities for students to follow along as a story is read aloud.

- Use strategies that are effective in a language arts classroom, such as building schema, teaching language-learning strategies, using graphic organizers, and incorporating pre- and post-reading tasks. Use the writing process to develop good writers.

- Encourage students to begin communicating, especially in writing. Have them write down their thoughts in the way they sound to them. Then have students work with the teacher or another student for corrections. Students can also look through textbooks and dictionaries to assist with error correction.

- Maintain high standards. Require students to focus on accuracy and proficient communication. Many heritage speakers experience frustration with reading and writing in the home language when they have good aural/oral skills. Building language skills takes time.

Teaching Heritage Speakers with *Auténtico A*

Auténtico A offers the ideal solution for heritage speakers who begin Spanish instruction with a first-year textbook. It is recommended that teachers use ***Auténtico A,*** Para hispanohablantes, with these students. This gives teachers three options: (1) the student textbook with English support; (2) the companion all-Spanish worktext on Realize; or (3) a combination of both.

Teaching All Students: Summary

The diverse needs of today's Spanish students pose a challenge to teachers, curriculum developers, and school administrators as they design programs to ensure that all students develop language proficiency. With ***Auténtico,*** teachers have at their disposal a variety of materials and strategies to enable them to provide access to Spanish for all learners. Clearly, some students will require additional tutoring and specialized services to reach their full learning potential. However, the activities and materials that accompany ***Auténtico,*** coupled with instructional strategies described within this article, constitute a viable framework for reaching and teaching all learners.

Teaching Heritage Speakers with *Para hispanohablantes*

Auténtico A provides extensive support for teaching heritage speakers.

STUDENT EDITION

Focused vocabulary and grammar

Integrated language and culture

Extensive reading and writing

PARA HISPANOHABLANTES ON **REALIZE**

All-Spanish companion worktext available as downloadable PDFs

All-Spanish grammar explanations

Companion PDFs for each section of Student Edition

Increased emphasis on reading and writing

Accompanying Teacher's Guide on Realize

ASSESSMENT PROGRAM: *PARA HISPANOHABLANTES* ON **REALIZE**

Direction lines in Spanish

Complete assessment support

Rubrics in Spanish

PLACEMENT TEST ON **REALIZE**

Leveled Placement Test with audio

Vocabulary, grammar, and proficiency assessment

Index of Cultural References

Cancha maya en Chichén Itzá

Index of Cultural References

Index of Cultural References

Index of Cultural References

La Catedral de Sevilla, España

Index of Cultural References

Una calle de Antigua

Auténtico

Boston, Massachusetts   Chandler, Arizona
Glenview, Illinois   New York, New York

Front cover: Margarita Island, Venezuela

Pearson, 330 Hudson Street, New York, NY 10013.

ISBN-13:   978-0-328-93440-9
ISBN-10:   0-328-93440-2

1 2 3 4 5 6 7 8 9 10   V082   20 19 18 17 16

A

Auténtico

Go **Online** to practice

PEARSON
realize™

PearsonSchool.com/Autentico

AUDIO VIDEO WRITING SPEAK/RECORD MAPA GLOBAL AUTÉNTICO FLASCHARDS ETEXT 2.0 GAMES

Peggy Palo Boyles
OKLAHOMA CITY, OK

Myriam Met
EDGEWATER, MD

Richard S. Sayers
LONGMONT, CO

Pearson

Auténtico Authors

Peggy Palo Boyles

During her foreign language career of over forty years, Peggy Palo Boyles has taught elementary, secondary, and university students in both private and public schools. She is currently an independent consultant who provides assistance to schools, districts, universities, state departments of education, and other organizations of foreign language education in the areas of curriculum, assessment, cultural instruction, professional development, and program evaluation. She was a member of the ACTFL Performance Guidelines for the K–12 Learners task force and served as a Senior Editor for the project. She served on the Advisory Committee for the ACTFL Assessment for Performance and Proficiency of Languages (AAPPL). Peggy is a Past-President of the National Association of District Supervisors of Foreign Language (NADSFL) and was a recipient of ACTFL's K–12 Steiner Award for Leadership in K–12 Foreign Language Education.

Myriam Met

For most of her professional life, Myriam (Mimi) Met has worked in the public schools, first as a high school teacher in New York, then as K–12 supervisor of language programs in the Cincinnati Public Schools, and finally as a Coordinator of Foreign Language in Montgomery County (MD) Public Schools. After a long career in the public schools, she joined the National Foreign Language Center, University of Maryland, where she worked on K–12 language policy and infrastructure development. She currently works with schools and school districts as an independent consultant.

Richard S. Sayers

Rich Sayers has been involved in world languages education since 1978. He taught Spanish at Niwot High School in Longmont, CO for 18 years, where he taught levels 1 through AP Spanish. While at Niwot High School, Rich served as department chair, district foreign language coordinator, and board member of the Colorado Congress of Foreign Language Teachers and the Southwest Conference on Language Teaching. In 1991, Rich was selected as one of the Disney Company's Foreign Language Teacher Honorees for the American Teacher Awards. Rich has served as a world languages consultant for Pearson since 1996. He is currently the Vice President of Humanities in Pearson's Sales division.

Carol Eubanks Wargin taught Spanish for 20 years. She also shared her knowledge and experiences with other Spanish teachers through publications and award-winning presentations. The *Auténtico* author team is grateful for Carol's contribution to the instructional foundation on which this program was built.

Contributing Writers

Eduardo Aparicio
Chicago, IL

Daniel J. Bender
New Trier High School, Winnetka, IL

Marie Deer
Bloomington, IN

Leslie M. Grahn
Howard County Public Schools, Ellicott City, MD

Thomasina Hannum
Albuquerque, NM

Nancy S. Hernández
World Languages Supervisor, Simsbury (CT) Public Schools

Patricia J. Kule
Fountain Valley School of Colorado, Colorado Springs, CO

Jacqueline Hall Minet
Upper Montclair, NJ

Alex Paredes
Simi Valley, CA

Martha Singer Semmer
Breckenridge, CO

Dee Dee Drisdale Stafford
Putnam City Schools, Oklahoma City, OK

Christine S. Wells
Cheyenne Mountain Junior High School, Colorado Springs, CO

Michael Werner
University of Chicago, Chicago, IL

Digital Course on Realize

AUTÉNTICO includes lots of online resources to help you learn Spanish! You'll find these resources highlighted with technology icons on the pages of your print or online Student Edition.

PEARSON
realize™

The digital course on Realize!

The program's digital course on Realize puts the Student Edition, workbooks, video, audio, flashcards, games, and more at your fingertips.

Look for these icons in your *Auténtico* textbook or digital course.

🔊 AUDIO
Audio to learn and practice vocabulary and pronunciation, and increase your listening skills

▶ VIDEO
Videocultura Cultural overviews of each theme

Videohistoria Vocabulary videos with an entertaining storyline to practice listening to new words in an authentic context

GramActiva Grammar explanations that present new concepts with humorous examples

Grammar Tutorials Clear explanations of grammar with comparisons to English

Animated Verbs Animations that highlight verb conjugations

✏ WRITING
Practice activities with writing

🎤 SPEAK/RECORD
Speak-and-record tool for speaking activities, you can save your recording

🌐 MAPA GLOBAL INTERACTIVO
Links to interactive maps for virtual exploration of the Spanish-speaking world. You can download .kmz files from PearsonSchool.com/Autentico and link to sites using Google Earth™ or other geographic information systems.

📁 AUTÉNTICO
Collection of authentic video, audio, and text resources organized by theme

🗐 FLASHCARDS
Practice for the new vocabulary

📖 ETEXT 2.0
Complete textbook online

🎮 GAMES
Interactive, fun practice and review games such as concentration, crosswords, word search and more

📄 PDF
Video scripts, readings

📚 WORKBOOK
Core and Guided practice activities

Learn Spanish Using Authentic Resources

To become proficient in Spanish, you need to learn to understand and speak it in real-world situations. In *Auténtico*, you will learn about the language and cultures of Spanish-speaking countries as you watch, read, and listen to material created for Spanish speakers.

The **Auténtico** pages in your textbook feature strategies that will help you build your language skills and increase your confidence as you watch videos, listen to audio, and read authentic articles and blogs. ▼

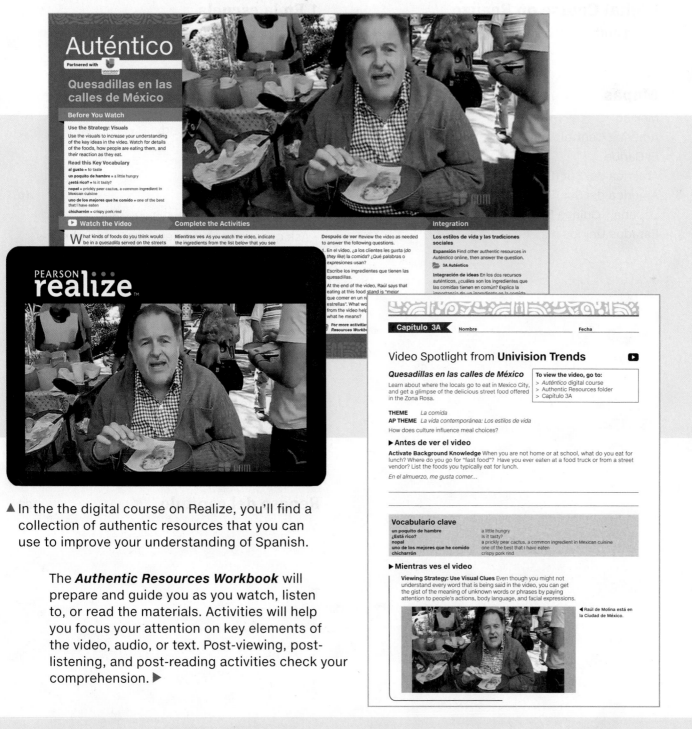

▲ In the the digital course on Realize, you'll find a collection of authentic resources that you can use to improve your understanding of Spanish.

The **Authentic Resources Workbook** will prepare and guide you as you watch, listen to, or read the materials. Activities will help you focus your attention on key elements of the video, audio, or text. Post-viewing, post-listening, and post-reading activities check your comprehension. ▶

Tabla de materias

México

ESTADOS UNIDOS

Tijuana

Ciudad Juárez

30° N

Río Bravo del Norte

Baja California

Golfo de California (Mar de Cortés)

SIERRA MADRE OCCIDENTAL

Chihuahua

Nuevo Laredo

Río Grande

SIERRA MADRE ORIENTAL

Monterrey

Golfo de México

Trópico de Cáncer

LEYENDA
Elevación

Metros	Pies
3,000	9,840
2,000	6,560
1,000	3,280
500	1,640
200	656

Frontera nacional
⯂ Capital
● Ciudad
▲ Volcán o montaña

0   200 Millas
0   200 Kilómetros

Proyección cónica conforme de Lambert

Guadalajara

Querétaro

Mérida

Península de Yucatán

20° N

Paracutín ▲

Ciudad de México ⯂ Iztaccíhuatl
▲ Puebla
Popocatépetl

Veracruz

Oaxaca

ISTMO DE TEHUANTEPEC

BELICE

SIERRA MADRE DEL SUR

Acapulco

GUATEMALA

EL SALVADOR

OCÉANO PACÍFICO

N
O   E
S

Baile en el día de la Guelaguetza
en Oaxaca, México

México

Capital México, D.F.

Population 121.7 million

Area 758,449 sq mi / 1,964,375 sq km

Languages Spanish (official), Nahuatl, various Mayan and other indigenous languages

Religions Roman Catholic, Protestant

Government federal republic

Currency *peso mexicano*

Exports manufactured products, oil and oil products, silver, coffee, cotton, fruit, vegetables

América Central

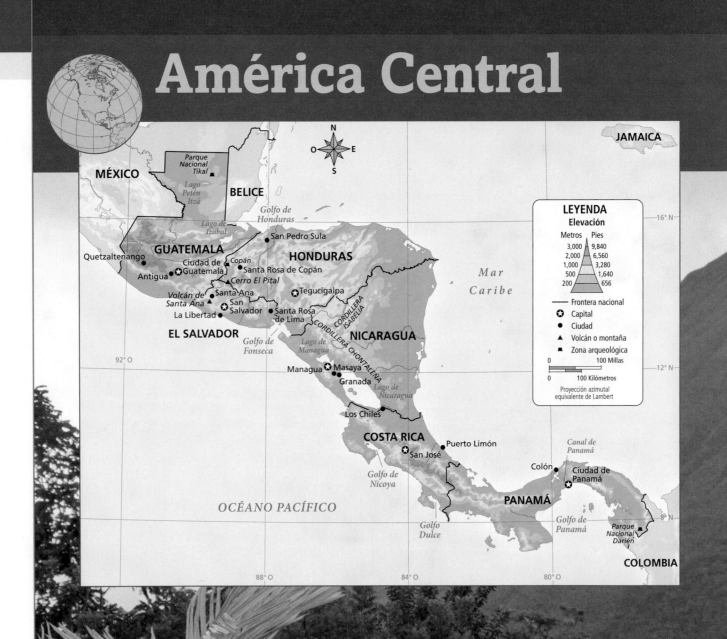

MÉXICO

GUATEMALA

Parque Nacional Tikal

Lago Petén Itzá

BELICE

Quetzaltenango

Ciudad de Guatemala

Antigua

Copán

Santa Rosa de Copán

Cerro El Pital

Volcán de Santa Ana

Santa Ana

La Libertad

San Salvador

EL SALVADOR

Golfo de Fonseca

Golfo de Honduras

San Pedro Sula

HONDURAS

Tegucigalpa

CORDILLERA ISABELIA

Santa Rosa de Lima

Lago de Managua

Lago de Izabal

JAMAICA

Mar Caribe

NICARAGUA

CORDILLERA CHONTALEÑA

Managua Masaya

Granada

Lago de Nicaragua

Los Chiles

COSTA RICA

San José

Puerto Limón

Golfo de Nicoya

OCÉANO PACÍFICO

Golfo Dulce

PANAMÁ

Canal de Panamá

Colón

Ciudad de Panamá

Golfo de Panamá

Parque Nacional Darién

COLOMBIA

LEYENDA
Elevación

Metros	Pies
3,000	9,840
2,000	6,560
1,000	3,280
500	1,640
200	656

Frontera nacional

✪ Capital

● Ciudad

▲ Volcán o montaña

■ Zona arqueológica

0   100 Millas

0   100 Kilómetros

Proyección azimutal equivalente de Lambert

16° N

92° O

12° N

88° O   84° O   80° O

8° N

Guatemala

Capital Ciudad de Guatemala

Population 14.9 million

Area 42,042 sq mi / 108,889 sq km

Languages Spanish (official), Quiche, Cakchiquel, Kekchi, Mam, Garifuna, Xinca, and other indigenous languages

Religions Roman Catholic, Protestant, traditional Mayan beliefs

Government constitutional democratic republic

Currency *quetzal*, U.S. dollar *(dólar)*

Exports coffee, sugar, petroleum, clothing, textiles, bananas, vegetables

El Salvador

Capital San Salvador

Population 6.1 million

Area 8,124 sq mi / 21,041 sq km

Languages Spanish (official), Nahua

Religions Roman Catholic, Protestant

Government republic

Currency U.S. dollar *(dólar)*

Exports offshore assembly parts, coffee, sugar, textiles, chemicals, electricity

Honduras

Capital Tegucigalpa

Population 8.7 million

Area 43,278 sq mi / 112,090 sq km

Languages Spanish (official), indigenous languages

Religions Roman Catholic, Protestant

Government democratic constitutional republic

Currency *lempira*

Exports coffee, bananas, shrimp, lobster, clothing, gold, wood

El volcán Arenal,
Costa Rica

Nicaragua

Capital Managua

Population 5.9 million

Area 50,336 sq mi / 130,370 sq km

Languages Spanish (official), English, Miskito, other indigenous languages

Religions Roman Catholic, Protestant

Government republic

Currency *córdoba*

Exports coffee, shrimp, lobster, cotton, tobacco, meat, sugar, gold

Costa Rica

Capital San José

Population 4.8 million

Area 19,730 sq mi / 51,100 sq km

Languages Spanish (official), English

Religions Roman Catholic, Protestant

Government democratic republic

Currency *colón*

Exports coffee, bananas, sugar, textiles, pineapple, electronic components

Panamá

Capital Ciudad de Panamá

Population 3.7 million

Area 29,120 sq mi / 75,420 sq km

Languages Spanish (official), other indigenous languages

Religions Roman Catholic, Protestant

Government constitutional democracy

Currency *balboa*, U.S. dollar *(dólar)*

Exports fruit, dried fruit, fish, iron, steel, wood

El Caribe

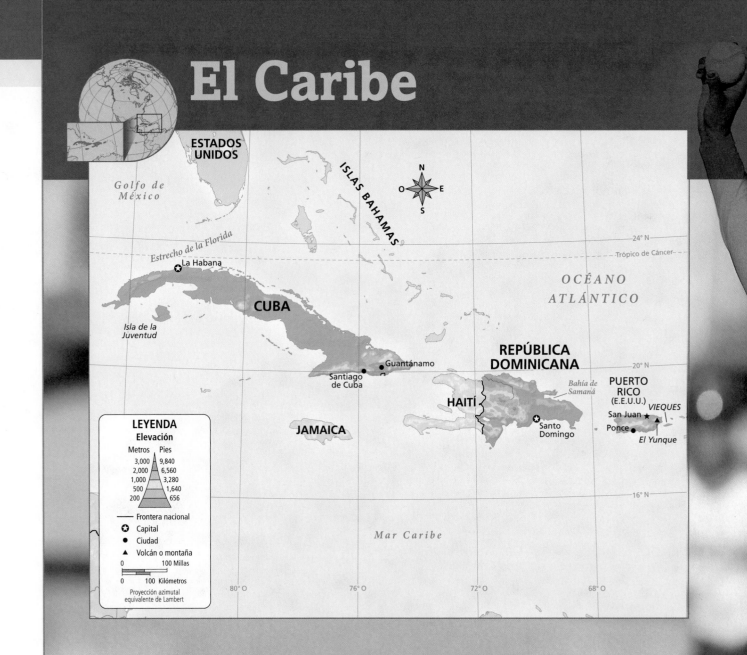

ESTADOS UNIDOS

Golfo de México

ISLAS BAHAMAS

Estrecho de la Florida

Trópico de Cáncer

24° N

La Habana

OCÉANO ATLÁNTICO

CUBA

Isla de la Juventud

Guantánamo

Santiago de Cuba

REPÚBLICA DOMINICANA

20° N

Bahía de Samaná

PUERTO RICO (E.E.U.U.)

VIEQUES

San Juan

HAITÍ

Ponce

JAMAICA

Santo Domingo

El Yunque

LEYENDA
Elevación

Metros	Pies
3,000	9,840
2,000	6,560
1,000	3,280
500	1,640
200	656

— Frontera nacional

✪ Capital

● Ciudad

▲ Volcán o montaña

0   100 Millas

0   100 Kilómetros

Proyección azimutal equivalente de Lambert

16° N

Mar Caribe

80° O   76° O   72° O   68° O

Cuba

Capital La Habana

Population 11 million

Area 42,803 sq mi / 110,860 sq km

Languages Spanish (official)

Religions Roman Catholic, Protestant, and other religions

Government Communist state

Currency *peso cubano*

Exports sugar, nickel, tobacco, shellfish, medical products, citrus, coffee

República Dominicana

Capital Santo Domingo

Population 10.5 million

Area 18,792 sq mi / 48,670 sq km

Languages Spanish (official)

Religions Roman Catholic, Protestant

Government democratic republic

Currency *peso dominicano*

Exports sugar, gold, silver, cocoa, tobacco, meat

Puerto Rico

Capital San Juan

Population 3.6 million

Area 5,325 sq mi / 13,791 sq km

Languages Spanish and English (both official)

Religions Roman Catholic, Protestant

Government commonwealth of the United States

Currency U.S. dollar

Exports chemicals, electronics, apparel, canned tuna, beverage concentrates, medical equipment

Go **Online** to practice
PEARSON
realize™
PearsonSchool.com/Autentico
MAPA GLOBAL

El equipo de béisbol de Cuba jugando un partido

América del Sur (PARTE NORTE)

Mar Caribe

Cartagena
Maracaibo
Caracas
Río Orinoco

VENEZUELA

Medellín
Río Magdalena

Cali
Bogotá

COLOMBIA

ECUADOR

Ecuador
Quito
Chimborazo
Guayaquil

Ecuador

0°

ISLAS
GALÁPAGOS
(Ecuador)

Golfo de
Guayaquil

PERÚ

BRASIL

Huascarán

Machu
Picchu

Callao
Cuzco
Lima

CORDILLERA DE LOS ANDES

BOLIVIA

La Paz
Cochabamba

Lago
Titicaca

ALTIPLANO

Sucre

Nevado
Sajama

Potosí

20° S

**OCÉANO
PACÍFICO**

PARAGUAY

Trópico de Capricornio

LEYENDA
Elevación

Metros	Pies
3,000	9,840
2,000	6,560
1,000	3,280
500	1,640
200	656

— Frontera nacional
✪ Capital
● Ciudad
▲ Volcán o montaña
▬ Zona arqueológica

0   400 Millas

0   400 Kilómetros

Proyección azimutal
equivalente de Lambert

CHILE

ARGENTINA

URUGUAY

N
O   E
S

**OCÉANO
ATLÁNTICO**

40° S

Colombia

Capital Bogotá

Population 44.7 million

Area 439,736 sq mi / 1,138,910 sq km

Languages Spanish (official)

Religion Roman Catholic

Government republic

Currency *peso colombiano*

Exports textiles, petroleum, coal, coffee, gold, emeralds, bananas, flowers, pharmaceuticals, sugar

Ecuador

Capital Quito

Population 15.9 million

Area 109,483 sq mi / 283,561 sq km

Languages Spanish (official), Quechua, other indigenous languages

Religion Roman Catholic protestant, and other religions

Government republic

Currency U.S. dollar (*dólar*)

Exports oil, bananas, flowers, shrimp, cocoa, coffee, wood

Una joven aymara
en Bolivia

Perú

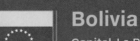

Capital Lima
Population 30.4 million
Area 496,225 sq mi / 1,285,216 sq km
Languages Spanish (official), Quechua (official), protestant and other indigenous languages
Religion Roman Catholic and other religions
Government constitutional republic
Currency *nuevo sol*
Exports gold, zinc, copper, fish and fish products, textiles

Venezuela

Capital Caracas
Population 27.6 million
Area 352,144 sq mi / 912,050 sq km
Languages Spanish (official), various indigenous languages
Religions Roman Catholic, Protestant
Government federal republic
Currency *bolívar fuerte*
Exports oil and oil products, aluminum, hydroelectricity

Bolivia

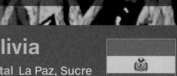

Capital La Paz, Sucre
Population 10.8 million
Area 424,164 sq mi / 1,098,581 sq km
Languages Spanish, Quechua, Aymara, Guaraní, and other indigenous languages
Religions Roman Catholic, Protestant
Government republic
Currency *boliviano*
Exports soy and soy products, natural gas, zinc, wood, tin, gold

América del Sur (PARTE SUR)

Mar Caribe

N O E S

VENEZUELA

COLOMBIA

Ecuador   Ecuador   0°

ECUADOR

PERÚ

BRASIL

OCÉANO
PACÍFICO

BOLIVIA

ALTIPLANO

CORDILLERA DE LOS ANDES

Río Paraguay

GRAN CHACO

PARAGUAY   20° S

Asunción ✪   Cataratas
del Iguazú   Trópico de Capricornio

CHILE

Río Paraná

LEYENDA
Elevación

Metros	Pies
3,000	9,840
2,000	6,560
1,000	3,280
500	1,640
200	656

—— Frontera nacional
✪ Capital
● Ciudad
▲ Volcán o montaña

0 ____ 400 Millas
0 ____ 400 Kilómetros

Proyección azimutal
equivalente de Lambert

ARGENTINA

Viña del Mar ●
Valparaíso ✪ ● Cerro
Santiago   Aconcagua

Rosario ●   URUGUAY

Buenos Aires ✪   Montevideo ✪
● Punta del
Este

PAMPAS   Río de la Plata   OCÉANO
● Mar del Plata   ATLÁNTICO

40° S

PATAGONIA

Cerro de
San Valentín ▲

Torres del ▲
Paine   TIERRA DEL
FUEGO
Estrecho de
Magallanes   ● Cabo de Hornos

Chile

Capital Santiago
Population 17.5 million
Area 291,933 sq mi / 756,102 sq km
Languages Spanish (official), English, and other indigenous languages
Religions Roman Catholic, Protestant
Government republic
Currency peso chileno
Exports copper, fish, fruit, paper and pulp, chemicals

La Casa Rosada en
Buenos Aires, Argentina

Paraguay

Capital Asunción

Population 6.8 million

Area 157,048 sq mi / 406,752 sq km

Languages Spanish and Guaraní (both official)

Religions Roman Catholic, Protestant

Government constitutional republic

Currency *guaraní*

Exports soy, cotton, meat, cooking oil, wood, leather

Argentina

Capital Buenos Aires

Population 43.4 million

Area 1,073,518 sq mi / 2,780,400 sq km

Languages Spanish (official), English, French, Italian, German, and indigenous languages

Religions Roman Catholic, Protestant, Jewish

Government republic

Currency *peso argentino*

Exports soy and soy products, petroleum, gas, motor vehicles, corn, wheat

Uruguay

Capital Montevideo

Population 3.3 million

Area 68,037 sq mi / 176,215 sq km

Languages Spanish (official), Portuñol/Brazilero

Religions Roman Catholic, Protestant, and other religions

Government constitutional republic

Currency *peso uruguayo*

Exports meat, soy, rice, wheat, wood, milk products, wool

España
Guinea Ecuatorial

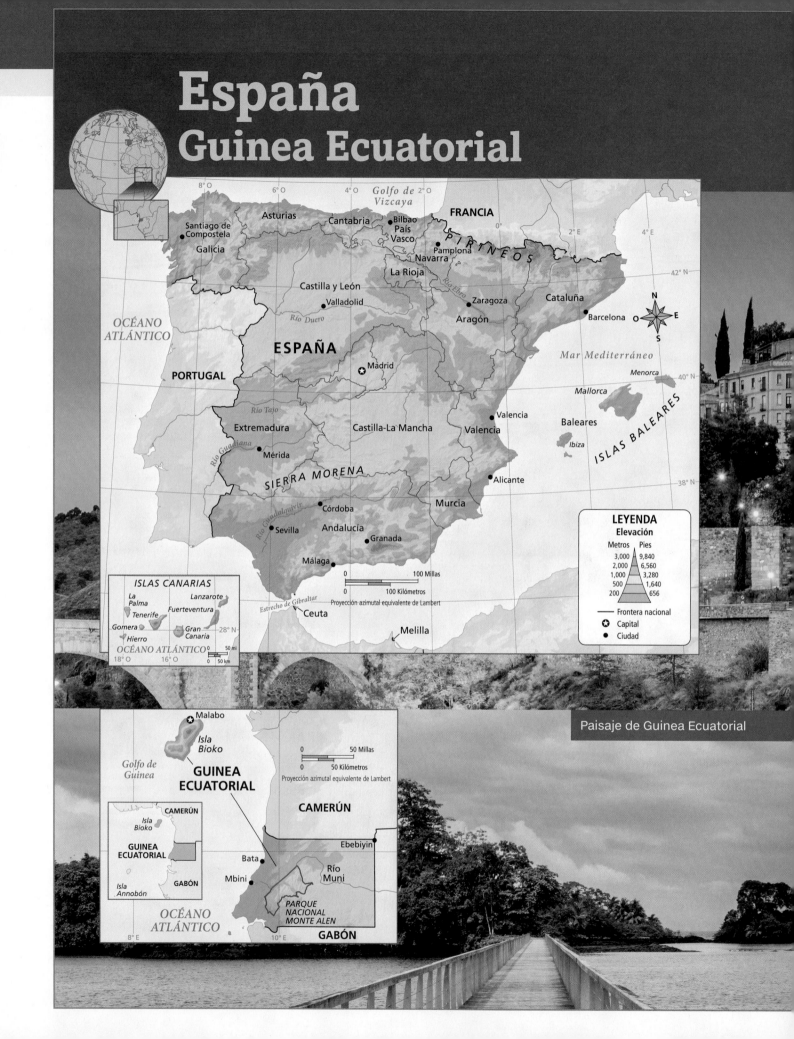

Golfo de Vizcaya

FRANCIA

8° O   6° O   4° O   2° O   0°   2° E   4° E

Asturias
Cantabria
Bilbao
País Vasco
Santiago de Compostela
Galicia
Pamplona
Navarra
La Rioja
PIRINEOS
42° N
Castilla y León
Valladolid
Zaragoza
Cataluña
Aragón
Río Ebro
Río Duero
Barcelona

OCÉANO ATLÁNTICO

N
O   E
S

ESPAÑA
Madrid

Mar Mediterráneo

PORTUGAL
Menorca
40° N
Mallorca
Río Tajo
Valencia
Baleares
Extremadura
Castilla-La Mancha
Valencia
Ibiza
ISLAS BALEARES
Mérida
Río Guadiana

SIERRA MORENA
38° N
Alicante
Córdoba
Murcia
Río Guadalquivir
Sevilla
Andalucía
Granada
Málaga

0   100 Millas
0   100 Kilómetros
Proyección azimutal equivalente de Lambert

LEYENDA
Elevación

Metros	Pies
3,000	9,840
2,000	6,560
1,000	3,280
500	1,640
200	656

Frontera nacional
⊛ Capital
● Ciudad

ISLAS CANARIAS
La Palma
Lanzarote
Tenerife
Fuerteventura
Gomera
Gran Canaria
Hierro
28° N
OCÉANO ATLÁNTICO
18° O   16° O
0   50 mi
0   50 km

Estrecho de Gibraltar
Ceuta
Melilla

Paisaje de Guinea Ecuatorial

Malabo
Isla Bioko
Golfo de Guinea
GUINEA ECUATORIAL
CAMERÚN

0   50 Millas
0   50 Kilómetros
Proyección azimutal equivalente de Lambert

CAMERÚN
Isla Bioko
GUINEA ECUATORIAL
GABÓN
Isla Annobón

Ebebiyin
Bata
Río Muni
Mbini
PARQUE NACIONAL MONTE ALEN

OCÉANO ATLÁNTICO
8° E   10° E   GABÓN

El Alcázar de Toledo, España

España

Capital Madrid

Population 48.1 million

Area 195,124 sq mi / 505,370 sq km

Languages Castilian Spanish (official); Catalan, Galician, Basque (official regionally), and other regional languages

Religion Roman Catholic

Government parliamentary monarchy

Currency *euro*

Exports food, machinery, motor vehicles, pharmaceutical products

Guinea Ecuatorial

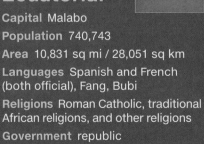

Capital Malabo

Population 740,743

Area 10,831 sq mi / 28,051 sq km

Languages Spanish and French (both official), Fang, Bubi

Religions Roman Catholic, traditional African religions, and other religions

Government republic

Currency *franco CFA*

Exports oil, timber

Estados Unidos

CANADÁ

Seattle

MONTAÑAS ROCOSAS

GRANDES LLANURAS

Grandes Lagos

Minneapolis

Detroit

Boston

Chicago

Cleveland

Nueva York

MONTES APALACHES

Filadelfia

ESTADOS UNIDOS

Washington, D.C.

OCÉANO ATLÁNTICO

San Francisco

Denver

▲ Mt. Elbert

St. Louis

Los Ángeles

San Diego

Phoenix

Atlanta

Dallas

OCÉANO PACÍFICO

Río Grande

Houston

San Antonio

MÉXICO

Golfo de México

Miami

Estrecho de la Florida

Trópico de Cáncer

CUBA

LEYENDA
Elevación

Metros	Pies
3,000	9,840
2,000	6,560
1,000	3,280
500	1,640
200	656

— Frontera nacional
⊗ Capital
● Ciudad
▲ Volcán o montaña

0   400 Millas
0   400 Kilómetros
Proyección cónica conforme de Lambert

ALASKA

CANADÁ

Mt. McKinley ▲

Mar de Bering

Golfo de Alaska

0   300 Millas
0   300 Kilómetros

OCÉANO PACÍFICO

HAWÁI

0   100 Millas
0   100 Kilómetros

N
O   E
S

Riverwalk en
San Antonio, Texas

xxvi

Go **Online** to practice
PearsonSchool.com/Autentico

MAPA GLOBAL

Estados Unidos

Capital Washington, D.C.

Population 321.4 million

Area 3,796,742 sq mi / 9,833,517 sq km

Languages English, Spanish, other Indo-European languages, Asian and Pacific Islander languages, other languages

Religions Protestant, Roman Catholic, Jewish, Muslim, Mormon, and other religions

Government federal republic

Currency U.S. dollar

Exports motor vehicles, aircraft, medicines, telecommunications equipment, electronics, chemicals, soybeans, fruit, corn

1 EN LA ESCUELA

Social interactions; Classroom directions; Numbers and telling time; Parts of the body

Vocabulary: greetings; introductions; leave-takings; numbers; time; body parts

Grammar: lexical use of **estar, ser,** and plural commands

Cultural Focus: appropriate behavior when greeting someone

2 EN LA CLASE

Classroom interactions; Spanish alphabet; The calendar

Vocabulary: classroom; date; asking for help

Grammar: nouns; singular definite articles; **hay; ¿cuántos, -as?**

Cultural Focus: the Aztecs and the Aztec calendar; the Maya and glyphs; holidays

3 EL TIEMPO

The weather; Seasons

Vocabulary: weather and seasons

Grammar: lexical use of **hacer**

Cultural Focus: reversed seasons in the Northern and Southern Hemispheres

Theme Support

Bulletin Boards

Theme: En la escuela

Ask students to cut out, copy, or download pictures of people greeting each other and saying good-bye, teachers interacting with students, and students interacting with each other. Cluster photos according to what the people are doing in each scene: saying hello, saying goodbye, socializing, asking questions, offering assistance, etc.

Hands-on Culture

Recipe: Guacamole

Guacamole is a popular dip from Mexico.

Ingredients:

2 ripe avocados	1 T. of chopped onion
1 small tomato	juice from 1 lemon
1 clove garlic, chopped	2 T. chopped cilantro
	salt

1. Cut the avocados in half, remove the pits, and scoop out the pulp with a spoon.
2. Mash the avocados with a fork.
3. Mix in the garlic, onion, lemon juice, and cilantro.
4. Dice the tomato and fold into mixture.
5. Add salt to taste and serve with tortilla chips.

Game

Número

This game practices numbers and is played like Bingo. Use it toward the end of *En la escuela,* after students have learned numbers 1–100.

Players: entire class

Materials: paper and pens with ink of different colors

Rules:

1. Students each prepare their own **Número** card by folding a sheet of paper to create 36 squares. To do this, students fold the paper in half vertically, then fold it in thirds. They unfold the paper and repeat the process horizontally. When students unfold the paper again, they should have 36 squares.
2. Students write **n-ú-m-e-r-o** in the top six squares. They then fill in the remaining 30 squares with any number from 1–100. The result should look like a Bingo card.
3. Call out a number from 1–100. Note the number you called on a sheet of paper that students can't see. If students have the number on their card, they cross it out. When a player has marked off an entire row of numbers, either vertically, horizontally, or diagonally, he or she calls out **Número,** then reads the numbers aloud in Spanish. If the numbers match the ones you have recorded, that student is the winner. If a number is incorrect, play continues until another student calls out **Número.**
4. Play again, having students use a pen of a different color to cross out numbers.

Variation: Instead of marking off a row, students mark off the four corners, the borders of the square, or the borders of a smaller square within the card.

21st Century Skills

Look for tips throughout *Para empezar* to enrich your teaching by integrating 21st Century Skills. Suggestions for the Project-Based Learning and Theme Culture follow below.

Project-Based Learning

Modify the Theme Project with one or more of these suggestions:

Information Literacy Have students research the climates in the four locations they choose and figure out what season it is in the current month. Their maps and weather reports should reflect those seasons. Have students think about the relationship between month and season in those locations, and compare to their own areas.

ICT Literacy Before students use Web sites to learn more about weather and climates in the Western Hemisphere, have them read the handout "Evaluate Web Sites" to help them analyze online materials. Have students think about possible ways to evaluate the accuracy of information in a Web site, and to observe how the material is presented and organized to convey its message.

Communication Have students working as partners review the four points from the handout "Give an Effective Presentation." Ask them to make sure to include these points in their feedback to their partners as they practice their presentations.

Theme Culture

Social and Cross-Cultural Skills Have students review their answers to the *Cultura* question on page 1, as well as the information about formal and informal greetings in the chapter. Ask them to discuss in small groups what they have learned so far about differences between their own culture and the culture of Spanish-speaking countries in this respect. Have students imagine they have to explain common forms of greeting in their own culture to a student from a Spanish-speaking country.

Project-Based Learning

Pronóstico del tiempo

Overview: Students write a video script and create maps for a weather forecast for four locations in the Western Hemisphere. They then record their forecast for the class to view.

Resources: online map, picture-editing software, poster board, markers, video equipment

Sequence: (suggestions for when to do each step appear throughout the chapter)

Step 1. Review instructions so students know what is expected of them. Hand out the Preliminary Unit Project Instructions and the rubric.

Step 2. Students write a rough draft of their weather forecast. They then exchange scripts with a partner for peer editing. Students make corrections based on their partner's comments.

Step 3. Students create one or more maps for their forecast on poster board. After completing their map(s), students add drawings or symbols that indicate the weather in each city they plan to talk about and the temperature there.

Step 4. Students rehearse their forecast with a partner. Partners give students feedback about the content, accuracy, and presentation of the forecast.

Step 5. Students record their weather forecast. Show video to the class.

Options

1. Students present their forecasts to the class "live" instead of recording them.
2. Students give a presentation on the weather of one location for each season.

Assessment

Here is a detailed rubric for assessing this project:

Preliminary Unit Project: *Pronóstico del tiempo*

Rubric	Score 1	Score 3	Score 5
Evidence of planning	You submitted no written draft.	Your draft was written, but not corrected.	You submitted a corrected draft.
Your use of illustrations	You included no map.	Your map was difficult to read, incomplete, and / or inaccurate.	Your map was easy to read, complete, and accurate.
Your presentation	You did not include the majority of the required elements.	You included some of the following: greeting, name, day, date, weather, and temperature for four locations.	You included all of the following: greeting, name, day, date, weather, and temperature for four locations.

AT A GLANCE

Objectives
- Listen to greetings and announcements
- Read a description of the weather and a list of school supplies
- Greet people at different times of the day
- Introduce yourself to others
- Respond to classroom directions
- Begin using numbers
- Tell time
- Identify parts of the body
- Talk about things in the classroom
- Ask questions about new words and phrases
- Use the Spanish alphabet to spell words
- Talk about things related to the calendar
- Learn about the Aztec calendar
- Describe weather conditions
- Identify the seasons
- Compare weather in the Northern and Southern Hemispheres

Vocabulary
- Greetings and leave-takings
- Introductions
- Forms of address
- Ask/tell how you and others are
- Classroom commands
- Numbers 1–100
- Body parts

Grammar
- Nouns
- Singular definite articles
- *cuántos, -as*
- *hay*

Culture
- Greetings, pp. 1, 2–4
- First names in the Spanish-speaking world, p. 3
- Mayan glyphs, p. 13
- Mexican holidays, p. 15
- *Los sanfermines,* p. 16
- The Aztecs and the Aztec calendar, p. 17
- Reversed seasons in the Northern and Southern Hemispheres, p. 20

RESOURCES

	FOR THE STUDENT	DIGITAL	PRINT	FOR THE TEACHER	DIGITAL	PRINT
Plan				Teacher's Edition	•	•
				Teacher's Resource Materials	•	
				Pre-AP® Resource Materials	•	
				Lesson Plans, pp. xxxiv-e, xxxiv-f	•	•
				Mapa global interactivo	•	
Introducción pp. xxxii–1						
Present	Student Edition, pp. xxxii–1	•	•	Teacher's Edition, pp. xxxii-1	•	•
	DK Reference Atlas	•		Teacher's Resource Materials	•	
	Para hispanohablantes	•				
En la escuela pp. 2–9						
Present & Practice	Student Edition, pp. 2–9	•	•	Interactive Whiteboard Vocabulary Activities	•	
	Technology: Audio	•		Teacher's Edition, pp. 2-9	•	•
	Canción de hip hop	•		Teacher's Resource Materials	•	
	Instant Check	•		Communicative Pair Activities, pp. 11, 14–15	•	
	Guided WB, pp. 1–10	•	•	Vocabulary Clip Art	•	
	Core WB, pp. 1–5	•	•	Technology: Audio	•	
	Communication Activities	•				
	Para hispanohablantes	•				
	Communicative Pair Activities	•				
Assess and Remediate				Prueba P–1 with Remediation	•	
				Prueba P–1: Assessment Program, p. 8	•	
				Assessment Program Para hispanohablantes, p. 8	•	

RESOURCES

FOR THE STUDENT	DIGITAL	PRINT	FOR THE TEACHER	DIGITAL	PRINT
En la clase pp. 10–17					
Present & Practice — Student Edition, pp. 10–17	•	•	Interactive Whiteboard Vocabulary Activities	•	
Audio	•		Teacher's Edition, pp. 10–17	•	•
Instant Check	•		Teacher's Resource Materials	•	
Guided WB, pp. 11–18	•	•	Communicative Pair Activities	•	
Core WB, pp. 6–8	•	•	Technology: Audio	•	
Communication Activities	•				
Para hispanohablantes	•				
Communicative Pair Activities	•				
Assess and Remediate			Prueba P–2 with Remediation	•	
			Prueba P–2: Assessment Program, p. 9	•	
			Assessment Program Para hispanohablantes, p. 9	•	
El tiempo, pp. 18–21					
Present & Practice — Student Edition, pp. 18–21	•	•	Interactive Whiteboard Vocabulary Activities	•	
Audio	•		Teacher's Edition, pp. 18–21	•	
Instant Check	•		Teacher's Resource Materials	•	
Canción de hip hop	•		Technology: Audio	•	
Guided WB, pp. 19–24	•	•			
Core WB, p. 9	•	•			
Communication Activities	•				
Para hispanohablantes	•				
			Prueba P–3 with Remediation	•	
			Prueba P–3: Assessment Program, p. 10	•	
			Assessment Program Para hispanohablantes, p. 10	•	
Repaso del capítulo pp. 22–23					
Review — Student Edition, pp. 22–23	•	•	Teacher's Edition, pp. 22–23	•	
Online Puzzles and Games	•		Teacher's Resource Materials	•	
Core WB, pp. 10–12	•	•	Technology: Audio	•	
Para hispanohablantes	•				
Instant Check	•				
Chapter Assessment					
Assess			Examen de Para empezar	•	
			Assessment Program, pp. 11–12	•	
			Alternate Assessment Program, pp. 1–2	•	
			Assessment Program Para hispanohablantes, pp. 11–12	•	
			Technology: Audio, *Para empezar* Examen	•	
			ExamView: Test Banks A and B questions only online	•	
			Heritage Learner Test Bank	•	
			Pre-AP® Test Bank	•	

LESSON PLAN

DAY	Warm-up / Assess	Preview / Present / Practice / Communicate		Wrap-up / Homework Options
1	**General Housekeeping** (15 min.) • Chapter Opener • Arte y cultura	**En la escuela** (30 min.) • Presentation: ¡Hola! ¿Cómo te llamas? • Presentation: Los nombres	• Exploración del lenguaje • Actividades 1, 2, 3	**Wrap-up and Homework Options** (5 min.) • Core Practice P-1
2	**Warm-up** (5 min.) • Homework check	**En la escuela** (40 min.) • Interactive Whiteboard Vocabulary Activities • Presentation: ¡Hola! ¿Cómo estás? • Exploración del lenguaje	• Actividades 4, 5, 6 • Presentation: ¡Atención, por favor! • Actividad 7	**Wrap-up and Homework Options** (5 min.) • Core Practice P-2, P-3
3	**Warm-up** (10 min.) • Homework check	**En la escuela** (35 min.) • Presentation: Los números • Actividades 8, 9, 10 • Communicative Pair Activity	• Presentation: ¿Qué hora es? • Actividades 11, 12	**Wrap-up and Homework Options** (5 min.) • Core Practice P-4
4	**Warm-up** (5 min.) • Homework check	**En la escuela** (25 min.) • Presentation: El cuerpo • Actividades 13, 14 • Communicative Pair Activity • Audio Activities 5, 6	**En la clase** (15 min.) • Objectives • Presentation: La sala de clases • Actividad 1	**Wrap-up and Homework Options** (5 min.) • Core Practice P-5 • Prueba PE-1 with Remediation: En la escuela
5	**Warm-up** (10 min.) • Writing Activity 10 • Homework check • **Formative Assessment** (10 min.) • Prueba PE-1 with Remediation: En la escuela	**En la clase** (25 min.) • Actividad 2 • Presentation: Nouns • Actividad 3 • Interactive Whiteboard Vocabulary Activities	• Presentation: El alfabeto • Actividad 4	**Wrap-up and Homework Options** (5 min.) • Core Practice P-6
6	**Warm-up** (10 min.) • Actividad 5 • Homework check	**En la clase** (35 min.) • Exploración del lenguaje • Cultura • Actividades 6, 7	• Presentation: El calendario y la fecha • Actividades 8, 9	**Wrap-up and Homework Options** (5 min.) • Core Practice P-7, P-8
7	**Warm-up** (10 min.) • Actividad 10 • Homework check	**En la clase** (20 min.) • Cultura • Audio Activity 7 • Actividades 11, 12	**El tiempo** (15 min.) • Presentation: ¿Qué tiempo hace? • Presentation: Las estaciones • Actividad 1	**Wrap-up and Homework Options** (5 min.) • Prueba PE-2 with Remediation: En la clase
8	**Warm-up** (10 min.) • Writing Activity 11 • **Formative Assessment** (10 min.) • Prueba PE-2 with Remediation: En la clase	**El tiempo** (25 min.) • Interactive Whiteboard Vocabulary Activities • Actividades 2, 3, 5, 6 • Audio Activities 8, 9		**Wrap-up and Homework Options** (5 min.) • Actividad 4 • Core Practice P-9 • Prueba PE-3 with Remediation: El tiempo
9	**Warm-up** (15 min.) • Writing Activities 12, 13 • Homework check • **Formative Assessment** (10 min.) • Prueba PE-3 with Remediation: El tiempo	**El tiempo** (5 min.) • Communicative Pair Activity **Repaso del capítulo** (15 min.) • Vocabulario • Preparación para el examen 1, 2, 3, 4	• Situation Cards • Communicative Pair Activities	**Wrap-up and Homework Options** (5 min.) • Core Practice P-10, P-11 • Instant Check • Examen del capítulo
10	**Warm-up** (10 min.) • Homework check • **Summative Assessment** (40 min.) • Examen del capítulo			

ALTERNATE LESSON PLAN

DAY	Warm-up / Assess	Preview / Present / Practice / Communicate	Wrap-up / Homework Options
1	**General Housekeeping** (15 min.) • Chapter Opener • Arte y cultura	**En la escuela** (70 min.) • Objectives • Presentation: ¡Hola! ¿Cómo te llamas? • Presentation: Los nombres • Exploración del lenguaje • Actividades 1, 2, 3 • Interactive Whiteboard Vocabulary Activities • Presentation: ¡Hola! ¿Cómo estás? • Exploración del lenguaje • Actividades 4, 5	**Wrap-up and Homework Options** (5 min.) • Audio Activity 1 • Core Practice: P-1, P-2
2	**Warm-up** (10 min.) • Homework check	**En la escuela** (75 min.) • Actividad 6 • Presentation: ¡Atención, por favor! • Actividad 7 • Presentation: Los números • Actividades 8, 9, 10 • Communicative Pair Activity • Presentation: ¿Qué hora es? • Actividades 11, 12 • Presentation: El cuerpo • Actividades 13, 14 • Communicative Pair Activity • Audio Activity 2	**Wrap-up and Homework Options** (5 min.) • Core Practice P-3, P-4, P-5 • Writing Activity 6 • Prueba PE-1 with Remediation: En la escuela
3	**Warm-up** (15 min.) • Homework check • Review: En la escuela • **Formative Assessment** (10 min.) • Prueba PE-1 with Remediation: En la escuela	**En la clase** (60 min.) • Objectives • Presentation: La sala de clases • Actividades 1, 2 • Presentation: Nouns • Actividad 3 • Interactive Whiteboard Vocabulary Activities • Audio Activity 3 • Presentation: El alfabeto • Actividades 4, 5, 6, 7 • Exploración del lenguaje • Cultura • Audio Activity 4 • Presentation: El calendario y la fecha • Presentation: Los meses del año • Actividades 8, 9	**Wrap-up and Homework Options** (5 min.) • Core Practice P-6, P-7, P-8 • Prueba PE-2 with Remediation: En la clase
4	**Warm-up** (20 min.) • Cultura • Actividad 10 • Homework check • **Formative Assessment** (10 min.) • Prueba PE-2 with Remediation: En la clase	**El tiempo** (55 min.) • Actividades 11, 12 • Writing Activity 7 • Objectives • Presentation: ¿Qué tiempo hace? • Presentation: Las estaciones • Actividades 1, 2, 3, 5, 6 • Interactive Whiteboard Vocabulary Activities • Audio Activity 5 • Writing Activity 8	**Wrap-up and Homework Options** (5 min.) • Actividad 4 • Core Practice P-9 • Prueba PE-3 with Remediation: El tiempo
5	**Warm-up** (20 min.) • Writing Activities 12, 13 • Homework check • Review: El tiempo • **Formative Assessment** (10 min.) • Prueba PE-3 with Remediation: El tiempo	**Repaso del capítulo** (55 min.) • Vocabulario • Preparación para el examen 1, 2, 3, 4 • Situation Cards • Communicative Pair Activities • Project-Based Learning: Begin	**Wrap-up and Homework Options** (5 min.) • Practice Workbook P-10, P-11 • Instant Check • Examen del capítulo
6	**Warm-up** (15 min.) • Homework check • Answer questions • **Summative Assessment** (45 min.) • Examen del capítulo		**Wrap-up and Homework Options** (30 min.) • Project-Based Learning: Finish

Can-Do Statements

Read the can-do statements in the chapter objectives with students. Then have students read Preparación para el examen on page 23 to preview what they will be able to do at the end of the chapter

Standards for Capítulo PE

To achieve the goals of the Standards, students will:

COMMUNICATION

1.1 Interpersonal
- Greet and introduce themselves to others
- Use correct leave-taking phrases
- Ask how others are
- Provide others with the correct numbers of things
- Ask and provide others the correct time
- Talk about classroom people and objects
- Ask for and provide others the date or day of the week
- Talk about the weather

1.2 Interpretive
- Read and listen to information about appropriate greetings, introductions, and leave-takings
- Read and listen to information about how to ask about how someone is
- Read and listen to information about classroom directions and commands
- Read and listen to information about numbers
- Read and listen to information about telling time
- Read and listen to information about parts of the body
- Read and listen to information about classroom people and objects
- Read and listen to information about the alphabet
- Read and listen to information about the calendar
- Read and listen to information about weather and seasons

1.3 Presentational
- Present information about appropriate greetings, introductions, and leave-takings
- Write the correct numbers of things
- Present information about people and things
- Present information about the Spanish alphabet
- Present information about dates and days of the week
- Present information about seasons and the weather

CULTURE

2.1 Practices to Perspectives
- Talk about los sanfermines

CONNECTIONS

3.1 Making Connections
- Discuss the hieroglyphics of the Maya
- Discuss the Aztec calendar
- Discuss geography and climatology in the Southern Hemisphere
- Reinforce math and metric conversion skills

Para empezar

Communication

By the end of *Para empezar* you will be able to:
- Listen to greetings and announcements.
- Read a description of the weather and a list of school supplies.

You will demonstrate what you know and can do:
- Repaso del capítulo: Preparación para el examen

You will also learn to:

1 En la escuela
- Greet people at different times of the day
- Introduce yourself to others
- Respond to classroom directions
- Begin using numbers
- Tell time
- Identify parts of the body

2 En la clase
- Talk about things in the classroom
- Ask questions about new words and phrases
- Use the Spanish alphabet to spell words
- Talk about things related to the calendar
- Learn about the Aztec calendar

3 El tiempo
- Describe weather conditions
- Identify the seasons
- Compare weather in the Northern and Southern Hemispheres

ARTE y CULTURA ◆ El mundo hispano

Greetings Social relations are somewhat more formal in Spanish-speaking countries than in the United States. New acquaintances usually greet one another with a handshake. Friends, however, greet each other with a hug or a kiss on the cheek.

▶ How does this compare with the way you greet people in the United States?

Enrich Your Teaching

The End in Mind

Have students preview the sample performance tasks on *Preparación para el examen,* p. 23, and connect them to the Chapter Objectives. Explain to students that by completing the sample tasks they can self-assess their learning progress.

Technology: Mapa global interactivo

Download the *Mapa global interactivo* files for *Para empezar* and preview the activities. Use *Actividad* 1 to travel to Mexico and compare Mayan ruins. *Actividad* 2 takes you to the streets of Pamplona, Spain. In *Actividad* 3, you look at North and South America and Ecuador, and you compare weather in the Northern and Southern hemispheres.

Go **Online** to practice

PEARSON
realize™

PearsonSchool.com/Autentico

🔊 AUDIO ▶ VIDEO ✏ WRITING 🎤 SPEAK/RECORD 🌐 MAPA GLOBAL 📁 AUTÉNTICO 🗂 FLASCHARDS 📖 ETEXT 2.0 🎮 GAMES

Preview   **PE**

Un grupo de amigos en el Parque Darío,
Matagalpa, Nicaragua

Para empezar • Uno **1**

COMPARISONS

4.1 Language
- Explain the difference between *tú* and *usted*
- Discuss that nouns are either masculine or feminine
- Discuss some rules of punctuation and accent marks

4.2 Cultural
- Compare customs of greetings and introductions
- Compare festivals in which animals play a role

Chapter Opener

Suggestions: As you go through the Objectives, ask volunteers to identify in English the ways people might introduce themselves, name common classroom objects, or describe the day's weather. Scan the section with students to help familiarize them with the structure of this unit (which follows a different pattern from the other chapters). Explain that the *Para empezar* is an introduction to their language learning that will help them communicate right away, and that the vocabulary and expressions they learn here will then be recycled throughout the book. The emphasis should be on recognition and limited use, not on mastery.

ARTE Y CULTURA

Standards: 4.1

Suggestions: Ask students about the different ways strangers, adults, young people, men, women, and family members greet each other in the United States.
Answers will vary.

Teaching with Photos

Have students look at the teens in the photo. What do they notice about how these young people are dressed? How does it compare with the way they dress?

Culture Note

Young people in the United States have many colloquialisms for greeting each other. *How's it going?*, *What's up?*, and *Hey!* are just a few of them. Teens in Latin America also have informal ways of greeting each other, such as *¿Cómo te va?*, *¿Qué onda?*, and *¿Quehúbole?*

Project-Based Learning

Pronóstico del tiempo

Have pairs of students role-play how two strangers who do not speak each others' languages might still "talk" to each other about weather. Then ask students to explain why their body language and gestures are so easily understood—weather is a universally shared experience. Have them repeat their discussions, this time substituting whatever Spanish words they know.

¡Hola! ¿Cómo te llamas?

Standards: 1.2

Resources: Teacher's Resource Materials: Input Script, Clip Art, Audio Script; Technology: Audio Cap. PE

Suggestions: Use the Input Script from the *Teacher's Resource Materials* any time you have new vocabulary to introduce, or use other ideas that work for you. Be sure students notice the age differences of the speakers and the different times of day the conversations take place. When students have become familiar with the conversations, ask them to greet you and one another. Point out the *Nota* and explain that these provide additional explanations and useful information.

EXPLORACIÓN DEL LENGUAJE

Suggestions: Write examples on the board such as **Señor Trujillo** and then write the abbreviation **Sr. Trujillo.** Point out the comparison in English to students. They may be surprised at the relative formality with which adults are addressed in Spanish. Have students identify school personnel with the new Spanish titles.

Technology: Interactive Whiteboard

Vocabulary Activities PE Use the whiteboard activities in your Teacher Resources as you progress through the vocabulary practice with your class.

---

1 En la escuela

OBJECTIVES
▶ Greet people at different times of the day
▶ Introduce yourself to others
▶ Respond to classroom directions
▶ Begin using numbers
▶ Tell time
▶ Identify parts of the body

🔊 **¡Hola! ¿Cómo te llamas?**

Nota
A woman or girl says *encantada*.
A man or boy says *encantado*.

07:00
—¡Buenos días, señor!
—¡Buenos días! ¿Cómo te llamas?
—Me llamo Felipe.

03:30
—¡Buenas tardes, señora!
—¡Buenas tardes! ¿Cómo te llamas?
—Me llamo Beatriz.
—Mucho gusto.
—Encantada.

09:40
—¡Buenas noches! ¿Cómo te llamas?
—¡Hola! Me llamo Graciela. ¿Y tú?
—Me llamo Lorenzo.
—Mucho gusto.
—Igualmente.

Exploración del lenguaje ▸ Señor, señora, señorita

The words *señor, señora,* and *señorita* mean "sir," "madam," and "miss" when used alone. When they are used with people's last names they mean "Mr.," "Mrs.," and "Miss," and are abbreviated *Sr., Sra.,* and *Srta.* Note that the abbreviations are capitalized.

In Spanish you should address adults as *señor, señora,* or *señorita,* or use the titles *Sr., Sra.,* and *Srta.* with their last names.

2 dos • En la escuela

Differentiated Instruction

Students with Learning Difficulties

If students have problems identifying individual phrases in context, provide them with a list of specific words and phrases that you want them to know. Model different ways in which they can combine the words and phrases for communication.

Challenge

Explain that *¿Cómo te llamas?* and *Me llamo...* do not literally mean "What's your name?" and "My name is...". Use this as an opportunity to demonstrate that languages cannot be translated on a word-to-word basis. Some students may also benefit from further explanation of the *Nota* and of agreement of adjectives.

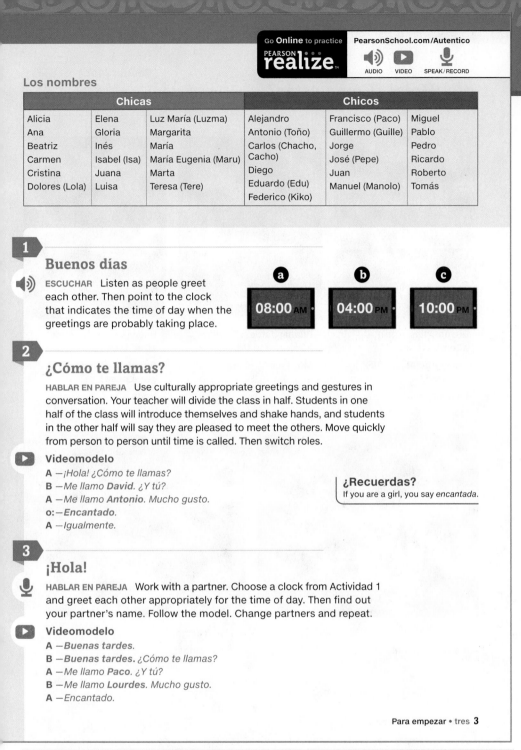

Los nombres

Chicas			Chicos		
Alicia	Elena	Luz María (Luzma)	Alejandro	Francisco (Paco)	Miguel
Ana	Gloria	Margarita	Antonio (Toño)	Guillermo (Guille)	Pablo
Beatriz	Inés	María	Carlos (Chacho, Cacho)	Jorge	Pedro
Carmen	Isabel (Isa)	María Eugenia (Maru)		José (Pepe)	Ricardo
Cristina	Juana	Marta	Diego	Juan	Roberto
Dolores (Lola)	Luisa	Teresa (Tere)	Eduardo (Edu)	Manuel (Manolo)	Tomás
			Federico (Kiko)		

1

Buenos días

ESCUCHAR Listen as people greet each other. Then point to the clock that indicates the time of day when the greetings are probably taking place.

a 08:00 AM **b** 04:00 PM **c** 10:00 PM

2

¿Cómo te llamas?

HABLAR EN PAREJA Use culturally appropriate greetings and gestures in conversation. Your teacher will divide the class in half. Students in one half of the class will introduce themselves and shake hands, and students in the other half will say they are pleased to meet the others. Move quickly from person to person until time is called. Then switch roles.

Videomodelo

A —¡Hola! ¿Cómo te llamas?
B —Me llamo **David**. ¿Y tú?
A —Me llamo **Antonio**. Mucho gusto.
o:—**Encantado**.
A —Igualmente.

> **¿Recuerdas?**
> If you are a girl, you say *encantada*.

3

¡Hola!

HABLAR EN PAREJA Work with a partner. Choose a clock from Actividad 1 and greet each other appropriately for the time of day. Then find out your partner's name. Follow the model. Change partners and repeat.

Videomodelo

A —*Buenas tardes.*
B —*Buenas tardes. ¿Cómo te llamas?*
A —*Me llamo Paco. ¿Y tú?*
B —*Me llamo Lourdes. Mucho gusto.*
A —*Encantado.*

Para empezar • tres **3**

Enrich Your Teaching

Culture Note

In Spain and many other Spanish-speaking countries, **Buenos días** is used until noon. **Buenas tardes** is used from noon until the evening meal. **Buenas noches** is considered both a greeting and a farewell.

21st Century Skills

Social and Cross-Cultural Skills
Suggest that students go online to discover the most common surnames in Spanish-speaking countries. Have them use online dictionaries and other resources to determine the meaning of some of the names. For example, have them list surnames that indicate an occupation.

Go **Online** to practice PearsonSchool.com/Autentico

PEARSON realize

AUDIO   VIDEO   SPEAK/RECORD

Interpersonal   PE

1

Standards: 1.2

Resources: Teacher's Resource Materials: Audio Script; Technology: Audio Cap. PE

Suggestions: In all *Escuchar* activities, you may either play the *audio* or read the script. Walk around the room to monitor comprehension and check that students are pointing to the correct clocks.

 Technology: Audio Script and Answers

1. —Buenas noches, señor Rodríguez.
   —Hola, Roberto. *(c)*
2. —Buenas tardes, Alicia.
   —Buenas tardes, señora. *(b)*
3. —Buenos días, señora Gómez.
   —Hola, Ana. *(a)*
4. —Buenos días, Pablo.
   —Buenos días, señor. *(a)*
5. —Buenas noches, Jorge.
   —Hola, María. *(c)*
6. —Hola, Juana.
   —Buenas tardes, Catalina. *(b)*

2

Standards: 1.1

Suggestions: Model a personalized version of the conversation with a volunteer and go over roles. Students will need to learn how to do paired practice. Point out that the *¿Recuerdas?* boxes will remind students of things they've already learned.

3

Standards: 1.1

Suggestions: If you wish, have students choose Spanish names to use in class. Allow students to repeat the activity with several partners.

Teacher-to-Teacher

Bring in a kitchen timer and set it for the time you want to allot for each paired activity. When the bell rings, stop the activity, review the task with students if necessary, and move on. The timer will help you keep track of the time and will help students focus.

3

¡Hola! ¿Cómo estás?

Standards: 1.2

Resources: Teacher's Resource Materials: Input Script, Audio Script; Technology: Audio Cap. PE

Suggestions: Use the dialogue to help students guess the meanings of the unfamiliar words in blue type. Direct attention to the *¿Recuerdas?* Play the *audio* or read the conversations beneath the pictures. Then role-play the conversations with students. Draw a rising sun at one end of the board, a noontime sun a little to the right with a dividing line under it, a setting sun a little further to the right, and a moon at the far end. Position pairs of students at various points along the board, and have the class identify whether they would say **Buenos días, Buenas tardes,** or **Buenas noches,** depending on where they are. Point out that **hasta + an expression of time** means that you're saying good-bye until that time.

Starter Activity

Ask students to prepare a short dialogue with a partner to represent one of the pairs of speakers pictured.

🔊 **¡Hola! ¿Cómo estás?**

> **¿Recuerdas?**
> *Señor, señora,* and *señorita* are abbreviated to **Sr., Sra.,** and **Srta.** before a person's last name.

—Buenos días, Adela.
¿Cómo estás?

—Bien, gracias, Sr. Ruiz.
¿Y usted?

—Bien, gracias.

—Buenas tardes, Sr. Ruiz.
¿Cómo está Ud.?

—Muy bien, gracias. ¿Y tú?

—Bien, gracias.

—Buenas noches, Miguel.
¿Qué tal?

—Regular. ¿Y tú, Carlos?
¿Qué pasa?

—Nada.

—¡Adiós, Srta. Moreno! ¡Hasta luego!

—¡Hasta mañana!

—¡Hasta luego, Juan!

—¡Nos vemos!

4 cuatro • En la escuela

Differentiated Instruction

Students with Learning Difficulties

Have students create a section in their notebook for vocabulary and a separate section for grammar. For each chapter, students can enter new vocabulary and grammar concepts into their respective sections. Allow students to accompany vocabulary words with pictures and English translations, as needed.

Heritage Speakers

Many students who already speak Spanish may have little or no formal experience with the written language. Ask these students to write new versions of the dialogues above, personalizing them in some way. Have them pay special attention to spelling. You can use this exercise to informally assess their written Spanish.

Exploración del lenguaje ‹ *Tú* vs. *usted*

For most Spanish speakers there are two ways to say "you": *tú* and *usted*. Use *tú* when speaking to friends, family, people your own age, children, and pets. *Usted* is formal. Use it to show respect and when talking to people you don't know well, older people, and people in positions of authority. In writing, *usted* is almost always abbreviated *Ud.*, with a capital *U*.

Would you say *tú* or *Ud.* when talking to the following people? With a partner, role play greeting these people using the correct form, *tú* or *Ud.*

• your brother
• your teacher
• your best friend
• your friend's mother
• your cat
• your principal
• a new acquaintance who is your age

4 ¿Hola o adiós?

🔊 ESCUCHAR Make a chart on your paper with two columns. Label one *Greeting,* the other *Leaving.* Number your paper from 1–8. As you hear each greeting or leave-taking, place a check mark in the appropriate column next to the number.

Greeting	Leaving
1.	
2.	
3.	

5 ¡Hola! ¿Qué tal?

🎤 HABLAR EN PAREJA Work with a partner. Greet each other appropriately, shake hands, and ask how your partner is. Say good-bye. Then change partners and repeat.

Videomodelo

A —*Hola, Luisa. ¿Qué tal?*
B —*Bien, Lupe. ¿Y tú?*
A —*Regular. ¡Hasta luego!*
B —*¡Adiós!*

6 Mucho gusto

✏️ LEER Read the conversation and then reply *sí* or *no* to the statements.

Profesor: Buenos días. Me llamo José Guzmán. ¿Y tú?

Estudiante: Me llamo María Hernández. Mucho gusto.

Profesor: Igualmente. ¿Cómo estás, María?

Estudiante: Bien, gracias. ¿Y Ud.?

Profesor: Muy bien, gracias. Hasta luego.

Estudiante: Adiós, señor.

1. The people knew each other.
2. The teacher is a man.
3. We know the last names of both people.
4. The student talks to the teacher in a formal tone.
5. Neither person is feeling well today.

Para empezar • cinco **5**

EXPLORACIÓN DEL LENGUAJE ‹

Standards: 4.1

Suggestions: Tell students to use **Ud.** for anybody that they call by their last name.

Answers:

1. tú; 2. usted; 3. tú; 4. usted; 5. tú; 6. usted;
7. tú

4

Standards: 1.2

Resources: Teacher's Resource Materials: Audio Script; Technology: Audio Cap. PE

Suggestions: Draw the chart on the board as a model.

🔊 **Technology: Audio Script and Answers**

1. Hola, Juan. ¿Qué pasa? *(greeting)*
2. Adiós, Miguel. *(leaving)*
3. Buenos días, señor García. *(greeting)*
4. Hola, Elena. *(greeting)*
5. Nos vemos. *(leaving)*
6. Hasta mañana, señor Pérez. *(leaving)*
7. Buenas noches, señora. *(greeting)*
8. Hasta luego, Ana. *(leaving)*

5

Standards: 1.1

Suggestions: Have students switch roles with one asking and one answering.

6

Standards: 1.2, 1.3

Suggestions: If the answer is "No," have students provide correct information.

Answers:

1. no 2. sí 3. sí 4. sí 5. no

Additional Resources

📶 **Technology: Online Resources**
• Communication Activities Audio Act. 1
• Teacher's Resource Materials: Audio Script, Communicative Pair Activity
• Technology: Audio Cap. PE

Print
• Core WB p. 2

¡Atención, por favor!

Standards: 1.2

Resources: Teacher's Resource Materials: Audio Script; Technology: Audio Cap. PE

Suggestions: Play the *audio* or refer to the text under the pictures. Dramatize the classroom commands while saying them aloud or playing the audio. Have students guess the commands. Then say them again and have the class respond as asked. Try to do as much classroom management in Spanish as possible.

7

Standards: 1.2

Resources: Teacher's Resource Materials: Audio Script; Technology: Audio Cap. PE

Suggestions: Play the *audio* or read the script. Have students simply listen the first time. Then play or read the script again, having students act out the commands.

🔊 Technology: Audio Script and Answers

1. Abran el libro. *(open the book)*
2. Levántense. *(stand up)*
3. Repitan: Buenas tardes. *(repeat)*
4. Siéntense. *(sit down)*
5. Cierren el libro. *(close the book)*
6. Saquen una hoja de papel. *(take out a sheet of paper)*

Extension: Provide additional commands for the students: *Pasen a la pizarra. Trabajen en parejas. Cierren la puerta. Abran la ventana.*

🔊 ¡Atención, por favor!

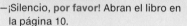

levántense

siéntense

—¡Silencio, **por favor!** Abran el libro en la página 10.

—Levántense, por favor.
—Siéntense, por favor.

—¡Atención! Cierren el libro.
—Repitan, por favor: Buenos días.
—Buenos días.

—Saquen una hoja de papel. Escriban los números.

—Entreguen sus hojas de papel.

7

¡Siéntense!

🔊 **ESCUCHAR** You will hear some classroom commands. Listen carefully and act them out.

6 seis • En la escuela

Differentiated Instruction

Special Needs

For students who find the commands difficult to act out, have them discuss with you other ways they might indicate comprehension of the commands. Depending on the students, these might include simple hand or arm movements.

Challenge

Have students turn to p. 100 in their textbook and then flip through the pages, randomly stopping ten times. They should say or write the page number each time they stop. Point out that the numbers are written out on each page.

🔊 Los números

0	cero	10	diez	20	veinte	40	cuarenta
1	uno	11	once	21	veintiuno	50	cincuenta
2	dos	12	doce		. . .	60	sesenta
3	tres	13	trece	30	treinta	70	setenta
4	cuatro	14	catorce	31	treinta y uno	80	ochenta
5	cinco	15	quince		. . .	90	noventa
6	seis	16	dieciséis			100	cien
7	siete	17	diecisiete				
8	ocho	18	dieciocho				
9	nueve	19	diecinueve				

8 Los números

🎤 **HABLAR** Supply the missing number. Then read the sequence in Spanish.

1. 1, ___, 3
2. 6, ___, 8
3. 7, ___, 9
4. 10, ___, 12
5. 14, ___, 16
6. 17, ___, 19
7. 23, ___, 25
8. 29, ___, 31

9 Más números

🎤 **HABLAR EN PAREJA** With a partner, provide the missing numbers in each sequence. Then say the number sequence aloud in Spanish.

1. 1, 2, 3, . . . 10
2. 2, 4, 6, . . . 20
3. 1, 3, 5, . . . 19
4. 5, 10, 15, . . . 60
5. 3, 6, 9, . . . 39
6. 10, 20, 30, . . . 100

10 Números y más números

🎤 **HABLAR EN PAREJA, ESCUCHAR, ESCRIBIR** Tell your partner these numbers in Spanish. He or she will write them using numerals, not words. Then check your partner's work.

1. the phone numbers used to dial for information and emergencies
2. the bar code number on the back of your Spanish book
3. your house or apartment number
4. number of minutes it takes you to get from your home to school
5. number of months until your next birthday

Azulejo *(tile)* de cerámica

Para empezar • siete **7**

Enrich Your Teaching

Teacher-to-Teacher

Give each student a number written large on a piece of paper. Have them tape the numbers to their shirts. Then have the class stand in a circle and clap their hands rhythmically. The student who is *uno* says his or her number and then calls out another number. The student who has that number says it, then calls out another number (e.g., *"¡uno, diez!"; diez* then responds, saying *"¡diez, cuatro!"*). All the while, students clap the rhythm. If someone makes a mistake, the person and number are out.

Interpersonal **PE**

Los números

Standards: 1.2

Resources: Teacher's Resource Materials: Audio Script; Technology: Audio Cap. PE

Suggestions: Have students practice numbers by playing bingo or by rolling number cubes.

8

Standards: 1.1

Suggestions: Have students read the entire sequence, not just the answer.

Answers:

1. dos	**4.** once	**7.** veinticuatro
2. siete	**5.** quince	**8.** treinta
3. ocho	**6.** dieciocho	

9

Standards: 1.1

Suggestions: Make sure students understand that each sequence represents a pattern. They have to identify the pattern before they can provide the missing numbers.

Answers:

1. cuatro, cinco, seis, siete, ocho, nueve
2. ocho, diez, doce, catorce, dieciséis, dieciocho
3. siete, nueve, once, trece, quince, diecisiete
4. veinte, veinticinco, treinta, treinta y cinco, cuarenta, cuarenta y cinco, cincuenta, cincuenta y cinco
5. doce, quince, dieciocho, veintiuno, veinticuatro, veintisiete, treinta, treinta y tres, treinta y seis
6. cuarenta, cincuenta, sesenta, setenta, ochenta, noventa

10

Standards: 1.1, 1.3

Suggestions: Have the students check each other's work.

Answers will vary.

Additional Resources

📶 **Technology: Online Resources**
• Teacher's Resource Materials: Communicative Pair Activity
Print
• Core WB p. 3

¿Qué hora es?

Resources: Teacher's Resource Materials: Audio Script; Technology: Audio Cap. PE

Suggestions: Ask the students: *¿Qué hora es?* Point to a clock, and have students tell you the time.

Pre-AP® Integration

- **Learning Objective:** Interpretive: Audio
- **Activity:** Have students number 1–8 on a sheet of paper. As you point to each clock, make true/false statements. Have students write C *(Cierto)* or F *(Falso)* to respond.
- **Pre-AP® Resource Materials:** Comprehensive guide to Pre-AP® writing skill development

11

Suggestions: Point to the classroom clock and prompt students to say what time it is.

Answers: 1. Son las siete; 2. Son las tres y media / treinta; 3. Es la una y cuarto / quince; 4. Son las dos y veinte; 5. Son las nueve y cuarenta. / Son las diez menos veinte; 6. Son las doce y cincuenta. / Es la una menos diez.

12

Resources: Teacher's Resource Materials: Audio Script; Technology: Audio Cap. PE

Suggestions: Repeat the activity and ask volunteers for the answers.

Technology: Audio Script and Answers

1. Es la una y media. *(1:30)*; 2. Son las diez. *(10:00)*; 3. Son las once y cinco. *(11:05)*; 4. Son las doce. *(12:00)*; 5. Son las seis y media. *(6:30)*; 6. Son las siete y cuarenta y cinco. *(7:45)*; 7. Son las nueve y veinte. *(9:20)*; 8. Son las tres y treinta y cinco. *(3:35)*

¿Qué hora es?

In Spanish, to ask what time it is, you say *¿Qué hora es?* Here are some answers:

Es la una.   Son las dos.   Son las tres y cinco.   Son las cuatro y diez.

Son las cinco y cuarto.   Son las seis y media.   Son las siete menos veinte.   Son las ocho y cincuenta y dos.

11

¿Qué hora es?

HABLAR EN PAREJA Work with a partner to ask and answer questions about the time. Use these clocks.

Videomodelo
A —*¿Qué hora es?*
B —*Son las diez.*

10:00

1 7:00   **2** 3:30   **3** 1:15

4 2:20   **5** 9:40   **6** 12:50

▲ "La persistencia de la memoria / The Persistence of Memory" (1931), Salvador Dalí
Oil on canvas, 9 1/2 x 13 in. (24.1 x 33 cm). Given anonymously.
© 2009 Salvador Dalí, Gala-Salvador Dalí Foundation/Artists Rights Society (ARS), New York./A.K.G., Berlin. Photo: Superstock.

12

La hora

ESCUCHAR Write the numbers 1–8 on a sheet of paper. Write the times you hear with numerals—1:00, 2:15, and so on.

8 ocho • En la escuela

Differentiated Instruction

Students with Learning Difficulties

Some students may be unable to read clocks with faces and hands. If so, provide times on digital clocks.

Challenge

Have students write a television program guide with the names and times of their favorite programs. Suggest that they use newspaper or internet listings as a model. Have students exchange program guides. One student will say a time, and the other student will say the name of the program.

El cuerpo

la cabeza

el ojo

la boca

la nariz

"¡Ay! Me duele el pie".

el brazo

el dedo

la mano

el estómago

la pierna

el pie

13

Señalen

ESCUCHAR You will hear some commands. Listen carefully and act out the commands. When you hear the word *señalen*, you should point to that part of the body.

14

Juego

ESCUCHAR Play the game *Simón dice . . .* (Simon Says). Listen and follow the leader's directions. Remember that if the leader does not say *"Simón dice,"* you should not do the action.

Para empezar • nueve **9**

Enrich Your Teaching

Teacher-to-Teacher

Have students create a poster of a "creature" using images cut from magazines or newspapers. Their creature can have six arms, four legs, etc. Have them label each of the body parts. Provide plurals as necessary. Display the art in the classroom and ask students true-or-false questions about each one, or have them list the body parts that they see.

21st Century Skills

ICT Literacy Encourage students to use online tools such as dictionaries to learn the new vocabulary, including multiple meanings. Have them write down the words and meanings and then use the words in a song, poem, or short written paragraph.

Interpretive PE

El cuerpo

Standards: 1.2

Resources: Teacher's Resource Materials: Audio Script; Technology: Audio Cap. PE

Suggestions: Play the *audio*. Pretend to be in pain and say: *¡Ay! Me duele el pie.* Continue with the rest of the vocabulary. Note that only singular body parts are used. Point out the use of the article to refer to body parts.

13

Standards: 1.2

Resources: Teacher's Resource Materials: Audio Script; Technology: Audio Cap. PE

Suggestions: Play the *audio* or read the script twice. Have students listen first and perform the action the second time.

Technology: Audio Script and Answers

1. Señalen la nariz. *(nose)*
2. Señalen el estómago. *(stomach)*
3. Señalen la mano. *(hand)*
4. Señalen la cabeza. *(head)*
5. Señalen el pie. *(foot)*
6. Señalen el brazo. *(arm)*

14

Standards: 1.2

Suggestions: Have students take turns playing leader in small groups.

Additional Resources

Technology: Online Resources
- Instant Check
- Guided, Core, Video, Audio
- *Para hispanohablantes*
- Communication Activities Audio Act. 2
- Teacher's Resource Materials: Audio Script
- Technology: Audio Cap. PE

Print
- Guided WB pp. 1–10
- Core WB p. 5

Assessment

Prueba P-1 with Remediation (online only)
Quiz: En la escuela
- Prueba P-1

9

Go **Online** to practice

PEARSON **realize**™

PearsonSchool.com/Autentico

AUDIO   VIDEO   SPEAK/RECORD

La sala de clases

Standards: 1.2

Resources: Teacher's Resource Materials: Input Script, Clip Art, Audio Script; Technology: Audio Cap. PE

Suggestions: Use the commands from p. 6 to introduce and practice these vocabulary items, using actual items in your classroom. Combine these with other commands for students to carry out. Tell students that for the rest of the year, if they want to know either the Spanish or English word for something, you will only respond if they use the questions presented here.

1

Standards: 1.2

Resources: Teacher's Resource Materials: Audio Script; Technology: Audio Cap. PE

Suggestions: Tell students that if an object is not visible in the classroom, they may point to the picture in the book. Explain the *También se dice...* but tell students that they will not have to remember these words.

🔊 Technology: Audio Script and Answers

1. la hoja de papel *(sheet of paper)*
2. el libro *(book)*
3. la profesora (el profesor) *(teacher)*
4. el pupitre *(student desk)*
5. el bolígrafo *(pen)*
6. el cuaderno *(notebook)*
7. el lápiz *(pencil)*
8. la carpeta *(folder)*

Starter Activity

Working in pairs, have students alternate saying classroom commands.

🖥 Technology: Interactive Whiteboard

Vocabulary Activities PE Use the whiteboard activities in your Teacher Resources as you progress through the vocabulary practice with your class.

---

2 En la clase

OBJECTIVES
▶ Talk about things in the classroom
▶ Ask questions about new words and phrases
▶ Use the Spanish alphabet to spell words
▶ Talk about things related to the calendar
▶ Learn about the Aztec calendar

🔊 La sala de clases

el estudiante

el profesor

la profesora

la estudiante

—¿Qué quiere decir *lápiz*?
—Quiere decir *pencil.*

—¿Cómo se dice *book* en español?
—Se dice *libro.*

el pupitre   el bolígrafo   la carpeta   el lápiz

También se dice . . .
In many Spanish-speaking countries or regions, you will hear different words for the same thing. Words like these are highlighted in the *También se dice . . .* sections. For example, in Spain a classroom is **el aula,** while in Mexico, it is **el salón de clases.**

el cuaderno   la hoja de papel   el libro

1

El libro, el lápiz, . . .

🔊 **ESCUCHAR** You will hear the names of classroom objects. After you hear each word, hold up the object if you have it on your desk or point to it if it is somewhere in the classroom.

10 diez • En la clase

Differentiated Instruction

Students with Learning Difficulties

The concept of grammatical gender is sometimes difficult for English speakers. Encourage students to always learn a noun with its article as a means of reinforcing the sound and rhythm. If they are copying new vocabulary into their notebooks, have them use a blue and a pink highlighter to color-code the words.

Heritage Speakers

Ask students if they use any words that are different from the vocabulary in the book, but that mean the same thing. For instance, in Spain, a pen is **el bolígrafo,** but in some other countries, people say *la pluma.* Be sure students understand that their words are valid, but that you may make other vocabulary choices for class.

2

¿Cómo se dice . . . ?

🎤 **HABLAR EN PAREJA** Talk with a partner about items and people in your classroom.

Videomodelo

A —¿Cómo se dice **book** en español?
B — Se dice **libro**.

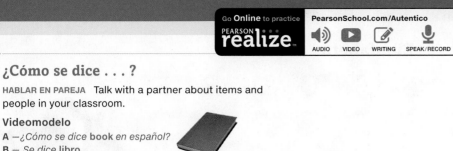

Videomodelo

mano
A —¿Qué quiere decir **mano**?
B — Quiere decir **hand**.

6. cuaderno   7. hoja de papel   8. cabeza   9. carpeta   10. brazo

---

Gramática ‹ Nouns

Nouns refer to people, animals, places, things, and ideas. In Spanish, nouns have gender. They are either masculine or feminine.

Most nouns that end in -o are masculine. Most nouns that end in -a are feminine.

The definite articles *el* and *la* also point out if a word is masculine or feminine. They both mean "the."

Spanish nouns that end in -*e* or a consonant must be learned as masculine or feminine. You should practice them with their definite articles, *el* or *la*.

Masculine	Feminine
el libro	la carpeta
el bolígrafo	la hoja de papel

Masculine	Feminine
el profesor	la noche
el lápiz	la conversación

3

¿Masculino o femenino?

✏️ **ESCRIBIR** Look at these words and decide whether each one is masculine or feminine. Rewrite each word and add the appropriate definite article *(el or la)*.

1. pierna   3. cuaderno   5. pupitre   7. profesora
2. nariz   4. hora   6. pie   8. estudiante

Para empezar • once **11**

Enrich Your Teaching

Teacher-to-Teacher

Since Spanish nouns have gender, a concept foreign to most native English speakers, students often make overgeneralizations when learning vocabulary. Point out exceptions to the gender rule: *la mano* (feminine even though it ends in *o*) and *el día* (masculine even though it ends in *a*), but stress that in most cases the *o / a* rule is accurate. Tell students that they should always learn nouns with the correct article.

2

Suggestions: Be sure students understand that they are to use the English word in items 1–5 because they are asking for the Spanish word. In items 6–10, they must use the Spanish word because they are asking for an English word.

Answers:

1. pen / bolígrafo   6. cuaderno / notebook
2. student / estudiante   7. hoja de papel / sheet of paper
3. notebook / cuaderno   8. cabeza / head
4. desk / pupitre   9. carpeta / folder
5. folder / carpeta   10. brazo / arm

Gramática

Suggestions: Have students identify the genders of various nouns.

3

Suggestions: Have students identify the genders of nouns ending in **-o** or **-a.** Point out that **estudiante** is tricky, and that **nariz** must simply be learned as feminine.

Answers:

1. la   3. el   5. el   7. la
2. la   4. la   6. el   8. el / la

Additional Resources

📶 **Technology: Online Resources**
- *Para hispanohablantes*
- Communication Activities: Audio Act. 3
- Teacher's Resource Materials: Audio Script; Communicative Pair Activity
- Technology: Audio Cap. PE
Print
- Core WB p. 6

El alfabeto

Standards: 1.2

Resources: Teacher's Resource Materials: Input Script, Clip Art, Audio Script; Technology: Audio Cap. PE

Suggestions: Develop a rap rhythm for the letters. Ask volunteers to say a letter, quickly moving from one student to the next.

4

Standards: 1.2, 1.3

Resources: Teacher's Resource Materials: Audio Script; Technology: Audio Cap. PE

Suggestions: Allow students to listen more than once.

🔊 Technology: Audio Script and Answers

1. ge-u-ese-te-o *(gusto)*
2. be-i-e-ene *(bien)*
3. ere-e-ge-u-ele-a-ere *(regular)*
4. o-ene-ce-e *(once)*
5. be-ere-a-zeta-o *(brazo)*
6. pe-i-e-ere-ene-a *(pierna)*
7. pe-u-pe-i-te-ere-e *(pupitre)*
8. ce-a-be-e-zeta-a *(cabeza)*

5

Standards: 1.1, 1.3

Suggestions: As students work, monitor their pronunciation.

Answers:

1. carpeta: *ce-a-ere-pe-e-te-a*
2. cuaderno: *ce-u-a-de-e-ere-ene-o*
3. libro: *ele-i-be-ere-o*
4. pupitre: *pe-u-pe-i-te-ere-e*
5. bolígrafo: *be-o-ele-i acento-ge-ere-a-efe-o*

Starter Activity

Have students choose a letter and say the letter and a word in Spanish that starts with that letter.

🔊 El alfabeto

A	B	C	D	E	F
a	be	ce	de	e	efe
G	H	I	J	K	L
ge	hache	i	jota	ka	ele
M	N	Ñ	O	P	Q
eme	ene	eñe	o	pe	cu
R	rr	S	T	U	V
ere	erre	ese	te	u	ve, uve
W	X	Y	Z		
doble ve, doble u	equis	i griega, ye	zeta		

—¿Cómo se escribe *libro*?
—Se escribe ele-i-be-ere-o.

4

Escucha y escribe

🔊 ESCUCHAR, ESCRIBIR On a sheet of paper, write the numbers 1–8. You will hear several words you know spelled aloud. Listen carefully and write the letters as you hear them.

5

Pregunta y contesta

🎤 HABLAR EN PAREJA, ESCRIBIR Work with a partner. Use the pictures to ask and answer according to the model. As Student B spells the words, Student A should write them out. When you are finished, check your spelling by looking at p. 10.

Videomodelo
A —¿Cómo se escribe **lápiz**?
B — *Se escribe ele-a acento-pe-i-zeta*.

12 doce • En la clase

Differentiated Instruction

Heritage Speakers

Have students look at Spanish newspapers or magazines and write a list of ten words that have accent marks. Then have students spell the words aloud. Remind them to include the accent marks in their spelling.

Challenge

Have students turn to p. 9, make a list of the labeled parts of *El cuerpo,* and then write or say the letters for each word.

Exploración del lenguaje ◂ Punctuation and accent marks

You have probably noticed that in Spanish, questions begin with an upside-down question mark (¿) and exclamations with an upside-down exclamation point (¡). This lets you know at the beginning of a sentence what kind of sentence you are reading.

You have probably also noticed the accent mark (el acento) on words like *días* and *estás*.

When you write in Spanish, you must include these accents and punctuation marks.

Try it out! Rewrite these sentences and insert the correct punctuation and accents.

Como estas	Que tal
Hasta luego	Y tu

6

🎤 **¿Cómo te llamas?**

HABLAR EN PAREJA Work with a partner. Follow the model to find out each other's names and how they are spelled. Then change partners and repeat.

▶️ **Videomodelo**

A —¿Cómo te llamas?
B —Me llamo **María**.
A —¿Cómo se escribe **María**?
B — Se escribe **eme-a-ere-i acento-a**.

> **Strategy**
> **Sustaining a conversation** If you need your partner to spell a word again, say *Repite, por favor.*

7

✏️ **Juego**

ESCRIBIR, HABLAR EN PAREJA, ESCUCHAR

1 Play this game in pairs. Each player makes a list of five Spanish words that you have learned. Don't let your partner see your words.

2 Spell your first word aloud in Spanish. Don't forget any accent marks. Your partner will write the word as you spell it. Then your partner will spell a word for you to write. Take turns until you have spelled all the words on your lists.

3 Check each other's papers. The winner is the player with the most words spelled correctly.

CULTURA ◂ **El mundo hispano**

Los mayas were among the early civilizations in the Western Hemisphere to develop a form of writing with symbols, known as hieroglyphics *(los jeroglíficos)*. Each symbol, or glyph, represents a word or an idea.

Pre-AP® Integration: Human Geography With what other hieroglyphic writing are you familiar?

🌐 **Mapa global interactivo** Compare ancient Mayan ruins in different locations in Mexico. What key details do you see in them?

Jeroglíficos mayas

Para empezar • trece **13**

Enrich Your Teaching

Teacher-to-Teacher

Have students write two sentences about themselves and then create their own hieroglyphs. Tell them to draw pictures that represent the sentences they wrote. Then have students exchange their glyphs with another student and try to read their hieroglyphic system.

Teacher-to-Teacher

In 1994, the Association of Spanish Language Academies eliminated *ch* and *ll* as separate letters from the Spanish alphabet. This simplified dictionaries and made the language more computer friendly. Spelling, pronunciation, and usage are not affected. Some sources treat *rr* as a sound and not a letter of the alphabet. In this text, the *rr* is listed as a letter.

6

Standards: 1.1

Suggestions: Direct students' attention to the *Strategy.* Explain that these are tips that will help in language learning. Have students change partners three or four times. When reviewing, call on pairs of students who did not work together to do the dialogue.

Answers will vary.

EXPLORACIÓN DEL LENGUAJE ◂

Standards: 4.1

Suggestions: If students need help, have them look at p. 4 to review the words. Stress that accent marks are required for correct meaning and pronunciation.

CULTURA ◂

Standards: 3.1

Suggestions: Explain that glyphs can be difficult to translate because they are not individual letters that form words, but pictures that represent something—an idea, a person, an action. Glyphs are closer in function to words than letters.

🌐 **Technology: Mapa global interactivo**, Actividad 1 Compare ancient Mayan ruins in different locations in Mexico.

7

Standards: 1.2

Suggestions: Suggest that students choose vocabulary words from different categories, rather than from a single group. This way, their partner will not be able to guess as easily.

Answers will vary.

Additional Resources

📶 **Technology: Online Resources**
- Communication Activities: Audio Act. 4
- Teacher's Resource Materials: Audio Script
- Technology: Audio Cap. PE

El calendario y la fecha

Standards: 1.2

Resources: Teacher's Resource Materials: Audio Script; Technology: Audio Cap. PE

Suggestions: You may want to present this vocabulary in three sets: days of the week, months of the year, and asking and telling the date. Show students a calendar, and explain that in most Spanish-speaking countries, calendars start with Monday. Prompt students to ask you: *¿Qué día es hoy?* Respond and point to the day at the top of the calendar, then ask students: *Y mañana, ¿qué día es mañana?* Repeat this exercise for each of the days of the week.

Use the question *¿Cuántos días hay en el mes de...?* to introduce the months in order. Students answer with a number. As they listen, ask students to raise their hand when they hear their birth month.

Direct attention to the *Nota.*

Use the dialogues to introduce how to ask the date. Practice other dates by flipping through a calendar and pointing to random dates. Direct attention to the second *Nota,* then include **el primero** in the practice. Each day at the beginning of class, ask students what the date is.

Starter Activity

Use flashcards to quickly drill students on numbers 1–31.

🔊 El calendario y la fecha

el mes — el día

			agosto			
lunes	**martes**	**miércoles**	**jueves**	**viernes**	**sábado**	**domingo**
				1	2	3
4	5	6	7	8	9	10
11	12	13	14	15	16	17
18	19	20	21	22	23	24
25	26	27	28	29	30	31

la semana

—¿Qué día es hoy?
—Hoy es lunes. Mañana es martes.
—¿Cuántos días hay en el mes de agosto?
—Hay treinta y un días.

Los meses del año

← agosto ∨ →

enero
l m m j v s d
1 2 3 4 5
6 7 8 9 10 11 12
13 14 15 16 17 18 19
20 21 22 23 24 25 26
27 28 29 30 31

febrero
l m m j v s d
1 2
3 4 5 6 7 8 9
10 11 12 13 14 15 16
17 18 19 20 21 22 23
24 25 26 27 28

marzo
l m m j v s d
1 2
3 4 5 6 7 8 9
10 11 12 13 14 15 16
17 18 19 20 21 22 23
24 25 26 27 28 29 30
31

abril
l m m j v s d
1 2 3 4 5 6
7 8 9 10 11 12 13
14 15 16 17 18 19 20
21 22 23 24 25 26 27
28 29 30

mayo
l m m j v s d
1 2 3 4
5 6 7 8 9 10 11
12 13 14 15 16 17 18
19 20 21 22 23 24 25
26 27 28 29 30 31

junio
l m m j v s d
1
2 3 4 5 6 7 8
9 10 11 12 13 14 15
16 17 18 19 20 21 22
23 24 25 26 27 28 29
30

julio
l m m j v s d
1 2 3 4 5 6
7 8 9 10 11 12 13
14 15 16 17 18 19 20
21 22 23 24 25 26 27
28 29 30 31

agosto
l m m j v s d
1 2 3
4 5 6 7 8 9 10
11 12 13 14 15 16 17
18 19 20 21 22 23 24
25 26 27 28 29 30 31

septiembre
l m m j v s d
1 2 3 4 5 6 7
8 9 10 11 12 13 14
15 16 17 18 19 20 21
22 23 24 25 26 27 28
29 30

octubre
l m m j v s d
1 2 3 4 5
6 7 8 9 10 11 12
13 14 15 16 17 18 19
20 21 22 23 24 25 26
27 28 29 30 31

noviembre
l m m j v s d
1 2
3 4 5 6 7 8 9
10 11 12 13 14 15 16
17 18 19 20 21 22 23
24 25 26 27 28 29 30

diciembre
l m m j v s d
1 2 3 4 5 6 7
8 9 10 11 12 13 14
15 16 17 18 19 20 21
22 23 24 25 26 27 28
29 30 31

14 catorce • En la clase

Nota

Notice that the days of the week and the months of the year are not capitalized in Spanish, except at the beginning of sentences.

The first day of the week in a Spanish-language calendar is *lunes.*

Differentiated Instruction

Heritage Speakers

Have students research and write down the names and dates of three important celebrations in their heritage countries. Give them the opportunity to describe the occasion and the festivities that occur during these celebrations. Check their written work for correct spelling, including use of accents.

Challenge/Pre-AP®

Have students make a twelve-month calendar using the Spanish names for months and days of the week. Students should note important days, such as school holidays and classmates' birthdays. You may want students to research and include important holidays in Spanish-speaking cultures. Post the calendars in the room.

＋		‹	agosto	›		🔍 ▭
lunes	martes	miércoles	jueves	viernes	sábado	domingo
			el primero	1	2	3
4	5	6	7	8	9	10
11	12	13	14	15	16	17
18	19	20	21	22	23	24
25	26	27	28	29	30	31

el 22 de agosto

—¿Cuál es la fecha?

—Es el 22 de agosto.

—¿Cuál es la fecha?

—Es **el primero** de agosto.

Nota
To say the first day of the month, use *el primero*. For the other days, use the numbers *dos, tres,* and so on.

8

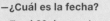

Hoy y mañana

🎤 HABLAR EN PAREJA Ask and answer according to the model.

Videomodelo
lunes
A —¿Qué día es hoy?
B —Hoy es *lunes.* Mañana es **martes.**

1. martes
2. sábado
3. jueves
4. miércoles
5. viernes
6. domingo

9

Días de fiesta

✏ LEER, ESCRIBIR Read the following sentences and rewrite them, making the necessary corrections.

1. El Día de San Patricio es el 14 de enero.
2. El Día de San Valentín es en junio.
3. Januká es en febrero.
4. La Navidad *(Christmas)* es el 25 de noviembre.
5. El Día de la Independencia de los Estados Unidos *(United States)* es el 4 de junio.
6. El Año Nuevo *(New Year's Day)* es en diciembre.
7. Hoy es el 3 de agosto.

Para empezar • quince **15**

Enrich Your Teaching

Culture Note

Cinco de mayo commemorates the victory of the Mexican army over the invading French army at the Battle of Puebla in 1862. It is not, as is commonly misunderstood, Mexican Independence Day, which is celebrated September 15 and 16. *Cinco de mayo* has become an occasion for parties and celebration in the United States, even among people of other heritages.

8

Standards: 1.1

Suggestions: Be sure students understand their roles. Have them switch roles and repeat the activity.

Answers:

Student B:
1. Hoy es martes. Mañana es miércoles.
2. ...domingo.
3. ...viernes.
4. ...jueves.
5. ...sábado.
6. ...lunes.

Extension: Create a spinner with the seven days of the week randomly placed. Have students spin and tell you the day that follows the day shown.

9

Standards: 1.3

Suggestions: Tell students to first read to identify the errors, then to read again, substituting the correct information before they write their sentences. When students are done, show the answers and have them correct their sentences if necessary.

Answers:
1. El Día de San Patricio es el 17 de marzo.
2. El Día de San Valentín es en febrero.
3. Januká es en diciembre.
4. La Navidad es el 25 de diciembre.
5. El Día de la Independencia de los Estados Unidos es el 4 de julio.
6. El Año Nuevo es en enero.
7. Hoy es el *(the current date).*

Teaching with Photos

Direct attention to the photo. Ask: *¿Qué día es?* Have students read the caption and answer. Encourage them to look for and read captions throughout the text, because they will give important information and will also use new words and structures. Explain how photos can support understanding of unfamiliar words.

10

Suggestions: Be sure students understand they are to answer based on the calendar in the book.

Answers:

1. Hoy es el 7 de julio.
2. Hoy es lunes.
3. Mañana es martes.
4. Mañana es el 8 de julio.
5. Hay 31 días en el mes de julio.
6. Hay 7 días en una semana.

Extension: Create calendars of other months and repeat the activity.

CULTURA

Suggestions: Explain that *los sanfermines* dates back to the Middle Ages. There are many other parts of this celebration, including music, dancing, and the Masquerade of the Giants, papiermâché figures of kings and queens that are paraded through the streets. Stress that the running of the bulls is a very dangerous activity that frequently results in injury or death.

Answers will vary, but may include events such as annual rodeos or the Kentucky Derby.

🌐 **Technology: Mapa global interactivo**, Actividad 2 Explore the narrow streets of Pamplona, Spain.

Additional Resources

🌐 **Technology: Online Resources**
- Instant Check
- *Para hispanohablantes*

Print
- Guided WB pp. 11–18
- Core WB pp. 7–8

10

El calendario

✏️ ESCRIBIR Answer the questions based on the calendar page below.

➕		‹	julio	›		🔍 🗒
lunes	martes	miércoles	jueves	viernes	sábado	domingo
	1	2	3	4	5	6
7 (hoy)	8	9	10	11	12	13
14	15	16	17	18	19	20
21	22	23	24	25	26	27
28	29	30	31			

1. ¿Cuál es la fecha hoy?
2. ¿Qué día de la semana es?
3. ¿Qué día es mañana?
4. ¿Cuál es la fecha de mañana?
5. ¿Cuántos días hay en este *(this)* mes?
6. ¿Cuántos días hay en una semana?

CULTURA ‹ España

Los sanfermines, or the "Running of the Bulls," is a popular two-week festival in Pamplona, Spain, named for the town's patron saint, San Fermín, who is commemorated on July 7 each year. The celebration includes daily bullfights, but before they begin the real excitement starts! As the bulls are released from their pens and run through the streets, many people run ahead or alongside them to the bullring.

Pre-AP® Integration: Entertainment What festivals are you familiar with in which animals play a role?

🌐 **Mapa global interactivo** Explore the narrow streets of Pamplona, Spain, and compare the city's layout with where you live.

La Fiesta de San Fermín, en Pamplona, España

16 dieciséis • En la clase

Differentiated Instruction

Challenge

Ask students to research Pamplona and *los sanfermines.* Remind them to include information on the other aspects of the two-week-long festival, not just on the running of the bulls. Suggest that they create print or digital visuals to share with the class.

Special Needs

Some students may have difficulty grasping the abstraction of pretending that it is a different date in *Actividad* 10. If so, make a calendar that shows today's date and have them answer the questions on that basis.

11

El calendario azteca

LEER The Aztecs were a nomadic tribe that finally settled in the valley of central Mexico in 1325. They established their capital, Tenochtitlán, on a swampy lake and built a mighty empire that dominated most of Mexico. The Aztec empire flourished until 1521, when it was defeated by the Spaniards, led by Hernán Cortés.

Conexiones ◀ La historia

One of the most famous symbols of Mexico is the monolith, or huge stone, carved by the Aztecs in 1479. Known today as the Aztec calendar or the Sun Stone, the carving weighs almost 24 tons and is approximately 12 feet in diameter. The Aztecs dedicated it to the sun, represented by the face in the center. The calendar represents a 260-day year.

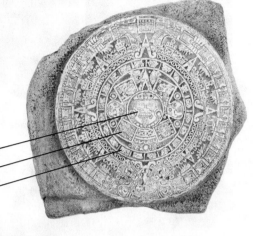

Representation of the sun, or Tonatiuh

One of the previous four world creations

This band shows the 20 days of the month.

12

Los símbolos aztecas

✏️ **ESCRIBIR** Here are several glyphs representing days found on the Sun Stone. Match the glyph with the Spanish word. What do you think each of the glyphs represents? Why do you think the Aztecs included those symbols on their calendar?

a. Jaguar

b. Perro

c. Movimiento

d. Serpiente

e. Cráneo

f. Agua

Enrich Your Teaching

Culture Note

After the Spaniards conquered the Aztec city of Tenochtitlán (now Mexico City) in 1521, the Sun Stone was buried. It was rediscovered December 17, 1790, in what is now the **Zócalo,** or main plaza, of Mexico City. The Sun Stone now sits in Mexico's National Museum of Anthropology.

21st Century Skills

Social and Cross-Cultural Skills

After students have read the *Conexiones: La historia* note on page 17, guide them in a brief investigation about different forms of time tracking and calendar models among Native American tribes in the United States. Have them find information about the importance of the Moon in the formation of calendars among these groups. Compare this to the central role played by the Sun in the Aztec calendar.

11

Standards: 3.1

Suggestions: Throughout the program, you will find *Conexiones* activities that link language study with other disciplines. Students are moved into working directly in Spanish as quickly as possible. The *Conexiones* will either include activities and questions or will be followed by a related activity. Ask: Why might a people like the Aztecs abandon a nomadic lifestyle, settle, and develop agriculture? How long did the Aztecs dominate Mexico? What does the Sun Stone suggest about the Aztec culture?

12

Standards: 3.1

Suggestions: Help students define the Spanish words before beginning the activity.

Answers:

1. d   **2.** e   **3.** f   **4.** b   **5.** a   **6.** c

Assessment

Prueba P-2 with Remediation (online only)
Quiz: En la clase
• Prueba P-2

¿Qué tiempo hace?

Standards: 1.2

Resources: Teacher's Resource Materials: Input Script, Clip Art, Audio Script; Technology: Audio Cap. PE

Suggestions: Use gestures to convey meaning. Bring in clothing or other items associated with each weather condition and use them in presenting and cueing the vocabulary. Have volunteers choose one of the items to hold up and ask their classmates ¿Qué tiempo hace? Make this a regular question that you ask at the beginning of each class period. After modeling each expression, ask questions like ¿Hace calor en diciembre? Say the name of a month and a region of the United States, and ask students for possible logical weather conditions.

To introduce the seasons, model pronunciation. Then say the months of a particular season (**septiembre, octubre, noviembre**) and ask students to choose which one it is.

Technology: Interactive Whiteboard

Vocabulary Activities PE Use the whiteboard activities in your Teacher Resources as you progress through the vocabulary practice with your class.

Additional Resources

Technology: Online Resources
- Instant Check
- Guided, Core, Audio, Writing, Reading
- *Para hispanohablantes*
- Teacher's Resource Materials: Audio Script
- Technology: Audio Cap. PE

Print
- Guided WB pp. 19–24
- Core WB p. 9

---

3 El Tiempo

OBJECTIVES
▶ Describe weather conditions
▶ Identify the seasons
▶ Compare weather in the Northern and Southern Hemispheres

🔊 ¿Qué tiempo hace?

Hace sol. ☀

Hace calor. 🌡

Hace frío. 🌡

Hace viento. 〰

Llueve. ☁

Nieva. ❄

Las estaciones

la primavera   el verano   el otoño   el invierno

Differentiated Instruction

Challenge/Pre-AP®
Assign students a city in the Spanish-speaking world, and have them follow the weather for one week. They can find weather conditions on the Internet and summarize their findings for the class. Make a bulletin board to track the weather. Have students provide additional facts about the cities and tell how weather may affect the lifestyle there.

Bodily/Kinesthetic Learner
Nonverbal cues can often help students retain new vocabulary and expressions. Ask students to work in pairs to pantomime each of the weather conditions and seasons. Have students guess what kind of weather or which season is being represented and say the vocabulary word.

1

El tiempo

ESCUCHAR You will hear six descriptions of different weather conditions. Write the numbers 1–6 on a sheet of paper. Then, next to each number, write the letter of the photo for which the weather is being described.

2

¿Qué tiempo hace?

HABLAR EN PAREJA Work with a partner. Ask and answer the questions based on the city and weather information for each item.

Videomodelo

Miami / julio / ☀
A —¿Qué tiempo hace en **Miami** en **julio**?
B —**Hace sol.**

1. Denver / enero / ❄
2. Chicago / octubre / 🌬
3. San Francisco / noviembre / 🌧
4. Washington, D.C. / junio / 🌡
5. Minneapolis / diciembre / 🌡
6. Dallas / agosto / 🌡

3

Las estaciones

HABLAR, ESCRIBIR Answer the questions based on where you live.

1. ¿Qué tiempo hace en la primavera? ¿En el otoño? ¿En el verano? ¿En el invierno?
2. ¿En qué estación hace frío? ¿Calor? ¿Sol? ¿Viento?
3. ¿En qué estación llueve?
4. ¿En qué estación nieva?

Para empezar • diecinueve **19**

Enrich Your Teaching

Teacher-to-Teacher

Make photocopies of a newspaper weather map. Have students use the symbols on the map or read the weather for various cities and then write a sentence indicating the weather for those cities.

21st Century Skills

Information Literacy Encourage teams of students to go online to gather weather and climate data from several cities in Spanish-speaking countries. Have them arrange the data in charts and tables and then use the graphics to compare at least two places.

Starter Activity

Standards: 1.2

Put these expressions on the board: *Hace calor, hace frío, hace viento, nieva, llueve, hace sol.* Ask students to draw a simple illustration. As a follow-up, have them point to the appropriate illustration as you say the expressions.

1

Standards: 1.2

Resources: Teacher's Resource Materials: Audio Script; Technology: Audio Cap. PE

Suggestions: Ask students to briefly describe in English the weather they see in each picture. Explain that there are six items, so some of the pictures will be used more than once.

Technology: Audio Script and Answers

1. Hace calor. (b)
2. Llueve. (d)
3. Nieva. (c)
4. Hace frío. (c)
5. Hace viento. (d)
6. Hace sol. No hace calor. (a)

2

Standards: 1.1

Suggestions: Ask students to think about what the weather is like in each city. Be sure they understand which words they need to replace in each item.

Answers:

1. Nieva. / Hace frío.
2. Hace viento.
3. Llueve.
4. Hace calor. / Hace sol.
5. Hace frío.
6. Hace calor. / Hace sol.

Extension: Ask: *¿Qué tiempo hace en* (your town) *en* (month)? Have volunteers ask questions of their classmates.

3

Standards: 1.2, 1.3

Suggestions: Have students write this activity in paragraph form, giving it a title such as *El tiempo en* (name of town).

Answers will vary.

19

4

Suggestions: Ask students to describe the location of Colorado and Chile. Ask them to look at the Mapa global interactivo. Refer students to the pictures. Be sure they understand the difference between the Northern and Southern Hemispheres. Have students share their answers with the class.

Answers:

1. En febrero hace calor en Chile.
2. En junio hace calor en Colorado.
3. Answers will vary.

Extension: Write on the board the names of ten places in the Northern and Southern Hemispheres and refer students to a world map or globe. Have students identify which hemisphere each place is in and ask them what the weather might be like during *enero, abril, junio, julio, septiembre,* and *noviembre.*

🌐 **Technology: Mapa global interactivo,** Actividad 3 Locate the continents of North and South America, the equator, and the country of Ecuador. Then compare weather north and south of the equator.

Teacher-to-Teacher

Using a world map or globe, ask students to follow these instructions: *Señalen dónde hace frío en enero; Señalen dónde hace calor en enero; Señalen dónde hace frío en julio; Señalen dónde hace calor en julio; Señalen dónde nieva en diciembre; Señalen dónde nieva en agosto.* Then have students work in pairs to think of more scenarios and give instructions to classmates.

4

Dos hemisferios

✏️ **LEER, ESCRIBIR, HABLAR** Read about the seasons in the Northern and Southern Hemispheres and then answer the questions.

Conexiones ⟨ **La geografía**

Did you know that the seasons for the Northern and Southern Hemispheres are reversed? When it's winter in the Northern Hemisphere, it's summer in the Southern Hemisphere and vice versa. So if you want to ski all year round, go from the slopes of the Rockies in Colorado in December to those of the Andes in Bariloche, Argentina in July. Or for a December getaway to a warmer climate, go to one of the coastal resorts at Viña del Mar, Chile.

🌐 **Mapa global interactivo** Locate North and South America and compare the weather north and south of the equator.

1. En febrero, ¿qué tiempo hace en Chile?
2. En junio, ¿qué tiempo hace en Colorado?
3. En tu comunidad, ¿qué tiempo hace en diciembre? ¿Y en agosto?

20 veinte • El tiempo

Differentiated Instruction

Students with Learning Difficulties

You might need to read this passage with students who struggle with reading. Encourage them to read through the questions at the bottom prior to reading. Converting temperatures might prove a challenge for students; the *Nota* on p. 21 could be an added task not required of all students.

Heritage Speakers

Have students research the climate and seasons of their heritage countries and write a short paragraph. They should note the country's hemisphere, compare the weather with that of your community, and distinguish the seasons and their temperatures in the two places.

Go Online to practice
PEARSON
realize™

PearsonSchool.com/Autentico

VIDEO · WRITING · SPEAK/RECORD · MAPA GLOBAL

Interpersonal PE

ciudad	diciembre	julio
Asunción, Paraguay	85° F / 29° C	75° F / 24° C
Bogotá, Colombia	66° F / 19° C	64° F / 17° C
Buenos Aires, Argentina	78° F / 26° C	50° F / 10° C
Caracas, Venezuela	80° F / 27° C	80° F / 27° C
Chicago	36° F / 2° C	75° F / 24° C
Ciudad de méxico, México	70° F / 21° C	74° F / 23° C
Guatemala, Guatemala	72° F / 22° C	74° F / 23° C
La Habana, Cuba	76° F / 24° C	82° F / 28° C
La Paz, Bolivia	58° F /15° C	55° F /13° C
Lima, Perú	76° F / 24° C	76° F / 24° C
Los Ángeles	67° F / 19° C	88° F / 31° C
Miami	76° F / 24° C	97° F / 36° C
Nueva York	41° F / 5° C	74° F / 23° C
Quito, Ecuador	65° F / 18° C	67° F / 19° C
San José, Costa Rica	78° F / 26° C	78° F / 26° C
San Juan, Puerto Rico	74° F / 23° C	80° F / 27° C
Santiago, Chile	82° F / 28° C	50° F / 10° C
Seattle	41° F / 5° C	66° F / 19° C
St. Louis	36° F / 2° C	81° F / 27° C
Tegucigalpa, Honduras	70° F / 21° C	81° F / 27° C

Los Ángeles

Tegucigalpa, Honduras   Asunción, Paraguay

Nota
In most parts of the world, people express temperatures in Celsius. A simple way to convert from Celsius to Fahrenheit is to multiply the temperature by $\frac{9}{5}$, then add 32.

$30°C = \underline{?}\ F$
$30 \times \frac{9}{5} = 54 + 32$
$30°C = 86°F$

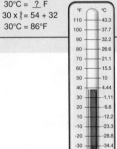

5 ¿Hace calor o hace frío?

🎤 **HABLAR EN PAREJA** Work with a partner. Discuss the weather in six different places on the chart.

▶ **Videomodelo**
A —¿Qué tiempo hace en **Chicago** en **diciembre**?
B —Hace **frío**.

6 ¿Y qué tiempo hace en . . . ?

🎤 **HABLAR EN PAREJA** Work with a partner. Ask about the temperature in six different places on the chart.

▶ **Videomodelo**
A —¿Cuál es la temperatura en **Quito** en **diciembre**?
B —Sesenta y cinco grados.
o: —Dieciocho grados.

Para decir más . . .
la temperatura = temperature
grados = degrees

Para empezar • veintiuno **21**

Starter Activity
Have students turn to p. 7 and review *Los números*.

5

Standards: 1.1, 3.1

Suggestions: Using the Mapa global interactivo, help students locate the countries and cities in the chart. Direct their attention to the *Nota*. To internalize the concept, have them practice one or two conversions using a calculator. Have students take turns asking and answering the questions. Both students should write the questions and the answers, indicating the cities they selected and their weather.

Answers will vary.

Extension: Students should point to the map and show the cities they chose.

6

Standards: 1.1

Suggestions: Point out that the words in *Para decir más....* are helpful for completing the activity but do not have to be memorized.

Answers will vary.

Pre-AP® Integration
- **Learning Objective:** Interpersonal Speaking
- **Activity 6:** Students practice informal speaking skills as they ask and answer questions about weather.
- **Pre-AP® Resource Materials:** Comprehensive guide to Pre-AP® speaking skill development

Additional Resources
📶 **Technology: Online Resources**
- Communication Activities Audio Act. 5
- Teacher's Resource Materials: Audio Script
- Technology: Audio Cap. PE

Assessment
Prueba P-3 with Remediation (online only)
Quiz: El tiempo
- Prueba P-3

Enrich Your Teaching

Culture Note
The highest temperature in the continental United States,134°F (57°C), was recorded on July 10, 1913, in Death Valley, California. The lowest recorded temperature, –70°F (–57°C), was at Roger's Pass, Montana, on January 20, 1954. In South America, the highest and lowest recorded temperatures were in Argentina: 120°F (49°C) at Rivadavia on December 11, 1905, and –27°F (–33°C) at Sarmiento on June 1, 1907. Remind students that the highest and lowest temperatures happen at opposite times of the year in North and South America. Write these dates and have students read them.

Review Activities

To greet someone and to say good-bye: Have students say greetings and leave-takings in pairs.

To ask and tell how someone is: Have students circulate from partner to partner asking and telling how they are doing.

To tell time: Have students list five times and take turns asking and answering *¿Qué hora es?*

To count up to 100: Have students write the numerals 1–9 on index cards. Shuffle the cards and place them face down. Each player draws two cards and says the number that is formed.

To talk about the body: Have students draw the outline of a person and identify the body parts, referring to p. 9 for help.

To talk about the classroom: Have students use the Clip Art in the *Teacher's Resource Materials* to make flashcards to identify classroom items.

To say the date: Have partners ask and answer *¿Qué día es hoy?* and *¿Cuál es la fecha?* while pointing to a calendar.

To ask for help: Have students quiz one another on word meanings using the questions shown.

To talk about the weather: Have students ask each other, *¿Qué tiempo hace?*

To talk about the seasons: Have students identify seasons using images.

Digital Portfolio

Have students select one or two items that they feel best demonstrate their achievements in Spanish to include in their portfolios. Have them also include the Chapter Checklist and Self Assessment Worksheet.

Pre-AP® Integration

- **Learning Objective:** Interpersonal speaking
- **Pre-AP® Resource Materials Activity Sheets, Tema PE:** Have students work in pairs, and choose from questions 1–10 to guide their conversation.

Additional Resources

Technology: Online Resources
- Instant Check
- Integrated Performance Assessment
- *Para hispanohablantes*

Print
- Core WB pp. 10–11
- Communication Activities: p. 226

Teacher Resources
- Teacher's Resource Materials: Situation Cards, Clip Art
- Assessment Program: Chapter Checklist and Self-Assessment Worksheet

---

Repaso del capítulo

OBJECTIVES
▶ Review the vocabulary
▶ Demonstrate you can perform the tasks on p. 23

🔊 Vocabulario

En la escuela

to greet someone

Buenos días.	Good morning.
Buenas noches.	Good evening.
Buenas tardes.	Good afternoon.
¡Hola!	Hello!
¿Cómo te llamas?	What is your name?
Me llamo . . .	My name is . . .
Encantado, -a.	Delighted.
Igualmente.	Likewise.
Mucho gusto.	Pleased to meet you.
señor, Sr.	sir, Mr.
señora, Sra.	madam, Mrs.
señorita, Srta.	miss, Miss

to ask and tell how someone is

¿Cómo está Ud.? *(formal)*	How are you?
¿Cómo estás? *(familiar)*	How are you?
¿Qué pasa?	What's happening?
¿Qué tal?	How are you?
¿Y tú? / ¿Y usted (Ud.)?	And you?
(muy) bien	(very) well
nada	nothing
regular	okay, so-so
gracias	thank you

to say good-bye

¡Adiós!	Good-bye!
Hasta luego.	See you later.
Hasta mañana.	See you tomorrow.
¡Nos vemos!	See you!

to tell time

¿Qué hora es?	What time is it?
Es la una.	It's one o'clock.
Son las . . . y / menos . . .	It's . . . (time).
y cuarto / menos cuarto	quarter past / quarter to
y media	thirty, half-past

to count up to 100 (Turn to p. 7.)

to talk about the body (Turn to p. 9.)

En la clase

to talk about the classroom

el bolígrafo	pen
la carpeta	folder
el cuaderno	notebook
el estudiante, la estudiante	student
la hoja de papel	sheet of paper
el lápiz	pencil
el libro	book
el profesor, la profesora	teacher
el pupitre	(student) desk
la sala de clases	classroom

to say the date

el año	year
el día	day
el mes	month
la semana	week
¿Qué día es hoy?	What day is today?
¿Cuál es la fecha?	What is the date?
Es el *(number)* de *(month)*.	It's the . . . of . . .
Es el primero de *(month)*.	It's the first of . . .
hoy	today
mañana	tomorrow

to say the days of the week and the months of the year (Turn to p. 14.)

other useful words

¿cuántos, -as?	how many?
en	in
hay	there is / there are
por favor	please

to ask for help

¿Cómo se dice . . . ?	How do you say . . . ?
Se dice . . .	You say . . .
¿Cómo se escribe . . . ?	How is . . . spelled?
Se escribe . . .	It's spelled . . .
¿Qué quiere decir . . . ?	What does . . . mean?
Quiere decir . . .	It means . . .

Differentiated Instruction

Students with Learning Difficulties

The *Repaso* page contains a lot of information, and may be too much for some students to absorb and understand at once. Help students take the review section by section. Show them how to focus on things they've not mastered.

Challenge

You may wish to ask students to facilitate review sessions within small groups. Suggest that they write five review questions to share with their group.

El tiempo

to talk about the weather

¿Qué tiempo hace?	What's the weather like?
Hace calor.	It's hot.
Hace frío.	It's cold.
Hace sol.	It's sunny.
Hace viento.	It's windy.
Llueve.	It's raining.
Nieva.	It's snowing.

to talk about the seasons

la estación	season
el invierno	winter
el otoño	fall, autumn
la primavera	spring
el verano	summer

Preparación para el examen

Interpretive

1 ESCUCHAR On the exam you will be asked to listen to and understand people as they greet each other and introduce themselves. To practice, listen to some students greet people in the school halls. Answer these questions about each greeting: Is it morning or afternoon? Was the greeting directed to an adult? How did that person respond?

To review, see pp. 2–5 and Actividades 1, 4.

Interpretive

2 ESCUCHAR You will be asked to listen to and understand someone announcing the current date and time. To practice, listen to the message and answer the questions: What is the time of day? What is the date?

To review, see pp. 7–8 and Actividad 12; pp. 14–16 and Actividad 10.

Interpretive

3 LEER You will be asked to read and understand a description of the weather for a given day. To practice, read the weather forecast below. Answer the questions: What is the date? What are the high and low temperatures? What is the weather like?

> El dos de septiembre
> Hoy en San Antonio hace sol. La temperatura máxima es
> 75 grados y la mínima es 54. No llueve.

To review, see pp. 18–21 and Actividades 2–6.

Interpretive

4 LEER You will be asked to read a list of school supplies and identify them. To practice, copy the school supply list below onto a sheet of paper. Please note: *un, una* mean "a" or "an." Then look to see whether you have any of the items on your desk right now. Make a check mark next to each item you have.

un cuaderno	un lápiz	una hoja de papel
un bolígrafo	una carpeta	un libro

To review, see p. 10.

Differentiated Assessment

Core Assessment
- Assessment Program: Examen de *Para empezar*
- Technology: Audio Cap. PE
- ExamView: Chapter Test, Test Banks A and B

Challenge/Pre-AP®
- ExamView: Pre-AP® Test Bank
- Pre-AP® Resource Materials

Extra Support
- Alternate Assessment Program: Examen del capítulo PE
- Technology: Audio Cap. PE

Heritage Speakers
- Assessment Program: *Para hispanohablantes:* Examen del capítulo PE
- ExamView: Heritage Learner Test Bank

Performance Tasks

Standards: 1.2, 1.3

Student Resource: *Para hispanohablantes*
Teacher Resources: Teacher's Resource Materials: Audio Script; Technology: Audio Cap. PE

Note that the test for the *Para empezar* does not ask for active communicative production.

1. Escuchar

Suggestions: Remind students of the greetings for different times of day and for greeting adults versus friends.

Script and Answers:
1. —Buenas tardes, Sr. Ruiz. ¿Cómo está Ud.?
2. —Bien, señor. *(afternoon; to an adult; he is well)*
3. —¡Hola, Elena!
4. — Buenos días. Nos vemos en la escuela. *(morning; to a teen; she said good morning)*
5. —Julio, ¿qué tal?
   —Regular, ¿y tú? *(either; to a teen; he's so-so)*

2. Escuchar

Suggestions: Play the *audio* or read the script.

Script and Answers:
1. Muy buenos días. Es el veintidós de septiembre. Son las ocho y media de la mañana. *(morning; September 22)*
2. Muy buenas tardes. Es el ocho de enero. Son las dos y veinte de la tarde. *(afternoon; January 8)*
3. Muy buenas noches. Es el cuatro de noviembre. Son las nueve y diez de la noche. *(evening/night; November 4)*

3. Leer

Suggestions: Have volunteers share their answers with the class.

Answers: September 2; high temperature 75°; the low is 54°; it's sunny and not raining

4. Leer

Suggestions: Have students try this activity without consulting the vocabulary list.
Answers will vary.

CAPÍTULO 1A

¿Qué te gusta hacer?

Activities you and others like and don't like to do

Vocabulary: activities and expressions for saying what you like and don't like to do

Grammar: infinitives; making negative statements

Cultural Perspectives: favorite activities of teens

Auténtico: Mariachi Music Academy

CAPÍTULO 1B

Y tú, ¿cómo eres?

Personality traits

Vocabulary: adjectives and vocabulary to ask about and describe someone's personality

Grammar: adjectives; definite and indefinite articles; word order

Cultural Perspectives: opinions about what makes a good friend

Auténtico: Nataliz Jiménez Gives You 3 Practical Tips to Make Your Personality Shine in an Audition

Theme Support

Bulletin Boards

Theme: Mis amigos y yo

Ask students to cut out, copy, or download photos of people from many different cultures engaged in a variety of academic, social, and leisure activities, sports, crafts, and artistic pursuits. Cluster photos according to the types of activities featured.

Game

¿Quién es?

This game is played like Twenty Questions. Use it in *Capítulo* 1B.

Players: entire class   **Materials:** scraps of paper, pen, a paper bag

Rules:

1. Students write their names on scraps of paper and place them in a paper bag.
2. Shake the paper bag to mix up the names. Then call on a volunteer to come to the front of the class. The volunteer draws the name of a student from the paper bag, then gives the paper to you.
3. Students take turns asking the volunteer yes / no questions in an attempt to determine the identity of the person listed on the scrap of paper.

   Student 1: ¿Es una chica?   **Leader:** Sí.
   Student 2: ¿Es deportista?   **Leader:** Sí.
   Student 3: ¿Le gusta montar en bicicleta?   **Leader:** No.
4. When a student correctly guesses the identity of the person on the paper, he or she becomes the new volunteer.

Hands-on Culture

Craft: Maracas

Maracas are very popular percussion instruments in Spanish-speaking countries. They can be made of many materials.

Materials: newspaper, 2 round balloons, 2 jars, white glue, scissors, foil pan, measuring cup, pin, masking tape, 24 dried beans or small pebbles, 2 paper towel tubes, paint, paintbrush, crepe paper

Directions:

1. Cover work area with newspapers.
2. Blow up balloons to grapefruit size.
3. Place each balloon in the mouth of a jar, with the tied end inside the jar.
4. Cut strips of newspaper 6" × ½".
5. In the foil pan, mix equal amounts of white glue and water (about ½ cup each). Dip newspaper strips in glue mixture and apply wet strips to balloons, criss-crossing them. Use five layers to make the maraca strong. Be sure only the bottom parts of the balloons show through.
6. Let dry overnight. Hold each balloon by the tied end and burst it with a pin.
7. Remove the balloon. Insert 12 beans or pebbles through the hole in each maraca and tape the hole closed.
8. To make handles, cut four parallel slits (about 3" long) into the end of each paper towel tube, running lengthwise. Circle the tubes with tape just below the slits to keep them from splitting further. Spread the slit pieces apart and fit the maraca onto them. Tape the slit pieces firmly to the maraca, taping all the way around and ½ to ¾ of the way up the maraca. Paint and let dry overnight.
9. Cut two strips of crepe paper about 3" wide and 14" long. To make a fringe, cut 1½" slits all along the edge of each strip, about ½" apart. Glue the uncut edge of one strip to the handle of one of the maracas, starting just below the maraca. Wind and glue the strip around the handle.

21st Century Skills

Look for tips throughout *Tema* 1 to enrich your teaching by integrating 21st Century Skills. Suggestions for the Project-Based Learning and Theme Support follow below.

Project-Based Learning

Modify the Project-Based Learning with one or more of these suggestions:

Information Literacy Have students come up with creative ideas for arranging the content of their albums, such as themes, seasons, favorite places, activities, or people. Encourage them to decide how to choose materials at the outset.

Critical Thinking and Problem Solving Have students develop their own timeline for accomplishing different stages of the project. They should study the rubric and anticipate which grammar and vocabulary tools they will need. The handout "Solve Problems" can help them develop a plan of action.

Collaboration Have students working as partners compare the activities in their albums with those presented in the chapter. Provide them with the handout "Compare and Contrast" to help them organize their ideas.

Theme Culture

Social and Cross-Cultural Skills Have students review the *Cultura* notes on pages 31 and 34, comparing responses with a partner's. They can investigate similarities and differences they notice regarding activities in the two countries. What could explain what they notice? Location? Climate?

▶ **Videocultura** View *Amigos y actividades* with the class to learn more about how friends like to spend their time.

Project-Based Learning

Álbum de recuerdos

Overview: Students create two pages for a digital photo album featuring photos of their friends and themselves with captions written underneath. They then give an oral presentation of their album, describing the people in the photos and telling what they like and don't like to do. Students can create decorations using physical materials and scan them to digital files.

Resources: electronic or print photos, image editing and presentation software and/or construction paper, magazines, colored pencils, markers, glue, scissors

Sequence: (suggestions for when to do each step appear throughout the chapters)

1A **Step 1.** Review instructions so students know what is expected of them. Hand out the Theme 1 Project Instructions and the rubric.

Step 2. Students submit a rough sketch of their photo album pages. Return the sketches with your suggestions. For vocabulary and grammar practice, ask students to work with a partner and present their drafts to each other.

Step 3. Students do layouts. Encourage students to try different arrangements before finalizing layouts and writing captions.

1B **Step 4.** Students submit a draft of their captions. Note your corrections and suggestions, then return the drafts to students.

Step 5. Students complete and present their albums to the class. They should describe the people in the photos and say what they like and don't like to do.

Options

1. Students feature fictitious friends in their scrapbook.
2. Students create scrapbook pages only about themselves.

Assessment

Here is a detailed rubric for assessing this project:

Theme 1 Project: *Álbum de recuerdos*

Rubric	Score 1	Score 3	Score 5
Evidence of planning	You provided no written draft or page layouts.	Your draft was written and layout created, but not corrected.	You corrected your draft and layout.
Your use of illustrations	You included no photos / visuals.	Your photos / visuals were included, but your layout was unorganized.	Your album was easy to read, complete, and accurate.
Your presentation	You included little of the required information for each photo.	You included most of the required information for each photo.	You included all the required information for each photo.

1A ¿Qué te gusta hacer?

AT A GLANCE

Objectives
- Listen to and read about activities people like and don't like to do
- Talk and write about what you and others like and don't like to do
- Describe your favorite activities and ask others about theirs
- Identify cultural practices in an authentic video about an after-school music program
- Describe dances and music from the Spanish-speaking world and compare them to dances you know
- Compare favorite activities of Spanish-speaking teens to those of teens in the United States

Vocabulary
- Activities
- Expressing likes and dislikes

Grammar
- Infinitives

- Negatives
- Expressing agreement or disagreement

Culture
- Pablo Picasso, p. 25
- Outdoor cafés, p. 31
- **La Plaza Mayor** in Salamanca, p. 31
- The **güiro** and rhythm instruments, p. 34
- Jaime Antonio González Colson, p. 34
- Music and dances of different Spanish-speaking countries, pp. 35, 42
- Spanish architecture, pp. 44–45

Authentic Resources
- Video about how students in a high school get to practice their pastime during the school day, pp. 44–45

Recycle
- Accent marks
- *nada*

RESOURCES

	FOR THE STUDENT	DIGITAL	PRINT	FOR THE TEACHER	DIGITAL	PRINT
Plan				Teacher's Edition	•	•
				Teacher's Resource Materials	•	
				Pre-AP® Resource Materials	•	
				Lesson Plans, pp. 24-e, 24-f	•	
				Mapa global interactivo	•	
Introducción pp. 24–50						
Present	Student Edition, pp. 24–25	•	•	Teacher's Edition, pp. 24–25	•	•
	DK Reference Atlas	•		Teacher's Resource Materials	•	
	Videocultura	•		Mapa global interactivo	•	
	Para hispanohablantes	•				
Vocabulario en contexto pp. 26–29						
Present & Practice	Student Edition, pp. 26–29	•	•	Teacher's Edition, pp. 26–29	•	•
	Audio	•		Teacher's Resource Materials	•	
	Videohistoria	•		Vocabulary Clip Art	•	
	Flashcards	•		Technology: Audio	•	
	Instant Check	•		Video Program: Videohistoria	•	
	Guided WB, pp. 25–32	•	•			
	Core WB, pp. 13–16	•	•			
	Communication Activities	•				
	Para hispanohablantes	•				
Assess and Remediate				Prueba 1A–1: Assessment Program, pp. 13–14	•	
				Assessment Program para hispanohablantes, pp. 13–14	•	

24-c

	FOR THE STUDENT	DIGITAL	PRINT	FOR THE TEACHER	DIGITAL	PRINT
Vocabulario en uso pp. 30–31						
Present & Practice	Student Edition, pp. 30–31	•	•	Interactive Whiteboard Vocabulary Activities	•	
	Instant Check	•		Teacher's Edition, pp. 30–31	•	•
	Communication Activities	•		Teacher's Resource Materials	•	
	Para hispanohablantes	•		Communicative Pair Activities	•	
	Communicative Pair Activities	•		Technology: Audio	•	
				Videomodelos	•	
Assess and Remediate				Prueba 1A-2 with Remediation	•	
				Prueba 1A-2: Assessment Program, pp. 15–16	•	
				Assessment Program para hispanohablantes, pp. 15–16	•	
Gramática pp. 32–39						
Present & Practice	Student Edition, pp. 32–39	•	•	Interactive Whiteboard Grammar Activities	•	
	Instant Check	•		Teacher's Edition, pp. 32–39	•	•
	Animated Verbs	•		Teacher's Resource Materials	•	
	Tutorial Video: Grammar	•		Communicative Pair Activities	•	
	Canción de hip hop	•		Technology: Audio	•	
	Guided WB, pp. 33–36	•	•	Videomodelos	•	
	Core WB, pp. 17–19	•	•	Video Program: GramActiva	•	
	Communication Activities	•				
	Para hispanohablantes	•				
	Communicative Pair Activities	•				
Assess and Remediate				Pruebas 1A–3 and 1A–4 with Remediation	•	
				Pruebas 1A–3, 1A–4: Assessment Program, pp. 17–18	•	
				Assessment Program para hispanohablantes, pp. 17–18	•	
Aplicación pp. 40–45						
Apply	Student Edition, pp. 40–45	•	•	Teacher's Edition, pp. 40–45	•	•
	Authentic Resources Workbook	•	•	Teacher's Resource Materials	•	
	Authentic Resources	•		Mapa global interactivo	•	
	Online Cultural Reading	•		Authentic Resources Lesson Plans with scripts, answer keys	•	
	Guided WB, pp. 37–38	•	•			
	Communication Activities	•				
	Para hispanohablantes	•				
Repaso del capítulo pp. 46–47						
Review	Student Edition, pp. 46–47	•	•	Teacher's Edition, pp. 46–47	•	•
	Online Puzzles and Games	•		Teacher's Resource Materials	•	
	Core WB, pp. 20–21	•	•	Technology: Audio	•	
	Communication Activities	•				
	Para hispanohablantes	•				
	Instant Check	•				
Chapter Assessment						
Assess				Examen del capítulo 1A	•	
				Assessment Program, pp. 19–25	•	
				Alternate Assessment Program, pp. 3–7	•	
				Assessment Program para hispanohablantes, pp. 19–25	•	
				Technology: Audio, Cap. 1A, Examen	•	
				ExamView: Test Banks A and B questions only online	•	
				Heritage Learner Test Bank	•	
				Pre-AP® Test Bank	•	

LESSON PLAN (50 MINUTES)

DAY	Warm-up / Assess	Preview / Present / Practice / Communicate		Wrap-up / Homework Options
1	**Warm-up** (10 min.) • Return Examen del capítulo	**Chapter Opener** (5 min.) • Objectives • Arte y cultura	**Vocabulario en contexto** (30 min.) • Presentation: Vocabulario en contexto • Actividades 1, 2	**Wrap-up and Homework Options** (5 min.) • Core Practice 1A-1, 1A-2
2	**Warm-up** (5 min.) • Homework check	**Vocabulario en contexto** (40 min.) • Presentation: Videohistoria *Bienvenidos a Codo a codo* • View: Videohistoria	• Interactive Whiteboard Vocabulary Activities • Video Activities 1, 2, 3, 4 • Actividades 3, 4	**Wrap-up and Homework Options** (5 min.) • Core Practice 1A-3, 1A-4 • Prueba 1A-1: Vocabulary recognition
3	**Warm-up** (10 min.) • Actividades 5, 6 • Homework check • **Formative Assessment** (10 min.) • Prueba 1A-1: Vocabulary recognition	**Vocabulario en uso** (25 min.) • Actividades 7, 8 • Cultura • Audio Activities 5, 6 • Communicative Pair Activity		**Wrap-up and Homework Options** (5 min.) • Writing Activity 10 • Prueba 1A-2 with Remediation: Vocabulary production
4	**Warm-up** (5 min.) • Homework check • **Formative Assessment** (10 min.) • Prueba 1A-2 with Remediation: Vocabulary production	**Gramática y vocabulario en uso** (30 min.) • Presentation: Infinitives • View: GramActiva video • Interactive Whiteboard Grammar Activities	• Actividades 9, 10, 12, 13 • Communicative Pair Activity • Audio Activity 7	**Wrap-up and Homework Options** (5 min.) • Core Practice 1A-5 • Actividad 11 • Prueba 1A-3 with Remediation: Infinitives
5	**Warm-up** (10 min.) • Writing Activity 11 • Homework check • **Formative Assessment** (10 min.) • Prueba 1A-3 with Remediation: Infinitives	**Gramática y vocabulario en uso** (25 min.) • Exploración del lenguaje • Cultura • Actividad 14 • Presentation: Negatives	• View: GramActiva video • Interactive Whiteboard Grammar Activities • Actividades 16, 17	**Wrap-up and Homework Options** (5 min.) • Core Practice 1A-6
6	**Warm-up** (10 min.) • Actividad 15 • Homework check	**Gramática y vocabulario en uso** (35 min.) • Audio Activity 8 • Writing Activity 12 • Communicative Pair Activity • Presentation: Expressing agreement or disagreement	• Interactive Whiteboard Grammar Activities • Actividades 18, 19	**Wrap-up and Homework Options** (5 min.) • Prueba 1A-4 with Remediation: Negatives
7	**Warm-up** (5 min.) • Review Negatives • **Formative Assessment** (10 min.) • Prueba 1A-4 with Remediation: Negatives	**Gramática y vocabulario en uso** (20 min.) • Audio Activity 9 • Writing Activity 13 • Pronunciación • El español en la comunidad	**Aplicación** (10 min.) • Lectura • ¿Comprendes?	**Wrap-up and Homework Options** (5 min.) • Core Practice 1A-7
8	**Warm-up** (10 min.) • Homework check	**Aplicación** (30 min.) • La cultura en vivo • Presentación oral: Steps 1, 2 • Auténtico		**Wrap-up and Homework Options** (10 min.) • Presentación oral: Step 2 • Preparación para el examen 3, 4, 5
9	**Warm-up** (5 min.) • Homework check	**Aplicación** (30 min.) • Presentación oral: Step 3	**Repaso del capítulo** (10 min.) • Vocabulario y gramática • Preparación para el examen 1, 2	**Wrap-up and Homework Options** (5 min.) • Core Practice 1A-8, 1A-9 • Instant Check • Examen del capítulo 1A
10	**Warm-up** (10 min.) • Homework check • **Summative Assessment** (40 min.) • Examen del capítulo 1A			

ALTERNATE LESSON PLAN (90 MINUTES)

DAY	Warm-up / Assess	Preview / Present / Practice / Communicate	Wrap-up / Homework Options
1	**Warm-up** (10 min.) • Return Examen del capítulo	**Chapter Opener** (15 min.) • Objectives • Arte y cultura **Vocabulario en contexto** (55 min.) • Presentation: Vocabulario en contexto • Actividades 1, 2 • Presentation: Videohistoria *Bienvenidos a Codo a codo* • View: Videohistoria • Video Activities 1, 2, 3, 4 • Actividades 3, 4	**Wrap-up and Homework Options** (10 min.) • Core Practice 1A-1, 1A-2, 1A-3, 1A-4 • Prueba 1A-1: Vocabulary recognition
2	**Warm-up** (10 min.) • Actividades 5, 6 • Homework check • **Formative Assessment** (10 min.) • Prueba 1A-1: Vocabulary recognition	**Vocabulario en uso** (10 min.) • Actividades 7, 8 • Cultura • Interactive Whiteboard Vocabulary Activities • Audio Activities 5, 6 **Gramática y vocabulario en uso** (55 min.) • Communicative Pair Activity • Presentation: Infinitives • View: GramActiva video • Interactive Whiteboard Grammar Activities • Actividades 9, 10, 12, 13 • Audio Activity 7 • Communicative Pair Activity	**Wrap-up and Homework Options** (5 min.) • Writing Activity 10 • Core Practice 1A-5 • Actividad 11 • Pruebas 1A-2, 1A-3 with Remediation: Vocabulary production, Infinitives
3	**Warm-up** (10 min.) • Homework check • Writing Activity 11 • **Formative Assessment** (15 min.) • Pruebas 1A-2, 1A-3 with Remediation: Vocabulary production, Infinitives	**Gramática y vocabulario en uso** (60 min.) • Exploración del lenguaje • Cultura • Actividad 14 • Presentation: Negatives • View: GramActiva video • Interactive Whiteboard Grammar Activities • Actividades 16, 17 • Audio Activity 8 • Writing Activity 12 • Communicative Pair Activity	**Wrap-up and Homework Options** (5 min.) • Core Practice 1A-6 • Prueba 1A-4 with Remediation: Negatives
4	**Warm-up** (5 min.) • Homework check • Actividad 15 • **Formative Assessment** (10 min.) • Prueba 1A-4 with Remediation: Negatives	**Gramática y vocabulario en uso** (35 min.) • Presentation: Expressing agreement or disagreement • Interactive Whiteboard Grammar Activities • Actividades 18, 19 • Audio Activity 9 **Aplicación** (35 min.) • Lectura • ¿Comprendes? • La cultura en vivo • Writing Activity 13 • Pronunciación • El español en la comunidad • Presentación oral: Steps 1, 2 • ¡Auténtico!	**Wrap-up and Homework Options** (10 min.) • Core Practice 1A-7
5	**Warm-up** (10 min.) • Homework check • **Formative Assessment** (10 min.)	**Aplicación** (45 min.) • Presentación oral: Step 3 **Repaso del capítulo** (25 min.) • Vocabulario y gramática • Preparación para el examen 1, 2, 3, 4, 5	**Wrap-up and Homework Options** (10 min.) • Core Practice 1A-8, 1A-9 • Instant Check • Examen del capítulo 1A
6	**Warm-up** (15 min.) • Homework check • Answer questions **Repaso del capítulo** (25 min.) • Situation Cards • Communicative Pair Activities • **Summative Assessment** (45 min.) • Examen del capítulo 1A		**Wrap-up and Homework Options** (5 min.) • Lectura • Auténtico

Can-Do Statements

Read the can-do statements in the chapter objectives with students. Then have students read *Preparación para el examen* on page 47 to preview what they will be able to do at the end of the chapter.

Standards for Capítulo 1A

To achieve the goals of the Standards, students will:

COMMUNICATION

1.1 Interpersonal
- Talk about preferences in leisure activities

1.2 Interpretive
- Read and listen to information about leisure activities and likes; read a picture-based story
- Listen to and watch a video about leisure activities
- Read about: leisure and recreational activities; traditional dances; snowboarding
- Listen to and understand information about infinitives
- Read information of general interest in Spanish language media

1.3 Presentational
- Present information on preferences in leisure activities

CULTURE

2.1 Practices to Perspectives
- Discuss outdoor *cafés* as popular places to relax with friends

2.2 Products to Perspectives
- Discuss Pablo Picasso; Jaime Antonio González Colson; a dance of the Dominican Republic, the *merengue;* musical instruments used in the Dominican Republic; traditional dances; the mambo; periods in Spain's history that affected its architecture

CONNECTIONS

3.1 Making Connections
- Discuss: important artists and their work: Picasso, Colson; musical instruments used in the Dominican Republic; traditional dances; current events from Spanish language media; historical foundations of Spanish language and architecture

3.2 Acquiring Information and Diverse Perspectives
- Acquire information about current events through Spanish language media sources

COMPARISONS

4.1 Language
- Talk about new vocabulary through the recognition of cognates
- Compare: Spanish and English infinitives; construction of negatives between English and Spanish; expressing agreement or disagreement in English and Spanish; the Spanish vowels *a, e,* and *i* to their English counterparts

4.2 Cultural
- Compare: places where teens gather to spend free time; the selection of news stories in Spanish language media

---

CAPÍTULO

¿Qué te gusta hacer?

Country Connections Explorar el mundo hispano

Estados Unidos · México · Costa Rica · España · República Dominicana · Puerto Rico · Colombia · Guinea Ecuatorial · Argentina

CHAPTER OBJECTIVES

Communication

By the end of this chapter you will be able to:
- Listen to and read about activities people like and don't like to do.
- Talk and write about what you and others like and don't like to do.
- Describe your favorite activities and ask others about theirs.

Culture

You will also be able to:
- **Auténtico:** Identify cultural practices in an authentic video about an after-school music program.
- Describe dances and music from the Spanish-speaking world and compare them to dances you know.

- Compare favorite activities of Spanish-speaking teens to those of teens in the United States.

You will demonstrate what you know and can do:
- Presentación oral: A mí me gusta mucho...
- Repaso del capítulo: Preparación para el examen

You will use:

Vocabulary
- Activities
- Expressing likes and dislikes

Grammar
- Infinitives
- Negatives
- Expressing agreement or disagreement

ARTE y CULTURA España

Pablo Picasso (1881–1973), one of the best-known Spanish artists of the twentieth century, had a long, productive career creating art in a wide range of styles and forms. He showed remarkable artistic talent as a child and had his first exhibition when he was 13 years old. "Three Musicians" is an example of Picasso's cubist painting style.

▶ Study this painting and list some characteristics that show why this style is known as "cubism."

"Musiciens aux masques / Three Musicians" ▶ (1921), Pablo Picasso

Oil on canvas, 6' 7'' X 7' 3 3/4''. Mrs. Simon Guggenheim Fund, #55.1949. © 2009 Estate of Pablo Picasso/Artists Rights Society (ARS), New York. Photo: © The Museum of Modern Art/Scala/Art Resource, NY.

24 veinticuatro • Tema 1 • Mis amigos y yo

Enrich Your Teaching

The End in Mind

Have students preview the sample performance tasks on *Preparación para el examen,* p. 47, and connect them to the Chapter Objectives. Explain to students that by completing the sample tasks they can self-assess their learning progress.

Technology: Mapa global interactivo

Download the *Mapa global interactivo* files for Chapter 1A and preview the activity. Students will explore the bustling Plaza Mayor in Salamanca, Spain.

Patinando en línea,
Barcelona, España

Videocultura **Amigos y actividades**

Capítulo 1A • veinticinco **25**

Project-Based Learning

Álbum de recuerdos

Ask students to start gathering pictures for their photo albums. The photos can be recent or when they were younger and should show them doing different activities. Photos can be of the student alone or with others and activities can be those they enjoy now, enjoyed when younger, or those that they might not like at all. Students can also include images from other sources if they do not have their own photos.

sources to those in media sources in English; Latin dances to those in the United States

COMMUNITIES

5.2 Lifelong Learning

- Utilize the language to experience news and entertainment available through print and electronic Spanish language media

Chapter Opener

Resources: Mapa global interactivo

Suggestions: Introduce students to the theme of the chapter and review the objectives. Explain to students that *Capítulo* 1A is the first of two chapters in *Tema* 1, *Mis amigos y yo*. In this chapter, students will learn language for talking about things they like and do not like to do and ways to express the negative.

Tell students that they will watch videos with people talking about what they like to do. The *Videohistoria* is about working for a volunteer organization called *Codo a codo*. The *GramActiva* videos will help them understand the grammar taught in the chapter.

▶ **Technology: Videocultura** View *Amigos y actividades* with the class to learn more about how friends like to spend their time.

ARTE Y CULTURA

Standards: 2.2, 3.1

Suggestions: Point out that "cubism" comes from the word "cube." Ask students to describe the properties of a cube before answering the question.

Answers will vary but might include: Objects in the painting are made up of squares and other geometric figures.

Teaching with Art

Suggestions: Explain that Picasso developed his cubist style after years of study and work in more traditional styles of painting. He felt he could express ordinary things best by using simple geometric shapes.

Culture Note

Direct students' attention to the large gold-colored sculpture of a fish in the background of the photo. This sculpture, *El Peix*, was commissioned by the city of Barcelona in preparation for the Summer Olympics in 1992. The fish looks out over the sea and is visible from different points along the city's coastline. It is one of many pieces of public art in Barcelona.

Vocabulario en contexto

Standards: 1.2

Resources: Teacher's Resource Materials: Input Script, Clip Art, Audio Script; Technology: Audio Cap. 1A

Suggestions: Use the Input Script from the *Teacher's Resource Materials* as a source of ideas for presentation of new vocabulary and comprehensible input. Keep in mind that this spread is designed for input of new words and lexical presentation of grammatical structures explained later in the chapter.

Tell students that pictures often help us understand the meanings of unfamiliar words. Tell students that the words in heavy blue type are the words they will be responsible for knowing.

Read each conversation and dramatize each sentence as you say it. Use gestures, facial expressions, and tone to convey meaning. Ask students to guess the meaning. When they understand the statements, begin substituting words from the visuals.

Ask students to raise their hands when they hear an activity they like. Ask a volunteer to track the responses and tally them on the board to see which are the most- and least-favored leisure activities.

Starter Activity

Have students practice greeting and introducing themselves to two other classmates.

Technology: Interactive Whiteboard

Vocabulary Activities 1A Use the whiteboard activities in your Teacher Resources as you progress through the vocabulary practice with your class.

Vocabulario en contexto

OBJECTIVES
Read, listen to, and understand information about activities people like and don't like to do

Ana: ¡Hola, Beatriz! ¿Qué te gusta hacer? ¿Te gusta bailar?

Beatriz: ¡Sí! ¡Me gusta mucho bailar! ¿Y a ti, Edgar?

Edgar: A mí no me gusta nada bailar. Me gusta mucho jugar videojuegos. También me gusta practicar deportes. Me gusta esquiar y nadar.

Ana   Beatriz   Edgar

correr

nadar

dibujar

esquiar

cantar

practicar deportes

bailar

escuchar música

26 veintiséis • Tema 1 • Mis amigos y yo

Differentiated Instruction

Heritage Speakers

Have students identify the leisure activities that are most popular with young people in their heritage countries. Are there any leisure activities preferred by people in Spanish-speaking countries that are not common in the United States? Are there differences in what the activities are called in various countries?

Students with Learning Difficulties

Use the Organizer from the *Core Workbook* to create a written vocabulary list for easy reference for oral, listening, and writing activities throughout the chapter. The list will help students to succeed with the activities. Encourage them to use their lists whenever they need them.

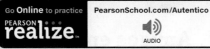

Ana: Pues, no me gusta jugar videojuegos. Me gusta montar en bicicleta o en monopatín.

Beatriz: A mí tampoco me gusta jugar videojuegos. Edgar, ¿qué te gusta más, usar la computadora o ver la tele?

Edgar: No me gusta ni usar la computadora ni ver la tele. ¡Me gusta escribir cuentos!

Ana: A mí también. ¡Me gusta mucho escribir!

jugar videojuegos
montar en monopatín
ver la tele
montar en bicicleta
usar la computadora
escribir cuentos

1

¿Te gusta o no te gusta?

🔊 ESCUCHAR Luz will say what she likes to do and doesn't like to do. Give a "thumbs-up" sign when you hear her say something she likes to do and a "thumbs-down" sign when she says something she doesn't like to do.

2

Me gusta...

🔊 ESCUCHAR Listen to what some people like to do. Point to the picture of the activity each describes.

Capítulo 1A • veintisiete **27**

Enrich Your Teaching

Culture Note

Because the climates and cultures of Spanish-speaking countries are so diverse, a variety of leisure activities are available. People in eastern Chile can engage in mountain climbing. In Caracas, Venezuela, free time can be spent surfing and swimming. Throughout Mexico, soccer is a common sport on any open field.

Teacher-to-Teacher

Have students make flashcards using the Clip Art from the *Teacher's Resource Materials*. Students can write a Spanish word on one side of each card and paste the picture on the other. For nonvisualized words, have students write the Spanish word.

1

Standards: 1.2

Resources: Teacher's Resource Materials: Audio Script; Technology: Audio Cap. 1A

Suggestions: Demonstrate the "thumbs-up" and "thumbs-down" signs. Play the audio or read the script to the class. Allow students to listen and display the signs several times.

🔊 **Technology: Audio Script and Answers**

1. A mí me gusta bailar. (*thumbs-up*)
2. También me gusta cantar y escuchar música. (*thumbs-up*)
3. No me gusta mucho esquiar. (*thumbs-down*)
4. Tampoco me gusta nadar. (*thumbs-down*)
5. Pues, me gusta mucho montar en bicicleta. (*thumbs-up*)
6. No me gusta nada montar en monopatín. (*thumbs-down*)

Extension: Choose other new vocabulary to vary and extend the activity.

2

Standards: 1.2

Resources: Teacher's Resource Materials: Audio Script; Technology: Audio Cap. 1A

Suggestions: Play the audio or read the script as students point to the pictures. Walk around the classroom and check that they select the correct pictures.

🔊 **Technology: Audio Script and Answers**

1. A mí me gusta mucho escribir cuentos. (*escribir cuentos*)
2. Me gusta practicar deportes. (*practicar deportes*)
3. A mí me gusta ver la tele. (*ver la tele*)
4. Me gusta montar en bicicleta. (*montar en bicicleta*)
5. A mí me gusta dibujar. (*dibujar*)
6. A mí me gusta mucho escuchar música. (*escuchar música*)

Additional Resources

📶 **Technology: Online Resources**
- Instant Check
- Guided, Core, Audio, Writing practice
- *Para hispanohablantes*
Print
- Guided WB pp. 25–28
- Core WB pp. 13–14

27

Vocabulario en contexto

Standards: 1.2

Resources: Technology: Audio Cap. 1A

Suggestions: Model the dialogue with a volunteer. Begin the reading again with volunteers playing the roles of the characters. Using the presentation, help students understand the new words in blue type.

Post-reading: Complete Actividad 3 to check comprehension.

3

Standards: 1.2, 1.3

Suggestions: You may wish to do this as a listening activity, reading the sentences to the students.

Extension: Use the sentences as a basis for a classroom survey, changing each sentence to start with *Me gusta....* For each item, have students give a "thumbs up" sign if they agree with the statement or a "thumbs down" if they disagree. Ask one student to count and tally responses for each item.

Answers
1. Sí
2. No
3. No
4. Sí

Pre-AP® Integration

- **Learning Objective:** Interpersonal Speaking
- **Activity:** Have students create a short conversation based on this written exchange. Students can play the roles of Rosa and José as they discuss the activities that they like or dislike. Have pairs of students recreate any dialogue substituting new vocabulary for actions that you point out.
- **Pre-AP® Resource Materials:** Comprehensive guide to Pre-AP® vocabulary skill development

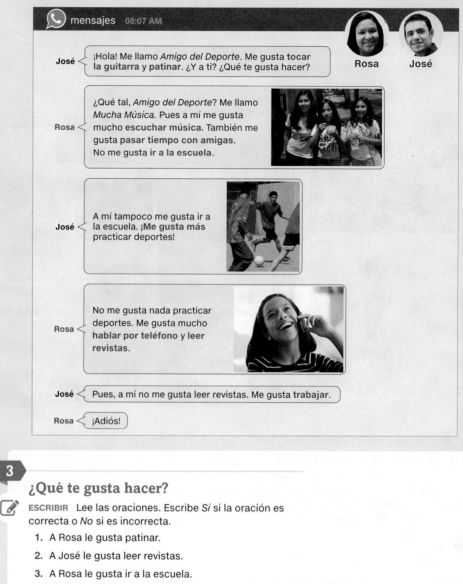

Amigos en Internet

José y Rosa escriben mensajes en Internet.

mensajes 08:07 AM

José ¡Hola! Me llamo *Amigo del Deporte*. Me gusta **tocar la guitarra** y **patinar**. ¿Y a ti? ¿Qué te gusta hacer?

Rosa José

Rosa ¿Qué tal, *Amigo del Deporte*? Me llamo *Mucha Música*. Pues a mí me gusta mucho **escuchar música**. También me gusta **pasar tiempo con amigas**. No me gusta **ir a la escuela**.

José A mí tampoco me gusta ir a la escuela. ¡Me gusta más **practicar deportes**!

Rosa No me gusta nada practicar deportes. Me gusta mucho **hablar por teléfono** y **leer revistas**.

José Pues, a mí no me gusta leer revistas. Me gusta **trabajar**.

Rosa ¡Adiós!

3

¿Qué te gusta hacer?

ESCRIBIR Lee las oraciones. Escribe *Sí* si la oración es correcta o *No* si es incorrecta.

1. A Rosa le gusta patinar.
2. A José le gusta leer revistas.
3. A Rosa le gusta ir a la escuela.
4. A José le gusta tocar la guitarra.

28 veintiocho • Tema 1 • Mis amigos y yo

Differentiated Instruction

Challenge

Have students research volunteer programs in Costa Rica. Tell students to choose a program to present to the class. They should look for pictures or other graphics showing the country or program to add visual interest to their written or oral presentation.

Verbal/Linguistic Learner

Ask students to bring in a photo of themselves doing a favorite activity. Have them use a post from *Amigos en Internet* as a model to write a brief caption that tells who they are and what they like to do. Post the photos and captions in the classroom.

Videohistoria

Go **Online** to practice

PEARSON
realize ™

PearsonSchool.com/Autentico

AUDIO   VIDEO   WRITING   SCRIPT

Bienvenidos a Codo a Codo

Before You Watch

Using visuals Focus on the images in a video to increase your understanding. Connect each visual with the narration. Look at the photos shown and watch for similar activities in the video.

Complete the Activity

Las actividades Look at the two photos. What volunteer activities are these teens doing? Use the phrase *trabajar de voluntario* and phrases you have just learned to say whether or not you like to do volunteer work.

▶ Watch the Video

What different kinds of activities can you do to help others and still have fun?

Go to **PearsonSchool.com/Autentico** to watch the video *Bienvenidos a Codo a Codo* and to view the script.

After You Watch

✎ **¿COMPRENDES?** Answer the following questions based on your understanding of the video.

1. ¿Qué actividades hay en el video?
2. What is *Codo a Codo*?
3. What can you infer about the purpose of the video?

Pregunta personal Answer these questions to see if you could be a candidate for *Codo a Codo*.

1. ¿Te gusta ver la tele o correr?
2. ¿Qué te gusta más, usar la computadora o pasar tiempo con amigos?
3. ¿Te gusta trabajar y ayudar (*help*)?

Capítulo 1A • veintinueve **29**

Enrich Your Teaching

Culture Note

Costa Rica, situated immediately north of Panama, is one of the southernmost countries in North America. It's home to almost five million people and an astonishing number of plant and animal varieties. Besides being renowned for its natural resources, Costa Rica is known for the fact that it has no military. With heavy investment in education, it has achieved a literacy rate of 96%, one of the highest in Latin America. Social volunteerism remains strong though, with many local and international organizations operating in the country.

Technology: Video

Standards: 1.2

Resources: Teacher's Resource Materials: Video Script

Before You Watch

Review the previewing strategy and activity with the students. Then ask students to talk or write about the pictures.

Watch the Video

Show the video without pausing. Show it again, pausing along the way to check comprehension. If there are words that students haven't learned yet, you may want to write those on the board. Show the segment a final time, without pausing.

After You Watch

Standards: 1.2

Suggestions: Discuss the questions with the class to confirm understanding of the video.

Answers

1. Usar la computadora, practicar deportes, ver la tele, correr, leer revistas, visitar lugares, hablar por teléfono, pasar el tiempo con los amigos.
2. *Codo a Codo* is a volunteer organization based in Costa Rica.
3. The purpose of the video is to promote activities that make a difference in the world.

Preguntas personales: Answers will vary. Sample answers:

1. Me gusta ver la tele y correr.
2. Me gusta pasar tiempo con mis amigos y usar la computadora.

Have the students complete additional Video activities online or print the activities from the Teacher's Resource Materials in the online course and pass out the activity sheets to the class.

Additional Resources

📶 **Technology: Online Resources**
- Instant Check
- Guided, Core, Video, Audio
- *Para hispanohablantes*

Print
- Guided WB pp. 29–32
- Core WB pp. 15–16

Assessment

Quiz: Vocabulary Recognition
- PRUEBA 1A-1

5

Suggestions: Call students' attention to the degrees of liking or not liking something expressed in the sentence beginnings. You might have them begin by selecting some activities and ordering them from what they like least to what they like most.

Answers will vary.

6

Suggestions: Be sure students understand that the words shown on the chart are models. They do not have to include them in their own charts. Remind them to save their charts for *Actividad* 7.

Answers will vary.

7

Suggestions: Help students understand that this is a real conversation, so they will need to listen to their partners carefully. Be sure Student B understands that he or she should answer truthfully.

Answers will vary.

Pair Extension: Have students work in pairs to exchange their opinions in writing about free time activities they like or do not like to do.

Active Classroom

Give each student at the beginning of a row a blank sheet of paper. Tell them to write a Spanish infinitive and pass the paper to the next person, who will write another infinitive, and so on. Call time. Have a student in one of the rows say one of the infinitives, and tell the rest of the class to pantomime the action. Do this several times.

Vocabulario en uso

OBJECTIVES
▸ Write and talk about activities you and others like and don't like to do
▸ Exchange information while comparing what you like to do
▸ Compare how you spend free time to teenagers in Spain

5

¿Te gusta o no te gusta?

ESCRIBIR Complete the following sentences with one of the activities shown, or with any of the other activities shown on pp. 26–29.

Modelo
*Me gusta **practicar deportes**.*

1. Me gusta ____.
2. No me gusta ____.
3. Me gusta mucho ____.
4. No me gusta nada ____.
5. Me gusta ____.
6. No me gusta ni ____ ni ____.

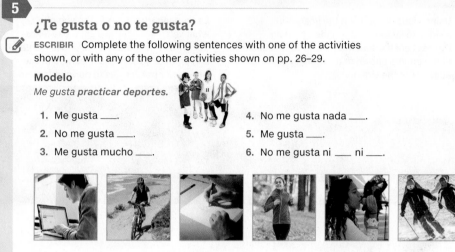

6

Me gusta o no me gusta

ESCRIBIR Find four activities on pp. 26–29 that you like to do and four that you don't like to do. Copy this chart on your paper and write the activities in the corresponding columns.

Modelo

Me gusta	No me gusta
correr	*cantar*

7

¡A mí también!

HABLAR EN PAREJA Express and exchange personal opinions with a partner. Using the information from Actividad 6, tell your partner three activities that you like to do. Your partner will agree or disagree with you. Follow the model. Then switch roles and repeat the activity.

ESCRIBIR EN PAREJA Repeat the activity, but send an email to a second student telling them the three activities you like. The second partner will agree or disagree with you. Switch roles and repeat.

Videomodelo
A —*Me gusta correr.*
B —*¡A mí también!*
o: —*¡A mí no me gusta!*

También se dice . . .
No me gusta nada = No me gusta para nada (*muchos países*)

30 treinta • Tema 1 • Mis amigos y yo

Differentiated Instruction

Students with Learning Difficulties

Review *¡A mí también!* and *¡A mí no me gusta!* as the two responses for *Actividad* 7. Students might need an immediate reminder in order to succeed.

Heritage Speakers

You may want to allow heritage language learners to include additional activities on their lists for *Actividad* 6. Use this as an informal opportunity to assess spelling skills. If you choose this option, pair heritage language learners for *Actividad* 7.

8

Go **Online** to practice

PEARSON
realize™

PearsonSchool.com/Autentico

VIDEO   WRITING   SPEAK/RECORD   MAPA GLOBAL

¿Qué te gusta hacer?

HABLAR EN PAREJA Exchange preferences with your partner about activities in everyday life. Ask whether he or she likes doing the activities below. Your partner will answer using one of the two responses shown. Then switch roles and answer your partner's questions.

Videomodelo

A —¿Te gusta **montar en monopatín**?
B —*Sí, me gusta mucho.*
o:—*No, no me gusta nada.*

Estudiante A
¿Te gusta . . . ?

Estudiante B

¡Respuesta personal!

CULTURA   El mundo hispano

Outdoor cafés are popular gathering places throughout the Spanish-speaking world. Friends go there to enjoy a snack or light meal, catch up with one another, or just watch people go by.

Pre-AP Integration: Lifestyles Where do you go to socialize with your friends or to meet new ones? What factors might affect the differences in where and how teens socialize?

Mapa global interactivo Explore the Plaza Mayor en Salamanca, Spain and describe the surrounding buildings.

En el verano, me gusta pasar tiempo con mis amigos en la ▶
Plaza Mayor de Salamanca, España.

Capítulo 1A • treinta y uno **31**

8

Standards: 1.1

Suggestions: Review the visualized vocabulary with the class, then role-play the model with a student. When students are paired, remind them that **Respuesta personal** in the Student B bubble means that their answer should express their own opinion. When finished, ask for volunteers to practice for the class.

Answers:

Student A
1. —¿Te gusta hablar por teléfono?
2. —¿Te gusta dibujar?
3. —¿Te gusta bailar?
4. —¿Te gusta pasar tiempo con amigos?
5. —¿Te gusta tocar la guitarra?
6. —¿Te gusta cantar?
7. —¿Te gusta correr?
8. —¿Te gusta escribir?

Student B: Answers will vary.

Common Errors: Students may forget to use proper intonation. Model appropriate intonation for questions and answers.

CULTURA

Standards: 2.1, 4.2

Suggestions: Have students study the photo and read the paragraph. Provide other information that you know about plazas and cafés.

Answers will vary.

Technology: Mapa global interactivo, Actividad 2 Visit the Plaza Mayor in Salamanca, Spain, and the area that surrounds it.

Additional Resources

Technology: Online Resources
• Technology: Audio Cap 1A
• Communication Activities: Audio Act. 6
• Communicative Pair Activity
• Teacher's Resource Materials: Audio Script

Assessment

Prueba 1A-2 with Remediation (online only)
Quiz: Vocabulary Production
• Prueba 1A-2

Enrich Your Teaching

Culture Note

The *Plaza Mayor* is one of Salamanca's most famous and popular meeting places. Built by order of Felipe V, the baroque-style plaza was completed in 1755 under the direction of the Churriguera family, famous Spanish architects. Ceremonies, festivities, and even bullfights have taken place there. In 1988, UNESCO made the Plaza Mayor of Salamanca a World Heritage Site.

21st Century Skills

ICT Literacy Remind students that whenever they do a speaking activity they will always have the opportunity to first watch and listen to native speakers in the *Videomodelos*. This way, they can use a native-speaker model to monitor their own progress.

Gramática

Standards: 4.1

Resources: Teacher's Resource Materials: Video Script; Technology: Video Cap. 1A

Technology: Interactive Whiteboard

Grammar Activities 1A Use the whiteboard activities in your Teacher Resources as you progress through the grammar practice with your class.

Suggestions: Ask students to brainstorm infinitives in English. Write them on the board, underlining *to* in each infinitive. Have students call out Spanish infinitives they've learned. Underline the endings in different colors. Play the *GramActiva* Video for reinforcement.

9

Standards: 1.3

Suggestions: You may want to do this activity with the whole class. Draw the chart on the board and have volunteers write the infinitives in the correct columns. Students should save this chart to use with *Actividad* 11.

Answers:

-*ar:* nadar, tocar, jugar, bailar
-*er:* leer, ver, correr
-*ir:* escribir

Extension: Have students write three *"Me gusta ____."* and *"No me gusta ____."* sentences using infinitives from the chart.

10

Standards: 1.2

Resources: Teacher's Resource Materials: Audio Script; Technology: Audio Cap. 1A

Suggestions: Have students use three colors of index cards so you can immediately see if answers are correct. Play the audio or read the script. After students have held up their papers, hold up the correct card.

Technology: Audio Script and Answers

1. patinar *(-ar)*   5. leer *(-er)*
2. correr *(-er)*   6. nadar *(-ar)*
3. trabajar *(-ar)*   7. ir *(-ir)*
4. escribir *(-ir)*   8. hacer *(-er)*

Gramática

OBJECTIVES
▶ Write about and discuss activities
▶ Listen to descriptions of what someone likes to do
▶ Read about, listen to, and write about different types of Latin music

Infinitives

Verbs are words that are most often used to name actions. Verbs in English have different forms depending on who is doing the action or when the action is occurring:

I **walk**, she **walks**, we **walked**, etc.

The most basic form of a verb is called the infinitive. In English, you can spot infinitives because they usually have the word "to" in front of them:

to swim, **to** read, **to** write

Infinitives in Spanish, though, don't have a separate word like "to" in front of them. Spanish infinitives are only one word, and always end in *-ar*, *-er*, or *-ir*:

na**dar**, le**er**, escrib**ir**

Más recursos ONLINE

▶ *GramActiva* Video
▶ **Tutorial:** Conjugation & Infinitive
▶ Animated Verbs
◀)) *Canción de hip hop: Mambo*
✎ *GramActiva* Activity

9

¿Cuál es?

ESCRIBIR On a sheet of paper, make a chart with three columns for the headings *-ar*, *-er*, and *-ir*. Then look at these pictures of activities. Write the infinitive for each activity under the corresponding head. Save your chart to use in Actividad 11.

Modelo

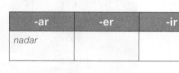

-ar	-er	-ir
nadar		

10

Tres papeles

ESCUCHAR Tear a sheet of paper into three equal parts. Write *-ar* on one piece, *-er* on another piece, and *-ir* on the third piece. You will hear several infinitives. Listen carefully to the endings. Hold up the paper with the ending that you hear.

`-ar` `-er` `-ir`

32 treinta y dos • Tema 1 • Mis amigos y yo

Differentiated Instruction

Students with Learning Difficulties

Give several examples of infinitives in English. Have students give examples themselves. Clarify the relationship between "to…" in English and **-ar, -er, -ir** in Spanish. You might have them add that to their "activity list" for quick reference until the fact is internalized.

Verbal/Linguistic Learner

Have students refer to pp. 26–28 and list all the infinitives and infinitive phrases (e.g. **pasar tiempo con mis amigos**) used in the *Vocabulario en contexto* presentations.

11

El verbo es . . .

ESCRIBIR Here are some verbs in English. Look them up in the English-Spanish glossary at the back of the book and write down the Spanish infinitives on the chart you made in Actividad 9.

> to walk   to live   to eat   to study   to have

It's easy to talk about the things you like to do once you know the infinitive, because you just add the infinitive to *Me gusta.* Try writing this sentence in Spanish: *I like to sleep.*

> **Strategy**
> **Using a dictionary or glossary** When you need to look up a verb, always look under the infinitive form.

12

Encuesta: ¿Qué te gusta hacer?

ESCRIBIR, HABLAR EN GRUPO

1 Ask four classmates to tell you two things they like to do (*¿Qué te gusta hacer?*) and two things they don't like to do (*¿Qué no te gusta hacer?*). Record their names and responses on a chart like this one.

2 Work in groups of four. Add up the results of your interviews to see which activities are the most popular and which ones are the least popular.

3 Share your results with the class.

   1. Las actividades más *(most)* populares:
   2. Las actividades menos *(least)* populares:

Modelo

Nombre	Me gusta	No me gusta
Beto	nadar ir a la escuela	patinar usar la computadora

Actividad	Me gusta	No me gusta
tocar la guitarra	|||		
cantar			|||
trabajar	||	||

13

Escucha y escribe

ESCUCHAR, ESCRIBIR Write the numbers 1–7 on a sheet of paper. You will hear Raúl say seven things that he likes to do. Write them down as he says them. Spelling counts!

> **¿Recuerdas?**
> Remember to include any accent marks when you spell a word.

Capítulo 1A • treinta y tres **33**

Enrich Your Teaching

Teacher-to-Teacher

Take time to explain the Glossaries to students. For most, this will be the first time they have used a dictionary with two languages. Point out that there are two sections, one that presents words from Spanish to English, and one that presents them from English to Spanish. Warn of the limitations of using dictionaries and glossaries, especially as this relates to words that have multiple meanings in one language but not the other.

11

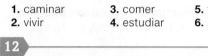
Standards: 1.3, 4.1

Suggestions: Help students locate the English-Spanish Vocabulary that starts on p. 496. Show them how to find the first item.

Answers:
1. caminar   3. comer   5. tener
2. vivir   4. estudiar   6. Me gusta dormir.

12

Standards: 1.1, 1.2, 1.3

Suggestions: Using the glossary on p. 496, have students make a list of their favorite leisure activities. Ask them to find their Spanish equivalent infinitives in the dictionary. Then ask them to make a list of their least favorite activities.

Answers will vary.

13

Standards: 1.2, 1.3

Resources: Teacher's Resource Materials: Audio Script; Technology: Audio Cap. 1A

Suggestions: Read the *¿Recuerdas?* and ask for three words that have accent marks. Play the audio or read the script.

Technology: Audio Script and Answers

1. Me gusta tocar la guitarra.
2. Me gusta ver la tele.
3. También me gusta jugar videojuegos.
4. Me gusta ir a la escuela.
5. Me gusta patinar.
6. Me gusta usar la computadora.
7. ¡Y me gusta mucho escuchar música!

Additional Resources

Technology: Online Resources
- Instant Check
- Guided, Core, Audio, Writing, Reading
- *Para hispanohablantes*
- Technology: Audio Cap. 1A
- Communication Activities, Audio Act. 7
- Teacher's Resource Materials: Audio Script

Print
- Guided WB p. 33
- Core WB p. 17

Assessment

Prueba 1A-3 with Remediation (online only)
Quiz: Infinitives
- Prueba 1A-3

EXPLORACIÓN DEL LENGUAJE

Standards: 4.1

Suggestions: Refer students to the *Strategy*. When they finish *Try it out!*, ask volunteers to identify the cognates. Have them find the cognates on these pages.

Answers: *Try it out!: música, practicar, esquiar, usar, computadora, bicicleta, tele, guitarra*

Starter Activity

Have students refer to the Mapa interactivo and locate the three islands in the Caribbean where Spanish is spoken, and their capitals.

CULTURA

Standards: 2.2, 3.1

Suggestions: Have students read the *Cultura*. Then have students find the Dominican Republic on the Mapa interactivo. Ask them to identify the musical instruments they see in the photo. Have students answer the question and discuss their responses.

Answers will vary.

Teaching with Art

Suggestions: Have students examine the painting *Merengue* by Jaime Antonio González Colson. The artist was born in the Dominican Republic in 1901. The indigenous peoples of the Dominican Republic were influenced by both Spanish and African cultures, and its music, dance, and art reflect these influences. Ask students: What words in Spanish do you know that describe the actions in the painting? *(hablar, tocar, cantar, bailar)*

Exploración del lenguaje — Cognates

Words that look alike and have similar meanings in English and Spanish are called **cognates** *(cognados)*. Here are examples from this chapter:

Spanish	English
popular	popular
usar	to use
guitarra	guitar
computadora	computer

Strategy
Recognizing cognates
Becoming skilled at recognizing cognates will help you understand what you read and will increase your vocabulary.

Try it out! Look at pp. 26–29 and make a list of seven cognates from the vocabulary on those pages.

CULTURA — República Dominicana

Jaime Antonio González Colson (1901–1975) was an artist from the Dominican Republic. His works usually focused on the people and culture of his homeland.

The *merengue*, the dance shown in this painting, originated in the Dominican Republic in the nineteenth century. One of the instruments used to accompany it is the *güiro* (shown at the top right), made from a gourd and played by scraping it with a stick.

Las maracas, el güiro, la cabassa y las claves son instrumentos típicos de la música del Caribe.

Pre-AP Integration: Visual and Performing Arts What details of the local culture does the artist include in his painting?

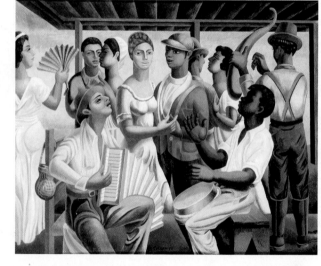

"Merengue" (1937), Jaime Antonio González Colson

Differentiated Instruction

Heritage Speakers

Students may have items from Spanish-speaking countries in their homes that they can share with their classmates. Ask if anyone has *maracas, un güiro, un rascador, una clave,* or *una cabassa* to bring to class. Emphasize, however, that students should not bring valuables or rare items.

Challenge

Have students research artist Jaime Antonio González Colson. Ask them to use the Internet and other resources to find information about his life, other artists who influenced his work, and additional examples of his work. Students can share their research with the class.

Go Online to practice
PearsonSchool.com/Autentico

PEARSON
realize™
AUDIO

Interpretive   1A

14

El baile y la música del mundo hispano

LEER, ESCUCHAR, ESCRIBIR Each country in the Spanish-speaking world has distinct musical styles and traditions. Many of the unique rhythms and dances of Spanish-speaking countries are now popular in the United States. This music features instruments such as guitars, violins, accordions, and various types of percussion such as *güiros,* sticks, cymbals, cow bells, and drums. As you read the captions, see how many words you can understand due to their similarity to English words. After you read, your teacher will play examples of each type of music. Listen for the different instruments used.

Conexiones ‹ La música

- Reread each of the captions and make a list of seven cognates.
- Make a list of instruments you heard in the different songs. You might need to listen to the music again.

☰ Artículo › Baile latino   ★★★★★ comentarios (1209)

En **Argentina, el tango** es muy popular. Es un baile romántico.

En **Puerto Rico, la salsa** es el baile preferido. El ritmo de la salsa es popular en la música de los Estados Unidos también.

En la **República Dominicana,** el baile tradicional es **el merengue.** El merengue tiene muchos ritmos africanos.

El flamenco es un baile típico de **España.** El instrumento más importante en el flamenco es la guitarra.

La cumbia es el baile más famoso de **Colombia.**

Capítulo 1A • treinta y cinco **35**

Enrich Your Teaching

Culture Note

Play samples of merengue music by Juan Luis Guerra, the Dominican Republic's foremost contemporary composer of songs with this rhythm. Tango rhythms by Carlos Gardel and Astor Piazzola, and salsa music by Celia Cruz or Tito Puente are good selections. Cumbia musicians Juan Madera, Wilson Choperena, José Barros, and Mario Gareña are also good choices. The local library may have music from Spanish-speaking countries, or you may be able to find short clips on the Internet. Search online with the words **merengue, tango, salsa,** and **cumbia** to read more about the history of these music genres and about how they are being mixed with modern music styles.

Standards: 1.2, 2.2, 3.1

14

Teacher's Resources: Teacher's Resource Materials: Audio Script; Technology: Audio Cap. 1A

Suggestions: Read through *El baile y la música del mundo hispano* with students. Then have them read each of the captions silently, using cognates and the photos to help with comprehension. Ask volunteers to share their understanding of the captions. Then have students complete the activity.

Answers:

Cognates: típico, música popular, romántico, República, tradicional, ritmo(s), africanos, preferido, famoso
Instruments: Answers will vary.

Common Errors: Some students may be confused by the general placement of adjectives and adjective phrases after the noun they modify. Explain to students that in Spanish, the noun usually comes first.

Pre-AP® Integration

- **Learning Objective:** Interpretive: Print and Audio
- **Activity 14:** Have students read the captions carefully as a homework assignment. In class the next day, read only a portion of the assigned page as a dictation. (A few sentences should be enough.) Have students write what they hear. After they finish writing, point out the selection that you read in the book and have students correct their answers.
- **Pre-AP® Resource Materials:** Comprehensive guide to Pre-AP® communication skill development

Project-Based Learning

Provide the instructions and rubrics for the Project-Based Learning to students. Review the tasks and rubrics with the class. (For more information, see p. 24-b.)

Teacher-to-Teacher

Bring to class a recording of merengue music. Although it originated in the 19th century, it is still very popular. If you have time, show students pictures of merengue performers, play a few songs, and have them listen for the rhythm, instruments, and any words they understand.

Gramática

Resources: Teacher's Resource Materials: Video Script, Video Program: Cap. 1A

Technology: Interactive Whiteboard

Grammar Activities 1A Use the whiteboard activities in your Teacher Resources as you progress through the grammar practice with your class.

Suggestions: Write on the board the affirmative sentence *Me gusta cantar*. Show students how to make the negative by adding **No** in front of **Me,** and changing capital *M* to lowercase. Do this with additional examples. Direct attention to the *¿Recuerdas?* Show the *GramActiva* Video to reinforce use of the negative. Note that the video also includes a discussion of **también** and **tampoco,** so you may want to stop it and use the second part with the grammar presentation on p. 38.

15

Standards: 1.2, 1.3

Suggestions: Have students silently read the conversation between Ana and Tomás and then write the words that belong in blanks 1–5. When they have finished the activity, have two students role-play the conversation for the class. If any of the answers are incorrect, ask the class to provide the correct negative.

Answers:

1. no   3. ni   5. tampoco
2. ni   4. nada

Active Classroom

Working in pairs, have students write ten infinitives for common activities. Have students use their lists to ask four other students about what they like to do aloud. Students should answer truthfully and express personal opinions or preferences in spoken conversation: *Me gusta mucho bailar* or *No me gusta nada bailar*.

Gramática

OBJECTIVES
▶ Read and write about other people's likes and dislikes
▶ Ask and answer questions about activity preferences

Negatives

To make a sentence negative in Spanish, you usually put *no* in front of the verb or expression. In English you usually use the word "not."

No me gusta cantar.   *I do not like to sing.*

To answer a question negatively in Spanish you often use *no* twice. The first *no* answers the question. The second *no* says, "I do not . . . (don't)." This is similar to the way you answer a question in English.

¿Te gusta escribir cuentos?   *Do you like to write stories?*
No, no me gusta.   *No, I don't.*

In Spanish, you might use one or more negatives after answering *"no."*

¿Te gusta cantar?   *Do you like to sing?*
No, no me gusta nada.   *No, I don't like it at all.*

If you want to say that you do not like either of two choices, use *ni . . . ni:*

No me gusta   *I don't like either*
  ni nadar ni dibujar.   *swimming or drawing.*
    I like neither swimming
      nor drawing.

¿Recuerdas?
Did you remember that *nada* has another meaning?
  ¿Qué pasa? **Nada.**
In this case, *nada* means "nothing."

Más recursos ONLINE
▶ *GramActiva* Video
▶ Tutorials: Affirmative and Negative, Making a Sentence Negative, Formation of Negative Sentences
✎ *GramActiva* Activity

15

Una persona muy negativa

LEER, ESCRIBIR Fill in the blanks in the dialogue with one of these expressions: *no, nada, tampoco, ni . . . ni.*

Tomás es un nuevo estudiante en la clase y es una persona muy negativa.

Ana: Hola, Tomás. ¿Te gusta escuchar música?
Tomás: No, __1.__ me gusta. ☹
Ana: Pues, ¿qué te gusta más, jugar videojuegos o usar la computadora?
Tomás: No me gusta __2.__ jugar videojuegos __3.__ usar la computadora.
Ana: ¿Te gusta practicar deportes?
Tomás: No, no me gusta __4.__ practicar deportes.
Ana: Pues, Tomás, no me gusta pasar tiempo con personas negativas.
Tomás: ¡A mí __5.__ !

36 treinta y seis • Tema 1 • Mis amigos y yo

Differentiated Instruction

Students with Learning Difficulties

To help visual learners grasp the pattern for negation, write *No, I don't like to sing.* and *No, no me gusta cantar*. Circle *No* and write the number 1, then circle *don't* and write the number 2. In the Spanish version, circle the first **No** and write the number 1, then circle the second **no** and write the number 2.

Challenge/Pre-AP®

Have students write a paragraph describing what they like to do, what they do not like to do, and what they do not like to do at all. When you hand back their corrected papers, have them rewrite the paragraphs and display them for the class to read.

¡No, no me gusta!

HABLAR EN PAREJA Respond to questions about everyday life. Today you feel very negative. With a partner, respond to each question saying that you don't like to do any of these activities.

Videomodelo
A —¿Te gusta *jugar videojuegos*?
B —No, no me gusta *jugar videojuegos*.

Estudiante A

Estudiante B

No, no me gusta . . .

¿Qué te gusta más?

HABLAR EN PAREJA Ask and respond to questions about everyday life and personal preferences with a partner. Find out what activities your partner likes more. Then switch roles.

Videomodelo
A —¿Qué te gusta más, *nadar* o *esquiar*?
B —Pues, me gusta más *nadar*.
o: —Pues, no me gusta ni *nadar* ni *esquiar*.

1.
2.

3.
4.

Enrich Your Teaching

Teacher-to-Teacher

Ask students to brainstorm a gesture for each of the vocabulary words. Then have students work in pairs to give and follow instructions using the vocabulary: Student A says *hablar por teléfono* and Student B acts out the expression. Student A gives instructions until Student B misses one. Then they switch roles.

21st Century Skills

Information Literacy Encourage students to make use of online dictionaries and other Internet resources to support their individual learning. Teams of students can also benefit by creating their own electronic or print flashcards, games, and quizzes and exchanging them with other teams.

Starter Activity

Ask students to name the activities shown in the Student A balloon.

Standards: 1.1

Suggestions: Remind pairs that Student B will always respond in the negative. When students finish, have them reverse roles and repeat the activity.

Answers:

1. patinar
2. montar en bicicleta
3. nadar
4. usar la computadora
5. dibujar
6. Ir a la escuela

Standards: 1.1

Suggestions: Review the visualized vocabulary with the class. Role-play the *Modelo* with a student. Stress the **ni … ni** to emphasize the negatives. When students have completed the activity, ask several pairs to present to the class.

Answers:

1. ¿Qué te gusta más, leer o cantar? Pues, me gusta más leer. o: Pues, no me gusta ni leer ni cantar.
2. ¿… ver la tele o tocar la guitarra?
3. ¿… jugar videojuegos o montar en monopatín?
4. ¿… hablar por teléfono o pasar tiempo con amigos?

Additional Resources

 Technology: Online Resources
- Instant Check
- Guided, Core, Video, Audio
- *Para hispanohablantes*
- Technology: Audio Cap. 1A
- Communication Activities, Audio Act. 8
- Teacher's Resource Materials: Audio Script

Print
- Guided WB pp. 34–35
- Core WB p. 18

Assessment

Prueba 1A-4 with Remediation (online only)
Quiz: Negatives
- Prueba 1A-4

1A Communication

Gramática

Standards: 4.1

🖰 Technology: Interactive Whiteboard

Grammar Activities 1A Use the whiteboard activities in your Teacher Resources as you progress through the grammar practice with your class.

Suggestions: Be sure students understand that they say **A mí también** to agree with an affirmative statement and **A mí tampoco** to agree with a negative statement. Use the second portion of the *GramActiva* Video on negatives.

18

Standards: 1.1, 1.3

Suggestions: First, ask students to brainstorm leisure activities they like and do not like to do while you write them on the board. Then have students work in pairs to exchange their opinions in writing.

Answers will vary.

19

Standards: 1.2, 1.3, 4.1

Suggestions: Explain to students that they do not know all these words and should use cognates, and context for overall comprehension.

Answers:
1. Alicia; sometimes
2. Enrique; with his friends
3. Sandra; it's bad for your eyes
4. Answers will vary.

Pre-AP® Integration

- **Learning Objective:** Interpersonal Writing
- **Activity 19:** Have students use their responses to the activity's questions to write an email to Alicia, Enrique, or Sandra expressing their personal opinion about videogames. Have them exchange their work with a classmate
- **Pre-AP® Resource Materials:** Comprehensive guide to Pre-AP® writing skill development

Gramática

OBJECTIVES
▶ Express agreement and disagreement about what you and others like to do
▶ Read and write opinions about activities

Expressing agreement or disagreement

To agree with what a person likes, you use *"a mí también."* It's like saying "me too" in English.

Me gusta pasar tiempo con amigos.	*I like to spend time with friends.*
A mí también.	*Me too.*

If someone tells you that he or she dislikes something, you can agree by saying *"a mí tampoco."* It's like saying "me neither" or "neither do I" in English.

No me gusta nada cantar.	*I don't like to sing at all.*
A mí tampoco.	*Me neither.*

18

¿También o tampoco?

✎ **ESCRIBIR EN PAREJA** Exchange text messages with a classmate expressing your opinion about free time activities. First, write a list of three things that you like to do and three things that you don't like to do. Tell your partner the activities on your list. Your partner will agree or disagree based upon his or her personal preferences. Follow the model.

Modelo
A —*Me gusta mucho bailar.*
B —*A mí también.*
o:—*Pues, a mí no me gusta nada bailar.*
A —*No me gusta nada cantar.*
B —*A mí tampoco.*
o:—*Pues, a mí me gusta cantar.*

19

Opiniones

✎ **LEER, ESCRIBIR** Read the opinions of three students on videogames and answer the questions.

1. Who thinks that videogames are neither good nor bad? How often does he or she play videogames?
2. Who likes videogames a lot? With whom does this person play them?
3. Who doesn't like videogames? Why not?
4. ¿A ti te gusta jugar videojuegos?

Jugar videojuegos: ¿bueno o malo[1]?

😐 **Alicia**
Ni lo uno ni lo otro
Jugar videojuegos no es ni bueno ni malo. Me gusta jugar a veces[2].

🙂 **Enrique**
¡Es fabuloso!
A mí también me gusta jugar videojuegos. Es fabuloso jugar con mis amigos.

🙁 **Sandra**
¡Es terrible!
Jugar videojuegos es malo para los ojos[3]. ¡No me gusta nada!

[1]bad [2]sometimes [3]eyes

38 treinta y ocho • Tema 1 • Mis amigos y yo

Differentiated Instruction

Students with Learning Difficulties

Some students may have difficulty understanding the two choices in the second model for *Actividad* 18. Explain that the first means that they agree with their partner, and the second means that they disagree. Write the model on the board and label the choices as "agree" and "disagree."

Heritage Speakers

Have students choose two leisure activities studied in this chapter and use the text in *Actividad* 19 as a model to express written opinions appropriate for their selections. Provide feedback on errors in standard Spanish.

38

Pronunciación ⟨ The vowels *a, e,* and *i*

The vowel sounds in Spanish are different from those in English. In Spanish, each vowel has just one sound. Spanish vowels are also quicker and shorter than those in English.

The letter *a* is similar to the sound in the English word *pop*. Listen to and say these words:

andar	cantar	trabajar
hablar	nadar	pasar

The letter *e* is similar to the sound in the English word *met*. Listen to and say these words:

tele   me   Elena   deportes

The letter *i* is similar to the sound in the English word *see*. As you have already seen, the letter *y* sometimes has the same sound as *i*. Listen to and say these words:

sí	patinar	ti
escribir	lápiz	mí

Try it out! Listen to and say this rhyme:

A-E-I   **El perro canta para ti.**

A-E-I   **El tigre baila para mí.**

Try it again, substituting *el gato* for *el perro* and *la cebra* for *el tigre.*

El español en la comunidad

Hispanics in the United States make up approximately 16 percent of the total population and are the fastest-growing minority group. By the year 2050, the Hispanic population is expected to be almost 29 percent of the total U.S. population. Because of this, there are an increasing number of Spanish-language electronic and print media sources—Internet, television, radio, magazines, and newspapers—available throughout the country.

- Make a list of Spanish-language media sources in your community. Try to find local, regional, national, or even international sources, as well as both electronic and print media. If possible, bring in examples. How much can you understand?

These sources will help you improve your Spanish, and you'll learn about Spanish-speaking cultures as well.

Capítulo 1A • treinta y nueve **39**

Enrich Your Teaching

Teacher-to-Teacher

Use this tongue twister to teach the vowels *a, e,* and *i: Mi mamá me mima y mimo a mi mamá.* ("My mom pampers me, and I pamper my mom.")

21st Century Skills

Media Literacy After students complete the suggested activity in *El español en la comunidad,* have them work in small groups to compare their findings. How much did the Spanish-language examples vary in form and content from English media? Ask them to try to identify specific forms of information in their examples, such as advertisements, public service announcements, etc.

Pronunciación

Standards: 4.1

Resources: Teacher's Resource Materials: Audio Script; Technology: Audio Cap. 1A

Suggestions: Go through the *Pronunciación* with students. Have them pronounce the vowels *a, e,* and *i* and the example words. Let students work individually to memorize the rhyme. Then ask volunteers to say the rhyme. Use the drawing to identify the animals. Regional variations in English pronunciation can affect sound models such as "pop." You may want to use other words like "father," "bother," or "potter" as examples.

Draw a chart on the board. Make three columns, one each for *a, e,* and *i* words. Have students work in pairs to list other words they have studied that contain these vowels. Have students go to the board and write their words on the chart.

El español en la comunidad

Standards: 1.2, 3.1, 3.2, 4.2, 5.2

Suggestions: Have the class suggest ideas for Spanish-language media sources while you write them on the board. Possible answers include local newspapers, radio and television stations, magazines they've seen on newsstands, etc.

Project-Based Learning

Students can perform Step 2 at this point. Be sure they understand your suggestions. (For more information, see p. 24-b.)

Additional Resources

Technology: Online Resources
- Instant Check
- Guided, Core, Audio, Writing, Reading
- *Para hispanohablantes*
- Teacher's Resource Materials: Audio Script, pp. 46–47, Communicative Pair Activity
- Technology: Audio Cap. 1A

Print
- Guided WB p. 36
- Core WB p. 19

Starter Activity

Ask students to explain what cognates are and give examples.

Lectura

Standards: 1.2, 1.3, 4.1

Suggestions

Pre-reading: Direct attention to the *Strategy*. Have students quickly scan the selection to see if they can identify any cognates. Remind them that cognates can help them to understand the notes as they read them.

Reading: Have students read each note without interruption. They can predict the meaning of the notes from the context and cognates. Stop after each note and ask volunteers to tell what activities were mentioned.

Post-reading: After students finish reading the four notes, review each one with them. Ask a volunteer to read the first note aloud. Ask: What things does Marisol like to do? Let students suggest activities until all volunteers have spoken. Make sure the class agrees on all of the activities and that they are correct. Ask students to explain how they arrived at their understanding. Repeat the exercise with all four notes.

Active Classroom

Divide the class into groups of three or four. Have them write as many cognates as they can in five minutes. Have them agree in their group what cognates are. Call time and ask a representative of each group to give their explanation.

Lectura

OBJECTIVES
▶ Read about favorite activities of some teenagers
▶ Use cognates to figure out new words

Strategy
Using cognates Use what you already know about cognates to figure out what new words mean.

¿Qué te gusta hacer?

Read these fictional posts from four students looking for e-pals. As you read their notes, focus on the key words *me gusta* and the key details of their activity preferences. Think about how their likes and interests compare to yours.

e-pals revista global

GUINEA ECUATORIAL
Pablo, 15 años

"Me gusta mucho jugar al vóleibol y al tenis. Me gusta escribir cuentos y también me gusta organizar fiestas con amigos. No me gusta ni jugar videojuegos ni ver la tele. ¡Hasta pronto!"

ESPAÑA
Silvia, 17 años

"Me gusta leer revistas, bailar y cantar. Soy fanática de la música alternativa. También me gusta hablar por teléfono con amigos. ¿Y a ti? ¿Qué te gusta hacer?"

40 treinta y ocho • Tema 1 • Mis amigos y yo

Differentiated Instruction

Verbal/Linguistic Learner

Have students research their favorite sport. When was it invented? Is it popular? Is it an Olympic sport? Students can present their findings in the form of a poster, a report, or an oral presentation.

Students with Learning Difficulties

Have students divide a sheet of paper into four equal sections. In each section, have them list what each student likes and doesn't like to do. They may wish to use this list as an aid in answering the questions in the *¿Comprendes?* section.

Go **Online** to practice

PEARSON
realize™

PearsonSchool.com/Autentico

WRITING

Interpretive Reading **1A**

PUERTO RICO
Marisol, 14 años

❝¿Te gusta practicar deportes y escuchar música? ¡A mí me gusta mucho! También me gusta jugar al básquetbol. ¡Hasta luego!❞.

COLOMBIA
Daniel, 13 años

❝Me gusta mucho ver la tele y escuchar música clásica. También me gusta tocar el piano y pasar tiempo con amigos en un café o en una fiesta. ¿Y a ti?❞.

✎ ¿Comprendes?

1. What key words or phrases help you understand what each teen likes to do?

2. Draw a bar graph. Indicate on the graph how many of the four young people like each of these types of activities: *televisión, música, deportes, pasar tiempo con amigos.* Which are the most popular?

3. Of the four students, with whom do you have the most in common?

4. Write a personal message similar to those in the magazine. Use one of them as a model.

Capítulo 1A • cuarenta y uno **41**

Enrich Your Teaching

Teacher-to-Teacher

Using a large wall map or the maps on pp. xxiv, xxvi, and xxxx, help students find *Puerto Rico, Colombia, España,* and *Guinea Ecuatorial*. Make sure students understand that *Puerto Rico* is not a country, but *un Estado libre asociado,* a territory—not a state—of the United States.

21st Century Skills

ICT Literacy Have students go online and visit Spanish-language Web sites that feature sports, dance, music, hobbies, and other activities of personal interest. Have them use the sites to list and learn new vocabulary and to read the new words in context. Ask them to share the new words and phrases they have learned.

¿Comprendes?

Standards: 1.1, 1.3

Suggestions: Make sure students understand how to make a bar graph. Have students complete the activity. Draw the bar graph on the board and ask a volunteer to fill it in. Students can compare their charts with the one on the board, suggest corrections, and check their own. After students write their own messages, have several students share their personal messages with the class by reading them or writing them on the board.

Answers:

1. Answers will vary.
2. Students' bar graphs should indicate:
   1 televisión; 3 música; 2 deportes;
   3 pasar tiempo con amigos.
3. Answers will vary.
4. Answers will vary.

Pre-AP® Integration

- **Learning Objective:** Interpersonal Speaking
- **Activity:** Have students create a short conversation, based on the responses of any two of the teens in the reading as models, and substituting their own likes and dislikes.
- **Pre-AP® Resource Materials:** Comprehensive guide to Pre-AP® speaking skill development

Teacher-to-Teacher

If you have the resources, students may enjoy having an e-pal with whom they can practice Spanish. This could take the form of a class-only chat if you have access to a lab or an arrangement with another Spanish class, or with students in a Spanish-speaking country. If Internet access is not available, students may enjoy having a secret pen pal in class. They can draw names and write notes that you collect and distribute.

For Further Reading

Student Resource: *Para hispanohablantes: Lectura 2*

Additional Resources

📶 **Technology: Online Resources**
- Guided, Writing, Reading
- *Para hispanohablantes*
- Cultural Reading Activity
Print
- Guided WB p. 37

La cultura en vivo

Standards: 2.2, 3.1

Resources: Teacher's Resource Materials: Audio Script; Technology: Audio Cap. 1A

Suggestions: Locate in advance some mambo music to play in class. Tell the class that dancing is popular in Spanish-speaking countries and some of the dances have been around for many years. People often learn popular national or regional dances as young children. Direct attention to the diagram. Explain that the dotted line shows the moving foot, and then demonstrate the steps with your back to the students. Have them follow along with you. After a little practice, play the music. Have students listen to the rhythm and the beat. Explain that this music is for dancing the **mambo,** a popular dance from Cuba.

Be sensitive to students who do not dance for religious reasons or because of physical limitations. Other students may be hesitant to dance, so create an inviting environment by not putting individuals on the spot. Show that this is fun. Clear a space in the classroom, or move to an open area where students have room to move. Demonstrate the steps slowly. Then, as a class, practice the steps slowly a few times. Try to move more quickly and smoothly each time.

Once students have acquired some proficiency, allow them to practice. Arrange students in pairs with partners facing each other. Have one partner begin the dance with the left foot moving forward and the other with the right foot going back at the same time. After a few minutes have each pair change partners.

Play a mambo tune and allow students to dance. If students have fun and become even mildly proficient, they may enjoy holding a dance contest.

Direct attention to *Comparación cultural* and have students answer the questions.

Answers will vary.

Online Cultural Reading

After doing the online activity, ask students to name some musical instruments in Spanish and identify the families of musical instruments to which they belong.

Additional Resources

📶 **Technology: Online Resources**
• Cultural Reading Activity
• *Para hispanohablantes*

La cultura en vivo   ¿Te gusta bailar?

Thanks to the worldwide popularity of Latin music, Latin dances have captured the attention of people of all ages. As a result, people all around the United States are learning dances such as the merengue, tango, and salsa. Here is a dance you can learn. It is called the mambo, and it originated in Cuba in the 1940s.

Comparación cultural How is doing the mambo with a partner different from dances you might do? What dances do you know from the United States that are danced with a partner?

Online Cultural Reading

Go to PearsonSchool.com/Autentico ONLINE to read about musical instruments in Spanish and learn how they are grouped in families.

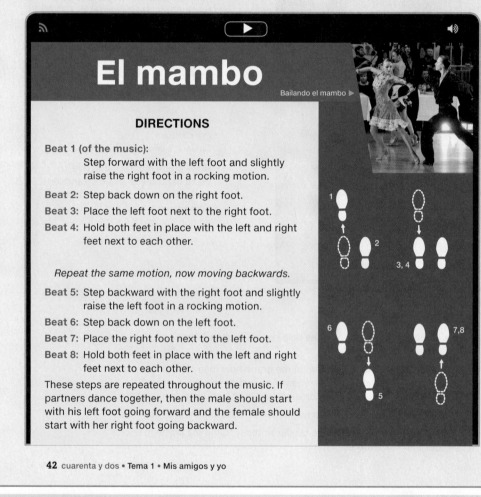

El mambo

Bailando el mambo ▶

DIRECTIONS

Beat 1 (of the music):
Step forward with the left foot and slightly raise the right foot in a rocking motion.

Beat 2: Step back down on the right foot.

Beat 3: Place the left foot next to the right foot.

Beat 4: Hold both feet in place with the left and right feet next to each other.

Repeat the same motion, now moving backwards.

Beat 5: Step backward with the right foot and slightly raise the left foot in a rocking motion.

Beat 6: Step back down on the left foot.

Beat 7: Place the right foot next to the left foot.

Beat 8: Hold both feet in place with the left and right feet next to each other.

These steps are repeated throughout the music. If partners dance together, then the male should start with his left foot going forward and the female should start with her right foot going backward.

42 cuarenta y dos • Tema 1 • Mis amigos y yo

Differentiated Instruction

Heritage Speakers

Some students may be familiar with the mambo and the music associated with it. If so, allow them to help teach the steps and to share personal experiences if they wish. Others may be familiar with other dances from Spanish-speaking countries and may have interesting stories to share with the class.

Musical/Rhythmic Learner

If students master the dance quickly, they may find other dances interesting too. Encourage them to research salsa, merengue, or tango and present their findings to the class, preferably demonstrating the dance.

Presentación oral

OBJECTIVES
▶ Talk about your likes and dislikes
▶ Use a diagram to organize your ideas

Go **Online** to practice
PearsonSchool.com/Autentico
PEARSON **realize**
SPEAK/RECORD

A mí me gusta mucho. . .

TASK You are a new student at school and have been asked to tell the class a little bit about your likes and dislikes.

Strategy
Creating visuals Making a diagram can help you organize a presentation.

1 Prepare Copy this diagram, then list at least five activities to include in the three different ovals.

Using your list, create a poster or other visual aid to illustrate the three categories and at least five activities. You can use drawings, pictures from magazines, or photos of yourself doing the activities. Make sure that each activity is easy to identify. You will use this visual as part of your presentation.

2 Practice Rehearse your presentation with classmates. Use your notes the first time or two, then practice using only the visuals.

Modelo *Me gusta mucho. . .*
Me gusta. . .
No me gusta nada. . .

3 Present Talk about yourself using your visuals. Look at the Evaluation rubric below to know what to emphasize in your presentation. Begin the presentation with your name, and try to:
• use complete sentences
• use visuals to stay focused
• speak clearly

4 Evaluation The following rubric will be used to grade your presentation.

Rubric	Score 1	Score 3	Score 5
How much information you communicate	You mention one detailed example in each category.	You mention four activities and all three categories.	You mention five activities and all three categories.
How easily you are understood	You are difficult to understand and have many patterns of grammatical errors.	You are fairly easy to understand with occasional patterns of grammatical errors.	You are easy to understand and have very few patterns of grammatical errors.
How clearly and neatly your visuals match what you are saying	You include three visuals that clearly connect to activities.	You include four visuals that clearly connect to activities.	You include five visuals that clearly connect to activities.

Capítulo 1A • cuarenta y tres **43**

Enrich Your Teaching

Teacher-to-Teacher
Display the students' visual presentations for the class. Make time for students to walk around, view each diagram, and take notes or write questions to ask their classmates. Provide time for a class discussion of the diagrams, comments, and questions.

21st Century Skills
Communication Using the *Presentación oral as* a model, find a student you don't know well in Spanish class, greet him or her, and ask about his or her favorite activities. Find one of your friends with an interest in common with the student, introduce them, and mention the interest they have in common.

Presentación oral

Standards: 1.3

Suggestions: Explain the task and the 4-step approach to students. Review the rubric with the class to explain how you will grade the performance task. Do a presentation of your own (an anchor) to model a top-scoring presentation. Have students work through each step of the speaking process.

Pre-AP® Integration

• **Learning Objective:** Interpersonal Speaking
• **Activity:** Have students interact, comparing likes and dislikes.
• **Pre-AP® Resource Materials:** Comprehensive guide to Pre-AP® speaking skill development

Digital Portfolio

Make video or audio recordings of student presentations in class, or assign the Speak and Record activity so they can record their presentations online. Include the recording in their portfolios.

Additional Resources

📶 **Technology: Online Resources**
• Guided
• *Para hispanohablantes*
Print
• Guided WB p. 38

Assessment

Presentación oral
• **Assessment Program:** Rubrics
Go over the descriptions of the different levels of performance. After assessing students, help individuals understand how their performance could be improved. (See Teacher's Resource Materials for suggestions on using rubrics in assessment.)

Auténtico

Standards: 2.2, 3.1

Resources: *Authentic Resources Wkbk*, Cap. 1A
Authentic Resources: Cap 1A: Videoscript
AP Theme: *La belleza y la estética: Las artes visuales y escénicas*

Before You Watch

Discuss the *Strategy* with students. Have students listen to the audio thinking about the global meaning of the video. Perhaps have them identify the main themes, such as education, heritage, or culture, and listen for key words that help them understand the main idea of the video. Then review the key vocabulary with the class. Have students comment on how they contribute to the main themes and the global meaning of the resource.

Technology: Watch the Video

Before starting the video, direct students' attention to the *Mientras ves* activity. Have students use the activity page from the *Authentic Resources Workbook*. Ask students to compare the ideas mentioned in the activity to the answers they provided in the *Auténtico Resources Workbook* activity page, and ask them to add any additional key words or information they would like to the list.

Play the video once completely through, without pausing, and tell students to listen for words and ideas they recognize in the video. Remind students that they will not understand every word, but that they should listen and watch for overall understanding. Replay the video, stopping as necessary for students to complete the listening activity and to check comprehension. Show the video a final time without pausing.

Auténtico

Partnered with **univision** COMMUNICATIONS INC

Conservatorio de Mariachi

Before You Watch

Use the Strategy: Listen for Global Meaning

As you watch the video, don't worry about what every word means. Focus on key words that you understand and also read the key vocabulary to help you get the general idea.

Read this Key Vocabulary
orgullo = pride
echarle ganas = put in effort
raíces mexicanas = Mexican roots
me siento = I feel
comunidad = community
plantar semillitas = plant seeds

▶ Watch the Video

What do you do for fun? What sorts of skills do you need to do that activity? How do you feel when you are doing that activity? Listen for the expression "me siento" and decide what the speaker would like to communicate about his emotions.

Go to **PearsonSchool.com/Autentico** and watch the video **Conservatorio de mariachi** to see how students in a high school get to practice their pastime during the school day.

Complete the Activities

Mientras ves As you watch the video, try to listen and see if you can understand the general meaning of the video. Number the ideas in the order that they occur in the video.

Aprender[1] a ser[2] un líder.
Es una música tradicional de México.
Ser parte de una familia.
Ofrecer clases de mariachi a la comunidad.

[1]to learn
[2]to be

Differentiated Instruction

Challenge

Have students choose a traditional instrument from a Spanish-speaking culture and using the Internet and other resources, find information about that instrument. Students can share their research with the class, including a picture of the instrument or a clip of the instrument being played.

Heritage Speakers

Students may be familiar with mariachi music or other musical traditions from Spanish-speaking cultures. Ask students to write a short description of mariachi or another traditional music that is part of their heritage, such as *norteño, cumbia, merengue,* or *salsa,* using their own knowledge or outside sources such as a family member or the Internet.

Integration

Después de ver Review the video as needed to answer the following questions.

1. Write in Spanish the musical activities students learn in the *Conservatorio*.

2. How might the teens from the video answer the question, *¿Qué te gusta hacer?*

3. Throughout the video the word *orgullo* is used to describe students playing mariachi. In the key vocabulary section, the word is defined as pride. Explain why you think the word is used to describe this pastime.

📖 **For more activities, go to the *Authentic Resources Workbook*.**

Los pasatiempos

Expansión Find other authentic resources in *Auténtico* online, then answer the question.

📁 **1A Auténtico**

Integración de ideas In the authentic resources other types of pastimes are described. Use the resources to write a statement that provides your opinion about the pastimes and to say which of the pastimes you prefer.

Comparación cultural Compare what you like to do with pastimes in Spanish-speaking culture that you have learned about in these resources.

Enrich Your Teaching

Culture Note

Mariachi are often travelling groups who perform in traditional dress and play a variety of instruments including guitars, *guitarrones* (deep-bodied Mexican guitar), violins, trumpets, flutes and even a harp, and the music of mariachi is well-known in many communities throughout the Spanish-speaking world and the United States. *Perspectivas*: What musical style is representative of your culture?

Using Authentic Resources

Using as many words and phrases from the chapter vocabulary as possible, have students write an interview for their classmates where they ask which of the activities in the authentic resources they like or do not like.

Complete the Activities

Mientras ves

Standards: 1.1, 1.2, 1.3, 4.2

Suggestions: Students' understanding will vary. Ask for volunteers to share and list the words and themes they understood on the board. Prompt students to listen for the key expressions listed in the activity.

Follow-up activities could include asking students to raise their hands when they hear key expressions.

Answers:

1. Es una música tradicional de México.
2. Ser parte de una familia.
3. Aprender a ser un líder.
4. Ofrecer clases de mariachi a la comunidad.

Después de ver

Standards: 1.1, 1.2, 1.3, 4.2

Suggestions: Students may need to look back at the Vocabulario en contexto page to recall the syntax of the expressions.

Allow students to view the video again or use the themes from the previous activity to develop their answer as they focus on identifying key words. Ask for multiple volunteers to provide their opinions.

Answers:

1. Tocar la guitarra / Tocar un instrumento / Ser parte de una banda / Cantar
2. Me gusta tocar la guitarra / Me gusta cantar / Me gusta ser parte de una banda/ Me gusta tocar la música tradicional de México
3. *Answers will vary.* Students should be able to make connections to activities that make one feel proud.

For more Authentic Resources: Assign the *Authentic Resources Workbook* activities for homework, so that students can play the video on their own and complete the workbook activities at their own pace.

Pre-AP® Integration

Standards: 1.1, 1.2, 1.3, 4.2

Resources: *Authentic Resources Workbook*, Cap. 1A; Authentic
Resources: Cap 1A; Videoscript

Suggestions: Before completing the Pre-AP® activity, have students go to the workbook and complete the worksheets for these two additional resources.

45

Review Activities

To talk about activities: Have students work in pairs to quiz each other on the vocabulary. Have them create flashcards. Creating and collecting these cards may prove helpful to students throughout the course.

To say what you like and don't like to do: Have students work in pairs and tell each other what they like to do and don't like to do. Students can respond with *A mí también* or *A mí tampoco*.

To ask others what they like to do: Have students interview each other about activities they like to do. Ask students to brainstorm a list of activities and write five questions using *¿Te gusta...?* Tell them to interview a different classmate for each question. Encourage students to use the phrases in *Other useful words and expressions* in their responses. After they have completed the interview, ask volunteers: *¿Qué te gusta hacer?*

Digital Portfolio

Invite students to review chapter activities, including written reports, posters or other visuals, and recordings of oral presentations, or other projects. Have them select one or two items that they feel best demonstrate their achievements in Spanish. Include these products in students' portfolios. Have them include this with the chapter checklist and Self-Assessment Worksheet.

Pre-AP® Integration

- **Learning Objective:** Interpersonal speaking
- **Pre-AP® Resource Materials Activity Sheets, Tema 1**

Additional Resources

Technology: Online Resources
- Instant Check
- *Para hispanohablantes*

Print
- Core WB pp. 20–21

Teacher Resources
- Teacher's Resource Materials: Situation Cards, Clip Art
- **Assessment Program:** Chapter Checklist and Self-Assessment Worksheet

---

Repaso del capítulo

OBJECTIVES
▸ Review the vocabulary and grammar
▸ Demonstrate you can perform the tasks on p. 47

🔊 Vocabulario

to talk about activities

bailar	to dance
cantar	to sing
correr	to run
dibujar	to draw
escribir cuentos	to write stories
escuchar música	to listen to music
esquiar	to ski
hablar por teléfono	to talk on the phone
ir a la escuela	to go to school
jugar videojuegos	to play video games
leer revistas	to read magazines
montar en bicicleta	to ride a bicycle
montar en monopatín	to skateboard
nadar	to swim
pasar tiempo con amigos	to spend time with friends
patinar	to skate
practicar deportes	to play sports
tocar la guitarra	to play the guitar
trabajar	to work
usar la computadora	to use the computer
ver la tele	to watch television

to say what you like to do

(A mí) me gusta ___.	I like to ___.
(A mí) me gusta más ___.	I like to ___ better. (I prefer to ___.)
(A mí) me gusta mucho ___.	I like to ___ a lot.
A mí también.	I do too.

to say what you don't like to do

(A mí) no me gusta ___.	I don't like to ___.
(A mí) no me gusta nada ___.	I don't like to ___ at all.
A mí tampoco.	I don't (like to) either.

For Vocabulario adicional, see pp. 472–473.

to ask others what they like to do

¿Qué te gusta hacer?	What do you like to do?
¿Qué te gusta más?	What do you like better (prefer)?
¿Te gusta ___?	Do you like to ___?
¿Y a ti?	And you?

Gramática

other useful words and expressions

ni . . . ni	neither . . . nor, not . . . or
o	or
pues . . .	well . . .
sí	yes
también	also, too
y	and

Differentiated Instruction

Students with Learning Difficulties

Have students review the *Repaso del capítulo* and create flashcards for any words that they do not know. Pair them with a student who is more confident with the vocabulary to practice. Before the test, provide students with a practice test, so they can become comfortable with the format.

Heritage Speakers

Have students write a few paragraphs telling about their perfect birthday celebration: Where are they going to have it? Whom are they going to invite? What food are they going to eat? What kind of music are they going to play? Encourage them to use as many vocabulary words from this chapter as they can.

Preparación para el examen

Más recursos   PearsonSchool.com/Autentico

☒ Games   🗏 Flashcards   ✎ Instant check
▶ Tutorials   *GramActiva* videos   ▶ Animated verbs

What you need to be able to do for the exam . . .	Here are practice tasks similar to those you will find on the exam . . .	For review go to your print or digital textbook . . .
Interpretive		
① ESCUCHAR I can listen to and understand a description of what someone likes to do.	Listen to a voice mail from a student looking for a "match-up" to the homecoming dance. a) What are two things this person likes doing? b) What is one thing this person dislikes doing?	pp. 26–29 *Vocabulario en contexto* p. 27 Actividades 1–2 p. 33 Actividad 13
Interpersonal		
② HABLAR I can talk about myself and what I like and don't like to do and ask the same of others.	You agreed to host a student from the Dominican Republic for a week. What can you tell him or her about yourself in a taped message? Include a brief description of what you like to do. How would you ask the student to tell you something about himself or herself?	p. 30 Actividad 7 p. 31 Actividad 8 p. 33 Actividad 12 p. 37 Actividades 16–17 p. 43 *Presentación oral*
Interpretive		
③ LEER I can read and understand someone's description of himself or herself.	Read this pen pal e-mail from a Spanish-language magazine. What types of things does the person like to do? Does this person have anything in common with you? What is it? ¡Hola! A mí me gusta mucho usar la computadora y tocar la guitarra. No me gusta ni ir a la escuela ni leer. En el verano me gusta nadar y en el invierno me gusta esquiar. ¿Y a ti? ¿Qué te gusta hacer?	pp. 26–29 *Vocabulario en contexto* p. 29 Actividad 3 p. 36 Actividad 15 p. 38 Actividad 19 pp. 40–41 *Lectura*, no. 3
Presentational		
④ ESCRIBIR I can write about myself with a description of things I like and don't like to do.	A school in the Dominican Republic wants to exchange e-mails with your school. Tell your e-pal your name and what you like to do and don't like to do.	p. 30 Actividades 5–6 p. 33 Actividad 12 p. 38 Actividad 18 p. 41 *¿Comprendes?*
Cultures		
⑤ EXPLICAR I can demonstrate an understanding of cultural differences regarding dancing.	How would you describe the Latin dances that have become popular in the United States? With what countries do you associate each dance? With what type of music or rhythms do you associate each dance?	p. 34 *Fondo cultural* p. 35 Actividad 14 p. 42 *La cultura en vivo*

Capítulo 1A • cuarenta y siete 47

Differentiated Assessment

Core Assessment

- Assessment Program: Examen del capítulo 1A
- Technology: Audio Cap. 1A
- ExamView: Chapter Test, Test Banks A and B

Challenge/Pre-AP®

- ExamView: Pre-AP® Test Bank
- Pre-AP® Resource Materials

Extra Support

- Alternate Assessment Program: Examen del capítulo 1A
- Technology: Audio Cap. 1A

Heritage Speakers

- Assessment Program: *Para hispanohablantes:* Examen del capítulo 1A
- ExamView: Heritage Speaker Test Bank

Performance Tasks

Standards: 1.3

Student Resource: *Para hispanohablantes*

Teacher Resources: Teacher's Resource Materials: Audio Script; Technology: Audio Cap. 1A

Suggestions: Explain the format of the chapter test to students. The first portion will assess their knowledge of vocabulary and grammar. The second portion is performance-based and will have tasks very similar to those shown here.

1. Escuchar

Suggestions: Play the audio or read the script.

Script and Answers

Pues, ... a mí me gusta practicar deportes y pasar tiempo con amigos. *(This person likes to practice sports and spend time with friends.)* ¿Y bailar? No me gusta nada bailar. ¿Y a ti? *(This person doesn't like to dance.)*

2. Hablar

Suggestions: Allow time for students to work in class. If they have difficulty speaking spontaneously, have them write their messages and practice them until they can say them without notes.

Answers will vary.

3. Leer

Suggestions: Remind students that cognates can help them understand unfamiliar words.

Answers: usar la computadora, tocar la guitarra, nadar, esquiar; answers will vary.

4. Escribir

Suggestions: Have students try this activity without consulting the vocabulary list, notes, or completed activities.

5. Explicar

Suggestions: Ask students to name the various dances. Elicit comments about rhythms, instruments, etc.

Y tú, ¿cómo eres?

Objectives

- Listen to and read descriptions of others
- Talk and write about your personality traits
- Describe your personality to others
- Identify cultural practices in an authentic video about personality traits
- Compare cultural perspectives on friendship

Vocabulary

- Personality traits
- Expressing likes and dislikes

Grammar

- Adjectives
- Definite and indefinite articles
- Word order: Placement of adjectives

Culture

- Frida Kahlo, p. 49
- Simón Bolívar, p. 58
- *huipil*, p. 65
- What makes a good friend in different cultures, p. 66

Recycle

- Gender
- Negatives
- *gustar*

Authentic Resources

- Video about how students can highlight their personality in an interview, an audition, or any other presentation, pp. 68–69.

	FOR THE STUDENT	DIGITAL	PRINT	FOR THE TEACHER	DIGITAL	PRINT
Plan				Teacher's Edition	•	•
				Teacher's Resource Materials	•	
				Pre-AP® Resource Materials	•	
				Lesson Plans, pp. 48-c, 48-d	•	
				Mapa global interactivo	•	
Introducción pp. 48–49						
Present	Student Edition, pp. 48–49	•	•	Teacher's Edition, pp. 48–49	•	•
	DK Reference Atlas	•		Teacher's Resource Materials	•	
	Para hispanohablantes	•		Mapa global interactivo	•	
Vocabulario en contexto pp. 50–53						
Present & Practice	Student Edition, pp. 50–53	•	•	Teacher's Edition, pp. 50–53	•	•
	Audio	•		Teacher's Resource Materials	•	
	Videohistoria	•		Vocabulary Clip Art		
	Flashcards			Technology: Audio		
	Instant Check	•		Video Program: Videohistoria	•	
	Guided WB, pp. 39–46	•	•			
	Core WB, pp. 22–25	•	•			
	Communication Activities	•				
	Para hispanohablantes	•				
Assess and Remediate				Prueba 1B–1: Assessment Program, pp. 26–27	•	
				Assessment Program para hispanohablantes, pp. 26–27	•	

RESOURCES	FOR THE STUDENT	DIGITAL	PRINT	FOR THE TEACHER	DIGITAL	PRINT
Vocabulario en uso p. 54						
Present & Practice	Student Edition, p. 54	•	•	Interactive Whiteboard Vocabulary Activities	•	
	Instant Check	•		Teacher's Edition, p. 54	•	•
	Communication Activities	•		Teacher's Resource Materials	•	
	Para hispanohablantes	•		Communicative Pair Activities	•	
	Communicative Pair Activities	•		Technology: Audio	•	
				Videomodelos	•	
Assess and Remediate				Prueba 1B-2 with Remediation	•	
				Prueba 1B-2: Assessment Program, pp. 28–29	•	
				Assessment Program para hispanohablantes, pp. 28–29	•	
Gramática pp. 55–63						
Present & Practice	Student Edition, pp. 55–63	•	•	Interactive Whiteboard Grammar Activities	•	
	Instant Check	•		Teacher's Edition, pp. 55–63	•	•
	Animated Verbs	•		Teacher's Resource Materials	•	
	Tutorial Video: Grammar	•		Communicative Pair Activities	•	
	Canción de hip hop	•		Technology: Audio	•	
	Guided WB, pp. 47–50	•	•	Videomodelos	•	
	Core WB, pp. 26–28	•	•	Video Program: GramActiva	•	
	Communication Activities	•				
	Para hispanohablantes	•				
	Communicative Pair Activities	•				
Assess and Remediate				Pruebas 1B-3 to 1B-5 with Remediation	•	
				Pruebas 1B-3 to 1B-5: Assessment Program, pp. 30–31	•	
				Assessment Program para hispanohablantes, pp. 30–31	•	
Aplicación pp. 64–69						
Application	Student Edition, pp. 64–69	•	•	Teacher's Edition, pp. 64–69	•	•
	Authentic Resources Workbook	•	•	Mapa global interactivo	•	
	Authentic Resources	•		Authentic Resources Lesson Plans with scripts, answer keys	•	
	Literacy Skills Workbook	•	•			
	Online Cultural Reading	•				
	Guided WB, pp. 51–52	•	•			
	Communication Activities	•				
	Para hispanohablantes	•				
Repaso del capítulo pp. 70–71						
Review	Student Edition, pp. 70–71	•	•	Teacher's Edition, pp. 70–71	•	•
	Online Puzzles and Games	•		Teacher's Resource Materials	•	
	Core WB, pp. 29–30	•	•	Technology: Audio	•	
	Communication Activities	•				
	Para hispanohablantes	•				
	Instant Check	•				
Chapter Assessment						
Assess				Examen del capítulo 1B	•	
				Assessment Program, pp. 33–40	•	
				Alternate Assessment Program, pp. 8–12	•	
				Assessment Program para hispanohablantes, pp. 33–40	•	
				Technology: Audio, Cap. 1B Examen	•	
				ExamView: Test Banks A and B questions only online	•	
				Heritage Learner Test Bank	•	
				Pre-AP® Test Bank	•	

LESSON PLAN (50 MINUTES)

DAY	Warm-up / Assess	Preview / Present / Practice / Communicate		Wrap-up / Homework Options
1	**Warm-up** (10 min.) • Return Examen del capítulo 1A	**Chapter Opener** (5 min.) • Objectives • Arte y cultura	**Vocabulario en contexto** (30 min.) • Presentation • Actividades 1, 2	**Wrap-up and Homework Options** (5 min.) • Core Practice 1B-1, 1B-2

2	**Warm-up** (5 min.)
	• Homework check
		Vocabulario en contexto (40 min.)
		• Presentation:
		  Videohistoria
		  ¿Cómo eres?
			• View: Videohistoria
			• Video Activities 1, 2, 3, 4
			• Actividades 3, 4
				Wrap-up and Homework Options (5 min.)
				• Core Practice 1B-3, 1B-4
				• Prueba 1B-1: Vocabulary recognition

3	**Warm-up** (10 min.) • Homework check • **Formative Assessment** (10 min.) • Prueba 1B-1: Vocabulary recognition	**Vocabulario en uso** (25 min.) • Actividades 5, 6 • Audio Activities 5, 6 • Communicative Pair Activity • Interactive Whiteboard Vocabulary Activities		**Wrap-up and Homework Options** (5 min.) • Writing Activity 10 • Prueba 1B-2 with Remediation Vocabulary production
4	**Warm-up** (5 min.) • Homework check • **Formative Assessment** (10 min.) • Prueba 1B-2 with Remediation Vocabulary production	**Gramática y vocabulario en uso** (30 min.) • Presentation: Adjectives • View: GramActiva video • Interactive Whiteboard Grammar Activities	• Actividades 8, 9, 10, 11	**Wrap-up and Homework Options** (5 min.) • Core Practice 1B-5 • Actividades 7, 12 • Prueba 1B-3 with Remediation Adjectives
5	**Warm-up** (10 min.) • Writing Activity 11 • Homework check • **Formative Assessment** (10 min.) • Prueba 1B-3 with Remediation Adjectives	**Gramática y vocabulario en uso** (15 min.) • Actividad 13 • Audio Activity 7 • Communicative Pair Activity	(10 min.) • Exploración del lenguaje • Cultura • Actividad 14	**Wrap-up and Homework Options** (5 min.) • Actividad 15 • Auténtico
6	**Warm-up** (5 min.) • Homework check	**Gramática y vocabulario en uso** (40 min.) • Presentation: Definite and indefinite articles • View: GramActiva video • Interactive Whiteboard Grammar Activities	• Actividades 16, 17 • Audio Activity 8 • Writing Activity 12 • Pronunciación	**Wrap-up and Homework Options** (5 min.) • Core Practice 1B-6 • Prueba 1B-4 with Remediation Definite and indefinite articles
7	**Warm-up** (10 min.) • Actividad 18 • Homework check • **Formative Assessment** (10 min.) • Prueba 1B-4 with Remediation Definite and indefinite articles	**Gramática y vocabulario en uso** (25 min.) • Presentation: Word order: Placement of adjectives • Interactive Whiteboard Grammar Activities • Actividades 20, 21	• Audio Activity 9 • Writing Activity 13 • El español en el mundo del trabajo	**Wrap-up and Homework Options** (5 min.) • Core Practice 1B-7 • Actividad 22 • Prueba 1B-5 with Remediation Placement of adjectives
8	**Warm-up** (10 min.) • Actividad 19 • Homework check • **Formative Assessment** (10 min.) • Prueba 1B-5 with Remediation Placement of adjectives	**Aplicación** (25 min.) • Lectura • ¿Comprendes? • Cultura	• Presentación escrita: Steps 1, 5 • Perspectivas del mundo hispano	**Wrap-up and Homework Options** (5 min.) • Presentación escrita: Step 2 • Preparación para el examen 3, 4, 5
9	**Warm-up** (5 min.) • Homework check	**Aplicación** (20 min.) • Presentación escrita: Step 3 • Auténtico	**Repaso del capítulo** (20 min.) • Vocabulario y gramática • Preparación para el examen 1, 2	**Wrap-up and Homework Options** (5 min.) • Presentación escrita: Step 4 • Core Practice 1B-8, 1B-9 • Instant Check • Examen del capítulo 1B
10	**Warm-up** (10 min.) • Homework check • **Summative Assessment** (40 min.) • Examen del capítulo 1B			

ALTERNATE LESSON PLAN

DAY	Warm-up / Assess	Preview / Present / Practice / Communicate		Wrap-up / Homework Options
1	**Warm-up** (10 min.) • Return Examen del capítulo 1A	**Chapter Opener** (10 min.) • Objectives • Arte y cultura **Vocabulario en contexto** (60 min.) • Presentation: Vocabulario en contexto	• Actividades 1, 2 • Presentation: Videohistoria *¿Cómo eres?* • View: Videohistoria • Video Activities 1, 2, 3, 4 • Actividades 3, 4	**Wrap-up and Homework Options** (10 min.) • Core Practice 1B-1, 1B-2, 1B-3, 1B-4 • Prueba 1B-1: Vocabulary recognition
2	**Warm-up** (10 min.) • Homework check • **Formative Assessment** (10 min.) • Prueba 1B-1: Vocabulary recognition	**Vocabulario en uso (65 min.)** • Interactive Whiteboard Vocabulary Activities • Actividades 5, 6 • Audio Activities 5, 6 • Communicative Pair Activity • Presentation: Adjectives	• View: GramActiva video • Interactive Whiteboard Grammar Activities • Actividades 7, 8, 9, 10, 11, 12	**Wrap-up and Homework Options** (5 min.) • Writing Activity 10 • Core Practice 1B-5 • Prueba 1B-2 with Remediation Vocabulary production
3	**Warm-up** (5 min.) • Homework check • **Formative Assessment** (10 min.) • Prueba 1B-2 with Remediation Vocabulary production	**Gramática y vocabulario en uso** (70 min.) • Exploración del lenguaje • Cultura • Actividades 13, 14 • Audio Activity 7 • Communicative Pair Activity • Presentation: Definite and indefinite articles • View: GramActiva video	• Interactive Whiteboard Grammar Activities • Actividades 15, 16, 17 • Audio Activity 8 • Writing Activity 11 • Writing Activity 12 • Pronunciación	**Wrap-up and Homework Options** (5 min.) • Core Practice 1B-6 • Pruebas 1B-3, 1B-4 with Remediation Adjectives, Definite and indefinite articles
4	**Warm-up** (10 min.) • Actividad 18 • Homework check • **Formative Assessment** (15 min.) • Pruebas 1B-3, 1B-4 with Remediation Adjectives, Definite and indefinite articles	**Gramática y vocabulario en uso** (40 min.) • Presentation: Word order: Placement of adjectives • Interactive Whiteboard Grammar Activities • Actividades 19, 20, 21, 22 • Audio Activity 9 • Writing Activity 13 • El español en el mundo del trabajo	**¡Adelante!** (20 min.) • Lectura • ¿Comprendes? • Cultura • Presentación escrita: Steps 1, 5 • Perspectivas del mundo hispano	**Wrap-up and Homework Options** (5 min.) • Core Practice 1B-7 • Actividad 22 • Presentación escrita: Step 2 • Lectura • Prueba 1B-5 with Remediation Placement of adjectives
5	**Warm-up** (5 min.) • Homework check • **Formative Assessment** (10 min.) • Prueba 1B-5 with Remediation Placement of adjectives	**Aplicación** (45 min.) • Presentación escrita: Step 3 • Auténtico	**Repaso del capítulo** (25 min.) • Vocabulario y gramática • Preparación para el examen 1, 2, 3, 4, 5	**Wrap-up and Homework Options** (5 min.) • Presentación escrita: Step 4 • Core Practice 1B-8, 1B-9 • Instant Check • Examen del capítulo 1B
6	**Warm-up** (15 min.) • Homework check • Answer questions **Repaso del capítulo** (25 min.) • Situation Cards • Communicative Pair Activities • **Summative Assessment** (45 min.) • Examen del capítulo 1B			**Wrap-up and Homework Options** (5 min.) • El mundo hispano

Can-Do Statements

Read the can-do statements in the chapter objectives with students. Then, have students read Preparación para el examen on page 71 to preview what they will be able to do at the end of the chapter.

Standards for Capítulo 1B

To achieve the goals of the Standards, students will:

COMMUNICATION

1.1 Interpersonal
- Talk about personality traits
- Talk about themselves and each other
- Talk about activities and personality traits
- Talk about familiar objects

1.2 Interpretive
- Listen to information about personality traits
- Read information about personality traits
- Read a picture-based story
- Listen to and watch a video about personality traits
- Listen to and identify the gender of nouns
- Read a personality quiz based on color association

1.3 Presentational
- Present descriptions of traits of themselves and others
- Use poetry to express and describe themselves

CULTURE

2.1 Practices to Perspectives
- Explain how friendships are formed and maintained in some Spanish-speaking countries.

2.2 Products to Perspectives
- Discuss Frida Kahlo and her painting
- Discuss how the *huipil* reveals facts about its wearer

CONNECTIONS

3.1 Making Connections
- Discuss important artists and their work: Frida Kahlo
- Talk about and write a type of poem known as the *diamante*

COMPARISONS

4.1 Language
- Talk about vocabulary through the recognition of cognates
- Discuss building vocabulary through the use of root words
- Explain gender-agreement rules with use of adjectives
- Compare cognates that begin with the letters *es* plus consonant
- Explain the use of definite and indefinite articles
- Talk about the pronunciation of the letters *o* and *u*
- Talk about the placement of adjectives

4.2 Cultural
- Compare Internet-based chat habits of teenagers
- Talk about and compare the influence of Simón Bolívar to other leaders
- Compare clothing choices that reflect personality

CAPÍTULO 1B
Y tú, ¿cómo eres?

Country Connections Explorar el mundo hispano

CHAPTER OBJECTIVES

Communication

By the end of this chapter you will be able to:
- Listen to and read descriptions of others.
- Talk and write about your personality traits.
- Describe your personality to others.

Culture

You will also be able to:
- **Auténtico**: Identify cultural practices in an authentic video about personality traits.
- Compare cultural perspectives on friendship.

You will demonstrate what you know and can do:
- Presentación escrita: Amigo por correspondencia
- Repaso del capítulo: Preparación para el examen

You will use:

Vocabulary	Grammar
• Personality traits	• Adjectives
• Expressing likes and dislikes	• Definite and indefinite articles
	• Word order: Placement of adjectives

ARTE y CULTURA México

Frida Kahlo (1907–1954) is one of the best-known Mexican painters. In spite of a childhood illness, a crippling traffic accident, and many hospital stays throughout her life, Kahlo was a successful painter and led a very active social life. She used her artwork as an outlet for her physical and emotional suffering.

▶ Frida Kahlo painted over fifty self-portraits. What is she saying about herself through this painting?

🌐 **Mapa global interactivo** Explore the Tlatelolco *barrio* of Mexico City and the Blue House where Frida lived, and examine connections with her art.

"Autorretrato con mono" (1938), Frida Kahlo ▶

Oil on masonite, 16 X 12 inches. Courtesy of Albright-Knox Art Gallery, Buffalo, NY. Bequest of A. Conger Goodyear, 1966. © 2009 Banco de México, Diego Rivera & Frida Kahlo Museums Trust. México, D.F./Artists Rights Society (ARS), New York.

48 cuarenta y ocho • Tema 1 • Mis amigos y yo

Enrich Your Teaching

The End in Mind

Have students preview the sample performance tasks on *Preparación para el examen,* p. 71 and connect them to the Chapter Objectives. Explain to students that by completing the sample tasks they can self-assess their learning progress.

Technology: Mapa global interactivo

Download the *Mapa global interactivo* files for Chapter 1B and preview the activities. In Activity 1, discover artist Frida Kahlo's world in Ciudad de México. Activity 2 looks at the countries Simón Bolívar liberated—Venezuela, Colombia, Ecuador, Peru, and Bolivia.

Un grupo de amigos,
San Juan del Sur, Nicaragua

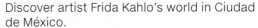
Videocultura **Amigos y actividades**

Capítulo 1B • cuarenta y nueve **49**

- Compare words used to identify friends and acquaintances
- Compare how friendships are formed and maintained
- Compare the African influence on music in the Americas

COMMUNITIES

5.1 School and Global Communities
- Reflect and discuss careers for which bilingualism is an asset

5.2 Lifelong Learning
- Communicate by e-mail in Spanish

Chapter Opener

Resources: Mapa global interactivo

Suggestions: Explain that students will learn language for identifying personality traits and describing what people are like. (Physical descriptions will be taught in *Capítulo* 5B in the context of family.) The *Videohistoria* focuses on the personality traits of various teens in the video. The *GramActiva* Videos will help students learn to describe things using adjectives.

▶ **Technology: Videocultura** View *Amigos y actividades* with the class to learn more about how friends like to spend their time.

ARTE Y CULTURA

Standards: 2.2, 3.1

Suggestions: After students have studied the paragraph and the painting, explain that Frida Kahlo chose to wear traditional Mexican clothing and jewelry, and this is reflected in her self-portraits. Have students comment on what the painter is wearing and her facial expression. Ask them what they would include in a self-portrait.

Answers will vary but may include personality traits, or that she displays some pain in the serious tone of the self-portrait.

🌐 **Mapa global interactivo, Actividad 1**
Discover artist Frida Kahlo's world in Ciudad de México.

Teaching with Art

Ask students: Why do you think Frida Kahlo chose a monkey as her partner in this self-portrait? Have you ever drawn a portrait of yourself?

Project-Based Learning

Álbum de recuerdos (continued)

Have students think about what the pictures available to them for their photo albums show about the type of person they were when they were younger, and the type of person they are now. Were they serious, fun-loving, quite, sociable, industrious, playful, energetic? Have students make a list of the adjectives they would use to describe themselves in each picture in order to compare what the pictures show about them then with how they perceive themselves now.

Go **Online** to practice
PEARSON
realize™
PearsonSchool.com/Autentico
AUDIO · VIDEO · WRITING · SPEAK/RECORD · MAPA GLOBAL · AUTÉNTICO · FLASHCARDS · ETEXT 2.0 · GAMES

Vocabulario en contexto

Standards: 1.2, 4.1

Resources: Teacher's Resource Materials: Input Script, Clip Art, Audio Script; Technology: Audio Cap. 1B

Suggestions: Use the Input Script from the *Teacher's Resource Materials* to present the new vocabulary, or use some of the suggestions here. Present the *Más vocabulario* using pantomime or exaggerated acting and explain to students that they will be held responsible for knowing these words.

Ask a female student to read the text in the first quote, from Sarita. She describes herself and her friend Marcos. Ask a male student to read the text in the second quote, from Marcos. Explain that many adjectives have different endings depending on whether they're describing a female or a male. Can students begin to deduce the rules? Encourage them to guess meanings of cognates. Can they guess the opposite of *paciente?*

Starter Activity

Put these letters for words for personality traits on the board and ask the students to unscramble them:

licoseba; rosie; utidosesa

(**Answers:** *sociable, serio, estudiosa*)

Active Classroom

Have students bring in pictures that represent the adjectives in this chapter. Have them cut out the pictures, paste them on poster board, and write the appropriate adjectives under each picture. Help students use correct gender endings.

🖥 Technology: Interactive Whiteboard

Vocabulary Activities 1B Use the whiteboard activities in your Teacher Resources as you progress through the vocabulary practice with your class.

Vocabulario en contexto

Vocabulario en contexto

OBJECTIVES
Read, listen to, and understand information about personality traits

> Me llamo Sarita. ¿Cómo soy? Pues, **yo soy** deportista y artística. También soy **muy** desordenada.
>
> ¿Y el chico? ¿Cómo se llama? Se llama Marcos. **Es mi amigo.** ¿Cómo es? Es ordenado y no es perezoso. **A veces** él no es muy **paciente,** y no es deportista. **No le gusta** nada practicar deportes.

impaciente

talentoso

atrevida

deportista

inteligente

estudiosa

graciosa

artística

50 cincuenta • Tema 1 • Mis amigos y yo

Differentiated Instruction

Students with Learning Difficulties

Give students English adjective examples that correspond to the Spanish ones shown on this page. Have them copy the list of new vocabulary into the Organizer from the *Core Workbook*.

Challenge

Have students bring in magazine or newspaper pictures of people in various professions, such as firefighters, judges, athletes, comedians, artists, etc. and write a list of personality traits for each profession. Students can use these as flashcards to review or expand their vocabulary.

" La chica es mi amiga Sarita. Ella es muy inteligente y le gusta estudiar. También es graciosa y **simpática**. Según ella, soy trabajador y estudioso. Pero según mi familia, ¡soy perezoso! ¿Y tú? ¿Cómo eres? "

Más vocabulario
reservado, -a = reserved

ordenado

trabajador

desordenado

perezoso

1

¿Marcos o Sarita?

ESCUCHAR   Listen to each word. If a word describes Sarita, turn your head to look to the right. If a word describes Marcos, turn your head to look left.

2

¿Cómo es?

ESCUCHAR   Listen to how people describe themselves. Point to the picture each adjective describes.

Capítulo 1B • cincuenta y uno **51**

Enrich Your Teaching

Teacher-to-Teacher

Have students draw a series of three pictures of themselves and label the pictures using vocabulary from pp. 50–51. Point out that adjectives usually have different endings when used to describe a female or a male. Ask volunteers to share drawings with the class.

21st Century Skills

Social and Cross-Cultural Skills Have students go online to social media and photo-sharing sites and read the profiles of other students from Spanish-speaking countries. As they read, have them list adjectives that the Spanish speakers use to describe themselves.

1

Standards: 1.2

Resources: Teacher's Resource Materials Audio Script; Technology: Audio Cap. 1B

Suggestions: Have students scan the photos and read the captions on pp. 50–51 before beginning the activity. Play the audio or read the script. Pause often to monitor that students are identifying the correct person. Have volunteers say the answers aloud.

Technology: Audio Script and Answers

1. impaciente *(Marcos-look left)*
2. artística *(Sarita-look right)*
3. ordenado *(Marcos-look left)*
4. simpática *(Sarita-look right)*
5. deportista *(Sarita-look right)*
6. inteligente *(Sarita-look right)*

2

Standards: 1.2

Resources: Teacher's Resource Materials Audio Script; Technology: Audio Cap. 1B

Suggestions: Play the audio or read the script. Be sure students pay attention to the key words that describe each person. Pause after each sentence if necessary.

Technology: Audio Script and Answers

1. Me llamo Sra. Martínez. Soy muy reservada. *(reservada)*
2. Mi buena amiga Liliana es muy graciosa. *(graciosa)*
3. Soy Joaquín. Mi familia dice que soy desordenado. *(desordenado)*
4. El chico se llama José. Es un chico atrevido. *(atrevido)*
5. ¿El chico? Es mi amigo David. Él es perezoso. *(perezoso)*
6. La chica es Sofía. Ella es trabajadora. *(trabajadora)*

Additional Resources

Technology: Online Resources
• Instant Check
• Guided, Core, Audio, Writing practice
• *Para hispanohablantes*
Print
• Guided WB pp. 39–42
• Core WB pp. 22–23

Vocabulario en contexto

Standards: 1.2

Resources: Teacher's Resource Materials Audio Script; Technology: Audio Cap. 1B

Suggestions: Begin the reading again with volunteers playing the roles of the characters. Using the presentation, help students understand the new words in bluetype.

Post-reading: Complete Actividad 3 to check comprehension.

3

Standards: 1.2, 1.3

Suggestions: You may wish to do this as a listening activity, reading the sentences and answers to the students.

Extension: Use the items as a basis for a classroom survey. For each couple of options, pick a student to answer the question "¿Cómo eres tú?"

Answers:
1. b
2. b
3. a
4. b

🔊 Las dos amigas

Jessica: Hola, Mariana. ¿Cómo estás?

Mariana: ¡Muy bien, gracias! Jessica, **eres** una chica muy simpática. ¿También eres muy **buena** estudiante?

Jessica · Mariana

Jessica: Sí. Me gusta ir a la escuela. ¡Soy muy estudiosa!

Mariana: Y, ¿cómo se llama tu profesor de inglés?

Jessica: Mi profesor es el señor Santos. No es sociable, es muy serio. **Pero** también es paciente. ¿Cómo es tu profesor?

Mariana: Mi profesora es la señora Brown. Es muy sociable y simpática, pero también es muy estricta.

Jessica: Mariana, ¿eres trabajadora?

Mariana: Sí, Jessica. Soy trabajadora. Pero **no soy** seria, ¡soy graciosa!

serio · sociable

3

¿Cómo es?

✏ **ESCRIBIR** Contesta a cada una de las siguientes preguntas.

1. ¿Cómo es el señor Santos?
   a. Él es sociable.
   b. Él es serio.

2. ¿Cómo es la señora Brown?
   a. Ella es trabajadora.
   b. Ella es simpática.

3. ¿Cómo es Jessica?
   a. Ella es muy estudiosa.
   b. Ella es paciente.

4. ¿Cómo es Mariana?
   a. Ella es seria.
   b. Ella es graciosa.

52 cincuenta y dos • Tema 1 • Mis amigos y yo

Differentiated Instruction

Heritage Speakers
Have students write a paragraph describing their best friend. Check to be sure they are making appropriate adjective agreements.

Bodily/Kinesthetic Learner
Ask students to come to the front of the class and role-play the parts of the two friends in the dialogue. Encourage them to be dramatic and act out any adjectives they can. Give them a few minutes to practice beforehand.

Go **Online** to practice

PEARSON **realize**™   PearsonSchool.com/Autentico

AUDIO   VIDEO   WRITING   SCRIPT

¿Cómo eres?

Before You Watch

Listening for key information What details would you include in a description of yourself? As you watch the video, listen for key details that each person uses to describe themselves.

Complete the Activity

¿Cómo eres? Describe tu personalidad con tres palabras.

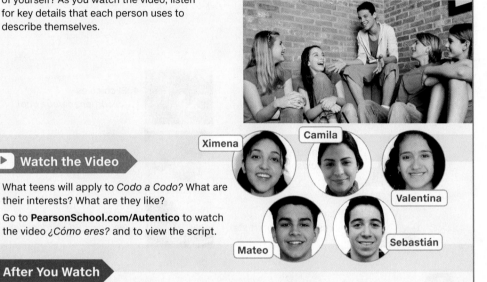

Ximena   Camila   Valentina   Mateo   Sebastián

▶ Watch the Video

What teens will apply to *Codo a Codo?* What are their interests? What are they like?

Go to **PearsonSchool.com/Autentico** to watch the video *¿Cómo eres?* and to view the script.

After You Watch

✎ **¿COMPRENDES?** Answer the following questions about the characters based on key details in the video.

Mateo, Camila, Ximena, Sebastián, Valentina

1. Read the sentences and indicate which character is being described.

   a. Es atrevido, sociable y paciente.

   b. No es paciente pero es curioso(a).

   c. Es inteligente y trabajador(a).

   d. Es deportista, sociable y gracioso(a).

   e. Es deportista, serio(a) y trabajador(a).

2. Según Ximena, uno de los chicos es gracios(a). ¿Quién es?

3. A uno de los chicos le gusta cantar y tocar la guitarra. ¿Quién es?

Pregunta personal Which video character interests you the most based on their personal descriptions? Why?

Capítulo 1B • cincuenta y tres **53**

Enrich Your Teaching

Culture Note

Different meanings The word *guapo* o *guapa* means handsome, pretty, good looking. In most Spanish-speaking countries when someone says, *¡Eres muy guapo!* it means you are very attractive. But also, when someone says *Él es muy guapo*, it could mean he is very brave. This word is yet used in

another way in the Dominican Republic, Puerto Rico, and Cuba where *guapo/ guapa* can mean something different. When someone says *Él siempre está guapo*, it means he is always angry. It all depends of the context and the country.

Technology: Video

Resources: Teacher's Resource Materials: Video Script

Before You Watch

Review the previewing strategy and activity with the students. Ask students for examples of personality traits your best friend has. Also point out the words about personality traits that will be discussed in the video. Review the Complete the Activity with the class. Ask for volunteers to write two sentences describing their own personality traits.

Watch the Video

Remind students that they do not need to understand every word in the video to understand what is happening, but they should consider the context of the video to guide their comprehension. Show the video once without pausing; then show it again, stopping to check comprehension.

After You Watch

Suggestions: Discuss the questions with the class to confirm understanding of the video.

Answers

1. a. Sebastián
   b. Ximena
   c. Valentina
   d. Mateo
   e. Camila

2. Sebastián
3. Daniel

Pregunta personal: Answers will vary. Sample answer: They all have interesting personality traits but I like Mateo because he is *deportista, sociable* and *gracioso*.

Have the students complete additional Video activities online or print the activities from the Teacher's Resources in the online course and pass out the activity sheets to the class.

Additional Resources

🛜 **Technology: Online Resources**
• Instant Check
• Guided, Core, Video, Audio
• *Para hispanohablantes*
Print
• Guided WB pp. 43–46
• Core WB pp. 24–25

Assessment

Quiz: Vocabulary Recognition
• Prueba 1B-1

5

Standards: 1.2, 1.3

Suggestions: Point out that students should look at the two adjective choices with each picture as well as at the pictures.

Answers:

1. artística	**3.** reservada	**5.** atrevida
2. perezoso	**4.** desordenado	**6.** estudiosa

Common Errors: Beginning students may forget to use the correct gender ending when they focus on vocabulary meanings.

Starter Activity

Put the following sentences on the board:
1) ____ es un chico ____ y ____
2) ____ es un chica ____ y ____
Have students refer to pp. 50–51 and fill in the blanks to describe classmates.

6

Standards: 1.2, 1.3, 4.1

Suggestions: This is a good homework assignment.

Answers:

1. deportista	**4.** desordenado	**6.** trabajador
2. gracioso	**5.** estudioso	**7.** bueno
3. sociable		

Additional Resources

📶 **Technology: Online Resources**
- Instant Check
- Guided, Core, Audio, Writing practice
- Teacher's Resource Materials: Audio Script
- Technology: Audio Cap. 1B
- Communication Activities: Audio Act. 6

Assessment

Prueba 1B-2 with Remediation (online only)
Quiz: Vocabulary Production
- Prueba 1B-2

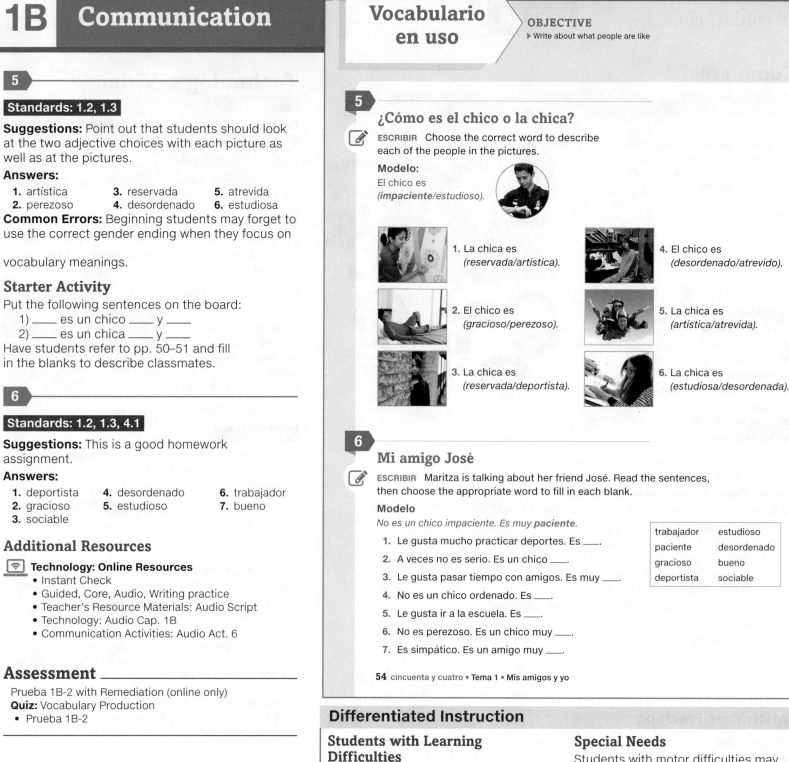

Vocabulario en uso

OBJECTIVE
▶ Write about what people are like

5

¿Cómo es el chico o la chica?

✏️ **ESCRIBIR** Choose the correct word to describe each of the people in the pictures.

Modelo:
El chico es
(*impaciente*/estudioso).

1. La chica es
(reservada/artística).

2. El chico es
(gracioso/perezoso).

3. La chica es
(reservada/deportista).

4. El chico es
(desordenado/atrevido).

5. La chica es
(artística/atrevida).

6. La chica es
(estudiosa/desordenada).

6

Mi amigo José

✏️ **ESCRIBIR** Maritza is talking about her friend José. Read the sentences, then choose the appropriate word to fill in each blank.

Modelo
*No es un chico impaciente. Es muy **paciente**.*

1. Le gusta mucho practicar deportes. Es ____.
2. A veces no es serio. Es un chico ____.
3. Le gusta pasar tiempo con amigos. Es muy ____.
4. No es un chico ordenado. Es ____.
5. Le gusta ir a la escuela. Es ____.
6. No es perezoso. Es un chico muy ____.
7. Es simpático. Es un amigo muy ____.

trabajador	estudioso
paciente	desordenado
gracioso	bueno
deportista	sociable

54 cincuenta y cuatro • Tema 1 • Mis amigos y yo

Differentiated Instruction

Students with Learning Difficulties

Have students study the word bank for *Actividad* 6 before starting the activity to be sure they understand all the words. Some students will benefit from writing the words on their own paper, then crossing them out as they are used.

Special Needs

Students with motor difficulties may find it easier to do *Actividad* 7 if you use colored string or yarn to make ovals on a tabletop. Write the words on index cards for them and have them sort the words into the ovals.

Gramática

OBJECTIVES
▶ Write about and discuss what you and others are like
▶ Describe your personality
▶ Read and write a self-descriptive poem

Go Online to practice
PEARSON realize™
PearsonSchool.com/Autentico
✎ WRITING

Adjectives

Words that describe people and things are called adjectives (*adjetivos*).

Masculine	Feminine
ordenad**o**	ordenad**a**
trabajad**or**	trabajad**ora**
pacient**e**	pacient**e**
deportist**a**	deportist**a**

• In Spanish, most adjectives have both masculine and feminine forms. The masculine form usually ends in the letter *-o* and the feminine form usually ends in the letter *-a*.

• Masculine adjectives are used to describe masculine nouns.

Marcos es ordenad**o** y simpátic**o**.   *Marcos is organized and nice.*

• Feminine adjectives are used to describe feminine nouns.

Marta es ordenad**a** y simpátic**a**.   *Marta is organized and nice*

• Adjectives that end in *-e* describe both masculine and feminine nouns.

Anita es inteligente.   *Anita is smart.*
Pedro es inteligente también.   *Pedro is also smart.*

• Adjectives whose masculine form ends in *-dor* have a feminine form that ends in *-dora*.

Juan es trabajad**or**.   *Juan is hardworking.*
Luz es trabajad**ora**.   *Luz is hardworking.*

• Some adjectives that end in *-a*, such as *deportista*, describe both masculine and feminine nouns. You will need to learn which adjectives follow this pattern.

Tomás es deportista.   *Tomás is sports-minded.*
Marta es deportista también.   *Marta is also sports-minded.*

Más recursos   ONLINE

▶ ***GramActiva* Video**
▶ **Tutorials:** Adjectives, Adjective clauses
🔊 ***Canción de hip hop:*** *¿Cómo soy yo?*
✎ ***GramActiva* Activity**

7

Roberto y Yolanda

✎ **ESCRIBIR**   Copy the Venn diagram on a sheet of paper. Which words from the list below could only describe Roberto? Write them in the oval below his name. Which words could only describe Yolanda? Write them in the oval below her name. Which words could describe either Roberto or Yolanda? Write them in the overlapping area.

artístico	deportista
graciosa	simpático
ordenada	perezosa
serio	talentosa
atrevida	estudiosa
impaciente	inteligente
paciente	reservado
sociable	trabajador

Modelo

artístico   atrevida

Roberto   **Yolanda**

Enrich Your Teaching

Teacher-to-Teacher

Give each student a blue, a yellow, and a pink index card. As you call out various adjectives, have students hold up the card whose color matches the gender of the word you've said. This allows for a quick check of comprehension.

Teacher-to-Teacher

Have students practice questions and answers with the classmates in their row of desks. Ask the first student in each row: *¿Cómo eres?* That student answers using an appropriate adjective, then asks the second student the same question. Continue until all students have participated.

Communication   1B

Gramática

Standards: 4.1

Resources: Teacher's Resource Materials Video Script; Technology: Video Cap. 1B

📲 Technology: Interactive Whiteboard

Grammar Activities 1B Use the whiteboard activities in your Teacher Resources as you progress through the grammar practice with your class.

Suggestions: Use the *GramActiva* Video as an initial introduction to adjectives or as a follow-up. Write **gracioso, estudiosa,** and **inteligente** on the board. Ask which one applies to a male, which one to a female, and which one can be applied to either. Change the genders of the characters and tell the story again. Once students grasp the concept of agreement, introduce invariable adjectives.

7

Standards: 1.3

Suggestions: Draw the Venn diagram on the board. Shade Roberto's oval blue, Yolanda's pink, and the overlapping portion yellow. Have volunteers write the answers in the diagram.

Answers: *Roberto:* artístico, serio, simpático, reservado, trabajador; *Yolanda:* graciosa, ordenada, atrevida, perezosa, talentosa, estudiosa; *Either:* impaciente, paciente, sociable, deportista, inteligente

Common Errors: Adjectives ending in **-ista** are mistaken as feminine. Remind students that they apply to both genders.

Assessment

Prueba 1B-3 with Remediation (online only)
Quiz: Adjectives
• Prueba 1B-3

8

Standards: 1.2

Suggestions: Remind Student B to pay attention to the adjective endings. When they have completed the activity, have students reverse roles.

Answers
1. Elena es graciosa.
2. Marcos es talentoso.
3. Felipe es perezoso.
4. Juan es desordenado.
5. Jaime es sociable.
6. Gloria es atrevida.

Extension: Have students bring in pictures of famous people and mount them on poster board. Label the pictures with an attribute of each person: *Pete Sampras es deportista.*

9

Standards: 1.2

Suggestions: Have students use words from *Vocabulario en contexto.* Tell students not to repeat an adjective. Remind students to use the correct endings.

Answers will vary.

10

Standards: 1.3, 4.1

Suggestions: Model a chart on the board that describes you. Be sure students use correct gender endings when they make their charts. Encourage them to use **muy** and **a veces** when applicable.

Answers will vary.

Extension: Have students create another chart with names of friends and family members at the top. For example, *Mi madre es / no es. . ., Mi amigo Brent es / no es. . .,* etc. Have students share their charts with the class. Tell students to save their charts to use in *Actividades* 11 and 12.

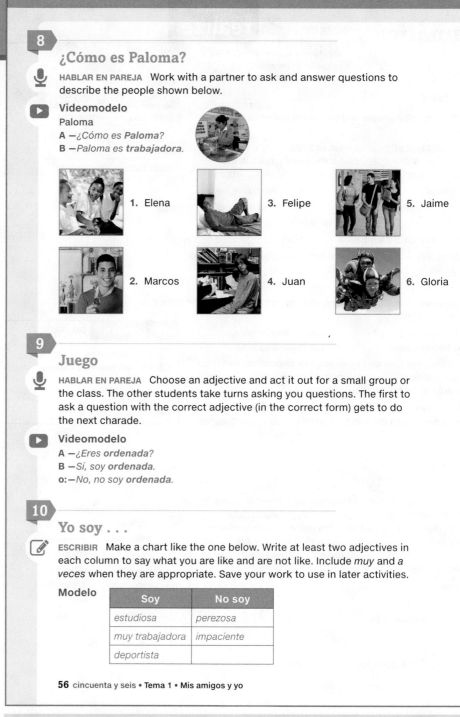

8

¿Cómo es Paloma?

🎤 **HABLAR EN PAREJA** Work with a partner to ask and answer questions to describe the people shown below.

▶ **Videomodelo**
Paloma
A —*¿Cómo es Paloma?*
B —*Paloma es trabajadora.*

1. Elena
2. Marcos
3. Felipe
4. Juan
5. Jaime
6. Gloria

9

Juego

🎤 **HABLAR EN PAREJA** Choose an adjective and act it out for a small group or the class. The other students take turns asking you questions. The first to ask a question with the correct adjective (in the correct form) gets to do the next charade.

▶ **Videomodelo**
A —*¿Eres ordenada?*
B —*Sí, soy ordenada.*
o: —*No, no soy ordenada.*

10

Yo soy . . .

✏️ **ESCRIBIR** Make a chart like the one below. Write at least two adjectives in each column to say what you are like and are not like. Include *muy* and *a veces* when they are appropriate. Save your work to use in later activities.

Modelo

Soy	No soy
estudiosa	perezosa
muy trabajadora	impaciente
deportista	

56 cincuenta y seis • Tema 1 • Mis amigos y yo

Differentiated Instruction

Heritage Speakers
Ask students to name a famous person from their heritage culture or someone they consider a role model and describe that person, using the vocabulary they have learned. Check that they are using appropriate gender endings.

Special Needs
Allow students to refer to their Organizer and/or their flashcards as they complete the activities. Some students may need to have someone transcribe for them. Having a fellow student do this can benefit both students.

11 ¿Eres estudioso(a)?

HABLAR EN PAREJA, ESCRIBIR Use your chart from Actividad 10. Talk with your partner about your personality traits. Take notes on what your partner tells you. Make another two-column chart, but with the headings *Es* and *No es*. Fill it in with information about your partner. You will use this chart in the next activity.

Videomodelo
A —*¿Cómo eres?*
B —*Soy estudiosa y muy trabajadora. También soy deportista. ¿Y tú?*
A —*Soy artístico. Según mis amigos, soy talentoso. No soy perezoso.*

12 Mi amigo(a)

ESCRIBIR, HABLAR EN GRUPO Use the information from the previous activity to write a short description of yourself and your partner. Read your description to a small group or the class.

Modelo
Me llamo Luisa. Soy estudiosa y trabajadora. Y soy deportista. Mi amiga se llama Susana. Ella es simpática. También es deportista y trabajadora.

Exploración del lenguaje ‹ Cognates that begin with *es* + consonant

Many words in Spanish that begin with *es* + consonant are easy to understand because they have the same meaning as English words. Knowing this pattern helps you recognize the meaning of new Spanish words and learn them quickly.

Try it out! Look at these words, then cover up the *e* at the beginning. Name the English words that come from the same root word.

estudiante	**es**tudioso
escuela	**es**pecial
esquiar	**es**tómago
estricto	**es**cena

Es muy estudioso.
Le encanta estudiar.

Capítulo 1B • cincuenta y siete **57**

Enrich Your Teaching

Teacher-to-Teacher
Have students write five names of real or fictional people on a piece of paper, such as Frida Kahlo, Abraham Lincoln, Rosa Parks, Sponge Bob, Superman, or Goldilocks. Then have them write a sentence using an adjective to describe each person or character.

21st Century Skills
Collaboration Work with teams of students to set up an e-mail exchange with an English class in a Spanish-speaking country. Have your students share with the Spanish-speaking class information about themselves and ask questions about those students' interests, likes, and dislikes.

13

Recycle: *Me/te gusta,* activities vocabulary

Suggestions: Students should answer according to what is true for them. Encourage them to use the **Respuesta personal**

Answers:

Student A:
1. ¿Te gusta trabajar?
2. ¿... practicar deportes?
3. ¿... dibujar?
4. ¿... esquiar?
5. ¿... pasar tiempo con los amigos?
6. ¿... cantar?
7. ¿... ir a la escuela?

Student B answers will vary.

CULTURA

Suggestions: Ask students what can be inferred from the picture about the time period and the person depicted. What is he grasping in his left hand? *(a sword)* Use the Mapa global Interactivo to show where Venezuela, Colombia, Ecuador, Peru, and Bolivia are located.

Answers will vary.

🌐 **Technology: Mapa global interactivo,** Locate the countries that Simón Bolívar liberated: Venezuela, Colombia, Ecuador, Peru, and Bolivia.

Active Classroom

Have students conduct Internet research on Simón Bolívar. Students can work in groups and choose different aspects of his life (family, education, the influence of Napoleon Bonaparte, liberation of Latin America, etc.) and prepare a short report. They can present their findings orally or in poster format.

13

¿Qué te gusta hacer?

🎤 **HABLAR EN PAREJA** Trabaja con otro(a) estudiante. Pregunta y contesta según el modelo. Luego, escribe una lista de las actividades que le gusta hacer a tu compañero(a) *(classmate).*

▶ **Videomodelo**
A —¿*Te gusta* **correr**?
B —*Sí, soy* **deportista**.
o:—*No, no soy* **deportista**.
o:—*Sí, pero no soy muy* **deportista**.

Estudiante A   Estudiante B

CULTURA ◀ El mundo hispano

Simón Bolívar (1783–1830) liberated the territory that is now Venezuela, Colombia, Ecuador, Peru, and Bolivia from Spanish rule. A daring military commander and statesman, Bolívar is revered in South America as *el Libertador* (the Liberator).

Pre-AP Integration: Heroes and Historical Figures
Compare Bolívar's role to that of another historical leader. What effect would liberation from Spain have had on the people in these South American countries?

🌐 **Mapa global interactivo** Explore the capital cities of Venezuela, Colombia, Ecuador, Peru, and Bolivia, and the routes between the cities, and reflect on the vastness of the territory that Bolívar covered on horseback.

"Simón Bolívar" (siglo xix), Anónimo ▶
Chromolitho. Private Collection / Archives Charmet / Bridgeman Art Library.

58 cincuenta y ocho • Tema 1 • Mis amigos y yo

Differentiated Instruction

Bodily/Kinesthetic Learner

Have students choose three or four words to describe themselves. For each of the words, have them write a sentence telling what they like or dislike doing. Example: ***artístico**—Me gusta tocar la guitarra.* Ask students to read their sentences to the class and act out their descriptions.

Go **Online** to practice

PearsonSchool.com/Autentico

VIDEO WRITING SPEAK/RECORD MAPA GLOBAL

14

El poema "Soy Elena"

LEER, ESCRIBIR The following poem is called a *poema en diamante*. Can you guess why? After you've read the poem, answer the questions.

Conexiones ◄ La literatura

Soy Elena

En general, soy

reservada y ordenada.

A veces, soy atrevida,

graciosa o impaciente.

No soy ni deportista

ni artística.

¡Yo soy yo!

1. Look for key words in the poem that describe Elena. Which of the following activities would you invite Elena to do based on her description of herself?

   dibujar   montar en monopatín   escuchar música

2. Rewrite the poem replacing *Soy Elena* with *Soy Tomás*.

15

Y tú, ¿qué dices?

ESCRIBIR Write *un poema en diamante* about yourself. Choose adjectives that best describe you. Look back at Actividad 10 for some ideas. Substitute your adjectives in the poem above. Be sure to write the poem in the form of a diamond. You might want to use calligraphy or an appropriate font on the computer and add pictures to illustrate your work.

Capítulo 1B • cincuenta y nueve **59**

Enrich Your Teaching

Teacher-to-Teacher

If students enjoy writing poems, you can have them bring photos of friends, family members, celebrities or pictures from magazine advertisements and use them to write similar poems. These should be in the third-person form:

Es _____. Ask students to decorate their finished poems and present them to the class. The class can vote for the best poem in categories such as **el más artístico, el más atrevido,** or **el más gracioso.** Display finished poems in the classrooms.

14

Standards: 1.2, 1.3, 3.1

Resources: Teacher's Resource Materials

Suggestions: Have students answer item 1 aloud. They can then complete item 2 on a sheet of paper, writing in the **diamante** form. Ask volunteers to share their poems with the class.

Answers:

1. *dibujar:* No. Elena no es artística. *montar en monopatín:* Sí. Elena es atrevida. *escuchar música:* No. Elena no es artística. o: Sí, es reservada.

2. Soy Tomás. En general soy reservado y ordenado. A veces, soy atrevido, gracioso o impaciente. No soy ni deportista ni artístico. ¡Yo soy yo!

Starter Activity

Complete these sentences about two classmates:

____ (Boy) ____ es ____ y ____.

____ (Girl) ____ es ____ y ____.

15

Standards: 1.3, 3.1

Suggestions: Point out that the title will still be *Soy* _____, and the last line will be *¡Yo soy yo!* Students can review the lesson, make a list of adjectives, and refer to the list as they write their poems. Encourage students to decorate their poems and display them in the classroom.

Answers will vary.

Project-Based Learning

Students can perform Step 4 at this point. Be sure students understand your corrections and suggestions. (For more information, see p. 24-b.)

Additional Resources

Technology: Online Resources
- Instant Check
- Guided, Core, Video, Audio
- Para hispanohablantes
- Teacher's Resource Materials: Audio Script
- Technology: Audio Cap. 1B

Print
- Guided WB pp. 47–48
- Core WB p. 26

Gramática

Standards: 4.1

Resources: Teacher's Resource Materials: Video Script; Technology: Video Cap. 1B

🔲 Technology: Interactive Whiteboard

Grammar Activities 1B Use the whiteboard activities in your Teacher Resources as you progress through the grammar practice with your class.

Suggestions: Some students will benefit from further clarification of the terms *definite* and *indefinite*. Direct attention to the *Strategy*. Use flashcards with familiar nouns and have students say **el** (or **un**) or **la** (or **una**) as they say each one.

16

Standards: 1.2

Resources: Teacher's Resource Materials: Audio Script; Technology: Audio Cap. 1B

Suggestions: You may want to bring thick markers to class so that students can write the articles in large, visible letters. Use blue and pink paper or index cards to reinforce the gender relationship and to allow for easy assessment of comprehension. Play the audio or read the script to students.

🔊 Technology: Audio Script and Answers

1. libro *(el)*
2. carpeta *(la)*
3. chica *(la)*
4. profesor *(el)*
5. escuela *(la)*
6. chico *(el)*
7. sábado *(el)*
8. amiga *(la)*

Active Classroom

Have students write a list of ten nouns, omitting the definite articles. Ask Student A to say a word on the list. Student B repeats the word, and adds the correct definite article. If the article is correct, Student B gets a point. When Student A finishes his or her list, the pair should reverse roles. When both lists have been practiced, the partner with the most points wins.

Gramática

OBJECTIVE
▶ Identify and write about people and things at your school

Definite and indefinite articles

El and *la* are called definite articles and are the equivalent of "the" in English. *El* is used with masculine nouns; *la* is used with feminine nouns. You've already seen words with definite articles:

| el libro | the book |
| la carpeta | the folder |

Un and *una* are called indefinite articles and are the equivalent of "a" and "an" in English. *Un* is used with masculine nouns; *una* is used with feminine nouns:

| un libro | a book |
| una carpeta | a folder |

| el | the |
| la | the |

| un | a, an |
| una | a, an |

Strategy
Learning by repetition When you learn a new noun, say it aloud, along with its definite article, as often as you get a chance. Eventually, you will find that words just "sound right" with the correct definite article and you will know whether nouns are masculine or feminine.

Más recursos ONLINE
- ▶ *GramActiva* Video
- ▶ **Tutorial:** Definite and Indefinite Articles
- 📝 *GramActiva* Activity

16

¿El o la?

🔊 ESCUCHAR Write the word *el* in large letters on a sheet of paper or an index card. Write *la* in large letters on another sheet. You will hear eight words you already know. When you hear a masculine word, hold up the paper with *el*. When you hear a feminine word, hold up the paper with the word *la* on it.

el	*la*

60 sesenta • Tema 1 • Mis amigos y yo

Differentiated Instruction

Students with Learning Difficulties

When teaching articles, provide very concrete examples that students can easily write in their Organizer or on flashcards. Students who struggle with writing might need the information provided on a handout that can be put directly into their notebooks.

Challenge/Pre-AP®

Have students review the *Vocabulario en contexto* and list all the nouns and their corresponding articles. Students can exchange lists to compare answers.

17

¿Qué es?

HABLAR EN PAREJA Tell your partner the names of the things pictured below.

Videomodelo
A —¿Qué es?
B —Es un brazo.

18

La escuela de Diego

ESCRIBIR Diego is talking about people at his school. Read the sentences and complete each one with *un* or *una*.

1. La Sra. Secada es ___ profesora simpática.
2. Alicia es ___ estudiante trabajadora.
3. Juan Carlos es ___ chico perezoso.
4. Germán es ___ chico sociable.
5. El Sr. Guzmán es ___ profesor gracioso.
6. Adriana es ___ chica muy seria.
7. La Srta. Cifuentes es ___ profesora paciente.
8. Arturo es ___ estudiante talentoso.

Pronunciación The vowels *o* and *u*

In Spanish, the pronunciation of the letter *o* is similar to the vowel sound in the English word "boat" but is always cut very short. Say these words, concentrating on making a short *o* sound.

bolígrafo	gracioso	cómo
teléfono	tampoco	otoño

In Spanish, the pronunciation of the letter *u* is similar to the vowel sound in the English word "zoo." Say these words.

mucho	lunes	usted
octubre	estudioso	según

¡Ojo! Careful! Sometimes the words we mispronounce most are the ones that remind us of English words.

El mundo

Try it out! Pronounce these words, concentrating on the Spanish vowel sounds:

agosto	regular	tropical	música
gusto	universidad	Uruguay	Cuba

Capítulo 1B • sesenta y uno **61**

17

Standards: 1.1

Recycle: School vocabulary; body parts
Suggestions: Have students reverse roles when they have completed the activity.
Answers:
1. Es un bolígrafo.
2. Es una carpeta.
3. Es un lápiz.
4. Es una hoja de papel.
5. Es un ojo.
6. Es un cuaderno.
7. Es un pupitre.
8. Es una pierna.

18

Standards: 1.2, 1.3

Suggestions: Remind students to read the whole sentence for clues to gender.
Answers:
1. una; **2.** una; **3.** un; **4.** un; **5.** un; **6.** una; **7.** una; **8.** un

PRONUNCIACIÓN

Standards: 4.1

Resources: Teacher's Resource Materials: Audio Script; Technology: Audio Cap. 1B
Suggestions: Have students say each word in the *Pronunciación* and in *Try it out!*

Additional Resources

Technology: Online Resources
- Instant Check
- Guided, Core, Video, Audio
- Para hispanohablantes
- Teacher's Resource Materials: Audio Script
- Technology: Audio Cap. 1B
- Communication Activities, Audio Act. 8

Print
- Guided WB p. 49
- Core WB p. 27

Assessment

Prueba 1B-4 with Remediation (online only)
Quiz: Definite and Indefinite Articles
- Prueba 1B-4

Enrich Your Teaching

Teacher-to-Teacher

For homework, have students write two columns with the headings *Masculine Nouns: **el / un*** and *Feminine Nouns: **la / una***. Instruct them to list ten objects or people, such as **un profesor,** in the appropriate columns. After the homework has been checked, students should keep their lists and add other nouns as they learn them, using this as an ongoing reference.

Gramática

Standards: 4.1

Technology: Interactive Whiteboard

Grammar Activities 1B Use the whiteboard activities in your Teacher Resources as you progress through the grammar practice with your class.

Suggestions: Contrast English and Spanish word order by having students give English equivalents of the sentences in the chart. Direct attention to the *¿Recuerdas?* Have students practice making negative sentences by placing the word ***no*** in the sample sentences.

19

Standards: 1.3

Suggestions: Help students identify the various parts of speech before they unscramble the sentences.

Answers:
1. Marina es una chica artística.
2. Tito es un chico perezoso.
3. Paquita es una chica deportista.
4. Marcos no es un chico reservado.
5. Rafael no es un chico estudioso.
6. Teresa no es una chica inteligente.

Extension: Write additional sentences on strips of paper and cut them apart. Have students work together to unscramble them.

20

Standards: 1.2, 1.3

Resources: Teacher's Resource Materials: Audio Script; Technology: Audio Cap. 1B

Suggestions: Play the audio or read the script as many times as necessary. Point out that two of the people described are female and one is male. Remind students to listen carefully and write the correct adjective endings. Have students check their work with a partner.

Technology: Audio Script and Answers

Arturo es un chico atrevido y serio. Le gusta mucho esquiar. Marta es una chica inteligente, paciente y trabajadora. Belinda es muy sociable. Le gusta hablar con los amigos.

Gramática

OBJECTIVES
▶ Write about and describe yourself and others
▶ Listen to and write a description of three teens

Word order: Placement of adjectives

In Spanish, adjectives usually come after the noun they describe. Notice how *artística* follows *chica* in the Spanish sentence.

> Margarita es **una chica artística**.
> *Margarita is **an artistic girl**.*

Did you notice that in the English sentence the adjective comes before the noun?

Here's a simple pattern you can follow when writing a sentence in Spanish.

¿Recuerdas?
To make a sentence negative you place the word *no* before the verb.
• Eduardo **no es** un chico serio.
• **No** me gusta jugar videojuegos.

Subject	Verb	Indefinite Article + Noun	Adjective
Margarita	es	una chica	muy artística.
Pablo	es	un estudiante	inteligente.
La Sra. Ortiz	es	una profesora	muy buena.

Más recursos ONLINE

▶ **Tutorial:** Position of Adjectives

19

Frases desordenadas

ESCRIBIR Rewrite these scrambled words to create a sentence. Follow the "building-blocks" pattern above and be sure to add a period at the end of each sentence.

Modelo
perezoso Antonio es chico un
Antonio es un chico perezoso.

1. artística es una chica Marina
2. es un Tito perezoso chico
3. deportista chica una es Paquita
4. Marcos chico un es reservado no
5. chico no Rafael es estudioso un
6. no una Teresa chica es inteligente

20

Escucha y escribe

ESCUCHAR, ESCRIBIR You will hear a description of Arturo, Marta, and Belinda. Write what you hear.

62 sesenta y dos • Tema 1 • Mis amigos y yo

Differentiated Instruction

Students with Learning Difficulties

Have students write female and male names, the verb form ***es,*** the indefinite articles ***un*** and ***una,*** along with appropriate nouns (***chico, chica estudiante***), and adjectives on individual index cards. They can use these cards to practice forming sentences using correct word order. Color-coding can help to reinforce the pattern.

Heritage Speakers

For homework, have students ask family members to describe the personality of their best friends and write down the description. Have students use different highlighters to mark the various parts of speech.

21

Go **Online** to practice

PearsonSchool.com/Autentico

PEARSON
realize™
🔊 ▶ 📝 🎤
AUDIO VIDEO WRITING SPEAK/RECORD

Interpersonal **1B**

¿Cómo es . . . ?

🎤 **HABLAR** You are sitting in your school cafeteria with a new exchange student from Costa Rica. Describe the other students based on their activities.

Modelo
Emilia es una chica talentosa.

Felipe

Emilia

Corina   Lilia

Carmen

Lucía

22

Y tú, ¿qué dices?

🎤 **ESCRIBIR, HABLAR**

1. Según tu familia, ¿cómo eres?

2. Según tu mejor *(best)* amigo(a), ¿cómo eres?

3. Y tú, ¿cómo eres?

El español en el mundo del trabajo

Paciente,
inteligente,
trabajador,
ordenado. . .

These four qualities will make you a good candidate for any job. And if you add *bilingüe* to the list, your job qualifications will be enhanced.

Make a list of careers in which your knowledge of Spanish would be an asset. Which of these careers are of interest to you?

Job Search

Apply Online   Add to My Job Cart

Job Description: Bilingual Paralega
Seeking college graduate with high GPA and excellent oral/written communication skills for paralegal position. Native English/Spanish or Spanish fluency preferred

Capítulo 1B • sesenta y tres **63**

Enrich Your Teaching

Teacher-to-Teacher

Make "human sentences" to reinforce word order. Give each student a color-coded sheet of paper with a word or phrase on it. Use one color for subjects, one color for verbs, one color for indefinite articles + objects, and one color for adjectives. At your signal, students must place themselves in the correct order so the class can read the sentences that are formed. Have one student be the negative who inserts himself or herself in the various sentences.

21

Standards: 1.3

Suggestions: Point out to students that they should use as many adjectives as apply to each person.

Answers will vary but may include:

Lilia es una chica talentosa *(graciosa, sociable)*. Felipe es un chico impaciente *(trabajador, inteligente)* Also accept negative statements.

Pre-AP® Integration

- **Learning Objective:** Interpersonal Writing
- **Activity 22:** Based on their answers to activity 22, have students write an e-mail describing themselves to one of the students pictured in activity 21.
- **Pre-AP® Resource Materials:** Comprehensive guide to Pre-AP® writing skill development

22

Standards: 1.2, 1.3

Suggestions: In items 1 and 2, point out that *tu* means "your."

Answers will vary.

El español en el mundo del trabajo

Standards: 5.1

Suggestions: Ask students how else bilingualism might be valuable, in addition to being an asset professionally.

Additional Resources

📶 **Technology: Online Resources**
- Instant Check
- Guided, Core, Video, Audio
- Para hispanohablantes
- Teacher's Resource Materials: Audio Script
- Technology: Audio Cap. 1B
- Communication Activities, Audio Act. 9

Print
- Guided WB p. 50
- Core WB p. 28

Assessment _____

Prueba 1B-5 with Remediation (online only)
Quiz: Word Order
- Prueba 1B-5

Lectura

Standards: 1.2, 1.3, 4.1

Suggestions

Pre-reading: Direct students' attention to the *Strategy* and discuss how visual clues often help in understanding a text. Help them identify the color names. Colors are formally taught in *Capítulo* 6A. You may want to use this as an opportunity to introduce them and demonstrate that color words are adjectives and must agree with the nouns they modify.

Reading: Pair students and have them take turns reading the text to each other. Encourage them to choose their favorite color and see what it reveals about them.

Post-reading: Have students tell what the quiz says about them. Do they agree with the quiz? Have them complete the *¿Comprendes?* to check comprehension.

Project-Based Learning

Students can perform Step 5 at this point. Record their presentations for inclusion in their portfolio. (For more information, see p. 24-b.)

Active Classroom

Colors have different meanings in different cultures. Have students work in small groups to discuss which colors are used to convey messages and feelings in the United States. Each group should summarize their discussion and share it with the class or make a collage showing colors and their cultural significance.

Lectura

OBJECTIVES
▶ Read and understand an article about personality traits
▶ Use visual clues to understand new words
▶ Learn how a Mayan item of clothing represents family and community

Strategy
Using visual clues to get meaning You have not yet learned the Spanish words for colors, but see if you can figure out what they are from the visual clues in the article.

Un *self-quiz*

¿Hay una relación entre los colores y la personalidad? Según un *self-quiz* de la revista *Amigos,* tus colores favoritos revelan perfectamente cómo eres.

¿Cómo eres tú?
¡Los COLORES revelan tu personalidad!

¿Eres una **chica**? ¿Te gusta el **ROJO**?	= Eres *muy apasionada*.
¿Eres un **chico**? ¿Te gusta el **ROJO**?	= Eres *atrevido*.
¿Eres una **chica**? ¿Te gusta el **VERDE**?	= Eres una chica *natural*.
¿Eres un **chico**? ¿Te gusta el **VERDE**?	= Eres muy *generoso*.
¿Eres una **chica**? ¿Te gusta el **AZUL**?	= Eres *muy talentosa*.
¿Eres un **chico**? ¿Te gusta el **AZUL**?	= Eres un chico *sociable*.
¿Eres una **chica**? ¿Te gusta el **ANARANJADO**?	= Eres una chica *artística*.
¿Eres un **chico**? ¿Te gusta el **ANARANJADO**?	= Eres *gracioso*.
¿Eres una **chica**? ¿Te gusta el **VIOLETA**?	= Eres una chica *muy independiente*.
¿Eres un **chico**? ¿Te gusta el **VIOLETA**?	= Eres un chico *romántico*.
¿Eres una **chica**? ¿Te gusta el **AMARILLO**?	= Eres una chica *muy trabajadora*.
¿Eres un **chico**? ¿Te gusta el **AMARILLO**?	= Eres *muy serio*.

64 sesenta y cuatro • Tema 1 • Mis amigos y yo

Differentiated Instruction

Challenge

Have students write a brief poem about themselves using the names of colors and other adjectives. Be sure they understand that the words in the poem do not have to rhyme. Students can decorate their papers using corresponding colors and pictures.

Heritage Speakers

Have students search the Internet to find additional personality quizzes. They can print these out and write summaries of what the tests say about them, changing from the second person to the first person.

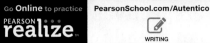

Go Online to practice
PearsonSchool.com/Autentico
PEARSON realize
WRITING

¿Comprendes?

1. You were probably able to understand the meaning of most of the unknown key words in the quiz. What is the English meaning that you can infer for these Spanish cognates in the reading?

- revelan
- generoso
- natural
- apasionada
- independiente
- romántico

2. According to the "self-quiz," what should be the favorite colors of these teenagers?

   a. A Beto le gusta estar con amigos.

   b. A Margarita le gusta dibujar.

   c. A Lorenzo le gusta el trabajo voluntario.

   d. A Lupe le gusta estudiar. Es muy seria.

   e. A Isabel le gusta estar con amigos, pero también le gusta estar sola *(alone)*.

3. Which of the colors in this reading best matches your personality? Why?

Modelo
Amarillo: *Soy una chica trabajadora. Me gusta ir a la escuela.*

CULTURA Guatemala • México

Huipil is the word for the colorful, hand-woven blouse worn by female descendants of the Maya. The color, design, and style of weaving are unique to each *huipil* and identify the background and specific village of the weaver. Hundreds of designs and styles of weaving have been identified in the Mayan regions, which are located principally in Guatemala and parts of Mexico.

Pre-AP Integration: National and Ethnic Identities What does choosing to wear a "huipil" today say about a person's connection to their national identity?

Una mujer de Guatemala con huipil ▶

Capítulo 1B • sesenta y cinco **65**

Standards: 1.1

Suggestions: Have students share their answers for items 1 and 2. Ask for volunteers to explain their answer for part three.

Answers

1. reveal, passionate, generous, independent, natural romantic
2. a) azul; b) anaranjado; c) verde; d) amarillo; e) violeta
3. Answers will vary.

CULTURA

Standards: 2.2, 4.2

Suggestions: Bring in photos or actual examples of clothing from various Spanish-speaking cultures. Help students recognize that even if they are purchasing clothing rather than making it, it nonetheless is a reflection of their values and personalities.

Answers will vary but might include t-shirts, team uniforms, particular colors or styles of clothing, etc.

Pre-AP® Integration

- **Learning Objective:** Interpretive: Print
- **Activity:** Have students bring to class a picture (from a magazine, the Internet, etc.) of a famous person and attach the picture to a sheet of construction paper that is the color associated in the article with that person's personality. Have them write a sentence below the picture identifying the personality traits.
- **Pre-AP® Resource Materials:** Comprehensive guide to Pre-AP® reading skill development

For Further Reading

Student Resource: *Para hispanohablantes, Lectura 2*

Additional Resources

📶 **Technology: Online Resources**
- Guided, Writing, Reading
- Cultural Reading Activity
- *Para hispanohablantes*

Print
- Guided WB p. 51
- Literacy Skills WB

Enrich Your Teaching

Culture Note

Crafting the *huipil* is a tradition kept by Mayan women. Other indigenous peoples have similar traditions. The Kuna, who live on small coral islands along the Atlantic coast of Panama, are famous for their *molas* (see p. 338). *Mola* is the Kuna word for the elaborate embroidered panels that make up the front and back of a Kuna woman's blouse.

21st Century Skills

Critical Thinking and Problem Solving Have students working in small groups tally their responses to the self-quiz. Was there a favorite color among female students? Among male students? Then, have all the groups compare their results. Was there a favorite color in the class? Ask students if they agree with the suggested relationship between color and personality trait.

Perspectivas del mundo hispano

Standards: 2.1, 4.2

Suggestions: Get students thinking about friendship and what it means to them by asking them to think about how many friends they have and the qualities they look for in a friend.

Have students read the page. Talk about the experiences of Marcos and Brianna. Do students feel these experiences are realistic? Have any of them had similar experiences? Ask if they differentiate between a friend and an acquaintance. If so, what terms do they use for this distinction?

Direct students to the Explicar section. After they have completed it, go over the Spanish terms and have students do the activity.

Some students may have personal experiences similar to those described because of having moved to a foreign country or to another city or community. Have students look at the photos and discuss what they see as compared to their own world.

Direct attention to the *Comparación cultural* section and have students discuss it.

Answers will vary.

Online Cultural Reading

After doing the online activity, ask students to describe the students they learned about.

Pre-AP® Integration

- **Learning Objective:** Presentational Speaking (Cultural Comparison)
- **Background:** This task prepares students for the Spoken Presentational Communication tasks that focus on cultural comparisons.
- **Activity:** Have students prepare a two-minute (maximum) presentation in English as to whether perspectives on friendship can vary between cultures. Think about the experiences shared by the teens in the reading. Then compare their experiences to your own and to perspectives about friendship in your own culture. In your opinion, could location (small town versus large city, for example) influence perspectives on friendship?
- **Pre-AP® Resource Materials:** Comprehensive guide to Pre-AP® speaking skill development

Additional Resources

📶 **Technology: Online Resources**
- Cultural Reading Activity
- *Para hispanohablantes*

Perspectivas del mundo hispano

¿Qué es un amigo?

Un amigo

Marcos, a Costa Rican student on an exchange program in the United States writes:

❝ When I arrived in the United States, I was amazed at all the friends my host brother and sister had. They knew a lot of people. These friends came to the house frequently, and we went out in groups. People were very open when meeting me. We'd spend some time together and get to know each other in a short amount of time. And once you got to know them, you ended up talking about everything! ❞

Brianna, a United States student on an exchange program in Colombia writes:

❝ After I spent my year in Colombia, I learned that the concept of friendship is a little different than in the United States. My host brother and sisters spent a lot of time with their family. They knew people at school and from after-school activities, but they had just a few close friends and we'd do things with them. It was definitely a smaller group than I was used to. It seems that it took longer to become close friends with people too. ❞

In Spanish, two expressions are used frequently to describe friendly relationships: *un amigo*, which means "friend," and *un conocido*, which means "acquaintance." You already know the word *amigo*. *Conocido* comes from the verb *conocer*, which means "to meet." Each expression implies a different type of relationship.

Explicar In many Spanish-speaking countries you'll find lots of expressions for someone who is your friend: *hermano, cuate (México), amigote (España),* and *compinche (Uruguay, Argentina, España).*

Actividad Write an email in Spanish to greet a friend in your class. Use one of these expressions.

Comparación cultural Compare how the United States perspective on friendship is different from that of a Spanish-speaking country. Use the terms *amigo* and *conocido* as you make the comparison.

> **Online Cultural Reading**
>
> **Go to PearsonSchool.com/Autentico** ONLINE to read and understand information about students from Texas.

Differentiated Instruction

Heritage Speakers

Students may have first-hand knowledge of the differences in friendships if they have moved from another country. If so, encourage them to share their experiences with the class.

Teacher-to-Teacher

e-amigos: Pair students to be *e-amigos*. Have them use e-mail to send each other short notes like the notes they write for the *Presentación escrita* on p. 67. Have students print out their e-mails or send them to you for your review.

Presentación escrita

OBJECTIVES
▶ Write an e-mail introduction
▶ Apply the steps of the writing process

Go Online to practice
PearsonSchool.com/Autentico

WRITING

Amigo por correspondencia

TASK Write an e-mail in which you introduce yourself to a new classmate using culturally appropriate register and style.

1 Prewrite To think about and organize the information you want to give, answer these questions:

- ¿Cómo te llamas?
- ¿Qué te gusta hacer?
- ¿Cómo eres?
- ¿Qué no te gusta hacer?

Strategy
Using the writing process To create your best work, follow each step in the writing process.

2 Draft Write a first draft of your e-mail answering the questions above. Decide if you will use *tú* or *usted*. Begin by introducing yourself: *¡Hola! Me llamo . . . .* End with *Escríbeme pronto.* ("Write to me soon.")

Modelo
¡Hola! Soy Pati. Soy atrevida y muy deportista. Me gusta mucho nadar y correr, pero me gusta más esquiar. ¡No me gusta nada jugar videojuegos! Escríbeme pronto y dime qué actividades te gusta y no te gusta hacer.

3 Revise Revise your first draft and share it with a partner. Ask yourself:

- Is it well organized?
- Does it answer the Prewrite questions?
- Are the spelling and adjective forms correct?
- Did you include the opening and the closing?

Decide whether or not to use your partner's suggestions and rewrite your draft.

4 Publish Type up your e-mail. Send it or print it for a classmate to answer.

5 Evaluation The following rubric will be used to grade your e-mail.

Rubric	Score 1	Score 3	Score 5
Completion of task	You provide some of the required information.	You provide most of the required information.	You provide all of the required information.
Following the writing process	You provide only the prewrite questions.	You provide the prewrite questions and rough draft.	You provide the prewrite, rough draft, and final product.
Using adjectives correctly	You use only one adjective with grammar errors.	You use two adjectives with some grammar errors.	You use more than two adjectives with very few grammar errors.

Capítulo 1B • sesenta y siete **67**

Enrich Your Teaching

21st Century Skills

Communication Before students write their e-mails, direct them to study the third step of the task, Revise. Using these questions as a pre-writing guide will make it easier for them to fulfill the requirements in the rubric for writing a better e-mail and getting a high score on the assignment.

Presentación escrita

Standards: 1.3

Suggestions: Introduce the *Presentación escrita* to the class and have students review the rubric. Then have them work through each step of the process.

Prewrite: Suggest to students that they make an outline or write a list of facts they want to include in their e-mail. Students should use the questions in Step 1 to guide their thinking.

Draft: Encourage students to be creative when they write their e-mail, but explain that they can use the example in Step 2 to format their own message.

Revise: Tell students to check their e-mail to identify errors or better ways to communicate before sharing it with a partner. When suggestions have been accepted, be sure students know to incorporate them and revise their message.

Publish: Remind students to reread their final copy of the e-mail for typing errors before they send it or give it to someone.

Evaluation: See Assessment below.

Pre-AP® Integration

Pre-AP® Resource Materials: Comprehensive guide to Pre-AP® writing skill development

Digital Portfolio

Have students create PDFs of their e-mails for inclusion in their digital portfolios.

Additional Resources

Technology: Online Resources
- Guided
- *Para hispanohablantes*

Print
- Guided WB, p. 52

Assessment

Presentación escrita
- **Assessment Program:** Rubrics
Go over the descriptions of the different levels of performance. After assessing students, help individuals understand how their performance could be improved. (See Teacher's Resource Materials for suggestions on using rubrics in assessment.)

Auténtico

Standards: 2.1, 2.2, 4.2

Resources: *Authentic Resources Wkbk*, Cap. 1B

Authentic Resources: Cap 1B: Videoscript

AP Theme: *Las identidades personales y públicas: La autoestima*

Before You Watch

Discuss the *Strategy* with students. Ask them to make a list of words they would use, and another of words they would not use, to describe themselves in Spanish at an interview or audition. Then have they discuss what they know about how to present themselves in formal situations. Then review the key vocabulary with the class. Ask students how the words listed fit into what they already know about interviews and auditions. Ask students to predict what tips they might learn in the video about auditioning for a talent show in the Spanish-speaking world, using the key vocabulary and image in their text. Make a list of tips on the board, as well as positive and negative descriptive words.

Technology: Watch the Video

Before starting the video, direct students' attention to the *Mientras ves* activity. Compare the list of descriptive words to the list the class compiled on the board and have students add any additional words to their list.

Play the video once completely through, without pausing, and tell students to listen for words they recognize in the video. Remind students that they will not understand every word, but that they should listen and watch for overall understanding. Replay the video, stopping as necessary for students to complete the listening activity and to check comprehension. Show the video a final time without pausing.

Auténtico

Partnered with

UNIVISION COMMUNICATIONS INC

Nataliz te da tres tips prácticos

Before You Watch

Use the Strategy: Use Background Knowledge to Increase Understanding

Think about ways that people might describe themselves in an audition, interview, or other similar situation. What are important personality traits to share? Do you think the importance of traits differs between cultures?

Read this Key Vocabulary

audición = audition   **concurso** = contest

bonita = pretty   **resaltar** = to standout, to highlight

bella = beautiful   **sueño** = dream

por dentro y por fuera = inside and out

▶ Watch the Video

Reporter Nataliz Jiménez gives three practical tips to help contestants highlight their personality traits during an audition for *Nuestra Belleza Latina*, a beauty pageant and reality show on Spanish television.

Go to **PearsonSchool.com/Autentico** and watch the video *Nataliz Jiménez te da tres tips prácticos para poder resaltar tu personalidad en las audiciones* to learn how you can highlight your personality in an interview, an audition, or any other presentation.

Complete the Activities

Mientras ves As you watch the video, listen for the following descriptive words and indicate the personality traits that Nataliz presents in her three tips. Which word does she repeat in each tip? Based on what you know about beauty pageants, why would this be an important trait to highlight?

tranquila	nerviosas
famosa	bella
bonitas	desordenado
tímida	fabulosas
diferente	práctico

Differentiated Instruction

Students with Learning Difficulties

Ask students to create a chart with three columns for Nataliz's three tips. They can label the columns for each tip as follows: *3 cosas*, *Quién soy*, *Relax*. In each column, have them write the vocabulary words that they recognize Nataliz use as she gives that tip.

Heritage Learners

In the video, some words in English are used. Have students identify these words, and offer alternative words in Spanish. Ask students to first reflect on their own experiences with code-switching, which is switching back and forth between two languages. Do they ever switch languages mid-sentence, or know anyone who does? Then have students write a few sentences considering what it means to mix languages, and how that affects the audience.

¡SUSCRÍBETE YA! ▶ You Tube

UNIVISION®
COMMUNICATIONS INC

Integration

Después de ver Answer the questions to demonstrate your understanding of the video and to identify cultural practices related to personal presentation.

1. ¿Cómo es Nataliz Jiménez? Usa tres adjetivos para describir a Nataliz.

2. Why does Nataliz NOT recommend describing yourself as beautiful on the inside and out, or as a fighter?

3. What strategies do you use to prepare for an important audition or interview? Compare your strategies to what Nataliz recommends.

📖 **For more activities, go to the *Authentic Resources Workbook*.**

Definiciones de la identidad y la belleza

Expansión Find other authentic resources in *Auténtico* online, then answer the questions.

📁 **1B Auténtico**

Integración de ideas How might we describe ourselves and present ourselves differently in different situations? In different cultures?

Comparación cultural Compare adjectives used in the resources to define *belleza latina* with adjectives that you use to define beauty.

Enrich Your Teaching

Culture Note

Nataliz Jiménez is a Domincan celebrity first known for her participation in *Nuestra Belleza Latina,* a US-based reality television beauty contest. Since she has worked as a correspondent for *Univision* and a radio show host based in Miami.

Perspectivas: Have students use Nataliz's tips from the video to present themselves to the class.

Using Authentic Resources

Ask students to identify the character or physical trait emphasized in each authentic source that they most identify with using the vocabulary from the chapter and the words used in the authentic sources. What does each source tell them about the culture it represents?

Interpret Authentic Resources **1B**

Completa las actividades

Mientras ves

Standards: 1.1, 1.2

Suggestions: Play the video several times, stopping after the introduction and after each tip to confirm what students understand. Remind students to listen for English words or possible cognates. Then ask students which Spanish adjectives describe themselves or someone they know. Ask them what other Spanish adjectives they could use to describe themselves or others.

Answers:

nerviosas, bonitas, tímida, interesante, diferente; Nataliz repeats 'diferente' in each tip.
Answers will vary.

Después de ver

Standards: 1.1, 1.2

Answers:

1. *Answers will vary. Possible answers include:* La chica (Nataliz) es talentosa, simpática y sociable.
2. Producers are looking for someone unique; We are all fighters/beautiful inside and out.
3. *Answers will vary.*

For more Authentic Resources: Assign the *Authentic Resources Workbook* activities for homework, so that students can play the video on their own and complete the workbook activities at their own pace.

Pre-AP® Integration

Standards: 1.3

Resources: *Authentic Resources Workbook,* Cap. 1B; Authentic
Resources: Cap 1B; Videoscript

Suggestions: Before completing the Pre-AP® activity, have students go to the workbook and complete the worksheets for these two additional resources.

Review Activities

To talk about what you and others are like: Have students work in pairs to quiz each other on the vocabulary. They can pantomime the adjectives and have classmates guess the words.

To ask people about themselves or others: Have students walk around the room and ask three people about themselves or another person. Each student should ask and answer three questions.

To talk about what someone likes or dislikes: Have students talk in pairs about what their friends like and dislike, using infinitives from the learned vocabulary in the structure *(No) Le gusta ___.*

To describe someone: Have students work in small groups to describe themselves or another person using *(No) Soy ___.* and *Es ___.* Tell them to use as many adjectives as possible.

To tell whom are you talking about: Have the class write short sentences *(Es un chico...)* using correct verb forms and gender endings to describe themselves or someone else.

Other useful words: Refer students to this section and remind them to practice these expressions as they create sentences.

Digital Portfolio

Invite students to review the activities they completed in this chapter, including written reports, posters or other visuals, and recordings of oral presentations or other projects. Have them select one or two items that they feel best demonstrate their achievements in Spanish. Include these products in students' portfolios. Have them include this with the Chapter Checklist and Self-Assessment Worksheet.

Additional Resources

Technology: Online Resources
- Instant Check
- *Para hispanohablantes*

Print
- Core WB pp. 29–30

Teacher Resources
- Teacher's Resource Materials: Situation Cards, Clip Art
- Assessment Program: Chapter Checklist and Self-Assessment Worksheet

---

Repaso del capítulo

OBJECTIVES
- Review the vocabulary and grammar
- Demonstrate you can perform the tasks on p. 71

🔊 Vocabulario

to talk about what you and others are like

artístico, -a	artistic
atrevido, -a	daring
bueno, -a	good
deportista	sports-minded
desordenado, -a	messy
estudioso, -a	studious
gracioso, -a	funny
impaciente	impatient
inteligente	intelligent
ordenado, -a	neat
paciente	patient
perezoso, -a	lazy
reservado, -a	reserved, shy
serio, -a	serious
simpático, -a	nice, friendly
sociable	sociable
talentoso, -a	talented
trabajador, -ora	hardworking

to ask people about themselves or others

¿Cómo eres?	What are you like?
¿Cómo es?	What is he / she like?
¿Cómo se llama?	What's his / her name?
¿Eres . . . ?	Are you . . . ?

to talk about what someone likes or doesn't like

le gusta . . .	he / she likes . . .
no le gusta . . .	he / she doesn't like . . .

to describe someone

soy	I am
no soy	I am not
es	he / she is

to tell whom you are talking about

el amigo	male friend
la amiga	female friend
el chico	boy
la chica	girl
él	he
ella	she
yo	I

other useful words

a veces	sometimes
muy	very
pero	but
según	according to
según mi familia	according to my family

Gramática

adjectives

Masculine	Feminine
ordenado	ordenada
trabajador	trabajadora
paciente	paciente
deportista	deportista

definite articles

el	the
la	the

indefinite articles

un	a, an
una	a, an

For *Vocabulario adicional,* see pp. 472–473.

Differentiated Instruction

Students with Learning Difficulties

Cut out magazine pictures of people who could be described using the vocabulary in this chapter. Hold up two of the pictures and give a short description of one of them. Have students tell you which one you are describing.

Logical-Mathematical Learner

Have students make a word-search puzzle with all the new adjectives mixed in among other letters. Instead of listing the words to search for, have students write clues. For example: *Me gustan los deportes.* **(Soy deportista.)**

Preparación para el examen

Más recursos PearsonSchool.com/Autentico

☒ Games   🗐 Flashcards   ✎ Instant check
▶ Tutorials   ▶ GramActiva videos   ▶ Animated verbs

What you need to be able to do for the exam . . .	Here are practice tasks similar to those you will find on the exam . . .	For review go to your print or digital textbook . . .
Interpretive		
1 ESCUCHAR I can listen to and understand a description of a friend.	Listen as a character in a Spanish soap opera describes his ex-girlfriend. What does he think her good qualities are? What does he think her shortcomings are? Can you understand why he broke up with her?	pp. 50–53 *Vocabulario en contexto* p. 57 *Actividades 11–12* p. 62 *Actividad 20*
Interpersonal		
2 HABLAR I can talk about myself in terms of how I see myself.	While you're talking to your Spanish teacher, you realize that she doesn't know the "real you." Tell her some things about yourself that would help her understand you.	pp. 50–53 *Vocabulario en contexto* p. 56 *Actividad 9* p. 57 *Actividad 11* p. 58 *Actividad 13* p. 63 *Actividad 22*
Interpretive		
3 LEER I can read and understand a description of someone.	In a popular Spanish magazine, you see an interview with the actor who plays the part of a teenager, Carlos, in a TV show you have been watching. See if you can understand what he is saying about the character he plays: ¡No me gusta nada el chico! Él es muy inteligente, pero le gusta hablar y hablar de NADA. Es ridículo. Es muy impaciente y perezoso. Él no es ni simpático ni gracioso. Yo soy un actor . . . ¡no soy como Carlos!	pp. 50–53 *Vocabulario en contexto* p. 59 *Actividad 14* pp. 64–65 *Lectura*
Presentational		
4 ESCRIBIR I can write a short paragraph describing myself.	The first issue of your school's online newspaper is called "Getting to Know You." Submit a brief profile of yourself. Mention what your family thinks of you and list some things you like to do. For example: Yo soy una chica deportista y muy sociable. Según mi familia, soy graciosa. Me gusta patinar y hablar por teléfono.	pp. 56–57 *Actividades 10–12* p. 59 *Actividad 15* p. 63 *Actividad 22* p. 67 *Presentación escrita*
Cultures		
5 Comparar I can demonstrate an understanding of cultural perspectives on friendship.	Explain the differences between the terms *amigo* and *conocido* in Spanish-speaking cultures. How does this compare to words that we use in the United States?	p. 66 *Perspectivas del mundo hispano*

Capítulo 1B • setenta y uno **71**

Differentiated Assessment

Core Assessment
- Assessment Program: Examen del capítulo 1B
- Technology: Audio Cap. 1B
- ExamView: Chapter Test, Test Banks A and B

Challenge/Pre-AP®
- ExamView: Pre-AP® Test Bank
- Pre-AP® Resource Materials

Extra Support
- Alternate Assessment Program: Examen del capítulo 1B
- Technology: Audio Cap. 1B

Heritage Speakers
- Assessment Program: Para hispanohablantes: Examen del capítulo 1B
- ExamView: Heritage Learner Test Bank

Performance Tasks

Standards: 1.1, 1.2, 1.3, 3.1

Student Resource: *Para hispanohablantes*
Teacher Resources: Teacher's Resource Materials
Audio Script; Technology: Audio Cap. 1B

1. Escuchar

Suggestions: Play the audio or read the script. Have students suggest answers.

Script

¿Cómo es María Elena? Pues... es una chica inteligente y talentosa, pero es muuuy seria. Y no es sociable. Yo soy un chico gracioso y muy sociable. A mí me gustan más las chicas atrevidas.

Answers: Elena is talented and intelligent, but very serious. Her shortcomings are that she is not sociable. He likes more outgoing or daring women.

2. Hablar

Suggestions: For more practice, have students describe themselves as the opposite of what they are like.

Answers will vary.

3. Leer

Suggestions: Remind students to look for cognates. Ask volunteers to point out the phrases that describe personality traits.

Answers:
1. Es ridículo. Es muy impaciente y perezoso. Él no es ni simpático ni gracioso.
2. Él es muy inteligente, pero le gusta hablar de nada.

4. Escribir

Suggestions: Encourage students to be creative. Tell them they can either describe themselves as they are, or write about a "person" they create as themselves.

Answers will vary.

5. Comparar

Suggestions: Allow students to speak spontaneously or from a short list of their thoughts.

Answers will vary.

CAPÍTULO 2A

Tu día en la escuela

School subjects and schedules

Vocabulary: class subjects; school activities; school supplies; ordinal numbers

Grammar: subject pronouns; the present tense of *-ar* verbs

Cultural Perspectives: comparing schools

Auténtico: What Advantages Do Children Who Master Math Have?

CAPÍTULO 2B

Tu sala de clases

Describing a classroom

Vocabulary: classroom items and furniture; parts of the classroom; prepositions of location

Grammar: the verb *estar;* plurals of nouns and articles

Cultural Perspectives: opinions about school

Auténtico: Overcoming the Nuisance of Homework

Theme Support

Bulletin Boards

Theme: La escuela

Ask students to cut out, copy, or download photos of school supplies, classroom items, schools from around the world, and scenes from different school settings. Cluster photos according to these four categories.

Hands-on Culture

Chant for choosing teams

When choosing teams to play a game, students in **América Latina** often sing a chant like the one that follows.

Directions:

1. Type out the words to the chant and distribute copies to students.
2. Have students repeat each line of the chant after you to practice pronunciation.
3. Begin the chant, or choose a leader. The entire class responds to the leader.
   Leader: Ambos a dos ... Matarile, rile, rile. Ambos a dos ... Matarile, rile, rile, ron.
   Class: ¿Qué quiere usted? Matarile, rile, rile. ¿Qué quiere usted? Matarile, rile, rile, ron.
   Leader: Yo quiero un paje. Matarile, rile, rile. Yo quiero un paje. Matarile, rile, rile, ron.
   Group: ¿Qué paje quiere usted? Matarile, rile, rile. ¿Qué paje quiere usted? Matarile, rile, rile, ron.
   Leader: Yo quiero a *(name of a student).* Matarile, rile, rile. Yo quiero a *(name of a student).* Matarile, rile, rile, ron.
   Group: Aquí tiene usted su paje. Matarile, rile, rile. Aquí tiene usted su paje. Matarile, rile, rile, ron.
4. The student who is named joins the leader, and the chant begins again to choose the next team member.

Game

¿Tienes...?

This game is similar to Go Fish. Have students play it after you present the vocabulary from *Capítulo* 2B.

Players: 2 to 4 **Materials:** index cards, colored pencils or markers

Rules:

1. The cards for this game should be prepared ahead of time. Have students draw on the index cards the classroom items listed on p. 120. There should be four index cards for each item, making a deck of 48 cards for each pair or group.
2. One student deals each player five cards, then places the remaining cards face down on the desk or table.
3. Players examine their cards to see whether they have any matching pairs. If they do, they remove the pairs and set them aside.
4. The dealer begins play by asking whether anyone has a card.
   Dealer: Linda, ¿tienes un reloj?
5. If the player has the card that the dealer is asking for, he or she responds affirmatively and gives the card to the dealer. The dealer then sets the pair aside and takes another turn. If the player doesn't have the card, the dealer must draw one from the pile and the next player takes a turn.
   Player: Sí, tengo un reloj. No, no tengo un reloj. Toma un naipe *(card).*
6. The game ends when one player puts down or gives away the last card. All players count their cards. The player with the most pairs wins.

Variation: Have students write the vocabulary words on index cards, then turn them face down on a large table or the floor to play Concentration. Students turn over two cards at a time to find matching pairs.

21st Century Skills

Look for tips throughout Tema 2 to enrich your teaching by integrating 21st Century Skills. Suggestions for Project-Based Learning and Theme Support follow below.

Project-Based Learning

Modify the Project-Based Learning with one or more of these suggestions:

Critical Thinking and Problem Solving Have students research several Web sites and decide which design features and arrangement of information will be best for their Web site. With help from the teacher, they might also decide what could be added to the site to best represent the values of the school.

ICT Literacy As students examine different Web sites, have them develop criteria that they can use now and in the future to judge the quality of the sites they research. The handout "Evaluate Web Sites" can help them analyze online materials.

Collaboration Each student in the group should have a role, and work should be equally distributed. For example, three roles are design, photo/text selection, and site set-up. To better understand collaboration, have students read together and discuss the handout "Work in Teams."

Theme Culture

Information Literacy Have students review the *Cultura* notes on pages 80 and 86 and then draft an e-mail to a U.S. student, pretending to be a Spanish speaker. The writer should discuss school activities that differ from those the U.S. student might be used to.

▶ **Videocultura** View *Los uniformes escolares* with the class to learn more about different types of uniforms.

Project-Based Learning

Página Web

Overview: Students create a Web page for their school featuring the school's name, address, and phone number and at least four symbols or photos that represent different classes. Under each symbol or photo, students write a description of the class represented. Students then present their Web page to the class, describing all the information featured on the page.

Resources: Web creation software, poster board, magazines, colored pencils, markers, glue, scissors, bilingual dictionary

Sequence: (suggestions for when to do each step appear throughout the chapters)

2A **Step 1.** Review instructions so students know what is expected of them. Hand out the Theme 2 Project Instructions and the rubric.

Step 2. Students submit a rough sketch of their Web page. Return the sketches with your suggestions. For vocabulary and grammar practice, ask students to partner and present their drafts to each other.

Step 3. Students create layouts on poster board. Encourage students to try different arrangements before drawing or gluing photos or symbols and writing descriptions. Encourage students to use as much of the vocabulary from *Capítulos* 2A and 2B as possible in the descriptions. Also, encourage them to use a bilingual dictionary for any words they would like to use, but do not yet know.

2B **Step 4.** Students submit a draft of their descriptions. Note your corrections and suggestions, then return the drafts to students.

Step 5. Students complete and present their Web page to the class, reading and / or describing all the information featured on the page.

Options

1. Students create a brochure for their school instead of a Web page.
2. Students create a virtual tour of a classroom, describing its contents.

Assessment

Here is a detailed rubric for assessing this project:
Theme 2 Project: *Página Web*

Rubric	Score 1	Score 3	Score 5
Evidence of planning	You provided no written draft or page layout.	Your draft was written and layout created, but not corrected.	You corrected your draft and layout.
Your use of illustrations	You included no photos or visuals.	You included photos or visuals, but your layout was unorganized.	Your Web page was easy to read, complete, and accurate.
Your presentation	You included little of the required information.	You included most of the required information.	You included all the required information.

Objectives

- Listen to and read descriptions of school subjects and schedules
- Talk and write about classes, school activities, and likes and dislikes
- Exchange information while explaining what classes and activities you and friends have in common
- Identify cultural practices listened to in an authentic audio about school subjects
- Compare your school day with those of students in Spanish-speaking countries
- Compare sports and attitudes towards sports in the Spanish-speaking world and the United States

Vocabulary

- School subjects and schedules
- School supplies
- Class descriptions

Grammar

- Subject pronouns
- Present tense of *-ar* verbs

Culture

- Cortada, Xavier, p. 72
- Courses students take in Spanish-speaking countries, p. 80
- Romans in Spain, p. 81
- Latin influence on Spanish, p. 81
- *el recreo,* p. 86
- The Mayan numbering system, p. 88
- Facts about Costa Rica, pp. 90–91
- The 24-hour clock, p. 91
- Soccer fan chants, p. 92

Recycle

- Titles used with adults
- Infinitives
- Negatives
- *gustar*

Authentic Resources

- Audio about proposed changes to math instruction in Latin America pp. 94–95

	FOR THE STUDENT	DIGITAL	PRINT	FOR THE TEACHER	DIGITAL	PRINT
Plan				Teacher's Edition	•	•
				Teacher's Resource Materials	•	
				Pre-AP® Resource Materials	•	
				Lesson Plans, pp. 72-e, 72-f	•	
				Mapa global interactivo	•	
Introducción pp. 72–73						
Present	Student Edition, pp. 72–73	•	•	Teacher's Edition, pp. 72–73	•	•
	DK Reference Atlas	•		Teacher's Resource Materials	•	
	Videocultura	•		Mapa global interactivo	•	
	Para hispanohablantes	•				
Vocabulario en contexto pp. 74–77						
Present & Practice	Student Edition, pp. 74–77	•	•	Teacher's Edition, pp. 74–77	•	•
	Audio	•		Teacher's Resource Materials	•	
	Videohistoria	•		Vocabulary Clip Art	•	
	Flashcards	•		Technology: Audio	•	
	Instant Check	•		Video Program: Videohistoria	•	
	Guided WB, pp. 53–62	•	•			
	Core WB, pp. 31–34	•	•			
	Communication Activities	•				
	Para hispanohablantes	•				
Assess and Remediate				Prueba 2A-1: Assessment Program, pp. 41–42	•	
				Assessment Program para hispanohablantes, pp. 41–42	•	

RESOURCES

	FOR THE STUDENT	DIGITAL	PRINT	FOR THE TEACHER	DIGITAL	PRINT
Vocabulario en uso pp. 78–81						
Present & Practice	Student Edition, pp. 78–81	•	•	Interactive Whiteboard Vocabulary Activities	•	
	Instant Check	•		Teacher's Edition, pp. 78–81	•	•
	Communication Activities	•		Teacher's Resource Materials	•	
	Para hispanohablantes	•		Communicative Pair Activities	•	
	Communicative Pair Activities	•		Technology: Audio	•	
				Videomodelos	•	
Assess and Remediate				Prueba 2A-2 with Remediation	•	
				Prueba 2A–2: Assessment Program, pp. 43–44	•	
				Assessment Program para hispanohablantes, pp. 43–44	•	
Gramática pp. 82–89						
Present & Practice	Student Edition, pp. 82–89	•	•	Interactive Whiteboard Grammar Activities	•	
	Instant Check	•		Teacher's Edition, pp. 82–89	•	•
	Animated Verbs	•		Teacher's Resource Materials	•	
	Tutorial Video: Grammar	•		Communicative Pair Activities	•	
	Canción de hip hop	•		Technology: Audio	•	
	Guided WB, pp. 63–66	•	•	Videomodelos	•	
	Core WB, pp. 35–37	•	•	Video Program: GramActiva	•	
	Communication Activities	•				
	Para hispanohablantes	•				
	Communicative Pair Activities	•				
Assess and Remediate				Pruebas 2A–3 and 2A-4 with Remediation	•	
				Pruebas 2A–3, 2A-4: Assessment Program, pp. 45, 46	•	
				Assessment Program para hispanohablantes, pp. 45, 46	•	
Aplicación pp. 90–95						
Apply	Student Edition, pp.90–95	•	•	Teacher's Edition, pp. 90-95	•	•
	Authentic Resources Workbook	•	•	Mapa global interactivo	•	
	Authentic Resources	•		Authentic Resources Lesson Plans with scripts, answer keys	•	
	Online Cultural Reading	•				
	Guided WB, pp. 67–68	•	•			
	Communication Activities	•				
	Para hispanohablantes	•				
Repaso del capítulo pp. 96–97						
Review	Student Edition, pp. 96–97	•	•	Teacher's Edition, pp. 96–97	•	•
	Online Puzzles and Games	•		Teacher's Resource Materials	•	
	Core WB, pp. 38–39	•	•	Technology: Audio	•	
	Communication Activities	•				
	Para hispanohablantes	•				
	Instant Check	•				
Chapter Assessment						
Assess				Examen del capítulo 2A	•	
				Assessment Program, pp. 47–53	•	
				Alternate Assessment Program, pp. 13–18	•	
				Assessment Program para hispanohablantes, pp. 47–53	•	
				Technology: Audio, Cap. 2A, Examen	•	
				ExamView: Test Banks A and B questions only online	•	
				Heritage Learner Test Bank	•	
				Pre-AP® Test Bank	•	

2A Lesson Plans

LESSON PLAN (50 MINUTES)

DAY	Warm-up / Assess	Preview / Present / Practice / Communicate		Wrap-up / Homework Options
1	**Warm-up** (10 min.) • Return Examen del capítulo 1B	**Chapter Opener** (5 min.) • Objectives • Arte y cultura	**Vocabulario en contexto** (30 min.) • Presentation: Vocabulario en contexto • Actividades 1, 2	**Wrap-up and Homework Options** (5 min.) • Core Practice 2A-1, 2A-2
2	**Warm-up** (5 min.) • Homework check	**Vocabulario en contexto** (40 min.) • Presentation: Videohistoria *Las clases hoy* • View: Videohistoria	• Video Activities 1, 2, 3, 4 • Actividad 3	**Wrap-up and Homework Options** (5 min.) • Core Practice 2A-3, 2A-4 • Prueba 2A-1: Vocabulary recognition
3	**Warm-up** (10 min.) • Actividad 4, 5 • Homework check • **Formative Assessment** (10 min.) • Prueba 2A-1: Vocabulary recognition	**Vocabulario en uso** (25 min.) • Interactive Whiteboard Vocabulary Activities • *Actividades* 6, 7, 8, 9 • Cultura • Audio Activities 5, 6		**Wrap-up and Homework Options** (5 min.) • Writing Activity 10 • Prueba 2A-2 with Remediation: Vocabulary production
4	**Warm-up** (10 min.) • Communicative Pair Activity • Homework check • **Formative Assessment** (10 min.) • Prueba 2A-2 with Remediation: Vocabulary production	**Gramática y vocabulario en uso** (25 min.) • Exploración del lenguaje • Cultura • Presentation: Subject pronouns • View: GramActiva Video	• Interactive Whiteboard Grammar Activities • Actividades 10, 12 • Audio Activity 7	**Wrap-up and Homework Options** (5 min.) • Core Practice 2A-5 • Actividad 11 • Prueba 2A-3 with Remediation: Subject pronouns
5	**Warm-up** (10 min.) • Writing Activity 11 • Homework check • **Formative Assessment** (10 min.) • Prueba 2A-3 with Remediation: Subject pronouns	**Gramática y vocabulario en uso** (25 min.) • Presentation: Present tense of *-ar* verbs • View: GramActiva video • Interactive Whiteboard Grammar Activities • Actividades 13, 14, 15 • Audio Activities 8, 9		**Wrap-up and Homework Options** (5 min.) • Core Practice 2A-6, 2A-7
6	**Warm-up** (15 min.) • Writing Activities 12, 13 • Homework check	**Gramática y vocabulario en uso** (30 min.) • Communicative Pair Activity	• Actividades 16, 17, 18, 19 • Cultura	**Wrap-up and Homework Options** (5 min.) • Prueba 2A-4 with Remediation: Present tense of *-ar* verbs
7	**Warm-up** (5 min.) • Review *-ar* verbs • **Formative Assessment** (10 min.) • Prueba 2A-4 with Remediation: Present tense of *-ar* verbs	**Gramática y vocabulario en uso** (15 min.) • Actividades 20, 21 • Pronunciación • El español en la comunidad	• Lectura • ¿Comprendes? • Cultura	**Wrap-up and Homework Options** (5 min.) • Auténtico • Lectura
8	**Warm-up** (10 min.) • Homework check	**Aplicación** (35 min.) • La cultura en vivo • Presentación oral: Step 1	• Situation Cards • Communicative Pair Activities	**Wrap-up and Homework Options** (5 min.) • Presentación oral: Step 2 • Preparación para el examen 3, 4, 5
9	**Warm-up** (5 min.) • Homework check	**Aplicación** (30 min.) • Presentación oral: Step 3	**Repaso del capítulo** (10 min.) • Vocabulario y gramática • Preparación para el examen 1, 2	**Wrap-up and Homework Options** (5 min.) • Core Practice 2A-8, 2A-9 • Instant check • Examen del capítulo 2A
10	**Warm-up** (10 min.) • Homework check • **Summative Assessment** (40 min.) • Examen del capítulo 2A			

ALTERNATE LESSON PLAN (90 MINUTES)

DAY	Warm-up / Assess	Preview / Present / Practice / Communicate	Wrap-up / Homework Options
1	**Warm-up** (10 min.) • Return Examen del capítulo 1B	**Chapter Opener** (5 min.) • Objectives • Arte y cultura **Vocabulario en contexto** (60 min.) • Presentation: Vocabulario en contexto • Actividades 1, 2 • Presentation: Videohistoria *Las clases hoy* • View: Videohistoria • Video Activities 1, 2, 3, 4 • Actividad 3 **Vocabulario en uso** (10 min.) • Actividad 6 • Cultura • Interactive Whiteboard Vocabulary Activities	**Wrap-up and Homework Options** (5 min.) • Core Practice 2A-1, 2A-2, 2A-3, 2A-4 • Prueba 2A-1: Vocabulary recognition
2	**Warm-up** (10 min.) • Actividad 4, 5 • Homework check • **Formative Assessment** (10 min.) • Prueba 2A-1: Vocabulary recognition	**Gramática y vocabulario en uso** (65 min.) • Actividades 7, 8, 9 • Audio Activities 5, 6 • Writing Activity 10 • Exploración del lenguaje • Cultura • Presentation: Subject pronouns • View: GramActiva video • Interactive Whiteboard Grammar Activities • Actividades 10, 11, 12 • Audio Activity 7	**Wrap-up and Homework Options** (5 min.) • Core Practice 2A-5 • Actividad 11 • Prueba 2A-2 with Remediation: Vocabulary production
3	**Warm-up** (5 min.) • Communicative Pair Activity • Homework check • **Formative Assessment** (10 min.) • Prueba 2A-2 with Remediation: Vocabulary production	**Gramática y vocabulario en uso** (70 min.) • Presentation: Present tense of *-ar* verbs • View: GramActiva video • Interactive Whiteboard Grammar Activities • Actividades 13, 14, 15 • Audio Activities 8, 9 • Writing Activities 11, 12, 13	**Wrap-up and Homework Options** (5 min.) • Core Practice 2A-6, 2A-7 • Pruebas 2A-3, 2A-4 with Remediation: Subject pronouns, Present tense of *-ar* verbs
4	**Warm-up** (10 min.) • Homework check • **Formative Assessment** (15 min.) • Pruebas 2A-3, 2A-4 with Remediation: Subject pronouns, Present tense of *-ar* verbs	**Gramática y vocabulario en uso** (35 min.) • Communicative Pair Activity • Actividades 16, 17, 18, 19 • Cultura • Actividades 20, 21 • Pronunciación • El español en la comunidad **Aplicación** (25 min.) • Lectura • ¿Comprendes? • Cultura	
5		**Aplicación** (50 min.) • La cultura en vivo • Situation Cards • Communicative Pair Activities • Presentación oral: Step 3 • Auténtico **Repaso del capítulo** (30 min.) • Vocabulario y gramática • Preparación para el examen 1, 2, 3, 4, 5	**Wrap-up and Homework Options** (5 min.) • Core Practice 2A-8, 2A-9 • Instant check • Examen del capítulo 2A
6	**Warm-up** (15 min.) • Homework check • Answer questions **Repaso del capítulo** (25 min.) • **Summative Assessment** (45 min.) • Examen del capítulo 2A		**Wrap-up and Homework Options** (5 min.) • Lectura

Can-Do Statements

Read the can-do statements in the chapter objectives with students. Then have students read Preparación para el examen on page 97 to preview what they will be able to do at the end of the chapter.

Standards for Capítulo 2A

To achieve the goals of the Standards, students will:

COMMUNICATION

1.1 Interpersonal
- Talk about: homework and classes; preferences in school subjects; preferences in activities; people and schedules at school

1.2 Interpretive
- Listen to information: on school subjects, schedules, supplies; about the present tense of -ar verbs; about activities during recreo
- Read: a picture-based story; information about school subjects, schedules, supplies; information about a language school in Costa Rica
- Listen to and watch a video about school schedules
- Listen to the use of subject pronouns

1.3 Presentational
- Present information about: work, home, and school activities; school subjects, schedules, supplies
- Present school cheers like those in Spanish-speaking countries

CULTURE

2.1 Practices to Perspectives
- Explain the focus on English language acquisition in Spanish-speaking countries
- Talk about: school sporting event celebrations and traditions; leisure time during school hours

2.2 Products to Perspectives
- Discuss about symbolism of Xavier Cortada mural painting.
- Read and talk about school cheers

CONNECTIONS

3.1 Making Connections
- Build vocabulary through an understanding of mathematics
- Explain influences of Roman Empire history on Spain; similarities between Mayan numbering system and Roman numerals; the impact Spanish exploration had on the Maya

3.2 Acquiring Information and Diverse Perspectives
- Read and recite school cheers

COMPARISONS

4.1 Language
- Talk about new vocabulary through the recognition of cognates; the present tense of -ar verbs
- Compare personalized school-related vocabulary
- Explain the use of subject pronouns; the pronunciation of the letter c

---

CAPÍTULO **2A**
Tu día en la escuela

Country Connections Explorar el mundo hispano

España
México
Costa Rica
Colombia
Argentina

CHAPTER OBJECTIVES

Communication

By the end of this chapter you will be able to:
- Listen to and read descriptions of school subjects and schedules.
- Talk and write about classes, school activities, and likes and dislikes.
- Exchange information while explaining what classes and activities you and friends have in common.

Culture

You will also be able to:
- **Auténtico:** Identify cultural practices listened to in an authentic audio about school subjects.
- Compare your school day with those of students in Spanish-speaking countries.

- Compare sports and attitudes towards sports in the Spanish-speaking world and the United States.

You will demonstrate what you know and can do:
- Presentación oral: Mis clases
- Repaso del capítulo: Preparación para el examen

You will use:

Vocabulary	Grammar
• School subjects and schedules	• Subject pronouns
• School supplies	• Present tense of -ar verbs
• Class descriptions	

ARTE y CULTURA United States

Xavier Cortada (1964-) is a Cuban–American painter born in Albany, New York. He now resides in Miami, Florida. His works have been exhibited around the world in prestigious museums and galleries. Cortada is also a social and environmental activist and writer. His artwork is known for being environmentally oriented and for creating social awareness.

▶ Based upon the painting, how could you describe Cortada's style?

Protecting America's Children: A National Message Mural (2005), Xavier Cortada ▶
Private Collection/Bridgeman Images

Enrich Your Teaching

The End in Mind
Have students preview the sample performance tasks on Preparación para el examen, p. 97, and connect them to the Chapter Objectives. Explain to students that by completing the sample tasks they can self-assess their learning progress.

Technology: Mapa global interactivo
Download the Mapa global interactivo files for Chapter 2A and preview the activities. In Activity 1, you visit Segovia, Spain. Activity 2 takes you to Costa Rica.

Unos estudiantes,
San Cristóbal de las Casas, México

Videocultura **Los uniformes escolares**

Capítulo 2A • setenta y tres **73**

Project-Based Learning

Página Web

Ask students to write a blog of their school schedule and school activities for a week. Ask them to upload some personal photos of themselves and their friends to make their blog more interesting Ask them to be ready to present their blog to the rest of the class.

4.2 Cultural
- Compare: motivations for foreign language learning; leisure periods during the school day; the use of the 24-hour clock to the 12-hour clock; school cheers and sporting event celebrations

COMMUNITIES

5.1 School and Global Communities
- Discuss why English-speakers in the community are interested in learning Spanish

Chapter Opener

Resources: Mapa global interactivo

Suggestions: Introduce students to the theme of the chapter, school schedules, and subjects by discussing what their school day is like now. Ask students to predict what some of the vocabulary words may be, based on the context. The *Videohistoria* is about a family getting ready to start the school day.

▶ **Technology: Videocultura** View *Los uniformes escolares* with the class to learn more about different types of uniforms.

ARTE Y CULTURA

Standards: 2.2, 3.1

Suggestions: Discuss with the students the fact that this is just one panel of a larger mural entitled *Protecting America's Children: A National Message Mural.* Ask students to search online for the full painting and discuss the symbolism of the faded image in the mural.

Answers will vary but may include adjectives such as *strange* or *unrealistic*.

Teaching with Art

Suggestions: Remind students that not all artists want to recreate an image exactly. You may wish to give examples of other artists who distort reality, such as Salvador Dalí, Pablo Picasso, or Joan Miró.

Vocabulario en contexto

Resources: Teacher's Resource Materials: Input Script, Clip Art, Audio Script; Technology: Audio Cap. 2A

Suggestions: Use the Input Script from the *Teacher's Resource Materials* to present the new vocabulary and grammar. Ask students by answering short questions. (Example: *¿Tomás tiene ciencias sociales o educación física en la tercera hora?*) Play *Lotería del horario.* Give students blank versions of the school schedule shown. Allow them to fill in the schedule with classes however they wish. Call out a class period and a course name. Students mark off the classes as you call them. The first to completely mark a schedule calls out: *¡Tengo mi horario!*

Starter Activity

Review telling time by dictating several clock times. Ask that one student work at the board for confirmation.

1

Resources: Teacher's Resource Materials: Audio Script; Technology: Audio Cap. 2A

Suggestions: Play the *audio* or read the script to the class. Allow students to listen more than once. Remind students that they should respond based on Tomás' statements about his classes on pp. 74–75.

 Technology: Audio Script and Answers

1. No me gusta mi horario. (*thumbs down*)
2. En la séptima hora tengo la clase de inglés. (*thumbs down*)
3. ¡La clase de español no me gusta! (*thumbs down*)
4. En la tercera hora tengo la clase de ciencias naturales. (*thumbs down*)
5. En la quinta hora tengo la clase de ciencias naturales. (*thumbs up*)
6. En la primera hora, tengo la clase de tecnología. (*thumbs down*)
7. En la segunda hora tengo la clase de arte. (*thumbs up*)
8. En la novena hora tengo la clase de inglés. (*thumbs up*)
9. En la cuarta hora tengo la clase de educación física. (*thumbs down*)
10. En la octava hora tengo la clase de matemáticas, y necesito una calculadora. (*thumbs up*)

Vocabulario en contexto

66 Me gusta mucho mi **horario**. En la primera hora, **tengo la clase de español** . . . ¡es mi clase **favorita**! Es **interesante** y **práctica**. Pero a veces es **difícil** 99.

1 primera hora
español

2 segunda hora
arte

3 tercera hora

4 cuarta hora
el almuerzo

5 quinta hora
ciencias naturales

educación física

6 sexta hora
ciencias sociales

7 séptima hora
tecnología

8 octava hora
matemáticas

9 novena hora
inglés

74 setenta y cuatro • Tema 2 • La escuela

Differentiated Instruction

Challenge/Pre-AP®

Have students prepare a schedule of their classes. Have them put their teachers' names under each subject, using **Profesor** + (name) and **Profesora** + (name). Ask students to write three sentences under their schedule: *Mi clase favorita es* (subject); (Subject) *es difícil;* (Subject) *es fácil.*

Students with Learning Difficulties

Have students write new words into the vocabulary section of their notebooks and encourage them to accompany each with a picture if possible.

" Tengo **más tarea** en la clase de matemáticas **que** en la clase de inglés. **Para** la clase de matemáticas **necesito** una calculadora y una carpeta de argollas. Para la clase de español necesito un diccionario **".

> **Más vocabulario**
> décimo, -a = tenth

la calculadora

la carpeta de argollas

un diccionario

1
¿Sí o no?

ESCUCHAR Listen to Tomás make several statements about his class schedule. If what he says is true, give a "thumbs up". If what he says is false, give a "thumbs down".

2
Verónica y Tomás

ESCUCHAR Listen to Verónica and Tomás talk about their classes. Touch the picture of each class as you hear it.

Capítulo 2A • setenta y cinco **75**

2

Resources: Teacher's Resource Materials: Audio Script; Technology: Audio Cap. 2A

Suggestions: Use the audio or read the script aloud. Pause to check students' progress after each item. Remind students that they should focus on the vocabulary for school subjects and schedules, and that they should not worry about understanding every word.

Technology: Audio Script and Answers

1. Verónica: La clase de inglés es muy interesante. (*inglés*)
2. Tomás: En la clase de español tengo mucha tarea. (*español*)
3. Verónica: La clase de matemáticas es difícil. (*matemáticas*)
4. Tomás: Me gusta la clase de tecnología, es mi clase favorita. (*tecnología*)
5. Verónica: A mí me gusta la clase de educación física. (*educación física*)
6. Tomás: El almuerzo es después de la clase de ciencias naturales. (*almuerzo, ciencias naturales*)

Additional Resources

Technology: Online Resources
- Instant Check
- Guided, Core, Audio, Writing practice
- *Para hispanohablantes*

Print
- Guided WB pp. 53–58
- Core WB pp. 31–32

Enrich Your Teaching

Culture Note

Explain to students that in some parts of Latin America students begin classes at 7 A.M. in order to end the day at 1 or 2 P.M. so they can go home for lunch. Lunch is the main meal of the day, and family members often gather to eat at home.

Teacher-to-Teacher

A great way to get students on task at the beginning of the class is to write on the board or project a short written exercise. Stand at the door as students enter and hand them papers with questions, so they can begin immediately. Set a time limit, and take attendance or collect homework while students work.

Vocabulario en contexto

Standards: 1.2

Resources: Technology: Audio Cap. 2A

Suggestions: Model the dialogue with a volunteer. Begin the reading again with volunteers playing the roles of the characters. Using the presentation, help students understand the new words in blue type.

Post-reading: Complete *Actividad* 3 to check comprehension.

3

Standards: 1.2, 1.3

Suggestions: You may wish to do this as a listening activity, reading the sentences to the students.

Extension: Ask students if they enjoy their math class, if they work hard at it, and if they ask for help from their teacher. Ask if they enjoy their science classes.

Answers

1. Sí
2. No
3. Sí
4. No
5. Sí

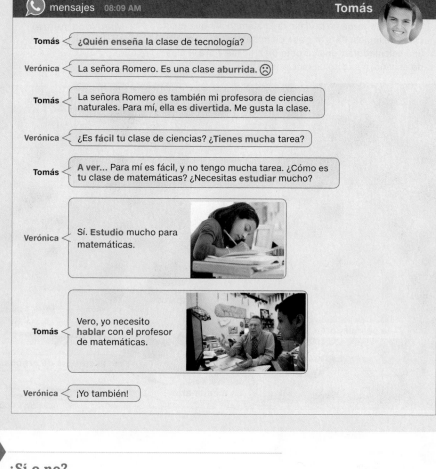

Verónica y Tomás escriben mensajes para hablar de sus clases.

mensajes 08:09 AM   **Tomás**

Tomás ¿Quién enseña la clase de tecnología?

Verónica La señora Romero. Es una clase **aburrida**. ☹

Tomás La señora Romero es también mi profesora de ciencias naturales. Para mí, ella es **divertida**. Me gusta la clase.

Verónica ¿Es fácil tu clase de ciencias? ¿**Tienes mucha tarea**?

Tomás **A ver...** Para mí es fácil, y no tengo mucha tarea. ¿Cómo es tu clase de matemáticas? ¿Necesitas **estudiar** mucho?

Verónica Sí. **Estudio** mucho para matemáticas.

Tomás Vero, yo necesito **hablar** con el profesor de matemáticas.

Verónica ¡Yo también!

3

¿Sí o no?

ESCRIBIR   Lee las oraciones. Escribe *Sí* si la oración es correcta o *No* si es incorrecta. *Corrige* (Correct) las oraciones incorrectas.

1. La señora Romero enseña la clase de teconología y la clase de ciencias naturales.
2. Para Tomás, la clase de ciencias es difícil.
3. Verónica estudia mucho para su clase de matemáticas.
4. La señora Romero no enseña la clase de tecnología.
5. Tomás y Verónica necesitan hablar con el profesor de matemáticas.

76 setenta y seis • Tema 2 • La escuela

Differentiated Instruction

Heritage Speakers

Have students write a letter to an imaginary friend telling about the first day of school. Then have students exchange letters and answer them. When reading and reviewing students' letters, discuss any necessary strategies for improving their writing skills.

Bodily/Kinesthetic Learner

Have students prepare a short dialogue based on the Vocabulario en contexto in which they discuss their school schedule, teachers, and their favorite classes. Then have the students present their dialogues to the class.

Videohistoria

Go **Online** to practice

PEARSON realize™

AUDIO · VIDEO · WRITING · SCRIPT

PearsonSchool.com/Autentico

Interpretive | 2A

Las clases hoy

Before You Watch

Connect with the context Think about what you do to get ready for school each day. Does someone help you? What do you discuss? Use your routine and these photos from a school day to connect to the video.

Complete the Activity

Para las clases ¿Qué necesitas para las clases? Describe los libros y los objetos que necesitas según tu horario de clases hoy.

▶ Watch the Video

What does Sebastián and his family do in the morning before school?

Go to **PearsonSchool.com/Autentico** to watch the video *Las clases hoy* and to view the script.

Sebastián

After You Watch

 ¿COMPRENDES?

1. Complete the sentences based on your understanding of the video.
   a. Daniel tiene las clases de _____ y _____.
   b. Gabriela necesita _____ y _____.
   c. La mamá de Sebastián necesita _____ con el profesor de ciencias.
   d. Sebastián tiene el primer almuerzo. Es a las _____.
   e. Al papá de los chicos le gusta _____ la música de Colombia.
2. ¿Quién hace los almuerzos de los chicos, la mamá o el papá?
3. ¿Quién hace la tarea con Gabriela y Daniel, la mamá, el papá o Sebastián?

Capítulo 2A • setenta y sietee **77**

Enrich Your Teaching

Culture Note

Ajiaco Santafereño is a traditional Colombian food from Santa Fe de Bogotá, former name of the capital of Colombia. For this reason, it was formerly called *ajiaco Santafereño*, although today it is simply called *ajiaco*. It is a chicken and potato soup delicately spiced with an herb called

guascas that gives the soup a wonderful flavor. It has chicken cut in small pieces and three different types of potatoes: red, white, and the *papa criolla*, which is a tiny potato with a buttery taste grown in Colombia. The *ajiaco* is served hot with capers and cream.

Technology: Video

Standards: 1.2

Resources: Teacher's Resource Materials: Video Script

Before You Watch

Review the previewing strategy and activity with the students. Ask students for examples of what they do each morning to get ready for school. Also point out the images of the different activities the family is doing that will be discussed in the video. Review the Complete the Activity with the class. Ask students to list all the activities they do before leaving home to ensure they have all they need with for school. Students can volunteer their responses orally or in writing.

Watch the Video

Show the video without pausing. Show it again, pausing along the way to check comprehension. If there are words that students haven't learned yet, you may want to write those on the board. Show the segment a final time, without pausing.

After You Watch

Standards: 1.2

Suggestions: Discuss the questions with the class to confirm understanding of the video.

Answers

1. a. matemáticas, inglés
   b. lápices y una carpeta
   c. hablar
   d. once menos cuarto (diez y cuarenta y cinco)
   e. escuchar
2. el papa
3. Sebastián

Additional Resources

📶 **Technology: Online Resources**
 • Instant Check
 • Guided, Core, Video, Audio
 • *Para hispanohablantes*
 Print
 • Guided WB pp. 59–62
 • Core WB pp. 33–34

Assessment

Quiz: Vocabulary Recognition
 • Prueba 2A-1

4

Suggestions: Have students review class names, and ask about those they cannot identify. Point out that "the arts" may refer to more than art class: the term includes performing as well as visual arts. Ask specific questions about word meanings, such as **artes plásticas** and **semanales.** Remind students to use strategies such as prior knowledge and cognate identification.

Answers:

1. once
2. tres horas
3. dos—historia universal y educación cívica y ética
4. dos—biología e introducción a la física
5. danza, teatro, artes plásticas, música

Extension: Have students design their own list of classes. Suggest that they total up the number of hours they spend on each subject. You will need to supply names for some classes. Discuss which classes are important, practical, fun, and interesting.

Starter Activity

Have students work in pairs to tell each other the names of their teachers using *Sr., Sra.,* and *Srta.* as well as what they teach.

5

Suggestions: Point out the *¿Recuerdas?* Write the names of several teachers in your school with the appropriate titles, for example: **el Sr. Hassan, la Srta. Chung, la Sra. McGuire.**
Answers will vary.

Vocabulario en uso

4

Un horario

 LEER, ESCRIBIR Read the list of classes offered at a high school in Querétaro, Mexico. This school has a special focus on the arts. Answer the questions about the schedule.

1. ¿Cuántas clases hay cada *(each)* semana?
2. ¿Cuántas horas de inglés hay?
3. ¿Cuántas clases de ciencias sociales hay?
4. ¿Cuántas clases de ciencias naturales hay?
5. Escribe los nombres de las diferentes clases de arte.

México

Centro de Educación Artística
"IGNACIO MARIANO DE LAS CASAS"

Primer Semestre		
	Español	5 h semanales
	Matemáticas	5 h semanales
	Historia universal	3 h semanales
	Educación cívica y ética	3 h semanales
	Biología	3 h semanales
	Introducción a la física	3 h semanales
	Inglés	3 h semanales
	Danza	3 h semanales
	Teatro	3 h semanales
	Artes plásticas	3 h semanales
	Música	3 h semanales
	TOTAL	37 h semanales

5

Mi horario

ESCRIBIR Write out your class schedule. Copy the chart and provide the information for each class.

Modelo

Hora	Clase	Profesor(a)
la primera hora	la clase de inglés	la Sra. Sánchez

¿Recuerdas?
Use *señor, señora,* and *señorita* when talking **to** adults. Use *el* in front of *señor* and *la* in front of *señora* or *señorita* when talking **about** adults.

Differentiated Instruction

Heritage Speakers

If students have attended school in other countries, ask them to describe any different scheduling and grading procedures. They may mention rotating schedules with different classes each day, and grading with numbers instead of letters. You may wish to discuss these differences with the rest of the class.

Students with Learning Difficulties

When practicing reading comprehension, as in *Actividad* 4, allow students with learning difficulties extra time to use the variety of reading strategies that are accessible. Comprehension may require two or three attempts at reading the questions and text.

6

Mucha tarea

HABLAR EN PAREJA Ask and respond to questions about everyday life. With a partner, ask and tell if you have a lot of homework in each class. Follow the model, then switch roles.

▶ **Videomodelo**

A —*¿Tienes mucha tarea en la clase de matemáticas?*
B —*Sí, tengo mucha tarea.*
o: —*No, no tengo mucha tarea.*
o: —*No estudio matemáticas.*

Estudiante A

Estudiante B

¡Respuesta personal!

7

Me gusta más . . .

ESCRIBIR Write sentences stating which of the two classes you like better and why. Use the list of adjectives to help with your response. Save your paper for Actividad 8.

Modelo
inglés/español
Me gusta más la clase de español. Es divertida.
o: *Me gusta más la clase de español. No es aburrida.*
o: *No me gusta ni la clase de español ni la clase de inglés.*

aburrida	divertida	interesante
difícil	fácil	práctica

1. inglés / español
2. arte / educación física
3. inglés / matemáticas

4. ciencias sociales / ciencias naturales
5. tecnología / música
6. matemáticas / ciencias sociales

Capítulo 2A • setenta y nueve **79**

6

Standards: 1.1

Suggestions: Briefly review which subject each object represents. Have volunteers read the model and be sure students understand their options. Have them take turns being Student A and Student B.

Suggestions: Student A:

1. ¿Tienes mucha tarea en la clase de español?
2. ¿ ... en la clase de inglés?
3. ¿ ... en la clase de tecnología?
4. ¿ ... en la clase de ciencias naturales?
5. ¿ ... en la clase de arte?
6. ¿ ... en la clase de educación física?
7. ¿ ... en la clase de ciencias sociales?

Student B: Answers will vary.

Common Errors: Students often have trouble understanding that **mucho(a)** is an adjective and must agree with the noun that follows it. Remind students that **tarea** is feminine; they should say **mucha tarea,** not **mucho tarea.**

7

Standards: 1.3

Suggestions: If students do not take all the classes listed, suggest alternatives. Remind students to save their answers to use in *Actividad 8.*

Answers will vary.

Extension: For homework, have students rewrite their opinions, this time comparing both classes. Provide a model to copy onto their papers. The sentences should be simple, for example: *La clase de inglés es divertida, pero la clase de español es difícil.*

Enrich Your Teaching

Culture Note

In Spanish-speaking countries, students often address teachers by their title to show respect: for example, **Profesor Rodríguez, Profesora Millán,** or simply **Profesor(a).** Occasionally, students will address their teacher as **profe,** short for **profesor(a).** Students in Spain, however, may actually call teachers by their first names.

Teacher-to-Teacher

When students see the words *¡Respuesta personal!* in an activity, encourage them to create phrases beyond what the model suggests.

8

Standards: 1.1

Suggestions: Remind students to use the information from *Actividad* 7. Point out that instead of using **me gusta** in the response, they will use **es más** (adjective) **que** to explain why they prefer one class to another.

Answers: Student A

1. ¿Te gusta más la clase de inglés o la clase de español?
2. ¿ ... la clase de arte o la clase de educación física?
3. ¿ ... la clase de inglés o la clase de matemáticas?
4. ¿ ... la clase de ciencias sociales o la clase de ciencias naturales?
5. ¿ ... la clase de tecnología o la clase de música?
6. ¿ ... la clase de matemáticas o la clase de ciencias sociales?

Student B: Answers will vary.

9

Standards: 1.1, 1.3

Suggestions: You may want to have students answer the questions in paragraph format, with the title *Mi clase favorita.*

Answers will vary.

CULTURA

Standards: 2.1, 4.2

Suggestions: Tell students that throughout the Spanish-speaking world, learning English is important to success both in school and at work. Students begin to learn English at an early age and by middle school are often quite competent.

Answers will vary.

Additional Resources

Technology: Online Resources
- Instant Check
- Guided, Core, Video, Audio
- Teacher's Resource Materials: Audio Script
- Technology: Audio Cap. 2A
- Communication Activities: Audio Act. 6

8

¿Qué te gusta más?

HABLAR EN PAREJA Work with a partner and exchange opinions about your classes. Use your notes from Actividad 7 to tell which classes you like best and why.

Videomodelo
A —¿Te gusta más la clase de inglés o la clase de español?
B —A ver . . . Para mí, la clase de español es más divertida que la clase de inglés.

9

Y tú, ¿qué dices?

ESCRIBIR, HABLAR Ask and respond to questions about everyday life with a partner.

1. ¿Qué clase te gusta más?
2. ¿Cómo es la clase?
3. ¿En qué hora tienes la clase?
4. ¿Quién enseña la clase?
5. ¿Tienes mucha tarea en la clase?

CULTURA El mundo hispano

Studying English While you're in Spanish class at your school, large numbers of Spanish-speaking students are studying to learn the most popular foreign language worldwide: English. Many children begin to study English in grade school and continue through high school. They often attend a special language school for additional English classes. When visiting a Spanish-speaking country, you might easily find someone who is eager to practice his or her English skills with you in exchange for helping you improve your Spanish.

Pre-AP Integration: Innovations How can technology help you learn another language?

Clase de inglés en México ▶

Differentiated Instruction

Heritage Speakers

Have students compare English and Spanish. Do the languages seem closely related? What specific structures in English are different in Spanish? What expressions are difficult to remember? Follow up their comments with a whole-class discussion on some of the challenges and rewards of learning a second language.

Challenge/Pre-AP®

Assign students a Spanish-speaking country and ask them to use the Internet to find information about the education system in that country. Suggest that they include details such as the format and size of schools, subjects offered, and languages of instruction. Have them share their findings with the class.

Go **Online** to practice

PEARSON
realize™

VIDEO   WRITING   SPEAK/RECORD   MAPA GLOBAL

PearsonSchool.com/Autentico

Exploración del lenguaje ⟩ Connections between Latin, English, and Spanish

Many words in English and Spanish are based on Latin. Seeing the relationship between these words will help expand your English or Spanish vocabulary. Look at the list of Latin root forms for the numbers 1 to 10.

Try it out! For each Roman numeral listed, choose one of the root forms (if more than one is listed) and write down a Spanish or English word you know that is based on that root.

Try it out! The Roman year used to begin with the month of March. Knowing that, can you explain why *septiembre, octubre, noviembre,* and *diciembre* use the Latin root forms for seven, eight, nine, and ten?

Roman numeral	root form
I	uni- prim-
II	du- bi- second-
III	tri-
IV	quadr- quart-
V	quint-
VI	sext-
VII	sept-
VII	oct- octav-
IX	novem-
X	dec- decim-

CULTURA ⟩ España

Many Spanish words are derived from Latin because Spain was once part of the Roman Empire. Rome occupied most of Spain from about 209 B.C. to 586 A.D. During that time, massive public structures, including aqueducts and theaters, were built. Some of these, such as the aqueduct that towers over the modern city of Segovia, are still standing. The Latin name for Spain was *Hispania.*

• Can you see the similarity between *Hispania* and the country's name in Spanish, *España?* Also compare both names to English and identify any similarities.

Mapa global interactivo Explore the beautiful city of Segovia in Spain and locate the aqueduct left by the Roman Empire.

El Acueducto de Segovia ▶

Capítulo 2A • ochenta y uno **81**

Standards: 3.1

Suggestions: To extend the second *Try it out!,* ask students to come up with other words in English or Spanish that use the roots *sept-, oct-, nov-, dic-* or *dec-.* Have students share their answers with the class.

Answers may include:

unisex, primary, dual, bicycle, secondary, tricycle, quadrant, quarter, quintuplets, sexto, September, séptimo, octagon, octavo, octave, November, decade, decimal; these months were named using ordinals, so September, October, November, and December were the seventh, eighth, ninth, and tenth months, respectively.

CULTURA

Standards: 3.1

Suggestions: Point out that the historical connection between Rome and Spain goes beyond language. Some of Rome's most successful leaders came from Spain, for example, Trajan (98–117 a.d.)

🌐 **Technology: Mapa global interactivo, Actividad 1**
Locate the Roman aqueduct in Segovia, Spain.

Pre-AP® Integration

• **Learning Objective:** Interpretive: Print
• **Activity:** Provide students with a short passage in Spanish about some aspect of the historical influence of the Roman Empire in Spain. Encourage students to identify the main idea and supporting details as they read. Clarify the language where necessary. Have students summarize the main ideas of the text and compare their responses.
• **Pre-AP® Resource Materials:** Comprehensive guide to Pre-AP® reading skill development

Teaching with Photos

Point out to students that this structure, like many of the Roman Empire remains, is significant because of its size and complexity. Remind students that lack of modern building tools made construction projects difficult.

Assessment

Prueba 2A-2 with Remediation (online only)
Quiz: Vocabulary Production
• Prueba 2A-2

Enrich Your Teaching

Culture Note

Spanish is one of the Romance languages, along with French, Italian, Portuguese, Romanian, and Romansch (one of the official languages of Switzerland). These languages are called "Romance" because they came from the language of ancient Rome, Latin. Spanish is considered the most similar to Latin. More than half of English words are derived from Latin or Greek, though most of these are relative latecomers to the English language.

Search online with the keyword ***Hispania*** to read more about the history of Spain during the time of the Roman Empire. For photos and information on Roman ruins in Spain, search with the keywords ***Segovia*** or ***Merida, Spain.***

2A Communication

Starter Activity
Before beginning, define subject pronouns and have students list them in English. Without looking at the chart, can students name Spanish subject pronouns they've seen so far?

Gramática

Standards: 4.1

Resources: Teacher's Resource Materials: Video Script; Technology: Video Cap. 2A

Suggestions: Use the *GramActiva* Video either as an initial introduction to subject pronouns or as a follow-up to your own explanation. Remind students of the distinction between *tú* and *usted.* Use groups of students standing at the front of the class to reinforce the concepts, pointing to them and moving them as necessary. Recall students' English language knowledge to introduce compound subjects in Spanish.

Technology: Interactive Whiteboard

Grammar Activities 2A Use the whiteboard activities in your Teacher Resources as you progress through the grammar practice with your class.

10

Standards: 1.2

Suggestions: Model this activity for your students, pointing to pre-designated people in the class. You will need to say the subject pronouns aloud. For example, point to yourself for **yo,** have students face each other and point for **tú,** point to a male or female student when saying **él** and **ella,** indicate an imaginary circle including yourself when saying **nosotros,** point directly to two or more students for **vosotros,** and point to a group of male or female students for **ellos / ellas.** You might want to draw several adult-like stick figures on the board so students can point to **ustedes.**

Gramática

> OBJECTIVE
> ▶ Identify, talk to, and write about different people

Subject pronouns

The subject of a sentence tells who is doing the action. You often use people's names as the subject:

Gregorio escucha música.   *Gregory listens to music.*
Ana canta y baila.   *Ana sings and dances.*

You also use subject pronouns *(I, you, he, she, we, they)* to tell who is doing an action. The subject pronouns replace people's names:

Él escucha música.   *He listens to music.*
Ella canta y baila.   *She sings and dances.*

Here are all the subject pronouns in Spanish:

yo	I	nosotros nosotras	we (masc., masc./fem.) we (fem.)
tú usted (Ud.)	you (familiar) you (formal)	vosotros vosotras ustedes (Uds.)	you (masc., masc./fem.) you (fem.) you (formal)
(él) (ella)	he she	ellos ellas	they (masc., masc./fem.) they (fem.)

Tú, usted, ustedes, and *vosotros(as)* all mean "you."

- Use *tú* with family, friends, people your age or younger, and anyone you call by his or her first name.
- Use *usted* with adults you address with a title, such as *señor, señora, profesor(a)*, etc. *Usted* is usually written as *Ud.*
- In Latin America, use *ustedes* when speaking to two or more people, regardless of age. *Ustedes* is usually written as *Uds.*
- In Spain, use *vosotros(as)* when speaking to two or more people you call *tú* individually: *tú* + *tú* = *vosotros(as)*. Use *ustedes* when talking to two or more people you call *usted* individually.

If a group is made up of males only or of both males and females together, use the masculine forms: *nosotros, vosotros, ellos.*

If a group is all females, use the feminine forms:

nosotras, vosotras, ellas.

You can combine a subject pronoun and a name to form a subject.

Alejandro y yo = **nosotros**   Pepe y tú = **ustedes**
Carlos y ella = **ellos**   Lola y ella = **ellas**

Más recursos ONLINE
- *GramActiva* Video
- Tutorials: Present indicative, Pronouns, Subject pronouns, Subjects
- *GramActiva* Activity

82 ochenta y dos • Tema 2 • La escuela

Differentiated Instruction

Heritage Speakers
Give students a paragraph or list of sentences. Ask them to underline the subjects of the sentences in one color and the subject pronouns in another.

Students with Learning Difficulties
Students often have difficulty substituting subject pronouns for proper nouns. Give students two or three examples in English of how they substitute subject pronouns, and then have them transfer this skill to Spanish. Start with individual nouns, then work up to full sentences.

¡Señala!

ESCUCHAR, HABLAR EN PAREJA   Your teacher will name several subject pronouns. Point to people in the classroom who represent the pronoun you hear. After you have practiced with your teacher, practice with a partner.

¿Es ella?

ESCRIBIR   What subject pronouns would you use to talk about these people?

Modelo
Gloria
Ella.

1. Carlos
2. Felipe y yo
3. María y Sarita
4. Pablo, Tomás y Anita
5. el señor Treviño
6. tú y Esteban

¿Tú, Ud. o Uds.?

HABLAR EN PAREJA   Tell whether you would use *tú, Ud.,* or *Uds.* with these people.

Capítulo 2A • ochenta y tres **83**

Standards: 1.3

Suggestions: Refer students to p. 82 to decide which subject pronoun is appropriate. Point out that item 6 has two possible responses.

Answers:

1. él	**4.** ellos
2. nosotros	**5.** él
3. ellas	**6.** vosotros / ustedes

Standards: 1.3

Suggestions: Remind students that *tú* is used informally, and **usted** is generally used for people who would be addressed by their last name. Point out that students will not use **vosotros(as)** in this activity. If you stress **vosotros,** however, allow that as an answer.

Answers:

1. Ud.	**4.** Uds.	**7.** tú
2. tú	**5.** Ud.	**8.** Ud.
3. Ud.	**6.** Uds.	

Project-Based Learning

Give students copies of the Project-Based Learning outline and rubric. Explain the task to them, and have the perform Step 1. (See p. 72-b.)

Additional Resources

Technology: Online Resources
- Instant Check
- Guided, Core, Video, Audio
- *Para hispanohablantes*
- Teacher's Resource Materials: Audio Script
- Technology: Audio Cap. 2A
- Communication Activities: Audio Act. 7

Print:
- Guided WB pp. 63–64
- Core WB p. 35

Assessment

Prueba 2A-3 with Remediation (online only)
Quiz: Subject Pronouns
- Prueba 2A-3: p. 45

Enrich Your Teaching

Teacher-to-Teacher

Often, confusion arises when the subject pronouns **yo** and **tú** are seen in an activity. When given such prompts, students generally should assume that they will stay the same in their answers. When an activity is "talking to" the students (for example, **Y tú, ¿qué dices?**), they need to change the **tú** in the question to **yo** in the answer in order to talk about themselves.

Teacher-to-Teacher

Have students prepare three pieces of paper, one labeled **tú,** one labeled **usted,** and one labeled **ustedes.** Have them cut out magazine pictures or download images showing individuals and groups of people whom they would address as **tú, usted,** or **ustedes,** and mount them on the correct sheet. These can be displayed on the bulletin board.

Gramática

Standards: 4.1

Resources: Teacher's Resource Materials: Video Script; Technology: Video Cap. 2A

Suggestions: Point out the *¿Recuerdas?* and remind students that they have seen **-ar** verbs before. Show the *GramActiva* Video as reinforcement. Give students several examples of how stems are derived. Show them that the stem of a verb carries the basic meaning, while the ending tells "who" and "when." Point out that the same thing happens in English, though the endings are not as helpful—which is why we cannot usually drop the subject. Demonstrate this difference with examples from the two languages: *canto/ canta* vs. *I sing/he sings*. Have students identify stems of other infinitives.

Technology: Interactive Whiteboard

Grammar Activities 2A Use the whiteboard activities in your Teacher Resources as you progress through the grammar practice with your class.

13

Standards: 1.2

Resources: Teacher's Resource Materials: Audio Script; Technology: Audio Cap. 2A

Suggestions: Before beginning, direct students' attention to the *Strategy*. Have students refer to the verb chart while doing this activity. Point out that the forms on the left side of the chart are singular (one person doing the action), and those on the right are plural.

Technology: Audio Script and Answers

1. hablo *(one hand)*
2. enseñan *(two hands)*
3. dibujamos *(two hands)*
4. trabaja *(one hand)*
5. cantas *(one hand)*
6. estudian *(two hands)*
7. necesitan *(two hands)*
8. practico *(one hand)*

Common Errors: Students hear the **-s** in the **tú** ending and think it is a plural. Remind them that the **-s** ending makes nouns plural, but not verbs.

Gramática

OBJECTIVES
▶ Write and exchange information about what you and others study and do
▶ Listen to a description of activities during recess
▶ Compare the Mayan numbering system to the one you use

Present tense of -ar verbs

You already know that the infinitive forms of Spanish verbs always end in *-ar, -er,* or *-ir.*

The largest group of verbs end in *-ar. Hablar* is one of these *-ar* verbs.

¿Recuerdas?
You already know many *-ar* verbs, such as *cantar* and *bailar.*

You will want to use verbs in ways other than in the infinitive form. To do this, you will drop the *-ar* ending and make changes.

To create the forms of most *-ar* verbs, you first drop the *-ar* from the infinitive, leaving the stem:

　　hablar ➜ habl-

Then you add the verb endings *-o, -as, -a, -amos, -áis,* or *-an* to the stem.

Here are the forms of *hablar:*

(yo)	habl**o**	(nosotros)(nosotras)	habl**amos**
(tú)	habl**as**	(vosotros)(vosotras)	habl**áis**
Ud.(él)(ella)	habl**a**	Uds.(ellos)(ellas)	habl**an**

Hablo can be translated into English in two ways:

Hablo español.　　*I speak Spanish.*
　　　　　　　　　　I am speaking Spanish.

The verb endings always indicate who is doing the action. In this case, they tell *who* is speaking. Because of this, you can often use the verb without a subject:

Hablo inglés.　　**¿Hablas** español?

Subject pronouns are often used for emphasis or clarification.

Ella habla inglés pero **él** habla español.

Más recursos ONLINE
▶ *GramActiva* Video
▶ **Tutorials:** -Subject and verb agreement, Verbs, -ar verbs, Singular and plural, Definite and indefinite articles
🔊 *Canción de hip hop: En la clase*
✏ *GramActiva* Activity

13

¿Una mano o dos?

🔊 ESCUCHAR You will hear eight *-ar* verbs. If the ending tells you one person is performing the action, raise one hand. If the ending tells you more than one person is doing something, raise both hands.

Strategy
Listening for information Always listen carefully for the endings on verbs to know who is doing the action.

84 ochenta y cuatro • Tema 2 • La escuela

Differentiated Instruction

Bodily/Kinesthetic Learner
Have students cut out magazine pictures that depict **-ar** verbs and paste them on construction paper to make posters. At the bottom of the poster have students write a sentence describing each action.

Heritage Speakers
Pay special attention to students' verb formation. Depending on their heritage, their pronunciation may vary from the "standard" ways of saying these endings. These differences may result in incorrect spelling or adding the wrong verb ending. Some students may also use forms such as the **voseo,** which should be recognized.

Go **Online** to practice
PEARSON
realize™
PearsonSchool.com/Autentico
🔊 AUDIO ▶ VIDEO ✍ WRITING

14

¿Qué estudian?

✎ **ESCRIBIR, HABLAR** Look at the pictures and tell what these people are studying.

Modelo
Tomás
Tomás estudia música.

1. Laura

2. Josefina, Elena y yo

3. tú

4. Catalina y José

5. Joaquín y tú

6. yo

15

Juego

ESCUCHAR, HABLAR EN PAREJA

① Work with a partner and tear a sheet of paper into eight pieces of equal size. Write a different subject pronoun on each piece *(yo, tú, él, ella, Ud., nosotros, ellas, Uds.)*. Place the subject pronouns face down in a pile.

② Your teacher will say an infinitive. One partner will select the top piece of paper from the pile, read the subject pronoun, and say the correct verb form. A correct answer earns one point. Place the "used" subject pronouns in a separate pile. Take turns selecting from the pile and answering.

③ When your teacher tells you to stop, shuffle the pieces of paper with subject pronouns and place them in a new pile face down. When the next verb is read aloud, continue playing. The partner with the most correct answers is the winner.

él	ella
ellas	Uds.
yo	Ud.
nosotros	tú

Capítulo 2A • ochenta y cinco **85**

Enrich Your Teaching

Culture Note
Look at the picture on p. 85 and point out that students are wearing uniforms. It is common practice to require uniforms in secondary schools in many Spanish-speaking countries. You might also mention that in some places students stay in the same room all day, and the teachers come to them.

21st Century Skills
Social and Cross-Cultural Skills
Several European countries require that, through high school, students study not one, but two foreign languages. Have students research the study of foreign languages from primary school through high school in other parts of the world. Which languages are popular?

14

Standards: 1.3

Suggestions: Review the school subjects quickly. Call on students to answer orally.

Answers:
1. Laura estudia matemáticas.
2. Josefina, Elena y yo estudiamos arte.
3. Tú estudias inglés.
4. Catalina y José estudian español.
5. Joaquín y tú estudian (estudiáis) tecnología.
6. Yo estudio ciencias sociales.

Extension: Have students replace the subjects with subject pronouns in the answers for items 1, 2, 4, and 5. Then have them write out all six answers in the negative, with the pronouns.

15

Standards: 1.1, 1.2

Resources: Teacher's Resource Materials: GramActiva

Suggestions: Tell students how much time they will have, and walk around the room to make sure students check their answers.

Teacher's Script:
1. estudiar
2. enseñar
3. trabajar
4. cantar
5. bailar
6. patinar
7. necesitar
8. usar

Answers will vary.

Additional Resources

📶 **Technology: Online Resources**
• Instant Check
• Guided, Core, Video, Audio
• *Para hispanohablantes*
• Teacher's Resource Materials: Audio Script
• Technology: Audio Cap. 2A
• Communication Activities: Audio Act. 8–9
Print
• Guided WB pp. 65–66
• Core WB pp. 36–37

Assessment

Prueba 2A-4 with Remediation (online only)
Quiz: Present tense of *-ar verbs*
• Prueba 2A-4: p. 46

16

Standards: 1.2, 1.3

Suggestions

Recycle: Meanings of **-ar** verbs

Suggestions: Refer students to the **-ar** verb chart on p. 84. Point out that they need both the correct form and meaning to get the right answer. They will not use all of the verbs in the word bank.

Answers:

1. dibujan
2. usas
3. necesito

4. practicamos
5. enseña
6. habla

17

Standards: 1.2, 1.3

Resources: Teacher's Resource Materials: Audio Script; Technology: Audio Cap. 2A

Suggestions: Play the *audio* or read the script more than once

🔊 **Technology: Audio Script and Answers**

1. Dos amigos y yo hablamos de las clases.
2. Tomás estudia español.
3. Ana canta.
4. Y María escucha música.

CULTURA

Standards: 2.1, 4.2

Suggestions: Have students look at the picture of **el recreo** and identify what the students are doing and where. Ask them to talk about what they do in the short breaks between classes.

Answers will vary.

Active Classroom

For *Actividad* 16, have students write out the sentences and underline the subjects. Then have them write eight more sentences or questions using the verbs listed. Encourage them to write at least two negative sentences.

16

En la escuela

✏️ **ESCRIBIR** Use the verbs in the list to complete the sentences about what different activities take place during school.

necesitar	hablar	dibujar
usar	practicar	enseñar
patinar	bailar	

Modelo
*Yo **estudio** mucho en la clase de español.*

1. Lupe y Guillermo ___ mucho en la clase de arte.
2. Tú ___ la computadora en la clase de tecnología.
3. Yo ___ una calculadora y una carpeta para la clase de matemáticas.
4. Tomás y yo ___ deportes en la clase de educación física.
5. ¿Quién ___ la clase de ciencias naturales?
6. Marta ___ mucho en la clase de español.

17

Escucha y escribe

🔊 **ESCUCHAR, ESCRIBIR** Listen to a student describe this picture of himself and other students during their *recreo*. Write what you hear.

CULTURA ◀ **El mundo hispano**

El recreo In Spanish-speaking countries, students usually have *el recreo* (recess or break) in the school *patio*. Students take time to relax and spend time with friends, eat a snack, or participate in activities such as a quick game of basketball, soccer, or volleyball.

Pre-AP Integration: Relationships Compare the *recreo* to the time you have to socialize in your school. How do you think this affects personal relationships among students?

Estudiantes en el recreo ▶

86 ochenta y seis • Tema 2 • La escuela

Differentiated Instruction

Visual/Spatial Learner

Have students create posters promoting activities that can be done during school free time. Explain that by using the **nosotros** form of the verb **ir,** minus the subject pronoun, they are expressing the command "Let's." For example, **¡Vamos a jugar!** they are suggesting, "Let's play!"

Special Needs

Before starting the *Actividades* for this section, review infinitives and the word bank in *Actividad* 16. Transcribing while listening can be difficult for some students. Have them listen and then discuss what they understood. For *Actividad* 18, review the activities in the word bank. Provide a copy of the Venn diagram graphic organizer.

18

Actividades y más actividades

ESCRIBIR, HABLAR EN PAREJA

Go **Online** to practice
PEARSON
realize.
PearsonSchool.com/Autentico
AUDIO VIDEO WRITING SPEAK/RECORD

1 Work with a partner. Copy the Venn diagram on a sheet of paper. Label the oval on the left *Yo.* Label the oval on the right with the name of your partner. Label the overlapping area *Nosotros* or *Nosotras.*

Modelo

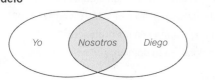

2 From the list below, choose five activities you do a lot. Write your activities in the oval labeled *Yo.* Be sure to conjugate the verb in the *yo* form.

montar en bicicleta	estudiar	hablar español	trabajar
hablar por teléfono	pasar tiempo con amigos	nadar	cantar
escuchar música	practicar deportes	usar la computadora	bailar
dibujar			

3 Interview your partner. Ask questions to find out the five activities your partner wrote in his or her diagram. When you find out an activity, write it in the right oval of your diagram. Be sure to conjugate the verb in the *él / ella* form. Save your diagram for Actividad 19.

Videomodelo

A —¿*Dibujas mucho?*
B —*A ver . . . No, no dibujo mucho.*
A —*Pues, ¿trabajas mucho?*
B —*Sí, trabajo mucho.*

¿Recuerdas?
When you answer in the negative, you often use *no* twice. The first *no* answers the question. The second *no* goes before the verb and means "not."

19

Nosotros(as) . . .

 ESCRIBIR Compare the two sides of your diagram. Write the activities you and your partner both do in the center. Be sure to use the *nosotros(as)* form. Then use your completed diagram from Actividad 18 to write about what you and/or your partner do. Write at least five complete sentences.

Modelo
Diego y yo trabajamos.
Yo dibujo.

Capítulo 2A • ochenta y siete **87**

18

Standards: 1.1, 1.3

Recycle: *-ar* verb meanings
Suggestions: Use the board to show students how to fill in the ovals. Point out that students must write the words in the **yo** form for Step 2, and in the **él/ella** form for Step 3. Have volunteers read the **Modelo** for Step 3, and then re-read it, this time personalizing it with their information. Encourage students to use other words besides **mucho,** such as **bien** or **con mis amigos.** Point out that they will not use the **nosotros** section of the Venn diagram until *Actividad* 19.
Answers will vary.

19

Standards: 1.3

Suggestions: Encourage students to write negative sentences about actions neither of them do: *Nosotros no dibujamos.* Ask them to then state who does the action and who doesn't. For example: *Diego dibuja pero yo no dibujo.*
Answers will vary.
Extension: Have pairs read a sentence aloud. Then have a third student repeat the information, using the **ellos/ellas** form.

Pre-AP® Integration

• **Learning Objective:** Interpersonal Writing
• **Activity 19:** Use the information from the center of your diagram to write an e-mail to another classmate, describing what you and your partner do. Be sure to ask your friend at least one question about what he or she does.
• **Pre-AP® Resource Materials:** Comprehensive guide to Pre-AP® writing skill development

Assessment

Evaluate students on both their written and spoken accuracy on Act. 18 and 19.

Enrich Your Teaching

Teacher-to-Teacher

Have students bring in action pictures of themselves, family, or friends, or pictures from magazines. They should prepare 3–5 sentences about the actions shown, using more than one picture if needed. The next day, they can present these orally to a partner, or volunteers can present them to the class.

21st Century Skills

Critical Thinking and Problem Solving After using all the tools for *-ar* verbs in this chapter, have students make a connection between the reading they did in Chapter 1B (p. 64) and the activities they learn in this chapter by connecting color preference, personality type, and preferred activities.

2A | Communication

Standards: 1.1, 1.3

Recycle: School subjects; meanings of **-ar** verbs

Suggestions: Before students answer the questions, remind them that the verb forms for the answers will differ from the verb forms in the questions. Suggest that sudents ask and answer the questions with a partner before reviewing their answers as a class.

Answers will vary.

Common Errors: Students often get confused about which subject to use when answering questions in Spanish. Write this chart on the board for students to copy into their notebooks as a reference. Remind them that this pattern is the same as in English.

Question		Answer
tú/Ud.	→	yo
Uds.	→	nosotros(as)
él/ella	→	él/ella
ellos/ellas	→	ellos/ellas
tú y _____	→	nosotros(as)

21

Standards: 3.1

Suggestions: Make up two or three additional numbers to review with students before having them decipher the ones in the book.

Answers will vary but may include the Roman numeral system.

Extension: Write simple addition or subtraction problems on the board using the Mayan number system. Have students give the answers in both Mayan symbols and Arabic numerals.

20

Y tú, ¿qué dices?

🎤 **HABLAR** State you opinions and preferences about school. Use the questions as a guide.

1. En tu escuela, ¿quién enseña la clase de arte? ¿Quién enseña la clase de educación física? ¿Cómo son los profesores?

2. En tu escuela, ¿quién canta muy bien *(well)*? ¿Quién dibuja muy bien?

3. ¿Escuchan tus amigos(as) mucha música? ¿Bailan bien tú y tus amigos(as)?

4. ¿Qué estudias en la primera hora? ¿Cómo son los profesores?

5. ¿Qué clase tienes en la tercera hora? En tu opinión, ¿cómo es la clase?

21

Los números mayas

✏️ **LEER, ESCRIBIR** Long before the Spaniards set foot in the Americas, many different civilizations already existed here. One of these, the Maya, lived in southern Mexico and Central America, where their decendants still make their home. One of the accomplishments of the ancient Maya was the development of a system of mathematics.

Conexiones ‹ **Las matemáticas**

The Maya used three symbols to write numbers:

a dot ●, a bar ▬▬▬ , and a drawing of a shell 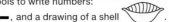 .

The dot equals 1, the bar equals 5, and the shell equals 0. Mayan numbers were written from bottom to top, not from left to right. Look at the Mayan numbers below.

What would these Mayan numbers be in our numbering system?

1. 2. 3.

Now write these numbers in the Mayan system.

4. 13   5. 16   6. 19

Are you familiar with any other numbering systems that remind you of the Mayan system?

Differentiated Instruction

Challenge

Have students use the Internet to do further research on the Mayan number system. They could also explore numbering systems used by other civilizations in the Americas.

Heritage Speakers

Ask students to share what they know from their families about the people who lived in the areas their families came from before the Europeans arrived. Ask if any are aware of languages other than Spanish (or English) being spoken in those regions.

Pronunciación › The letter *c*

In Spanish the pronunciation of the letter *c* depends on the letter that follows it.

When the letter *c* comes before *a, o, u,* or another consonant, it is pronounced like the *c* in "cat." Listen to and say these words:

computadora	**ca**ntar	es**cu**ela
tampo**co**	**có**mo	to**car**
correr	practi**car**	**Ca**rlos

When the letter *c* comes before *e* or *i*, most Spanish speakers pronounce it like the *s* in "Sally." Listen to and say these words:

ve**ce**s	so**ci**able	gra**ci**oso	gra**ci**as
ha**cer**	on**ce**	do**ce**	tre**ce**

Try it out! Listen to this rhyme. Listen particularly for the sound of the letter *c*. Then repeat the rhyme.

Cero más cuatro,
o cuatro más cero,
siempre[1] son cuatro.
¿No es verdadero[2]?

$$0 + 4 = 4$$
$$4 + 0 = 4$$

Say the rhyme again, first replacing *cuatro* with *doce*, then replacing *cuatro* with *trece*. Then say the rhyme quickly several times.

[1]always [2]true

El español en la comunidad

Do you know about opportunities to learn Spanish in your community outside of your school? Do some research using the Internet. Consult the web pages of local colleges, universities, libraries, or language schools to find out about Spanish classes or private lessons offered in your community. Make a list of your findings. Why do you think people in your community want to study Spanish?

Capítulo 2A • ochenta y nueve **89**

Enrich Your Teaching

Teacher-to-Teacher

If you know of older students who have traveled abroad on an exchange program, invite them to speak to the class describing how their language skills improved during the trip. If you participated in an exchange program yourself, you may want to share your experiences with learning Spanish. This will serve as a good introduction to the reading on p. 90.

21st Century Skills

Critical Thinking and Problem Solving
Guide students in a brief investigation about the numbering system developed by the Inca in Perú. Discuss with the class the basic idea of a system of knots tied on strings, as the Inca had no written language. Have students think about the advantages and disadvantages of such a numbering system. Which is more similar to our own, the Mayan or the Incan?

Standards: 4.1

Resources: Teacher's Resource Materials: Audio Script; Technology: Audio Cap. 2A

Suggestions: You should explain that some Spanish speakers pronounce a *c* before *e* or *i* with a "th" sound. For the *Try it out!*, read the rhyme first, then have student volunteers read it aloud. Have volunteers say the variations with ***doce*** and ***trece.*** Students can compete to say the rhyme the fastest.

El español en la comunidad

Suggestions: Ask if students know of anyone who is taking Spanish classes outside of your school. If so, have them inquire about the courses. Why does the person want to learn Spanish? What methods and activities does the teacher use? What are some of the topics covered? If these answers are available, have students compare the community class with their own class.

Answers will vary but may include:

Spanish classes are offered by adult education centers, community colleges, private language institutes, and private tutors. Reasons for studying Spanish may include for travel, business, and being able to talk with family or friends.

Project-Based Learning

Students can perform Step 2 at this point. Be sure they understand your corrections and suggestions. (See p. 72-b.)

Teacher-to-Teacher

Communities: Invite a Spanish professor from a local community college or university to talk to your students about college courses and class schedules using the words and expressions in this chapter.

Lectura

Standards: 1.2, 1.3

🔊 **Technology: Mapa global interactivo, Actividad 2**

Explore the topography of Costa Rica.

Suggestions

Pre-reading: Have students look at the title and subtitle and ask them to predict what the reading is about. Direct attention to the Strategy and point out that the photos will help identify the context of the reading.

Reading: Pair students and have them take turns reading the text to each other. Encourage students to deduce the meaning of the passage from context and cognates. Have students share words they could not figure out and write them on the board. Ask volunteers to guess the meanings and explain how they deduced them.

Post-reading: Answer the *¿Comprendes?* questions in class or have students write their answers as homework.

Starter Activity

Put these letters on the board representing the days of the week. Ask that students unscramble the letters as they write the days in correct order.

J M S M V D L

Teaching with Photos

Before reading, have students guess what some of the activities offered by the school, based on the climate and atmosphere depicted in the photos. Brainstorm a list of activities that would be done in such an environment, and then have the class check the list as you review the reading.

Active Classroom

Have students choose a destination in the United States and create a brochure for an English language institute similar to *La Escuela Español Vivo.* Have them include a schedule of classes and other possible activities that students can participate in. They may illustrate their piece with drawings or photos.

Lectura

OBJECTIVES
- Read about a language school in Costa Rica
- Use photos to help you understand what you read
- Analyze how the 24-hour clock is used in Spanish-speaking countries

Strategy
Using photos Look at the photos to help you understand the contents of a brochure or advertisement.

Consider what an immersion experience in Spanish would be like for you as you read this brochure from a Spanish language school in Costa Rica.

Costa Rica

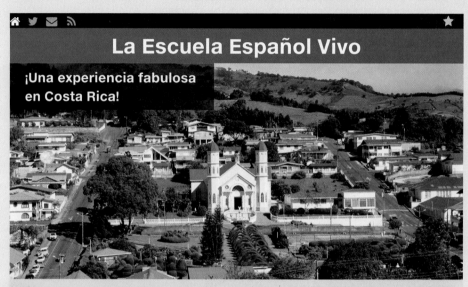

La Escuela Español Vivo

¡Una experiencia fabulosa en Costa Rica!

¡Estudia español con nosotros en la Escuela Español Vivo!

Es verano, el mes de junio. Eres estudiante en Santa Ana, un pueblo en las montañas de Costa Rica.

¿Y cómo es una clase? Hay cinco estudiantes en tu clase. Uds. escuchan, hablan y practican el español todo el día. También usan la computadora.

En la escuela hay estudiantes de muchos países: Estados Unidos, Inglaterra, Francia, Brasil, Canadá, Japón, India, Sudáfrica y otros. ¡Todos estudian español!

Differentiated Instruction

Heritage Speakers

If applicable, ask students to comment on the idea of immersion. If they came from another country, did they know English at all before coming to the United States? If not, or if their English skills were limited, ask them to list the advantages and disadvantages of being immersed in an English-speaking culture.

Logical-Mathematical Learner

Have students rewrite their own schedules in Spanish, including after-school activities, using the 24-hour clock. Have them use a chart format.

Los sábados y los domingos hay actividades muy interesantes: visitar un volcán o un parque nacional, nadar en el océano Pacífico. . . ¡y más!

El horario de clases en la escuela es:		sábados/domingos	¿Por qué la Escuela Español Vivo?
hora	**lunes a viernes**	• visitar un volcán	• La naturaleza de Costa Rica en el pueblo de Santa Ana
08:00–10:30	Clases de español	• visitar un parque nacional	• Amigos de muchos países
10:30–11:00	Recreo	• nadar en el océano Pacífico	• Mucha práctica y conversación en español
11:00–13:00	Clases de español		• Clases de música y baile
13:00–14:00	Almuerzo		• Excursiones los sábados y domingos
14:00–15:30	Conversaciones		
15:30–16:30	Clase de música y baile		

¿Comprendes?

1. When does the program take place?
2. Describe what a class is like.
3. What key words tell you which activities are offered on the weekends?
4. How many hours are spent on learning and using Spanish each week?
5. Would you like to study Spanish in Costa Rica? Why or why not?

Mapa global interactivo Explore Costa Rica's geography and investigate its mountains, volcanoes and national parks.

CULTURA El mundo hispano

La hora in Spanish-speaking countries is usually shown using the 24-hour clock on official schedules and timetables. Times in the morning are shown as 00:00 (midnight) through 11:59 (11:59 A.M.), 1:00 P.M. is shown as 13:00, 2:00 p.m. is 14:00, and so on.

Pre-AP Integration: Innovations How does new technology make it easier to access schedules and understand time differences in other countries?

En una estación de trenes de Madrid

Enrich Your Teaching

Culture Note

In Spanish-speaking countries, the 24-hour clock is used for public events such as concerts, bullfights, sports events, and radio and television schedules, as well as for invitations to private events such as graduations and weddings. It may also be used in ordinary conversation to specify that an event people are talking about is occurring in the evening.

Teacher-to-Teacher

Look at Spanish-language Web sites, newspapers, magazines, or travel guides to find examples of how times of events are listed using the 24-hour clock. Post these scheduled events on a bulletin board.

¿Comprendes?

Standards: 1.2, 1.3

Suggestions: Have students share their answers for items 1–4. Ask volunteers to explain their answers for item 5.

Answers:

1. In the summer, in June.
2. There are five students in a class. They listen, speak, and practice Spanish all day, and also use the computer.
3. You can visit a volcano or a park, or you can swim in the ocean.
4. Six hours a day.
5. Answers will vary.

CULTURA

Standards: 4.2

Suggestions: Read the text to the class and give students some extra examples of schedules in the 24-hour format. Point out that the 24-hour clock is used in the United States Armed Forces, and therefore is often referred to as military time. Ask students what the benefits are of using this system.

Answers will vary.

Pre-AP® Integration

• **Learning Objective:** Interpretive: Print and Audio
• **Activity:** Write on the board the words: *"En la clase"* and *"Los sábados y los domingos."* Read several teacher-made statements indicating where/when the activities usually take place. Students raise their left hand if the answer is *"en la clase"* and their right hand if the answer is *"los sábados y los domingos."* (Ex. *Visitamos un parque nacional.*)
• **Pre-AP® Resource Materials:** Comprehensive guide to Pre-AP® communication skill development

For Further Reading

Student Resource: *Para hispanohablantes*

Additional Resources

Technology: Online Resources
• Guided, Writing, Reading
• Cultural Reading Activity
• *Para hispanohablantes*
Print
• Guided WB pp. 67

La cultura en vivo

Standards: 1.3, 2.1, 2.2, 3.2, 4.2

Suggestions: Before reading, poll students to determine their favorite sports. List them on the board and have students arrive at a class favorite. After noting the favorite sport of the class, ask what they think the favorite sport is in the entire world.

Direct attention to the opening paragraph. After students have finished reading, find out if any correctly predicted the world's most popular sport. If your school has a soccer team, talk about it.

Many teams have cheerleaders who cheer the team on enthusiastically, boost spirits, and help create a winning attitude. Have students think about cheers they know and their meaning, if any. Point out those in the book. Read one aloud with enthusiasm. Emphasize the rhythm. Have students repeat after you. Move on to the second and do the same. Direct students to the *Presentar*. Allow them to work on their cheers and present them another day.

Some students will have no interest in soccer (or perhaps in any sport at all). You may find it helpful to allow them to focus on the rhyme scheme of the cheers. Perhaps grouping them with students who are enthusiastic will help. Also, when working in a group, these students may prefer to record the group's ideas.

Direct attention to the *Comparación cultural* section and have students discuss the questions.

Answers will vary.

Online Cultural Reading

After doing the online activity, ask students to describe how the school shown on the web site seems similar to and different from your school.

Additional Resources

📶 **Technology: Online Resources**
  • Cultural Reading Activity
  • *Para hispanohablantes*

La cultura en vivo — Aficionados al fútbol

El fútbol (soccer) is the favorite sport in most Spanish-speaking countries. In fact, it is the most popular sport in the entire world. It has grown in popularity in the United States over the past years. As with other sports you are familiar with, *fútbol* has loyal fans, cheers, team songs, and sometimes cheerleaders. If you attended a game in Venezuela at the Escuela Secundaria Bolívar you might hear the following chant:

🎵 *Chiquitibúm a la bim bom bam*
  A la bio
  A la bao
  A la bim bom bam
  ¡Bolívar! ¡Bolívar!
  ¡Ra, ra, ra!

Except for the school name, the words of this chant do not have any meaning.

Here's another cheer:

¡Se ve! ¡Se siente!	You see it, you feel it!
¡Bolívar está presente!	Bolívar is here!
¡Que sí, que no!	Oh, yes, oh, no!
¡Bolívar ya ganó!	Bolívar has already won!
¡A la bio, a la bao!	¡A la bío! ¡A la bao!
¡El otro está cansao!	The other team is tired!

Aficionados al fútbol, Bogotá, Colombia

Presentar In groups of five, select one of the chants and use it for a model to create a chant for one of your school teams. Present it to the class.

Comparación cultural How are these cheers and fan enthusiasm similar to or different from the cheers at your school?

Online Cultural Reading

Go to PearsonSchool.com/Autentico ONLINE to explore the web site of a school in a Spanish-speaking country.

92 noventa y dos • **Tema 2** • La escuela

Differentiated Instruction

Bodily-Kinesthetic Learner

Encourage students to make up moves to accompany their cheers. Allow them to present their cheers to the class.

Heritage Speakers

Some students may be familiar with cheers from their heritage country. Allow them time to ask family and friends about them, and then to bring the information to share with the class.

Presentación oral

OBJECTIVES
▶ Describe your classes and schedule
▶ Use a chart to organize your ideas

 Go **Online** to practice **PEARSON realize**™
PearsonSchool.com/Autentico
 🎤 SPEAK/RECORD

Mis clases

TASK Imagine there is a new student from Costa Rica at your school. Tell the student your opinion about some of your classes.

Strategy
Using graphic organizers Simple charts can help you organize your main ideas and supporting opinions for a presentation.

1 **Prepare** Fill in a chart with information and your opinion about three of your classes. Use this chart to plan what you want to say about these classes.

Hora	Clase	Comentarios	Profesor(a)
primera	español	me gusta hablar español	la Sra. Salinas
cuarta	arte	difícil	el Sr. Highsmith
octava	ciencias naturales	divertida	la Sra. Huerta

2 **Practice** Go through your presentation several times. You can use your notes in practice, but your teacher may not want you to use them when presenting. Try to:
- mention the information about your classes and teachers
- use complete sentences and speak clearly

Modelo
En la primera hora tengo la clase de español. Me gusta hablar español. La clase es muy divertida. La Sra. Salinas es la profesora.

3 **Present** Describe the three classes you selected and give your opinion of each one.

4 **Evaluation** The following rubric will be used to grade your presentation.

Rubric	Score 1	Score 3	Score 5
How complete your preparation is	You have information written down but without the use of the chart.	You used the chart, but only partially completed it.	You used the chart and provided all the information.
Amount of information you give	You describe three classes but only provide one piece of information about each class.	You describe three classes but only provide two pieces of information about each class.	You describe five classes and include all requested information.
How easily you are understood	You are very difficult to understand, using only isolated words and phrases.	You are understandable but have frequent errors in vocabulary and/or grammar.	You are easily understood. Your teacher does not have to "decode" what you are trying to say.

Capítulo 2A • noventa y tres **93**

Enrich Your Teaching

21st Century Skills
Critical Thinking and Problem Solving Have teams of students come up with a model for a simple brochure for their own school, inspired by the brochure about the school in Costa Rica in the *Lectura.* Encourage students to use the materials for their *Presentación oral,* as well as the information in the reading, to propose the text and layout for their brochure.

Teacher-to-Teacher
Have students visit other Spanish classes and present the school cheers they created. Students might want to present their Spanish cheer at a school pep rally or assembly.

Starter Activity
Create and display a document like the one on the page, with the names of classes and the hour or period as an ordinal number.

Presentación oral

Standards: 1.3

Suggestions: Review the task and the four steps with students. You might want to model a top-scoring presentation. Then, to get students started, have them brainstorm vocabulary they can use to describe classes. Have students practice their presentation with a partner, focusing on fluency and pronunciation.

Digital Portfolio
Make video or audio recordings of student presentations in class, or assign the Speak and Record activity so they can record their presentations online. Include the recording in their portfolios.

Additional Resources
📶 **Technology: Online Resources**
- Guided
- *Para hispanohablantes*
Print
- Guided WB p. 68

Assessment _____

Presentación oral
- **Assessment Program:** Rubrics, Review the rubric with students. Go over the descriptions of the different levels of performance. After assessing students, help individuals understand how their performance could be improved. (See Teacher's Resource Materials for suggestions on using rubrics in assessment.)

Auténtico

Standards: 2.1, 2.2, 3.2, 4.2

Resources: *Authentic Resources Wkbk,* Cap. 2A
Authentic Resources: Cap 2A: Audioscript
AP Theme: *La vida contemporánea: La educación y las carreras profesionales*

Before You Listen

Discuss the *Strategy* with students. Have them make a list of words they know that relate to the topic of teaching math. Have them study the picture, and say words that they can use to describe details of the image in Spanish. Then review the key vocabulary with the class. Again, have students add the words to their list. Ask students to predict the discussion they might hear in the audio, using the key vocabulary and details from the image in their text. Note these predicted ideas on the board.

Technology: Listen to the Audio

Standards: 1.2

Before starting the audio, direct students' attention to the *Mientras escuchas* activity. Compare their answers to the activities to the word lists they made, and ask them if they would like to add any words to their lists.

Play the audio completely through, without pausing, and tell students to listen for the words and details on their lists and others that they recognize in the audio. Remind students that they will not understand every word, but that they should listen for overall understanding. Listen again to the audio, stopping as necessary for students to complete the listening activity and to check comprehension. Play the audio a final time without pausing.

Auténtico

Partnered with ⬛IDB

Ventajas de dominar las matemáticas

Before You Listen

Use the Strategy: Listen for Key Details

The speaker suggests changes to the way math is taught in Latin America. Use the key vocabulary, the Spanish you know, and your experience to increase your understanding of the key details in the audio.

Listen for this Key Vocabulary
ventajas = advantages
dominar = master
validar teorías = validate theories
**encontrar sus
propias respuestas** = find their own answers
camino hacia el éxito = path to success

🔊 Listen to the Audio

Think of the ways in which you use math in daily life. What changes does the speaker propose so that students in Latin America may also apply math skills in daily life? How do these changes reflect cultural changes towards education? Use your experience and the key details you understand from the audio to help you infer the speaker's message.

Go to **PearsonSchool.com/Autentico** and listen to the audio **¿Qué ventajas tienen los niños que dominan matemáticas?** to hear about proposed changes to math instruction in Latin America.

Complete the Activities

Mientras escuchas As you listen to the audio, identify which of the following are key details from the speaker's suggestions.

pensar por sí mismo   **resolver problemas**
usar experiencias reales   **aprender más**
encontrar respuestas   **usar fórmulas**

Differentiated Instruction

Students with Special Needs

You may wish to provide hearing impaired students with a copy of the script so that they may follow along and engage in activities.

Heritage Speakers

Ask students to research math terminology in Spanish, and then to write out a simple math word problem using chapter vocabulary. Are any of these words familiar to them? How similar or different are these Spanish words to English words? Ask them to present their word problems, and to work through the answers. Pay careful attention to spelling and correct use of accents in written language.

Integration

Después de escuchar Answer the following questions to demonstrate your understanding of key details in the audio.

1. What is one of the speaker's suggestions?

2. The speaker states that schools should present an *idea positiva de matemáticas*. Based on that, what can you infer about how math is presented now?

3. The speaker says that math is a *path to success*. Do you agree or disagree? Support your answer with ideas you inferred from the audio.

📖 **For more activities, go to the *Authentic Resources Workbook*.**

Escuelas en Latinoamérica

Expansión Find other authentic resources about schools in *Auténtico* online, then answer the question.

📁 **2A Auténtico**

Integración de ideas The authentic resources present schools in Spanish-speaking countries. Write a sentence to describe a detail of a school that you find interesting.

Comparación cultural What similarities and differences are there between these schools and your own school?

Interpret Authentic Resources

2A

Complete the Activities

Mientras escuchas

`Standards: 1.2`

Ask students to identify phrases in the audio by listening for breaks in speech. Call attention to the words that begin a new phrase, or that are stressed within a phrase, to help find key details and main ideas. Have students write out words that they hear, but that they may not be familiar with, using their understanding of the Spanish alphabet and its pronunciation.

Answers:

pensar por sí mismo	resolver problemas
usar experiencias reales	~~aprender más~~
encontrar respuestas	~~usar formulas~~

Después de escuchar

`Standards: 1.2`

Students' answers may vary based on their comprehension.

For additional discussion, you might ask students: *¿Te gusta estudiar las matemáticas? ¿Tienes clase de matemáticas hoy? ¿Cómo es la clase de matemáticas? ¿Tienes mucha tarea en la clase de matemáticas? ¿Es difícil o fácil? ¿Cómo es el/la profesor(a)? ¿Cómo es un estudiante de matemáticas?*

Answers:

1. *Answers will vary.* Students should think for themselves; they should validate theories; they should apply math to real and practical experiences.
2. *Answers will vary.* Students have negative experiences during math instruction.
3. *Answers will vary.*

For more Authentic Resources: Assign the *Authentic Resources Workbook* activities for homework, so that students can play the video on their own and complete the workbook activities at their own pace.

Enrich Your Teaching

Culture Note

The school system in Latin America does not mirror the school system in the United States. In most Latin American countries, secondary education is five to six years in duration, but in some countries, such as El Salvador, as few as three years is all that is officially required

Perspectivas: Which of the teaching techniques mentioned sounds the most useful to you?

Using Authentic Resources

Have students create a map of a school based on the authentic resources. In each room, have students list the relevant vocabulary from the chapter and the resources to describe the activities that happen in that room.

Pre-AP® Integration

`Standards: 1.3`

Resources: *Authentic Resources Workbook,* Cap. 2A; Authentic
Resources: Cap 2A; Audioscript

Suggestions: Before completing the Pre-AP® activity, have students go to the workbook and complete the worksheets for these two additional resources.

Review Activities

To talk about your school day: Have students bring in books from other classes. Randomly select a few and call on volunteers to tell what class each is from. For example, using the Spanish book, ask: *¿Es para la clase de ciencias naturales?* (*No. Es para la clase de español.*)

To talk about the order of things and things you need for school: Have students make a list of their classes for that day, numbering them in order. Have Student A point to a specific class on Student B's list and have Student B say what time it is and then describe it. For example, *En la tercera hora tengo la clase de matemáticas. Es divertida.* Be sure to have students include items they need from the list in *To talk about things you need for school.*

To describe your classes and other useful words: Using the list created above, have students work in pairs to compare classes. For example, *La clase de tecnología es más difícil que la clase de inglés.* Be sure they use a variety of descriptions and comparisons.

Digital Portfolio

Invite students to review the activities they completed in this chapter, including written reports, posters or other visuals, and recordings of oral presentations, or other projects. Have them select one or two items that they feel best demonstrate their achievements in Spanish to include in their portfolios. Have them include this with the Chapter Checklist and Self-Assessment Worksheet.

Pre-AP® Integration

- **Learning Objective:** Interpersonal speaking
- **Pre-AP® Resource Materials Activity Sheets, Tema 2** Have students work in pairs, and choose from questions 1–10 to guide their conversation.

Additional Resources

Technology: Online Resources
- Instant Check
- Integrated Performance Assessment

Print
- Core WB pp. 38–39

Teacher Resources
- Teacher's Resource Materials: Situation Cards, Clip Art
- Assessment Program: Chapter Checklist and Self-Assessment Worksheet

---

Repaso del capítulo

OBJECTIVES
▸ Review the vocabulary and grammar
▸ Demonstrate you can perform the tasks on p. 97

🔊 Vocabulario

to talk about your school day

el almuerzo	lunch
la clase	class
la clase de . . .	. . . class
arte	art
español	Spanish
ciencias naturales	science
ciencias sociales	social studies
educación física	physical education
inglés	English
matemáticas	mathematics
tecnología	technology/computers
el horario	schedule
en la . . . hora	in the . . . hour (class period)
la tarea	homework

to describe school activities

enseñar	to teach
estudiar	to study
hablar	to talk

to talk about the order of things

primero*, -a	first
segundo, -a	second
tercero*, -a	third
cuarto, -a	fourth
quinto, -a	fifth
sexto, -a	sixth
séptimo, -a	seventh
octavo, -a	eighth
noveno, -a	ninth
décimo, -a	tenth

*Changes to primer, tercer before a masculine singular noun.

For *Vocabulario adicional*, see pp. 472–473.

to talk about things you need for school

la calculadora	calculator
la carpeta de argollas	three-ring binder
el diccionario	dictionary
necesito	I need
necesitas	you need

to describe your classes

aburrido, -a	boring
difícil	difficult
divertido, -a	amusing, fun
fácil	easy
favorito, -a	favorite
interesante	interesting
más . . . que	more . . . than
práctico, -a	practical

other useful words

a ver . . .	Let's see
mucho	a lot
para	for
¿Quién?	Who?
(yo) tengo	I have
(tú) tienes	you have

Gramática

subject pronouns

yo	I	nosotros	we (masc., masc. / fem.)
		nosotras	we (fem.)
tú	you (fam.)	vosotros	you (masc. masc. / fem.)
usted (Ud.)	you (form.)	vosotras	you (fem.)
		ustedes (Uds.)	you (form.)
él	he	ellos	they (masc., masc. / fem.)
ella	she	ellas	they (fem.)

hablar *to talk*

hablo	hablamos
hablas	habláis
habla	hablan

Differentiated Instruction

Students with Learning Difficulties

Have students review the *Repaso del capítulo* and create flashcards for any words that they do not know. Pair them with a student who is more confident with the vocabulary to practice. Before the test, provide students with a practice test, so they can become comfortable with the format.

Heritage Speakers

Have students write a few paragraphs telling about their perfect school and class schedule: Where do they go to school? With whom do they attend classes? What classes do they take? What are their classes and teachers like? Encourage them to use as many vocabulary words from this chapter as they can.

Preparación para el examen

Más recursos PearsonSchool.com/Autentico

▣ Games   🗎 Flashcards   ✎ Instant check
▶ Tutorials   ▶ GramActiva videos   ▶ Animated verbs

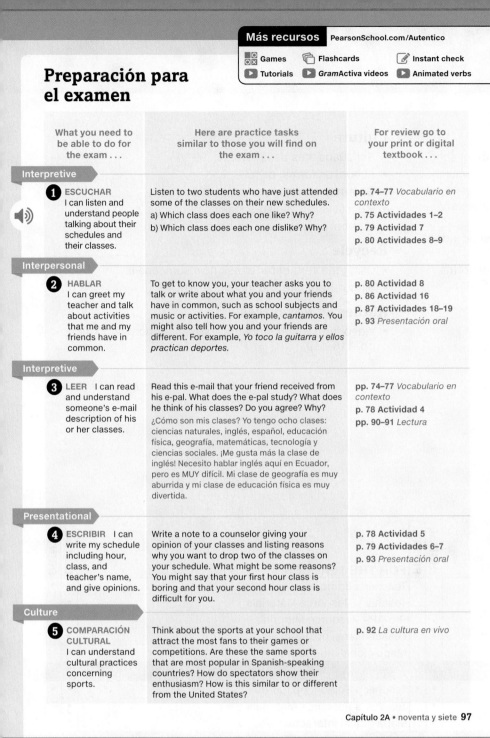

What you need to be able to do for the exam . . .	Here are practice tasks similar to those you will find on the exam . . .	For review go to your print or digital textbook . . .
Interpretive ① **ESCUCHAR** I can listen and understand people talking about their schedules and their classes.	Listen to two students who have just attended some of the classes on their new schedules. a) Which class does each one like? Why? b) Which class does each one dislike? Why?	**pp. 74–77** *Vocabulario en contexto* **p. 75** Actividades 1–2 **p. 79** Actividad 7 **p. 80** Actividades 8–9
Interpersonal ② **HABLAR** I can greet my teacher and talk about activities that me and my friends have in common.	To get to know you, your teacher asks you to talk or write about what you and your friends have in common, such as school subjects and music or activities. For example, *cantamos.* You might also tell how you and your friends are different. For example, *Yo toco la guitarra y ellos practican deportes.*	**p. 80** Actividad 8 **p. 86** Actividad 16 **p. 87** Actividades 18–19 **p. 93** *Presentación oral*
Interpretive ③ **LEER** I can read and understand someone's e-mail description of his or her classes.	Read this e-mail that your friend received from his e-pal. What does the e-pal study? What does he think of his classes? Do you agree? Why? ¿Cómo son mis clases? Yo tengo ocho clases: ciencias naturales, inglés, español, educación física, geografía, matemáticas, tecnología y ciencias sociales. ¡Me gusta más la clase de inglés! Necesito hablar inglés aquí en Ecuador, pero es MUY difícil. Mi clase de geografía es muy aburrida y mi clase de educación física es muy divertida.	**pp. 74–77** *Vocabulario en contexto* **p. 78** Actividad 4 **pp. 90–91** *Lectura*
Presentational ④ **ESCRIBIR** I can write my schedule including hour, class, and teacher's name, and give opinions.	Write a note to a counselor giving your opinion of your classes and listing reasons why you want to drop two of the classes on your schedule. What might be some reasons? You might say that your first hour class is boring and that your second hour class is difficult for you.	**p. 78** Actividad 5 **p. 79** Actividades 6–7 **p. 93** *Presentación oral*
Culture ⑤ **COMPARACIÓN CULTURAL** I can understand cultural practices concerning sports.	Think about the sports at your school that attract the most fans to their games or competitions. Are these the same sports that are most popular in Spanish-speaking countries? How do spectators show their enthusiasm? How is this similar to or different from the United States?	**p. 92** *La cultura en vivo*

Capítulo 2A • noventa y siete **97**

Differentiated Assessment

Core Assessment
- Assessment Program: Examen del capítulo 2A, pp. 47–53
- Technology: Audio Cap. 2A
- ExamView: Chapter Test, Test Banks A and B

Challenge/Pre-AP®
- ExamView: Pre-AP® Test Bank
- Pre-AP® Resource Materials

Extra Support
- Alternate Assessment Program: Examen del capítulo 2A
- Technology: Audio Cap. 2A

Heritage Speakers
- Assessment Program: Para hispanohablantes: Examen del capítulo 2A
- ExamView: Heritage Learner Test Bank

Performance Tasks

Standards: 1.2, 1.3, 2.1, 4.2

Student Resource: *Para hispanohablantes*
Teacher Resources: Teacher's Resource Materials: Audio Script; Technology: Audio Cap. 2A

1. Escuchar

Suggestions: Use the audio or read the script.

Script:

Boy: Me gusta mucho la clase de arte. Me gusta dibujar. Es una clase fantástica. Pero la clase de matemáticas... ¡Uf! Es mucho más difícil que mi clase de arte. A veces hay mucha tarea.

Girl: ¡La clase de matemáticas no es difícil! La tarea es muy fácil. Me gusta mucho el profesor. Él es muy divertido. Pero no me gusta la clase de educación física. No soy atlética.

Answers

Boy: a) Art class, because he likes to draw. b) Math, because it's difficult and has lots of homework. Girl: a) Math: the homework is easy and she likes the teacher. b) Physical education: she's not athletic.

2. Hablar

Standards: 1.2

Suggestions: Brainstorm possible vocabulary with students.

Answers will vary.

3. Leer

Suggestions: Remind students that almost all the vocabulary can be found on p. 96.

Answers:

He studies science, English, Spanish, physical education, geography, math, technology, and social studies. He likes English and thinks that geography is boring. Answers will vary.

4. Escribir

Suggestions: Brainstorm with students words to use for this activity.

Answers will vary.

5. Comparación cultural

Suggestions: Suggest students use a Venn diagram to organize their writing.

Answer will vary

2B Tu sala de clases

Objectives

- Listen to and read conversations and notes about school
- Talk and write about classes, classrooms, and where things are located
- Exchange information while describing someone's location
- Identify cultural practices viewed in an authentic video about school
- Compare perspectives towards school and uniforms in the Spanish-speaking world and the United States

Vocabulary

- Classroom items and furniture
- Computers
- Words to describe location

Grammar

- The verb *estar*
- Plurals of nouns and articles

Culture

- Sor Juana Inés de la Cruz, p. 99
- School uniforms, p. 106
- Currency exchange rates, p. 109
- P.E. class in Spanish-speaking countries, p. 113
- Cultural perspectives on school, p. 116

Recycle

- Using the verb *estar* to ask how someone is
- Singular definite and indefinite articles

Authentic Resources

- Video from which students learn about homework tips, pp. 118–119

	FOR THE STUDENT	DIGITAL	PRINT	FOR THE TEACHER	DIGITAL	PRINT
Plan				Teacher's Edition	•	•
				Teacher's Resource Materials	•	
				Pre-AP® Resource Materials	•	
				Lesson Plans, pp. 98-c, 98-d	•	
				Mapa global interactivo	•	
Introducción pp. 98–99						
Present	Student Edition, pp. 98–99	•	•	Teacher's Edition, pp. 98–99	•	•
	DK Reference Atlas	•		Teacher's Resource Materials	•	
	Para hispanohablantes	•		Mapa global interactivo	•	
Vocabulario en contexto pp. 100–103						
Present & Practice	Student Edition, pp. 100–103	•	•	Teacher's Edition, pp. 100–103	•	•
	Audio	•		Teacher's Resource Materials	•	
	Videohistoria	•		Vocabulary Clip Art	•	
	Flashcards	•		Technology: Audio	•	
	Instant Check	•		Video Program: Videohistoria	•	
	Guided WB, pp. 69–76	•	•			
	Core WB, pp. 40–43	•	•			
	Communication Activities	•				
	Para hispanohablantes	•				
Assess and Remediate				Prueba 2B–1: Assessment Program, pp. 54–55	•	
				Assessment Program para hispanohablantes, pp. 54–55	•	

RESOURCES

	FOR THE STUDENT	DIGITAL	PRINT	FOR THE TEACHER	DIGITAL	PRINT
Vocabulario en uso pp. 104–106						
Present & Practice	Student Edition, pp. 104–106	•	•	Interactive Whiteboard Vocabulary Activities	•	
	Instant Check	•		Teacher's Edition, pp. 104–106	•	•
	Communicative Activities	•		Teacher's Resource Materials	•	
	Para hispanohablantes	•		Communicative Pair Activities	•	
	Communicative Pair Activities	•		Technology: Audio	•	
				Videomodelos	•	
Assess and Remediate				Prueba 2B–2 with Remediation	•	
				Prueba 2B–2: Assessment Program, pp. 56–57	•	
				Assessment Program para hispanohablantes, pp. 56–57	•	
Gramática pp. 107–113						
Present & Practice	Student Edition, pp. 107–113	•	•	Interactive Whiteboard Grammar Activities	•	
	Instant Check	•		Teacher's Edition, pp. 107–113	•	•
	Animated Verbs	•		Teacher's Resource Materials	•	
	Tutorial Video: Grammar	•		Communicative Pair Activities	•	
	Canción de hip hop	•		Technology: Audio	•	
	Guided WB, pp. 77–80	•	•	Videomodelos	•	
	Core WB, pp. 44–46	•	•	Video Program: GramActiva	•	
	Communication Activities	•				
	Para hispanohablantes	•				
	Communicative Pair Activities	•				
Assess and Remediate				Pruebas 2B–3 and 2B–4 with Remediation	•	
				Pruebas 2B–3, 2B–4: Assessment Program, pp. 58, 59	•	
				Assessment Program para hispanohablantes, pp. 58, 59	•	
Aplicación pp. 114–119						
Apply	Student Edition, pp. 114–119	•	•	Teacher's Edition, pp. 114–119	•	•
	Authentic Resources Workbook	•	•	Mapa global interactivo	•	
	Authentic Resources	•		Authentic Resources Lesson Plans with scripts, answer keys	•	
	Literacy Skills Workbook	•	•			
	Online Cultural Reading	•				
	Guided WB, pp. 81–82	•	•			
	Communication Activities	•				
	Para hispanohablantes	•				
Repaso del capítulo pp. 120–121						
Review	Student Edition, pp. 120–121	•	•	Teacher's Edition, pp. 120–121	•	•
	Online Puzzles and Games	•		Teacher's Resource Materials	•	
	Core WB, pp. 47–48	•	•	Technology: Audio	•	
	Communication Activities	•				
	Para hispanohablantes	•				
	Instant Check	•				
Chapter Assessment						
Assess				Examen del capítulo 2B	•	
				Assessment Program, pp. 60–66	•	
				Alternate Assessment Program, pp. 19–24	•	
				Assessment Program para hispanohablantes, pp. 60–66	•	
				Technology: Audio, Cap. 2B Examen	•	
				ExamView: Test Banks A and B questions only online	•	
				Heritage Learner Test Bank	•	
				Pre-AP® Test Bank	•	

	LESSON PLAN (50 MINUTES)		
DAY	**Warm-up / Assess**	**Preview / Present / Practice / Communicate**	**Wrap-up / Homework Options**

1	**Warm-up** (10 min.)
	• Return Examen del capítulo 2A
		Chapter Opener (5 min.)
		• Objectives
		• Arte y cultura **Vocabulario en contexto** (30 min.)
		    • Presentation: Vocabulario en contexto
		    • Actividades 1, 2
			Wrap-up and Homework Options (5 min.)
			• Core Practice 2B-1, 2B-2

2	**Warm-up** (5 min.) • Homework check	**Vocabulario en contexto** (40 min.) • Presentation: Videohistoria *Enseñar en Guatemala* • View: Videohistoria • Video Activities 1, 2, 3, 4 • Actividad 3	**Wrap-up and Homework Options** (5 min.) • Core Practice 2B-3, 2B-4 • Prueba 2B-1: Vocabulary recognition
3	**Warm-up** (10 min.) • Actividades 4, 5 • Homework check • **Formative Assessment** (10 min.) • Prueba 2B-1: Vocabulary recognition	**Vocabulario en uso** (25 min.) • Interactive Whiteboard Vocabulary Activities • Actividades 6, 7, 8 • Audio Activities 5, 6 • Communicative Pair Activity	**Wrap-up and Homework Options** (5 min.) • Writing Activity 10 • Prueba 2B-2 with Remediation: Vocabulary production
4	**Warm-up** (5 min.) • Cultura • Homework check • **Formative Assessment** (10 min.) • Prueba 2B-2 with Remediation: Vocabulary production	**Gramática y vocabulario en uso** (30 min.) • Exploración del lenguaje • Presentation: The verb *estar* • View: GramActiva video • Interactive Whiteboard Grammar Activities • Actividades 9, 10, 11	**Wrap-up and Homework Options** (5 min.) • Core Practice 2B-5
5	**Warm-up** (10 min.) • Writing Activity 11 • Homework check	**Gramática y vocabulario en uso** (35 min.) • View: GramActiva video • Actividades 12, 13, 14 • Audio Activity 7 • Communicative Pair Activity	**Wrap-up and Homework Options** (5 min.) • Prueba 2B-3 with Remediation: The verb *estar* • Auténtico
6	**Warm-up** (5 min.) • Homework check • **Formative Assessment** (10 min.) • Prueba 2B-3 with Remediation: The verb *estar*	**Gramática y vocabulario en uso** (30 min.) • Presentation: The plurals of nouns and articles • Actividades 15, 16, 17, 18 • View: GramActiva video • El español en el mundo del trabajo • Interactive Whiteboard Grammar Activities	**Wrap-up and Homework Options** (5 min.) • Core Practice 2B-6
7	**Warm-up** (10 min.) • Writing Activity 12 • Homework check	**Gramática y vocabulario en uso** (35 min.) • View: GramActiva video • Audio Activities 8, 9 • Actividades 19, 20 • Pronunciación • Cultura	**Wrap-up and Homework Options** (5 min.) • Core Practice 2B-7 • Prueba 2B-4 with Remediation: The plurals of nouns and articles
8	**Warm-up** (10 min.) • Writing Activity 13 • Homework check • **Formative Assessment** (10 min.) • Prueba 2B-4 with Remediation: The plurals of nouns and articles	**Aplicación** (25 min.) • Lectura • ¿Comprendes? • Presentación escrita: Steps 1, 5 • Perspectivas del mundo hispano	**Wrap-up and Homework Options** (5 min.) • Presentación escrita: Step 2 • Preparación para el examen 3, 4, 5

9	**Warm-up** (5 min.)
	• Homework check
		Aplicación (20 min.)
		• Presentación escrita: Step 3 **Repaso del capítulo** (20 min.)
		    • Vocabulario y gramática
		    • Preparación para el examen 1, 2
			Wrap-up and Homework Options (5 min.)
			• Presentación escrita: Step 4 • Instant Check
			• Core Practice 2B-8, 2B-9 • Examen del capítulo 2B

10	**Warm-up** (10 min.) • Homework check • **Summative Assessment** (40 min.) • Examen del capítulo 2B		

ALTERNATE LESSON PLAN

DAY	Warm-up / Assess	Preview / Present / Practice / Communicate		Wrap-up / Homework Options
1	**Warm-up** (10 min.) • Return Examen del capítulo 2A	**Chapter Opener** (5 min.) • Objectives • Arte y cultura **Vocabulario en contexto** (60 min.) • Presentation: Vocabulario en contexto • Actividades 1, 2 • Presentation: Videohistoria *Enseñar en Guatemala* • View: Videohistoria • Video Activities 1, 2, 3, 4 • Actividad 3	**Vocabulario en uso** (10 min.) • Interactive Whiteboard Vocabulary Activities • Actividades 4, 5	**Wrap-up and Homework Options** (5 min.) • Core Practice 2B-1, 2B-2, 2B-3, 2B-4 • Prueba 2B-1: Vocabulary recognition
2	**Warm-up** (10 min.) • Homework check • **Formative Assessment** (10 min.) • Prueba 2B-1: Vocabulary recognition	**Gramática y vocabulario en uso** (65 min.) • Actividades 6, 7, 8 • Audio Activities 5, 6 • Communicative Pair Activity • Exploración del lenguaje • Cultura • Presentation: The verb *estar*	• View: GramActiva video • Interactive Whiteboard Grammar Activities • Actividades 9, 10, 11	**Wrap-up and Homework Options** (5 min.) • Core Practice 2B-5 • Writing Activity 10 • Prueba 2B-2 with Remediation: Vocabulary production
3	**Warm-up** (10 min.) • Homework check • Writing Activity 11 • **Formative Assessment** (10 min.) • Prueba 2B-2 with Remediation: Vocabulary production	**Gramática y vocabulario en uso** (65 min.) • Actividades 12, 13, 14 • Audio Activity 7 • Communicative Pair Activity • Presentation: The plurals of nouns and articles • View: GramActiva video • Interactive Whiteboard Grammar Activities • Actividades 15, 16, 17, 18 • El español en el mundo del trabajo • Pronunciación		**Wrap-up and Homework Options** (5 min.) • Core Practice 2B-6, 2B-7 • Pruebas 2B-3, 2B-4 with Remediation: The verb *estar*, The plurals of nouns and articles
4	**Warm-up** (10 min.) • Homework check • Writing Activity 13 • **Formative Assessment** (15 min.) • Pruebas 2B-3, 2B-4 with Remediation: The verb *estar*, The plurals of nouns and articles	**Gramática y vocabulario en uso** (30 min.) • Audio Activities 8, 9 • Actividades 19, 20 • Cultura • Writing Activity 13	**Aplicación** (30 min.) • Lectura • ¿Comprendes? • Presentación escrita: Steps 1, 5	**Wrap-up and Homework Options** (5 min.) • Presentación escrita: Step 2 • Lectura
5	**Warm-up** (5 min.) • Homework check	**Aplicación** (50 min.) • Perspectivas del mundo hispano • Auténtico • Presentación escrita: Step 3	**Repaso del capítulo** (30 min.) • Vocabulario y gramática • Situation Cards • Communicative Pair Activities • Preparación para el examen 1, 2, 3, 4, 5	**Wrap-up and Homework Options** (5 min.) • Presentación escrita: Step 4 • Core Practice 2B-8, 2B-9 • Instant Check • Examen del capítulo 2B
6	**Warm-up** (15 min.) • Homework check • Answer questions **Repaso del capítulo** (25 min.) • **Summative Assessment** (45 min.) • Examen del capítulo 2B			**Wrap-up and Homework Options** (5 min.) • Auténtico

Can-Do Statements

Read the can-do statements in the chapter objectives with students. Then have students read *Preparación para el examen* on page 121 to preview what they will be able to do at the end of the chapter.

Standards for Capítulo 2B

To achieve the goals of the Standards, students will:

COMMUNICATION

1.1 Interpersonal
- Talk about personal and classroom items and furniture
- Talk about the locations of: objects in a classroom setting; people in a photo

1.2 Interpretive
- Listen to information about: classroom items and furniture; the use of location words
- Read: a picture-based story; information about classroom items and furniture; a dialogue requiring understanding of the irregular verb *estar*; a dialogue requiring understanding of articles; a journalistic article about UNICEF; a note about a students request for information
- Listen to and watch a video about a classroom prank
- Compare a photo to oral descriptions of a Spanish club

1.3 Presentational
- Present information about classroom items and furniture
- Retell portions of a story they have heard
- Present a dialogue requiring understanding of articles
- Compose: a paragraph about their classroom; a letter to a pen pal
- Write a fictional e-mail to a friend about classes

CULTURE

2.1 Practices to Perspectives
- Discuss women's access to education in seventeenth century Mexico; the widespread use of school uniforms; how physical education classes and team sports are conducted
- Explain that school demands a high percentage of students' time

2.2 Products to Perspectives
- Explain the structure educational systems

CONNECTIONS

3.1 Making Connections
- Discuss the seventeenth-century Mexican intellectual, Sor Juana Inés de la Cruz; currency of Spanish-speaking countries
- Read a journalistic article about UNICEF

CAPÍTULO **2B**
Tu sala de clases

Country Connections Explorar el mundo hispano

CHAPTER OBJECTIVES

Communication

By the end of this chapter you will be able to:
- Listen to and read conversations and notes about school.
- Talk and write about classes, classrooms, and where things are located.
- Exchange information while describing someone's location.

Culture

You will also be able to:
- **Auténtico:** Identify cultural practices viewed in an authentic video about school homework.
- Compare perspectives towards school and uniforms in the Spanish-speaking world and the United States

You will demonstrate what you know and can do:
- Presentación escrita: Tu sala de clases
- Repaso del capítulo: Preparación para el examen

You will use:

Vocabulary	Grammar
• Classroom items and furniture	• The verb *estar*
• Computers	• Plurals of nouns and articles
• Words to describe location	

ARTE y CULTURA ▸ México

Sor Juana Inés de la Cruz (1648–1695), born near Mexico City, was one of the greatest intellectuals of her time. She wrote poetry, essays, music, and plays. Sor Juana also defended a woman's right to an education at a time when few women had access to it. She entered a convent at the age of 19 and over the years built a library of several thousand books. Sor Juana's living quarters in the convent became a meeting place for other writers and intellectuals, who were drawn to her because of her intelligence and knowledge.

▸ How are various aspects of Sor Juana's life represented in this painting? If you were to pose for a portrait, what objects would you include that represent you and your interests?

Retrato de Sor Juana Inés de la Cruz, siglo XVII ▸
Foto: Archivo Agencia EL UNIVERSAL.

98 noventa y ocho • Tema 2 • La escuela

Enrich Your Teaching

The End in Mind

Have students preview the sample performance tasks on *Preparación para el examen,* p. 121, and connect them to the Chapter Objectives. Explain to students that by completing the sample tasks they can self-assess their learning progress.

Go **Online** to practice
PEARSON
realize.
PearsonSchool.com/Autentico

AUDIO · VIDEO · WRITING · SPEAK/RECORD · MAPA GLOBAL · AUTÉNTICO · FLASCHARDS · ETEXT 2.0 · GAMES

Estudiantes mexicanas

▶ Videocultura **Los uniformes escolares**

Capítulo 2B • noventa y nueve **99**

COMPARISONS

4.1 Language
* Talk about vocabulary through the recognition of cognates; the verbal and nonverbal expression, *¡Ojo!*; about the irregular verb *estar;* the pronunciation of the letter *g*
* Explain number agreement with nouns and articles

4.2 Cultural
* Compare: the use of school uniforms; influence of women writers on perspectives; the design of physical education class; commitments to and behavior in school
* Consider the hypothetical result of United States expansion south to Panama in the nineteenth century

COMMUNITIES

5.1 School and Global Communities
* Consider the need for Spanish speakers in different types of jobs in the educational field

Chapter Opener

Resources: Mapa global interactivo

Suggestions: Review the objectives. Explain to students that they will be learning to talk about classroom objects and locations. The *Videohistoria* is about a school in Guatemala. The *GramActiva* Video will help students learn the present tense of **estar** and the plurals of nouns and articles.

▶ **Technology: Videocultura** View *Los uniformes escolares* with the class to learn more about different types of uniforms.

ARTE Y CULTURA

Standards: 2.1, 2.2, 4.2

Suggestions: Point out the dates of Sor Juana's birth and death and ask students what they know about that era (science, arts, and historical events). What opportunities did women have in the seventeenth century to be independent professionals, artists, and scientists?
Answers will vary.

Culture Note
Direct attention to the photo and point to the insignia that the students have on their sweaters and vests. In addition to uniforms (see *Cultura*, p.106) some schools require their students to wear the official school seal. Others may require school-specific uniform colors.

Project-Based Learning

Página Web (continued)
Ask students to work in pairs to draw a layout of their classroom. It should include the position of all the classroom objects, with clear labels of where they are, objects like the whiteboard, clock, etc. If there is time you can ask the class to work in small groups to provide a new layout for their ideal classroom.

Vocabulario en contexto

Standards: 1.2

Resources: Teacher's Resource Materials: Input Script, Clip Art, Audio Script; Technology: Audio Cap. 2B

Suggestions: Use the Input Script from the *Teacher's Resource Materials* to introduce the new vocabulary. Have students look at the picture of the classroom in their books and touch the pictures as you describe the scene. Use the new vocabulary to name items in your classroom and have volunteers move around the room to touch the objects you name. If possible, use your classroom computer to identify its parts.

Starter Activity

Review the school subjects in Spanish with the students. Ask students to name another subject they take and describe an object in that classroom.

Active Classroom

Have students put their heads down on their desks while one student moves an object in the classroom. When done, everyone raises their heads, and the student who moved the object asks: *¿Dónde está (la papelera)?* The first student to spot it must accurately describe its location and then becomes "It."

Technology: Interactive Whiteboard

Vocabulary Activities 2B Use the whiteboard activities in your Teacher Resources as you progress through the vocabulary practice with your class.

Vocabulario en contexto

OBJECTIVES
Read, listen to, and understand information about the classroom and where objects are located

🔊 **❝Estamos en mi clase de español. El escritorio de la profesora está delante de la clase. Aquí está el escritorio de mi profesora, al lado de una ventana.**

El sacapuntas está encima del escritorio. Detrás del escritorio hay una bandera, y debajo hay un reloj. ¡La profesora es muy ordenada! Me gusta estudiar en la clase de español. Y a ti, ¿te gusta tu clase de español? ❞

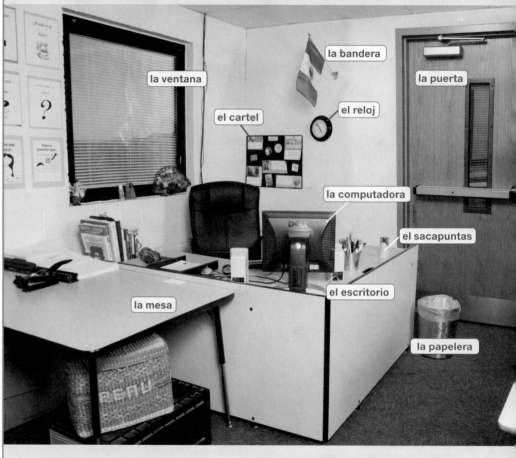

100 cien • Tema 2 • La escuela

Differentiated Instruction

Heritage Speakers

Have students make their own vocabulary lists of classroom objects, adding other words they know. If necessary, help them with spelling.

Logical/Mathematical Learner

Have students count objects in their classroom for which they've learned words. Have them write sentences: *Hay tres computadoras en la sala de clases. Hay treinta pupitres,* etc. The class can listen to the sentences and tell whether they are accurate.

"Me gusta estudiar aquí, pero hay muchos estudiantes y es importante ser ordenada. Mi **mochila** está debajo de la mesa. Mi ratón está al lado de mi teclado. Es bueno estudiar aquí. ¿A ti dónde te gusta estudiar?".

Más vocabulario
el disco compacto = compact disc
el DVD = DVD (disc)

la pantalla
el ratón
el teclado
la silla

1

¿Está en la clase de español?

🔊 ESCUCHAR Listen to the statements about school items while looking at the two photos. If you see the item in either photo, give a "thumbs up". If it isn't there, give a "thumbs down".

2

¿Dónde están las cosas?

🔊 ESCUCHAR Listen to descriptions of where things are located in the two school photos. Pay attention to the key details. Touch the item(s) mentioned in each description.

Capítulo 2B • ciento uno **101**

Enrich Your Teaching

Teacher-to-Teacher

Have students make decorative labels for objects in the classroom. Have them place the labels as they tell where the object is located: *El sacapuntas está al lado del diccionario.*

21st Century Skills

Critical Thinking and Problem Solving After students have worked with the digital tools for this section of the chapter, have them work with a partner to compare their current classroom to the one pictured on page 100. They should use a graphic organizer, such as a Venn diagram, to summarize the similarities and differences.

1

Standards: 1.2

Resources: Teacher's Resource Materials: Audio Script; Technology: Audio Cap. 2B

Suggestions: Explain to students that they will be listening for the name of the objects, and that it might appear in either of the large pictures. Allow students to listen more than once.

🔊 **Technology: Audio Script and Answers**

1. Hay una calculadora. *(thumbs down)*
2. Hay una computadora. *(thumbs up/thumbs down)*
3. Hay una mesa. *(thumbs up)*
4. Hay un sacapuntas. *(thumbs up)*
5. Hay un teclado. *(thumbs up/thumbs down)*
6. Hay una silla. *(thumbs up)*

2

Standards: 1.2

Resources: Teacher's Resource Materials: Audio Script; Technology: Audio Cap. 2B

Suggestions: Tell students that some of the objects referred to in this exercise are pictured on p.100.

🔊 **Technology: Audio Script and Answers**

1. La mesa está delante del escritorio de la profesora. *(point to the teacher's desk)*
2. El ratón está al lado de la computadora. *(point to the computer mouse)*
3. La silla está detrás de la mesa. *(point to the desk)*
4. El sacapuntas está encima de la mesa. *(point to the pencil)*
5. La papelera está allí. *(point to the wastepaper basket)*
6. El cartel está al lado del reloj. *(point to the poster)*

Additional Resources

📶 **Technology: Online Resources**
• Instant Check
• Guided, Core, Audio, Writing practice
• *Para hispanohablantes*
Print
• Guided WB pp. 69–72
• Core WB pp. 40–41

Vocabulario en contexto

Standards: 1.2, 4.1

Resources: Technology: Audio Cap. 2B

Suggestions: Model the dialogue with a volunteer. Begin the reading again with volunteers playing the roles of the characters. Using the presentation, help students understand the new words in blue type.

Post-reading: Complete Actividad 3 to check comprehension.

3

Standards: 1.2, 1.3

Suggestions: You may wish to do this as a listening activity, reading the sentences to the students.

Extension: Use the sentences as a model for students to create their own. Have students take turns making similar statements and, as a class, say *Sí* or *No* to express whether the sentence is correct or not.

Answers

1. Sí
2. No
3. Sí
4. No
5. Sí

Pre-AP® Integration

- **Learning Objective:** Interpretive Audio
- **Activity:** Have students create a short conversation based on this written exchange. Students can play the roles of Rosi and the teacher as they further discuss the distraction vs. the academic benefits of having a phone in school.
- **Pre-AP® Resource Materials:** Comprehensive guide to Pre-AP® vocabulary skill development

🔊 Un teléfono en la clase

Profesor:	Rosi, ¿qué es esto?
Rosi:	¿Dónde?
Profesor:	Allí, en tu mochila.
Rosi:	Es un teléfono.
Profesor:	¿Un teléfono en mi clase?
Rosi:	Sí, profesor.
Profesor:	No me gustan **los** teléfonos en mi clase.
Rosi:	Pero necesito mi teléfono para estudiar.
Profesor:	¿Qué?
Rosi:	Sí. Mi teléfono tiene un diccionario muy práctico.
Profesor:	Rosi, hablamos en mi oficina.
Rosi:	Sí, señor.

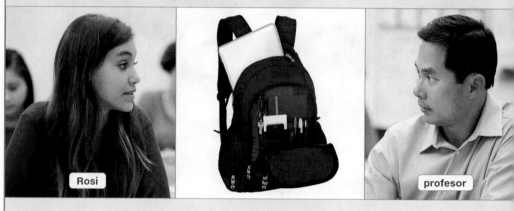

Rosi   profesor

3

¿Sí o no?

✏️ **ESCRIBIR** Lee las oraciones. Escribe *Sí* si la oración es correcta o *No* si es incorrecta. *Corrige* (Correct) las oraciones incorrectas.

1. Rosi tiene un teléfono en la clase.
2. El teléfono está encima del libro.
3. Al profesor no le gustan los teléfonos en su clase.
4. Rosi necesita la calculadora de su teléfono.
5. El profesor necesita hablar con Rosi en su oficina.

102 ciento dos • Tema 2 • La escuela

Differentiated Instruction

Heritage Speakers

Have students extend the story by writing what the **Profesor** tells Rosi at his office. Check students' work and provide feedback as necessary.

Videohistoria

Go **Online** to practice
PEARSON
realize™

PearsonSchool.com/Autentico

🔊 ▶️ ✏️ 📄
AUDIO VIDEO WRITING SCRIPT

Interpretive 2B

Enseñar en Guatemala

Before You Watch

Predicting Read the questions in *After You Watch* to predict what you will learn in the video. Based on key words from the questions, what do you think this episode is about? What will you see?

Complete the Activity

En Guatemala Describe la escuela oficial rural de Guatemala que ves en las fotos.

▶️ Watch the Video

What do you think schools are like in other Spanish-speaking countries?

Go to **PearsonSchool.com/Autentico** to watch the video *Enseñar en Guatemala* and to view the script.

Ximena   Camila

After You Watch

✏️ **¿COMPRENDES?** Listen for these key words. Indicate if each statement is *cierto* or *falso* based on the video.

1. uniforme: Los niños no necesitan uniformes para ir a la escuela.
2. pizarrón: Hay un pizarrón y una pantalla en las salas de clase.
3. computación: No hay videojuegos en la sala de computación.
4. cafetería: Los niños siempre pasan el almuerzo en la cafetería.
5. deportes: Practican deportes en una sala grande.

Comparación cultural ¿Qué hay en la escuela de Guatemala en el video que también hay en tu escuela? ¿Qué no hay?

Capítulo 2B • ciento tres **103**

Enrich Your Teaching

Culture Note

Most private and public schools in Spanish-speaking countries require their students to wear a full uniform. Sometimes the uniform consists of a smock that is worn over a student's regular clothes to protect them from getting dirty or torn during the school day. Some uniforms are of the same color for girls and boys, and even secondary school students wear uniforms. It gives them a sense of school pride, it is believed to encourage discipline, and avoid peer pressure.

Technology: Video

Standards: 1.2

Resources: Teacher's Resource Materials: Video Script

Before You Watch

Review the previewing strategy and activity with the students. Ask students to predict what they will see in the video. Review the Complete the Activity with the class. Ask students to talk or write about the school and students presented in the photos.

Watch the Video

Show the video once without pausing. Show it again, stopping to ask questions and check comprehension. Remind students that they may not understand every word in the video, but that they should listen and watch for overall understanding. Show the segment a final time without pausing.

After You Watch

Standards: 1.2

Suggestions: Discuss the questions with the class to confirm understanding of the video.

Answers
1. falso
2. cierto
3. falso
4. falso
5. falso

Comparación cultural: Answers will vary and may include the use of uniforms.

Have the students complete additional Video activities online or print the activities from the Teacher's Resources in the online course and pass out the activity sheets to the class.

Additional Resources

📶 **Technology: Online Resources**
- Instant Check
- Guided, Core, Video, Audio
- *Para hispanohablantes*
Print
- Guided WB pp. 73–76
- Core WB pp. 42–43

Assessment

Quiz: Vocabulary Recognition
- Prueba 2B-1

4

Standards: 1.3

Suggestions: Remind students that **hay** means "there is" or "there are," and that no other verb is required.

Answers:

1. Hay un sacapuntas.
2. ...un reloj.
3. ...una silla.
4. ...una mochila.
5. ...un cartel.
6. ...una papelera.
7. ...una ventana.
8. ...una mesa.

Extension: Have students tell what items they have in their backpacks.

Starter Activity

Use the objects pictured in *Actividad* 4 to quickly review indefinite articles.

5

Standards: 1.2

Recycle: Classroom vocabulary

Suggestions: Remind students that they need to analyze the logic of the word grouping to decide which word does not belong.

Answers:

1. Una mochila—¡No! Un pupitre—¡Sí!
2. La sala de clase—¡No! Debajo de—¡Sí!
3. Un diccionario... Un sacapuntas...
4. Bailar... Enseñar...
5. Necesitan... Necesita, sí.
6. La chica... El chico...

Extension: Have students create their own sets of items like those in the activity.

Vocabulario en uso

OBJECTIVES
▶ Write and talk about objects in a classroom
▶ Describe a bedroom and a classroom
▶ Exchange information about school supplies and their location

4

¿Qué hay?

ESCRIBIR Describe these objects. Write the names of the things you see.

Modelo
Hay una bandera.

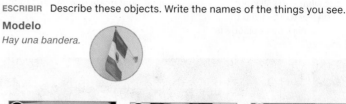

5

¿Es lógico o no?

ESCRIBIR Write the word that doesn't belong in each group. Then supply a word that logically belongs.

Modelo
el ratón   el teclado   la pantalla   la ventana
La ventana: ¡No! La computadora: ¡Sí!

1. una mesa   una silla   una mochila   un escritorio
2. la sala de clases   al lado de   detrás de   encima de
3. un diccionario   una calculadora   un reloj   una computadora
4. leer   estudiar   escribir   bailar
5. está   habla   necesitan   trabaja
6. el profesor   la chica   el estudiante   el señor

104 ciento cuatro • Tema 2 • La escuela

Differentiated Instruction

Students with Learning Difficulties

Students with language processing difficulties may need extra help with *Actividad* 5. Go item by item and ask them to tell you the characteristics of each. Guide them to see what the categories are that link the items.

Actividad 7, and others like it, are perfect for cooperative learning; however, it is very important that students with learning difficulties are matched up with the appropriate partners.

6

¿Dónde está?

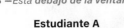

HABLAR EN PAREJA Take turns with a partner to ask and tell where various items in Beto's bedroom are located.

Videomodelo

A —¿Dónde está *el escritorio*?
B —Está *debajo de la ventana*.

Estudiante A

¿Dónde está . . . ?

Estudiante B

al lado de   detrás de
delante de   encima de
debajo de

Nota

When the preposition *de* is followed by the masculine definite article *el*, the contraction *del* must be used.
- La papelera está al lado del escritorio.

7

Juego

HABLAR, ESCUCHAR

1. Work with a partner. Your partner will face away from you and have a blank piece of paper and a pen or a pencil.

2. Choose four classroom items and arrange them on your desk, putting objects on top of others, next to each other, and so forth.

Videomodelo

A —¿Tienes un sacapuntas?
B —No, no tengo un sacapuntas.
A —¿Tienes una calculadora?
B —Sí, tengo una calculadora.
A —¿Dónde está?
B —Está encima de la carpeta.

3. Your partner will ask you questions about what is on your desk and how the items are positioned. You will use the vocabulary key words to answer. Based on your answers, he or she will try to draw the arrangement on your desk.

4. When your teacher tells you to stop, see how closely the picture matches the actual arrangement. Then switch roles.

Para decir más . . .
a la izquierda de = to the left of
a la derecha de = to the right of

Capítulo 2B • ciento cinco **105**

Standards: 1.1

Suggestions: Help Student A see that there are multiple items to choose from, and that they can be chosen in any order. This can also be turned into a whole-class guessing game.

Answers will vary. Items will include:
la ventana, la computadora, el escritorio, la mochila, la silla, la papelera, la mesa, el reloj, el cartel.

Standards: 1.1, 1.2

Resources: Teacher's Resource Materials
Recycle: Classroom vocabulary:
Suggestions: Remind students that vocabulary in the *Para decir más...* will be helpful to them in completing an activity, but that it is not tested. Demonstrate how to play the game. Walk around the room, prompting students if necessary and monitoring their accuracy.
Answers will vary.

Pre-AP® Integration

- **Learning Objective:** Presentational Speaking
- **Activity:** Ask students to bring a sketch of their room, or a picture of a classroom downloaded from the Internet, showing the position of various items. Have students briefly describe their sketch or picture in front of the class using the vocabulary from this chapter.
- **Pre-AP® Resource Materials:** Comprehensive guide to Pre-AP® speaking skill development

Teacher-to-Teacher

Give the following classroom instructions for students to follow: *Pongan la mochila encima de la silla, pongan la papelera debajo de la ventana, pongan el bolígrafo encima del escritorio del profesor/de la profesora,* etc. Have students work in small groups to write additional instructions to give to other groups to follow.

Enrich Your Teaching

Culture Note

Since many Spanish-speaking countries have an evening class schedule (in addition to a day schedule), most evening school students will do their homework in the morning. Ask students to imagine doing their homework at 8:00 A.M., instead of later in the day. What advantages and disadvantages are there?

Teacher-to-Teacher

Provide pairs of students two very similar pictures of a classroom but with five or six differences. Without looking at each other's pictures, have the students ask one another questions about the objects and their locations until they have identified all the differences.

EXPLORACIÓN DEL LENGUAJE

Standards: 4.1

Suggestions: Demonstrate the *¡Ojo!* gesture. Have students discuss what kinds of gestures they use to communicate or are familiar with. Do different age groups have different types of body language? Are there different types of body language to indicate different relationships between people?

CULTURA

Standards: 2.1, 4.2

Suggestions: Have students look at the picture. Ask them to discuss the advantages and disadvantages of uniforms. Remind them about the insignias on the chapter opener photo.

Answers will vary.

8

Standards: 1.2, 1.3

Suggestions: Have students take notes and organize their answers to the questions at the beginning of the class period while you take attendance.

Answers will vary but will include:

1. La puerta está...
2. Hay un/una...al lado de la puerta.
3. *Sí / No* hay ventanas en la clase. Hay...ventana(s).
4. *Sí / No* hay un reloj en la clase. El reloj está...
5. Hay...escritorios y...sillas.
6. Hay...

Standards: 1.2, 1.3

Expansion: This activity can be used to create a written presentation.

Additional Resources

📶 **Technology: Online Resources**
Print
- Teacher's Resource Materials: Audio Script
- Technology: Audio Cap. 2B
- Communication Activities: Audio Act. 6

Assessment

Prueba 2B-2 with Remediation (online only)
Quiz: Vocabulary Production
- Prueba 2B-2

Exploración del lenguaje ⟨ Language through gestures

In Spanish, just as in English, nonverbal body language in the form of gestures, or *gestos*, is very important to communication.

Do you know the expression *¡Ojo!*? The word literally means "eye," but it is used to mean "be careful" or "pay attention." It is usually accompanied by a gesture, and often people use the *¡Ojo!* gesture without saying the word.

- Can you show other gestures that are used to communicate? What do they mean?

CULTURA ⟨ El mundo hispano

School uniforms Many schools in Spanish-speaking countries require their students to wear uniforms. Often students wear a full uniform, like the ones you see in the photo. Sometimes the uniform consists of something more like a smock that is worn over a student's regular clothes and helps protect them from becoming dirty or torn during the school day.

Pre-AP Integration: Education Communities How does wearing a uniform affect a person's connection to a school community as compared to not wearing a uniform?

Estudiantes durante el descanso
Santa Clara, Cuba ▶

8

Y tú, ¿qué dices?

🎤 ESCRIBIR/HABLAR   Describe your classroom and the objects in it. Use the questions as a guide. Write the description or present orally to the class.

✏️
1. ¿Dónde está la puerta?
2. ¿Qué hay al lado de la puerta?
3. ¿Hay ventanas en la clase? ¿Cuántas?
4. ¿Hay un reloj en la clase? ¿Dónde está?
5. ¿Cuántos escritorios y sillas hay?
6. ¿Qué más *(What else)* hay?

106 ciento seis • Tema 2 • La escuela

Differentiated Instruction

Students with Learning Difficulties

From time to time, allow students to refer to the vocabulary section of their notebooks when doing activities that require memorization. For *Gramática,* have them write all forms of **estar** into their grammar notebook section. Understanding and mastering verb forms can prove difficult and may require numerous reinforcement exercises.

Heritage Speakers

Have students make a list of appropriate gestures used in Spanish-speaking communities. Then have them compare these with body language used by people in the United States.

Gramática

> **OBJECTIVES**
> ▸ Write about and discuss the location of people and things
> ▸ Listen to a description of the position of people in a photo
> ▸ Compare prices for backpacks in Spanish-speaking countries

Go **Online** to practice
PearsonSchool.com/Autentico
PEARSON realize
WRITING   VIDEO   SPEAK/RECORD

Interpersonal   2B

The verb *estar*

The *-ar* verbs you have used until now are called **regular verbs** because they follow a regular pattern. Verbs that do not follow a regular pattern are called **irregular verbs.**

Estar is irregular because the *yo* form doesn't follow a regular pattern and because the forms *estás, está,* and *están* require accent marks.

Use *estar* to tell how someone feels or where someone or something is located.

> **¿Recuerdas?**
> You have used the verb *estar* to ask how someone is.
> ¿Cómo **estás**?
> ¿Cómo **está** Ud.?

(yo)	est**oy**	(nosotros) (nosotras)	est**amos**
(tú)	est**ás**	(vosotros) (vosotras)	est**áis**
Ud. (él) (ella)	est**á**	Uds. (ellos) (ellas)	est**án**

> **Más recursos**   ONLINE
> ▶ *GramActiva* Video
> ▶ Tutorial: *Estar*
> ▶ Animated Verbs
> ✎ *GramActiva* Activity

9

¡Hola! ¿Cómo estás?

✎ ESCRIBIR Write the correct forms of *estar* on a separate sheet of paper.

Marcos: ¡Buenos días! ¿Cómo __1.__ Uds.?

Paula y Roberta: ¡Hola, Marcos! Nosotras __2.__ bien, gracias. ¿Y tú?

Marcos: __3.__ muy bien. ¿Dónde __4.__ Pedro y Juana?

Roberta: Pedro __5.__ en la sala de clases. Juana __6.__ en la oficina.

10

¿En qué clase están?

🎤 HABLAR EN PAREJA Take turns with a partner to give the correct forms of *estar* as you tell what class each person is in.

Modelo
Ella
Ella está en la clase de tecnología.

1. yo

2. los profesores

3. la profesora

4. nosotros

5. ella

6. tú

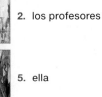

Enrich Your Teaching

Challenge/Pre-AP®

Demonstrate how important body language can be by telling students a story using only Spanish. Even though students don't have the vocabulary or grammar to understand the entire story, use gestures to help them. For example: *¡Vamos! Ya es tarde* (point to your watch impatiently) *y tengo hambre* (rub your stomach). *Tengo ganas de comer* (place your fingertips together and bring your hand up close to your mouth. Repeat the motion several times). See p. 442 for more gestures.

Gramática

Standards: 4.1

Resources: Teacher's Resource Materials: Video Script; Technology: Video Cap. 2B

Suggestions: Direct attention to the *¿Recuerdas?* Point out additional examples of *estar* that students have encountered. Show the *GramActiva* Video to reinforce the presentation. Ask questions for each verb form: *¿Cómo estás? Yo estoy muy bien. ¿Cómo está(n) usted(es)?* Be sure students notice the accents, and that they understand the importance of including them when writing.

Technology: Interactive Whiteboard

Grammar Activities 2B Use the whiteboard activities in your Teacher Resources as you progress through the grammar practice with your class.

9

Standards: 1.2

Suggestions: Have students read the exercise before answering and identify the subject of each statement. Have volunteers perform the dialogue.

Answers:

1. están
2. estamos
3. Estoy
4. están
5. está
6. está

10

Standards: 1.1

Recycle: Names of classes

Suggestions: Review the school subjects before students begin the activity.

Answers:

1. (Yo) estoy en la clase de español.
2. Los profesores están en la clase de ciencias naturales.
3. La profesora está en la clase de matemáticas.
4. Nosotros estamos en la clase de inglés.
5. Ella está en la clase de arte.
6. Tú estás en la clase de educación física.

Extension: Use names of students in some of the sentences to practice matching subject pronouns and names.

Starter Activity

Go around the room and have students state where they are in relation to another student or a classroom object. Example: *Yo estoy al lado de la ventana.*

11
Standards: 1.2

Resources: Teacher's Resource Materials: Audio Script; Technology: Audio Cap. 2B

Suggestions: Have students examine the photograph, saying the names of the people, indicating what they are doing, and identifying objects that appear. Allow students to listen more than once.

Technology: Audio Script and Answers

1. Yo estoy detrás de Sara. *(cierto)*
2. El señor Salas está debajo del escritorio. *(falso)*
3. Julián y Mateo están delante de Rosa. *(falso)*
4. Sara y yo estamos al lado del escritorio. *(cierto)*
5. José y Lucita están encima del escritorio. *(cierto)*
6. Benito está delante del señor Salas. *(cierto)*

12
Standards: 1.1

Suggestions: Be sure students understand that they are describing locations from Javier's perspective.

Answers will vary but may include:

1. Julián y Mateo están detrás de Rosa.
2. Rosa está al lado del escritorio.
3. Sara está delante de mí.
4. Yo estoy detrás de Sara.
5. El Sr. Salas está delante del escritorio.
6. Lucita y José están encima del escritorio.
7. Benito está delante del escritorio.
8. Sara y yo estamos a la izquierda del escritorio.

Active Classroom

Have students stand in two facing lines. The first student in Group A will name a person or people, such as **Carmen y Mateo.** The first student in Group B will answer with **Ellos están.** Tally points on the board.

11
¿Cierto o falso?

ESCUCHAR Write the numbers 1–6 on a sheet of paper. Listen to the statements about Javier's Spanish club photo and write *cierto* or *falso* based on the key details provided as you view the photograph from *your* perspective.

12
¿Y dónde están todos?

HABLAR EN PAREJA Work with a partner. Using the club picture above, find out where the various students are located from *Javier's* perspective. Follow the model.

▶ **Videomodelo**
A —*¿Y dónde está* **Lucita***?*
B —*Lucita está* **encima del escritorio***.*

1. Julián y Mateo	5. el Sr. Salas
2. Rosa	6. Lucita y José
3. Sara	7. Benito
4. yo	8. Sara y yo

108 ciento ocho • Tema 2 • La escuela

Differentiated Instruction

Heritage Speakers

Have students bring in photographs. Ask them to break into small groups to describe the location of people and things in the photos. Encourage students to indicate location by using **estar** and vocabulary they have learned.

Special Needs

Some students may have difficulty visualizing spatial relationships from a photo. Bring in small dolls, name them, and place them in order in front of the student. This will make the relationships more concrete.

13

Juego

ESCRIBIR, HABLAR EN PAREJA Work with a partner. Write down the name of someone in the classroom. Your partner can ask only *sí / no* questions to find out the name. When your partner has guessed the mystery student's identity, change roles.

Videomodelo

A —*¿Es una estudiante?*
B —*Sí.*
A —*¿Está al lado de Tomás?*
B —*No.*
A —*¿Está detrás de mí?*
B —*Sí.*
A —*¿Es Patricia?*
B —*Sí.*

> **Para decir más . . .**
> **detrás de mí** = behind me
> **detrás de ti** = behind you

14

Los precios de mochilas

LEER, ESCRIBIR

Conexiones ‹ **Las matemáticas**

Most countries have their own currencies. In Mexico, people pay for their purchases in *pesos,* in Peru they use *nuevos soles,* and so on. The value of each currency can go up or down daily in relation to other countries' currencies. For example, a dollar might be worth 10 Mexican *pesos* one day and 11 *pesos* the following day. Read the prices for una *mochila* in six different countries.

1. How much does a typical *mochila* cost in your community?

2. Convert the prices for *una mochila* into dollars. You can find a currency converter on the Internet.

3. How do these prices compare to those in your community? Why might the same item have different values in different countries?

Los precios de mochilas en el mundo hispano	
País	**Precio**
España	24 euros
Perú	80 nuevos soles
Puerto Rico	25 dólares
México	425 pesos
Venezuela	110 bolívares fuertes
Guatemala	200 quetzales

Capítulo 2B • ciento nueve **109**

Enrich Your Teaching

Culture Note

The official currency of Venezuela, the **bolívar,** is named after Simón Bolívar, the "Great Liberator." The **quetzal,** the official unit of money in Guatemala, is named after a rare, exotic bird found only in Central American rain forests. Have students research these and other currencies to see what they look like.

21st Century Skills

ICT Literacy If students do research on the Internet for *Actividad* 14, remind them that the Web sites they use should be compared and evaluated to find those that have the best and most accurate information, and the best, most accessible design.

Starter Activity

Ask students to use their Classroom Layout from the Project-Based Learning on p. 99 to quickly review location of classroom objects. Instead of having students write sentences, you may want to have them say where the object is.

13

Standards: 1.1

Suggestions: Point out the *Para decir más...* and demonstrate the words. Model the questions before students begin.

Answers will vary but may include:

al lado de, delante de, detrás de.

14

Standards: 3.1

Suggestions: Bring in prices of other school supplies that you've found on the Internet (or have students do a search themselves) to reinforce the concept that items not only have different prices but different values in various countries.

Answers will vary.

Additional Resources

Technology: Online Resources
- Instant Check
- Guided, Core, Video, Audio
- *Para hispanohablantes*
- Teacher's Resource Materials: Audio Script
- Technology: Audio Cap. 2B
- Communication Activities: Audio Act. 7
Print
- Guided WB pp. 77–78
- Core WB p. 44

Assessment

Prueba 2B-3 with Remediation (online only)
Quiz: The verb *estar*
- Prueba 2B-3

Gramática

Standards: 4.1

Resources: Teacher's Resource Materials: Video Script; Technology: Video Cap. 2B

Suggestions: Direct attention to the *¿Recuerdas?* Show the *GramActiva* Video to reinforce the presentation. **Unos / unas** is difficult for many English speakers to grasp, so you will want to give additional examples.

Technology: Interactive Whiteboard

Grammar Activities 2B Use the whiteboard activities in your Teacher Resources as you progress through the grammar practice with your class.

15

Standards: 1.2

Recycle: School vocabulary

Suggestions: Encourage students to try chanting the singular and then the plural with a rap-like cadence to make the pattern second-nature: **el cuaderno, los cuadernos, la bandera, las banderas,** etc. Then have them go back and forth between definite and indefinite articles.

Answers:

1. los cuadernos
2. las banderas
3. las papeleras
4. los profesores
5. unas clases
6. unas mochilas
7. unos escritorios
8. unos pupitres

16

Standards: 1.2, 1.3

Recycle: School supplies

Suggestions: Encourage students to work together to select the appropriate articles before they carry on the conversation. Be sure they use the definite article in all cases.

Answers:

1. los	**3.** los	**5.** la	**7.** los	**9.** la
2. la	**4.** los	**6.** las	**8.** las	**10.** las

Extension: Have students create their own dialogues based on real objects.

Gramática

OBJECTIVES
▸ Identify and describe the location of objects around school
▸ Exchange information about the location of things in a classroom

The plurals of nouns and articles

To make nouns plural you usually add -s to words ending in a vowel and -es to words ending in a consonant.

silla → sillas   teclado → teclados   cartel → carteles

Singular nouns that end in *z* change the *z* to *c* in the plural.

el lápiz → los lápices

The plural definite articles are *los* and *las*. Like *el* and *la*, they both mean "the."

las sillas → *the chairs*

The plural indefinite articles are *unos* and *unas*. They both mean "some" or "a few."

unos carteles → *some posters*

Singular		Plural	
el reloj	**la** ventana	**los** reloj**es**	**las** ventana**s**
un cuaderno **una** mesa		**unos** cuaderno**s** **unas** mesa**s**	

¿Recuerdas?
You have used definite and indefinite articles in the singular:
el, la = the
un, una = a, an

Más recursos ONLINE

▶ *GramActiva* Video
▶ **Tutorials:** Noun-adjective agreement, Singular plural formation
🔊 *Canción de hip hop: ¿Qué hay?*
✎ *GramActiva* Activity

15

Palabras plurales

✎ **ESCRIBIR** Write the plural forms of the articles and nouns below.

1. el cuaderno
2. la bandera
3. la papelera
4. el profesor
5. una clase
6. una mochila
7. un escritorio
8. un pupitre

16

¡A estudiar!

✎ **LEER, ESCRIBIR, HABLAR EN PAREJA** Marta and Berta are getting ready for school. Read the dialogue with a partner and fill in the blanks with the correct definite articles.

Marta: ¿Dónde están __1.__ lápices?

Berta: Aquí están, en __2.__ mochila.

Marta: ¿Y tienes __3.__ bolígrafos y __4.__ libros?

Berta: No. Están allí, encima de __5.__ mesa, debajo de __6.__ ventanas.

Marta: Ah, sí. ¿Y __7.__ cuadernos y __8.__ carpetas? ¿Dónde están?

Berta: Están encima de __9.__ mesa, detrás de __10.__ computadoras.

Differentiated Instruction

Students with Learning Difficulties

Provide students with a two-column graphic organizer. Have them write examples of singular nouns in one column and the corresponding plural forms in the next. Have them record this information in their grammar notebook section. Provide numerous examples of situations in which **el, la, los,** and **las** are used.

Bodily/Kinesthetic Learner

Have students prepare a short dialogue in which they ask a parent to help them find their things before they leave for school. Then have students present their dialogues to the class.

17

Más palabras plurales

ESCUCHAR, HABLAR You will hear eight words. Say the plural form of each word as you hear it.

Modelo
You will hear: *el libro*
You will say: *los libros*

18

Es el cuaderno de . . .

HABLAR EN GRUPO Describe an object and its location orally to a group. Work in groups of four. Each of you should choose a classroom object you have brought to class. Show your group your object. Your teacher will collect all the items, then place them in view in different parts of the classroom. Ask your group where your object is. Take turns until all objects and their location have been described.

> **Nota**
> In Spanish, you express possession by using *de* and the name of the owner of the item.
> el escritorio **de** la profesora
> *the teacher's desk*

Videomodelo
A —*¿Dónde está mi calculadora?*
B —*Tu calculadora está debajo de la silla de Margarita.*

El español en el mundo del trabajo

School districts in the United States have many positions in which employees need to speak Spanish. For example, school counselors work with new students and parents from Spanish-speaking countries. Counselors help them set up schedules, talk about school policies, and answer questions. Both the parents and the new students feel much more comfortable when the counselor can communicate with them in Spanish.

* Does your district need employees who speak Spanish? In what other jobs within a school system would speaking Spanish be helpful?

Capítulo 2B • ciento once **111**

Enrich Your Teaching

Teacher-to-Teacher

Use the Clip Art from the *Teacher's Resource Materials* to create flashcards to practice articles and plurals. Some should show single objects. Others should show multiple copies of one object.

21st Century Skills

Collaboration Have students work in pairs to research online about jobs requiring Spanish in their community. Have the students develop a basic plan of study that would give them the qualifications they would need to be eligible for such jobs. After completing their research have them make a short presentation of their findings.

17

Standards: 1.2

Resources: Teacher's Resource Materials: Audio Script; Technology: Audio Cap. 2B

Suggestions: Play the audio or read the script and have the class respond with the appropriate plural.

Technology: Audio Script and Answers

1. la mesa *(las mesas)*
2. la ventana *(las ventanas)*
3. el escritorio *(los escritorios)*
4. la mochila *(las mochilas)*
5. el teclado *(los teclados)*
6. el reloj *(los relojes)*
7. la bandera *(las banderas)*
8. el estudiante *(los estudiantes)*

18

Standards: 1.1, 1.2

Suggestions: Be sure students don't volunteer anything of any value. Return all items to students before the end of the class period. Remind them of the *Nota* on p. 111.
Answers will vary.

El español en el mundo del trabajo

Standards: 5.1

Suggestions: Have school employees who speak Spanish in their jobs tell students about what they do and why Spanish is important.

Answers will vary but may include:

secretary, principal, teacher, nurse, social worker.

Project-Based Learning

Students can perform Step 4 at this point. Be sure they understand your corrections and suggestions. (For more information, see p. 72-b.)

19

Standards: 1.1, 1.2

Suggestions: Be sure students understand that they can choose among the options to create their questions.

Answers will vary.

Suggestions: Have students compare their classroom to the one in the picture. Or, bring in other photos of classrooms to have students describe.

20

Standards: 1.3

Suggestions: Assign this as homework. Students should list or outline what they want to talk about and some of the words they want to use.

Answers will vary.

Pre-AP® Integration

• **Learning Objective:** Interpersonal Writing
• **Activity 19:** Have students expand on their questions and answers to the activity by writing an email to one of the students in the picture asking for more details about their classroom, and about the class they are taking.
• **Pre-AP® Resource Materials:** Comprehensive guide to Pre-AP® writing skill development

Additional Resources

Technology: Online Resources
• Instant Check
• Guided, Core, Audio, Writing, Reading
• *Para hispanohablantes*
• Technology: Audio Cap. 2B
• Communication Activities: Audio Acts. 8–9
• Teacher's Resource Materials: Audio Script

Print
• Guided WB pp. 79–80
• Core WB pp. 45–46

Assessment

Prueba 2B-4 with Remediation (online only)
Quiz: The plural of nouns and articles
• Prueba 2B-4

19

Una clase de inglés

ESCRIBIR, HABLAR EN PAREJA Look at this picture of a high school class in Cuba.

1 Study the photograph and make a list in Spanish of items you can name.

2 Write two questions about the photograph, then ask your partner the questions. Use the models below.

Videomodelo

A —¿Cuántos estudiantes hay en la clase?
B —Hay seis estudiantes.
A —¿Hay banderas en la clase?
B —No, no hay banderas.

¿Qué es esto?	¿Quién está . . . ?
¿Cuántos(as) . . . hay?	¿Hay . . . ?
¿Dónde está(n) . . . ?	¿Qué hay

20

Y tú, ¿qué dices?

ESCRIBIR Look around your classroom and write five sentences to describe it.

Modelo
En mi clase de español hay 33 estudiantes. Hay 35 pupitres y un escritorio. El escritorio está delante de los pupitres. La computadora está encima del escritorio. No hay bandera en mi clase.

112 ciento doce • Tema 2 • La escuela

Differentiated Instruction

Students with Learning Difficulties

Students might need to use their vocabulary notebook section to do *Actividad* 19. You might need to modify *Actividad* 20, having students write three sentences, instead of five. For *Pronunciación,* have students put the rule for **g** in their grammar notebook section.

Challenge

Have students choose a Spanish-speaking country and research the educational system. They should include information about requirements for attendance, whether schools are primarily private or public, how schools are divided based on ages, and the country's literacy rate.

Communication 2B

Pronunciación › The letter *g*

In Spanish, the letter *g* sounds like *g* in "go" when it is followed by *a, o,* or *u,* although it often has a slightly softer sound than in English. Listen to and say the following words and sentences:

Gustavo	domin**go**	ten**go**
a**go**sto	pre**gu**nta	lue**go**
ami**go**	ar**go**llas	**ga**to

In Spanish, the letter *g* sounds like the letter *h* in "hot" when it is followed by *e* or *i.* Listen to and say the following words. Some of these words you have not yet heard or seen. Can you guess the meanings of the cognates?

inteli**ge**nte	**ge**neroso	**ge**neral
gimnasio	tecnolo**gí**a	biolo**gí**a

Try it out! See if you can guess how to pronounce the following Spanish first names. Keep in mind the pronunciation rules for the *g* sound.

Estudiantes en un gimnasio

Gabriela	Ángela	Gerardo
Gilberto	Gustavo	Rodrigo
Olga	Rogelio	Gregorio

CULTURA › El mundo hispano

School gyms are rare in Spanish-speaking countries. Students usually have physical education classes in the school's *patio*. High school students usually have P.E. one or two times a week, sometimes before or after regular school hours. School sports teams are also less common than in the United States.

Pre-AP Integration: Education and Careers What are some reasons that schools in Spanish-speaking countries might place less emphasis on physical education, sports, and gymnasiums?

Una clase de educación física de una escuela primaria, México ▶

Capítulo 2B • ciento trece **113**

Lectura

Standards: 1.2, 3.1

Suggestions

Pre-reading: Direct students' attention to the *Strategy.* Have students scan the reading for cognates and to tell what the main ideas are in this text. Ask students to take a good look at the illustrations and predict how they might relate to the reading.

Reading: Have students read the article, stopping to make note of the important information in each paragraph.Tell students to refer to their list of predictions as they read and make a checkmark next to each one that is mentioned in the article.

Post-reading: Invite students to share which of their predictions were mentioned in the article. Then have them complete the *¿Comprendes?* questions in class or as homework.

Starter Activity

Write these cognates on the board and ask students to tell what the English equivalent is:

dignidad   protección   dieta   familia

(**Answers:** dignity, protection, diet, family)

Active Classroom

Have students discuss the list of items that children in every nation should have. Do they feel these are privileges or necessities? Do they feel that these goals are being met where they live?

Lectura

OBJECTIVES
▶ Read about a United Nations program for children
▶ Make predictions about what you will read

Strategy
Predicting outcomes Think about what you would consider to be basic rights for children around the world. Jot down four of them on a piece of paper. As you read the article, see if your ideas are included.

Lee este artículo sobre UNICEF.

UNICEF y una convención para los niños[1]

¿Sabes que es un privilegio estar en una escuela, tener una mochila con libros, unos lápices, una calculadora, unas hojas de papel y un profesor bueno? En ciertas[2] naciones, ir a la escuela es difícil o no es posible.

UNICEF es la organización internacional de las Naciones Unidas que trabaja para los niños. UNICEF es una sigla[3] inglesa que significa "Fondo Internacional de Emergencia de las Naciones Unidas para los Niños". Tiene siete oficinas regionales en diversas naciones y un Centro de Investigaciones en Italia. El 20 de noviembre de 1989, la Organización de las Naciones Unidas escribió[4] "una convención para los niños" en inglés, árabe, chino, ruso y francés.

[1]children [2]some [3]acronym [4]wrote

114 ciento catorce • Tema 2 • La escuela

Differentiated Instruction

Students with Learning Difficulties

Point out the *Strategy* and provide examples of the concept of "basic rights." Before reading, go through *¿Comprendes?* highlighting key words and phrases. Students might need to read through passage a number of times to comprehend information. Doing guided reading with students may be useful.

Challenge

Have students research other organizations that provide aid to children. Can they find information in Spanish about the organizations? Have them bring in examples to share with the class.

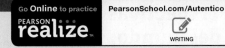

Go **Online** to practice   **PearsonSchool.com/Autentico**

PEARSON realize™

WRITING

Esta convención dice que[5] los niños de todas[6] las naciones necesitan:

- dignidad
- una casa
- protección
- una buena dieta
- la práctica de deportes
- atención especial para los niños con problemas físicos
- amor y la comprensión de la familia
- expresar sus opiniones
- una comunidad sin[7] violencia
- ir a la escuela para ser inteligentes y sociables

[5]says that [6]all [7]without

¿Comprendes?

1. Para los estudiantes de todas las naciones es fácil estar en una escuela y tener una mochila. ¿Cierto o falso?
2. ¿Cuántas oficinas regionales tiene UNICEF?
3. ¿Qué significa la sigla UNICEF?
4. ¿Dónde está el Centro de Investigaciones?
5. La convención es para los niños de todas las naciones. ¿Cierto o falso?
6. ¿Qué palabras clave indican cuatro cosas que necesitan todos los niños?

Capítulo 2B • ciento quince **115**

Enrich Your Teaching

Culture Note

UNICEF is a private, nonprofit organization supported by volunteers who help raise funds selling the well-known UNICEF greeting cards and conducting the "Trick or Treat for UNICEF" program. The agency seeks to generate understanding of the rights and needs of children everywhere. UNICEF helps children get the care they need as infants and encourages families to educate girls as well as boys. Funds are used to reduce infant deaths and illnesses and to protect children from war or natural disasters.

¿Comprendes?

Standards: 1.2, 1.3

Suggestions: Help students understand the questions that contain cognates and decodable words. Have students discuss the questions and answers in small groups.

Answers:

1. falso
2. siete
3. Fondo Internacional de Emergencia de las Naciones Unidas para los Niños (United Nations International Children's Emergency Fund).
4. El Centro de Investigaciones está en Italia.
5. cierto
6. Answers will vary but will include any of the items in the list on p. 115.

Pre-AP® Integration

- **Learning Objective:** Interpretive: Print
- **Activity:** Have students read each paragraph of the *Lectura* text silently. Pause after each paragraph to read teacher-made true/false statements.
- **Pre-AP® Resource Materials:** Comprehensive guide to Pre-AP® reading skill development

For Further Reading

Student Resource: *Para hispanohablantes, Lectura 2*

Additional Resources

Technology: Online Resources
- Guided, Writing, Reading
- Cultural Reading Activity
- *Para hispanohablantes*
- Communication Activities
Print
- Guided WB p. 97
- Literacy Skills WB

Perspectivas del mundo hispano

Standards: 2.1, 2.2, 4.2

Presentation: Have students vote about whether they spend too much time, too little time, or just the right amount of time in school. Tally the results on the board. Tell them that the school year in Spanish-speaking countries is usually longer than in the United States. Call attention to the graph. Point out the variations. Tell students that the way classes are run is different, too. Have volunteers read the bulleted items. Are there any that students find preferable to what they experience? Have students complete the *Comparación cultural.*

Suggestions: Most students will not like the idea of spending more time in school, but have them enumerate possible benefits to a longer school year. How would they like the added time spent? Ask how the rules might affect students and classes. Find out if students like the idea of wearing a uniform or having class lectures instead of class discussion, and why.

Direct attention to the *Investigar* section and have students discuss the questions.

Answers will vary.

Culture Note

In the United States it is common to use a letter grading system, where generally A = 90–100%, B = 80–90%, and so on. In the majority of Spanish-speaking countries, however, the grading system is generally based on the numbers 1–10, rather than on letter grades.

Teacher-to-Teacher

e-amigos: Have students e-mail descriptions of their Spanish classes to their *e-amigos.* Have them print out or e-mail you their messages.

Online Cultural Reading

Standards: 1.2

After doing the online activity, ask students to describe how the school supplies shown on the Web site seem similar to and different from the supplies you use or buy.

Additional Resources

🛜 **Technology: Online Resources**
- Cultural Reading Activity
- *Para hispanohablantes*

Perspectivas del mundo hispano

¿Cómo es la escuela?

Did you know that students in many Spanish-speaking countries spend more time in school than you do? The graph below shows the length of the school year in various countries.

School Facts You May Not Know

- In many schools, when a teacher enters the classroom, the students stand.
- The teacher may call the students by their last name.
- The students, on the other hand, are more likely to address their teacher simply as *maestro(a), profesor(a),* or just *profe,* without a last name.
- Class time is generally spent with the teacher lecturing rather than with class discussion.
- Many public and private schools require uniforms.

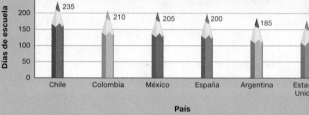

Días de escuela (vertical axis): 250, 200, 150, 100, 50, 0

Chile 235 | Colombia 210 | México 205 | España 200 | Argentina 185 | Estados Unidos

País

Comparación cultural Based on the information above, what might you assume are the attitudes toward school in Spanish-speaking cultures? How are these the same as or different from attitudes in your community? List five suggestions that might help an exchange student from Mexico City adjust to your school.

Investigar How are other schools in your area similar to or different from yours? How are they similar to or different from those in Spanish-speaking countries? Make a list of schools in your area and describe these similarities and differences. Are some schools more formal? Do students take classes that are different from the ones you take?

Online Cultural Reading

Go to PearsonSchool.com/Autentico ONLINE to read and understand a website selling school supplies.

Strategy: Scan the web page for categories and words you understand in order to find information you need.

Inténtalo: Demonstrate your understanding of the site by identifying the products you need for school and their cost.

Differentiated Instruction

Logical/Mathematical Learner

Have students find out about the length of the school day and year in a Spanish-speaking country not included in the graph. Ask them to compare their own curriculum with that of students of the same age in the country of their choice. Have them present this information to the class in the form of a graph.

Heritage Speakers

Some students may have gone to school in their heritage country. If so, ask them to tell what adjustments they found difficult when they came to school in the United States. Ask them to share what they prefer about each system.

Presentación escrita

OBJECTIVES
▶ Write a description of your classroom
▶ Make a sketch to remember ideas

Go **Online** to practice
PEARSON **realize**™

PearsonSchool.com/Autentico
✏ WRITING

Tu sala de clases

TASK Your pen pal from Mexico is coming to visit your school. Write him or her a note describing your Spanish classroom.

1 **Prewrite** Sketch your classroom, showing and labeling the items you intend to describe.

2 **Draft** Write the first draft of your note. Use your sketch to remember which items you want to describe and where they are. Use the model to organize your draft.

Modelo

En mi sala de clases hay cuatro ventanas. Mi pupitre está delante del escritorio de la profesora. La bandera está al lado de la puerta. Las computadoras están encima de la mesa.

3 **Revise** Check your note for correct spelling, as well as for the categories under Evaluation. Share your note with a partner, who will check for the following:

- Is your note easy to understand?
- Could you add other information?
- Are there any errors?

Rewrite your note making any necessary changes.

4 **Publish** Make a final copy of your note for display in the classroom or for your portfolio.

5 **Evaluation** The following rubric will be used to grade your note.

Strategy

Creating visuals Creating a sketch or a drawing can help you remember the things you want to write about in a description.

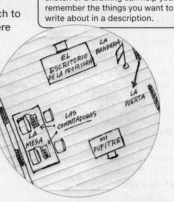

Rubric	Score 1	Score 3	Score 5
Use of newly acquired vocabulary	You use very little variation of vocabulary with frequent usage errors.	You use limited vocabulary with some usage errors.	You use an extended variety of vocabulary with very few usage errors.
Correct use of the verb *estar*	You use many repetitions of incorrect verb forms.	You use frequent repetitions of incorrect verb forms.	You use very few incorrect verb forms.
Amount of information	You provide information about two or fewer items in the classroom.	You provide information about three or fewer items in the classroom.	You provide information about four or more items in the classroom.

Enrich Your Teaching

Teacher-to-Teacher

Careers: *Tema 2* has focused on school and classes. Have students work in small groups to talk about a career as a Spanish teacher. Have them list words and expressions they have learned that would be helpful and share them.

21st Century Skills

ICT Literacy Help students conduct an Internet search to find photos and graphics to illustrate the items they describe in their notes. They can scan their sketches and devise ways to link visuals to them.

Presentación escrita

Standards: 1.3

Suggestions: Introduce the task to the class and then have them work through each step of the process. You may want to provide a model of a top-scoring note.

Digital Portfolio

Have students include their notes in their portfolios.

Pre-AP® Integration

- **Learning Objective:** Interpersonal Writing
- **Activity:** Have students convert their notes into e-mails to their pen pals in Mexico. Expand the task by asking students to include at least one question for the recipient of the communication.
- **Pre-AP® Resource Materials:** Comprehensive guide to Pre-AP® writing skill development

Teacher-to-Teacher

Pen pal Web sites serve to connect pen pals from different countries; some are geared for classrooms and students. Find out about setting students up with pen pals through school or home computers. You may contact a school in a Spanish-speaking city and set up a "sister" class for exchanging letters through regular mail service.

Additional Resources

🔊 **Technology: Online Resources**
- Guided
- *Para hispanohablantes*

Print
- Guided WB pp. 82

Self Assessment

Presentación escrita
- **Assessment Program:** Rubrics

Review the rubric with students. Go over the descriptions of the different levels of performance. After assessing students, help individuals understand how their performance could be improved. (See Teacher's Resource Materials for suggestions on using rubrics in assessment.)

Auténtico

Standards: 1.2, 1.3

Resources: *Authentic Resources Wkbk*, Cap. 2B
Authentic Resources: Cap 2B Videoscript
AP Theme: *Las familias y las comunidades: Las comunidades educativas*

Before You Watch

Discuss the *Strategy* with students. Have them use the words from the chapter vocabulary to identify possible study tips. Ask them to discuss tips they might expect to hear in English. Then review the key vocabulary with the class. Again, have students predict the kinds of tips they might see in the video, using the key vocabulary and image in their text. Note these tips on the board.

Technology: Watch the Video

Before starting the video, direct students' attention to the *Mientras ves* activity. Compare their answers in the activities to the discussions they had previously, anticipating study tips. Add any new tips to the board.

Play the video once completely through, without pausing, and tell students to watch for the tips and key words they discussed in the video. Remind students that they will not understand every word, but that they should listen and watch for overall understanding. Replay the video, stopping as necessary for students to complete the listening activity and to check comprehension. Show the video a final time without pausing.

Auténtico

Partnered with **NBC LEARN**

Vencer las molestias de la tarea

Before You Watch

Use the Strategy: Anticipate

The video provides homework tips to parents. Use information that you know to anticipate what the study tips might be in Spanish. Also review Spanish key words related to school you have already learned.

Read this Key Vocabulary

vencer = overcome   **la habitación** = bedroom
la molestia = annoyance   **mejor** = best
los consejos = tips   **el esfuerzo** = effort
el lugar = place
concentrarse = to concentrate

▶ Watch the Video

Think about the challenges you face while doing your homework. What tips *(consejos)* does the speaker give parents so they can help their children with homework?

Go to **PearsonSchool.com/Autentico** and watch the video *Vencer las molestias de la tarea* to learn about homework tips.

Complete the Activities

Mientras ves As you watch the video, indicate which of the following words are included and note which kind of tip they support in the video. Write a three column chart with the heads: *Lugar / Concentrarse / Rutina*, to organize the words you hear.

calculadora   bolígrafos
escuela   tarea
lápices   tiempo
escritorio   hablar por teléfono
mesa   les gusta

Differentiated Instruction

Logical/Mathematical Learner

Have students create a chart with categories based on their school day schedule, looking up any words they don't know. Then, have students organize the vocabulary words within the chart. Have them identify which vocabulary words fall under more than one category and which words don't seem to fit any of their categories.

Heritage Speakers

Ask students to write a paragraph describing their own homework routines, using as much chapter vocabulary as possible. Ask them to include what guidance they would like to receive in their Spanish homework from Spanish speakers in their lives, such as parents, guardians, or older siblings. Have students edit each other's work for spelling and vocabulary usage.

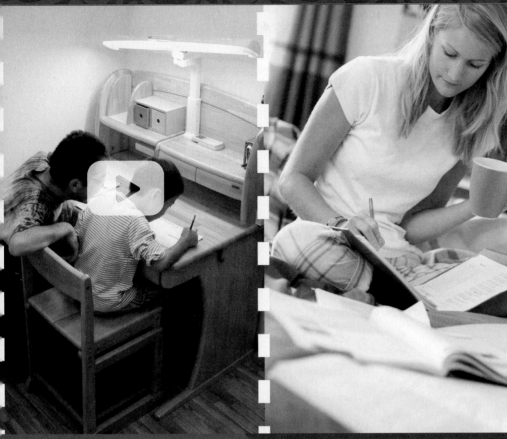

Integration

Después de ver Review the video as needed to answer the following questions.

1. According to the video, what do students need to have nearby before they start their homework?

2. What time management tips can you understand from the video?

3. In the final scene, the word *perseverancia* appears. What might perseverance have to do with overcoming the *molestias de la tarea*?

📖 **For more activities, go to the *Authentic Resources Workbook*.**

Las escuelas en Latinoamérica

Expansión Find other authentic resources in *Auténtico* online, then answer the question.

📁 **2B Auténtico**

Integración de ideas The authentic resources present information about studying in Spanish-speaking countries. Write a sentence to describe an aspect of education that you find interesting.

Comparación cultural Write about the similarities and differences of education as compared to your own experience.

Complete the Activities

Mientras ves

Standards: 1.2

Confirm that students have checked off the words and have organized them in to the chart. Discuss each subcategory for comprehension, and have students add their own ideas (using vocab words) to each category.

Answers:

Lugar	Concentrarse	Rutina
escritorio	calculadora	les gusta
mesa	bolígrafos	tarea
tarea	lápices	tiempo
	hablar por teléfono	escuela
	tarea	

Después de ver

Standards: 1.2, 1.3

Students' answers may vary based on their comprehension. Review school supply and routine words with students. Ask students to discuss their own homework routines, work places, and supplies in Spanish.

Answers:

1. Tener en mano lápices, bolígrafos, y calculadoras (útiles escolares) / Have pencils, pens, and calculators on hand.
2. Eliminate distractions and establish a routine
3. *Answers will vary.*

For more Authentic Resources: Assign the *Authentic Resources Workbook* activities for homework, so that students can play the video on their own and complete the workbook activities at their own pace.

Pre-AP® Integration

Standards: 1.2, 1.3

Resources: *Authentic Resources Workbook,* Cap. 2B; Authentic
Resources: Cap 2B; Videoscript

Suggestions: Before completing the Pre-AP® activity, have students go to the workbook and complete the worksheets for these two additional resources.

Enrich Your Teaching

Culture Note

In many Latin American countries, the school day is divided into sessions or shifts to accommodate more students in a single facility. Many public schools require their students to wear uniforms, and use a numbered grading system of either 1-10 or 1-20.

Perspectivas: What might an English class look like in a Spanish-speaking country?

Using Authentic Resources

Using the authentic resources and the chapter vocabulary, have students create a class schedule based on what they have learned about the school day in Spanish-speaking countries.

Review Activities

To talk about classroom items: Point to classroom items and have students identify them by name. Call on volunteers to tell what vocabulary items are not in their classroom. For example: *En la sala de clase hay una mesa pero no hay un sacapuntas.*

To talk about classroom furniture: Have students make a list of the furniture that can be in a classroom. Have Student A point to a specific piece of furniture and have Student B say what it is. For example, *¿Es una mesa? No. Es una silla.*

To talk about parts of a classroom and to indicate location: Using the list created above, have students work in pairs, asking and telling where different items are located relative to the parts of the classroom. For example: *¿Dónde está el escritorio? Está al lado (debajo de) la ventana.*

To indicate possession, to identify (description, quantity) and **to identify gender and quantity of nouns:** Have students work in groups. Tell them to put several classroom objects in front of them. Have Student A point to an item and ask what it is and Student B will name the item and say whose it is. For example, *¿Qué es esto? Es una calculadora; es tu calculadora.*

Estar: Ask volunteers to give the forms of **estar** by briefly reviewing the stem and verb endings. You may want them to create sentences for each form.

Digital Portfolio

Invite students to review the activities they completed in this chapter, including written reports, posters or other visuals, and recordings of oral presentations, or other projects. Have them select one or two items that they feel best demonstrate their achievements in Spanish to include in their digital portfolios. Have them include this with the Chapter Checklist and Self-Assessment Worksheet.

Additional Resources

Technology: Online Resources
- Instant Check
- Integrated Performance Assessment
- *Para hispanohablantes*

Print
- Core WB pp. 45–46

Teacher Resources
- Teacher's Resource Materials: Situation Cards, Clip Art
- Assessment Program: Chapter Checklist and Self-Assessment Worksheet

---

Repaso del capítulo

OBJECTIVES
- Review the vocabulary and grammar
- Demonstrate you can perform the tasks on p. 121

🔊 Vocabulario

to talk about classroom items

la bandera	flag
el cartel	poster
la computadora	computer
la mochila	bookbag, backpack
la pantalla	(computer) screen
la papelera	wastepaper basket
el ratón	(computer) mouse
el reloj	clock
el sacapuntas	pencil sharpener
el teclado	(computer) keyboard

to talk about classroom furniture

el escritorio	desk
la mesa	table
la silla	chair

to talk about parts of a classroom

la puerta	door
la ventana	window

to indicate location

al lado de la / del	next to, beside
allí	there
aquí	here
debajo de la / del	underneath
delante de la / del	in front of
detrás de la / del	behind
¿Dónde?	Where?
en	in, on
encima de la / del	on top of

For *Vocabulario adicional*, see pp. 472–473.

to indicate possession

de	of
mi	my
tu	your

to identify (description, quantity)

Es un(a) . . .	It's a . . .
Hay	There is, There are
¿Qué es esto?	What is this?

Gramática

estar *to be*

estoy	estamos
estás	estáis
está	están

to identify gender and quantity of nouns

los, las	the
unos, unas	some

Differentiated Instruction

Students with Learning Difficulties

Have students review the *Repaso del capítulo* and create flashcards for any words that they do not know. Pair them with a student who is more confident with the vocabulary to practice. Before the test, provide students with a practice test, so they can become comfortable with the format.

Heritage Speakers

Have students write a few paragraphs telling about the classroom of their favorite class: What things are in the classroom? Where is their desk? Where is the teacher's desk? Where are the computers, posters, etc.? Encourage them to use as many vocabulary words from this chapter as they can.

Preparación para el examen

What you need to be able to do for the exam . . .	Here are practice tasks similar to those you will find on the exam . . .	For review go to your print or digital textbook . . .
Interpretive		
① ESCUCHAR I can listen to and identify classrooms and locations.	Listen as a student frantically asks some of his friends where he left his homework. Can you identify all of the classrooms and places they suggest that he look?	**pp. 100–103** *Vocabulario en contexto* **p. 105** *Actividades 6–7* **p. 111** *Actividad 18*
Interpersonal		
② HABLAR, ESCRIBIR I can talk or write about where someone is located by describing where that person is in relation to objects in the classroom.	You are trying to find out the name of someone in your class. You ask the person next to you, but he doesn't understand whom you are talking about. Give at least three statements that would help him identify the person. You might include where he or she is in relation to the teacher's desk, the window, someone else's desk, and so on.	**pp. 100–103** *Vocabulario en contexto* **p. 105** *Actividades 6–7* **p. 108** *Actividades 11–12* **p. 109** *Actividad 13* **p. 111** *Actividad 18*
Interpretive		
③ LEER I can read and understand a letter that contains questions and concerns about school issues.	The school counselor has asked you to help him read a note written by a new Spanish-speaking student at school. After reading it, tell the counselor what the problem is and the kinds of questions the student asks. **Necesito una clase para la primera hora. ¿Cómo es la clase de tecnología, fácil o difícil? ¿Qué necesito para la clase? ¿Cuántos estudiantes hay en la clase? ¿Hay mucha tarea?**	**pp. 100–103** *Vocabulario en contexto* **p. 112** *Actividad 19* **p. 114** *Lectura*
Presentational		
④ ESCRIBIR I can write an email to a friend about one of her classes.	You have just moved to a new town and are sending an e-mail to a friend from your old school. You have lots of questions about her classes. Write at least three questions about one of her classes: whether she likes it, how many students are in it, where her desk is in the room, what else is in the room, etc.	**pp. 100–103** *Vocabulario en contexto* **p. 112** *Actividad 19*
Cultures		
⑤ COMPARAR I can demonstrate an understanding of cultural differences in schools.	Think about how students and teachers interact within a typical classroom in a Spanish-speaking country. What are at least four things you might find different from most schools in the United States?	**p. 106** *Fondo cultural* **p. 113** *Fondo cultural* **p. 116** *Perspectivas del mundo hispano*

Capítulo 2B • ciento veintiuno **121**

Differentiated Assessment

Core Assessment
- Assessment Program: Examen del capítulo 2B
- Technology: Audio Cap. 2B
- ExamView: Chapter Test, Test Banks A and B

Challenge/Pre-AP®
- ExamView: Pre-AP® Test Bank
- Pre-AP® Resource Materials

Extra Support
- Alternate Assessment Program: Examen del capítulo 2B
- Technology: Audio Cap. 2B

Heritage Speakers
- Assessment Program: *Para hispanohablantes*: Examen del capítulo 2B
- ExamView: Heritage Learner Test Bank

Performance Tasks

Standards: 1.1, 1.2, 1.3, 4.2

Student Resource: *Para hispanohablantes*
Teacher Resources: Teacher's Resource Materials: Audio Script; Technology: Audio Cap. 2B

1. Escuchar

Suggestions: Play the audio or read the script.

Script:

Juan: ¡Ay! Mi tarea...¿Dónde está? Necesito mi tarea para la clase de matemáticas. Ana, ¿dónde está mi tarea?

Ana: ¿Tu tarea? Está en la clase de ciencias sociales, en el escritorio del profesor.

Juan: Gracias, Ana. ¡Ay! No está aquí. Daniel, ¿dónde está mi tarea de matemáticas?

Daniel: Está en la clase de tecnología...al lado de la computadora.

Juan: Gracias.

Answers:

Clase de matemáticas, clase de ciencias sociales—en el escritorio del profesor, clase de tecnología—al lado de la computadora

2. Hablar

Suggestions: Pair students for this activity. Give them time to prepare before they speak.
Answers will vary.

3. Leer

Suggestions: If students have difficulty reading and understanding this note, refer them to the vocabulary list to study words they do not recognize.

4. Escribir

Suggestions: Have students try this activity without consulting the vocabulary list, notes, or completed activities.

5. Comparar

Suggestion: Encourage students to read the *Perspectivas del mundo hispano* and *Cultura* features to prepare for this task.

CAPÍTULO 3A

¿Desayuno o almuerzo?

Foods and beverages for breakfast and lunch

Vocabulary: foods; beverages; adverbs of frequency; expressions to show surprise

Grammar: present tense of *-er* and *-ir* verbs; *me gusta(n), me encanta(n)*

Cultural Perspectives: meals in the Spanish-speaking world

Auténtico: The Delectable Street Food of Mexico City

CAPÍTULO 3B

Para mantener la salud

Foods and beverages for dinner; food, health, and exercise choices

Vocabulary: food; beverages; expressions to discuss health and indicate preference, agreement, disagreement, and quantity; adjectives to describe food

Grammar: the plural of adjectives; the verb *ser*

Cultural Perspectives: opinions regarding diet and health

Auténtico: A Healthy Diet

Theme Support

Bulletin Boards

Theme: La comida

Ask students to download, cut out or copy photos of foods and beverages from around the world, people engaged in various forms of exercise, and recipes in Spanish. Cluster photos according to the following themes: healthy foods and beverages, unhealthy foods and beverages, exercise, and recipes.

Hands-on Culture

Recipe: Tortilla española

This popular dish from Spain can be eaten at breakfast, as an appetizer, or as a light supper.

Ingredients:

4 eggs	1 small onion	1/2 c. olive oil
3 potatoes	3/8 T. salt	

1. Scrub the potatoes and peel the onion. Slice the potatoes and onion.
2. In a frying pan, sauté the potatoes and onion in the olive oil until they are lightly browned. Add salt.
3. Beat the eggs thoroughly. Pour them over the potatoes and onion.
4. Cook the mixture over low heat for three to four minutes, until the eggs set.
5. Place a plate over the frying pan, and flip the **tortilla** onto the plate. Slide the **tortilla** back into the pan, the uncooked side down. Continue cooking over low heat for three to four minutes.
6. Place the **tortilla** on a serving plate and let it cool before serving.

Game

Categorías

This game is a timed relay race. Play it to review vocabulary before the Vocabulary production quiz.

Players: the entire class

Materials: paper, pens

Rules:

1. Arrange students' desks in five rows. Ask students to clear their desks. Give the first student in each row a sheet of paper and a pen.
2. Call out one of the following categories: **desayuno, almuerzo, cena, bebidas,** or **salud.** Tell students they have one minute to write as many words from the category as they can on their row's sheet of paper.
3. After you say **"empiecen,"** the first student in each row writes a word, then passes the paper and pen to the next student. That student writes another word, then passes it to the third student, and so on until the paper reaches the end of the row. The last student brings the paper to the first student and the relay begins again until you call time.
4. Rows exchange papers for correction. The team with the most words spelled correctly wins a point.
5. Continue play until all the categories have been completed. If there is a tie at the end of play, have students define each word on their row's list. The winner is the row that defines all words correctly first.

Variation: Have a relay spelling bee. Call out a vocabulary word or expression, and have each student in a row write one letter of the word.

21st Century Skills

Look for tips throughout *Tema 3* to enrich your teaching by integrating 21st Century Skills Cross-Disciplinary Standards. Suggestions for the Project-Based Learning and Theme Support follow below.

Project-Based Learning

Project Modify the Project-Based Learning with one or more of these suggestions:

ICT Literacy Beforehand, students should select several Web sites that provide accurate information about their resort. Knowing about climate, geography, and locally-grown foods will help them craft their Web page.

Information Literacy Have students think about their audience. Is the Web page aimed at a specific age group, or at people in a challenging situation? How will factors such as age affect the material included and the language used?

ICT Literacy Encourage students to think outside the box when planning their Web pages. They can, for example, create a Web page that combines different kinds of media: text, photos, video. The more creative the presentation of the material, the more appealing it will be to different audiences.

Theme Culture

Social and Cross-Cultural Skills

Have students review the *Cultura* on page 134 and then plan a public service announcement about the importance of breakfast. Have them devise a slogan and include food examples from traditional breakfasts in the United States and from the Spanish-speaking world.

▶ **Videocultura** View *El maíz: comida esencial* with the class to find out how corn is prepared in Spanish-speaking countries.

Project-Based Learning

Para la salud: Vacaciones

Overview: Students create a Web page describing a day at a health resort. The Web page includes a schedule of the day's activities and descriptions of breakfast, lunch, and dinner with photos or drawings of each meal and one of the activities. Students present the Web pages to the class as if they were sales representatives from the resort.

Resources: Internet access, Web page creation tools

Sequence: (suggestions for when to do each step are found throughout the chapters)

3A **Step 1.** Review instructions so students know what is expected of them. Hand out the Theme 3 Project-Based Learning Instructions and the rubric.

Step 2. Students submit a rough draft of their Web page. Give students your feedback and your suggestions. For vocabulary and grammar practice, ask students to partner and present their drafts to each other.

Step 3. Students design their Web page. Encourage students to try different design templates and different styles of writing for the content of the Web page.

3B **Step 4.** Students submit a draft of their meal descriptions and schedule. Note your corrections and suggestions.

Step 5. Students complete and present their Web page to the class, trying to "sell" their health package to classmates.

Options

1. Students design a one-week lunch plan for the school cafeteria. Suggest that students use the U.S. Department of Agriculture's ChooseMyPlate Web site as a resource.
2. Students create a diet and exercise guide for someone wanting to get in shape.

Assessment

Here is a detailed rubric for assessing this project:

Theme 3 Project: Para la salud: Vacaciones

Rubric	Score 1	Score 3	Score 5
Evidence of Planning	You provided no written draft or design plan.	Your draft was written and the design planned, but not corrected.	You corrected your draft text and design plan.
Your use of visuals	You included no visuals.	You included photos / visuals, but your page design was unorganized.	Your Web page was easy to read, complete, and accurate.
Your presentation	You included little of the required information for the Web page and made no attempt to "sell" the product.	You included most of the required information for the Web page and made some attempt to "sell" the product.	You included all of the required information for the Web page and tried to "sell" the product.

AT A GLANCE

Objectives
- Listen to and read descriptions of meals and menus
- Talk and write about foods you and others like and dislike
- Exchange information about food preferences
- Identify cultural practices viewed in an authentic video about food
- Trace the history of some foods originally native to the Americas and Europe

Vocabulary
- Foods and beverages for breakfast and lunch
- Expressions of frequency

Grammar
- Present tense of *-er* and *-ir* verbs
- *Me gustan, me encantan*

Culture
- Bartolomé Murillo, p. 123
- Fruits and vegetables from the Americas, p. 131
- Typical breakfasts in Spanish-speaking countries, p. 134
- Fruits imported from Chile, p. 139
- Popular snacks in Spanish-speaking countries, p. 140.

Recycle
- Present tense of *-ar* verbs
- Expressions of agreement and disagreement

Authentic Resources
- Video about the rich variety of street foods in Mexico City pp. 142–143

RESOURCES

	FOR THE STUDENT	DIGITAL	PRINT	FOR THE TEACHER	DIGITAL	PRINT
Plan				Teacher's Edition, pp. 122a–122f	•	•
				Teacher's Resource Materials	•	
				Pre-AP® Resource Materials	•	
				Lesson Plans, pp. 122-e, 122-f	•	•
				Mapa global interactivo	•	
Introducción pp. 122–123						
Present	Student Edition, pp. 122–123	•	•	Teacher's Edition, pp. 122–123	•	•
	DK Reference Atlas	•		Teacher's Resource Materials	•	
	Videocultura	•		Mapa global interactivo	•	
	Para hispanohablantes	•				
Vocabulario en contexto pp. 124–127						
Present & Practice	Student Edition, pp. 124–127	•	•	Teacher's Edition, pp. 124–127	•	•
	Audio	•		Teacher's Resources	•	
	Videohistoria	•		Vocabulary Clip Art	•	
	Flashcards	•		Technology: Audio	•	
	Instant Check	•		Video Program: Videohistoria	•	
	Guided WB, pp. 83–92	•	•			
	Core WB, pp. 49–52	•	•			
	Communication Activities	•				
	Para hispanohablantes	•				
Assess and Remediate				Prueba 3A–1: Assessment Program, pp. 67–68	•	
				Assessment Program para hispanohablantes, pp. 67–68	•	

RESOURCES

	FOR THE STUDENT	DIGITAL	PRINT	FOR THE TEACHER	DIGITAL	PRINT
Vocabulario en uso pp. 128–131						
Present & Practice	Student Edition, pp. 128–131	•	•	Interactive Whiteboard Vocabulary Activities	•	
	Instant Check	•		Teacher's Edition, pp. 128–131	•	•
	Communication Activities	•		Teacher's Resource Materials	•	
	Para hispanohablantes	•		Communicative Pair Activities	•	
	Communicative Pair Activities	•		Technology: Audio	•	
				Videomodelos	•	
Assess and Remediate				Prueba 3A–2 with Remediation	•	
				Prueba 3A–2: Assessment Program, pp. 69–70	•	
				Assessment Program para hispanohablantes, pp. 69–70	•	
Gramática pp. 132–137						
Present & Practice	Student Edition, pp. 132–137	•	•	Interactive Whiteboard Grammar Activities	•	
	Instant Check	•		Teacher's Edition, pp. 132–137	•	•
	Animated Verbs	•		Teacher's Resource Materials	•	
	Tutorial Video: Grammar	•		Communicative Pair Activities	•	
	Canción de hip hop	•		Technology: Audio	•	
	Guided WB, pp. 93–96	•	•	Videomodelos	•	
	Core WB, pp. 53–55	•	•	Video Program: GramActiva	•	
	Communication Activities	•				
	Para hispanohablantes	•				
	Communicative Pair Activities	•				
Assess and Remediate				Pruebas 3A–3 and 3A–4 with Remediation	•	
				Pruebas 3A–3, 3A–4: Assessment Program, pp. 71, 72	•	
				Assessment Program para hispanohablantes, pp. 71, 72	•	
Aplicación pp. 138–139						
Apply	Student Edition, pp.138–143	•	•	Teacher's Edition, pp. 138–143	•	•
	Authentic Resources Workbook	•	•	Mapa global interactivo	•	
	Authentic Resources	•		Authentic Resources Lesson Plans with scripts, answer keys	•	
	Online Cultural Reading	•				
	Literacy Skills Workbook	•	•			
	Guided WB, pp. 97–98	•	•			
	Communication Activities	•				
	Para hispanohablantes	•				
Repaso del capítulo pp. 144–145						
Review	Student Edition, pp. 144–145	•	•	Teacher's Edition, pp. 144–145	•	•
	Online Games	•		Teacher's Resource Materials	•	
	Core WB, pp. 56–57	•	•	Technology: Audio	•	
	Communication Activities	•				
	Para hispanohablantes	•				
	Instant Check	•				
Chapter Assessment						
Assess				Examen del capítulo 3A	•	
				Assessment Program, pp. 73–79	•	
				Alternate Assessment Program, pp. 25–29	•	
				Assessment Program para hispanohablantes, pp. 73–79	•	
				Technology: Audio, Cap. 3A, Examen	•	
				ExamView: Test Banks A and B questions only online	•	
				Heritage Learner Test Bank	•	
				Pre-AP® Test Bank	•	

DAY	Warm-up / Assess	Preview / Present / Practice / Communicate		Wrap-up / Homework Options
		LESSON PLAN		
1	**Warm-up** (10 min.) • Return Examen del capítulo 2B	**Chapter Opener** (5 min.) • Objectives • Arte y cultura	**Vocabulario en contexto** (30 min.) • Presentation: Vocabulario en contexto • Actividades 1, 2	**Wrap-up and Homework Options** (5 min.) • Core Practice 3A-1, 3A-2
2	**Warm-up** (5 min.) • Homework check	**Vocabulario en contexto** (40 min.) • Presentation: Videohistoria *El almuerzo* • View: Videohistoria	• Video Activities 1, 2, 3, 4 • Actividad 3	**Wrap-up and Homework Options** (5 min.) • Core Practice 6, 9, 10, 11 • Prueba 3A-1: Vocabulary recognition
3	**Warm-up** (10 min.) • Actividad 4 • Homework check • **Formative Assessment** (10 min.) • Prueba 3A-1: Vocabulary recognition	**Vocabulario en uso** (25 min.) • Interactive Whiteboard Vocabulary Activities • Actividades 5, 7, 8 • Exploración del lenguaje • Audio Activities 5, 6		**Wrap-up and Homework Options** (5 min.) • Actividades 6, 9, 10, 11 • Prueba 3A-2 with Remediation: Vocabulary production
4	**Warm-up** (15 min.) • Writing Activity 10 • Communicative Pair Activity • Homework check • **Formative Assessment** (10 min.) • Prueba 3A-2 with Remediation: Vocabulary production	**Gramática y vocabulario en uso** (20 min.) • Presentation: Present tense of **-er** and **-ir** verbs • View: GramActiva video • Interactive Whiteboard Grammar Activities • Actividades 12, 13 • Audio Activity 7		**Wrap-up and Homework Options** (5 min.) • Core Practice 3A-5
5	**Warm-up** (10 min.) • Writing Activity 11 • Homework check	**Gramática y vocabulario en uso** (35 min.) • Actividades 14, 15, 16 • Cultura • Communicative Pair Activity		**Wrap-up and Homework Options** (5 min.) • Prueba 3A-3 with Remediation: Present tense of **-er** and **-ir** verbs
6	**Warm-up** (5 min.) • Review of **-er** and **-ir** verbs • **Formative Assessment** (10 min.) • Prueba 3A-3 with Remediation: Present tense of **-er** and **-ir** verbs	**Gramática y vocabulario en uso** (30 min.) • Presentation: Me gustan, me encantan • View: GramActiva video • Interactive Whiteboard Grammar Activities	• Actividades 17, 18, 19 • Audio Activities 8, 9	**Wrap-up and Homework Options** (5 min.) • Core Practice 3A-6, 3A-7 • Actividad 20 • Prueba 3A-4 with Remediation: Me gustan, me encantan
7	**Warm-up** (15 min.) • Writing Activities 12, 13 • Homework check • **Formative Assessment** (10 min.) • Prueba 3A-4 with Remediation: Me gustan, me encantan	**Gramática y vocabulario en uso** (10 min.) • Pronunciación • El español en la comunidad • Aplicación (10 min.) • Lectura • ¿Comprendes?		**Wrap-up and Homework Options** (5 min.) • La cultura en vivo: Make recipe • Lectura
8	**Warm-up** (5 min.) • Cultura	**Aplicación** (40 min.) • La cultura en vivo: Finish • Auténtico • Presentación oral: Step 1	• Situation Cards • Communicative Pair Activities	**Wrap-up and Homework Options** (5 min.) • Presentación oral: Step 2 • Preparación para el examen 3, 4, 5
9	**Warm-up** (5 min.) • Homework check	**Aplicación** (30 min.) • Presentación oral: Step 3	**Repaso del capítulo** (10 min.) • Vocabulario y gramática • Preparación para el examen 1, 2	**Wrap-up and Homework Options** (5 min.) • Core Practice 3A-8, 3A-9 • Instant Check • Auténtico • Examen del capítulo 3A
10	**Warm-up** (10 min.) • Homework check • Answer questions • **Summative Assessment** (40 min.) • Examen del capítulo 3A			

ALTERNATE LESSON PLAN (90 MINUTES)

DAY	Warm-up / Assess	Preview / Present / Practice / Communicate	Wrap-up / Homework Options
1	**Warm-up** (10 min.) • Return Examen del capítulo 2B	**Chapter Opener** (5 min.) • Objectives • Arte y cultura **Vocabulario en contexto** (55 min.) • Presentation: Vocabulario en contexto • Actividades 1, 2 • Presentation: Videohistoria *El almuerzo* • View: Videohistoria • Video Activities 1, 2, 3 • Actividad 3 **Vocabulario en uso** (15 min.) • Interactive Whiteboard Vocabulary Activities • Actividades 5, 6, 7	**Wrap-up and Homework Options** (5 min.) • Core Practice 3A-1, 3A-2, 3A-3, 3A-4 • Prueba 3A-1: Vocabulary recognition
2	**Warm-up** (10 min.) • Actividad 4 • Homework check • **Formative Assessment** (10 min.) • Prueba 3A-1: Vocabulary recognition	**Gramática y vocabulario en uso** (65 min.) • Actividades 8, 9, 11 • Exploración del lenguaje • Audio Activities 5, 6 • Writing Activity 10 • Communicative Pair Activity • Presentation: Present tense of **-er** and **-ir** verbs • View: GramActiva video • Interactive Whiteboard Grammar Activities • Actividades 12, 13 • Audio Activity 7	**Wrap-up and Homework Options** (5 min.) • Actividad 10 • Core Practice 3A-5 • Prueba 3A-2 with Remediation: Vocabulary production
3	**Warm-up** (5 min.) • Homework check • **Formative Assessment** (10 min.) • Prueba 3A-2 with Remediation: Vocabulary production	**Gramática y vocabulario en uso** (70 min.) • Actividades 14, 15, 16 • Cultura • Communicative Pair Activity • Writing Activity 11 • Presentation: Me gustan, me encantan • View: GramActiva video • Interactive Whiteboard Grammar Activities • Actividades 17, 18, 19 • Writing Activities 12, 13	**Wrap-up and Homework Options** (5 min.) • Core Practice 3A-6, 3A-7 • Actividad 20 • Pruebas 3A-3, 3A-4 with Remediation: Present tense of **-er** and **-ir** verbs, Me gustan, me encantan
4	**Warm-up** (10 min.) • Homework check • **Formative Assessment** (15 min.) • Pruebas 3A-3, 3A-4 with Remediation: Present tense of **-er** and **-ir** verbs, Me gustan, me encantan	**Gramática y vocabulario en uso** (20 min.) • Pronunciación • El español en la comunidad • Audio Activities 8, 9 **Aplicación** (40 min.) • Lectura • ¿Comprendes? • Cultura • La cultura en vivo: Churros y chocolate • Presentación oral: Step 1	**Wrap-up and Homework Options** (5 min.) • Presentación oral: Step 2 • La cultura en vivo: Make recipe • Lectura
5	**Warm-up** (5 min.) • Homework check	**Aplicación** (50 min.) • Auténtico • Presentación oral: Step 3 **Repaso del capítulo** (30 min.) • Vocabulario y gramática • Preparación para el examen 1, 2, 3, 4, 5	**Wrap-up and Homework Options** (5 min.) • Core Practice 3A-8, 3A-9 • Instant Check • Examen del capítulo 3A
6	**Warm-up** (15 min.) • Homework check • Answer questions **Repaso del capítulo** (25 min.) • Situation Cards • Communicative Pair Activities • **Summative Assessment** (45 min.) • Examen del capítulo 3A		**Wrap-up and Homework Options** (5 min.) • Auténtico

Can-Do Statements

Read the can-do statements in the chapter objectives with students. Then have students read Preparación para el examen on page 145 to preview what they will be able to do at the end of the chapter.

Standards for Capítulo 3A

To achieve the goals of the Standards, students will:

COMMUNICATION

1.1 Interpersonal
• Talk about: preferences concerning foods and beverages; eating habits during different meals; favorite activities; *churros y chocolate*

1.2 Interpretive
• Listen to and understand information about food items
• Listen to information about breakfast and lunch
• Read: a picture-based story; recipes for meals and beverages in Spanish; information about eating habits during different meals; a restaurant menu; about fruits and vegetables of Spanish-speaking countries
• Listen to and watch a video about breakfast foods
• Read and be able to respond to a magazine food quiz

1.3 Presentational
• Present information about: foods and beverages; eating habits during meals; the origins of food items; a restaurant menu; food and drink preferences

CULTURE

2.1 Practices to Perspectives
• Interpret the value of fresh fruit from a historical, socioeconomic perspective
• Explain breakfast habits in Spanish-speaking countries
• Talk about the ingredients of *enchiladas*

2.2 Products to Perspectives
• Discuss Bartolomé Murillo and his painting; *churros y chocolate*
• Interpret that many Latin American meals result from the Columbian Exchange of produce items; the connection between produce exports and economics in Latin American countries

CONNECTIONS

3.1 Making Connections
• Discuss Bartolomé Murillo; the ingredients of *enchiladas*; the nutritional values of tropical fruits
• Make *churros y chocolate*

COMPARISONS

4.1 Language
• Talk about new vocabulary through the recognition of cognates; the usage of *me gustan* and *me encantan*
• Explain that nouns can modify other nouns
• Explain the present tense of *-er* and *-ir* verbs
• Explain the pronunciation of the letters *h* and *j*

CAPÍTULO **3A**
¿Desayuno o almuerzo?

Country Connections Explorar el mundo hispano

España
México
Venezuela
Costa Rica
Ecuador
Colombia
Perú
Bolivia
Chile

CHAPTER OBJECTIVES

Communication
By the end of this chapter you will be able to:
• Listen to and read descriptions of meals and menus.
• Talk and write about foods you and others like and dislike.
• Exchange information about food preferences.

Culture
You will also be able to:
• **Auténtico:** Identify cultural practices viewed in an authentic video about food.
• Analyze the exchange of native foods between the Americas and Europe.

You will demonstrate what you know and can do
• Presentación oral: ¿Qué te gusta comer?
• Repaso del capítulo: Preparación para el examen

You will use
Vocabulary
• Foods and beverages for breakfast and lunch
• Expressions of frequency

Grammar
• Present tense of *-er* and *-ir* verbs
• *Me gustan, me encantan*

ARTE y CULTURA España

Bartolomé Murillo (1617–1682) was the first Spanish painter to become famous throughout Europe. Several of his early paintings featured children from his native Sevilla. Murillo used color, light, and a natural portrayal of his subjects to create memorable masterpieces.

▶ Study the painting and come up with three adjectives that describe it. Would you say the impression Murillo gives of the boys is positive or negative? Why?

🌐 **Mapa global interactivo** Explore Sevilla, Spain and the home of Bartolomé Murillo and examine the connections between the city and the artist

"Niños comiendo fruta" (ca. 1650) Bartolomé Murillo ▶
© ARS, NY. Copyright Scala/Art Resource, NY. Alte Pinakothek, Munich, Germany

122 ciento veintidós • Tema 3 • La comida

Enrich Your Teaching

The End in Mind
Have students preview the sample performance tasks on *Preparación para el examen,* p. 145, and connect them to the Chapter Objectives. Explain to students that by completing the sample tasks they can self-assess their learning progress.

Technology: Mapa global interactivo
Download the *Mapa global interactivo* files for Chapter 3A and preview the activities. Use Activity 1 to travel to Sevilla, Spain. Activity 2 takes you to Chile.

Un almuerzo con toda la familia

 Videocultura **El maíz:** *comida esencial*

Capítulo 3A • ciento veintitrés **123**

4.2 Cultural
- Explain the Columbian Exchange of produce items
- Compare: typical breakfast habits; *churros y chocolate* to popular food and drink combinations in the United States; the creation of environmentally protected areas

COMMUNITIES

5.1 School and Global Communities
- Discover the local availability of foods from Spanishspeaking countries

5.2 Lifelong Learning
- Realize the value of being able to read a restaurant menu

Chapter Opener

Resources: Mapa global interactivo: Regional maps

Suggestions: Point out the chapter title. Students already know the word **almuerzo**. Can they guess the meaning of **desayuno**? As students read through the Objectives, tell them that they will be learning vocabulary for different foods and beverages and how to say what they like and don't like for breakfast and lunch. In the *Videohistoria* students will see different kinds of foods from Spanish-speaking cultures. Explain that different cultures have different practices associated with meals, and students will explore these in this chapter.

▶ **Technology: Videocultura** View *El maíz: comida esencial* with the class to find out how corn is prepared in Spanish-speaking countries.

ARTE Y CULTURA

Standards: 2.1, 2.2, 3.1

Suggestions: To help students answer the question, remind them of the techniques and themes mentioned in the reading.

Answers will vary, but may include adjectives such as touching, simple, or realistic. Students may suggest that Murillo's painting is positive, as the boys appear content, despite their possible hardships.

⊕ **Technology: Mapa global interactivo,** Actividad 1 Discover Sevilla, Spain and the seventeenth-century artist Bartolomé Murillo.

Teaching with Art

Ask students: How old do you think the boys are? What do you think their relationship is to one another? What is the feeling that they give off in the painting? How is that feeling portrayed?

Project-Based Learning

Para la salud: Vacaciones

Ask students to create a Web page describing a day at a health resort. The Web page should include a schedule of the day's activities and descriptions of breakfast, lunch, and dinner with photos or drawings of each meal and one of the activities.

Ask the students to present the Web pages to the class as if they were sales representatives from the resort.

123

Vocabulario en contexto

Standards: 1.2

Resources: Teacher's Resource Materials: Input Script, Clip Art, Audio Script; Technology: Audio Cap. 3A

Suggestions: Use the Input Script for Capítulo 3A. Tell students what you like and don't like to eat for breakfast, using p. 124 as a framework. Project the vocabulary presentation for the class. Have students point to the items on the screen or in their books as they hear them to confirm students' understanding. Then ask a volunteer to read the narrative. Make a list on the board of words that cannot be identified through visuals. Have the class work together to understand their meanings. Point out the footnote about the word *agua*.

Extension: Tell students to imagine they need to bring in two food items for a class breakfast. Ask them what they would bring.

Starter Activity

To review numbers, put these number sequences on the board and ask that students complete the sequences:

1. 1, ___, 5,___, 9
2. 13,___,19, 22
3. 30,___, 40, 45,___, 55

Active Classroom

Have students write the new vocabulary for food and beverage items in Spanish on individual index cards. Collect the cards and put them into a box. Then assign each student either breakfast or lunch. Students should choose three cards and tell you if the food is logical for the meal you assigned them.

Technology: Interactive Whiteboard

Vocabulary Activities 3A Use the whiteboard activities in your Teacher Resources as you progress through the vocabulary practice with your class.

Vocabulario en contexto

OBJECTIVES

Read, listen to, and understand information about foods and beverages for breakfast and lunch

los plátanos   el yogur de fresa   la salchicha   la limonada   el té

la ensalada de frutas   el jugo de naranja   el pan   el jamón   el cereal   el café   el queso   los huevos   el té

" El desayuno es mi **comida** favorita. **En el desayuno, yo como** cereal **con leche, tocino y pan tostado. Todos los días bebo** jugo de naranja. **Nunca bebo té sin leche. Y tú, ¿qué comes** en el desayuno? "

Más vocabulario
la pizza = pizza
el té helado = iced tea

124 ciento veinticuatro • Tema 3 • La comida

Differentiated Instruction

Students with Learning Difficulties

You may wish to have students create a two-column chart to help them organize vocabulary. Have students label the columns *Para beber* and *Para comer*, and the rows *El desayuno* and *El almuerzo.*

Logical/Mathematical Learner

Have students create a chart organizing the vocabulary. Students can choose their own categories such as meat, drinks, etc., looking up any words they don't know. Then, have students organize the vocabulary words within the chart. Have them identify which vocabulary words fall under more than one category and which words don't seem to fit any of their categories.

Me encanta el Restaurante de la Plaza. La comida es muy buena. **En el almuerzo,** como una ensalada de frutas o un sándwich de jamón y queso. **Siempre** bebo agua. Es importante **beber** mucha agua, ¿verdad?

las galletas

el perrito caliente

la hamburguesa

el agua*

el jugo de manzana

los refrescos

el tocino

las papas fritas

la sopa de verduras

la leche

el sándwich de jamón y queso

*Note that *agua* is a feminine noun. However, you use the masculine article *el* to make it easier to say.

1
¿Beber o comer?
ESCUCHAR Listen to the names of ten foods and beverages. If an item is a food, pantomime eating. If it's a beverage, pantomime drinking.

2
¿El desayuno o el almuerzo?
ESCUCHAR Listen as different people tell what they are eating. Hold up one hand if the meal is *el desayuno* and hold up both hands if it is *el almuerzo*.

Capítulo 3A • ciento veinticinco **125**

Enrich Your Teaching

Culture Note
Often, soft drinks from Spanish-speaking cultures tend to be fruitier and sweeter than drinks produced in the United States. Drinks with natural ingredients are very popular. For example, **horchata** is a well-known drink in Spain and Mexico. Throughout Mexico, it is possible to find **horchata** made with water or milk, rice, almonds, cinnamon, and sugar; while in Valencia, Spain, **horchata** is made with **chufa** (also known as tiger nut), water, a touch of cinnamon, and sugar.

1

Standards: 1.2

Resources: Teacher's Resource Materials: Audio Script; Technology: Audio Cap. 3A

Suggestions: Use the audio or read the script. You may want to decide on standard gestures for eating and drinking, then model them for the class.

Technology: Audio Script and Answers

1. la pizza (*eating*)
2. el perrito caliente (*eating*)
3. el agua (*drinking*)
4. el jamón (*eating*)
5. el té (*drinking*)
6. el pan (*eating*)
7. el queso (*eating*)
8. la limonada (*drinking*)
9. la leche (*drinking*)
10. el cereal (*eating*)

2

Standards: 1.2

Resources: Teacher's Resource Materials: Audio Script; Audio Cap. 3A

Suggestions: Use the audio or read the script aloud. Pause to check students' progress after each item. Remind students that they should focus on the vocabulary for food and beverages, and that they should not worry about understanding every word.

Technology: Audio Script and Answers

1. Como un sándwich de jamón y queso. (*both hands*)
2. Yo como el pan tostado y jugo de naranja. (*one hand*)
3. Y yo como los huevos con tocino. ¡Mmmm! (*one hand*)
4. Me gusta comer las hamburguesas. (*both hands*)
5. Yo como la ensalada de frutas y pan. (*both hands*)
6. Y yo siempre como el cereal con leche y salchichas. (*one hand*)

Additional Resources

Technology: Online Resources
• Instant Check
• Guided, Core, Audio, Writing practice
• Communication Activities
• *Para hispanohablantes*
Print
• Guided WB pp. 83–85
• Core WB pp. 49–50

Vocabulario en contexto

Standards: 1.2, 1.3

Resources: Technology: Audio Cap. 3A

Suggestions: Model the dialogue with a volunteer. Begin the reading again with volunteers playing the roles of the characters. Using the presentation, help students understand the new words in blue type.

Post-reading: Complete Actividad 3 to check comprehension.

3

Standards: 1.2, 1.3

Suggestions: You may wish to do this as a listening activity, reading the sentences to the students.

Extension: Use the sentences as a basis for a classroom survey. For each item, have students give a "thumbs up" sign if they agree with the statement or a "thumbs down" if they disagree. Ask one student to count and tally responses for each item.

Answers:

1. C
2. F
3. F
4. C

Pre-AP® Integration

- **Learning Objective:** Interpersonal Speaking
- **Activity:** Have students create a short conversation based on this written exchange. Students can play the roles of Carlos and María Rosario as they discuss their food preferences, replacing theitems mentioned with others they like or dislike.
- **Pre-AP® Resource Materials:** Comprehensive guide to Pre-AP® vocabulary skill development

---

🔊 María y Carlos mandan mensajes para hablar de las bebidas y comidas. María es de México pero está en San Antonio.

📞 mensajes 08:07 AM

María — ¿**Cuál** es tu almuerzo favorito?

Carlos — **Me encantan** los sándwiches. ☺

María — A mí me encantan las **tortas**.

Carlos — **No comprendo.** ❓ ¿Qué es una torta?

María — En México, una torta es un sándwich, pero el pan es especial.

Carlos — ¿Hay tortas de salchicha?

María — **Por supuesto.** Las tortas de huevo con salchicha son deliciosas. También me gusta comer **ensalada** de verduras, de frutas o de huevos.

Carlos — ¿Ensalada de huevos? **¡Qué asco!** ☹ No me gusta nada.

María — ¿Qué **bebes** con los sándwiches? ¿Te gustan los jugos?

Carlos — **Más o menos.** 😐

María — Me encantan las **aguas frescas.** Es como jugo pero con menos fruta. Mañana, yo **comparto** mi bebida y tú **compartes** tu sándwich.

3

El almuerzo favorito

✏️ **ESCRIBIR** Lee las frases. Escribe *C (cierto)* si la frase es correcta o *F (falso)* si la frase es incorrecta.

1. A María le encantan las tortas.
2. En México, una torta es un taco.
3. A Carlos le encantan los jugos.
4. Las aguas frescas tienen fruta.

126 ciento veintiséis • Tema 3 • La comida

Differentiated Instruction

Special Needs

You may wish to provide hearing-impaired students with a copy of the *Videohistoria* videoscript so that they may follow along and engage in post-viewing activities.

Bodily/Kinesthetic Learner

Have students prepare a short dialogue based on the *Vocabulario en contexto* in which they change the foods that are discussed. Encourage them to be comical in their selections. Then have students present their dialogues to the class.

Videohistoria

Go Online to practice — **PearsonSchool.com/Autentico**

PEARSON realize™

🔊 AUDIO ▶ VIDEO ✎ WRITING 📄 SCRIPT

El almuerzo

Before You Watch

Using visuals to infer meaning Use the images to help you infer the meaning of unknown words in the descriptions of traditional foods. Have you ever had foods similar to those in the photos?

Complete the Activity

Tu comida favorita Escribe una lista de las comidas que te gusta comer y las bebidas que te gusta beber en el almuerzo.

▶ Watch the Video

What foods will Valentina present as typical lunches in other Spanish-speaking countries?

Go to **PearsonSchool.com/Autentico** to watch the video *El almuerzo* and to view the script.

Valentina   Sebastián

After You Watch

✎ **¿COMPRENDES?** Complete the following sentences based on what you infer from the video.

1. Valentina estudia la comida de otros países en la clase de _____.
2. El ajiaco y el locro son _____ tradicionales en los países de Colombia y Ecuador.
3. En España, un bocadillo es un tipo de _____.
4. Un ejemplo de comida chatarra es _____.
5. En Argentina, un alfajor es una _____ popular.

Comparación cultural Según la presentación de Valentina, ¿es la comida en el almuerzo de otros países diferente a la comida que tú comes? ¿Por qué?

Capítulo 3A • ciento veintisiete **127**

Interpretive 3A

Technology: Video

Standards: 1.2, 1.3

Resources: Teacher's Resource Materials: Video Script

Before You Watch

Review the previewing strategy and activity with the students. Ask students for examples of the foods they have for lunch. Also point out the images of foods that will be discussed in the video.

Review the Complete the Activity with the class. Ask students to mention the foods and drinks they like for lunch. Students can speak or write their responses.

Watch the Video

Show the video once without pausing, then go back and show it again, pausing along the way to check for comprehension of new vocabulary.

After You Watch

Standards: 1.2, 1.3

Answers

1. ciencias
2. sopas (alt: comidas)
3. sándwich
4. la hamburguesa, el perrito caliente, la pizza
5. galleta

Comparación cultural: Answers will vary. Students should recognize that a typical lunch has more food, a variety of foods, and different ingredients than in the US.

Have the students complete additional Video activities online or print the activities from the Teacher's Resources in the online course and pass out the activity sheets to the class.

Additional Resources

📶 **Technology: Online Resources**
- Instant Check
- Guided, Core, Video, Audio
- *Para hispanohablantes*

Print
- Guided WB pp. 89–92
- Core WB pp. 51–92

Assessment _____

Quiz: Vocabulary Recognition
- Prueba 3A-1

Enrich Your Teaching

Culture Note

Meals in Spanish-speaking countries vary by country and region. In some cities, it is common to have a light breakfast and to have lunch as the main meal. In rural areas, however, families tend to eat what they produce for themselves. Breakfast might include steak, corn, milk, eggs, or beans. In Mexico, breakfast foods can vary by region. Corn tortillas are common at breakfast and are often filled with eggs, sauce, tomato and onion. Also popular are sweet breads, and tropical fruits and juices.

4

Suggestions: Ask questions such as *¿Comes una hamburguesa en el desayuno? ¿Comes yogur en el almuerzo?* By answering these questions, students will begin to classify the foods. Once they have two or three examples, they can fill in the rest of the vocabulary.

Answers will vary but should include:

el desayuno: los huevos, el tocino
el almuerzo: el jamón, los refrescos, las verduras
Both: el yogur de fresa, el jamón, los plátanos, el agua, la leche, la mantequilla, las naranjas, las manzanas

Starter Activity

To review prepositions, provide a word bank of prepositions on the board. Placing a food prop on, in front of, behind a desk, ask: *¿Dónde está...?*

5

Resources: Teacher's Resource Materials: Audio Script; Technology: Audio Cap. 3A

Focus: Listening to descriptions of foods

Recycle: Prepositions of location

Suggestions: Use the audio or read the script aloud. Explain that items near the bottom of the page are in the front, and those near the top are in the back.

Script and Answers:

1. Los huevos están delante de la mantequilla y el yogur. (*F*)
2. La leche está al lado de las manzanas. (*F*)
3. La leche está delante de los plátanos. (*C*)
4. Las manzanas están detrás de los plátanos. (*F*)
5. El tocino está detrás del jamón. (*C*)
6. El jamón y el tocino están debajo de las manzanas y las naranjas. (*C*)
7. Las naranjas están al lado del refresco. (*F*)
8. El yogur está encima del agua y del refresco. (*C*)

Vocabulario en uso

4

El desayuno o el almuerzo

✎ **PENSAR, ESCRIBIR** Think about the breakfast and lunch items that you have in your kitchen. Now look at the photo and list the foods and beverages that would typically be for breakfast, lunch or both.

desayuno
Modelo *los huevos*

desayuno y almuerzo

almuerzo
Modelo *el refresco*

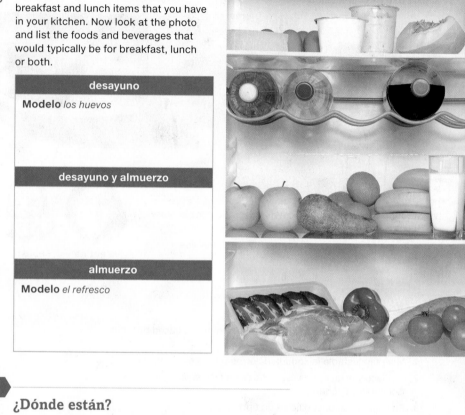

5

¿Dónde están?

🔊 **ESCUCHAR, ESCRIBIR** Vas a escuchar ocho descripciones sobre la foto de esta página. Escribe los números del 1 al 8 en una hoja de papel y escribe C si la descripción es cierta y *F* si es falsa.

Differentiated Instruction

Challenge/Pre-AP®

Ask students to think of three brand names of food or drink items. Have them say only the brand name, and call on a volunteer to explain what it is. The student who responds should continue the game by saying another brand name and calling on another volunteer to describe it.

Special Needs

For *Actividad* 4, pair visually-impaired students with other students who will say the Spanish names of the items pictured. Then have the visually impaired students say whether or not the item is appropriate for **desayuno**, **almuerzo**, or **los dos**.

Go **Online** to practice
PearsonSchool.com/Autentico

PEARSON
realize™

WRITING   AUDIO   SPEAK/RECORD   VIDEO

Interpersonal | **3A**

6

¿Qué bebes?

ESCRIBIR

1. On a sheet of paper, make three columns with these headings:

   Todos los días, A veces, Nunca. Write the names of these or other beverages under the appropriate heading based on how often you drink them.

2. Write complete sentences telling how often you drink these or other beverages.

Modelo

Bebo limonada todos los días.
Bebo jugo de manzana a veces.
Nunca bebo café.

También se dice...
beber = tomar *(México)*
el jugo = el zumo *(España)*
la naranja = la china *(Puerto Rico)*
las papas = las patatas *(España)*
el plátano = la banana, el guineo *(Puerto Rico)*
el sándwich = el bocadillo *(España)*, la torta *(México)*

7

¿Qué comes?

HABLAR EN PAREJA   Trabaja con otro(a) estudiante y habla de lo que comes.

Videomodelo

A —*¿Comes cereal?*
B —*Sí, como cereal todos los días.*
o: *No, nunca como cereal.*

Estudiante A

Estudiante B

Sí, todos los días.
Sí, a veces.
Sí, siempre.
No, nunca.
No, ¡qué asco!

Capítulo 3A • ciento veintinueve **129**

6

Standards: 1.3

Suggestions: Review the meanings of **todos los días, a veces**, and **nunca**. When students have finished Step 1, ask a volunteer to read the *Modelo* for Step 2. Direct students to the *También se dice...* and encourage them to be creative in using these regional variations as you do the activity in class.

Answers will vary.

7

Standards: 1.1

Suggestions: Have volunteers read the model on the page. Then have them use a vocabulary word not given in the activity to personalize the roles of Student A and Student B. They can also add **en el desayuno** or **en el almuerzo** to their questions and answers: *¿Comes cereal en el desayuno? Sí, a veces como cereal en el desayuno.*

Answers:

Student A
¿Comes pan?
¿Comes sopa?
¿Comes frutas?
¿Comes yogur?
¿Comes pan tostado?
¿Comes tocino?
¿Comes sándwiches?
Student B
Answers will vary.

Enrich Your Teaching

Culture Note

Sandwiches in Spain and Mexico differ in more than just name. In Spain, **un bocadillo** may be composed of a hard roll with a piece of cheese, cured beef, or **tortilla española**—a Spanish omelette. In Mexico, **una torta** almost always contains refried beans, chilies, lettuce, tomato, and ham, chicken, or cheese.

21st Century Skills

Information Literacy Have students work in small groups to discuss the merits of the different types of meals presented in this section: light breakfast vs. heavier type breakfast; light lunch vs. heavier lunch. Ask them to think about why such choices are made, and how the type of meals one eats regularly affects one's overall health.

8

Suggestions: Ask pairs of volunteers to read the *Modelo* once as it is in the book. Then have Student A ask the question and select any student to respond. Remind Student B that he or she can select any response from the Estudiante B balloon, but that it should reflect his or her own opinion.

Answers for Student B will vary. Student A answers:

1. Te gustan los huevos, ¿verdad?
2. Te gustan las galletas, ¿verdad?
3. Te gustan los refrescos, ¿verdad?
4. Te gustan las papas fritas, ¿verdad?
5. Te gustan las hamburguesas, ¿verdad?
6. Te gustan las salchichas, ¿verdad?
7. Te gustan los perritos calientes, ¿verdad?

Extension: Have students repeat the activity using drinks, which are sometimes singular. They should say *me gusta* and *me encanta*, when appropriate. You may want to project the vocabulary to remind students of vocabulary options.

EXPLORACIÓN DEL LENGUAJE

Suggestions: Provide an example of a noun modifying another noun in English, such as *peanut butter sandwich*. Have students come up with additional examples in English in order to internalize the concept. Refer students to the vocabulary presented on pp. 124–126 to complete the *Try it out!* Ask volunteers to share their answers.

You may want to point out that *la ensalada de frutas* and *la sopa de verduras* have plural modifiers because they are made from a combination of ingredients, while *la sopa de tomate* uses the singular because there is only one main ingredient.

Answers will vary but should include:

el yogur de fresa; el jugo de naranja; el jugo de manzana; la ensalada de frutas; el sándwich de jamón y queso; la sopa de verduras
la ensalada de lechuga   el jugo de piña
el sándwich de pollo   la sopa de tomate

8

Mis comidas favoritas

🎤 **HABLAR EN PAREJA** Trabaja con otro(a) estudiante y habla de las comidas que te gustan y que no te gustan.

Videomodelo
A —*Te gustan los plátanos, ¿verdad?*
B —*Sí, ¡por supuesto! Me encantan.*

Estudiante A

Estudiante B

Sí, ¡por supuesto! Me encantan.
Sí, más o menos.
No, no me gustan.
No, ¡qué asco!

Exploración del lenguaje — Using a noun to modify another noun

In English, one noun is often used to describe another noun: *vegetable soup, strawberry yogurt*. Notice that the noun that is being described comes second.

In Spanish, however, the noun that is being described comes first and is followed by *de* + the describing noun: *la sopa de verduras, el yogur de fresa*. Notice that you don't use a definite article in front of the second noun.

The form of the noun following *de* does not change even when the first noun becomes plural.

el sándwich de **jamón**
los sándwiches de **jamón**

Try it out! Name five examples of foods or beverages from this chapter that follow this pattern.

Now that you know the pattern, say what these foods and beverages are called in Spanish:

la lechuga   la piña   el pollo   el tomate

Differentiated Instruction

Visual/Spatial Learner

Have students illustrate some of the word combinations in the *Exploración del lenguaje* by cutting images from a magazine and pasting them on a poster board. For example, students could illustrate **un sándwich de queso** by using a photo of a sandwich, the word **de**, and a photo of cheese.

Challenge

To further increase rigor, have students use the **Conexiones: La historia** reading in *Actividad* 9 to begin a research project about the development of the Spanish colonies in Central and South America after the arrival of Columbus. Have students focus on the trade that occurred between Spain and the New World.

9

El intercambio entre dos mundos

LEER

Conexiones ◂ La historia

Think about how your meals would be different without corn, beans, squash, tomatoes, avocados, chiles, peanuts, cashews, turkey, pineapples, potatoes, vanilla, and chocolate. What do these foods have in common? They all had their origin in the Americas and were unknown in Europe until Columbus brought them there from his voyages in the fifteenth century. Today these foods are found in dishes in many countries.

The product exchange benefited both sides of the Atlantic Ocean. The Europeans brought to the Americas a wide range of foods including chicken, pork, beef, milk, cheese, sugar, grapes, and grains such as wheat and barley.

• What factors must have contributed to the successful establishment of crops or animals in the new countries?

10

Las enchiladas

LEER, ESCRIBIR Read the list of ingredients for a traditional Mexican dish of *enchiladas*. Based upon the information you just read and saw on the map, write which ingredients had their origins in the Americas and which came from Europe.

Ingredientes > Enchiladas de pollo¹ con salsa de tomate

12	tortillas de maíz ²
1	taza³ de pollo
1	taza de queso fresco ⁴
6	tomates grandes ⁵
2	cebollas ⁶ no muy grandes
	crema
	aceite ⁷ de maíz

¹chicken ²corn ³cup ⁴fresh ⁵large ⁶onions ⁷oil

11

Y tú, ¿qué dices?

HABLAR EN PAREJA Express and exchange opinions and preferences about food with a partner.

1. ¿Cuál es tu comida favorita, el desayuno o el almuerzo?
2. ¿Cuál es tu almuerzo favorito? ¿Y tu desayuno favorito?
3. ¿Qué frutas te gustan más?

Capítulo 3A • ciento treinta y uno **131**

Go **Online** to practice
PEARSON
realize™
PearsonSchool.com/Autentico
WRITING   SPEAK/RECORD   VIDEO

9

Standards: 2.2, 4.2

Suggestions: Make a list of some of the foods mentioned, and ask students if they have any insights into their origins. Check to see if students were correct in their predictions. Ask students to tell who they think benefited more from the exchange, the Europeans or the Americans.

10

Standards: 1.2, 1.3, 2.2, 3.1

Suggestions: Tell students you're going to be making **enchiladas de pollo** for dinner tonight. Have volunteers tell you what to put on your shopping list as you write it on the board.

Answers:

• Americas: tortillas de maíz, tomates, aceite de maíz
• Europe: pollo, queso, cebollas, crema

11

Standards: 1.1, 1.3

Suggestions: When students have completed the activity, have volunteers ask the questions and call on other classmates.

Answers will vary.

Additional Resources

Technology: Online Resources
• Instant Check
• Guided, Core, Video, Audio
• *Para hispanohablantes*
• Teacher's Resource Materials: Audio Script
• Technology: Audio Cap. 3A
• Communication Activities: Audio Act. 6
Print
• Guided WB pp. 89–92
• Core WB pp. 51–52

Assessment

Prueba 3A-2 with Remediation (online only)
Quiz: Vocabulary Production
• Prueba 3A-2

Enrich Your Teaching

Culture Note

Corn, tomatoes, and chilies are staples of the Mexican kitchen. Tortillas are present at every meal and are even made into a delicious soup. Chilies, tomatoes, and onions are used in many different ways, both raw and cooked, to make a variety of **salsas** that may be included in any meal, even breakfast.

Teacher-to-Teacher

Have each student find a recipe for a traditional dish from a Spanish-speaking culture. Have them write the recipe in English, tell the country it is from, and illustrate the page. Then compile all of the recipes, and ask a volunteer to design a cover. Make copies, bind the recipes, and distribute them to students in the class.

Starter Activity

Write an **-ar** verb on the board, and ask a volunteer to review the conjugation process.

Gramática

Standards: 4.1

Resources: Teacher's Resource Materials: Video Script; Technology: Video Cap. 3A

Suggestions: Direct students' attention to ¿Recuerdas? Use the Animated verbs or other video resources to reinforce the verb forms. Use the lists of familiar infinitives to have students practice creating the forms of the verbs. Use the GramActiva Video to introduce the grammar or reinforce your explanation.

Technology: Interactive Whiteboard

Grammar Activities 3A Use the whiteboard activities in your Teacher Resources as you progress through the grammar practice with your class.

12

Standards: 1.2, 1.3

Suggestions: Point out that each sentence will use a form of the verb **compartir**. Students may need to be reminded that **tú + yo** requires the **nosotros(as)** form of the verb.

Answers:

1. Tomás comparte una pizza con María.
2. Tú compartes unos sándwiches con Ramón.
3. Nosotros compartimos unas papas fritas con los estudiantes.
4. Uds. comparten unas galletas con el profesor.
5. Ellas comparten unos perritos calientes con nosotros.
6. Tú y yo compartimos unos plátanos con Luis y Roberta.
7. Yo comparto (student's choice) con mi amigo.

Pre-AP® Integration

- **Learning Objective:** Interpersonal Writing
- **Activity:** As a warm-up activity for five days, have students list what they have eaten for breakfast or lunch. At the end of the week, have them write a short email to a nutritionist asking for tips to improve their eating habits–or indicating how well they follow healthy eating guidelines.
- **Pre-AP® Resource Materials:** Comprehensive guide to Pre-AP® writing skill development

---

Gramática

OBJECTIVES
▶ Read, write, and talk about what you and others eat for breakfast and lunch, and about everyday activities
▶ Exchange information with classmates about favorite foods and drinks

Present tense of -er and -ir verbs

To create the present-tense forms of -er and -ir verbs, drop the endings from the infinitives, then add the verb endings -o, -es, -e, -emos / -imos, -éis / -ís, or -en to the stem.

Here are the present-tense forms of -er and -ir verbs using comer and compartir:

¿Recuerdas?
The pattern of present-tense -ar verbs is:

toco	tocamos
tocas	tocáis
toca	tocan

(yo)	com**o**	(nosotros) (nosotras)	com**emos**
(tú)	com**es**	(vosotros) (vosotras)	com**éis**
Ud. (él) (ella)	com**e**	Uds. (ellos) (ellas)	com**en**

(yo)	compart**o**	(nosotros) (nosotras)	compart**imos**
(tú)	compart**es**	(vosotros) (vosotras)	compart**ís**
Ud. (él) (ella)	compart**e**	Uds. (ellos) (ellas)	compart**en**

- Regular -er verbs that you know are beber, comer, comprender, correr, and leer.
- Regular -ir verbs that you know are compartir and escribir.
- You also know the verb ver. It is regular except in the yo form, which is veo.

Más recursos ONLINE

- ▶ GramActiva video
- ▶ Tutorials: -er verbs, -ir verbs, Regular verbs, Stem-endings
- ▶ Animated verbs
- 🔊 Canción de hip hop: ¿Qué comes?
- 📝 GramActiva Activity

12

¿Quiénes comparten el almuerzo?

ESCRIBIR On a sheet of paper, write complete sentences saying what each person is sharing and with whom. Follow the model.

Modelo
Elena / una manzana / Raúl
Elena comparte una manzana con Raúl.

1. Tomás / una pizza / María
2. tú / unos sándwiches / Ramón
3. nosotros / unas papas fritas / los estudiantes
4. Uds. / unas galletas / el profesor
5. ellas / unos perritos calientes / nosotros
6. tú y yo / unos plátanos / Luis y Roberta
7. yo / ¿-? / mi amigo

132 ciento treinta y dos • Tema 3 • La comida

Differentiated Instruction

Students with Learning Difficulties

When presenting the Gramática, point out the infinitives and demonstrate how the **-er** and **-ir** are removed and new endings added. Ask students to recall the process of changing verb forms with **-ar** verbs. Some students may benefit from repeating the conjugations with new endings until they have internalized the process.

Visual/Spatial Learner

Have students draw pictures to illustrate the **-er** and **-ir** verbs they know. Ask them to write a subject pronoun for each illustration. Have pairs exchange papers and say what the people are doing in the drawings.

Go **Online** to practice
PearsonSchool.com/Autentico

PEARSON
realize™

WRITING SPEAK/RECORD VIDEO

Interpersonal 3A

13

¿Qué beben y qué comen?

 HABLAR EN PAREJA Work with a partner. Use the verbs comer and beber to ask questions.

 Videomodelos

Juan / desayuno
A —¿Qué come Juan en el desayuno?
B —Juan come pan tostado.

Miguel y Carlos / almuerzo
A —¿Qué beben Miguel y Carlos en el almuerzo?
B —Miguel y Carlos beben limonada.

1. Raúl y Gloria / desayuno

2. tú / almuerzo

3. Graciela y Carlos / desayuno

4. Carolina / almuerzo

5. tu familia y tú / desayuno

6. ¿?
   tú / almuerzo
   ¡Respuesta personal!

14

Un blog

 LEER, ESCRIBIR Lee el blog de una amiga de Venezuela. En una hoja de papel, escribe la forma correcta del verbo apropiado que está entre paréntesis. Escribe un comentario al blog en el que expreses tus opiniones.

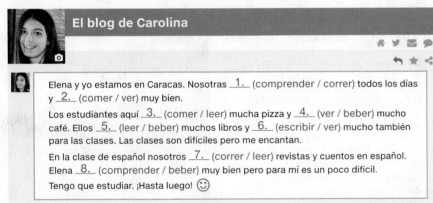

El blog de Carolina

Elena y yo estamos en Caracas. Nosotras __1.__ (comprender / correr) todos los días y __2.__ (comer / ver) muy bien.

Los estudiantes aquí __3.__ (comer / leer) mucha pizza y __4.__ (ver / beber) mucho café. Ellos __5.__ (leer / beber) muchos libros y __6.__ (escribir / ver) mucho también para las clases. Las clases son difíciles pero me encantan.

En la clase de español nosotros __7.__ (correr / leer) revistas y cuentos en español. Elena __8.__ (comprender / beber) muy bien pero para mí es un poco difícil. Tengo que estudiar. ¡Hasta luego! ☺

Capítulo 3A • ciento treinta y tres **133**

Enrich Your Teaching

Culture Note

In Latin America, to say what they eat for breakfast, people often use the verb **desayunar**, e.g., *Desayunamos huevos con tocino.* **Comer** can be used for any meal, but it's generally used when referring to lunch, and **cenar** is used to refer to the evening meal. **Almuerzo** is another word used throughout Latin America to describe lunch.

21st Century Skills

ICT Literacy Have students access the digital technology available in Realize for this section (like the *GramActiva* Video, and the *Canción de hip hop*). After reviewing, ask them to work in small groups to compose a reply to Carolina's blog in *Actividad* 14.

13

Standards: 1.1, 1.2

Suggestions: Ask volunteers to demonstrate the models. Point out that no article is necessary in front of the names of the foods and drinks.

Answers:
1. ¿Qué comen Raúl y Gloria en el desayuno?
   Raúl y Gloria comen huevos.
2. ¿Qué comes tú en el almuerzo?
   Yo como hamburguesas.
3. ¿Qué comen Graciela y Carlos en el desayuno?
   Graciela y Carlos comen cereal.
4. ¿Qué come Carolina en el almuerzo?
   Carolina come yogur.
5. ¿Qué beben tu familia y tú en el desayuno?
   Nosotros bebemos jugo de naranja.
6. ¿Qué comes tú en el almuerzo?
   Yo como (answers will vary).

14

Standards: 1.2, 1.3

Suggestions: Encourage students to scan the paragraph before writing the verb forms.

Answers:
1. corremos	4. beben	7. leemos
2. comemos	5. leen	8. comprende
3. comen	6. escriben	

Additional Resources

Technology: Online Resources
• Instant Check
• Guided, Core, Video, Audio
• Communication Activities
• *Para hispanohablantes*
• Teacher's Resource Materials: Audio Script
• Technology: Audio Cap. 3A
Print
• Guided WB pp. 93–94
• Core WB p. 53

Assessment

Prueba 3A-3 with Remediation (online only)
Quiz: Present tense of *-er* and *-ir* verbs
• Prueba 3A-3

Starter Activity

Review with student the vocabulary for food and drinks. Give students sentences such as *Yo como hamburguesas en el desayuno,* and have students tell you if each sentence is **lógica** or **ilógica**.

Standards: 1.1, 1.3

Suggestions: Have each student create a copy of the chart. Direct attention to the *Para decir más...* for additional words. You might also provide a list of other words that students want to use. Tell students to keep their charts for *Actividad* 16.

Answers will vary.

16

Standards: 1.3

Suggestions: Remind students to use the chart from *Actividad* 15 to complete this activity. Be sure that sentences include correct verb forms. Write a sample sentence on the board to get students started. Ask volunteers to say their completed sentences for the class.

Answers will vary.

CULTURA

Standards: 1.2, 2.1, 4.2

Suggestions: Have students discuss what they typically eat for breakfast, and tell what their idea of an American breakfast is.

Answers will vary but may include cereal, bacon, eggs, sausages, waffles, and pancakes.

Project-Based Learning

Give students copies of the project outline and rubric. Explain the task to them, and have them perform Step 1. (For more information, see p. 122-b.)

15

Los sábados y la comida

 ESCRIBIR, HABLAR What do you and your classmates eat and drink for breakfast and lunch on Saturdays? Make a chart like the one below on a sheet of paper and complete each box with information about yourself. Then survey two classmates to find out what their habits are. Record the information in the chart.

Para decir más...
la crema de cacahuate = peanut butter
el pan dulce = breakfast pastry
el panqueque = pancake
el pollo = chicken

Modelo
Los sábados, ¿qué comes en el desayuno? ¿Qué bebes? ¿Qué comes en el almuerzo? ¿Qué bebes?

	¿Qué comes?	¿Qué bebes?
el desayuno	Yo: huevos, pan tostado, tocino Sandra: cereal, plátanos, pan tostado	
el almuerzo		

16

Los hábitos de la clase

 ESCRIBIR Use your completed chart from Actividad 15 to write summary statements based on your survey. Be prepared to read your sentences to the class.

Modelo
Sandra y yo comemos huevos y cereal en el desayuno.
Gregorio no bebe jugo de naranja en el desayuno y le gusta mucho la leche.
Sofía come cereal y bebe leche en el desayuno.

CULTURA **El mundo hispano**

El desayuno Existe una gran variedad de alimentos en el desayuno en los países hispanos. En España se desayunan los churros con chocolate caliente; en Colombia comen las arepas de maíz o los patacones (de plátano verde). En muchos países la gente[1] prefiere un desayuno ligero[2]: pan dulce[3] o panecillos, café o té, y jugo. El cereal, los huevos, el jamón y las salchichas son menos comunes.

Pre-AP Integration: Los estilos de vida Compara lo que tú comes en la mañana con los desayunos en los países hispanos.

Pan dulce, México

[1]people [2]light [3]sweet

Differentiated Instruction

Students with Learning Difficulties

For *Actividad* 15, provide students with colored pencils. Make sure that students fill in their charts with their own information first. For each classmate that they include, have them write with a different color. This will help them to keep their information more organized.

Special Needs

For *Actividad* 17, some students may have difficulty manipulating three pieces of paper. You may want to provide students with four different index cards, labeled ***me gusta, me gustan, no me gusta,*** and ***no me gustan.***

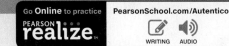

OBJECTIVES
▶ Indicate and write about what you like and don't like to eat
▶ Read and answer questions about a food survey and a menu
▶ Exchange information about food preferences

Go **Online** to practice
PEARSON **realize** ™
PearsonSchool.com/Autentico
✏️ WRITING   🔊 AUDIO

Me gustan, me encantan

Use *me gusta* and *me encanta* to talk about a singular noun.

Me gusta **el té** pero me encanta **el té helado**.

Use *me gustan* and *me encantan* to talk about plural nouns.

Me encantan **las fresas** pero no me gustan mucho **los plátanos**.

When you use *me gusta(n)* and *me encanta(n)* to talk about a noun, include *el*, *la*, *los*, or *las*.

Me encanta **el** jugo de naranja pero no me gusta **la** leche.

¿Qué te gustan más, **las** hamburguesas o **los** perritos calientes?

Más recursos	ONLINE
▶ *GramActiva* video	
▶ Tutorials: -er verbs	
✏️ *GramActiva* Activity	

17

¿Gusta o gustan?

🔊 ESCUCHAR, GRAMACTIVA

1. Tear a sheet of paper in thirds. On the first piece, write *No*. On the second piece write *me gusta*. On the third piece, write *n*.

2. You will hear eight food items. Indicate whether you like each item by holding up one, two, or all three pieces of paper. Remember to use *me gustan* when the item you hear is plural!

No ⟩ me gusta ⟩ n

18

¿Qué te gusta?

✏️ ESCRIBIR EN PAREJA   Exchange text messages with a classmate to express your opinions and preferences about foods. Write a text message for each food pictured.

Modelo
Me gustan las manzanas.
o: *No me gustan nada las manzanas.*
o: *Me encantan las manzanas.*

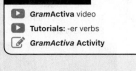

① ② ③ ④ ⑤ ⑥

Enrich Your Teaching

Teacher-to-Teacher

For more practice with the concepts of *me gustan* and *me encantan,* write a list of specific people, places, and things that students can identify, such as sports teams, individual athletes, singers, musical groups, or celebrities. Have students work in pairs to ask and say whether or not they like the items on the list.

21st Century Skills

Communication Have two students write a short play. One student will play a summer camp counselor. The other will play a camper. The camper tells the camp counselor his/her food preferences. After hearing what the camper likes to eat, the counselor will offer eating suggestions, addressing both what the camper likes to eat, and what would be the healthier choice.

Gramática

Standards: 4.1

Resources: Teacher's Resource Materials: Video Script; Technology: Video Cap. 3A

Suggestions: Use the *GramActiva* Video either as an initial introduction or as a follow-up to your explanation. Have students brainstorm foods and drinks and write them in the plural on the board. Ask volunteers to tell their likes and dislikes using *me gusta(n), no me gusta(n),* or *me encanta(n)* and the words listed on the board. Then provide some singular nouns to show the contrast.

🖥️ Technology: Interactive Whiteboard

Grammar Activities 3A Use the whiteboard activities in your Teacher Resources as you progress through the grammar practice with your class.

17

Standards: 1.2

Resources: Teacher's Resource Materials: Audio Script; Technology: Audio Cap. 3A

Suggestions: Use the audio or read the script aloud. Pause after each item to check the responses.

🔊 Script

1. la sopa	5. el pan
2. las hamburguesas	6. el yogur
3. el tocino	7. las galletas
4. las fresas	8. los huevos

Answers will vary but should include:

1. gusta	4. gustan	7. gustan
2. gustan	5. gusta	8. gustan
3. gusta	6. gusta	

18

Standards: 1.3

Suggestions: When students have finished the sentences, ask volunteers to express their opinions to the class. For each statement, ask a follow-up question to another student, such as *¿Y a ti? ¿Te gustan también...?*

Answers will vary but should include:

Me gusta(n)...
No me gusta(n) nada...
Me encantan...

19

Standards: 1.1, 1.2, 1.3

Recycle: Definite articles; *ni...ni, a mí también, a mí tampoco*; vocabulary from previous chapters

Suggestions: Have students read the entire survey for comprehension before writing their answers. You may wish to provide your own preferences as a model for the students.

Answers will vary.

Extension: Using the survey as a model, have students create their own survey, consisting of five to seven questions. They should include items that have to do with food, school, and leisure time activities.

PRONUNCIACIÓN

Standards: 4.1

Resources: Teacher's Resource Materials: Audio Script; Technology: Audio Cap. 3A

Suggestions: Use an exaggerated tone to emphasize the pronunciation distinctions as you read through the list. If you choose to use the audio, pause it after each word and repeat the word. Have students say it with you a third time.

Try it out! Have the class refer to pp. 124–125 for food vocabulary. Ask volunteers to say examples of **h** and **j** words.

Try it out! Read through the *trabalenguas* slowly with class. Use the picture to help students grasp the meaning. You may want to explain that **había** means "there was." Then have them read it together a few times. Finally, ask volunteers to say the *trabalenguas* for the class.

Project-Based Learning

Students can perform Step 2 at this point. Be sure students understand your suggestions. (For more information, see p. 122-b.)

19

¿Qué te gusta más?

LEER, ESCRIBIR EN PAREJA Read a survey and exchange opinions and preferences with a partner.

1. A popular magazine has provided this survey to see how much you and a friend have in common. On a sheet of paper, write the numbers 1–7 and then write your preferences.

2. Take turns exchanging emails with your partner about the survey items. Keep track of your similarities and differences. See how the magazine rates you.

Videomodelo

¿La comida mexicana o la comida italiana?
A —¿Qué te gusta más, la comida mexicana o la comida italiana?
B —Me gusta más la comida italiana.
o:—No me gusta ni la comida mexicana ni la comida italiana.
A —A mí también.
B —A mí me gusta la comida mexicana.
o:—A mí tampoco.

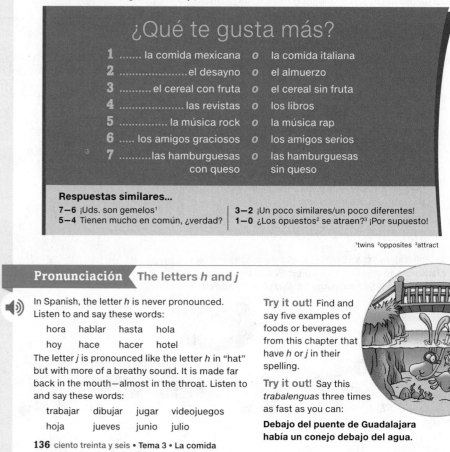

¿Qué te gusta más?

1	.... la comida mexicana	o	la comida italiana
2	.................el desayno	o	el almuerzo
3	.... el cereal con fruta	o	el cereal sin fruta
4	.... las revistas	o	los libros
5	.... la música rock	o	la música rap
6	..... los amigos graciosos	o	los amigos serios
7	.........las hamburguesas con queso	o	las hamburguesas sin queso

Respuestas similares...

7–6 ¡Uds. son gemelos[1]
5–4 Tienen mucho en común, ¿verdad?

3–2 ¡Un poco similares/un poco diferentes!
1–0 ¿Los opuestos[2] se atraen?[3] ¡Por supuesto!

[1]twins [2]opposites [3]attract

Pronunciación The letters *h* and *j*

In Spanish, the letter *h* is never pronounced. Listen to and say these words:

hora   hablar   hasta   hola
hoy   hace   hacer   hotel

The letter *j* is pronounced like the letter *h* in "hat" but with more of a breathy sound. It is made far back in the mouth—almost in the throat. Listen to and say these words:

trabajar   dibujar   jugar   videojuegos
hoja   jueves   junio   julio

Try it out! Find and say five examples of foods or beverages from this chapter that have *h* or *j* in their spelling.

Try it out! Say this *trabalenguas* three times as fast as you can:

Debajo del puente de Guadalajara había un conejo debajo del agua.

136 ciento treinta y seis • Tema 3 • La comida

Differentiated Instruction

Students with Learning Difficulties

To reinforce the vocabulary in Act. 19, suggest specific examples that students might know, rather than just giving them the word in English. Take extra time with the model, as it may be confusing to students. For Act. 20, have students read the *¿Comprendes?* questions first, then refer to the visuals before reading the menu.

Heritage Speakers

Be careful to emphasize the distinction between **h** and **j** to students, especially in writing. It is not uncommon to see the silent **h** left out in writing, so monitor this carefully when checking student work.

20

¿Qué comida hay en el Ciberc@fé @rrob@?

✎ LEER, ESCRIBIR, HABLAR   Lee el menú y contesta las preguntas.

Strategy
Skimming Look quickly through the menu. What meal is it for? Find three dishes you recognize and two that are new to you.

Desayunos

Menú del Ciberc@fé @rrob@		**Tel: 212 03 95** #65 Col. Centro

No. 1 Huevos: *(jamón, tocino, chorizo¹)* $27.00
Con cóctel de fruta $30.00

No. 2 Sincronizadas: *(tortilla de harina,²* $33.00
queso amarillo, jamón)
Con cóctel de fruta $36.00

No. 3 Cuernitos: *(jamón, queso, tomate* $30.00
y lechuga)
Con cóctel de fruta $33.00

No. 4 Chilaquiles: *verdes o rojos* $21.00
Con cóctel de fruta $24.00

No. 5 Omelet: *(con pollo, jamón, tomate* $27.00
cebolla, champiñones³ o queso)

No. 6 Crepas (champiñones, jamón, pollo) $19.00

Refrescos *$7.50*   Café *$6.00*   Jugos *$11.50*   Té o té helado *$6.00*

Crepas de cuitlacoche

Chilaquiles

¹spicy sausage ²flour ³mushrooms

¿Comprendes?

1. Comes el desayuno No. 1, con un jugo de naranja. ¿Cuál es el precio *(price)* del desayuno?
2. Comes un omelet con un café. ¿Cuál es el precio?
3. No te gustan nada los huevos. ¿Qué comes del menú?
4. No te gusta ni el café ni el té helado. ¿Qué bebes?

El español en la comunidad
Foods from different Spanish-speaking countries have become very popular in the United States. Visit a local grocery store and make a list of different types of foods that come from Spanish-speaking countries. Which of these foods have you tried?

Capítulo 3A • ciento treinta y siete **137**

Enrich Your Teaching

Culture Note
There are several Mexican dishes made from leftover tortillas, including one called **chilaquiles**. The tortillas are cut into strips, dried, fried, and then cooked in a sauce made from tomato, onion, and chile. They are then covered with cheese and heavy cream. This is a

popular breakfast favorite. **Cuernitos** are croissants and are often served as a sandwich with ham, cheese, and tomato. **Sincronizadas** are two flour tortillas with ham and cheese in the middle. They are first grilled on both sides, then cut into four even pieces.

20

Standards: 1.2, 1.3, 4.1, 5.2

Suggestions: Direct students' attention to the Strategy. Have the class list familiar foods and identify new ones using the footnotes at the bottom of the menu.

Answers:
1. $38.50 (treinta y ocho dólares y cincuenta centavos)
2. $33.00 (treinta y tres dólares)
3. Como sincronizadas, chilaquiles o cuernitos.
4. Bebo jugos.

Pre-AP® Integration
- **Learning Objective:** Interpretive: Print
- **Activity 20:** Students use reading comprehension skills to answer questions about a menu.

El español en la comunidad

Standards: 5.1

Suggestions: Have students talk about items they have eaten that are typical of Spanish-speaking cultures. Ask them to brainstorm a list of items that might not be well-known in the United States. Compile students' findings into one list, type it, and distribute copies to each student as a shopping list of new items to try.

Additional Resources

📶 **Technology: Online Resources**
- Instant Check
- Guided, Core, Audio, Writing, Reading
- Communication Activities
- *Para hispanohablantes*
- Teacher's Resource Materials: Audio Script
- Communicative Pair Activity
- Technology: Audio Cap. 3A

Print
- Guided WB pp. 95–96
- Core WB pp. 54–55

Assessment _____

Prueba 3A-4 with Remediation *(online only)*
Quiz: *Me gustan, me encantan*
- Prueba 3A-4

Lectura

Standards: 1.2, 1.3, 3.1, 4.1

Suggestions

Pre-reading: Direct students' attention to the *Strategy*. Have students look at the photos and ask if they recognize the fruits and vegetables. Have them look at the recipe on p. 139 and identify which part lists ingredients and which part is the instructions.

Reading: Remind students that it is not important to understand every word, but rather the passage as a whole. Have students discuss the question about which of these fruits they enjoy eating, or if they've not tried them, which ones look interesting. Have students predict what the recipe is for. As they read, ask them to write down unknown words on a separate sheet of paper. Then have them go back and attempt to find the meaning of these words based on their background knowledge and visual cues.

Post-reading: Have students write their answers to the *¿Comprendes?* questions as homework and then share them in class the next day.

Starter Activity

Show large flashcards (from Clip Art) for several fruits, vegetables, and dairy products. Have students name each item aloud in unison.

Pre-AP® Integration

- **Learning Objective:** Interpretive: Print
- **Activity:** Read to the class the first paragraph followed by several true/false statements. Then, read each fruit description aloud to model the pronunciation. Have volunteers repeat each description.
- **Pre-AP® Resource Materials:** Comprehensive guide to Pre-AP® reading skill development

---

Lectura

OBJECTIVES
- Read about fruits native to the Americas
- Use cognates and context to understand unknown words
- Learn about produce imported from Chile

Strategy
Making guesses When you find an unknown word, try to guess the meaning. Is it a cognate? What might it mean within the context of the reading and other words around it? Keep reading and the meaning may become clear.

Frutas y verduras de las Américas

Hay muchas frutas y verduras que son originalmente de las Américas que hoy se comen en todos los países. Las verduras más populares son la papa, el maíz, los frijoles y muchas variedades de chiles. También hay una gran variedad de frutas como la papaya, la piña y el aguacate. Estas frutas y verduras son muy nutritivas, se pueden preparar fácilmente y son muy sabrosas. La papaya y la piña son frutas que se comen en el desayuno o de postre. ¿Cuáles de estas frutas comes?

el aguacate
La pulpa del aguacate es una fuente de energía, proteínas, vitaminas y minerales. Tiene vitaminas A y B.

el mango
Aunque[1] el mango es originalmente del Asia, se cultiva en las regiones tropicales de muchos países de las Américas. Tiene calcio y vitaminas A y C, como la naranja.

[1]Although

la papaya
Es una fruta con mucha agua. Es perfecta para el verano. Tiene más vitamina C que la naranja.

138 ciento treinta y ocho • Tema 3 • La comida

Differentiated Instruction

Students with Learning Difficulties

When students are given longer reading passages, it may be beneficial to pair students with learning difficulties with a more skillful reader, who can help them apply the reading strategies that they have learned. These strategies might include using prior knowledge, visual cues, or cognates to deduce meaning.

Visual/Spatial Learner

Have students research fruits from Latin America and prepare a poster showing pictures and informative captions in Spanish.

Go **Online** to practice

PEARSON realize™

PearsonSchool.com/Autentico

WRITING MAPA GLOBAL

Interpretive Reading

3A

☰ **la receta** › Licuado de plátano

Licuado de plátano

El licuado es una bebida muy popular en los países tropicales. ¡Es delicioso y muy nutritivo!

★ ★ ★ ★ ☆ comentarios (129)

1 porción **5** minutos

Ingredientes

1 plátano
2 vasos de leche
1 cucharadita de azúcar
hielo

Preparación

1. Cortar el plátano.
2. Colocar los ingredientes en la licuadora.
3. Licuar por unos 5 ó 10 segundos.

✎ **¿Comprendes?**

1. ¿Qué vitaminas tienen las frutas en la página anterior?
2. De las frutas y verduras del artículo, ¿cuáles *(which ones)* te gustan? ¿Cuáles no te gustan?
3. ¿Qué otras frutas te gustan? ¿Comes estas frutas en el desayuno o en el almuerzo?
4. ¿Qué fruta no es originalmente de las Américas?

CULTURA ‹ Chile

Frutas y verduras Los Estados Unidos importan una variedad de frutas. Durante el invierno importan manzanas, duraznos y uvas de Chile. Todo el año importan frutas tropicales, como[1] la papaya o el mango, de México, la República Dominicana y otros países de Centro y Sudamérica.

Pre-AP Integration: Los temas económicos
¿Es importante el clima de un país en la importación de las frutas y verduras? ¿Por qué?

🌐 **Mapa global interactivo** Explore the geography of Chile and locate the agricultural regions.

Chile

Uvas de Chile

[1]like

Capítulo 3A • ciento treinta y nueve **139**

Enrich Your Teaching

Culture Note

In Latin America there are many little shops that sell *licuados* made from different fruits. A *licuado* can serve as a quick meal any time during the day.

Teacher-to-Teacher

If you plan to prepare a variety of foods and beverages for your students, you may want to submit your class lists to the school nurse first. Ask him or her to check for any allergies that are on record for your students. That way, you'll know who needs to avoid anything you are preparing.

Licuado de plátano

Suggestions: If possible, have volunteers bring in the ingredients and supplies to make the recipe in class. Be absolutely certain that students do not have food allergies before doing this. Have students read the recipe and point to each item. Ask the class to read the recipe and tell you what to do. Provide them with the phrase **Ud. necesita...** so that they are able to give you instructions.

¿Comprendes?

Standards: 1.2, 1.3

Suggestions: Have students read each question and then re-read the text, looking for key words to answer the questions. When students have completed the activity, have one student ask the questions and volunteers give their answers.

Answers:

1. Las frutas tienen vitaminas A, B y C.
2. Answers will vary.
3. Answers will vary.
4. el mango

CULTURA

Standards: 2.2, 5.1

Suggestions: After reading the passage, you may wish to ask students to begin a sticker collection. Reward them with a point or other compensation for every sticker that they bring in from fruits imported from a Spanish-speaking country. Title a blank piece of poster board **Las frutas importadas**, have students add the stickers, and display it in class.

Answers will vary but may include how weather, geography, and seasons, affect produce availability.

🌐 **Technology: Mapa global interactivo**, Actividad 2 Explore the geography and topography of Chile.

For Further Reading

Student Resource: *Para hispanohablantes*, Lectura 2

Additional Resources

💻 **Technology: Online Resources**
 • Guided, Writing, Reading
 • Cultural Reading Activity
 • Communication Activities
 • *Para hispanohablantes*
 Print
 • Guided WB pp. 97

La cultura en vivo

Standards: 2.2, 3.1, 4.2

Suggestions: Begin a class discussion about snack foods. Talk about foods sold by sidewalk vendors in the United States, such as soft pretzels and hot dogs. Encourage students to talk about what snacks they like, where and when they tend to eat them, and whether alone or in a group. Introduce the idea of *churros* and chocolate. Have students read the first paragraph. If students have personal experience with *churros*, let them share with the class.

Continue the discussion and remind students that people in Spanish-speaking countries often sit and socialize with friends and enjoy a snack. *Churros* are not as sweet as doughnuts and are often dipped in hot chocolate. The chocolate mentioned here is thicker and richer than that usually served in the United States. Point out the recipe. Tell students they might like to try making this at home with an adult.

Direct attention to the *Comparación cultural* section and have students discuss the questions.

Answers will vary.

Preparing hot foods in the classroom may not be an option. However, you may be able to get some *churros* for the students to taste. Another option is to prepare *churros* and chocolate for a food festival. Some parents may be willing to participate and help prepare the food.

Point out that *churros* are brought in a *churrería*, not a grocery store. Compare *churrerías* to doughnut shops. Ask why people might prefer to get doughnuts from a doughnut shop rather than an all-purpose grocery store. (Answers will vary but may include more variety: it's their specialty and so it is apt to be better; freshness; a place to sit and chat.)

Online Cultural Reading

Standards: 1.2

After doing the online activity, ask students to identify and list three cultural practices that differ from their own.

Additional Resources

📶 **Technology: Online Resources**
- Cultural Reading Activity
- *Para hispanohablantes*

La cultura en vivo — Churros y chocolate

Empezar el día con churros y chocolate es una tradición muy española y también de otros países de habla hispana. Hay restaurantes o cafés que se llaman churrerías y se especializan en los churros o puedes comprar los churros en puestos de la calle.

Los churros son pastas *(pastries)* que se fríen *(are fried)* en aceite *(oil)*. Lo típico es comer los churros con chocolate caliente, una bebida rica y espesa *(thick)*. Puedes tomar esta comida deliciosa en el desayuno o una merienda *(snack)*. Pero cuidado… no debes comer muchos porque tienen grasa.

Comparación cultural ¿Qué combinaciones de comida o bebida les gustan a ti y a tus amigos? ¿Comen algo parecido *(like)* a los churros y chocolate?

Online Cultural Reading

Go to PearsonSchool.com/Autentico
ONLINE to read and understand a website with information about meals on a day trip

Strategy: Use background knowledge to identify cultural differences. Notice information in a website that differs from your own experience.

Aplicación: Find the section about food on the web site and identify cultural practices related to food and mealtimes. Identify the meals and foods for purchase and compare the times of each meal to times you eat and foods you typically have.

Churros

1 cup water	1/2 cup unsalted butter (= 1 stick)
1/4 teaspoon salt	1 cup all-purpose flour
4 large eggs	oil for deep frying
1 cup sugar	

In a heavy saucepan, bring water, butter, and salt to a full boil. Remove from heat. Add the flour all at once, stirring briskly. Stir until the mixture pulls away from the side of the pan and forms a ball. Put the mixture in a bowl. With an electric mixer on medium speed, add one egg at a time. After adding the last egg, beat the mixture for one more minute.

With adult supervision, heat 2–3 inches of oil to 375° F in a deep, heavy pan. Fit a pastry bag or cookie press with a 1/2 inch star tip. Pipe out 6 inch-long tubes of dough into the oil. ***Be extremely cautious adding dough to the oil, because the oil may spatter and burn you!*** Fry, turning a few times, for 3–5 minutes or until golden brown. Place the sugar on a plate. Drain the *churros* well on paper towels and then roll them in the sugar.

Churros y chocolate

Chocolate caliente

To make hot chocolate in Mexico, cacao beans are ground to a powder. Cinnamon, powdered almonds, and sugar are then added, and hot milk is poured in. The mixture is whipped with a wooden whisk called *un molinillo* or *un batidor*. You can find Mexican-style chocolate for making *chocolate caliente* in many supermarkets.

Chocolate caliente

140 ciento cuarenta • Tema 3 • La comida

Differentiated Instruction

Heritage Speakers

Students may be familiar with other snacks from Spanish-speaking countries. If so, allow them to describe the snack and tell whether there is a special way to eat it. If not, they might enjoy researching such a food from their heritage culture.

Presentación oral

OBJECTIVES
▶ Role-play an interview about classes, favorite activities, and favorite foods
▶ Use a list of questions to get the information you want

Go **Online** to practice
PEARSON realize™

PearsonSchool.com/Autentico

🎙 SPEAK/RECORD

¿Y qué te gusta comer?

TASK You and a partner will role-play a telephone conversation between an exchange student from the United States and a member of his or her host family in Uruguay.

1 Prepare Be sure to prepare for both roles. Here's how:

Host student: List at least four questions for the exchange student. Find out what he or she likes to study, eat and drink for breakfast and lunch, and his or her favorite activities.

Exchange student: Write some possible answers to questions from the host student and be prepared to give information about yourself.

Strategy

Making lists Making lists of questions can help you in conversations where you need to find out specific information.

2 Practice Work with a partner to practice different questions and different responses. Here's how you might start your conversation:

> **Host student:** ¡Hola, Pablo! Soy Rosa.
>
> **Exchange student:** ¡Hola, Rosa! ¿Cómo estás?
>
> **Host Student:** Bien, gracias. Pues Pablo, ¿te gusta . . . ?

Continue the conversation. Use your notes in practice, but not to present.

3 Present You will be paired with another student, and your teacher will assign roles. The host student begins the conversation. Listen to your partner's questions and responses and keep the conversation going.

4 Evaluation The following rubric will be used to grade your presentation.

Rubric	Score 1	Score 3	Score 5
Completion of task	You ask or answer two questions during the conversation.	You ask or answer three questions during the conversation.	You ask or answer four or more questions during the conversation.
How easily you are understood	You are extremely difficult to understand. Your teacher could only recognize isolated words and phrases.	You are understandable, but have frequent errors in vocabulary and/or grammar that hinder your comprehensibility.	You are easily understood. You teacher does not have to "decode" what you are trying to say.
Your ability to keep the conversation going	You provide no conversational response or follow-up to what your partner says.	You provide frequent response or follow-up to what your partner says.	You always provide a response to your partner, listen and ask follow-up questions or volunteer additional information.

Enrich Your Teaching

21st Century Skills

Media Literacy Have two students prepare a script for an interview for a "foodie" radio program. One student is the interviewer and conducts a phone interview with a celebrity. The questions and answers deal with what the celebrity does to keep fit and to maintain a high energy level.

Interpersonal · 3A

Presentación oral

Standards: 1.1, 1.3

Suggestions: Point out the *Strategy*. Read through the assignment and the 4-step approach with students.

1. Prepare Provide time for students to complete this step individually. Students may need to refer to Capítulos 1A and 1B to guide them while writing their questions and answers. Students may want to keep their written questions and answers to add to their portfolio.

2. Practice Pair up students and have them work with another pair of students.

3. Present Students should not use their notes for this step. Remind them to listen carefully to the questions and answers so they can answer accurately.

4. Evaluation Your students may want to place a copy of your comments and their grade, along with the questions they prepared in advance, in their portfolios.

Pre-AP® Integration

Pre-AP® Resource Book: Comprehensive guide to Pre-AP® speaking skill development

Digital Portfolio

Make video or audio recordings of student presentations in class, or assign the Speak and Record activity so they can record their presentations online. Include the recording in their portfolios.

Additional Resources

📶 **Technology: Online Resources**
• Guided
• *Para hispanohablantes*
Print
• Guided WB pp. 98

Self Assessment

Presentación oral
• **Assessment Program:** Rubrics
Review the rubric with students. Go over the descriptions of the different levels of performance. After assessing students, help individuals understand how their performance could be improved. (See Teacher's Resource Materials for suggestions on using rubrics in assessment.)

Auténtico

Standards: 1.2, 2.1, 2.2

Resources: *Authentic Resources Wkbk,* Cap. 3A
Authentic Resources: Cap 3A: Videoscript
AP Theme: *La vida contemporánea: Los estilos de vida*

Before You Watch

Discuss the *Strategy* with students. Have them look at the image from the video and ask them to use Spanish to identify what they recognize in the scene. Students should be able to talk about some foods they see in Spanish, but discussion of the details of the people and food stand may need to be in English. Ask if there are any foods shown that they do not recognize. Then review the key vocabulary with the class. Again, have students comment on any food items that differ from their usual meal items, and see if they can identify any new food items using the key vocabulary. Ask students to predict the kinds of foods they might expect to see in the video, using the key vocabulary and image in their text. Note these foods in a list on the board.

Technology: Watch the Video

Before starting the video, direct students attention to the *Mientras ves* activity. Compare this food list to the list the class compiled on the board and have students add any additional foods to their list.

Play the video once completely through, without pausing, and tell students to watch for gestures people make and foods they recognize to increase their understanding of the video. Remind students that they will not understand every word, but that they should listen and watch for overall understanding. Replay the video, stopping as necessary for students to complete the listening activity and to check comprehension. Show the video a final time without pausing.

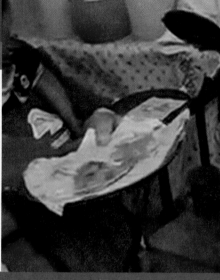

Auténtico

Partnered with UNIVISION COMMUNICATIONS INC

Quesadillas en las calles de México

Before You Watch

Use the Strategy: Visuals

Use the visuals to increase your understanding of the key ideas in the video. Watch for details of the foods, how people are eating them, and their reaction as they eat.

Read this Key Vocabulary

al gusto = to taste
un poquito de hambre = a little hungry
¿está rico? = Is it tasty?
nopal = prickly pear cactus, a common ingredient in Mexican cuisine
uno de los mejores que he comido = one of the best that I have eaten
chicharrón = crispy pork rind

▶ Watch the Video

What kinds of foods do you think would be in a *quesadilla* served on the streets of Mexico City?

Go to **PearsonSchool.com/Autentico** and watch the video **Raúl de Molina se dio gusto comiendo quesadillas en las calles de México** to see how eating street food can be a cultural experience for the senses.

Complete the Activities

Mientras ves As you watch the video, indicate the ingredients from the list below that you see or hear in the different food items.

queso	**chile**
carne	**nopal**
tortilla	**croquetas**
chicharrón	**cereal**
café	**arroz**

Differentiated Instruction

Heritage Speakers

Students may be familiar with other street food from Spanish-speaking countries. If so, allow them to describe the food and tell whether there is a special way to eat it. If not, they might enjoy researching such a food from their heritage culture.

Challenge

To increase the rigor of the activity, have students choose a new food from the video and find a recipe online to share with the class. They should include an explanation or pictures of new or unknown ingredients.

Integration

Después de ver Review the video as needed to answer the following questions.

1. En el video, ¿a los clientes les gusta (*do they like*) la comida? ¿Qué palabras o expresiones usan?

2. Escribe los ingredientes que tienen las quesadillas.

3. At the end of the video, Raúl says that eating at this food stand is "mejor que comer en un restaurante de cinco estrellas". What words and visual clues from the video help you to understand what he means?

📖 **For more activities, go to the *Authentic Resources Workbook*.**

Los estilos de vida y las tradiciones sociales

Expansión Find other authentic resources in *Auténtico* online, then answer the question.

📁 **3A Auténtico**

Integración de ideas En los dos recursos auténticos, ¿cuáles son los ingredientes que las comidas tienen en común? Explica la importancia de un ingrediente en la comida mexicana.

Comparación cultural Compara la comida típica en tu casa con la comida mexicana.

Complete the Activities

Mientras ves

Standards: 1.2, 2.2

Suggestions: Confirm that students have indicated all the correct foods shown or discussed in the video. Ask students what other foods they saw or heard in the video that were not on their list. Discuss what foods they expected to see and did not.

Answers:

queso, chile, nopal, tortilla, croquetas, chicharrón

Después de ver

Standards: 1.2, 1.3, 2.1, 2.2

Suggestions: Discuss the questions with the class. Ask for multiple volunteers to respond to each question in order to gauge overall understanding. Students' answers may vary based on their comprehension.

Answers:

1. Sí, les gusta la comida. *Answers will vary.* Está rico. Está fresquito. Está caliente. Está bueno.
2. chile, nopal, chicharrón
3. *Answers will vary.* Students may mention that customers say they like the food, that Raúl makes sounds to indicate that the food tastes good, that Raúl says that the food is very good.

For more Authentic Resources: Assign the *Authentic Resources Workbook* activities for homework, so that students can play the video on their own and complete the workbook activities at their own pace.

Pre-AP® Integration

Standards: 1.2, 1.3, 2.1, 2.2

Resources: *Authentic Resources Wkbk,* Cap. 3A; Authentic Resources: Cap 3A; Videoscript

Suggestions: Before completing the Pre-AP® Integration activity, have students go to the workbook and complete the worksheet(s) for the additional resource(s).

Enrich Your Teaching

Culture Note

Mexico City is known for its delicious street food. Vendors set up carts on street corners and have regular customers who visit them daily. Foods include *Tacos al pastor* made with pork, *barbacoa* often of roasted lamb, and *pescado a la talla,* a whole fish, split and grilled. These meats are served in corn tortillas with additions such as onions, cilantro, avocado, and salsas.

Using Authentic Resources

Have students create a personal vocabulary list with additional food words from the authentic resources. Suggest that they include foods that interest them or ones that would be useful if visiting a Mexican restaurant or preparing foods at home.

Review Activities

To talk about breakfast and lunch, to talk about beverages: Have students work in pairs to quiz each other on the vocabulary. They may find it useful to create flashcards with pictures on them.

To talk about eating and drinking: Have students ask others what they like to eat and drink.

To indicate how often: Have students make a list of their favorite foods and beverages and talk about how often they eat them.

To show surprise, to say that you like / love something: Have students brainstorm a list of foods and beverages that they like and dislike. Ask them to read their lists to a partner and react using one of these phrases.

Digital Portfolio

Invite students to review the activities they have completed in this chapter, including written reports, posters or other visuals, recordings of oral presentations, or other projects. Have them select one or two items that they feel best demonstrate their achievements in Spanish. These products should be included in students' portfolios. Have them include this with the Chapter Checklist and Self-Assessment Worksheet.

Pre-AP® Integration

- **Learning Objective:** Interpersonal speaking
- **Pre-AP® Resource Materials Activity Sheets, Tema 3.** Have students work in pairs, and choose from questions 1–10 to guide their conversation.

Additional Resources

Technology: Online Resources
- Instant Check
- *Para hispanohablantes*
- Integrated Performance Assessment

Print
- Core WB pp. 56–57

Teacher Resources
- Teacher's Resource Materials: Situation Cards, Clip Art
- Assessment Program: Chapter Checklist and Self-Assessment Worksheet

---

Repaso del capítulo

OBJECTIVES
▶ Review the vocabulary and grammar
▶ Demonstrate you can perform the tasks on p. 145

🔊 Vocabulario

to talk about breakfast

en el desayuno	for breakfast
el cereal	cereal
el desayuno	breakfast
los huevos	eggs
el pan	bread
el pan tostado	toast
el plátano	banana
la salchicha	sausage
el tocino	bacon
el yogur	yogurt

to talk about lunch

en el almuerzo	for lunch
la ensalada	salad
la ensalada de frutas	fruit salad
las fresas	strawberries
la galleta	cookie
la hamburguesa	hamburger
el jamón	ham
la manzana	apple
la naranja	orange
las papas fritas	French fries
el perrito caliente	hot dog
la pizza	pizza
el queso	cheese
el sándwich de jamón y queso	ham and cheese sandwich
la sopa de verduras	vegetable soup

to talk about beverages

el agua f.	water
el café	coffee
el jugo de manzana	apple juice
el jugo de naranja	orange juice
la leche	milk
la limonada	lemonade
el refresco	soft drink
el té	tea
el té helado	iced tea

to talk about eating and drinking

beber	to drink
comer	to eat
la comida	food, meal
compartir	to share

to indicate how often

nunca	never
siempre	always
todos los días	every day

to say that you like / love something

Me / te encanta(n) ____.	I / you love (____).
Me / te gusta(n) ____.	I / you like (____).

other useful words

comprender	to understand
con	with
¿Cuál?	Which? What?
más o menos	more or less
por supuesto	of course
¡Qué asco!	How awful!
sin	without
¿Verdad?	Right?

Gramática

present tense of -er verbs

como	comemos
comes	coméis
come	comen

present tense of -ir verbs

comparto	compartimos
compartes	compartís
comparte	comparten

For *Vocabulario adicional,* see pp. 472–473.

Differentiated Instruction

Extra Support

Have students review the *Repaso del capítulo* and create flashcards for any words that they do not know. Pair them with a student who is more confident with the vocabulary to practice. Before the test, provide students with a practice test, so they can become comfortable with the format.

Heritage Speakers

Have students write a few paragraphs telling about their perfect lunch: Where are they going to eat? Whom are they going to invite to eat with them? What food are they going to eat? What will they have to drink? Encourage them to use as many vocabulary words from this chapter as they can.

Preparación para el examen

Más recursos PearsonSchool.com/Autentico

- Games
- Flashcards
- Instant check
- Tutorials
- *Gram*Activa videos
- Animated verbs

What you need to be able to do for the exam...	Here are practice tasks similar to those you will find on the exam...	For review go to your print or digital textbook...
Interpretive		
1 ESCUCHAR I can understand descriptions of what people eat and drink for lunch.	Listen as three students describe what they typically eat and drink for lunch. Which is most like the kind of lunch you eat? Did they mention anything you could not buy in your school cafeteria?	pp. 124–127 *Vocabulario en contexto* p. 125 *Actividades 1–2* p. 128 *Actividad 5*
Interpersonal		
2 HABLAR I can tell someone what I typically eat for breakfast and ask them the same.	Your Spanish club is meeting for breakfast before school next week. Find out what other people in your class typically eat for breakfast. After you tell at least two people what you eat for breakfast, ask what they like to eat. Does everyone eat the same kind of breakfast or do you all like to eat different things?	p. 129 *Actividad 7* p. 130 *Actividad 8* p. 131 *Actividad 11* p. 133 *Actividad 13* p. 134 *Actividades 15–16* p. 141 *Presentación oral*
Interpretive		
3 LEER I can read and understand words on a menu.	You are trying to help a child order from the lunch menu below, but he is very difficult to please. He doesn't like anything white. And he refuses to eat anything that grows on trees. Which items from the menu do you think he would refuse to eat or drink? **Almuerzo** hamburguesa plátanos pizza manzana ensalada leche	pp. 124–127 *Vocabulario en contexto* p. 131 *Actividad 10* p. 137 *Actividad 20* pp. 138–139 *Lectura*
Presentational		
4 ESCRIBIR I can write a list of the foods that I like and dislike.	Your Spanish club is sponsoring a "Super Spanish Saturday." Your teacher wants to know what foods the class likes and dislikes so that the club can buy what most people like. Write the headings *Me gusta(n)* and *No me gusta(n)* in two columns. List at least four items that you like to eat and drink for breakfast and four items for lunch. Then list what you don't like to eat and drink for these same meals.	p. 128 *Actividad 4* p. 129 *Actividad 6* p. 131 *Actividad 11* p. 134 *Actividad 16* p. 135 *Actividad 18* p. 137 *Actividad 20*
Culture		
5 COMPARAR I can understand some cultural differences regarding snacks.	Think about popular food combinations in the United States, such as a cup of coffee and a doughnut. What is a similar combination that is popular in many Spanish-speaking countries, and where are you able to buy it?	p. 140 *La cultura en vivo*

Capítulo 3A • ciento cuarenta y cinco **145**

Differentiated Assessment

Core Assessment
- Assessment Program: Examen del capítulo 3A
- Technology: Audio Cap. 3A
- ExamView: Chapter Test, Test Banks A and B

Challenge/Pre-AP®
- ExamView: Pre-AP® Test Bank
- Pre-AP® Resource Materials

Extra Support
- Alternate Assessment Program: Examen del capítulo 3A
- Technology: Audio Cap. 3A

Heritage Speakers
- Assessment Program: *Para hispanohablantes:* Examen del capítulo 3A
- ExamView: Heritage Learner Test Bank

Performance Tasks

Standards: 1.3

Student Resource: Para hispanohablantes
Teacher Resources: Teacher's Resource Materials: Audio Script; Technology: Audio Cap. 3A

1. Escuchar

Suggestions: Play the audio or read the script.
Script

Marco: Siempre como una hamburguesa y papas fritas en el almuerzo. Por supuesto, necesito comer frutas y verduras, pero no me gustan.

Elena: ¡Qué asco! ¡Una hamburguesa y papas fritas! Nunca como papas fritas. Todos los días como una ensalada de frutas o sopa de verduras, ¡con una galleta, claro!

Tomás: ¿Cuál es mi comida favorita? Pues, no como mucho en el almuerzo. Como pizza o un perrito caliente y bebo un refresco.

Answers will vary.

2. Hablar

Suggestions: Allow time for students to work on this task in class. If students have difficulty with spontaneous conversation, have them write their messages first.

Answers will vary.

3. Leer

Suggestions: Have students read their answers to the class. Ask which items the boy would eat or drink.

Answers:
  Eat: ensalada, hamburguesa y pizza
  Not eat: plátanos, manzana y leche
Extension: Have students list items from p. 144 that the boy would eat or drink.

4. Escribir

Suggestions: Have students try this activity without the vocabulary list or notes.

5. Comparar

Suggestions: Remind students that in the United States we often snack on packaged foods. How does this differ from Spanish-speaking cultures?

Answers: ***Churros*** and ***chocolate*** can be purchased in ***churrerías*** or at street stands.

AT A GLANCE

Objectives

- Listen to and read descriptions of healthy and unhealthy lifestyles
- Talk and write about food, health, and exercise choices
- Exchange information while expressing your opinions about food choices and health
- Read and understand an authentic text about healthy foods
- Understand cultural perspectives on medicines and health care
- Compare traditional foods, markets, and festivals in the Spanish-speaking world with those in the United States

Vocabulary

- Food groups
- Healthy activities
- Ways to describe foods

Grammar

- Plurals of adjectives
- The verb *ser*

Culture

- Diego Rivera's mural of *el tianguis*, p. 147
- *el mate,* p. 152
- *la Tomatina,* p. 156
- *los mercados,* p. 160
- Soccer and the World Cup, p. 163
- Herbal remedies, p. 164

Authentic Resources

- Infographic providing ten nutrition tips, pp. 166–167

Recycle

- Gender agreement of adjectives and nouns
- Using *ser* to talk about what a person is like
- Present tense of *-ar* verbs
- *me gusta(n)*

RESOURCES

	FOR THE STUDENT	DIGITAL	PRINT	FOR THE TEACHER	DIGITAL	PRINT
Plan				Teacher's Edition	•	•
				Teacher's Resource Materials	•	
				Pre-AP® Resource Materials	•	
				Lesson Plans, pp. 146-c. 146-d	•	•
				Mapa global interactivo	•	
Introducción pp. 146–147						
Present	Student Edition, pp. 146–147	•	•	Teacher's Edition, pp. 146–147	•	•
	DK Reference Atlas	•		Teacher's Resource Materials	•	
	Para hispanohablantes	•		Mapa global interactivo	•	
Vocabulario en contexto pp. 148–151						
Present & Practice	Student Edition, pp. 148–151	•	•	Teacher's Edition, pp. 148–151	•	•
	Audio	•		Teacher's Resource Materials	•	
	Videohistoria	•		Vocabulary Clip Art	•	
	Flashcards	•		Technology: Audio	•	
	Instant Check	•		Video Program: Videohistoria	•	
	Guided WB, pp. 99–108	•				
	Core WB, pp. 58–61	•				
	Communication Activities	•				
	Para hispanohablantes	•				
Assess and Remediate				Prueba 3B–1: Assessment Program, pp. 80–81	•	
				Assessment Program para hispanohablantes, pp. 80–81	•	

RESOURCES

	FOR THE STUDENT	DIGITAL	PRINT	FOR THE TEACHER	DIGITAL	PRINT
Vocabulario en uso pp. 152–155						
Present & Practice	Student Edition, pp. 152–155	•	•	Interactive Whiteboard Vocabulary Activities	•	
	Instant Check	•		Teacher's Edition, pp. 152–155	•	•
	Communication Activities	•		Teacher's Resource Materials	•	
	Para hispanohablantes	•		Communicative Pair Activities	•	
	Communicative Pair Activities	•		Technology: Audio	•	
				Videomodelos	•	
Assess and Remediate				Prueba 3B–2 with Remediation	•	
				Prueba 3B–2: Assessment Program, pp. 82–83	•	
				Assessment Program para hispanohablantes, pp. 82–83	•	
Gramática pp. 156–161						
Present & Practice	Student Edition, pp. 156–161	•	•	Interactive Whiteboard Grammar Activities	•	
	Instant Check	•		Teacher's Edition, pp. 156–161	•	•
	Animated Verbs	•		Teacher's Resource Materials	•	
	Tutorial Video: Grammar	•		Communicative Pair Activities	•	
	Canción de hip hop	•		Technology: Audio	•	
	Guided WB, pp. 109–112	•	•	Videomodelos	•	
	Core WB, pp. 62–64	•	•	Video Program: GramActiva	•	
	Communication Activities	•				
	Para hispanohablantes	•				
	Communicative Pair Activities	•				
Assess and Remediate				Pruebas 3B–3 and 3B–4 with Remediation	•	
				Pruebas 3B–3, 3B–4: Assessment Program, pp. 84, 85	•	
				Assessment Program para hispanohablantes, pp. 84, 85	•	
Aplicación pp. 162–167						
Application	Student Edition, pp.162–167	•	•	Teacher's Edition, pp. 162–167	•	•
	Authentic Resources Workbook	•	•	Mapa global interactivo	•	
	Authentic Resources	•		Authentic Resources Lesson Plans with scripts, answer keys	•	
	Online Cultural Reading	•	•			
	Literacy Skills Workbook	•	•			
	Guided WB, pp. 113–114	•				
	Communication Activities	•				
	Para hispanohablantes	•				
Repaso del capítulo pp. 168–169						
Review	Student Edition, pp. 168–169	•	•	Teacher's Edition, pp. 168-169	•	•
	Online Games and Puzzles	•		Teacher's Resource Materials	•	
	Core WB, pp. 65–66	•	•	Technology: Audio	•	
	Communication Activities	•				
	Para hispanohablantes	•				
	Instant Check	•				
Chapter Assessment						
Assess				Examen del capítulo 3B	•	
				Assessment Program, pp. 86–92	•	
				Alternate Assessment Program, pp. 30–34	•	
				Assessment Program para hispanohablantes, pp. 86–92	•	
				Technology: Audio, Cap. 3B, Examen	•	
				ExamView: Test Banks A and B questions only online	•	
				Heritage Learner Test Bank	•	
				Pre-AP® Test Bank	•	

LESSON PLAN (50 MINUTES)

DAY	Warm-up / Assess	Preview / Present / Practice / Communicate		Wrap-up / Homework Options
1	**Warm-up** (10 min.) • Return Examen del capítulo 3A	**Chapter Opener** (5 min.) • Objectives • Arte y cultura	**Vocabulario en contexto** (30 min.) • Presentation: Vocabulario en contexto • Actividades 1, 2	**Wrap-up and Homework Options** (5 min.) • Core Practice 3B-1, 3B-2
2	**Warm-up** (5 min.) • Homework check	**Vocabulario en contexto** (40 min.) • Presentation: Videohistoria *Comida tropical* • View: Videohistoria	• Video Activities 1, 2, 3, 4 • Actividad 3	**Wrap-up and Homework Options** (5 min.) • Core Practice 3B-3, 3B-4 • Prueba 3B-1: Vocabulary recognition
3	**Warm-up** (10 min.) • Actividades 4, 5 • Homework check • **Formative Assessment** (10 min.) • Prueba 3B-1: Vocabulary recognition	**Vocabulario en uso** (25 min.) • Cultura • Interactive Whiteboard Vocabulary Activities • Actividades 6, 7, 8, 10 • Audio Activities 5, 6		**Wrap-up and Homework Options** (5 min.) • Writing Activity 10 • Prueba 3B-2 with Remediation: Vocabulary production
4	**Warm-up** (5 min.) • Actividad 9 • Homework check • **Formative Assessment** (10 min.) • Prueba 3B-2 with Remediation: Vocabulary production	**Gramática y vocabulario en uso** (30 min.) • Actividad 11 • Presentation: The plurals of adjectives • View: GramActiva video	• Interactive Whiteboard Grammar Activities • Actividades 12, 13, 14 • Cultura	**Wrap-up and Homework Options** (5 min.) • Core Practice 3B-5 • Prueba 3B-3 with Remediation: The plurals of adjectives
5	**Warm-up** (15 min.) • Writing Activity 11 • Audio Activity 7 • Homework check • **Formative Assessment** (10 min.) • Prueba 3B-3 with Remediation: The plurals of adjectives	**Gramática y vocabulario en uso** (20 min.) • Communicative Pair Activity • Pronunciación • Presentation: The verb *ser* • View: GramActiva video • Interactive Whiteboard Grammar Activities • Actividad 16		**Wrap-up and Homework Options** (5 min.) • Writing Activities 12, 13
6	**Warm-up** (5 min.) • Homework check	**Gramática y vocabulario en uso** (40 min.) • View: GramActiva video • Actividades 15, 17, 18 • Audio Activities 8, 9	• Communicative Pair Activity • El español en el mundo del trabajo	**Wrap-up and Homework Options** (5 min.) • Core Practice 3B-6, 3B-7 • Prueba 3B-4 with Remediation: The verb *ser*
7	**Warm-up** (10 min.) • Cultura • Homework check • **Formative Assessment** (10 min.) • Prueba 3B-4 with Remediation: The verb *ser*	**Gramática y vocabulario en uso** (25 min.) • Exploración del lenguaje • Actividades 19, 20		**Wrap-up and Homework Options** (5 min.) • Perspectivas del mundo hispano
8	**Warm-up** (5 min.) • Homework check	**Aplicación** (40 min.) • Lectura • ¿Comprendes? • Cultura	• Presentación escrita: Steps 1, 5 • Auténtico	**Wrap-up and Homework Options** (5 min.) • Presentación escrita: Step 2 • Preparación para el examen 3, 4, 5 • Lectura • Auténtico
9	**Warm-up** (5 min.) • Homework check	**Aplicación** (20 min.) • Presentación escrita: Step 3	**Repaso del capítulo** (20 min.) • Vocabulario y gramática • Preparación para el examen 1, 2	**Wrap-up and Homework Options** (5 min.) • Presentación escrita: Step 4 • Core Practice 3B-8, 3B-9 • Instant Check • Examen del capítulo 3B
10	**Warm-up** (10 min.) • Homework check • **Summative Assessment** (40 min.) • Examen del capítulo 3B			

ALTERNATE LESSON PLAN (90 MINUTES)

DAY	Warm-up / Assess	Preview / Present / Practice / Communicate		Wrap-up / Homework Options
1	**Warm-up** (10 min.) • Return Examen del capítulo 3A	**Chapter Opener** (5 min.) • Objectives • Arte y cultura **Vocabulario en contexto** (60 min.) • Presentation: Vocabulario en contexto • Actividades 1, 2 • Presentation: Videohistoria *Comida tropical* • View: Videohistoria	• Video Activities 1, 2, 3, 4 • Actividad 3 **Vocabulario en uso** (10 min.) • Actividades 6, 7	**Wrap-up and Homework Options** (5 min.) • Core Practice 3B-1, 3B-2, 3B-3, 3B-4 • Prueba 3B-1: Vocabulary recognition
2	**Warm-up** (10 min.) • Actividades 4, 5 • Homework check • **Formative Assessment** (10 min.) • Prueba 3B-1: Vocabulary recognition	**Vocabulario en uso** (65 min.) • Cultura • Interactive Whiteboard Vocabulary Activities • Actividades 8, 9, 10, 11 • Audio Activities 5, 6 • Pronunciación • Communicative Pair Activity		**Wrap-up and Homework Options** (5 min.) • Writing Activity 10 • Prueba 3B-2 with Remediation: production
3	**Warm-up** (5 min.) • Homework check • **Formative Assessment** (10 min.) • Prueba 3B-2 with Remediation: Vocabulary production	**Gramática y vocabulario en uso** (70 min.) • Presentation: The plurals of adjectives • View: GramActiva video • Actividades 12, 13, 14 • Cultura • Audio Activity 7 • Writing Activity 11 • Presentation: The verb *ser*	• View: GramActiva video • Interactive Whiteboard Grammar Activities • Actividades 15, 16, 17, 18 • Audio Activities 8, 9 • Communicative Pair Activity	**Wrap-up and Homework Options** (5 min.) • Core Practice 3B-5, 3B-6, 3B-7 • Writing Activities 12, 13 • Pruebas 3B-3, 3B-4 with Remediation: The plurals of adjectives, The verb *ser*
4	**Warm-up** (15 min.) • Homework check • **Formative Assessment** (15 min.) • Pruebas 3B-3, 3B-4 with Remediation: The plurals of adjectives, The verb *ser*	**Gramática y vocabulario en uso** (20 min.) • Cultura • El español en el mundo del trabajo • Exploración del lenguaje • Actividades 19, 20 **Aplicación** (35 min.) • Lectura • ¿Comprendes? • Cultura	• Presentación escrita: Steps 1, 5	**Wrap-up and Homework Options** (5 min.) • Presentación escrita: Step 2 • Lectura
5	**Warm-up** (5 min.) • Homework check	**Aplicación** (50 min.) • Presentación escrita: Step 3 • Perspectivas del mundo hispano • Auténtico **Repaso del capítulo** (30 min.) • Vocabulario y gramática • Preparación para el examen 1, 2, 3, 4, 5		**Wrap-up and Homework Options** (5 min.) • Presentación escrita: Step 4 • Core Practice 3B-8, 3B-9 • Instant Check • Examen del capítulo 3B
6	**Warm-up** (15 min.) • Homework check • Answer questions **Repaso del capítulo** (25 min.) • Situation Cards • Communicative Pair Activities • **Summative Assessment** (45 min.) • Examen del capítulo 3B			**Wrap-up and Homework Options** (5 min.) • Auténtico

Can-Do Statements

Read the can-do Statements in the chapter objectives with students. Then have students read Preparación para el examen on page 168 to preview what they will be able to do at the end of the chapter.

Standards for Capítulo 3B

To achieve the goals of the Standards, students will:

COMMUNICATION

1.1 Interpersonal
- Talk about food groups and healthy diet
- Talk about food preferences and meals
- Talk about healthy lifestyle choices
- Talk about the personality traits of various people

1.2 Interpretive
- Read and listen to information about food groups
- Read and listen to information about health habits
- Listen to ways to describe food
- Read a picture-based story
- Listen to and watch a video about healthy diet

1.3 Presentational
- Present information about foods and beverages
- Present information about healthy lifestyle choices
- Present information about personality traits of people

CULTURE

2.1 Practices to Perspectives
- Explain past and present open-air markets
- Talk about the communal nature of *mate*
- Talk about *La Tomatina* festival

2.2 Products to Perspectives
- Talk about Diego Rivera and his painting
- Talk about *mate*

CONNECTIONS

3.1 Making Connections
- Discuss Diego Rivera
- Discuss nutrition
- Reinforce math and graphing abilities skills

3.2 Acquiring Information and Diverse Perspectives
- Watch and listen to a video

COMPARISONS

4.1 Language
- Talk about new vocabulary through the recognition of cognates
- Explain gender agreement in use of adjectives
- Explain the pronunciation of the letters *l* and *ll*
- Explain number agreement in use of adjectives
- Explain the present tense of the irregular verb *ser*

4.2 Cultural
- Compare *mate* to its counterpart in the United States
- Compare *La Tomatina* to festivals in the United States
- Compare places people shop for produce

CAPÍTULO **3B**
Para mantener la salud

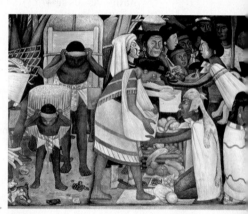

Country Connections Explorar el mundo hispano

España
México
Guatemala
Costa Rica
Chile
Paraguay
Uruguay
Argentina

CHAPTER OBJECTIVES

Communication

By the end of this chapter you will be able to:
- Listen to and read descriptions of healthy and unhealthy lifestyles.
- Talk and write about food, health, and exercise choices.
- Exchange information while expressing your opinions about food choices and health.

Culture

You will also be able to:
- **Auténtico:** Read an authentic text about healthy foods and identify cultural practices.
- Understand cultural perspectives on medicines and health care.

- Compare traditional foods, markets, and festivals in the Spanish-speaking world with those in the United States.

You will demonstrate what you know and can do:
- Presentación escrita: Para mantener la salud
- Repaso del capítulo: Preparación para el examen

You will use:

Vocabulary
- Food groups
- Healthy activities
- Ways to describe foods

Grammar
- Plurals of adjectives
- The verb *ser*

ARTE y CULTURA México

Diego Rivera (1886–1957) This detail of a mural entitled "La Gran Tenochtitlán" by Mexican artist Diego Rivera is located in the Palacio Nacional in Mexico City. It shows *el tianguis,* the bustling marketplace at Tenochtitlán, capital of the Aztec Empire. In the center right there are many kinds of food being traded, including tomatoes, squash, and different varieties of chile peppers. This mural is one of many by Rivera that focus on pre-Columbian life and civilizations.

- What impression do you think Rivera is giving about life in the pre-Columbian civilizations?

Mapa global interactivo Explore downtown Mexico City, and locate the Zócalo and Palacio Nacional.

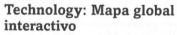

Detalle de *"La Gran Tenochtitlán"* (1945), Diego Rivera ▶
The Great City of Tenochtitlan, detail of a woman selling vegetables, 1945 (mural), Rivera, Diego (1886-1957)/Palacio Nacional, Mexico City, Mexico/Giraudon/The Bridgeman Art Library.

146 ciento cuarenta y seis • Tema 3 • La comida

Enrich Your Teaching

The End in Mind

Have students preview the sample performance tasks on *Preparación para el examen*, p. 169, and connect them to the Chapter Objectives. Explain to students that by completing the sample tasks they can self-assess their learning progress.

Technology: Mapa global interactivo

Download the *Mapa global interactivo* files for Chapter 3B and preview the activities. Activity 1 takes you to the Zócalo and the Palacio Nacional in Ciudad de México. Activity 2 visits Spain, winner of the 2010 World Cup.

Mercado de la Boquería,
Barcelona, España

▶ Videocultura **El maíz:** *comida esencial*

Capítulo 3B • ciento cuarenta y siete **147**

COMMUNITIES

5.1 School and Global Communities
• Understand the value of Spanish-speaking ability in a career such as culinary arts

Chapter Opener

Resources: Mapa global interactivo

Suggestions: Introduce students to the chapter theme and review the objectives. Tell them they will be learning to talk about healthy eating and health habits. Brainstorm a list of healthy foods and "junk" food that students eat, and discuss some of their eating habits. The *Videohistoria* for this chapter is about shopping for ingredients for Cuban recipes.

▶ **Technology: Videocultura** View *El maíz: comida esencial* with the class to find out how corn is prepared in Spanish-speaking countries.

ARTE Y CULTURA

Standards: 2.1, 2.2, 3.1

Suggestions: Explain that **el tianguis** was a central marketplace for the Aztecs. In modern Mexico these markets have the same name and many of the same goods are traded. Have students provide examples of markets in the United States. Do any traditional markets exist near you? What goods are sold?

Answers will vary.

🌐 **Technology: Mapa global interactivo, Actividad 1** Find the Zócalo and the Palacio Nacional in Ciudad de México.

Teaching with Art

Share with students that Tenochtitlán was located in what is now Mexico City. It was the capital of the Aztec civilization until 1521, when the Spanish defeated the Aztecs. After the Mexican Revolution (1910–1920), Diego Rivera and other artists were asked to paint large murals in Mexico City to convey a sense of pride in Mexico's past and hope for her future.

Project-Based Learning

Para la salud: Vacaciones
(continued)

Have students find information online in Spanish about healthy food choices to include in their health resort menus. Have students make a Web page based on what they have found. The Web page can consist of pictures and captions naming each food, with some brief statement of its health benefits.

Vocabulario en contexto

Standards: 1.2, 3.1

Resources: Teacher's Resource Materials: Input Script, Clip Art, Audio Script; Technology: Audio Cap. 3B

Suggestions: Use the Input Script from the *Teacher's Resource Materials* to present the new vocabulary and grammar. Bring plastic foods to class like those you would find in a child's toy kitchen. Present the vocabulary in three sets: fruits and vegetables, proteins and grains, and words to discuss health. Have students look at the pictures and guess what the words mean.

Ask questions that require a limited verbal response: *¿Te gustan las verduras? ¿Comes muchas uvas? ¿Los pasteles son buenos para la salud?* Have students "shop" for the plastic food items. Be sure they take foods from each of the food groups. Have them organize the items as you call out food groups.

Hand out copies of the Vocabulary Clip Art. Have students tear the images into individual food items. Describe different meals to students and have them group the foods as they would on a cafeteria tray. (If your class is small, you might be able to borrow real trays from the cafeteria.) Then ask if the meal you described is good or bad for one's health.

Technology: Interactive Whiteboard

Vocabulary Activities 3B Use the whiteboard activities in your Teacher Resources as you progress through the vocabulary practice with your class.

Vocabulario en contexto

Vocabulario en contexto

OBJECTIVES

Read, listen to, and understand information about
▶ food groups
▶ healthy activities
▶ ways to describe food

Paco y Tía Adela hablan de la comida.

Paco: Tengo hambre. Necesito comer **algo** bueno, por ejemplo, unos huevos rancheros.

Tía: Sí. Los huevos rancheros **son muy sabrosos.** Pero no **debes** comer **muchas grasas,** Paco. **¿Por qué no comes** una ensalada de tomates y cebollas?

Paco: ¡Qué **horrible! Prefiero** un helado o un pastel.

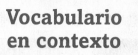

Tía Adela / Paco

las uvas · los tomates · las zanahorias · las cebollas · la lechuga · las grasas · la mantequilla · las papas · las judías verdes · los guisantes · la carne · el bistec · el pollo · el pescado

148 ciento cuarenta y ocho • Tema 3 • La comida

Differentiated Instruction

Students with Learning Difficulties

Have students write the new vocabulary in the vocabulary section of their notebook, accompanied by pictures and English translations, if needed. For *Actividad* 1, you might prepare students by naming individual items and having the students touch them before they hear them in context.

Heritage Speakers

Have students make two lists: one of their favorite foods and the other of foods they think they should be eating. Using their lists, have students discuss what they know about diet and activities to maintain good health. Check the lists for spelling.

Go **Online** to practice
PearsonSchool.com/Autentico
PEARSON
realize.
🔊 AUDIO

Paco:	Mi familia dice que mi dieta es **mala**. ¿Qué **hago**?
Tía:	**Para mantener la salud,** debes comer de **todo**. Come muchas verduras, frutas y también cereales. Paco, ¿haces ejercicio?
Paco:	Pues sí, **cada día**. Me gusta caminar y a veces levanto pesas.
Tía:	¡Muy bien!

caminar · los espaguetis · el helado · los cereales · los pasteles · el arroz · levantar pesas

1

¿Qué debe comer Paco?

🔊 ESCUCHAR Listen to Paco's friend giving him advice on his diet. Touch the photo of each item she mentions.

2

Una salud perfecta

🔊 ESCUCHAR Listen to a student describing his health habits. Raise one hand if he is describing things that are healthy and two hands if he is describing things that are unhealthy.

Capítulo 3B • ciento cuarenta y nueve **149**

Enrich Your Teaching

Culture Note

Food items may have many different names across cultures. Green beans, for example, may be called **judías verdes, ejotes, habas, alubias,** and **habichuelas.** Some may assume the term **judías verdes** is a reference to Jewish people. It is in fact from the Arabic *yudiyaa,* the word for "bean."

21st Century Skills

Communication Work with a partner in a role-play as nutritional counselor and elderly client. The counselor creates a plan for the client that includes both nutrition and exercise. Have students think about how the regimens would differ if the client were a teenager.

1

Standards: 1.2, 3.1

Resources: Teacher's Resource Materials: Audio Script; Technology: Audio Cap. 3B

Suggestions: Play the audio or use the script to read the activity aloud. Tell students that some of the sentences contain more than one food item.

🔊 **Technology: Audio Script and Answers**

1. Paco, hay que comer más zanahorias. (*carrots*)
2. También debes comer pescado. (*fish*)
3. No debes comer muchas grasas o mantequilla. (*butter*)
4. El arroz es bueno para la salud. (*rice*)
5. No es bueno comer muchos pasteles. (*pastries*)
6. Necesitas comer guisantes. (*peas*)
7. Debes comer uvas. (*grapes*)

2

Standards: 1.2, 3.1, 4.1

Resources: Teacher's Resource Materials: Audio Script; Technology: Audio Cap. 3B

Suggestions: Play the audio or read the script. Repeat the activity until students indicate understanding.

🔊 **Technology: Audio Script and Answers**

1. Mis amigos y yo corremos cada día. (*one hand*)
2. Nunca como fruta. (*both hands*)
3. No me gusta beber agua. (*both hands*)
4. Me gusta comer helados cada día. (*both hands*)
5. Me gusta levantar pesas en el gimnasio. (*one hand*)
6. Me encantan las verduras. (*one hand*)
7. Siempre desayuno fruta. (*one hand*)
8. Como judías verdes cada noche. (*one hand*)

Additional Resources

📶 **Technology: Online Resources**
• Instant Check
• Guided, Core, Audio, Writing practice
• *Para hispanohablantes*
Print:
• Guided WB pp. 99–104
• Core WB pp. 58–59

Vocabulario en contexto

Standards: 1.2

Resources: Technology: Audio Cap. 3A

Suggestions: Model the dialogue with a volunteer. Begin the reading again with volunteers playing the roles of the characters. Using the presentation, help students understand the new words in blue type.

Post-reading: Complete Actividad 3 to check comprehension.

3

Standards: 1.1, 1.3

Suggestions: You may wish to do this as a listening activity, reading the sentences to the students.

Extension: Use the sentences as a basis for a classroom survey. For each item, have students give a "thumbs up" sign if they agree with the statement or a "thumbs down" if they disagree. Ask one student to count and tally responses for each item.

Answers:

1. C
2. C
3. F
4. F

Pre-AP® Integration

- **Learning Objective:** Interpersonal Speaking
- **Activity:** Have students create a short conversation based on this written exchange. Students can play the roles of Celia and her father as they discuss what Celia would like to order and what in her father's mind is best for her.
- **Pre-AP® Resource Book:** Comprehensive guide to Pre-AP® vocabulary skill development

---

🔊 La cena con papá

Celia   Papá

Celia: **Tengo sed**, papá. Necesito una leche con chocolate para **la cena**.

Papá: Celia, nunca bebes agua. Debes beber más agua.

Celia: Sí papá, pero **prefiero** la leche con chocolate. Es más sabrosa.

Papá: **Estoy de acuerdo**, pero mucho chocolate es malo **para la salud**. ¿Qué **bebida prefieres**: agua, agua fresca o jugo?

Celia: Está bien, papá. Entonces, para beber, un agua fresca de mango **porque** tengo mucha, mucha sed. Y para comer, una sopa, unas enchiladas de pollo y...

Papá: **Creo que** es mucha comida.

Celia: ¡Yo **creo que no**! Tengo hambre, papá.

Papá: Está bien, Celia. Por favor, dos aguas frescas para beber. Y para comer, una sopa y unas enchiladas de pollo para ella. Y para mí... A ver... una ensalada de frijoles. Gracias.

3

Celia tiene sed y hambre

✏️ ESCRIBIR Lee las frases. Escribe C (cierto) si la frase es correcta o F (falso) si la frase es incorrecta.

1. Celia bebe agua fresca de mango.
2. No es bueno para la salud comer mucho chocolate.
3. A Celia le gusta comer enchiladas de pescado.
4. Celia y su papá comparten una cena de sopa, ensalada y leche con chocolate.

150 ciento cincuenta • Tema 3 • La comida

Differentiated Instruction

Special Needs

Some students may have difficulty matching the characters' speech in the *Videohistoria* dialogues with the people in the photos. As students read, have them point to the characters in their books.

Visual/Spatial Learner

Ask students to create a poster with foods they eat and exercises they do to stay healthy. Have them include activities from *Capítulo* 1A. The poster should include information about why the foods and exercises are healthy. Display the posters in class.

Comida tropical

Before You Watch

Using prior experience Think about what you see in the supermarket. Have you tried all the fruits and vegetables there? Which ones does your family typically eat most often?

Complete the Activity

Las verduras y frutas ¿Cuáles son las frutas y verduras que más come tu familia? ¿Comes las frutas, verduras y comidas de las fotos?

▶ Watch the Video

What different foods does Teo buy at the market for his Dad's Cuban recipes?

Go to **PearsonSchool.com/Autentico** to watch the video *Comida tropical* and to view the script.

Camila   Mateo

After You Watch

✎ **¿COMPRENDES?** Answer the following questions based on the video.

1. ¿Dónde está Teo? ¿Cómo habla con Camila?
2. ¿Qué verduras necesita Teo para la receta de ropa vieja?
3. ¿Qué más necesita para la ropa vieja?
4. Para hacer el flan, ¿necesita cocos o plátanos?
5. ¿Quién come muchas manzanas?
6. ¿Quién prefiere comidas con grasa?

Comparación cultural Compara las comidas cubanas de la familia de Teo con la comida de tu familia. ¿Comes las verduras, frutas o carnes que come la familia de Teo?

Enrich Your Teaching

Culture Note

Ropa vieja is a traditional and delicious dish from Cuba that everyone loves. The meat is cooked with carrots, celery, and bay leaves. Then the meat is shredded, and cooked again for a short time with a **sofrito** of onions, garlic, green peppers. *Ropa vieja* is served with rice and black beans. There are similar dishes in every country of Central and South America, but in Cuba it is called *Ropa vieja* perhaps because the meat is shredded just like old clothes.

Technology: Video

Standards: 1.2, 1.3

Resources: Teacher's Resource Materials: Video Script

Before You Watch

Review the previewing strategy and activity with the students. Ask students for examples of the fruits and vegetables they see in the supermarket. Also point out the images of types of foods that will be discussed in the video. Review the Complete the Activity with the class. Have students speak or write as many food names as they can.

Watch the Video

Show the video without pausing. Show it again, pausing along the way to check comprehension. If there are words that students haven't learned yet, you may want to write those on the board. Show the segment a final time, without pausing.

After You Watch

Standards: 1.2, 1.3

Suggestions: Discuss the questions with the class to confirm understanding of the video.

Answers

1. Teo está en el supermercado. Habla por teléfono con Camila.
2. Teo necesita cebolla, ajo y tomate.
3. También necesita carne.
4. Necesita coco.
5. Camila come muchas manzanas.
6. Teo prefiere las comidas con grasa.

Comparación cultural: Answers will vary. Students should recognize that most noon day meals are similar to their own dinner. There is more food, a variety of foods, and different ingredients than in a typical US lunch.

Have the students complete additional Video activities online or print the activities from the Teacher's Resources in the online course and pass out the activity sheets to the class.

Additional Resources

📶 **Technology: Online Resources**
- Instant Check
- Guided, Core, Video, Audio
- *Para hispanohablantes*

Print
- Guided WB pp. 105–108
- Core WB pp. 60–61

Assessment _____

Quiz: Vocabulary Recognition
- Prueba 3B-1

4

Standards: 1.3

Suggestions: To help students organize their answers have them make a two-column chart labeled **No** and **Sí**. Have volunteers give answers for each item. Accept any logical answer for the replacement items.

Answers: The second item in each set may vary.

1. el arroz...el bistec
2. los pasteles...la lechuga
3. ver la televisión...levantar pesas
4. sabroso...¡Qué asco!
5. comer mucho...mantener la salud
6. los tomates...el arroz
7. un día...siempre
8. las papas...el pescado
9. el pescado...el pastel

5

Standards: 1.3

Recycle: Foods and beverages

Suggestions: Tell students to use words from both *Capítulo* 3A and *Actividad* 4.

Answers will vary but may include:

En el refrigerador:
pescado, pollo, bistec, helado, pan, leche, jugo, salchichas, tocino, jamón, queso, yogur, ensalada, lechuga, refrescos, limonada, té helado, mantequilla
No necesitan refrigerador:
cereal, té, agua, café, cebollas, guisantes, papas, uvas, espaguetis, arroz, judías verdes, tomates, zanahorias, pasteles

CULTURA

Standards: 2.1, 2.2, 4.2

Suggestions: Explain that leaves from the **yerba mate** tree are used to make the herbal tea. The **bombilla** is a filtered metal straw to strain leaf fragments. The gourd is passed from person to person. Ask: What qualifies a beverage or food as "national"?

Answers will vary, but may include coffee, iced tea, or soft drinks.

Vocabulario en uso

OBJECTIVES
▸ Identify foods from the different groups
▸ Discuss food preferences and healthy food choices
▸ Exchange information while giving advice about staying healthy
▸ Read and write about healthy activities

4

¡Claro que no!

LEER, ESCRIBIR For each group of words, choose the word or expression that doesn't belong and write it down on a sheet of paper. Then think of one more word or expression that does fit with the group and write it down beside the first word you wrote.

Modelo
la cebolla / la lechuga / la uva
la uva   la zanahoria

1. el pollo / el pescado / el arroz
2. las zanahorias / los pasteles / las judías verdes
3. caminar / correr / ver la televisión
4. malo / horrible / sabroso
5. comer mucho / levantar pesas / hacer ejercicio
6. los tomates / el pan / los espaguetis
7. cada día / un día / todos los días
8. el bistec / las papas / el pollo
9. la mantequilla / el helado / el pescado

5

¿En el refrigerador o no?

ESCRIBIR Escribe dos listas. En la primera lista, escribe las comidas y bebidas que deben estar en el refrigerador. En la segunda lista, escribe las comidas y bebidas que no necesitan estar en el refrigerador.

CULTURA El mundo hispano

El mate es la bebida nacional de Argentina, Paraguay y Uruguay. Este té de hierbas[1] es bueno para beber con la familia y con los amigos. Las personas ponen el té en una calabaza hueca[2], que se llama mate. Beben el té con una paja[3] que se llama una bombilla.

Pre-AP Integration: Las tradiciones y los valores sociales ¿En los Estados Unidos hay una bebida nacional o una bebida favorita (popular)? ¿Cuál es?

[1]herb [2]hollow gourd [3]straw

Una mujer toma mate, Buenos Aires, Argentina. ▶

152 ciento cincuenta y dos • Tema 3 • La comida

Differentiated Instruction

Heritage Speakers

Have students ask family members or research herbs or spices that are important ingredients in heritage cooking (e.g., **chipotle, cilantro, comino, coco**). Have students find out if these ingredients are readily available in your area. What dishes are prepared with these ingredients? Have students prepare their research in written form. Be sure to correct spelling.

Students with Learning Difficulties

For *Actividad* 4, have students describe the characteristics of each item to help them see the categories. For *Actividad* 5, provide a sheet with a simple drawing of a refrigerator and have students write the words that belong in the refrigerator inside the picture, with the others outside.

6

¿Qué prefieres?

🎤 **HABLAR EN PAREJA** Ask your partner which of two foods he or she prefers. Your partner will state his or her preference and ask you which one you prefer.

▶️

Videomodelo

A —¿Qué prefieres, **carne o pescado**?
B —Prefiero **carne**. Y tú, ¿qué prefieres?
o: —No como ni **carne** ni **pescado**. Y tú, ¿qué prefieres?
A —Prefiero **pescado**.

Estudiante A

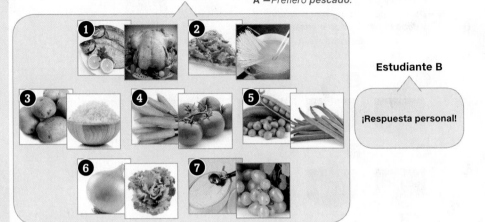

Estudiante B

¡Respuesta personal!

7

¿Sí o no?

🎤 **HABLAR EN PAREJA** Pregunta a tu compañero(a) qué debe comer y beber para mantener su salud. Luego, dile otras recomendaciones que debe hacer según su respuesta.

Modelo

A —¿Debes **beber leche** cada día para mantener la salud?
B —**Creo que sí**. Necesitas beber mucha leche.
o: —**Creo que no**. No necesitas beber mucha leche.

Estudiante A

Estudiante B

Creo que . . .

Capítulo 3B • ciento cincuenta y tres **153**

Go **Online** to practice
PearsonSchool.com/Autentico
PEARSON realize™
▶️ VIDEO   ✏️ WRITING   🎤 SPEAK/RECORD

6

Standards: 1.1

Suggestions: Discuss the options in the *Modelo* with students. Be sure they understand that they are to answer truthfully.

Answers will vary but will include:

1. ¿Qué prefieres, pescado o pollo?
2. ¿...pizza o espaguetis?
3. ¿...papas o arroz?
4. ¿...zanahorias o tomates?
5. ¿...guisantes o judías verdes?
6. ¿...cebollas o lechuga?
7. ¿...helado o uvas?

7

Standards: 1.1, 3.1

Suggestions: Discuss what kinds of foods should be eaten daily and which should not be eaten in excess. Ask volunteers to perform their conversations.

Answers:

1. —¿Debo comer papas fritas cada día para mantener la salud?
   —Creo que no.
2. ¿...verduras...? Creo que sí.
3. ¿...pan y mantequilla...? Creo que no.
4. ¿...frutas...? Creo que sí.
5. ¿...helado...? Creo que no.
6. ¿...yogur...? Creo que sí.
7. ¿...beber agua...? Creo que sí.

Extension: Have students reverse roles and use **necesito** instead of **debo**.

Pre-AP® Integration

- **Learning Objective:** Presentational Writing
- **Activity:** Have students turn the lists of foods they created for Activity 5 into a persuasive paragraph explaining why the foods on each list should or should not be in the refrigerator. Student may cite health, taste, or other reasons in their arguments.
- **Pre-AP® Resource Materials:** Comprehensive guide to Pre-AP® writing skill development

Enrich Your Teaching

Culture Note

The names of many foods in Mexico come from **náhuatl**, the ancient language of the Aztecs that is still spoken today in various dialects. Words from **náhuatl** often end in **-te** (formerly **-tl**). Examples include: **chocolate, cacahuate** (peanut), **ejote** (green bean), **elote** (corn), and **tomate**.

Challenge/Pre-AP®

Create a "refrigerator" out of a cardboard box with a flap for the door. Bring real food items, or empty packaging that suggests these items, to class. Place several of the items in the refrigerator, then open the door for students to see for three seconds. Close the door and have them list as many items as they can remember.

8

Standards: 1.1

Recycle: Telling time

Suggestions: Point out the *Para decir más....* Students are not held responsible for these words, but should use them in their answers. Point out that Student B should give a personal response.

Answers will vary but will include:

1. Son las doce (es mediodía)...
2. Son las diez de la noche...
3. Son las nueve de la mañana...
4. Son las siete de la mañana...
5. Son las seis de la tarde (*or* de la mañana)...
6. Son las tres de la tarde...

9

Standards: 1.2, 1.3

Suggestions: While students are working, walk around the room to support students who need assistance. Remind students to keep their work for *Actividad* 10.

Answers will vary.

10

Standards: 1.1

Suggestions: When students have discussed all seven items, have them reverse roles and practice again.

Answers will vary.

8

¿Hay algo para comer?

🎤 **HABLAR EN PAREJA** Pregunta a tu compañero(a) qué debe comer y beber a las horas indicadas. Luego, dile otras recomendaciones que debe hacer según su respuesta.

Para decir más...
de la mañana = in the morning
de la tarde = in the afternoon
de la noche = in the evening

Videomodelo

A —*Son las* **ocho de la mañana** *y tienes hambre y sed. ¿Qué debes comer y beber?*
B —*Debo comer* **cereal y pan tostado,** *y debo beber* **jugo de manzana**.

Estudiante A

Estudiante B

¡Respuesta personal!

9

Los buenos consejos

✏️ **LEER, ESCRIBIR** Da consejos *(Give advice)* sobre lo que una persona debe o necesita hacer para mantener la salud. Copia y completa las frases. Necesitas tus frases para la Actividad 10.

1. Para mantener la salud, debes _____ todos los días.
2. Necesitas beber _____ cada día.
3. Debes comer _____ en la cena.
4. _____ es malo para la salud.
5. El jugo de zanahoria es _____.
6. Debes comer _____ todos los días.
7. Nunca debes comer _____.

10

¿Estás de acuerdo?

✏️ **ESCRIBIR EN PAREJA** Intercambia tus consejos de la Actividad 9 con otro(a) estudiante por e-mail. ¿Está de acuerdo con tus consejos? Escribe la respuesta en otro e-mail.

Modelo

A —*Hola, Cristina: ¿Estás de acuerdo con lo que debes hacer para mantener la salud? ¿Debes practicar deportes todos los días?*
B —*No estoy de acuerdo...*

También se dice...
los guisantes = los chícharos *(México)*, las arvejas *(Argentina, Bolivia)*
el tomate = el jitomate *(México)*

154 ciento cincuenta y cuatro • **Tema 3** • La comida

Differentiated Instruction

Special Needs

Some students may be unable to read the clock faces in *Actividad* 8, so you may want to give them pictures of digital clocks instead. Others may need help filling in the blanks in *Actividad* 9. Offer a list of three choices for each blank and allow students to choose the one they prefer.

Verbal/Linguistic Learner

Have students research fast-food restaurants in Spanish-speaking countries. How many are there? Are they popular? Where do most people prefer to eat? What are some of the slogans used to sell the food? Students can present their findings in the form of a poster, a report, or an oral presentation.

11

Go Online to practice
PEARSON realize™
PearsonSchool.com/Autentico
🔊 AUDIO ▶ VIDEO ✏ WRITING 🎤 SPEAK/RECORD

¿Qué haces . . . ?

LEER, ESCRIBIR EN PAREJA Take this test on healthy activities to see how you rate.

1 Write your answers in complete sentences on a sheet of paper.

2 Write an email to ask a partner each question. Tally your partner's *sí* and *no* answers.

3 Send an email to your partner with three recommendations that he or she should follow based on the survey score. Ask what else he or she needs to do to stay healthy.

Modelo
Debes caminar o correr todos los días.

¿Qué haces para mantener la salud?

Contesta las preguntas según las actividades que haces cada día. Cada "sí" = 1 punto.

sí no
1. ¿Haces ejercicio?
2. ¿Practicas deportes?
3. ¿Comes verduras?
4. ¿Comes frutas?
5. ¿Caminas o corres?
6. ¿Comes un buen desayuno?
7. ¿Comes comida que es buena para la salud?
8. ¿Bebes cinco vasos* de agua?
9. ¿Pasas tiempo con amigos?
10. ¿Ves tres horas o menos de televisión?

9–10 puntos
¡Felicidades! ¡Haces mucho para mantener la salud!

6–8 puntos
Bien, pero debes hacer más para mantener la salud.

0–5 puntos
¡Ay, ay, ay! Necesitas hacer algo para mantener la salud.

*glasses

Pronunciación ◀ The letters *l* and *ll*

🔊 In Spanish, the letter *l* is pronounced much like the letter *l* in the English word "leaf." Listen to and say these words:

🎤 lechuga lunes pasteles helado
almuerzo sol abril difícil

For most Spanish speakers, the letter combination *ll* is similar to the sound of the letter *y* in "yes." Listen to and say these words:

llamo silla allí llueve
cebolla pollo ella mantequilla

Try it out! Listen to this song and then sing it.

Canta el gallo, canta el gallo

con el kiri, kiri, kiri, kiri, kiri;

La gallina, la g allina

con el cara, cara, cara, cara, cara;

Los polluelos, los polluelos

con el pío, pío, pío, pío, pío, pío, pí.

Capítulo 3B • ciento cincuenta y cinco **155**

11

Standards: 1.1, 1.2, 1.3

Suggestions: Have students skim the questionnaire and clarify any difficulties with the vocabulary. You may want to do the reading as a class.

Answers will vary.

Extension: Have students interview family members and report to the class.

PRONUNCIACIÓN ▶

Standards: 4.1

Resources: Teacher's Resource Materials: Audio Script; Technology: Audio Cap. 3B

Suggestions: Demonstrate the difference between the pronunciation of *l* and *ll*. Have students repeat the words. Play the song from the audio.

Try it out! Before listening to the song, have students look at the picture and match **gallo**, **gallina**, and **polluelos** with the correct images.

Additional Resources

🛜 **Technology: Online Resources**
• Technology: Audio Cap 3B: Comm. Audio Act. 6
• Teacher's Resource Materials: Audio Script

Assessment

Prueba 3B-2 with Remediation (online only)
Quiz: Vocabulary Production
• Prueba 3B-2

Enrich Your Teaching

Teacher-to-Teacher

Tell students that the song uses onomatopoeia (**onomatopeya**), words formed by imitating sounds. Students may enjoy learning how Spanish represents the sounds made by other animals. These provide very good pronunciation practice.

21st Century Skills

Information Literacy Working in small groups, have students compare their responses to the survey in Activity 11 and draw conclusions about the group's habits. Do their classmates eat well? Do they eat the right foods at the right time of day? Do they exercise regularly? After comparing the results for the whole class, students should come up with a plan for overall improvement of health habits, if necessary.

Gramática

Resources: Teacher's Resource Materials: Video Script, Video Program Cap. 3B

Technology: Interactive Whiteboard

Grammar Activities 3B Use the whiteboard activities in your Teacher Resources as you progress through the grammar practice with your class.

Suggestions: Remind students that adjectives agree in gender with nouns and point out the *¿Recuerdas?* Explain that adjectives also agree in number with the noun they modify. Remind students that a mixed-gender group of people also takes the masculine form. Reinforce the use of the plurals of adjectives by showing the *GramActiva* Video.

12

Suggestions: Have students copy the verb stems and endings onto note cards. When doing the activity, allow adequate time for students to select the correct cards.

Answers will vary.

CULTURA

Suggestions: Ask: Would you participate in a festival like this? Why or why not? How might a celebration like *La Tomatina* be good or bad for a community?

Answers will vary.

Gramática

The plurals of adjectives

Just as adjectives agree with a noun depending on whether it's masculine or feminine, they also agree according to whether the noun is singular or plural. To make adjectives plural, just add an *-s* after the vowel at the end of the adjective. If the adjective ends in a consonant, add *-es*.

La hamburguesa es sabrosa. Las hamburguesas son sabrosas.

El pastel es muy popular. Los pasteles son muy populares.

When an adjective describes a group including both masculine and feminine nouns, use the masculine plural form.

La lechuga, las zanahorias y los tomates son buenos para la salud.

Don't forget that the singular form of *mucho* means "much" or "a lot of," but that the plural form, *muchos(as),* means "many."

No como mucha carne, pero como muchas verduras.

¿Recuerdas?

Adjectives agree in gender with the masculine or feminine nouns they describe.

El bistec es sabroso.
La ensalada es sabrosa.

Más recursos ONLINE

▶ *GramActiva* Video
◀)) *Canción de hip hop:*
¿Sabroso o malo?
✎ *GramActiva* Activity

12

¿Sabroso o sabrosa?

✎ LEER Copy the different adjective stems and endings shown here onto note cards. Then your teacher will show you pictures of several foods. Show how you feel about each food item by holding up the appropriate adjective stem and the appropriate ending.

buen	sabros	mal

-o	-a	-os	-as

CULTURA | España

La Tomatina ¿Te gusta la idea de un festival con una gran pelea[1] con tomates? Así es la fiesta anual de La Tomatina en Buñol, España. El consejo[2] municipal distribuye más de 130 toneladas de tomates maduros[3]. Los participantes del festival tiran[4] los tomates durante una hora.

• Describe los festivales de comida de tu comunidad o tu estado. ¿Son como La Tomatina?

[1]fight [2]council [3]ripe [4]throw

La Tomatina, en Buñol, España

Differentiated Instruction

Heritage Speakers

Have students write ten adjectives used to describe foods. They should think of taste, color, and texture. Have them write sentences using the adjectives and hand them in for correction.

Students with Learning Difficulties

Have students refer to pp. 70 and 96 for a list of adjectives to add to the following nouns. Students should select adjectives appropriate for the noun and make sure that the endings are correct in number and gender. (Nouns: **las señoritas; los profesores; las calculadoras; las clases**)

13

¿Cómo son?

ESCRIBIR, HABLAR EN PAREJA

1 For each of these adjectives, name two famous people, cartoon characters, or people in your school whom the adjective fits. Then write a sentence that describes both of them.

Videomodelo
A —*Creo que Cameron Diaz y Antonio Banderas son talentosos.*

1. artístico, -a
2. deportista. -a
3. atrevido, -a
4. gracioso, -a
5. serio, -a
6. talentoso, -a
7. divertido, -a
8. trabajador, -a

2 Use your sentences to describe people orally. Speak with a partner and exchange personal opinions about who fits the adjectives. Who fits the adjectives in your partner's opinion?

Videomodelo
B —*Estoy de acuerdo. Julia Roberts y Tom Cruise son talentosos también.*
o:—*Sí, pero Julia Roberts y Tom Cruise son más talentosos que Cameron Diaz y Antonio Banderas.*

14

¿Qué prefieres?

ESCRIBIR, HABLAR EN GRUPO   Your class will be divided into groups of five to see what foods and beverages you prefer.

Conexiones Las matemáticas

1 Ask your group members what their favorites are from each of the following groups: *frutas, verduras, carnes,* and *bebidas.* Write the answers on a sheet of paper.

Videomodelo
A —*¿Qué **verdura** prefieres?*
B —*Prefiero las **zanahorias.***

2 Tally the results to see which foods and beverages are the most popular in each group. Indicate these favorites on a bar graph as shown. As a group, write four sentences that summarize your results. Compare your group's preferences to those of the other groups.

Prefieren...

	0	1	2	3	4	5
frutas	manzanas					
verduras	papas					
carnes	bistec					
bebidas	refrescos					

Número de estudiantes

Modelo
Del grupo de las verduras, cuatro estudiantes prefieren las papas.

Capítulo 3B • ciento cincuenta y siete **157**

13

Standards: 1.1, 1.3

Recycle: Adjectives to describe people
Suggestions: Brainstorm a list of people for Step 1. After Step 2, have several pairs of students share their opinions with the class.
Answers will vary.
Common Errors: Some students will try to assign gender to adjectives that are neutral, such as *deportista*.

14

Standards: 1.1, 1.3

Recycle: Food and beverage vocabulary
Suggestions: Students can refer to the *Repaso* in *Capítulos* 3A and 3B to review names of foods and beverages.
Answers will vary.
Extension: Divide the class into four groups: *frutas, verduras, proteínas, bebidas.* Have each group make a poster classifying foods from *Capítulos* 3A and 3B.

Project-Based Learning
Students can perform Step 4 at this point. Be sure they understand your corrections and suggestions. (See p. 122-b.)

Additional Resources
📶 **Technology: Online Resources**
• Instant Check
• Guided, Core, Audio
• *Para hispanohablantes*
• Technology: Audio Cap 3B
• Communication Activities: Audio Act. 7
• Teacher's Resource Materials: Audio Script
Print:
• Guided WB pp. 109–110
• Core WB p. 62

Assessment
Prueba 3B-3 with Remediation (online only)
Quiz: The plurals of adjectives
• Prueba 3B-3

Enrich Your Teaching

Culture Note
The tomato has been cultivated in the Andes since prehistoric times. Tomato growing spread from South America to Mexico more than 3,000 years ago. Tomatoes were then brought to Europe. By 1550, tomatoes were being grown in Italy.

Teacher-to-Teacher
Some students might enjoy creating a slideshow using presentation software with pictures of people well known to the class. They can have graphics appear that include plural forms of adjectives. Place strict limits: No unkind characterizations are allowed, except for fictional characters.

Gramática

Standards: 4.1

Resources: Teacher's Resource Materials: Video Script; Video Program Cap. 3B

⌨ Technology: Interactive Whiteboard

Grammar Activities 3B Use the whiteboard activities in your Teacher Resources as you progress through the grammar practice with your class.

Suggestions: Direct attention to the *¿Recuerdas?* Have students practice **ser** by first saying their own names (**Soy...**). Then point to or group other students to demonstrate the other forms.

15

Standards: 1.2, 1.3

Suggestions: Have students scan the paragraph and identify the subjects before writing their answers.

Answers:

1. eres	**4.** somos	**7.** somos
2. soy	**5.** son	**8.** es
3. son	**6.** es	**9.** somos

16

Standards: 1.2

Resources: Teacher's Resource Materials: Audio Script; Technology: Audio Cap. 3B

Suggestions: Play the audio or read the script two or three times to allow students to focus on the comments before they write.

🔊 Technology: Audio Script and Answers

1. Las zanahorias son muy buenas.
2. La papa es sabrosa.
3. Las cebollas son malas.
4. Señor, los guisantes son horribles.
5. El pescado no es bueno.

Gramática

OBJECTIVES
▶ Listen to descriptions of food in a market
▶ Describe people, places, and foods
▶ Compare opinions about food with a classmate
▶ Read and write about pizza

The verb *ser*

Ser, which means "to be," is an irregular verb. Use *ser* to describe what a person or thing is like. Here are the present-tense forms:

(yo)	**soy**	(nosotros) (nosotras)	**somos**
(tú)	**eres**	(vosotros) (vosotras)	**sois**
Ud. (él) (ella)	**es**	Uds. (ellos) (ellas)	**son**

¿Recuerdas?
In previous chapters, you learned how to talk about what a person is like.
—Tú **eres** muy deportista, ¿no?
—Sí, **soy** deportista.
—Mi amigo Pablo **es** deportista también.

Más recursos ONLINE
▶ *Gram*Activa Video
▶ Tutorials: *ser*
▶ Animated verbs
✎ *Gram*Activa Activity

15

Línea romántica

✎ **LEER, ESCRIBIR** Rafa has to tell his father why the cell phone bill was so high. Complete his explanations by using the correct form of the verb *ser*.

Para	papá@casa.com	✕
Asunto	Mis conversaciones	

¡Ay, Papá!
¡Tú __1.__ muy estricto! ¡Yo __2.__ un chico *muuuy* sociable! Hablo con mis amigas porque todas __3.__ muy simpáticas. Hablo con Lidia porque nosotros __4.__ muy deportistas. Mis conversaciones con ella siempre __5.__ muy interesantes. Fátima __6.__ muy estudiosa. Hablamos mucho porque ella y yo __7.__ inteligentes y hablamos de las clases. Y hablo con Lorena porque __8.__ muy graciosa y nosotros __9.__ muy buenos amigos.

✉ ✎ ▾ B I T! ≛ ≡ ≡ ≡ ↱ ↰ ☺

16

Escucha y escribe

🔊 **ESCUCHAR, ESCRIBIR** You will hear comments from five customers about the food being sold in a market. On a sheet of paper, write the numbers 1–5. As you listen, write the comments next to the numbers.

158 ciento cincuenta y ocho • Tema 3 • La comida

Differentiated Instruction

Students with Learning Difficulties

For *Actividad* 17, provide a limited list of possible adjectives for each person or item. As a first step, so students can focus on the verb form, give them adjectives that already agree. Then have them choose another adjective from the list and make the agreement themselves.

Challenge

Some students may notice that *¿Cómo estás?* and *¿Cómo está Ud.?* use a different verb for "to be" from the one shown above. If so, it is appropriate to go ahead and give them a limited explanation of the difference between **ser** and **estar**. The formal explanation is in *Capítulo* 5B, p. 258.

17

En tu escuela

HABLAR Describe orally the people and places in your school.

Modelo
el / la profesor(a) de tu clase de español
La profesora de mi clase de español es muy simpática.

1. tu clase de español
2. las chicas en tu clase de español
3. los chicos en tu clase de español
4. el / la director(a) de tu escuela
5. la comida de la cafetería
6. tú y tus amigos

18

¿Sabroso o malo?

HABLAR EN PAREJA En tu opinión, ¿cómo son las comidas y las bebidas? Habla con un(a) compañero(a). Usa los verbos *comer* o *beber*.

Videomodelo
A —¿Comes zanahorias en la cena?
B —No, no como zanahorias en la cena porque son horribles.
o:—Sí, como zanahorias en la cena porque son buenas para la salud.

Estudiante A

Estudiante B

(muy) sabroso
bueno para la salud
malo para la salud
horrible
¡Respuesta personal!

Capítulo 3B • ciento cincuenta y nueve **159**

Standards: 1.2, 1.3

Recycle: Adjectives

Suggestions: Remind students that *tu clase* becomes *mi clase* and *tú y tus amigos* becomes *mis amigos y yo*. Remind them to write full sentences and to watch for agreement.

Answers:
1. Mi clase de español es...   4. ...es...
2. ...son...   5. ...es...
3. ...son...   6. ...somos...

Common Errors: Students may forget to make subject-verb and noun-adjective agreements. Model the correct forms.

Starter Activity

Have students call out the names of the foods in *Actividad* 18 as you call out the numbers in random order.

18

Standards: 1.1

Recycle: Foods and beverages

Suggestions: Model the options in the answers.

Answers will include:
1. ¿Comes pescado en la cena?   7. ¿...agua...?
2. ¿...uvas...?   8. ¿...pasteles...?
3. ¿...guisantes...?   9. ¿...papas...?
4. ¿Bebes leche...?   10. ¿...tocino...?
5. ¿Comes mantequilla...?   11. ¿...fresas...?
6. ¿...judías verdes...?

Additional Resources

Technology: Online Resources
- Instant Check
- Guided, Core, Audio
- *Para hispanohablantes*
- Technology: Audio Cap 3B
- Communication Activities: Audio Acts. 8–9
- Teacher's Resource Materials: Audio Script

Print:
- Guided WB pp. 111–112
- Core WB pp. 63–64

Assessment

Prueba 3B-4 with Remediation (online only)
Quiz: The verb *ser*
- Prueba 3B-4

Enrich Your Teaching

Culture Note

The variety of fresh fruits and vegetables sold in open-air and interior markets in Spanish-speaking countries is amazingly assorted. A number of markets also serve hot meals at reasonable prices. Many people like to visit the markets during lunchtime.

21st Century Skills

Communication Have students imagine they are visiting the open-air market pictured in Activity 16. Have them compose a postcard to a Spanish-speaking friend describing what they see and hear around them.

CULTURA

Standards: 2.1, 4.2

Suggestions: Ask students what they find interesting about the picture. Discuss the differences between open-air markets and supermarkets. Ask if there are open-air markets in your community.

Answers will vary.

EXPLORACIÓN DEL LENGUAJE

Standards: 4.1

Suggestions: You may want to discuss word origins in English with the class before reading the *Exploración del lenguaje*. Have students match the obvious words first, and discuss the similarities between the words.

Answers:

1. agua...aqua
2. arroz...*óryza*
3. pan...*pane*
4. bistec...*beefsteak*
5. salchichas...*salciccia*
6. pescado...*piscatu*
7. café...*kahvé*
8. pollo...*pullu*

EL ESPAÑOL EN EL MUNDO DEL TRABAJO

Standards: 5.1

Suggestions: Have students research the names of restaurants in your area that serve food from Spanish-speaking cultures.

Answers will vary.

Project-Based Learning

Students can perform Step 5 at this point. (For more information, see p. 122-b.)

Active Classroom

Have students look at a newspaper's food section to get ideas for their own food article or advertisement. They can write a recipe, draw a food comic strip, or create supermarket ads.

CULTURA   El mundo hispano

Los mercados son comunes en América Latina. Un día a la semana, hay un mercado central; es posible comprar[1] comida, flores, artesanías[2] y ropa[3].

Pre-AP® Integration: Las tradiciones y los valores sociales ¿Cómo venden[4] las frutas y las verduras en tu comunidad? Compara la foto con los mercados en tu comunidad.

[1]to buy [2]crafts [3]clothes [4]to sell

Un mercado guatemalteco ▶

Exploración del lenguaje   Where did it come from?

The names of many foods in Spanish come from Latin as well as from other languages as diverse as Arabic, Italian, Greek, Turkish, and English. While it's clear that the word *espaguetis* comes from the Italian word *spaghetti*, it's not obvious that the word *zanahoria* comes from the Arabic word *safunariya*.

Try it out! Read the Spanish words in the first column and match them up to their counterparts in their language of origin.

agua	*piscatu* (latín)
arroz	*aqua* (latín)
pan	*beefsteak* (inglés)
bistec	*panis* (latín)
salchichas	*pullu* (latín)
pescado	*kahvé* (turco)
café	*salciccia* (italiano)
pollo	*óryza* (griego)

El español en el mundo del trabajo

Rick Bayless's career as a world-class Mexican chef began at the age of 14, when he visited Mexico and decided to study Spanish. Since 1987, Rick has opened gourmet Mexican restaurants, created and starred in cooking shows, written cookbooks, and won many awards.

* How would Rick's Spanish skills be helpful in his career?

Un molcajete (*mortar and pestle*) de México

160 ciento sesenta • Tema 3 • La comida

Differentiated Instruction

Verbal/Linguistic Learner

Ask students why food items often have names borrowed from other cultures. Have them research the origins of some of their favorite food items and the etymology of the names. Have them present their findings to the class.

Heritage Speakers

Have students choose four food items and explore the different names they have in different Spanish-speaking countries. How did these differences arise? Where did the names come from? If the name is borrowed from another language, what is the historical connection?

Interpretive   **3B**

Una pizza para la buena salud

LEER, ESCRIBIR   Lee este anuncio *(ad)* de una pizzería y contesta las preguntas.

1. Find and list three cognates in this ad.
2. Write three recommendations in Spanish for a healthier pizza. Send your recommendations in a text message to a classmate to tell them the kinds of pizza they should eat.

Strategy
Using cognates Be sure to look for cognates to help you read this ad.

≡   PIZZAS SALUDABLES   🔍

Pizzería Lilia
¡Pizzas saludables!

A veces la pizza tiene muchas calorías y grasas que no son buenas para la salud.

La Pizzería Lilia tiene una variedad de pizzas con ingredientes que son buenos y saludables.

🍴 Menos queso
🍴 Usamos ingredientes nutritivos
  • Más verduras (tienen pocas calorías y son muy nutritivas)
🍴 Evita[1] la combinación de carnes
  • Las carnes tienen mucho sodio y grasas
  • El pollo o el jamón son mejores[2] que las salchichas

¡Llámanos!
¡Estamos aquí para servirte!
372 42 89
Calle Independencia, 28

[1]Avoid [2]better

20

Y tú, ¿qué dices?

HABLAR   Expresa y explica tus preferencias personales sobre las comidas y la salud.

1. Describe tu pizza favorita.
2. ¿Crees que la pizza es buena o mala para la salud? ¿Por qué?
3. ¿Qué verduras prefieres? ¿Qué verduras no te gustan?
4. ¿Qué ejercicio haces con los brazos? ¿Qué ejercicio haces con las piernas?

Capítulo 3B • ciento sesenta y uno   **161**

19

Standards: 1.2

Suggestions: Point out the *Strategy* and have students scan the text for cognates. Have students read the ad and list the health benefits of each ingredient. Can students guess the meaning of *saludable*?

Answers will vary but may include:

1. pizza, ingredientes, calorías, variedad, usamos, nutritivos, combinación, sodio
2. Answers will vary.

Extension: Have students write their own ads for a vegetarian restaurant, a juice bar, or a gourmet sandwich shop. Have students list words related to health and food, and then work in pairs to draft the ad. Ads should include a name for the business, address, and telephone number.

Pre-AP® Integration

• **Learning Objective:** Interpretive: Print
• **Activity 19:** Students practice reading comprehension skills as they answer questions about an ad.
• **Pre-AP® Resource Materials:** Comprehensive guide to Pre-AP® reading skill development

Starter Activity

Have the class brainstorm foods that belong to each category: *carnes, frutas, bebidas, verduras* with *comida* in the center.

20

Standards: 1.1, 1.2

Suggestions: Students may like ingredients not listed in the vocabulary from *Capítulos* 3A or 3B. Encourage them to use a dictionary to find words such as **jalapeño, pimiento, piña, aceituna, oliva**, and **hongo**.

Answers will vary.

Enrich Your Teaching

Culture Note
The mortar and pestle has different names in different countries. The **molcajete** pictured on p. 160 is used in Mexico to grind chiles, spices, and grain, and to make guacamole, among other things. In other countries, it may be called a **mortero y mano de moler** or **pilón y maceta**.

Teacher-to-Teacher
Have students think about milk or orange juice ads they have seen. Have them create an ad that endorses a vegetable or fruit from this chapter. Display their posters in the room.

Lectura

Standards: 1.2, 1.3

Suggestions

Pre-reading: Point out the *Strategy* and be sure students understand skimming. Remind them that using prior knowledge and prediction will help them understand new texts. Have students also find cognates.

Reading: Have students read the pie chart. As they read, have them tell you in which segment the various food items fall.

Post-reading: Have students review their skimming predictions and see how accurate they were. Have them identify cognates they noticed in the reading.

Teacher-to-Teacher

Have students keep a weekly list of what they eat to track carbohydrate, protein, and fat intake. At the end of the week, ask them to draw a pie chart to display the information.

Pre-AP® Integration

- **Learning Objective:** Interpretive: Audio
- **Activity:** Have students carefully read the captions under each of the pictures as a homework assignment. In class the next day, have students work in groups of three and alternate reading one of the captions to the other two members as a dictation activity, writing what they hear. After they finish writing, have the groups confirm their work.
- **Pre-AP® Resource Materials:** Comprehensive guide to Pre-AP* reading skill development

---

Lectura

OBJECTIVES
- Read about a sports diet and learn about an athlete
- Skim what you read to find specific information
- Learn about soccer in Spanish-speaking countries and compare attitudes towards soccer with those in the United States

La comida de los atletas

Lee este artículo *(article)* de una revista deportiva. ¿Qué comen y qué beben los atletas profesionales para mantener la salud y estar en buena forma?

Strategy
Skimming List three things that you would expect to find in an article about athletes' eating habits. Skim the article to find the information.

¿Qué come un jugador de fútbol?

Los jugadores[1] de fútbol comen comidas equilibradas con muchos carbohidratos, minerales y vitaminas. Ellos consumen cerca de 5.000 calorías en total todos los días.

13% Grasas
17% Proteínas
70% Carbohidratos

Para el desayuno el día de un partido[2], un jugador come mucho pan con mantequilla y jalea[3], yogur y té.

Para el almuerzo antes del[4] partido, come pan, pasta, pollo sin grasa, verduras, frutas y una ensalada.

Para la cena después del[5] partido, el atleta come papas, carne sin grasa y más verduras y frutas.

También es muy importante beber muchos líquidos. La noche antes del partido, el jugador bebe un litro de jugo de naranja y durante el partido bebe hasta[6] dos litros de agua y bebidas deportivas.

[1]players [2]game [3]jam [4]before the [5]after the [6]up to

---

Differentiated Instruction

Heritage Speakers

Remind students to pay close attention to the correct spelling of words that that are frequently spelled incorrectly: ***mantequilla*** (not *mantequiya*), ***pollo*** (not *poyo*), ***jalea*** (not *jallea*), and ***atleta*** (not *athleta*). Keep track of words that give them spelling difficulties and do a dictation periodically to check them.

Students with Learning Difficulties

Many students have problems skimming. Suggest that they move their fingers along the lines to find any information they understand. The strategy of using expectations to aid in reading can be very helpful. Stress that they will not understand every word, nor will they need to.

Interpretive Reading

3B

Nombre: Lionel Messi

Fecha de nacimiento: 24 de junio de 1987

Lugar de nacimiento: Rosario

País de nacimiento: Argentina

Nacionalidad: argentino/español

Equipo[7]: FC Barcelona

Función: delantero

En esta foto, Messi representa al equipo nacional de Argentina.

Argentina

✎ ¿Comprendes?

1. ¿Qué debe comer Lionel Messi antes de un partido de fútbol?

2. ¿Qué debe beber?

3. ¿Qué comida no debe comer Messi?

4. ¿Es tu dieta diferente de la dieta de un jugador de fútbol profesional? ¿Cómo?

5. ¿Cuál es la fecha de nacimiento *(birth date)* de Messi? Escribe tu fecha de nacimiento como lo hacen en los países hispanohablantes.

¿Qué debes comer?

Habla con un(a) compañero(a) sobre los deportes que practican. Basándose en la lectura, haz *(ask)* preguntas y responde sobre lo que debe comer cada uno(a) según los deportes que practican.

CULTURA ▶ El mundo hispano

¡Gooooooooooool! Hacer el gol ganador[1] en el fútbol es muy emocionante. El fútbol es el deporte más popular del mundo, y en países donde la gente habla español, el fútbol es parte de la cultura. Cada cuatro años, equipos[2] de todo el mundo compiten en el evento deportivo más popular del mundo: la Copa Mundial.

• ¿Es muy popular el fútbol en Estados Unidos? ¿Es más o menos popular que en los países donde la gente habla español?

🌐 **Mapa global interactivo** Ubica y explora los estadios de fútbol más importantes de España, ganadora de la Copa Mundial de 2010.

[1] winner [2] teams

España gana la Copa Mundial, 2010.

Capítulo 3B • ciento sesenta y tres **163**

Enrich Your Teaching

Culture Note

Soccer is quickly gaining a strong following in the United States, and many youth soccer clubs have developed across the country. Soccer historians give the credit to Pelé, the star soccer player from Brazil who, in the 1970s, fascinated sports fans in the United States with his finesse and agility.

Teacher-to-Teacher

It might be fun to have students make a poster showing a soccer field with the players' positions labeled. Have students search the Internet for the Spanish names of the positions, such as: **delantero** ("forward"), **centrocampista** ("center"), and **portero** or **arquero** ("goalie" or "goalkeeper"). This may be a project for soccer enthusiasts in the class.

¿Comprendes?

Standards: 1.2, 1.3

Suggestions: Review the verb **deber** with students. Have students refer back to the reading as they write their answers.

Answers:

1. pan y mantequilla y jalea, yogur, pasta, pollo, verduras, frutas y una ensalada

2. Debe beber un litro de jugo de naranja y hasta dos litros de agua y bebidas deportivas.

3. Answers will vary.

4. Answers will vary.

5. El 2 de mayo. Answers will vary.

¿Qué debes comer?

Standards: 1.2

Suggestions: Have students think about whether there is much difference between what the players of one sport might eat over another. Students can discuss what foods they think best help their performance.

CULTURA ◀

Standards: 2.2, 3.1, 4.2

Suggestions: Ask if students have seen a World Cup soccer match. Discuss how soccer has become popular in the United States. Find out who plays soccer in your class and invite them to talk about the sport.

Answers will vary.

🌐 **Technology: Mapa global interactivo, Actividad 2** Explore Spain, home of the winners of the 2010 World Cup in soccer.

Teacher-to-Teacher

Careers: *Tema* 3 has focused on food that is good and bad for health. Have students work in small groups to talk about a career in the field of nutrition. Have them write a list of foods in Spanish that a 5-year-old child might eat and categorize them as healthful and unhealthful. Ask groups to share their lists.

Additional Resources

Technology: Online Resources
• Guided, Writing, Reading
• *Para hispanohablantes*
• Cultural Reading Activity

Print:
• Guided WB p. 113
• Literacy Skills WB

Perspectivas del mundo hispano

Standards: 2.1, 3.1, 4.2

Suggestions: Point out that finding ways to stay healthy is a perennially popular topic. Natural remedies and herbs are among those often mentioned. Neither of them is really new and many, such as eating chicken soup for a cold, have passed down from generation to generation. Have students read the text. Discuss what they may know about the remedies mentioned. Also discuss researching herbal remedies as modern-day solutions. Assign the *Analizar* section for homework. Discuss their responses at a later time.

Locate the Amazon rainforest on a map. Point out that a great deal of research into the benefits of herbal remedies takes place there. Discuss how scientists feel the rainforest has so much to offer because of its abundance of plants and animals, many of which are still not generally known elsewhere.

Direct attention to the *Comparación cultural* section and have students discuss the questions.

Answers will vary.

Online Cultural Reading

After doing the online activity, ask students to choose foods from the menus that seem different from what they are used to but that they would be curious to try. Have the students explain why these particular choices sound appetizing.

Pre-AP® Integration

- **Learning Objective:** Presentational Speaking (Cultural Comparison)
- **Background:** This task prepares students for the Spoken Presentational Communication tasks that focus on cultural comparisons.
- **Activity:** Have students prepare a two-minute (maximum) presentation on the following topic: Use of herbal remedies to supplement traditional medicine across cultures. Think of the use of *yerbabuena* in Mexico. Compare this to home remedies people in your family or community use to treat different ailments. Give your opinion on the use of herbs to treat illnesses.
- **Pre-AP® Resource Materials:** Comprehensive guide to Pre-AP® speaking skill development

Additional Resources

📶 **Technology: Online Resources**
- Cultural Reading Activity
- *Para hispanohablantes*

Perspectivas del mundo hispano

¿Qué haces para mantener la salud?

Have you ever eaten chicken soup when you have a cold? How about putting aloe on a sunburn? In many countries, including those in the Spanish-speaking world, traditional remedies consisting of medicinal herbs have been used for centuries to treat common medical problems. In Mexico, a mint known as *yerbabuena* may be made into tea and given to someone with a stomachache. Remedies such as these may not be prescribed by licensed physicians, but people have confidence in them because they have been passed down through the generations.

Online Cultural Reading

Go to Auténtico ONLINE to read and understand a website with menus from the Spanish-speaking world.

Researchers study traditional herbal remedies to find modern-day medical solutions. In the Amazon rainforest in South America, an amazing abundance of plant life may hold the key to treating a wide variety of common ailments and diseases. Drug companies are looking for cures found in these plants and herbs that could be reproduced in today's modern drugs.

Increasingly, medicinal herbs are accepted not only as the basis for pharmaceutical drugs, but also for their own inherent healing qualities. In many countries, including the United States, herbal remedies are sometimes used in combination with conventional health care.

Analizar In many Spanish-speaking cultures, herbal remedies have been accepted for centuries. Do you think that medicinal herbs can provide relief and cures? Why or why not?

Comparación cultural What special foods or drinks do you like to have when you don't feel well? Answer the following questions, then write a statement explaining what, if any, foods or drinks help you when you feel sick.

Modelo
Cuando estoy enfermo (*sick*) prefiero comer sopa de pollo.

1. Cuando estoy enfermo, prefiero comer _____.

2. Cuando estoy enfermo, me gusta beber _____.

3. Cuando me duele el estómago, (no) me gusta _____.

4. Cuando me duele la cabeza, prefiero _____.

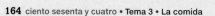

En un mercado de Guanajuato, México ▶

Differentiated Instruction

Challenge

Have students learn about the Amazon rainforest, where it is located, and why scientists are interested in the plants and animals that live there. Ask students to give a short explanation about possible medicines and cures that might come from the region.

Heritage Speakers

Students may be familiar with traditional remedies. Are there any that have been passed down in their family or in families they know? Encourage them to share their stories with the class.

Presentación escrita

<table>
<tr><td>**Presentación
escrita**</td><td>OBJECTIVES
▶ Create a poster
promoting healthy choices
▶ Gather information from a number
of sources</td><td>Go **Online** to practice
PEARSON
realize
AUDIO</td><td>PearsonSchool.com/Autentico</td></tr>
</table>

Para mantener la salud

TASK You are researching good eating and exercise habits for your health class. Make a poster in Spanish in which you state your opinion with five supporting suggestions about how to lead a healthier life.

1 **Prewrite** Ask people at school and home about good eating and exercise habits for teens. List their ideas under these headings to organize your information.

- *Debes comer . . .*
- *Debes beber . . .*
- *Debes . . . para mantener la salud*
- *No debes beber mucho(a) . . .*
- *No debes comer mucho(a) . . .*

> **Strategy**
> **Gathering information** Use information and opinions from a variety of sources to help you support your presentation on a topic.

2 **Draft** Decide how to present the information logically as you write your first draft. Use visuals for clarity and give your poster a title.

3 **Revise** Share your draft with a partner. Your partner should check the following:

- Have you communicated your opinion and supporting statements well?
- Do the visuals convey meaning? Is the poster attractive?
- Are the vocabulary and grammar correct?

Rewrite your poster making any necessary changes.

4 **Publish** Make a final copy for posting in the nurse's office, a community center, your classroom, or your portfolio.

5 **Evaluation** The following rubric will be used to grade your presentation.

Rubric	Score 1	Score 3	Score 5
Completion of task	You included at least three opinions about how to follow a healthy lifestyle.	You included at least four opinions about how to follow a healthy lifestyle.	You included five or more opinions about how to follow a healthy lifestyle.
Accuracy of vocabulary and grammar	You had very little variation of vocabulary use with many grammar errors.	You had limited usage of vocabulary and some grammar errors.	You had extended use of a variety of vocabulary with very few grammar errors.
Effective use of visuals	You included only three visuals that clearly connect to information.	You included only four visuals that clearly connect to information.	You included five visuals that clearly connect to information.

Capítulo 3B • ciento sesenta y cinco **165**

Presentación escrita

Standards: 1.3

Suggestions: Review the task, steps, and rubric with students. Point out that students should use reliable sources that know about health. Encourage students to make their posters visually appealing as well as persuasive. Review the rubric with the class to explain how you will grade the posters. Make and display a poster of your own as a model. Use a sample poster and show how it would be graded.

Have students present their posters to the class. Ask them how they might change their habits after completing this project.

Pre-AP® Integration

- **Learning Objective:** Presentational Writing
- **Activity:** You've created your healthy-living suggestions poster. Now, write a brief, persuasive paragraph to explain your recommendations. Why should people follow these suggestions? How would their health benefit from doing so?
- **Pre-AP® Resource Materials:** Comprehensive guide to Pre-AP® writing skill development

Digital Portfolio

Have students include their posters in their portfolios.

Additional Resources

Technology: Online Resources
- Guided
- *Para hispanohablantes*

Print:
- Guided WB, p. 114

Self Assessment

Presentación escrita
- **Assessment Program:** Rubrics

Go over the descriptions of the different levels of performance. After assessing students, help individuals understand how their performance could be improved. (See Teacher's Resource Materials for suggestions on using rubrics in assessment.)

Enrich Your Teaching

Teacher-to-Teacher

e-amigos: Have students write their *e-amigos* with suggestions for ways students at their school could improve their health. Have students print out or e-mail you the exchanges.

21st Century Skills

Creativity and Innovation Have students create a "Biggest Winner" program for the school—a contest to find the student able to establish and follow the healthiest nutrition and fitness regimen, developing rules, an eating plan, and an exercise plan for contestants to follow. Have the students write an announcement and create a web page to publicize the contest.

Auténtico

Standards: 1.2

Resources: *Authentic Resources Wkbk*, Cap. 3B
Authentic Resources: Cap 3B
AP Theme: *Los desafíos mundiales: El bienestar social*

Before You Read

Discuss the *Strategy* with students. Have them look at all the words in the image, and use their knowledge of cognates to infer meaning. Ask them to use Spanish to identify different foods, ingredients, and other key details that they recognize in the image. Ask if there are any foods shown that they think of as healthy, or as unhealthy. Then review the key vocabulary with the class. Have students comment on any food items pictured that differ from what they eat at home. Point out the image of the plate that has been quartered into sections, each labeled with a cognate. Ask them what they think it means. Have students put foods that they see and others that they know in to each section, and keep a list of these words on the board.

Technology: Read the Text

Before reading the text, direct students' attention to the *Mientras lees* activity. Compare these food lists to the lists the class compiled on the board and have students add any additional foods to their lists.

Read the text once completely through, without pausing, and tell students to watch and listen for the foods they recognize in the text. Remind students that they will not understand every word, but that they should read and listen for overall understanding. Read the text again, stopping as necessary for students to complete the reading activity and to check comprehension.

Auténtico

Alimentación saludable

Before You Read

Use the Strategy: Using Cognates
Use cognates to increase understanding and to help identify key words and details in a text. What words look just like a similar word in English?

Read this Key Vocabulary

la alimentación = nutrition	**las bayas** = berries
saludable = healthy	**logre su meta** = reach your goal
estilo de vida = lifestyle	
lo conducirán = will lead you to	
integrales = whole grain	
enriquezca = enrich	
legumbres = legumes (beans and peas)	

Read the Text

A*limentación saludable para un estilo de vida activa* is an infographic from the USDA that offers suggestions for diet and lifestyle. Think about 10 tips *(consejos)* that might help you lead a healthy lifestyle. See if they match with the 10 tips given here.

Go to **PearsonSchool.com/Autentico** and read the infographic *Alimentación saludable para un estilo de vida activa* to read nutrition tips.

Complete the Activities

Mientras lees As you read, identify words that are similar to English words. How do these cognates help you to infer key details of the text? Identify in the reading the key words listed here and provide their English equivalents. Write down additional cognates you find.

educación	enriquezca
optimizar	combinar
nutrición	productos lácteos
balancee	física
proteína	dieta
yogur	seleccione

Differentiated Instruction

Special Needs

Pair visually-impaired students with other students who will read the headers of each section. Then have the visually impaired students name foods that might fall into that category using chapter and key vocabulary. Have other student read the information that follows the header, and both students can confirm which foods best fit in a category.

Heritage Speakers

Have students list foods from their cultural heritage or home-life that fall into each healthy food category covered in the text. Then ask them to research a recipe of one, either by talking to a family member or using the Internet or other resources, and present it to the class.

Integration

Después de leer Demonstrate your understanding of the text by answering the following questions.

1. ¿Qué tipo de proteína es buena para la salud?

2. ¿Qué productos lácteos menciona el texto?

3. Estos consejos *(tips)* hablan de dos aspectos principales de un estilo de vida. ¿Cuáles son los dos aspectos?

📖 **For more activities, go to the *Authentic Resources Workbook*.**

Estilo de vida saludable

Expansión Find other authentic resources in *Auténtico* online, then answer the question.

📁 **3B Auténtico**

Integración de idea En los dos recursos auténticos, ¿qué recomendaciones hay para un estilo de vida saludable?

Comparación cultural Compara el estilo de vida de los recursos auténticos con tu estilo de vida.

Complete the Activities

Mientras lees

Standards: 1.2

Ask students to share additional cognates that they found. Confirm student understanding of each cognate.

Answers:

education	enrich
optimize	combine
nutrition	dairy (lacteal) products
balance	physical
protein	diet
yogurt	select

Después de leer

Standards: 1.2, 1.3

Students' answers may vary based on their comprehension.

Answers:

1. La proteína baja en grasa es buena para la salud.
2. El texto habla de la leche, el queso, el yogur, y la leche de soya.
3. El texto habla de la comida (alimentación/ dieta) y el ejercicio (actividad física).

For more Authentic Resources: Assign the *Authentic Resources Workbook* activities for homework, so that students can play the video on their own and complete the workbook activities at their own pace.

Pre-AP® Integration

Standards: 1.2, 1.3

Resources: *Authentic Resources Workbook,* Cap. 3B; Authentic Resources: Cap 3B

Suggestions: Before completing the Pre-AP® activity, have students go to the workbook and complete the worksheets for these two additional resources.

Enrich Your Teaching

Culture Note

Many traditional dishes from Spanish-speaking cultures reflect the good eating habits recommended in the reading. For example, shakes made with milk and natural tropical fruits like mango, papaya, and guava. Traditional dishes of black or red beans with rice, very popular throughout Latin America, are also a healthy nutritional choice.
Perspectivas: What healthy foods do you enjoy as meals and snacks?

Using Authentic Resources

Ask students to compile a list of the healthy living examples and suggestions presented in the resources that they find most useful. Ask them to add any suggestions that they think should be added to the list.

167

Review Activities

To talk about food and beverages: Have students work in pairs to quiz each other on the vocabulary. They may use flashcards. Use classroom posters, plastic foods, or magazines to help students review the vocabulary. Have them include *Tengo hambre* and *Tengo sed* in practicing the foods and beverages.

To discuss health: Have students work in pairs and give each other recommendations using *Para mantener la salud ____*. Have them agree or disagree, saying what is good or bad.

To indicate preference or agreement / disagreement: Give students choices of two items and ask their preference. Then have them agree or disagree with statements you make about whether something is good or bad for health.

To describe something: Give names of activities or foods and have students describe them.

Digital Portfolio

Invite students to review the activities they completed in this chapter, including written reports, posters or other visuals, and recordings of oral presentations or other projects. Have them select one to two items that they feel best demonstrate their achievements in Spanish to include in their portfolios. Have them include this with the Chapter Checklist and Self-Assessment Worksheet.

Pre-AP® Integration

- **Learning Objective:** Interpersonal speaking
- **Pre-AP® Resource Book:** Activity Sheets, Tema 3

Additional Resources

Technology: Online Resources
- Instant Check
- *Para hispanohablantes*

Print
- Core WB pp. 65–66

Teacher Resources
- Teacher's Resource Materials: Situation Cards, Clip Art
- Assessment Program: Chapter Checklist and Self-Assessment Worksheet

---

Repaso del capítulo

OBJECTIVES
▸ Review the vocabulary and grammar
▸ Demonstrate you can perform the tasks on p. 169

🔊 Vocabulario

to talk about food and beverages

la cena	dinner
el bistec	beefsteak
la carne	meat
el pescado	fish
el pollo	chicken
la cebolla	onion
los guisantes	peas
las judías verdes	green beans
la lechuga	lettuce
las papas	potatoes
los tomates	tomatoes
las uvas	grapes
las zanahorias	carrots
el arroz	rice
los cereales	grains
los espaguetis	spaghetti
las grasas	fats
la mantequilla	butter
el helado	ice cream
los pasteles	pastries
las bebidas	beverages

to talk about being hungry and thirsty

Tengo hambre.	I'm hungry.
Tengo sed.	I'm thirsty.

to discuss health

caminar	to walk
hacer ejercicio	to exercise
(yo) hago	I do
(tú) haces	you do
levantar pesas	to lift weights
para la salud	for one's health
para mantener la salud	to maintain one's health

to indicate a preference

(yo) prefiero	I prefer
(tú) prefieres	you prefer
deber	should, must

to indicate agreement or disagreement

creer	to think
Creo que . . .	I think . . .
Creo que sí / no.	I (don't) think so.
(No) estoy de acuerdo.	I (don't) agree.

to ask a question or give an answer

¿Por qué?	Why?
porque	because

to express quantity

algo	something
muchos, -as	many
todos, -as	all

to describe something

horrible	horrible
malo, -a	bad
sabroso, -a	tasty, flavorful

other useful words

cada día	every day

Gramática

plurals of adjectives

Masculine	Feminine
Singular / Plural	Singular / Plural
sabroso / sabrosos	sabrosa / sabrosas
popular / populares	popular / populares

ser *to be*

soy	somos
eres	sois
es	son

For *Vocabulario adicional,* see pp. 472–473.

Differentiated Instruction

Students with Learning Difficulties

Have students review the *Repaso del capítulo* and create flashcards for any words that they do not know. Pair them with a student who is more confident with the vocabulary to practice. Before the test, provide students with a practice test, so they can become comfortable with the format.

Heritage Speakers

Have students write a few paragraphs telling about their perfect dinner celebration: Where are they going to have it? Whom are they going to invite? What food are they going to eat? Encourage them to use as many vocabulary words from this chapter as they can.

Preparación para el examen

What you need to be able to do for the exam . . .	Here are practice tasks similar to those you will find on the exam . . .	For review go to your print or digital textbook . . .
Interpretive		
❶ **ESCUCHAR** I can listen and understand as people describe a healthy or unhealthy lifestyle.	Listen as two people are interviewed about their habits. See if you can tell which one is an Olympic skier and which one is a drummer. Be prepared to explain your "educated guesses."	**pp. 148–151** *Vocabulario en contexto* **p. 149 Actividad 2**
Interpersonal		
❷ **HABLAR** I can express my opinion about food preferences.	During a telephone survey, you are asked some questions in Spanish about your food preferences. Say whether you think each food choice is good or bad for your health.	**p. 153 Actividades 6–7** **p. 154 Actividades 8, 10** **p. 157 Actividad 14** **p. 159 Actividad 18**
Interpretive		
❸ **LEER** I can read and compare what people do and eat in order to determine whether they lead a healthy or unhealthy lifestyle.	Read the online conversation that you have just joined in a chat room. Decide whether each person has a healthy or unhealthy lifestyle, based on what they tell each other. Chato: ¿Qué hago yo? Cuando hace buen tiempo, corro por treinta minutos. Cuando llueve, levanto pesas. Chispa: No me gusta hacer ejercicio. Prefiero comer papas fritas. Son muy sabrosas. Andrés: ¿Papas fritas? Son horribles para la salud. Para mantener la salud, nunca debes comer papas fritas.	**pp. 148–151** *Vocabulario en contexto* **p. 154 Actividad 9** **p. 155 Actividad 11** **p. 161 Actividad 19** **pp. 162–163** *Lectura*
Presentational		
❹ **ESCRIBIR** I can write a list of things a person should do to maintain a healthy lifestyle.	Many people think that teens don't know anything about a healthy lifestyle. You and your friends are compiling a top-ten list of ways to improve teens' health. Write at least three suggestions for the list.	**p. 154 Actividad 9** **p. 155 Actividad 11** **p. 161 Actividad 19** **p. 165** *Presentación escrita*
Cultures		
❺ **COMPARAR** I can demonstrate an understanding of cultural perspectives regarding health care.	Give an example of an herbal remedy that is accepted in a Spanish-speaking country as a remedy for a common ailment. Compare this with a similar herbal/natural remedy believed by many in the United States to be a cure for a common ailment.	**p. 164** *Perspectivas del mundo hispano*

Differentiated Assessment

Core Assessment

- Assessment Program: Examen del capítulo 3B
- Technology: Audio Cap. 3B
- ExamView: Chapter Test, Test Banks A and B

Challenge/Pre-AP®

- ExamView: Pre-AP® Test Bank
- Pre-AP® Resource Materials

Extra Support

- Alternate Assessment Program: Examen del capítulo 3B
- Technology: Audio Cap. 3B

Heritage Speakers

- Assessment Program: *Para hispanohablantes*: Examen del Capítulo 3B
- ExamView: Heritage Learner Test Bank

Performance Tasks

Standards: 1.2, 1.3, 2.1, 4.2

Student Resource: *Para hispanohablante*
Teacher Resources: Teacher's Resource Materials: Audio Script; Technology: Audio Cap. 3B

1. Escuchar

Suggestions: Play the audio or read the script.

🔊 **Technology: Audio Script and Answers**

1. Cada día, a las cinco y media de la mañana, levanto pesas por treinta minutos y camino por una hora. Nunca como pasteles ni papas fritas porque son malos para la salud. (*Olympic skier*)
2. Nunca como el desayuno porque no tengo tiempo para comer. Para el almuerzo prefiero la comida rápida: una hamburguesa con un refresco. (*drummer*)

2. Hablar

Suggestions: Remind students that adjectives must agree with nouns in gender and number.
Answers will vary.

3. Leer

Suggestions: Have students list the clues to the answers as they read.
Answers:

Chato and Andrés lead a healthy lifestyle. Chispa leads an unhealthy lifestyle.

4. Escribir

Suggestions: Have students write their suggestions, then exhange their answers with a partner and correct any mistakes.
Answers will vary.

5. Comparar

Suggestions: Have students re-read the *Perspectivas del mundo hispano* information as homework.

CAPÍTULO 4A

¿Adónde vas?

Leisure activities and locations in your community

Vocabulary: leisure activities; places; expressions to tell where and with whom you go; expressions to talk about when things are done

Grammar: the verb *ir;* interrogative words

Cultural Perspectives: leisure activities in the Spanish-speaking world

Auténtico: Little Oaxaca

CAPÍTULO 4B

¿Quieres ir conmigo?

Activities outside of school and invitations

Vocabulary: leisure activities; feelings; expressions for extending, accepting, and declining invitations; expressions to tell when something happens

Grammar: *ir + a + infinitive;* the verb *jugar*

Cultural Perspectives: opinions on after-school activities

Auténtico: Sports, Culture, and Innovation

Theme Support

Bulletin Boards

Theme: Tiempo libre

Ask students to cut out, copy, or download photos of buildings and outdoor locations in Spanish-speaking countries and people engaged in leisure activities. Cluster photos of activities around photos of places where the activities might take place.

Hands-on Culture

Craft: Migajón

Migajón is the soft part of bread. It is used throughout Latin America as the base for a modeling material to create decorations and miniature toys.

Materials:

2 slices of white bread per student	2 tablespoons of white glue per student
acrylic paints	paint brushes

Steps:

1. Trim the crust from the bread and tear it into pieces.
2. Knead the glue into the bread until the bread feels like soft clay.
3. Shape the *migajón* into a small figure, such as an animal, car, or flower.
4. Set the figure aside for two to three days to let it air dry and become hard.
5. Decorate the figure with paint.

Game

Pregúntame

Play this game after you present *Gramática: Asking questions* in *Capítulo* 4A.

Players: the entire class

Materials: paper, pens, 2 paper bags

Steps:

1. Write all the question words and phrases from the *Gramática* on the chalkboard.
2. Divide the class into two teams. Teams write 11 sentences that would answer questions using the words and phrases from the board. Teams write one sentence for each question word or phrase.

   Question word: ¿Adónde?
   Team writes: Voy a la biblioteca.
   Question phrase: ¿Con quién?
   Team writes: Ella va con Roberto.

3. Collect the strips of paper and place them in two paper bags, one for each team.
4. Toss a coin to determine which team begins the game.
5. Draw a sentence from the Team 1 bag and read it aloud. Students from Team 2 have ten seconds to confer, then ask a question the sentence would answer. If the question is correct, Team 2 earns a point. If more than one question is possible, Team 2 may ask a second question to earn another point.
6. Repeat Step 5 for the other team.
7. The winner is the team with the most points after both bags have been emptied.

Variation: You write the sentences, making some of them simple and others more complex. Begin play with the simple sentences and progress to the more complex ones.

21st Century Skills

Look for tips throughout *Tema* 4 to enrich your teaching by integrating 21st Century Skills. Suggestions for the Project-Based Learning and Theme Support follow below.

Project-Based Learning

Modify the Project-Based Learning with one or more of these suggestions:

Creativity and Innovation Invite students to design a novel weekend entertainment guide using digital, print, and other media. The handout "Innovate" will help them develop, plan, and implement their groundbreaking guide.

Critical Thinking and Problem Solving Have students think about their audience. Would they rather attract a small and specific group of people, or a more general group? How would the target audience affect their plans for the guide? The handout "Make Decisions" can help them analyze their options.

ICT Literacy Have students consider advertising for their guide. Mention elements of an ad campaign, such as street signs, newspaper ads, radio, television, and Internet. Which advertising elements would work best to reach the audience they chose, and why?

Reading across the Curriculum

Social and Cross-Cultural Skills Have students review *Cultura* on pages 177 and 181 and compare what they do in their free time to what teens in Spanish-speaking countries do. Have them write a paragraph about how to adapt their free time activities to living or visiting in another country.

▶ **Videocultura** View *Los pasatiempos* online with the class to learn more about leisure time in Spanish-speaking countries.

Project-Based Learning

Guía para el tiempo libre

Overview: Students create a weekend entertainment guide for digital or print delivery, featuring the times and locations of six different events and an illustration of each event. They then present their guide to the class.

Resources: online or print samples of weekend entertainment guides; website creation software, image editing and page layout software and/or construction paper, magazines, scissors, glue, colored markers

Sequence: (suggestions for when to do each step appear throughout the chapters)

4A

Step 1. Review instructions so students know what is expected of them. Hand out the Theme 4 Project Instructions and the rubric.

Step 2. Students look at examples of entertainment guides on the Internet or in their local newspaper. They then brainstorm what to include in their guide.

Step 3. Students submit a rough sketch of their guide. Return the sketches with your suggestions.

4B

Step 4. Students create layouts. Encourage students to think through the details of their designs before implementing them and before writing the content of the guide.

Step 5. Students submit a draft of the information in their guide. Note your corrections and suggestions, then return the drafts to students. For additional oral practice, students use their guides to invite a partner to one of the events.

Step 6. Students complete and present their guide to the class, describing each of the events featured.

Options

1. Students write and act out a script for a T.V. entertainment show describing upcoming events.
2. Students make a collage or slide show of their favorite leisure activities and write a paragraph about when and where they do them.

Assessment

Here is a detailed rubric for assessing this project:

Theme 4 Project: *Guía para el tiempo libre*

Rubric	Score 1	Score 3	Score 5
Evidence of planning	You provided no written draft or page layout.	Your draft was written and layout created, but not corrected.	You corrected your draft and layout.
Your use of illustrations	You included no photos or illustrations.	You included photos or illustrations, but your layout was unorganized.	Your guide was easy to read, complete, and accurate.
Your presentation	Your guide and presentation included little of the required information.	Your guide and presentation included most of the required information.	Your guide and presentation included all of the required information.

AT A GLANCE

Objectives

- Listen and read about leisure activities and schedules
- Talk and write about places to go and activities to do during free time
- Exchange information about weekend plans
- Understand the meaning and role of children's rhymes from the Spanish-speaking world
- Compare leisure activities in the Spanish-speaking world and the United States
- Identify cultural practices in an authentic video about community

Vocabulary

- Leisure activities
- Places in the community

Grammar

- The verb *ir*
- Asking questions

Culture

- Francisco de Goya, p. 170
- Pedro Lázaro, p. 177
- *la plaza,* p. 177
- Popularity of sports clubs and gyms, p. 181
- Tradition of going to the movies, p. 185
- Old San Juan, pp. 186, 187
- Andean music, p. 189
- Chants and songs, p. 190

Recycle

- The verb *ir*
- The present tense of *-ar* verbs
- The present tense of *-er* and *-ir* verbs
- Infinitives

Authentic Resources

- Video showing the attractions and pastimes of a neighborhood in Carlsbad, California, pp. 192–193

RESOURCES

	FOR THE STUDENT	DIGITAL	PRINT	FOR THE TEACHER	DIGITAL	PRINT
Plan				Teacher's Edition	•	•
				Teacher's Resource Materials	•	
				Pre-AP® Resource Materials	•	
				Lesson Plans, pp. 170-e, 170-f	•	
				Mapa global interactivo	•	
Introducción pp. 170–171						
Present	Student Edition, pp. 170–171	•	•	Teacher's Edition, pp. 170–171	•	•
	DK Reference Atlas	•		Teacher's Resource Materials	•	
	Videocultura	•		Mapa global interactivo	•	
	Para hispanohablantes	•				
Vocabulario en contexto pp. 172–175						
Present & Practice	Student Edition, pp. 172–175	•	•	Teacher's Edition, pp. 172–175	•	•
	Audio	•		Teacher's Resource Materials	•	
	Videohistoria	•		Vocabulary Clip Art	•	
	Flashcards	•		Technology: Audio	•	
	Instant Check	•		Video Program: Videohistoria	•	
	Guided WB, pp. 115–124	•	•			
	Core WB, pp. 67–70	•	•			
	Communication Activities	•				
	Para hispanohablantes	•				
Assess and Remediate				Prueba 4A–1: Assessment Program, pp. 93–94	•	
				Assessment Program para hispanohablantes, pp. 93–94	•	

RESOURCES		FOR THE STUDENT	DIGITAL	PRINT	FOR THE TEACHER	DIGITAL	PRINT
Vocabulario en uso pp. 176–179							
Present & Practice		Student Edition, pp. 176–179	•	•	Interactive Whiteboard Vocabulary Activities	•	
		Instant Check	•		Teacher's Edition, pp. 176–179	•	•
		Communication Activities	•		Teacher's Resource Materials	•	
		Para hispanohablantes	•		Communicative Pair Activities	•	
		Communicative Pair Activities	•		Technology: Audio	•	
					Videomodelos	•	
Assess and Remediate					Prueba 4A–2 with Remediation	•	
					Prueba 4A–2: Assessment Program, pp. 95–96	•	
					Assessment Program para hispanohablantes, pp. 95–96	•	
Gramática pp. 180–187							
Present & Practice		Student Edition, pp. 180–187	•	•	Interactive Whiteboard Grammar Activities	•	
		Instant Check	•		Teacher's Edition, pp. 180–187	•	•
		Animated Verbs	•		Teacher's Resource Materials	•	
		Tutorial Video: Grammar	•		Communicative Pair Activities	•	
		Canción de hip hop	•		Technology: Audio	•	
		Guided WB, pp. 125–129	•	•	Videomodelos	•	
		Core WB, pp. 71–73	•	•	Video Program: GramActiva	•	
		Communication Activities	•		Mapa global interactivo	•	
		Para hispanohablantes	•				
		Communicative Pair Activities	•				
Assess and Remediate					Pruebas 4A–3 and 4A–4 with Remediation	•	
					Pruebas 4A–3, 4A–4 Assessment Program, pp. 97, 98	•	
					Assessment Program para hispanohablantes, pp. 97, 98	•	
Aplicación pp. 188–193							
Apply		Student Edition, pp. 188–193	•	•	Teacher's Edition, pp. 188–193	•	•
		Authentic Resources Workbook	•	•	Mapa global interactivo	•	
		Authentic Resources	•		Authentic Resources Lesson Plans with scripts, answer keys	•	
		Online Cultural Reading	•				
		Literacy Skills Workbook	•	•			
		Guided WB, pp. 130–132	•	•			
		Communication Activities	•				
		Para hispanohablantes	•				
Repaso del capítulo pp. 194–145							
Review		Student Edition, pp. 194–195	•	•	Teacher's Edition, pp. 194–195	•	•
		Online Puzzles and Games	•		Teacher's Resource Materials	•	
		Core WB, pp. 74–75	•	•	Technology: Audio	•	
		Communication Activities	•				
		Para hispanohablantes	•				
		Instant Check	•				
Chapter Assessment							
Assess					Examen del capítulo 4A	•	
					Assessment Program, pp. 99–104	•	
					Alternate Assessment Program, pp. 35–39	•	
					Assessment Program para hispanohablantes, pp. 99–104	•	
					Audio Program, Cap. 4A, Examen	•	
					ExamView: Test Banks A and B questions only online	•	
					Heritage Learner Test Bank	•	
					Pre-AP® Test Bank	•	

LESSON PLAN (50 MINUTES)

DAY	Warm-up / Assess	Preview / Present / Practice / Communicate		Wrap-up / Homework Options
1	**Warm-up** (10 min.) • Return Examen del capítulo 3B	**Chapter Opener** (5 min.) • Objectives • Arte y cultura	**Vocabulario en contexto** (30 min.) • Presentation: Vocabulario en contexto • Actividades 1, 2	**Wrap-up and Homework Options** (5 min.) • Core Practice 4A-1, 4A-2
2	**Warm-up** (5 min.) • Homework check	**Vocabulario en contexto** (40 min.) • Presentation: Videohistoria *Tiempo libre* • View: Videohistoria • Video Activities 1, 2, 3, 4 • Actividad 3		**Wrap-up and Homework Options** (5 min.) • Core Practice 4A-3, 4A-4 • Prueba 4A-1: Vocabulary recognition
3	**Warm-up** (10 min.) • Actividad 5 • Homework check • **Formative Assessment** (10 min.) • Prueba 4A-1: Vocabulary recognition	**Vocabulario en uso** (25 min.) • Actividades 4, 6, 7 • Cultura • Interactive Whiteboard Vocabulary Activities • Exploración del lenguaje • Audio Activities 5, 6		**Wrap-up and Homework Options** (5 min.) • Writing Activity 10 • Prueba 4A-2 with Remediation Vocabulary production
4	**Warm-up** (10 min.) • Actividad 9 • Homework check • **Formative Assessment** (10 min.) • Prueba 4A-2 with Remediation Vocabulary production	**Gramática y vocabulario en uso** (25 min.) • Actividad 8 • Communicative Pair Activity • Presentation: The verb *ir*	• View: GramActiva video • Interactive Whiteboard Grammar Activities • Actividades 11, 12	**Wrap-up and Homework Options** (5 min.) • Writing Activity 11
5	**Warm-up** (10 min.) • Actividad 10 • Homework check	**Gramática y vocabulario en uso** (35 min.) • Actividades 13, 14 • Audio Activity 7 • Cultura	• El español en la comunidad • Pronunciación	**Wrap-up and Homework Options** (5 min.) • Core Practice 4A-5 • Prueba 4A-3 with Remediation The verb *ir*
6	**Warm-up** (5 min.) • Homework check • **Formative Assessment** (10 min.) • Prueba 4A-3 with Remediation The verb *ir*	**Gramática y vocabulario en uso** (30 min.) • Presentation: Asking questions • View: GramActiva video • Interactive Whiteboard Grammar Activities	• Actividades 15, 17, 18 • Audio Activities 8, 9	**Wrap-up and Homework Options** (5 min.) • Core Practice 4A-6, 4A-7 • Actividad 16 • Prueba 4A-4 with Remediation Asking questions
7	**Warm-up** (15 min.) • Writing Activities 12, 13 • Homework check • **Formative Assessment** (10 min.) • Prueba 4A-4 with Remediation Asking questions	**Gramática y vocabulario en uso** (20 min.) • Communicative Pair Activity • Cultura • Actividad 19		**Wrap-up and Homework Options** (5 min.) • La cultura en vivo
8	**Warm-up** (5 min.) • Homework check	**Aplicación** (40 min.) • Lectura • ¿Comprendes? • Cultura	• Auténtico • Presentación oral: Step 1	**Wrap-up and Homework Options** (5 min.) • Presentación oral: Step 2 • Preparación para el examen 3, 4, 5 • Lectura
9	**Warm-up** (5 min.) • Homework check	**Aplicación** (30 min.) • Presentación oral: Step 3	**Repaso del capítulo** (10 min.) • Vocabulario y gramática • Preparación para el examen 1, 2	**Wrap-up and Homework Options** (5 min.) • Core Practice 4A-8, 4A-9 • Instant Check • Examen del capítulo 4A
10	**Warm-up** (10 min.) • Homework check • Answer questions • **Summative Assessment** (40 min.) • Examen del capítulo 4A			

ALTERNATE LESSON PLAN (90 MINUTES)

DAY	Warm-up / Assess	Preview / Present / Practice / Communicate		Wrap-up / Homework Options
1	**Warm-up** (10 min.) • Return Examen del capítulo 3B	**Chapter Opener** (5 min.) • Objectives • Arte y cultura **Vocabulario en contexto** (50 min.) • Presentation: Vocabulario en contexto • Actividades 1, 2 • Presentation: Videohistoria *Tiempo libre*	• View: Videohistoria • Video Activities 1, 2, 3, 4 • Actividad 3 **Vocabulario en uso** (20 min.) • Interactive Whiteboard Vocabulary Activities • Actividades 4, 5, 6, 7 • Cultura	**Wrap-up and Homework Options** (5 min.) • Core Practice 4A-1, 4A-2, 4A-3, 4A-4 • Prueba 4A-1: Vocabulary recognition
2	**Warm-up** (10 min.) • Actividad 10 • Homework check • **Formative Assessment** (10 min.) • Prueba 4A-1: Vocabulary recognition	**Gramática y vocabulario en uso** (65 min.) • Exploración del lenguaje • Audio Activities 5, 6 • Actividades 8, 9 • Communicative Pair Activity • Presentation: The verb *ir* • View: GramActiva video	• Interactive Whiteboard Grammar Activities • Actividades 11, 12, 13 • Audio Activity 7	**Wrap-up and Homework Options** (5 min.) • Writing Activity 10 • Core Practice 4A-5 • Prueba 4A-2 with Remediation Vocabulary production
3	**Warm-up** (5 min.) • Homework check • **Formative Assessment** (10 min.) • Prueba 4A-2 with Remediation Vocabulary production	**Gramática y vocabulario en uso** (70 min.) • Cultura • Actividad 14 • El español en la comunidad • Pronunciación • Presentation: Asking questions • View: GramActiva video • Interactive Whiteboard Grammar Activities • Actividades 15, 17, 18 • Audio Activities 8, 9 • Writing Activities 12, 13		**Wrap-up and Homework Options** (5 min.) • Writing Activity 11 • Core Practice 4A-6, 4A-7 • Pruebas 4A-3, 4A-4 with Remediation The verb *ir,* Asking questions
4	**Warm-up** (10 min.) • Actividad 16 • Homework check • **Formative Assessment** (15 min.) • Pruebas 4A-3, 4A-4 with Remediation The verb *ir,* Asking questions	**Gramática y vocabulario en uso** (25 min.) • Cultura • Communicative Pair Activity • Actividad 19	**Aplicación** (35 min.) • Lectura • ¿Comprendes? • Cultura • Presentación oral: Step 1	**Wrap-up and Homework Options** (5 min.) • La cultura en vivo • Presentación oral: Step 2
5	**Warm-up** (5 min.) • Homework check	**Aplicación** (50 min.) • Auténtico • Presentación oral: Step 3 **Repaso del capítulo** (30 min.) • Vocabulario y gramática • Preparación para el examen 1, 2, 3, 4, 5		**Wrap-up and Homework Options** (5 min.) • Core Practice 4A-8, 4A-9 • Instant Check • Examen del capítulo 4A
6	**Warm-up** (15 min.) • Homework check • Answer questions **Repaso del capítulo** (25 min.) • Situation Cards • Communicative Pair Activities • **Summative Assessment** (45 min.) • Examen del capítulo 4A			**Wrap-up and Homework Options** (5 min.) • Lectura

Can-Do Statements

Read the can-do statements in the chapter objectives with students. Then have students read Preparación para el examen on page 195 to preview what they will be able to do at the end of the chapter.

Standards for Capítulo 4A

To achieve the goals of the Standards, students will:

COMMUNICATION

1.1 Interpersonal
- Talk about leisure activities and locations
- Talk about where they go on different days of the week

1.2 Interpretive
- Read and listen to information about leisure activities
- Read a picture-based story; a letter telling how an exchange student spends her time; about Old San Juan, Puerto Rico; a mall advertisement about scheduled activities
- Listen to and watch a video about leisure activities
- Listen to information about a plaza

1.3 Presentational
- Present information about: leisure activities and locations; the history of Puerto Rico
- Reply to an e-mail message
- Perform a short skit about a student's first day of school

CULTURE

2.1 Practices to Perspectives
- Explain leisure enjoyment in the eighteenth-century Spanish aristocracy
- Talk about: the use of the town square in Spanish-speaking cultures; school-based exercise; movie-going habits; restoration of historic districts in Puerto Rico

2.2 Products to Perspectives
- Discuss Francisco de Goya and his painting; Pedro Lázaro and his painting; Andean music and instruments; about Spanish architecture in the United States

CONNECTIONS

3.1 Making Connections
- Discuss Francisco de Goya; the history of Puerto Rico; the influence of Spain's colonial history on the United States
- Reinforce math and graphing abilities skills

3.2 Acquiring Information and Diverse Perspectives
- Recite the Mexican folk song, "La Bamba"
- Practice songs to games played by children

COMPARISONS

4.1 Language
- Talk about new vocabulary through the recognition of cognates; the correct placement of stress and accents; origins of the Spanish days of the week
- Explain the verb ir; the use of interrogatives

CAPÍTULO **4A**
¿Adónde vas?

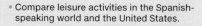

Country Connections Explorar el mundo hispano

CHAPTER OBJECTIVES

Communication

By the end of this chapter you will be able to:
- Listen and read about leisure activities and schedules.
- Talk and write about places to go and activities to do during free time.
- Exchange information about weekend plans.

Culture

You will also be able to:
- **Auténtico:** Identify cultural practices in an authentic video about community.
- Understand the meaning and role of children's rhymes from the Spanish-speaking world.

- Compare leisure activities in the Spanish-speaking world and the United States.

You will demonstrate what you know and can do:
- Presentación oral: Un estudiante nuevo
- Repaso del capítulo: Preparación para el examen

You will use:

Vocabulary
- Leisure activities
- Places in the community

Grammar
- The verb ir
- Asking questions

ARTE y CULTURA España

"El quitasol" is a work by Spanish painter Francisco de Goya (1746–1828). He made this painting in 1777 as a design to be used in the manufacture of a royal tapestry. At that time Goya was already famous for the elegance of his artwork and his ability to capture ordinary events in realistic detail. The brilliant colors of this painting suggest a happy moment of relaxation for two young people.

▶ Why do people who live in the city go out to the country to relax?

Mapa global interactivo Discover places of interest in Madrid, Spain and make a list of your favorite ones.

"El quitasol" (1777), Francisco de Goya ▲
Oil on canvas, 104 x 152 cm. Museo Nacional del Prado, Madrid, Spain.
Photo credit: Scala / Art Resource, NY.

170 ciento setenta • Tema 4 • Los pasatiempos

Enrich Your Teaching

The End in Mind

Have students preview the sample performance tasks on *Preparación para el examen,* p. 195, and connect them to the Chapter Objectives. Explain to students that by completing the sample tasks they can self-assess their learning progress.

Technology: Mapa global interactivo

Download the *Mapa global interactivo* files for Chapter 4A and preview the activities. Use Activity 1 to travel to Madrid, Spain. Activity 2 takes you to Chicago's Pilsen neighborhood. In Activity 3, you visit historic San Juan, Puerto Rico.

Go **Online** to practice

PearsonSchool.com/Autentico

PEARSON
realize

AUDIO · VIDEO · WRITING · SPEAK/RECORD · MAPA GLOBAL · AUTÉNTICO · FLASCHARDS · ETEXT 2.O · GAMES

Preview **4A**

En el Parque Nacional Torres
del Paine, Patagonia, Chile

 Videocultura **Los pasatiempos**

Capítulo 4A • ciento setenta y uno **171**

4.2 Cultural
- Compare: social gathering places to plazas; school-based sports and exercise activities; movie going habits of teens; restoration of historic districts; the influence of musical intruments; songs sung during children's games

COMMUNITIES

5.1 School and Global Communities
- Identify opportunities to explore local Spanish-speaking communities

Chapter Opener

Resources: Mapa global interactivo

Suggestions: Have students list the places in your community where they go for leisure activities. Explain that in this chapter they will be learning to talk about the places they go for fun. They will also learn to ask questions of others.

 Technology: Videocultura View *Los pasatiempos* online with the class to learn more about leisure time in Spanish-speaking countries.

ARTE Y CULTURA

Standards: 2.1, 2.2, 3.1

Suggestions: Explain that Goya is one of the great Spanish painters. Bring in additional examples of his work to share with students.

Answers will vary but may include that people enjoy being in a quieter, less polluted environment, surrounded by nature.

🌐 **Technology: Mapa global interactivo, Actividad 1** Discover places of interest in Madrid, Spain.

Culture Note

The *Parque Nacional Torres del Paine* was established in 1959. It lies in the Patagonian region of southern Chile. Within the park borders, visitors can view glaciers and mountains, and hike alongside rivers and lakes. The park was designated a World Biosphere Reserve by UNESCO in 1978.

Project-Based Learning

Guía para el tiempo libre

Have students research outdoor public events such as concerts or dance performances in public spaces in a specific city in a Spanish-speaking country. Sites of the events might include city parks or plazas.

171

Vocabulario en contexto

Standards: 1.2, 4.1

Resources: Teacher's Resource Materials: Input Script, Clip Art, Audio Script; Technology: Audio Cap. 4A

Suggestions: Use the Input Script from the *Teacher's Resource Materials* to present the new vocabulary and grammar. Present the vocabulary in two sets: places to go during the week and places to go on weekends. Draw a map of your town on the board or overhead and locate the various locales as you describe them. Have students raise their hands if you mention a place that they go. Remind students that they will be held responsible for the words in the *Más vocabulario*.

Pre-AP® Integration

- **Learning Objective:** Interpretive: Audio
- **Activity:** Have students copy from the board the following chart:

Nombre del estudiante	Actividad

Have four pairs of students volunteer to re-create and read aloud to the class one of the dialogs presented on pp. 172–173. Then, the rest of the class completes the chart from what they hear.

- **Pre-AP® Resource Materials:** Comprehensive guide to Pre-AP® vocabulary skill development,

Active Classroom

Divide students into groups of five or six. Allow each group to have one open book. Students take turns secretly writing down one of the places shown. The others ask, ***¿Vas a(l)...?*** until they guess the destination. When it is guessed, the first student confirms the answer: ***Sí, voy a(l)....*** Continue until all have had a turn.

⫶⃝ Technology: Interactive Whiteboard

Vocabulary Activities 4A Use the whiteboard activities in your Teacher Resources as you progress through the vocabulary practice with your class.

Vocabulario en contexto

OBJECTIVES
Read, listen to, and understand information about places to go when you're not in school, and plans for leisure time.

🔊

Julia:	En tu tiempo libre, después de las clases, ¿vas a la biblioteca?
Carmen:	No todos los días. **Los lunes** y viernes **voy** a mi trabajo. ¿Y tú?
Julia:	**Generalmente,** voy a mi clase de piano y **después,** al parque **para caminar** o **al** gimnasio **con** mis amigos.
Carmen:	Después de trabajar, **¿vamos al** centro comercial?
Julia:	¡Uf!, no puedo. Necesito ir **a casa** a estudiar.

Julia   Carmen

el gimnasio · la playa · la lección de piano · el trabajo · la biblioteca · el centro comercial · el parque · el restaurante

Differentiated Instruction

Students with Learning Difficulties

To help students acquire the structure ***a + el = al,*** use the Clip Art from the *Teacher's Resource Materials* and provide each student with copies of the various pictures. Help them label the pictures with the appropriate prepositions: ***al, a la,*** and ***a las.*** They can use these as flashcards for drill. Be sure to point out the Nota on p. 177.

Challenge

Have students create a calendar for the coming month on which they label where they are going and at what times. They can quiz one another: *¿Qué haces los (domingos)? ¿Qué haces el (18)?*

Julia: El fin de semana voy con mis amigos al cine a ver una película.

Carmen: ¿Con quién vas?

Julia: Con José. ¿Y tú?

Carmen: Me quedo en casa. O mejor, ¡voy a la playa o a la montaña! Me encanta nadar o caminar.

Más vocabulario
la iglesia = church
la mezquita = mosque
la sinagoga = synagogue
el templo = temple, Protestant church

el campo

el cine

las montañas

ir de compras

ver una película

la piscina

1

Un fin de semana especial

🔊 ESCUCHAR You will hear Julia describe where she does seven activities. If a statement is logical, lift your right hand. If it is not logical, leave both hands on your desk.

2

¿Adónde van?

🔊 ESCUCHAR Identify key words for locations. Listen to students discuss where they go in their free time. Point to the picture of the location.

Capítulo 4A • ciento setenta y tres **173**

Enrich Your Teaching

Culture Note
On Sundays in many Spanish-speaking countries, it is common for entire families to go out together. Often they will attend a religious service, then have something to eat at a restaurant, and then spend time in a park or at the movies. They may also gather at the home of a family member or friend.

Teacher-to-Teacher
Prepare a map handout with various places in your community pictured on it. Include places where your students work. As you describe an imaginary itinerary for one of your students, have students trace the route on the map. Project an online map of your community so that they can check their work.

1

Standards: 1.2

Resources: Teacher's Resource Materials: Audio Script; Technology: Audio Cap. 4

Suggestions: Play the audio or read the script. Repeat the activity. Then ask the class to name the seven activities that Elena describes.

🔊 **Technology: Audio**
Script and Answers

1. Me gusta esquiar en la biblioteca. *(leave hands on desk)*
2. Me gusta ir al cine a ver películas. *(lift right hand)*
3. Practico deportes en el restaurante. *(leave hands on desk)*
4. Nado en el cine. *(leave hands on desk)*
5. Bailamos en casa. *(lift right hand)*
6. Tomo lecciones de piano en la escuela. *(lift right hand)*
7. Estudiamos en la biblioteca. *(lift right hand)*

2

Standards: 1.2

Resources: Teacher's Resource Materials: Audio Script; Technology: Audio Cap. 4A

Suggestions: Play the audio or read the script. Explain that some sentences contain two activities or places.

🔊 **Technology: Audio**
Script and Answers

1. Voy a la biblioteca todos los viernes. *(point to library)*
2. Generalmente voy al cine los lunes. *(point to movie theater)*
3. En mi tiempo libre voy al campo. *(point to the countryside)*
4. Los domingos voy a la playa con mi familia. *(point to beach)*
5. Voy al centro comercial todos los días. *(point to mall)*
6. Después de la escuela voy al parque. *(point to park)*
7. Me gusta comer en un restaurante bueno todos los domingos. *(point to restaurant)*

Additional Resources

📶 **Technology: Online Resources**
• Instant Check
• Guided, Core, Audio, Writing practice
• *Para hispanohablantes*
• Communication Activities
Print
• Guided WB pp. 115–120
• Core WB pp. 67–68

Vocabulario en contexto

Standards: 1.2

Resources: Technology: Audio Cap. 4A

Suggestions: Model the dialogue with a volunteer. Begin the reading again with volunteers playing the roles of the characters. Using the presentation, help students understand the new words in blue type.

Post-reading: Complete Actividad 3 to check comprehension.

3

Standards: 1.2, 1.3

Suggestions: You may wish to do this as a listening activity, reading the sentences to the students.

Extension: Use the dialogue as a model to ask students about their weekend plans. Have students give a "thumbs up" if the plans match their own, or a "thumbs down" if the plans are different than theirs.

Answers:

1. C
2. F
3. F
4. F
5. C

Pre-AP® Integration

- **Learning Objective:** Interpersonal Speaking
- **Activity:** Have students create a short conversation based on this written exchange. Students can play the roles of Adrián and Mateo as they discuss their weekend plans, replacing the places mentioned with other places where they might go.
- **Pre-AP® Resource Materials:** Comprehensive guide to Pre-AP® vocabulary skill development

Adrián y Mateo escriben mensajes sobre sus actividades para el fin de semana.

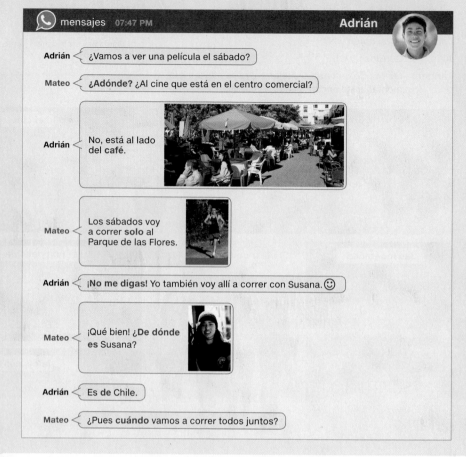

3

Un fin de semana especial

✎ ESCRIBIR Lee las frases. Escribe C (cierto) si la frase es correcta o F (falso) si la frase es incorrecta.

1. Adrián escribe a Mateo para ir al cine.
2. Adrián va al cine que está en el centro comercial.
3. Mateo va a correr con amigos al Parque de las Flores.
4. Mateo va al gimnasio todos los sábados.
5. Susana es de Chile.

Differentiated Instruction

Challenge

Have students rewrite the dialogue for the various characters, substituting other activities or places that they've learned. They could also personalize it using names of classmates. Have them perform their dialogues for the class. Encourage creativity.

Heritage Speakers

Have students write a short paragraph telling what they usually do each day of the week. Allow them to use vocabulary that has not yet been taught, if they desire. Verify their spelling and have them make necessary corrections before placing the paragraphs in their portfolios.

Videohistoria

Go **Online** to practice
PEARSON realize.
AUDIO   VIDEO   WRITING   SCRIPT

PearsonSchool.com/Autentico

Tiempo libre

Before You Watch

Watch and listen for key details If you were going to spend time somewhere new, what key information about places and activities do you need to enjoy your free time? How might these photos connect to free time in Costa Rica?

Complete the Activity

Tu tiempo libre ¿Adónde vas y qué haces en tu tiempo libre? Escribe una lista de cuatro lugares y las actividades que te gusta hacer allí.

Ximena   Camila   Valentina
Mateo   Sebastián

▶ **Watch the Video**

How do volunteers with *Codo a Codo* spend their free time?

Go to **PearsonSchool.com/Autentico** to watch the video *Tiempo libre* and to view the script.

After You Watch

✎ **¿COMPRENDES?**   Watch for key details in the video.

1. How does one *Codo a codo* volunteer spend his free time? For each place or activity, indicate if he likes to go there. If so, what he does and what day or time of day he goes.

   a. el centro comercial   b. el mercado local
   c. el gimnasio   d. el parque
   e. el cine   f. los restaurantes y los cafés
   g. el centro   h. los parques nacionales

2. ¿Con quién comparte el video Ximena?

Comparación cultural   ¿Es posible hacer tus actividades favoritas en la comunidad que ves en el video? ¿Por qué?

Capítulo 4A • ciento setenta y cinco **175**

Enrich Your Teaching

Culture Note

El tortuguero National Park in Costa Rica main attraction are the green sea turtles or tortuga verde, the leatherback or tortuga baula, and the Hawksbill or Tortuga Carey nest on the beaches. Located in the Caribbean coast of Costa Rica with over 20 miles of coastline, it provides the sea turtles

a safe place to lay their eggs. The park is also a migratory stopover for about one million of birds per year. Tortuguero was declared a protected nesting sanctuary in 1963 and declared National Park in 1970 by the Caribbean Conservation Corporation.

Technology: Video

Standards: 1.2

Resources: Teacher's Resource Materials: Video Script

Before You Watch

Review the previewing strategy and activity with the students. Ask students for examples of how they prepare before visiting a new place or job. Also point out the images of places that will be discussed in thew video.

Review the Complete the Activity with the class. Have students talk about what they do and where they go in their free time.

Watch the Video

Show the video without pausing. Show it again, pausing along the way to check comprehension. If there are words that students haven't learned yet, you may want to write those on the board. Show the segment a final time, without pausing.

After You Watch

Standards: 1.2, 1.3

Suggestions: Discuss the questions with the class.

Answers

1. **a.** No
   b. No
   c. Sí, levanta pesas, monta en bicicleta, dos veces por semana, por la tarde
   d. Sí, juega fútbol, fines de semana, por la tarde
   e. Sí, viernes
   f. Sí, desayunar, sábados temprano en la mañana
   g. Sí, pasea por la ciudad, casi todos los días
   h. Sí, visita parques nacionales, algunos fines de semana
2. Ximena comparte el video con todos los voluntarios.

Comparación cultural: Answers will vary.

Print and distribute the activity sheets from the Teacher's Resources. Or have students complete the additional video activities online.

Additional Resources

📶 **Technology: Online Resources**
  • Instant Check
  • Guided, Core, Video, Audio
  • *Para hispanohablantes*
  Print
  • Guided WB pp. 121–124
  • Core WB pp. 69–70

Assessment

Quiz: Vocabulary Recognition
  • Prueba 4A-1

4A | Communication

4

Standards: 1.2, 1.3

Suggestions: Review the places pictured before students begin. Brainstorm logical responses for the **Respuesta personal.**

Answers:

1. ... el gimnasio *(el parque)*.
2. ... la piscina *(la playa)*.
3. ... el cine.
4. ... la biblioteca *(casa, la escuela)*.
5. ... el centro comercial.
6. ... las montañas.
7. ... el restaurante *(casa, el café)*.

Extension: Have students create illogical sentences, e.g., *Nado en la biblioteca*. Ask volunteers to write theirs on the board and have the class correct them.

Starter Activity

Review with students the vocabulary in *Vocabulario en contexto* using pictures, photographs or magazine cut outs. Ask them about which places they like to go to when they are not in school.

5

Standards: 1.3

Resources: Teacher's Resource Materials: Video Program: GramActiva

Recycle: Expressions of frequency

Suggestions: Have students identify each picture before they begin. As students work, walk around the room, checking that they understand what to do.

Answers will vary.

Extension: Draw the line diagram on the board and have volunteers write places they go under the correct time expression.

Vocabulario en uso

OBJECTIVES
▶ Write and talk about places you go in your free time
▶ Listen to a description of a plaza
▶ Discuss and compare where you go and how often

4

¿Qué haces en . . . ?

ESCRIBIR, HABLAR   Completa las frases lógicamente.

1. Hago ejercicio en . . .
2. Nado en . . .
3. Veo películas en . . .
4. Leo libros y revistas en . . .
5. Voy de compras en . . .
6. Esquío en . . .
7. Como el desayuno en . . .

¡Respuesta personal!

5

¿Vas mucho a . . . ?

ESCRIBIR   On a sheet of paper, copy the diagram below and write the names of the places you go under the appropriate expression of frequency.

todos los días	mucho	a veces	nunca
		la playa	

176 ciento setenta y seis • Tema 4 • Los pasatiempos

Differentiated Instruction

Special Needs

Students who have difficulty writing can be given copies of the pictures from the Clip Art in the *Teacher's Resource Materials*. Prepare a large version of the diagram and have them place the pictures under the appropriate expressions.

Challenge/Pre-AP®

Have students write an original sentence using each one of the places mentioned in *Actividad* 5. Ask students to read their sentences to the class.

6

¡No me digas!

HABLAR EN PAREJA Work with a partner. Using what you wrote for Actividad 5, take turns saying where you go and how often. React to your partner's statements. Follow the model.

▶ **Videomodelo**

A —*Voy a la playa a veces.*
B —*¡No me digas! Yo voy a la playa a veces también.*
o:—*¡No me digas! Yo nunca voy a la playa.*
o:—*Pues, yo voy a la playa todos los días.*

Nota

When *a* is used before *el*, the two words form the contraction *al* (to the):

a + el = al

• Voy **al** centro comercial a veces, pero voy **a la** piscina mucho.

También se dice...

la piscina = la alberca (México); la pileta (América del Sur)
el restaurante = el restaurán (América del Sur)

7

Escucha y escribe

ESCUCHAR, ESCRIBIR Look at the painting of the plaza below. On a sheet of paper, write the numbers 1–6. You will hear six statements about the painting. Write what you hear.

CULTURA ◀ El mundo hispano

Pasear o caminar por la plaza mayor[1] de muchos pueblos y ciudades hispanos es una actividad popular para las personas. Una plaza mayor tiene tiendas, cafés, iglesias y edificios importantes. La gente va allí para comer, ir de compras, hacer negocios[2] y reunirse en celebraciones y festivales. Este cuadro de Pedro Lázaro (1956–) celebra la belleza y la importancia de la plaza en la cultura hispana.

Pre-AP® Integration: Los estilos de vida ¿Qué lugar de reunión social similar a una plaza hay en tu comunidad?

[1]main square [2]conduct business

"La plaza" (1981), Pedro Lázaro ▲
Lázaro, Pedro born 1956. "La plaza" (The Plaza), 1981.
Painting. Madrid, Private Collection.
Copyright akg-images/Joseph Martin/Newscom.

Capítulo 4A • ciento setenta y siete **177**

6

Standards: 1.1

Recycle: Expressions of frequency
Suggestions: Point out the *Nota* if you have not already explained this concept. Remind students of the examples they saw earlier. Have students tell you the preposition for each place or activity. Be sure Student B understands the options in the *Modelo*.

Answers will vary.

7

Standards: 1.2, 1.3

Resources: Teacher's Resource Materials: Audio Script; Technology: Audio Cap. 4A
Suggestions: Play the audio or read the script. Allow students to listen several times.

🔊 **Technology: Audio Script and Answers**

1. Hay muchas personas en la plaza.
2. Hace buen tiempo hoy.
3. ¿Ves la casa amarilla?
4. Muchas personas hablan en la plaza.
5. Voy a la plaza con mis amigos.
6. Me encanta la iglesia.

CULTURA

Standards: 2.1, 4.2

Suggestions: Point out that the main *plaza* is the hub of most towns or cities, and that people often arrange to meet at the *plaza*, both for business and pleasure.

Answers will vary but may include such places as malls, post offices, etc.

Teaching with Art

Artist Pedro Lázaro has depicted village life in a way that is representational without being photographic. His art is similar in style to American Primitive artists such as Grandma Moses. Bring in examples for students to compare.

Enrich Your Teaching

Culture Note

Lázaro's painting captures an essential feature of Hispanic towns: they are often built around the central focal point of the *plaza mayor*. Point out to students that the themes of *plaza* and community have been depicted by numerous artists in the Spanish-speaking world. You might show students paintings such as "Plaza Morazán en Tecucigalpa" by José Antonio Velásquez, sections of the "El Tianguis" mural by Diego Rivera, or contemporary works by Ernest Descals and Carmen Lomas Garza representing plazas and gatherings. Why do students think that this theme is important in Hispanic painting?

EXPLORACIÓN DEL LENGUAJE

Standards: 4.1

Suggestions: Remind students that what is now Spain was a Roman province for centuries. Have students research the origins of the English days of the week and make comparisons with the Latin / Spanish versions.

Answers:

1. c	**5.** b
2. e	**6.** f
3. a	**7.** d
4. g	

The Latin word for day is *dies*.

8

Standards: 1.1

Recycle: Vocabulary for leisure activities

Suggestions: Direct attention to the *Nota*. Point out that the article is required, unlike in English. Go through possible answers that Student B might give before students begin.

Answers will vary.

Common Errors: Students often try to use *en* before days of the week. To reinforce the correct structure, have Student B include the article and day of the week in the answers.

Extension: Have the class brainstorm places and activities they have learned and write them on the board. Then write, ***¿Cuándo vas...?*** and give a possible answer (***los jueves, los sábados,*** etc.). Then have volunteers ask and answer the question.

Exploración del lenguaje ◀ Origins of the Spanish days of the week

The word *sábado*, like many Spanish words, is based on Latin. The Spanish days of the week come from the Latin names for the gods, planets, sun, and moon, all of which were important in Roman daily life.

Try it out! Match the Spanish days of the week with their Latin origins.

	a. *dies Mercurii* named after Mercury, the god of commerce and travelers
	b. *dies Veneris* named after Venus, the goddess of beauty and love
1. lunes	
2. martes	**c.** *dies lunae* the day dedicated to the moon *(luna)*
3. miércoles	**d.** *dies solis* named after the sun *(sol)*, but later changed to *dies Dominicus*, which means "the Lord's day"
4. jueves	
5. viernes	**e.** *dies Martis* dedicated to Mars, the god of war
6. sábado	
7. domingo	**f.** *dies Saturni* named after Saturn; also called *dies Sabbati,* based on the Hebrew word *shabbath*, or "day of rest"
	g. *dies Jovis* named after Jove, or Jupiter, the ruler of the gods

• Since you know *día* means "day" in Spanish, what is the word for "day" in Latin?

8

¿Adónde vas?

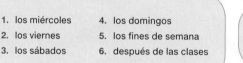

HABLAR EN PAREJA Hacer y contestar preguntas sobre la vida diaria. Habla con otro(a) estudiante sobre los lugares *(about the places)* adonde vas y cuándo vas allí.

Videomodelo

los lunes

A —¿Adónde vas **los lunes**?

B —Generalmente voy **a mi lección de piano**.

o:—Generalmente **me quedo en casa**.

Nota

To say that something usually happens on a certain day every week, use *los* with the day of the week:

• Generalmente ellos van al campo **los viernes** o **los sábados**.

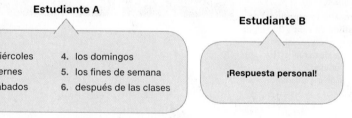

Estudiante A

1. los miércoles	4. los domingos
2. los viernes	5. los fines de semana
3. los sábados	6. después de las clases

Estudiante B

¡Respuesta personal!

Differentiated Instruction

Students with Learning Difficulties

If students have trouble with mathematics skills in *Actividad* 9, give them the formula for converting percentages: the number of students who gave a particular answer is divided by the total number of students in the class. Allow students to use calculators as necessary.

Challenge

Have students research the origins of the Spanish names of the months. Have them prepare a poster or handout with a two-column chart like the one in the *Exploración del lenguaje*. They could also create a matching exercise like the one there.

9

Cuando no estamos en la escuela . . .

HABLAR EN GRUPO, ESCRIBIR ¿Cómo pasan el tiempo tus compañeros de clase cuando no están en la escuela? Sigue *(follow)* los pasos.

Conexiones ⟨ **Las matemáticas**

1 Working in groups of four, take turns asking each person how often he or she does the activities listed below. Answer using *mucho, a veces,* or *nunca.* Keep a group tally of the responses.

ver películas	ir de compras
correr	ir a un trabajo
usar la computadora	ir a la biblioteca

Videomodelo

A —¿*Con qué frecuencia* (How often) **usas la computadora**?

B —*Uso la computadora* **mucho.**

2 Get together with another group of four and combine the results of your tally sheets. Prepare summary statements to report to the class.

3 Report your summary statements to the class and make a class total. Convert each total to a percentage.

4 Create a bar graph like the one shown for each activity that shows the class's frequency of participation.

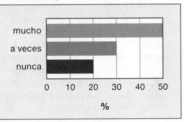
Un grupo de amigos en Lima, Perú

Frecuencia con que levantan pesas

10

Y tú, ¿qué dices?

ESCRIBIR, HABLAR

1. ¿Dónde ves más películas, en casa o en el cine?
2. Cuando vas de compras, ¿adónde vas?
3. ¿Adónde vas los fines de semana? ¿Vas solo(a) o con tus amigos?

Capítulo 4A • ciento setenta y nueve **179**

9

Standards: 1.1, 1.2, 1.3, 3.1

Recycle: Leisure activities

Suggestions: Give students the directions for each step just before it is done. Encourage speed in gathering the information in Step 1. You might give students a prepared checklist for tracking the answers. Help students with the mathematical operation, if necessary, or have students explain it to others. Create and project the format for a table students could use for creating the bar graph in Step 4.

Answers will vary.

10

Standards: 1.1, 1.2

Suggestions: Have students deduce the meaning of *solo(a)* in item 3 using cognate recognition or context clues (it's the opposite of *con tus amigos*).

Answers will vary but will include: ves, veo, corres, corro, usas, uso, vas, voy.

Additional Resources

Technology: Online Resources
- *Para hispanohablantes*
- Teacher's Resource Materials: Audio Script
- Technology: Audio Cap. 4A
- Communication Activities: Audio Act. 6

Assessment

Prueba 4A-4 with Remediation (online only)
Quiz: Vocabulary Production
- Prueba 4A-2

Enrich Your Teaching

Teacher-to-Teacher

Some students might enjoy doing a more extensive survey of their classmates' leisure preferences. Help them create lists of activities or places that are popular in your community. They can include some humorous choices. Ask them to use their lists to create a written survey with questions for everyone to answer. Have them compile the information and give a presentation of their findings to the class, complete with bar charts produced using presentation software.

Gramática

Standards: 4.1

Resources: Teacher's Resource Materials: Video Script; Technology: Video Cap. 4A

Suggestions: Direct attention to the *¿Recuerdas?* Write the verb forms on the board. Ask the question *¿Adónde vas?* of several students. Then point to another student and ask, *¿Adónde va?* Continue through the verb forms. For additional reinforcement, play the *GramActiva* Video.

Technology: Interactive Whiteboard

Grammar Activities 4A Use the whiteboard activities in your Teacher Resources as you progress through the grammar practice with your class.

11

Standards: 1.2, 3.1

Suggestions: Have students number their papers 1–6 and complete the assignment. Walk around the room as they work, assisting with comprehension. When students have finished, ask volunteers to read a sentence using the correct form of the verb.

Answers:

1. voy
2. va
3. van
4. van
5. vamos
6. vas

Active Classroom

Have students write a list of five places they go. Divide the class into groups of five. Name a leader in each group. The leader asks the person to the right, *¿Vas a (la biblioteca)?* The person responds with **Sí, voy...** or **No, no voy...** according to his or her list. The leader continues asking questions twice around the circle, and then must try to restate where everyone is going without making any errors. Play continues around the circle.

Gramática

OBJECTIVES
▶ Talk, read, and write about where you and others go
▶ Exchange information about where to go to do leisure activities

¿Recuerdas?
You have used the infinitive *ir* to talk about going to school.
• Me gusta **ir** a la escuela.

The verb *ir*

To say where someone is going, use the verb *ir*. Here are its present-tense forms:

(yo)	**voy**	(nosotros) (nosotras)	**vamos**
(tú)	**vas**	(vosotros) (vosotras)	**vais**
Ud. (él) (ella)	**va**	Uds. (ellos) (ellas)	**van**

The verb *ir* is almost always followed by *a*. To ask where someone is going, use *¿Adónde?*

¿Adónde vas? **Where are you going (to)?**

• You will often hear people say *¡Vamos!* This means, "Let's go!"

Más recursos ONLINE
▶ *GramActiva* Video
▶ Animated Verbs
◀) *Canción de hip hop: ¿Adónde vas?*
✎ *GramActiva* Activity

11

Un invierno en Chile

✎ LEER, ESCRIBIR

1 María, una estudiante de Chicago, Illinois, pasa un año en Santiago, Chile, con una familia chilena. Lee el email y escribe las formas apropiadas del verbo *ir*.

Para | sonia@email.net

Querida Sonia:

¿Cómo estás? Yo, bien. Generalmente paso tiempo en casa los fines de semana, pero a veces yo __1__ a Portillo con la familia para esquiar. Hace mucho frío allí y por eso mi "mamá" chilena no __2__ siempre con nosotros. En Portillo hay una escuela para los esquiadores y muchos chicos simpáticos __3__ a las lecciones. También hay un cibercafé con computadoras. Muchas personas __4__ allí para pasar tiempo con los amigos. Nosotros __5__ el domingo. Y tú, ¿__6__ a la playa todos los días con tus amigos?

Hasta luego,

María

Portillo, Chile ▶

2 Escribe el email de Sonia para responder a María.

Differentiated Instruction

Students with Learning Difficulties

In *Actividad* 13, some students may have difficulty with the compound subjects and with going from **tú** to the first person. They may also confuse **tus** with **tú**. You may want to provide them with a chart showing the transformations necessary for completing the sentences.

Verbal/Linguistic Learner

Have students research places to go in Chile and present their information as a postcard telling where they are going with their Chilean friends. Students can use pictures from magazines or the Internet to make the postcard look authentic.

Go Online to practice   PearsonSchool.com/Autentico

PEARSON realize
VIDEO   WRITING   SPEAK/RECORD

12 El email

LEER, ESCRIBIR, HABLAR   Lee el email de María en la Actividad 11 y contesta las preguntas.

1. ¿Quién no va a veces con la familia a Portillo?
2. ¿Por qué a María le gusta ir a las lecciones de esquí?
3. ¿Adónde van para usar las computadoras?
4. ¿Cuándo van al cibercafé?
5. ¿Adónde van muchas personas para pasar tiempo con los amigos?

13 ¿Adónde van todos?

LEER, HABLAR EN PAREJA, ESCRIBIR

1 Read the sentence and determine who does the activity. Using the correct form of *ir,* ask where they go to do the activity. Your partner will answer with the most logical place.

Videomodelo

A —Te gusta esquiar. *(tú) ¿Adónde vas?*
B —*Voy a las montañas para esquiar.*

1. Te gusta levantar pesas.
2. Tú y tu amigo corren mucho.
3. Tus amigos y tú ven muchas películas.
4. A tu amigo le gusta comer bistec.
5. Tus amigas nadan muy bien.
6. Tus amigos hacen ejercicio todos los días.

2 Now write four sentences about yourself and your friends, saying where you go and for what purpose.

Modelo
Vamos a . . . para . . .

CULTURA El mundo hispano

Los clubes de deportes y los gimnasios son muy populares en los países hispanos. Hay pocos equipos deportivos[1] en las escuelas y muchos estudiantes van a gimnasios privados para hacer ejercicio. También practican deportes en equipos privados.

Pre-AP® Integration: Los intereses personales ¿Adónde vas para practicar deportes o hacer ejercicio? ¿Es privado o público?

[1]sport teams [2]daily

Capítulo 4A • ciento ochenta y uno **181**

12

Standards: 1.2, 1.3

Suggestions: Have students take turns reading the letter in *Actividad* 11 aloud. Then ask the class the questions.

Answers:
1. La "mamá" chilena no va a veces con la familia.
2. Porque muchos chicos simpáticos van a las lecciones.
3. Van a un cibercafé.
4. Van el domingo.
5. Van a la playa.

Starter Activity
Name a place and ask students what one does there: *Vas a (la biblioteca). ¿Qué haces allí?* Students answer: *Leo libros y revistas. Estudio.* Continue asking about other places.

13

Standards: 1.1, 1.2, 1.3

Suggestions: For Step 1, you may want to state the item and ask the **¿Adónde...?** question for each item so that students hear what they should respond to. For Step 2, be sure students know that they can use any of the items in their responses or can create new ones.

Answers:
1. ¿Adónde vas? Voy al gimnasio para levantar pesas.
2. ¿Adónde van Uds.? Vamos al parque para correr.
3. ¿Adónde van Uds.? Vamos al cine para ver películas.
4. ¿Adónde va? Va al restaurante.
5. ¿Adónde van? Van a la piscina.
6. ¿Adónde van? Van al gimnasio.

Extension: Repeat Step 1 of the activity, but have students work in pairs.

CULTURA

Standards: 2.1, 4.2

Suggestions: Students may have difficulty imagining the situation posed in the question. Point out that students in other countries find outlets for exercise and sports despite the lack of school-sponsored competitions.

Answers will vary.

Enrich Your Teaching

Culture Note
Portillo is recognized as one of the finest resorts in South America, but it offers much more than just skiing and snowboarding. You can relax in one of the two lodges, take a yoga class, go to the movie theater, visit the game room, or use the gym. Portillo provides a relaxing vacation atmosphere for skiers and non-skiers alike.

21st Century Skills
ICT Literacy Have students view online videos about travel to review the verb *ir* and its conjugations through fun and exciting digital formats. Have students take notes on the phrases and expressions they hear.

14

Standards: 1.1, 1.2, 1.3

Suggestions: Point out to students that they need to write ten sentences, five stating what they like to do and five telling where they do each activity. Stress that they should not let other teams see their sentences. As students work in groups of four, walk around the room to monitor understanding, and correct sentence formation, speaking, and pronunciation.
Answers will vary.

El español en la comunidad

Suggestions: Ask a student to read *El español en la comunidad*. When students discuss the questions, ask: If you have not visited a neighborhood with a Spanish-speaking community, what would you expect to find in one? Correct any misconceptions.
Answers will vary.

🌐 **Technology: Mapa global interactivo,** Actividad 2 Explore Chicago's Pilsen neighborhood.

Pre-AP® Integration

- **Learning Objective:** Interpersonal Writing
- **Activity:** Have students bring to class three personal photos (or pictures from a magazine) of places they might go to after school or on weekends. Have them "send" an email to a classmate, with the photos as attachments. The subject of the email is 'mis actividades favoritas'. Have student recipients draft replies, asking a different question about each photo.
- **Pre-AP® Resource Materials:** Comprehensive guide to Pre-AP® communication skill development

---

14

Juego

🎤 **ESCRIBIR, HABLAR EN GRUPO** Play this game in teams of two.

1 With a partner, write five sentences saying what the two of you like to do in your free time and when. Also write sentences saying where you go for these activities.

Modelo
Nosotros corremos después de las clases. (Vamos al gimnasio.)

2 Read one of your statements about activities to another team of classmates, but don't read the part that tells where you go. Then have one person try to guess where you go to do this activity. If the student answers correctly, his or her team wins a point. The team that earns the most points wins.

▶ **Videomodelo**
A —*Nosotros corremos después de las clases.*
B —*Uds. van al gimnasio, ¿verdad?*
A —*Sí, vamos al gimnasio para correr.*
o: —*No, no vamos al gimnasio para correr. Vamos al parque.*

El español en la comunidad

In many businesses and neighborhoods in the United States, you can hear Spanish being spoken. For example, the Pilsen neighborhood in Chicago, Illinois, is home to one of the nation's largest Mexican communities. The colorful murals, thriving businesses, and popular restaurants give Pilsen its own character.

• Are there areas near you where you can see expressions of community for Spanish speakers? What are they?

Mapa global interactivo Explore the city of Chicago and find the Pilsen neighborhood on a map.

En la comunidad de Pilsen, en Chicago

182 ciento ochenta y dos • Tema 4 • Los pasatiempos

Differentiated Instruction

Special Needs
Students with hearing impairments may benefit from seeing hand signals to indicate where syllabic stress falls. You might use an open hand to indicate a stressed syllable and a closed one to indicate an unstressed one.

Heritage Speakers
Students may have trouble remembering to use written accents on words. Dictate a mixture of words that require accent marks and those that do not. Ask students to write the words, inserting necessary accent marks based on the rules they've learned.

Pronunciación — Stress and accents

How can you tell which syllable to stress, or emphasize, when you see words written in Spanish? Here are some general rules.

1. **When words end in a vowel, *n*, or *s*,** place the stress on the **next-to-last syllable.** Copy each of these words and draw a line under the next-to-last syllable. Then listen to and say these words, making sure you stress the underlined syllable:

centro   pasteles   piscina
computadora trabajo   parque
mantequilla escriben   generalmente

2. **When words end in a consonant (*except n or s*),** place the stress on the **last syllable.** Listen to and say these words, making sure you stress the last syllable:

señor   nariz   escribir
profesor   reloj   arroz
trabajador comer   español

3. **When a word has a written accent,** place the stress on the **accented syllable.** One reason for written accents is to indicate exceptions to the first two rules. Listen to and say these words. Be sure to emphasize the accented syllable.

café   número   teléfono
difícil   película   lápiz
fácil   plátano   artístico

Try it out! Listen to the first verse of the song "La Bamba" and say each word with the stress on the correct syllable. Then listen to the recording again and see if you can sing along with the first verse. What do you think the song is about? Why?

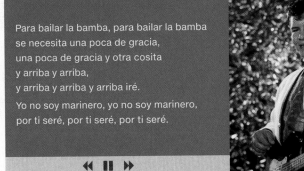

La Bamba   *de Richie Valens*

Para bailar la bamba, para bailar la bamba
se necesita una poca de gracia,
una poca de gracia y otra cosita
y arriba y arriba,
y arriba y arriba y arriba iré.

Yo no soy marinero, yo no soy marinero,
por ti seré, por ti seré, por ti seré.

CULTURA — El mundo hispano

La Bamba es una canción folk mexicana del estado de Veracruz. La primera versión famosa es de Richie Valens, que fusiona[1] la canción tradicional con el *rock and roll*. Combina elementos musicales españoles, indígenas y africanos. Salió en una película llamada también

La Bamba en 1987. Es una canción conocida[3] en todo el mundo y es muy importante en la historia del *rock and roll* en español.

• Según la historia de La Bamba, ¿son importantes las tradiciones folclóricas en la música mexicana? ¿Por qué?

[1]fuses [2]any

Capítulo 4A • ciento ochenta y tres **183**

Enrich Your Teaching

Culture Note

"La Bamba" is a folk song popularized by Ritchie Valens (1941–1959), a young singer from a Mexican American family in California. His last name was Valenzuela, but he changed it when he became a performer. Valens died in a small-plane crash with Buddy Holly, shortly before his eighteenth birthday.

21st Century Skills

Social and Cross-Cultural Skills
Have students research the folkloric influences evident in the song "La Bamba." Have them find out what instruments and rhythms characterize the style of music from which "La Bamba" arose.

PRONUNCIACIÓN

Standards: 3.2, 4.1

Resources: Teacher's Resource Materials: Audio Script; Technology: Audio Cap. 4A

Suggestions: Take each of the rules separately. Spend time drilling each stress pattern and its rules before moving on to the next step. Play the audio as many times as necessary.

Try it out! After students have completed the activity, ask two students to read one line at a time together. Correct pronunciation errors. Play the song and encourage students to sing.

Have students write the words to the song *"La Bamba"* and highlight accent and stress points mentioned in Steps 1, 2, and 3.

Teaching with Music

Songs are an excellent means of teaching rhythm and stress as students acquire a second language. Bring in other music from your collection or from libraries. Choose songs that have easy, singable lyrics.

Project-Based Learning

Give students copies of the Project-Based Learning outline and rubric. Explain the task to them, and have them perform Step 1. (For more information, see p. 170-b.)

Additional Resources

Technology: Online Resources
• Instant Check
• Guided, Core, Audio, Writing, Reading
• *Para hispanohablantes*
• Teacher's Resource Materials Audio Script
• Technology: Audio Cap. 4A
• Communication Activities: Audio Act. 7
Print
• Guided WB pp. 125–126
• Core WB pp. 71

Assessment

Prueba 4A-4 with Remediation (online only)
Quiz: The verb *-ir*
• Prueba 4A–3

Gramática

Standards: 4.1

Resources: Teacher's Resource Materials: Video Script; Technology: Video Cap. 4A

Suggestions: Be sure that students understand how questions are formed in English, and the relationship between the kind of information you are seeking and the way a question is asked. Go through the list of questions. Point out the use of the double question marks. Then point out the written accent marks on question words and explain that they are extra clues to the fact a question is being asked. When students seem to be grasping the concept, give them a statement and see if they can tell you what question they would ask to get that answer.

Technology: Interactive Whiteboard

Grammar Activities 4A Use the whiteboard activities in your Teacher Resources as you progress through the grammar practice with your class.

15

Standards: 1.2, 1.3

Suggestions: Write the words on strips of paper and show students how to resequence them. Tell them to be sure to capitalize appropriate words. Be sure they understand that they are to answer the questions truthfully.

Answers:
1. ¿De dónde eres tú?
2. ¿Adónde van Uds. los fines de semana?
3. ¿Cuándo van Uds. al centro comercial?
4. ¿Cuántas clases tienes?
5. ¿Qué haces tú después de las clases?
6. ¿Con quién vas tú al centro comercial?

Answers to the questions will vary.

Gramática

OBJECTIVES
▸ Write and answer questions about leisure activities
▸ Exchange information about where you and others go in your free time
▸ Read and write about places in San Juan, Puerto Rico

Asking questions

You use interrogative words (*who, what, where,* and so on) to ask questions.

¿Qué?	What?	¿Adónde?	(To) Where?
¿Cómo?	How?, What?	¿De dónde?	From where?
¿Quién?	Who?	¿Cuál?	Which?, What?
¿Con quién?	With whom?	¿Por qué?	Why?
¿Dónde?	Where?	¿Cuándo?	When?
¿Cuántos, -as?	How many?		

In Spanish, when you ask a question with an interrogative word you put the verb before the subject.

¿Qué **come Elena** en el restaurante? — *What does Elena eat at the restaurant?*

¿Adónde **van Uds.** después de las clases? — *Where do you go after classes?*

¿Por qué **va Ignacio** a la playa todos los días? — *Why does Ignacio go to the beach every day?*

You have already used several interrogative words. Notice that all interrogative words have a written accent mark.

For simple questions that can be answered by *sí* or *no,* you can indicate with your voice that you're asking a question:

¿Ana va a la biblioteca?

OR: ¿Va Ana a la biblioteca?

OR: Ana va a la biblioteca, ¿verdad?

Más recursos ONLINE

▸ *GramActiva* Video

▸ **Tutorials:** Questions with Interrogative Words, Question-word Questions, Formation of yes-no questions

✎ *GramActiva* Activity

15

Preguntas revueltas

✎ **LEER, ESCRIBIR EN PAREJA** Exchange written messages with a classmate to ask and answer questions about everyday life. First unscramble the questions. Then write them in the correct order and send them to a classmate to answer. Your classmate should send you responses and ask you similar questions.

1. ¿ / eres / de dónde / tú / ?
2. ¿ / Uds. / adónde / van / los fines de semana / ?
3. ¿ / al centro comercial / cuándo / van / Uds. / ?
4. ¿ / clases / tienes / cuántas / ?
5. ¿ / tú / qué / después de las clases / haces / ?
6. ¿ / vas / tú / con quién / al centro comercial / ?

Differentiated Instruction

Heritage Speakers

Using the interrogative words taught on this page, have students prepare a list of questions that they would like to ask their favorite singer, actor, athlete, or other person. Have students exchange lists and answer the questions as if they were the well-known individuals.

Special Needs

Write the words in *Actividad* 15 on individual cards and help students sort them into proper order. Use a different color card for the interrogative words so that they stand out. Emphasize the accent marks so students notice them.

Go Online to practice
PearsonSchool.com/Autentico

PEARSON
realize™

✎ WRITING

16

¿Cómo es el cine?

✎ **LEER, ESCRIBIR** Lee este anuncio del cine.

🔍

🏠 ✉ 📶

Cine Parque Arauco

★ Excelente calidad de proyección
★ Estacionamientos iluminados, gratis
★ Para su comodidad, aire acondicionado
★ Las únicas butacas reclinables de la ciudad
★ Excelentes instalaciones para discapacitados

★ Diariamente funciones continuadas desde el mediodía
★ Funciones de trasnoche los miércoles, viernes y sábados
★ Palomitas recién preparadas
★ Servicio amable y eficiente
★ Precios especiales para grupos y arriendos de salas de cine

Situado delante del Centro Comercial Gigante

Según el anuncio del Cine Parque Arauco, escribe la palabra apropiada para cada pregunta.

1. ¿____ es la calidad de la proyección en el cine? *Excelente.*
2. ¿____ comen muchas personas allí? *Palomitas.*
3. ¿____ es el nombre del cine? *Cine Parque Arauco.*
4. ¿____ van las personas a ver películas muy tarde *(late)* por la noche? *Los miércoles, viernes y sábados.*
5. ¿____ está el cine? *Delante del Centro Comercial Gigante.*

Cuándo	Por qué
Cómo	Cuál
Dónde	Qué

CULTURA ◀ El mundo hispano

Las películas son una forma popular de entretenimiento[1] para los adolescentes en los países hispanos. España, México, Colombia y Venezuela tienen industrias del cine importantes, pero las películas de los Estados Unidos también son populares. Los adolescentes de habla hispana[2] van al cine en grupos.

Pre-AP® Integration: El entretenimiento y la diversión Compara tus hábitos de ir al cine con los de los adolescentes de habla hispana. ¿Vas con amigos o solo(a)? ¿Son las películas de países hispanos populares en tu comunidad? ¿Por qué?

[1]entertainment [2]Spanish-speaking

Los actores españoles Penélope Cruz y Javier Bardem

Capítulo 4A • ciento ochenta y cinco **185**

16

Standards: 1.2, 1.3

Suggestions: Read through the ad with the class, activating prior knowledge, using cognates, and using context to help with meaning. Remind students that they do not have to know the meaning of every word to understand the general message. Point out the interrogatives in the word bank. Help students see how the words in italics are key to knowing which interrogative to choose.

Answers:

1. Cómo
2. Qué
3. Cuál
4. Cuándo
5. Dónde

Common errors: Students often forget to write accent marks on question words. Demonstrate that omitting them can often change meaning.

CULTURA ◀

Standards: 2.1, 4.2

Suggestions: Ask students to describe their movie-going habits. Have any students seen foreign films? Which ones? Were they dubbed or subtitled?
Answers will vary.

Enrich Your Teaching

Teacher-to-Teacher

Tell students that they are going to match up perfect friends in the class. To do so, they must create a survey questionnaire with questions that reveal people's personalities and interests, where they like to go, etc. Have them work in small groups to come up with six questions in each group. When they're done, have the groups report their questions as you write them on the board or overhead. Have the class vote on the ten best questions. Create a survey form that students can answer for homework. Have volunteers tally the results and match up the people who have the most similar answers.

Standards: 1.1, 1.3

Presentational: Describe simple situations orally using a mixture of words, phrases and simple sentences. (also 3.B.6)

Suggestions: Allow students to choose the three classmates for Step 1, but pair students for Step 2. Give them copies of the chart to fill out to save time. If they are drawing their own charts, be sure that they understand to omit the information shown in the example.

Answers will vary.

Starter Activity

Call out simple questions and have students give possible answers.

Standards: 1.1

Suggestions: Have students work individually on Step 1. While students are answering their messages for Step 2, walk around the room to monitor correct word usage, syntax, and spelling. As a follow-up, have volunteers ask their questions in front of the class while others answer.

Answers will vary.

Pre-AP® Integration

- **Learning Objective:** Interpersonal Speaking
- **Activity 18:** Students practice informal conversation skills as they ask and answer questions about a photo.
- **Pre-AP® Resource Materials:** Comprehensive guide to Pre-AP® speaking skill development

CULTURA

Standards: 4.2

Suggestions: If yours is a relatively new community, suggest that students think of places they have seen on vacations or other trips.

Answers will vary.

Los fines de semana

ESCRIBIR, HABLAR EN PAREJA

1 Ask questions about everyday life. Copy a chart like this one on a separate sheet of paper and fill in information about one activity you do on the weekends. Then find out the same information from three classmates.

Nombre	¿Adónde vas?	¿Con quién?
yo	a mi lección de guitarra	solo(a)
Laura	al centro comercial	con Selena

Videomodelo
A —¿Adónde vas los fines de semana?
B —Voy **al centro comercial**.
A —¿Con quién vas?
B —Voy **con Selena**.
o:—Voy **solo(a)**.

2 Describe situations orally. Tell the class or a classmate where you and each of the three people you interviewed are going and with whom.

Videomodelo
Yo voy a mi lección de guitarra solo(a).
Laura va al centro comercial con Selena.

Y tú, ¿qué preguntas?

ESCRIBIR EN PAREJA, HABLAR Escribe mensajes de texto a otro estudiante para hacer y contestar preguntas sobre la vida diaria.

1 Escribe un mensaje de texto a tu compañero(a) con tres preguntas sobre lo que va a hacer este fin de semana.

2 Tu compañero debe contestar tus preguntas y hacer tres preguntas más. Responde sus preguntas para hacer planes.

CULTURA Puerto Rico

El Viejo San Juan es una parte popular y llena de vida de la capital de Puerto Rico, San Juan. El gobierno[1] de Puerto Rico trabaja para preservar las casas y edificios[2] coloniales y devolverles[3] su condición original.

Pre-AP® Integration: La arquitectura
¿Hay áreas o casas históricas en tu comunidad? ¿Están en buenas condiciones o necesitan reparación? ¿Es importante preservar casas históricas en tu comunidad o en el Viejo San Juan?

El Viejo San Juan, Puerto Rico

[1]government [2]buildings [3]return

Differentiated Instruction

Students with Learning Difficulties

If students have trouble deciding what to ask about weekend activities or plans, you might give them a list of statements from which they can derive questions. If this is still difficult, help them identify the appropriate interrogative words and have them create the questions from those.

Bodily/Kinesthetic Learner

Have students list weekend activities they do often that are physical, such as walking, sports, dancing, physical work, or any other type of exercise. For one example from their list, have students describe where they engage in this activity and sensations they experience during the activity.

19

¡Vamos al Viejo San Juan!

LEER, ESCRIBIR Puerto Rico has been a commonwealth of the United States since 1952. It is an island with a fascinating past. Look at the photos and read about a historic section of Puerto Rico's capital. Then answer the questions below.

Conexiones ▸ La historia

El Viejo[1] San Juan es una zona histórica, pintoresca, colonial y muy popular en la capital de Puerto Rico. Los jóvenes[2] pasan el tiempo con sus amigos en los parques, cafés y plazas. Allí cantan, bailan y comen en los restaurantes típicos.

▸ **La Catedral de San Juan** tiene muchas obras de arte[3]. Allí descansan[4] los restos[5] de Juan Ponce de León, famoso explorador de la Florida.

▸ **El Morro** Construido en el siglo[6] XVI para combatir los ataques de los piratas ingleses y franceses[7]

Datos importantes

• Cristóbal Colón llega[8] aquí durante su segunda visita a las Américas en 1493.

• El Viejo San Juan llega a ser[9] la capital de Puerto Rico en 1521.

[1]Old [2]young people [3]works of art [4]lie [5]remains [6]century [7]French [8]arrives [9]becomes

1. For how many years has San Juan been the capital of Puerto Rico?

2. On which of his voyages did Christopher Columbus land on Puerto Rico?

3. Why did the Spaniards build El Morro?

4. What are two things you'll see when you visit the cathedral?

🌐 **Mapa global interactivo** Explore the geography of Puerto Rico and locate its capital, San Juan.

Capítulo 4A • ciento ochenta y siete **187**

Enrich Your Teaching

Culture Note

Puerto Ricans are American citizens. However, they do not have the right to vote for president or for full representation in Congress. Puerto Rico does send an observer to the U.S. House of Representatives. This individual cannot vote on laws but does vote in Congressional committees. The question of Puerto Rico becoming the 51st state has been debated for some time, and Puerto Ricans remain divided on the issue.

Teacher-to-Teacher

Have students plan a trip to Puerto Rico using guidebooks, encyclopedias, and the Internet. Students can work in small groups to write sentences saying where they plan to go while they are there.

19

Standards: 1.2, 1.3, 3.1

Suggestions: Refer to the *Mapa global interactivo* for another view of Puerto Rico. Have students read the questions in English before they begin to read. Be sure they know that they are to answer in English.

Answers:

1. San Juan has been the capital of Puerto Rico since 1521.

2. Christopher Columbus landed on Puerto Rico during his second voyage to the Americas.

3. Spaniards built El Morro to combat the attacks of English and French pirates.

4. Two things that one can see in the cathedral are the remains of Juan Ponce de León and many works of art.

🌐 **Technology: Mapa global interactivo**, Visit San Juan, Puerto Rico, and locate the historic fort Castillo del Morro.

Project-Based Learning

Students can perform Step 2 at this point. Be sure students understand the task. (For more information, see p. 170-b.)

Additional Resources

📶 **Technology: Online Resources**
  • Instant Check
  • Guided, Core, Video, Audio
  • *Para hispanohablantes*
  • Teacher's Resource Materials: Audio Script
  • Technology: Audio Cap. 4A
  • Communication Activites: Audio Acts. 8-9
  Print
  • Guided WB pp. 127–129
  • Core WB pp. 72-73

Assessment

Prueba 4A-4 with Remediation (online only)
Quiz: Asking Questions
  • Prueba 4A-4

Lectura

Suggestions

Pre-reading: Direct students' attention to the *Strategy*. Point out the words in the glosses. To activate students' prior knowledge, bring in brochures from a local mall with similar information and have students identify the events. Have them scan the *Lectura* to see if any of the events are similar. Have them identify the calendar organization of the brochure.

Reading: Have students take turns reading sections of the brochure. Remind them that context and cognates can help them understand what they read. Help them decode unfamiliar words.

Post-reading: Have students answer the *¿Comprendes?* questions to check comprehension. When they have finished, discuss the questions and answers in class.

Pre-AP® Integration

- **Learning Objective:** Presentational Writing
- **Activity:** Have students research a cultural calendar for their community or city on the Internet. Have them write a brief, persuasive paragraph about one of the upcoming events attempting to convince a friend or relative to attend this event.
- **Pre-AP® Resource Materials:** Comprehensive guide to Pre-AP® writing skill development

Lectura

OBJECTIVES
- Read about after-school and weekend activities at a mall
- Use prior knowledge to better understand what you read
- Compare the instruments used in Andean music to those used in music you enjoy

Strategy
Using prior knowledge Think about what you know about special-event weeks at shopping centers. List key words for events that you think might be offered at a mall.

Al centro comercial

Lee las actividades diferentes que puedes hacer en la semana del 11 al 17 de enero durante tu tiempo libre.

¡Vamos a la Plaza del Sol!

Aquí en la Plaza del Sol, ¡siempre hay algo que hacer!

Actividades para el 11 al 17 de enero

lunes 11		
8.00 P.M.	Música andina	
martes 12		
7.00 P.M.	Clase de yoga	
miércoles 13		
8.00 P.M.	Noche de jazz	
jueves 14		
7.00 P.M.	Clase de repostería[1]	
viernes 15		
8.00 P.M.	Música andina	
sábado 16		
1.30 P.M.	Exposición de fotografía	
2.00 P.M.	Show infantil	
4.00 P.M.	Exhibición de yoga	
8.00 P.M.	Sábado flamenco	
domingo 17		
1.30 P.M.	Exposición de fotografía	
2.00 P.M.	Show infantil	
4.00 P.M.	Exhibición de yoga	
8.00 P.M.	Noche de tango	

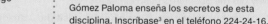

Música andina
Un grupo toca música andina fusionada con bossa nova y jazz el lunes a las 8.00 P.M. Abierto[2] al público.

Clase de yoga
La práctica de yoga es todos los martes desde las 7.00 hasta las 9.00 P.M. La instructora Lucía Gómez Paloma enseña los secretos de esta disciplina. Inscríbase[3] en el teléfono 224-24-16. Vacantes limitadas.

[1]pastry making [2]Open [3]Register

Differentiated Instruction

Students with Learning Difficulties

Some students may have difficulty sorting out information when it is presented in an advertisement like this. Help them identify that it's a calendar by pointing out the days and dates. Help them see that the four featured events are among those mentioned in the calendar portion.

Challenge

Have students go on the Internet to find shopping malls or cultural centers in Spanish-speaking countries that feature activities similar to those in the reading. Have them print out the schedules and identify in English the basic information.

Go **Online** to practice
PEARSON
realize™
PearsonSchool.com/Autentico
WRITING

Interpretive Reading

4A

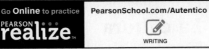

Sábado flamenco

El Sábado flamenco es el programa más popular de la semana. María del Carmen Ramachi baila acompañada por el guitarrista Ernesto Hermoza el sábado a las 8.00 P.M. Es una noche emocionante y sensacional de música y danza. Abierto al público.

Clase de repostería

Inscríbase gratis⁴ en la clase de repostería programada para el jueves a las 7.00 P.M. Preparamos unos pasteles deliciosos gracias a la Repostería Ideal y al maestro Rudolfo Torres. Inscríbase en el teléfono 224-24-16. Vacantes limitadas.

⁴free

✎ ¿Comprendes?

1. You will be in town from January 9 through February 2. Which activities will you be able to attend?

2. Which events require you to sign up in advance? Which do not? What key phrases provide this information?

3. Which day(s) would be best to go with a six-year-old child?

4. Según los intereses de estos chicos, ¿a qué eventos van ellos?

Raquel: Me gusta mucho hacer ejercicio.

Roberto: Me encantan los pasteles.

Teresa: Estudio baile. Tomo lecciones todos los jueves.

Alejandro: Me gusta escuchar música; toda clase de música.

5. ¿Qué actividad es más interesante para ti?

CULTURA ◄ Bolivia · Chile · Ecuador · Perú

La música andina es muy popular en todo el mundo. Este interesante estilo de música se originó en las montañas de los Andes en Perú, Ecuador, Bolivia y Chile. Los artistas a veces llevan trajes¹ tradicionales andinos. En la música andina los músicos tocan instrumentos especiales: los tambores² de materiales naturales, la flauta³ quena, la guaira⁴ o quena y una guitarra pequeña llamada charango.

• En la música andina los instrumentos son diferentes a los instrumentos de la música clásica. ¿Qué instrumentos usan en la música que te gusta a ti?

¹wear clothing ²drums ³flute ⁴panpipes

Músicos en la Plaza de Armas, Cuzco, Perú

Capítulo 4A • ciento ochenta y nueve **189**

¿Comprendes?

Standards: 1.3

Answers:

1. Yes, in all of them.
2. Yoga and the pastry class have limited spaces available; the Andean music and flamenco are open to the public.
3. Saturday the 16th and Sunday the 17th, because there's a children's show.
4. Raquel: yoga; Roberto: pastry making class; Teresa: flamenco and tango; Alejandro: Andean music and jazz
5. Answers will vary.

CULTURA

Standards: 2.2, 4.2

Suggestions: Focus an online map on the Andean region. Bring in or access online examples of Andean music for students to enjoy. Explain that flutes like the **quena** and **siku** are very ancient, and that similar instruments exist in many parts of the world.

Answers will vary.

Teaching with Music

Play some Andean music for the class and point out the instruments mentioned in the *Cultura*.

Project-Based Learning

Students can perform Step 3 at this point. Be sure that students understand your suggestions. (For more information, see p. 170-b.)

For Further Reading

Student Resource: *Para hispanohablantes*: Lectura 2

Additional Resources

📶 **Technology: Online Resources**
• Guided, Writing, Reading
• Cultural Reading Activity
• *Para hispanohablantes*

Enrich Your Teaching

Culture Note

Shopping malls are common in many parts of the Spanish-speaking world. You will find very elegant ones, for example, in cities like Mexico City. Many of the stores would be familiar to students, either because they are American chain stores or because they are similar in style.

21st Century Skills

Social and Cross-Cultural Skills
Remind students of the resources available online for acquiring and learning to use new vocabulary, including videos and personal travel blogs in Spanish.

La cultura en vivo

Standards: 3.2, 4.2

Resources: Technology: Audio Cap. 4A

Suggestions: Begin class by reciting a few words from an English nursery rhyme that students would likely know. Ask them to identify it. Ask if they remember any jump-rope rhymes. If students are unfamiliar with these, elicit something they do know and use it. Direct attention to the top photo of children jumping rope. Point out that it is easier to jump rope to a chant, as it helps you keep the beat and jump at the right time. Have students read the first two paragraphs. Practice the rhyme and the chant with the class.

If you can, go outdoors for this activity. A real jump rope works best. In the classroom, use a short piece of rope or string with a paper clip in the middle and a volunteer to demonstrate how a song helps to keep the beat while jumping rope. Students will hear the rope or paper clip hit the desk or floor.

Have students work in three groups. For the first chant, one student can say it, indicating another group member with each word, and the last person is "it." That person takes the role of saying the rhyme and the first one moves on to group 2. Students in group 2 jump rope to the chant, moving on to group 3 when their turn is over. Students in group 3 play the game described while singing the song. Each moves on to group 1 when the turn is over. Students continue until all have had a turn.

Direct attention to the *Comparación cultural* section and have students discuss the questions.

Answers will vary.

Online Cultural Reading

After doing the online activity, ask students to identify and list three cultural practices that differ from their own.

Additional Resources

📶 **Technology: Online Resources**
- Cultural Reading Activity
- *Para hispanohablantes*

La cultura en vivo — Rimas infantiles

¿Recuerdas las canciones que aprendiste de niño? ¿Y las rimas[1] para saltar a la cuerda?

Estas son algunas canciones que los niños del mundo hispano cantan al jugar. La primera es el equivalente español a "Eenie, meenie, minie, moe...". Es una rima sin sentido[2] que se usa para seleccionar a una persona para un juego.

> Tin Marín de dopingüé
> cucaramanga titirifuera
> yo no fui,
> fue Teté.
> pégale, pégale,
> que ella fue.

Los niños cantan esta canción cuando saltan a la cuerda:

Salta, salta la perdiz	*The partridge jumps and jumps*
por los campos de maíz.	*Through the cornfields.*
¡Ten cuidado, por favor,	*Be careful, please!*
porque viene el cazador!	*Here comes the hunter!*
	(The jump rope then turns faster.)

Comparación cultural ¿Qué rimas y canciones conoces en inglés? ¿Son similares a las canciones en español? ¿Cómo reflejan la cultura?

[1]rhymes [2]nonsense

Niña saltando a la cuerda

Online Cultural Reading

Go to Auténtico ONLINE to read and learn about a list of movies playing at a cinema in Guadalajara, Mexico.

Here's a traditional game that combines Spanish, math, and hopping over a board. Place a long, narrow board on the floor. Take turns hopping with both feet from one side of the board to the other. Go forward as you hop. When you get to the end of the board, jump and turn in the air, facing the direction you came from. Continue hopping from side to side back to the other end. Be very careful! Try this in an area where you won't hurt yourself. As you are hopping, sing this song:

Brinca la tablita	*Jump over the board*
que yo la brinqué.	*That I already jumped.*
Bríncala tú ahora	*Now you jump*
que yo me cansé.	*Since I'm tired.*
Dos y dos son cuatro,	*Two and two are four,*
cuatro y dos son seis.	*Four and two are six.*
Seis y dos son ocho,	*Six and two are eight,*
y ocho dieciséis,	*And eight are sixteen,*
y ocho veinticuatro,	*And eight are twenty-four,*
y ocho treinta y dos.	*And eight are thirty-two.*
Y diez que le sumo	*And ten that I add*
son cuarenta y dos.	*Equals forty-two.*

Differentiated Instruction

Musical/Rhythmic Learner

Have students learn other songs or rhymes from a Spanish-speaking country. Have them research this topic, learn one rhyme or song, and present it to the class, telling where it came from and when children use it.

Heritage Speakers

Students may be familiar with these or other children's songs and rhymes. If so, allow them to present them to the class with an explanation of when and how the song or rhyme is used.

Presentación oral

OBJECTIVES
- Role-play a conversation with another student about how you spend your free time
- Use models to prepare for your performance

Go Online to practice
PearsonSchool.com/Autentico
SPEAK/RECORD

Un estudiante nuevo

TASK Ask and answer questions about everyday life. You and a partner will play the roles of a new student and a student who has been at the school for a while. Find out information about the new student and answer any questions.

1 Prepare You will need to prepare for both roles.

Current student: List at least four questions. Greet the student and introduce yourself. Find out where the new student is from, what activities he or she likes to do and on what days, and where he or she goes and with whom.

New student: Look at the questions the current student will ask you and note your answers. Prepare two questions of your own.

Strategy

Using models It helps to go back and review models that prepare you for a task like this role play. Reread *Vocabulario en contexto* (pp. 172–175). Pay attention to the different questions and answers that will help you with this task.

2 Practice Work with a partner to practice different questions and responses. Be sure you are comfortable in both roles as you go through your presentation. Use your notes in practice, but not to present. Try to:
- get and give information
- keep the conversation going
- speak clearly

3 Present You will be paired with another student and your teacher will assign roles. The current student begins by greeting the new student. Listen to your partner's questions and responses and keep the conversation going.

4 Evaluation The following rubric will be used to grade your presentation.

Rubric	Score 1	Score 3	Score 5
Completion of task	You ask or answer two questions.	You ask or answer three questions.	You ask or answer four or more questions.
Your ability to keep the conversation going	You have no response or follow-up to what your partner says.	You have frequent response or follow-up to what your partner says.	You always respond to your partner and ask follow-up questions.
How easily you are understood	You are very difficult to understand. The teacher could only recognize isolated words and phrases.	You are understandable, but have frequent errors in vocabulary and/or grammar that hinder understanding.	You are easily understood. Your teacher does not have to "decode" what you are trying to say.

Capítulo 4A • ciento noventa y uno **191**

Presentación oral

Standards: 1.1, 1.3

Suggestions: Go over the task, the 4-Step, and the rubric with students. Point out the *Strategy*. Give students time to do the review suggested. Help them identify the questions that will be most important for them. Review the rubric with the class to explain how you will grade the performance task. Do a presentation of your own to model a top-scoring presentation.

Step 1: Pair up students and have them work with another pair of students.

Step 2: Allow students time to practice both roles. Monitor their progress.

Step 3: Students should not use their notes for this part. Remind the new student to listen carefully in order to answer accurately.

Step 4: Students can add the written questions and answers to their portfolio.

Pre-AP® Integration

Pre-AP® Resource Materials: Comprehensive guide to Pre-AP® speaking skill development

Digital Portfolio

Make video or audio recordings of student presentations in class, or assign the Speak and Record activity so they can record their presentations online. Include the recording in their digital portfolios.

Additional Resources

Technology: Online Resources
- Guided
- *Para hispanohablantes*

Print
- Guided WB p. 132

Assessment

Presentación oral
- **Assessment Program:** Rubrics

Go over the descriptions of the different levels of performance. After assessing students, help individuals understand how their performance could be improved.

Enrich Your Teaching

21st Century Skills

Communication Have students use what they have learned while preparing for their *Presentación oral* about meeting new people to introduce themselves to one Spanish-speaking student at their school whom they don't know well. Students should use the questions they prepared for this task to initiate the conversation. Have students practice their questions and answers in pairs before starting the activity

Auténtico

Standards: 1.2

Resources: *Authentic Resources Wkbk*, Cap. 4A
Authentic Resources: Cap 4A: Videoscript
AP Theme: *Las identidades personales y públicas: La identidad nacional y la identidad étnica*

Before You Watch

Discuss the *Strategy* with students. Have students identify words and details that they associate with their community, their neighborhood and their home. Tell them that that these words will guide them in listening and watching the video with a focus: why residents feel at home in this new neighborhood. Then review the key vocabulary with the class. Again, have students comment on any additional words and details that they would add to their lists, using the key vocabulary and image in their text.

Technology: Watch the Video

Before starting the video, direct students' attention to the *Mientras ves* activity. Compare this place list to the list the class compiled and have students add any additional words to their list.

Play the video once completely through, without pausing, and tell students to watch for the words and places they recognize in the video. Remind students that they will not understand every word, but that they should listen and watch for overall understanding. Replay the video, stopping as necessary for students to complete the listening activity and to check comprehension. Show the video a final time without pausing.

Auténtico

Partnered with **UNIVISION** COMMUNICATIONS INC.

Pequeña Oaxaca

Before You Watch

Use the Strategy: Listen with a Focus

As you watch the video, *Pequeña Oaxaca,* listen for key details to understand the reasons why Carslbad, California, feels like home for residents with roots from Oaxaca, Mexico.

Read this Key Vocabulary
barrio = neighborhood
Oaxaqueña = Oaxacan
clima = climate
seguridad = security
solidaridad = solidarity
plato típico = traditional dish

▶ Watch the Video

What makes a community? What places and practices make a neighborhood feel like home?

Go to **PearsonSchool.com/Autentico** and watch the video **Pequeña Oaxaca** to see the attractions and pastimes of a neighborhood in Carlsbad, California.

Complete the Activities

Mientras ves As you watch the video, focus on key words and details to identify the ways in which Carlsbad, California, is appealing to residents originally from Oaxaca. Indicate which of the places from your chapter vocabulary are mentioned or shown in the video.

la biblioteca	**el parque**
el centro commercial	**la playa**
la iglesia	**el gimnasio**
el restaurante	

Differentiated Instruction

Visual learners

Based on the information in the video, have students draw a map of how they imagine the community is laid out. Have them label, using chapter vocabulary, each place on the map.

Heritage Speakers

Have students write a paragraph that identifies and describes the places from the video that residents visit to remind them of their cultural heritage, and the adjustments that the residents have made to accommodate their new living situations. Or, students can write about their own experiences or those of a family member in their communities.

Integration

Después de ver
Review the video as needed to infer meaning and answer the following questions about the residents of Carlsbad.

1. ¿Qué les gusta de la ciudad de Carlsbad?

2. ¿Adónde van para los platos típicos?

3. At the end of the video one of the speakers explains that the Oaxacan community in Carlsbad maintains its traditions such as a kermés, a street fair held for fundraising. Why might the residents continue these traditions in their new home?

📖 **For more activities, go to the *Authentic Resources Workbook*.**

La communidad

Expansión Find other authentic resources for this chapter in *Auténtico* online, then answer the questions.

📁 **4A Auténtico**

Integración de ideas In the authentic resources you will learn about other communities. Describe one place you like in each community and explain why you like it.

Comparación cultural Compare the community in Carlsbad to your own community. What features make it feel like home to you?

Complete the Activities

Mientras ves

Standards: 1.2

Suggestions: Students should be able to identify the places that are supported with a visual image. Students may want to refer to the **Vocabulario en contexto** page for additional wording. Have students identify other images and places beyond what is on the list.

Answers:

la biblioteca	el parque
~~el centro commercial~~	la playa
~~la iglesia~~	~~el gimnasio~~
el restaurante	

Después de ver

Standards: 1.2, 1.3

Suggestions: Students may need to refer to other resources to recall the appropriate syntax or the use of the verb *ir*. Students may need prompting as to the meaning of *les gusta*. Encourage students to recall that they are being asked about the residents of Carlsbad and their prior experience with the verb *gustar*. Ask them to make a guess as to the meaning of the phrase and share answers. Identify the correct answer and then model the syntax for the answer before students answer the question.

Students' answers to the third question may vary.

Answers:

1. Les gustan las escuelas, la playa y los restaurantes de la ciudad.
2. Van a los restaurantes para los platos típicos de Oaxaca.
3. Answers may vary.

For more Authentic Resources: Assign the *Authentic Resources Workbook* activities for homework, so that students can play the video on their own and complete the workbook activities at their own pace.

Pre-AP® Integration

Standards: 1.2, 1.3

Resources: *Authentic Resources Workbook,* Cap. 4A; Authentic Resources: Cap 4A; Videoscript

Suggestions: Before completing the Pre-AP® activity, have students go to the workbook and complete the worksheets for these two additional resources.

Enrich Your Teaching

Culture Note

The official name of Mexico is *Estados Unidos Mexicanos,* and the country is made up of 31 states and a federal district. Oaxaca is a southern state, and the capital city of that state. Oaxaca is known for its seven unique varieties of *mole,* a sauce made with local chilies.

Perspectivas: Why is food such an important part of cultural identity?

Using Authentic Resources

Have students create an agenda for a day in a Spanish-speaking community using the resources and the chapter vocabulary. Suggest that they include points of interest for visitors, so that their agenda could serve as a guide.

Review Activities

To talk about leisure activities and places: Have students work in pairs to quiz each other on the vocabulary. They can create flashcards, writing the Spanish word on one side of an index card and the English meaning on the other. Provide copies of the Clip Art for this purpose.

To ask and tell where, with whom, and when you go: Have students work in pairs to practice asking and answering questions about their leisure activities.

Digital Portfolio

Invite students to review the activities they completed in this chapter, including written reports, posters or other visuals, recordings of oral presentations, or other projects. Have them select one or two items that they feel best demonstrate their achievements in Spanish to include in their digital portfolios. Have them include this with the Chapter Checklist and Self-Assessment Worksheet.

Pre-AP® Integration

- **Learning Objective:** Interpersonal speaking
- **Pre-AP® Resource Materials Activity Sheets, Tema 4,** Have students work in pairs, and choose from questions 1–10 to guide their conversation.

Additional Resources

Technology: Online Resources
- Instant Check
- Integrated Performance Assessment
- *Para hispanohablantes*

Print
- Core WB pp. 74–75

Teacher Resources
- Teacher's Resource Materials: Situation Cards, Clip Art
- Assessment Program: Chapter Checklist and Self-Assessment Worksheet

---

Repaso del capítulo

OBJECTIVES
▶ Review the vocabulary and grammar
▶ Demonstrate you can perform the tasks on p. 195

◀)) Vocabulario

to talk about leisure activities

ir de compras	to go shopping
ver una película	to see a movie
la lección de piano	piano lesson (class)
Me quedo en casa.	I stay at home.

to talk about places

la biblioteca	library
el café	café
el campo	countryside
la casa	home, house
en casa	at home
el centro comercial	mall
el cine	movie theater
el gimnasio	gym
la iglesia	church
la mezquita	mosque
las montañas	mountains
el parque	park
la piscina	swimming pool
la playa	beach
el restaurante	restaurant
la sinagoga	synagogue
el templo	temple, Protestant church
el trabajo	work, job

to tell where you go

a	to (prep.)
a la, al (a + el)	to the
¿Adónde?	(To) Where?
a casa	(to) home

to tell with whom you go

¿Con quién?	With whom?
con mis / tus amigos	with my / your friends
solo, -a	alone

to talk about when things are done

¿Cuándo?	When?
después	afterwards
después (de)	after
los fines de semana	on weekends
los lunes, los martes . . .	on Mondays, on Tuesdays . . .
tiempo libre	free time

to talk about where someone is from

¿De dónde eres?	Where are you from?
de	from, of

to indicate how often

generalmente	generally

other useful words and expressions

¡No me digas!	You don't say!
para + infinitive	in order to + infinitive

Gramática

ir *to go*

voy	vamos
vas	vais
va	van

For *Vocabulario adicional*, see pp. 472–473.

Differentiated Instruction

Students with Learning Difficulties

Have students review the *Repaso del capítulo* and create flashcards for any words that they do not know. Pair them with a student who is more confident with the vocabulary to practice. Before the test, provide students with a practice test, so they can become comfortable with the format.

Heritage Speakers

Have students write a few paragraphs telling about their perfect weekend: Where are they going to go? Whom are they going to invite to go with them? What are they going to do? Encourage them to use as many vocabulary words from this chapter as they can.

Preparación para el examen

□ Games   □ Flashcards   ✎ Instant check
▶ Tutorials   ▶ *GramActiva* videos   ▶ Animated verbs

Preparación para el examen

What you need to be able to do for the exam . . .	Here are practice tasks similar to those you will find on the exam . . .	For review go to your print or digital textbook . . .
Interpretive		
① ESCUCHAR I can listen and understand as people ask questions about weekend events.	Two friends are trying to make plans for the weekend. Based on their dialogue, what do they finally agree on? Listen for key words about: a) Who is going? b) Where are they going? c) When are they going?	pp. 172–175 *Vocabulario en contexto* p. 186 Actividad 17
Presentational		
② HABLAR I can talk about places to go and things to do on the weekend.	Describe what you're doing this weekend. Mention at least three places you plan to go or things you plan to do. For example, you might say *Voy de compras con mis amigos*.	pp. 172–175 *Vocabulario en contexto* p. 177 Actividad 6 p. 178 Actividad 8 p. 181 Actividad 13 p. 182 Actividad 14 p. 186 Actividad 17
Interpretive		
③ LEER I can read and understand information about what a person does on particular days of the week.	Someone has left his or her planner at your house. Read the schedule for two days to try to figure out what type of person owns it. Indicate whether you agree or disagree with the statements about the person. MARTES: 6:00 Desayuno 4:00 Lección de piano 5:00 Trabajo 8:30 Clase aeróbica JUEVES: 3:30 Gimnasio 4:30 Piscina 6:00 Trabajo 8:00 Biblioteca *¿Estás de acuerdo o no?* a) *Es muy perezoso(a);* b) *Es atlético(a);* c) *Le gusta ir de compras.*	pp. 172–175 *Vocabulario en contexto* p. 176 Actividad 4 p. 180 Actividad 11 pp. 188–189 Lectura
Presentational		
④ ESCRIBIR I can write a short note to a friend to let him or her know where I am going after school.	Your friend is taking a make-up test after school, so you need to write her a short note to tell her what you are doing after school today. In the note, tell her where you are going and then at what time you are going home.	p. 176 Actividad 4 p. 179 Actividad 10 p. 181 Actividad 13 p. 182 Actividad 14 p. 186 Actividad 18
Culture		
⑤ COMPARAR I can demonstrate an understanding of rhymes, songs, and games from Spanish-speaking cultures.	Think about your favorite childhood game. How does it compare to the children's games you learned about in this chapter? Describe a traditional game from a Spanish-speaking country.	p. 190 *La cultura en vivo*

Capítulo 4A • ciento noventa y cinco **195**

Differentiated Assessment

Core Assessment
- Assessment Program: Examen del capítulo 4A
- Technology: Audio Cap. 4A
- ExamView: Chapter Test, Test Banks A and B

Challenge/Pre-Ap®
- ExamView: Pre-AP® Test Bank
- Pre-AP® Resource Materials

Extra Support
- Alternate Assessment Program: Examen del capítulo 4A
- Technology: Audio Cap. 4A

Heritage Speakers
- Assessment Program: *Para hispanohablantes*: Examen del capítulo 4A
- ExamView: Heritage Learner Test Bank

Performance Tasks

Standards: 1.1, 1.2, 1.3, 4.2

Student Resource: *Para hispanohablantes*
Teacher Resources: Teacher's Resource Materials: Audio Script; Technology: Audio Cap. 4A

1. Escuchar
Standards: 1.1, 1.2, 1.3

Suggestions: Play the audio or read from the script until all students know the answers. Ask students to suggest answers to the questions.

Script:
—¿Adónde vas el fin de semana?
—El sábado me quedo en casa, pero el domingo voy al cine.
—¿A qué hora vas?
—A las nueve y media. Y tú, ¿qué haces el fin de semana?
—Yo también voy al cine el domingo.
—¿Por qué no vamos a las nueve y media?
—Yo prefiero ir a las siete.
—Bien… estoy de acuerdo. ¡A las siete!

Answers:
a) two boys   **b)** to the movies   **c)** Sunday at 7:00

2. Hablar
Standards: 1.1, 1.2, 1.3, 4.2

Suggestions: Allow individual study time in class. If students have difficulty with spontaneous conversation, have them write what they're going to say and practice until they can say it without consulting their notes.

Answers will vary.

3. Leer
Suggestions: Some students will understand this better if they transcribe it in planner form.

Answers: a) no   **b)** sí   **c)** no

4. Escribir
Suggestions: Have students try this activity without consulting the vocabulary list, notes, or completed activities.

Answers will vary.

5. Comparar
Suggestions: Have students reread *La cultura en vivo* if they need to.

Answers will vary.

AT A GLANCE

Objectives

- Listen to and read invitations and responses
- Discuss and write an invitation and an activity plan
- Exchange information while responding to an invitation
- Understand cultural differences regarding extracurricular activities
- Compare and contrast the careers of two athletes
- Identify cultural perspectives in an authentic video about sports and free-time activities

Vocabulary

- Sports and activities outside of school
- Telling time
- Extending, accepting, and declining invitations

Grammar

- *Ir* + *a* + infinitive
- The verb *jugar*

Culture

- The Paralympics, p. 197
- *fiestas,* p. 205
- Sergio García and Paola Espinosa, pp. 212, 213
- Rebecca Lobo, p. 213
- Leisure activities, p. 214

Recycle

- Telling time
- The verb *estar*
- The verb *ir*
- Infinitives

Authentic Resources

- Video of a teen program in Uruguay, pp. 216–217

RESOURCES

	FOR THE STUDENT	DIGITAL	PRINT	FOR THE TEACHER	DIGITAL	PRINT
Plan				Teacher's Edition	•	•
				Teacher's Resource Materials	•	
				Pre-AP® Resource Materials	•	
				Lesson Plans, pp. 196-c, 196-d	•	•
				Mapa global interactivo	•	
Introducción pp. 196–197						
Present	Student Edition, pp. 196–197	•	•	Teacher's Edition, pp. 196–197	•	•
	DK Reference Atlas	•		Teacher's Resource Materials	•	
	Para hispanohablantes	•		Mapa global interactivo	•	
Vocabulario en contexto pp. 198–201						
Present & Practice	Student Edition, pp. 198–201	•	•	Teacher's Edition, pp. 198–201	•	•
	Audio	•		Teacher's Resource Materials	•	
	Videohistoria	•		Vocabulary Clip Art	•	
	Flashcards	•		Technology: Audio	•	
	Instant Check	•		Video Program: Videohistoria	•	
	Guided WB, pp. 133–142	•	•			
	Core WB, pp. 76–79	•	•			
	Communication Activities	•				
	Para hispanohablantes	•				
Assess and Remediate				Prueba 4B–1: Assessment Program, pp. 105–106	•	
				Assessment Program para hispanohablantes, pp. 105–106	•	

RESOURCES

	FOR THE STUDENT	DIGITAL	PRINT	FOR THE TEACHER	DIGITAL	PRINT
Vocabulario en uso pp. 202–205						
Present & Practice	Student Edition, pp. 202–205	•	•	Interactive Whiteboard Vocabulary Activities	•	
	Instant Check	•		Teacher's Edition, pp. 202–205	•	•
	Communication Activities	•		Teacher's Resource Materials Communicative Pair Activities	•	
	Para hispanohablantes	•		Technology: Audio	•	
	Communicative Pair Activities	•		Videomodelos	•	
				Mapa global interactivo	•	
Assess and Remediate				Prueba 4B–2 with Remediation	•	
				Prueba 4B–2: Assessment Program, pp. 107–108 Assessment Program para hispanohablantes, pp. 107–108	• •	
Gramática pp. 206–211						
Present & Practice	Student Edition, pp. 206–211	•	•	Interactive Whiteboard Grammar Activities	•	
	Instant Check	•		Teacher's Edition, pp. 206–211	•	•
	Animated Verbs	•		Teacher's Resource Materials Communicative Pair Activities	•	
	Tutorial Video: Grammar	•				
	Canción de hip hop	•		Technology: Audio	•	
	Guided WB, pp. 143–146	•	•	Videomodelos	•	
	Core WB, pp. 80–82	•	•	Video Program: GramActiva	•	
	Communication Activities	•		Mapa global interactivo	•	
	Para hispanohablantes	•				
	Communicative Pair Activities	•				
Assess and Remediate				Pruebas 4B–3 and 4B–4 with Remediation	•	
				Pruebas 4B–3, 4B–4: Assessment Program, pp. 109, 110 Assessment Program para hispanohablantes, pp. 109, 110	• •	
Aplicación pp. 212–217						
Apply	Student Edition, pp. 212–217	•	•	Teacher's Edition, pp. 212–217	•	•
	Authentic Resources Workbook	•	•	Mapa global interactivo	•	
	Authentic Resources	•		Authentic Resources Lesson Plans with scripts, answer keys	•	
	Literacy Skills WB	•	•			
	Online Cultural Reading	•				
	Guided WB, pp. 147–148	•	•			
	Communication Activities	•				
	Para hispanohablantes	•				
Repaso del capítulo pp. 218–219						
Review	Student Edition, pp. 218–219	•	•	Teacher's Edition, pp. 218–219	•	•
	Online Puzzles and Games	•		Teacher's Resource Materials	•	
	Core WB, pp. 83–84	•	•	Technology: Audio	•	
	Communication Activities	•				
	Para hispanohablantes	•				
	Instant Check	•				
Chapter Assessment						
Assess				Examen del capítulo 4B Assessment Program, pp. 111–117 Alternate Assessment Program, pp. 40–45 Assessment Program para hispanohablantes, pp. 111–117	• • •	
				Audio Program, Cap. 4B, Examen	•	
				ExamView: Test Banks A and B questions only online Heritage Learner Test Bank Pre-AP® Test Bank	• • •	

4B | Lesson Plans

LESSON PLAN (50 MINUTES)

	Warm-up / Assess	Preview / Present / Practice / Communicate		Wrap-up / Homework Options
1	**Warm-up** (10 min.) • Return Examen del capítulo 4A	**Chapter Opener** (5 min.) • Objectives • Arte y cultura	**Vocabulario en contexto** (30 min.) • Presentation: Vocabulario y gramática en contexto • Actividades 1, 2	**Wrap-up and Homework Options** (5 min.) • Practice Workbook 4B-1, 4B-2
2	**Warm-up** (5 min.) • Homework check	**Vocabulario en contexto** (40 min.) • Presentation: Videohistoria *¿Te gustaría ir de camping?* • View: Videohistoria	• Video Activities 1, 2, 3, 4 • Actividad 3	**Wrap-up and Homework Options** (5 min.) • Practice Workbook 4B-3, 4B-4 • Prueba 4B-1: Vocabulary recognition
3	**Warm-up** (10 min.) • Actividad 7 • Homework check • **Formative Assessment** (10 min.) • Prueba 4B-1: Vocabulary recognition	**Vocabulario en uso** (25 min.) • Interactive Whiteboard Vocabulary Activities • Actividades 4, 5, 6, 8, 9 • Audio Activities 5, 6		**Wrap-up and Homework Options** (5 min.) • Writing Activity 10 • Para hispanohablantes 4B-1, 4B-2
4	**Warm-up** (10 min.) • Actividad 12 • Homework check	**Gramática y vocabulario en uso** (35 min.) • Actividades 10, 11 • Exploración del lenguaje • Cultura • Presentation: *ir + a + infinitive*	• View: GramActiva video • Interactive Whiteboard Grammar Activities • Actividades 13, 14, 15	**Wrap-up and Homework Options** (5 min.) • Practice Workbook 4B-5, 4B-6 • Prueba 4B-2 with Remediation: Vocabulary production
5	**Warm-up** (10 min.) • Communicative Pair Activity • Homework check • **Formative Assessment** (10 min.) • Prueba 4B-2 with Remediation: Vocabulary production	**Gramática y vocabulario en uso** (25 min.) • Actividad 17 • Audio Activity 7 • Presentation: The verb *jugar* • View: GramActiva video • Interactive Whiteboard Grammar Activities • Actividades 18, 20		**Wrap-up and Homework Options** (5 min.) • Writing Activities 11, 12, 13 • Prueba 4B-3 with Remediation: *ir + a + infinitive*
6	**Warm-up** (10 min.) • Actividad 16 • Homework check • **Formative Assessment** (10 min.) • Prueba 4B-3 with Remediation: *ir + a + infinitive*	**Gramática y vocabulario en uso** (25 min.) • Actividad 19 • Audio Activities 8, 9 • Communicative Pair Activity	• Pronunciación • El español en el mundo del trabajo	**Wrap-up and Homework Options** (5 min.) • Practice Workbook 4B-7 • Para hispanohablantes 4B-4, 4B-5 • Prueba 4B-4 with Remediation: The verb *jugar*
7	**Warm-up** (10 min.) • Actividad 21 • Homework check • **Formative Assessment** (10 min.) • Prueba 4B-4 with Remediation: The verb *jugar*	**Gramática y vocabulario en uso** (5 min.) • Actividad 22 **Aplicación** (20 min.) • Lectura • Cultura		**Wrap-up and Homework Options** (5 min.) • ¿Comprendes?
8	**Warm-up** (5 min.) • Homework check	**Aplicación** (30 min.) • Perspectivas del mundo hispano • Auténtico • Presentación escrita: Steps 1, 5	**Repaso del capítulo** (10 min.) • Vocabulario y gramática	**Wrap-up and Homework Options** (5 min.) • Presentación escrita: Step 2 • Preparación para el examen 3, 4, 5
9	**Warm-up** (5 min.) • Homework check	**Aplicación** (20 min.) • Presentación escrita: Step 3	**Repaso del capítulo** (20 min.) • Preparación para el examen 1, 2	**Wrap-up and Homework Options** (5 min.) • Presentación escrita: Step 4 • Practice Workbook 4B-8, 4B-9 • Instant Check • Examen del capítulo 4B
10	**Warm-up** (10 min.) • Homework check • **Summative Assessment** (40 min.) • Examen del capítulo 4B			

ALTERNATE LESSON PLAN (90 MINUTES)

DAY	Warm-up / Assess	Preview / Present / Practice / Communicate	Wrap-up / Homework Options
1	**Warm-up** (10 min.) • Return Examen del capítulo 4A	**Chapter Opener** (5 min.) • Objectives • Arte y cultura **Vocabulario en contexto** (60 min.) • Presentation: Vocabulario y gramática en contexto • Actividades 1, 2 • Presentation: Videohistoria *¿Te gustaría ir de camping?* • View: Videohistoria • Video Activities 1, 2, 3, 4 • Actividad 3 **Vocabulario en uso** (10 min.) • Actividades 4, 5, 6	**Wrap-up and Homework Options** (5 min.) • Practice Workbook 4B-1, 4B-2, 4B-3, 4B-4 • Para hispanohablantes 4B-1, 4B-2 • Prueba 4B-1: Vocabulary recognition
2	**Warm-up** (10 min.) • Homework check • **Formative Assessment** (10 min.) • Prueba 4B-1: Vocabulary recognition	**Vocabulario en uso** (65 min.) • Actividades 7, 8, 9, 10, 11, 12 • Cultura • Audio Activities 5, 6 • Exploración del lenguaje • Communicative Pair Activity • Interactive Whiteboard Vocabulary Activities	**Wrap-up and Homework Options** (5 min.) • Writing Activity 10 • Prueba 4B-2 with Remediation: Vocabulary production
3	**Warm-up** (5 min.) • Homework check • **Formative Assessment** (10 min.) • Prueba 4B-2 with Remediation: Vocabulary production	**Gramática y vocabulario en uso** (70 min.) • Presentation: *ir + a + infinitive* • View: GramActiva video • Actividades 13, 14, 15, 17 • Audio Activity 7 • Writing Activity 11 • Communicative Pair Activity • Presentation: The verb *jugar* • View: GramActiva video • Actividades 18, 19 • Audio Activities 8, 9 • Interactive Whiteboard Grammar Activities	**Wrap-up and Homework Options** (5 min.) • Practice Workbook 4B-5, 4B-6, 4B-7 • Para hispanohablantes 4B-4, 4B-5 • Writing Activities 12, 13 • Pruebas 4B-3, 4B-4 with Remediation: *ir + a + infinitive*, The verb *jugar*
4	**Warm-up** (15 min.) • Actividades 16, 20 • Homework check • **Formative Assessment** (15 min.) • Pruebas 4B-3, 4B-4 with Remediation: *ir + a + infinitive*, The verb *jugar*	**Gramática y vocabulario en uso** (20 min.) • Pronunciación • El español en el mundo del trabajo • Actividades 21, 22 **Aplicación** (35 min.) • Lectura • ¿Comprendes? • Cultura • Presentación escrita: Steps 1, 5 • Interactive Whiteboard Grammar Activities	**Wrap-up and Homework Options** (5 min.) • Presentación escrita: Step 2 • Lectura
5	**Warm-up** (5 min.) • Homework check	**Aplicación** (45 min.) • Presentación escrita: Step 3 • Perspectivas del mundo hispano • Auténtico **Repaso del capítulo** (35 min.) • Vocabulario y gramática • Preparación para el examen 1, 2, 3, 4, 5	**Wrap-up and Homework Options** (5 min.) • Presentación escrita: Step 4 • Practice Workbook 4B-8, 4B-9 • Instant Check • Examen del capítulo 4B
6	**Warm-up** (15 min.) • Homework check • Answer questions **Repaso del capítulo** (25 min.) • Situation Cards • Communicative Pair Activities • **Summative Assessment** (45 min.) • Examen del capítulo 4B		**Wrap-up and Homework Options** (5 min.) • Auténtico

Can-Do Statements

Read the can-do statements in the chapter objectives with students. Then have students read *Preparación para el examen* on page 219 to preview what they will be able to do at the end of the chapter.

Standards for Capítulo 4B

To achieve the goals of the Standards, students will:

COMMUNICATION

1.1 Interpersonal

- Talk about: sports and pastimes; emotions and states of being; when certain events and activities occur; cellular phone usage; experiences of family immigration
- Extend, accept, or decline invitations

1.2 Interpretive

- Read and listen to information about sports and pastimes
- Listen to information about how people are feeling
- Read: a picture-based story; about emotions and states of being; an advertisement for a sports training school; an advertisement for a campground; about athletes Sergio García and Paola Espinosa
- Listen to and watch a video about sports and pastimes

1.3 Presentational

- Present information about: sports and pastimes; emotions and states of being; when certain activities occur; a sports training school; Sergio García and Paola Espinosa
- Write about cellular phone usage
- Present an account of an interview about immigration

CULTURE

2.1 Practices to Perspectives

- Talk about the festival, *La Noche de los rábanos;* how students traditionally engage in activities outside of school

2.2 Products to Perspectives

- Talk about the elaborate radish-sculpting of *La Noche de los rábanos*

CONNECTIONS

3.1 Making Connections

- Reinforce math and metric conversion skills
- Apply knowledge of geography and current events

3.2 Acquiring Information and Diverse Perspectives

- Read an advertisement for a sports training school

COMPARISONS

4.1 Language

- Talk about new vocabulary through the recognition of cognates; the use of *ir* in conjunction with *a* and an infinitive; the pronunciation of the letter *d*
- Explain that words are borrowed across languages
- Compare the use of *jugar* idioms with English

CAPÍTULO **4B**
¿Quieres ir conmigo?

Country Connections Explorar el mundo hispano

Texas · Nueva York · Florida · España · México · Chile

CHAPTER OBJECTIVES

Communication

By the end of this chapter you will be able to:

- Listen to and read invitations and responses.
- Discuss and write an invitation and an activity plan.
- Exchange information while responding to an invitation.

Culture

You will also be able to:

- **Auténtico:** Identify cultural perspectives in an authentic video about sports and free-time activities.
- Understand cultural differences regarding extracurricular activities.
- Compare and contrast the careers of two athletes.

You will demonstrate what you know and can do:

- Presentación escrita: Una invitación
- Repaso del capítulo: Preparación para el examen

You will use:

Vocabulary
- Sports and activities outside of school
- Telling time
- Extending, accepting, and declining invitations

Grammar
- *Ir + a +* infinitive
- The verb *jugar*

ARTE y CULTURA ◁ El mundo hispano

Paralympic Games Starting with the first Paralympic Games in Rome in 1960, the International Paralympics Committee has organized summer and winter games that follow the regular Olympic Games and are hosted by the same city. Athletes with all types of disabilities compete in the Paralympics. In the most recent Summer and Winter Paralympics, more than 150 nations participated, with over 4,200 athletes worldwide.

▶ How do you think athletes with disabilities benefit from competing in the Paralympics or in similar local events?

Spanish swimmer Teresa Perales, posing with her bronze medal at the London 2012 Paralympic Games ▶

196 ciento noventa y seis • Tema 4 • Los pasatiempos

Enrich Your Teaching

The End in Mind

Have students preview the sample performance tasks on *Preparación para el examen,* p. 219, and connect them to the Chapter Objectives. Explain to students that by completing the sample tasks they can self-assess their learning progress.

Technology: Mapa global interactivo

Download the *Mapa global interactivo* files for Chapter 4B and preview the activities. Activity 1 takes you to Oaxaca, México. Activity 2 visits the coastal areas of Spain.

Pablo Javier Robledo, de Argentina, en los Juegos Paralímpicos de Sochi 2014

Videocultura **Los pasatiempos**

Capítulo 4B • ciento noventa y siete **197**

Project-Based Learning

Guía para el tiempo libre
(continued)

As part of their weekend guides, encourage students to research local professional, amateur, and school sports teams. Many local teams now have social media sites or Web pages. Have students discuss and plan the format for listing the sports events and providing information about the venues.

4.2 Cultural
- Compare: specialized, regional crafts and products; how students engage in activities outside of school

COMMUNITIES

5.1 School and Global Communities
- Consider local opportunities for Spanish-speakers in the health care professions
- Interview a Spanish-speaker about the immigrant experience

5.2 Lifelong Learning
- Read about athletes Sergio García and Paola Espinosa
- Explain the current influence of Spanish-speakers in areas like politics, music, poetry, and science

Chapter Opener

Resources: Mapa global interactivo

Suggestions: As you go over the objectives of the chapter, point out that the video segments will introduce more leisure-time vocabulary. Introduce the theme of the chapter by asking students what they like to do in their free time. How many enjoy concerts? How many participate in sports or other outdoor activities? Brainstorm a list of activities.

Help students locate the cities, states, and countries featured in the chapter by using the interactive map.

▶ **Technology: Videocultura** View *Los pasatiempos* with the class to learn more about leisure time in Spanish-speaking countries.

ARTE Y CULTURA

Standards: 3.1

Suggestions: Emphasize that the Paralympic Games promote international competition and fellowship among athletes with disabilities. Ask students to name similar local competitions and the events in which those athletes compete.

Answers will vary.

Vocabulario en contexto

Resources: Teacher's Resource Materials: Input Script, Clip Art, Audio Script; Technology: Audio Cap. 4B

Suggestions: Use the Input Script from the *Teacher's Resource Materials* to help present the new vocabulary and grammar. Ask such questions as: *¿Qué te gusta practicar más, el béisbol o el fútbol americano?* Continue the questions until students seem comfortable with the vocabulary.

Have students predict what is happening in the pictures on p.199. Ask volunteers to read the parts of Jazmín and her friends. Then have students list words they recognize in the conversation.

Starter Activity

Review the 24-hour clock by writing these times on the board and asking students to tell you the times using the 12-hour clock: *14:45 16:30 18:15 23:10.*

Active Classroom

Have students create advertisements for a sports club or outdoor recreation facility. They should include a variety of activities, hours of operation, and contact information. Suggest that they illustrate the advertisements, then post them in the room to be used to guide further conversations.

Technology: Interactive Whiteboard

Vocabulary Activities 4B Use the whiteboard activities in your Teacher Resources as you progress through the vocabulary practice with your class.

Additional Resources

Technology: Online Resources
- Instant Check
- Guided, Core, Audio, Writing practice
- *Para hispanohablantes*

Print
- Guided WB pp. 133–138
- Core WB pp. 76–77

Vocabulario en contexto

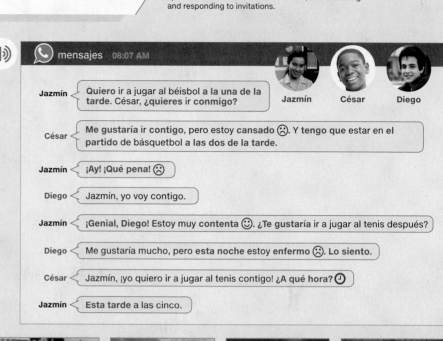

mensajes 08:07 AM

Jazmín: Quiero ir a jugar al béisbol a la una de la tarde. César, ¿quieres ir conmigo?

César: Me gustaría ir contigo, pero estoy cansado 😟. Y tengo que estar en el partido de básquetbol a las dos de la tarde.

Jazmín: ¡Ay! ¡Qué pena! 😟

Diego: Jazmín, yo voy contigo.

Jazmín: ¡Genial, Diego! Estoy muy contenta 🙂. ¿Te gustaría ir a jugar al tenis después?

Diego: Me gustaría mucho, pero esta noche estoy enfermo 😟. Lo siento.

César: Jazmín, ¡yo quiero ir a jugar al tenis contigo! ¿A qué hora? 🕐

Jazmín: Esta tarde a las cinco.

jugar al fútbol | jugar al golf | jugar al tenis | jugar al básquetbol

jugar al béisbol | jugar al fútbol americano | jugar al vóleibol

---

Differentiated Instruction

Special Needs
If students are unable to act out the vocabulary for *Actividad* 2 on p. 199, ask them to write each adjective on a sheet of paper or say it aloud.

Students with Learning Difficulties
Have students add new words to their vocabulary notebook section and accompany these words with pictures and English translations if needed. For *Actividad* 2, provide students with a few examples of what is expected of them.

mensajes 05:20 PM

César — ¡Oye, Diego!, ¿vas de pesca también?

Diego — ¡Qué buena idea! ¡Voy de pesca, sí! Puedo ir a las ocho de la mañana.

Jazmín — Estoy triste 😞 porque no puedes ir con nosotros, Diego. Siempre estás demasiado ocupado.

Diego — ¡Pero puedo ir a la fiesta con ustedes este fin de semana!

César — Entonces, nos vemos pronto.

el concierto

la fiesta

el baile

ir de cámping

ir de pesca

el partido

1

Hoy yo estoy...

🔊 ESCUCHAR You will hear people talk about how they are feeling today. Act out the appropriate feeling when you hear it.

2

¡Genial!

🔊 ESCUCHAR Juan Antonio is making plans for his week. As he lists the activities, point to the appropriate picture.

Capítulo 4B • ciento noventa y nueve **199**

Enrich Your Teaching

Culture Note

The musical sounds of Latin America have a variety of origins, most linked to regional history. Instruments include panpipes, steel drum, marimba, maracas, and **guitarrón.** Ask students to list some singers who have a distinct Latin American sound.

21st Century Skills

ICT Literacy Have students create a monthly calendar for the class Web site showing all activities that class members might be interested in. Have them use the calendar to promote a class discussion of any activities in which the class might want to participate.

1

Standards: 1.2

Resources: Teacher's Resource Materials: Audio Script; Technology: Audio Cap. 4B

Suggestions: First agree on the body language to represent the different feelings. In a large class, you may wish to have volunteers act out the words, and ask the rest of the class whether or not they agree with what they see.

🔊 **Technology: Audio Script and Answers:**

1. Tengo mucho trabajo y estoy cansada. *(tired)*
2. No puedo ir a la fiesta. Estoy triste. *(sad)*
3. Me gustaría ir al concierto de rock esta noche, pero estoy ocupado. *(busy)*
4. Voy de pesca con mi familia este fin de semana. Estoy muy contenta. *(happy)*
5. No me gusta ir de cámping. No voy a estar contenta. *(unhappy)*
6. No puedo jugar al tenis hoy. Estoy muy enfermo. *(sick)*

Extension: Give students three situations using known vocabulary, such as *Tengo que estudiar* or *No hay clases.* Ask them to give you at least one adjective to describe how they might feel in each situation.

2

Standards: 1.2

Resources: Teacher's Resource Materials: Audio Script; Technology: Audio Cap. 4B

Suggestions: Play the audio or read the script. Monitor to verify that students are correctly identifying the sports.

🔊 **Technology: Audio Script and Answers:**

1. Pues, el viernes a las tres de la tarde juego al béisbol. *(point to baseball)*
2. Por la noche voy al concierto de Maná en el parque. *(point to concert)*
3. El sábado a las diez de la mañana voy de pesca con mi amigo Julio. *(point to fishing)*
4. A la una, juego un poco de tenis. *(point to tennis)*
5. A las ocho de la noche, voy al baile con María. *(point to dance)*
6. El domingo, a las nueve de la mañana, voy al partido con mis papás. *(point to game)*
7. A las cuatro de la tarde, voy a una fiesta contigo. *(point to party)*

Vocabulario en contexto

Standards: 1.2

Resources: Technology: Audio Cap. 4B

Suggestions: Model the dialogue with a volunteer. Begin the reading again with volunteers playing the roles of the characters. Using the presentation, help students understand the new words in blue type.

Post-reading: Complete Actividad 3 to check comprehension.

3

Standards: 1.2, 1.3

Suggestions: You may wish to do this as a listening activity, reading the sentences to the students.

Answers:

1. *No*
2. *Sí*
3. *No*
4. *No*
5. *Sí*

¿Quieres hacer algo?

Santiago y Cristina hablan de sus planes este fin de semana.

Santiago: Cristina, ¿vas al baile de la escuela el sábado? Yo quiero ir.

Cristina: ¿Quieres ir al baile? ¿Por qué? Yo **sé** que no te gusta bailar.

Santiago: Es verdad, no me gusta bailar. Pero me gustaría mucho hablar con Marina.

Cristina: Ay, lo siento, pero Marina está ocupada el sábado. Vamos al concierto en el centro comercial.

Santiago: ¡No me digas! Entonces, creo que voy a estar **mal** y **un poco** enfermo. Me quedo en casa el sábado, hay un partido de béisbol que **puedo** ver en la televisión.

Cristina: Santiago, tú **sabes** que Marina y yo somos amigas. **Puedes** ir a la fiesta conmigo el viernes. ¿Te gustaría? Allí puedes hablar mucho con Marina.

Santiago: ¡Genial! ¡Qué buena idea! ¿A qué hora?

Cristina: A las siete **de la noche** en el parque central. Ok, tengo que ir a mi lección de piano. ¡Hasta pronto!

Santiago: ¡Chao!

Cristina   Santiago

3

¿Sí o no?

ESCRIBIR Contesta a las preguntas con *Sí* o *No*.

1. El baile es en el centro comercial.
2. A Santiago no le gusta bailar.
3. Marina está enferma.
4. Cristina va al concierto con Santiago.
5. Santiago está contento porque va a hablar con Marina en la fiesta.

200 doscientos • Tema 4 • Los pasatiempos

Differentiated Instruction

Heritage Speakers

Have students write three sentences about their favorite sport, including teams and athletes that they follow. Collect the first draft of their sentences, and correct any spelling and grammar mistakes.

Verbal/Linguistic Learner

Ask students to write a few short lines of dialogue to change the ending of the dialogue. In the new ending, Santiago should not accept the invitation to the party, and he should give two or three reasons why he will not go.

Videohistoria

Go **Online** to practice
PEARSON
realize™
PearsonSchool.com/Autentico
AUDIO VIDEO WRITING SCRIPT

Interpretive **4B**

¿Te gustaría ir de cámping?

Before You Watch

Focus on key words As you watch the video, focus on the use of the verb *ir a* with a place, or *ir a* and *ir de* with an activity, to understand each character's plans. What phrase with *ir* describes each photo?

Complete the Activity

¿Qué vas a hacer? ¿Qué vas a hacer este fin de semana? ¿Vas a jugar un deporte o ir a un evento especial? Describe tres actividades que vas a hacer y el día y la hora del evento.

▶ Watch the Video

What are Valentina and Yoojee planning to do this weekend?

Go to **PearsonSchool.com/Autentico** to watch the video *¿Te gustaría ir de cámping?* and to view the script.

Valentina

After You Watch

✎ **¿COMPRENDES?** Answer the following questions by focusing on the different conjugations of the key word *ir*.

1. ¿Quién va a estos lugares o hace estas actividades, Valentina or Yoojee?

   a. al campo
   b. acampar
   c. de pesca
   d. jugar al básquetbol
   e. de compras
   f. a la iglesia
   g. a un concierto
   h. al baile

2. ¿Cuál de las dos chicas va a estar más ocupada este fin de semana? ¿Por qué?

Capítulo 4B • doscientos uno **201**

Enrich Your Teaching

Culture Note

In Costa Rica, *gallo pinto,* the national dish of fried rice and black beans is served as a breakfast food. Many meals are derivatives of *gallo pinto,* including *arroz con pollo* or *arroz con atún.* At lunch, *gallo pinto* becomes *casado* which is rice and beans accompanied by cabbage and tomato salad, fried plantains, and meat.

Technology: Video

Standards: 1.2

Resources: Teacher's Resource Materials: Video Script

Before You Watch

Review the previewing strategy and activity with the students. Also point out the images of activities that will be discussed in the video. Review the Complete the Activity with the class. Invite volunteers to talk or write about activities they do on weekends with their families.

Watch the Video

Show the video, telling students to focus on identifying key details of the plot and a few key words from the dialogue. Then, in a class discussion, review these key details before showing the video a second time.

After You Watch

Standards: 1.2, 1.3

Suggestions: Discuss the questions with the class to confirm understanding of the video.

Answers

1. a. Valentina
   b. Valentina
   c. Valentina
   d. Yoojee
   e. Yoojee
   f. Yoojee
   g. Yoojee
   h. Valentina y Yoojee
2. Yoojee va a estar más ocupada que Valentina. Ella va a ir a más actividades.

Print and distribute the activity sheets from the Teacher's Resources. Or have students complete the additional video activities online.

Additional Resources

🛜 **Technology: Online Resources**
• Instant Check
• Guided, Core, Video, Audio
• *Para hispanohablantes*
Print
• Guided WB pp. 139–142
• Core WB pp. 78–79

Assessment _____

Quiz: Vocabulary Recognition
• Prueba 4B-1

4

Standards: 1.1

Suggestions: Emphasize that students will be using **Me gustaría** ("I would like") as opposed to **Me gusta** ("I like").

Answers will vary but should include:

(No) me gustaría ...
1. ir a un concierto.
2. ir al baile.
3. ir al partido.
4. ir de cámping.
5. ir de pesca.

5

Standards: 1.1, 1.2

Suggestions: Tell students that they will need this information for *Actividad* 6.

Answers will vary but should include:

Sé / No sé jugar al...
1. básquetbol.
2. fútbol americano.
3. vóleibol.
4. tenis.
5. golf.
6. fútbol

6

Standards: 1.1

Suggestions: Have students move around the room and interact with several different classmates.

Answers will vary.

Active Classroom

Have students in small groups dramatize going to a sports event. They should decide what event they will go to, who will go with them, and when they will go.

Suggestions: Have students articulate requests (inviting a friend) and offering alternatives (come up with another plan) if refused.

Vocabulario en uso

OBJECTIVES
▶ Write and talk about activities you would like to do, and sports you know how to play
▶ Listen to invitations and responses
▶ Discuss what activities you and others will do and at what time
▶ Exchange information while extending, accepting, and declining invitations

4

Me gustaría ir . . .

ESCRIBIR, HABLAR   Say whether or not you would like to do these things this weekend.

Modelo
Me gustaría ir a una fiesta este fin de semana.
o: *No me gustaría ir a una fiesta este fin de semana.*

5

No sé jugar . . .

ESCRIBIR, HABLAR   Indica si sabes o no sabes jugar estos deportes.

Modelo
Sé jugar al béisbol muy bien.
o: *No sé jugar al béisbol.*

6

¿Qué deportes practicas?

HABLAR EN PAREJA   Using the information from Actividad 5, ask and tell about which sports you know, or don't know, how to play.

Videomodelo
A —¿Sabes jugar al béisbol?
B —¡Por supuesto! Sé jugar al béisbol muy bien.
o:—No, no sé jugar al béisbol.

202 doscientos dos • Tema 4 • Los pasatiempos

Differentiated Instruction

Challenge

Ask students to use the Internet to research a well-known athlete of Spanish-speaking origin. Have them present a short profile of the athlete, including which sports he or she plays, his or her statistics, and what team he or she plays for, if appropriate.

Students with Learning Difficulties

Actividad 9 requires students to listen, process, and write at the same time, which can be challenging. You may want to divide this into two separate tasks: first listening for the event, then listening for the response.

7

¿Cómo estás?

LEER, ESCRIBIR You've asked your friends how they are. Now read each friend's reply and write the correct form of the missing word from the list.

cansado, -a	contento, -a
enfermo, -a	mal
ocupado, -a	triste

Tú: ¿Cómo estás?

Felipe: Muy __1.__. Voy a un concierto esta noche con mis amigos.

Miguel: ¡ __2.__ ! Mi clase de ciencias es muy aburrida y no me gusta nada el profesor.

Marta: Estoy __3.__. Me duele la cabeza. Hoy no puedo jugar al tenis ni patinar.

Carlos: Estoy __4.__. Todos mis amigos van a la playa el sábado pero tengo que trabajar.

Gabriela: Un poco __5.__. Todas las noches trabajo en el centro comercial.

Dolores: Demasiado __6.__. Juego al básquetbol después de las clases, tomo lecciones de piano y practico cada día y tengo un trabajo también.

8

Lo siento

HABLAR EN PAREJA Make plans with a partner. Ask your partner if he or she wants to do these activities with you. Your partner can't go, and will offer excuses to explain why.

Videomodelo

A —¡Oye! ¿Quieres **patinar** conmigo esta tarde?
B —Lo siento. Hoy no puedo. Estoy **demasiado enfermo(a)**.

Estudiante A

Estudiante B

muy	ocupado, -a
demasiado	enfermo, -a
un poco	cansado, -a
	triste
	mal
¡Respuesta personal!	

9

Escucha y escribe

ESCUCHAR, ESCRIBIR You will hear three invitations to events and the responses given. On a sheet of paper, write the numbers 1–3. As you listen, write down what each invitation is for and whether the person accepted it (write *sí*) or turned it down (write *no*).

Capítulo 4B • doscientos tres **203**

Enrich Your Teaching

Culture Note

If you are invited to a party, a dinner, or other event in a Spanish-speaking country and you cannot accept the invitation, it is usually best to offer an explanation. Just saying *Lo siento. Ya tengo planes.* ("I'm sorry. I already have plans."), may be seen as rude. It is also customary to bring the host or hostess a gift.

Teacher-to-Teacher

Using photos of activities, have students write three sentences saying why they cannot do certain things. Tell them to make their excuses logical or illogical. For example, students may say *No puedo montar en monopatín. Estoy demasiado contenta.* Then have the class decide whether or not the excuse makes sense.

7

Standards: 1.2, 1.3

Suggestions: Have students read the entire dialogue before answering.

Answers:
1. contento
2. mal
3. enferma
4. triste
5. cansada
6. ocupada

8

Standards: 1.1

Recycle: The body; school subjects

Suggestions: Be sure students can think of an excuse for why they can't do each activity.

Answers will vary but should include:
1. ir de pesca
2. jugar al básquetbol
3. ir de compras
4. montar en bicicleta
5. jugar al fútbol

9

Standards: 1.2

Resources: Teacher's Resource Materials: Audio Script; Technology: Audio Cap. 4B

Suggestions: Before the activity, remind students to listen for intonations that indicate a positive or negative reaction.

Technology: Audio Script and Answers:

1. —¿Puedes ir conmigo al baile esta noche? *(ir al baile)*
   —¡Qué pena! Tengo que trabajar. *(no)*
2. —¿Te gustaría ir conmigo al partido esta tarde? *(ir al partido)*
   —¡Qué buena idea! Me gustaría mucho. *(sí)*
3. —Voy a jugar al golf el domingo. ¿Quieres jugar? *(jugar al golf)*
   —¿Contigo? ¡Genial! *(sí)*

Standards: 1.1

Recycle: Telling time

Suggestions: Review the vocabulary. Go over the *Nota,* reminding students to refer to it as they do the activity. Review the *Modelo* to reinforce the structure.

Answers:

1. —¿A qué hora es el concierto?
   —A las nueve de la noche.
2. —¿A qué hora es la fiesta?
   —A las dos y media de la tarde.
3. —¿A qué hora es el partido?
   —A la una y media de la tarde.
4. —¿A qué hora es el baile?
   —A las ocho y media de la noche.
5. —¿A qué hora es la cena?
   —A las siete y media de la noche.
6. —¿A qué hora es el desayuno?
   —A las siete de la mañana.

Common Errors: Students may say ¿Qué hora? instead of ¿A qué hora? and **en la mañana** instead of **de la mañana.**

Pre-AP® Integration

- **Learning Objective:** Interpersonal Writing
- **Activity 10:** Have pairs of students select one of the activities pictured, and draft an enthusiastic e-mail inviting their partner to attend. The partner will reply, apologizing for not being able to go.
- **Pre-AP® Resource Materials:** Comprehensive guide to Pre-AP® communication skill development

Standards: 1.1

Recycle: *ir;* place names

Suggestions: Review the responses, making sure students know how to accept and decline an invitation.

Answers:

1. ir al baile; A las siete y media de la noche.
2. ir a la fiesta; A las ocho y media de la noche.
3. ir al cine; A las cinco y media de la tarde.
4. ir a la piscina; A la una de la tarde.
5. ir al partido de fútbol; A las cuatro y cuarto de la tarde.
6. ir de compras (ir al centro comercial); A las once de la mañana.

Project-Based Learning

Students can perform Step 4 at this point. (For more information, see p. 170-b.)

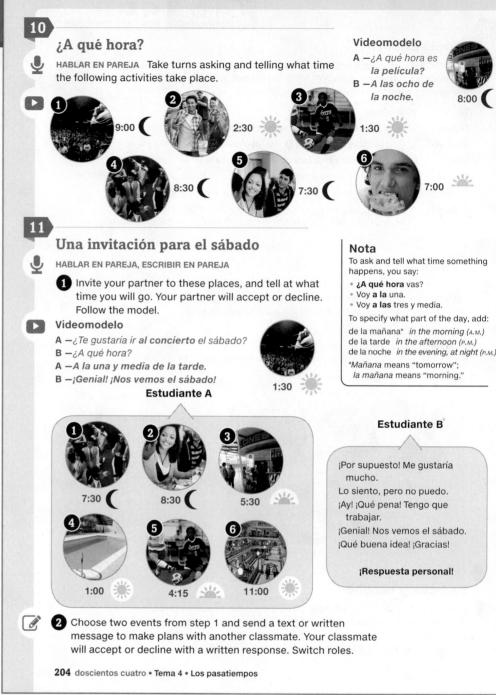

10

¿A qué hora?

🎤 **HABLAR EN PAREJA** Take turns asking and telling what time the following activities take place.

Videomodelo
A —¿A qué hora es la película?
B —A las ocho de la noche.

8:00

1. 9:00
2. 2:30
3. 1:30
4. 8:30
5. 7:30
6. 7:00

11

Una invitación para el sábado

🎤 **HABLAR EN PAREJA, ESCRIBIR EN PAREJA**

1 Invite your partner to these places, and tell at what time you will go. Your partner will accept or decline. Follow the model.

▶ **Videomodelo**
A —¿Te gustaría ir **al concierto** el sábado?
B —¿A qué hora?
A —A la una y media de la tarde.
B —¡Genial! ¡Nos vemos el sábado!

1:30

Estudiante A

1. 7:30
2. 8:30
3. 5:30
4. 1:00
5. 4:15
6. 11:00

Nota
To ask and tell what time something happens, you say:
- **¿A qué hora** vas?
- Voy **a la** una.
- Voy **a las** tres y media.

To specify what part of the day, add:
de la mañana* in the morning (A.M.)
de la tarde in the afternoon (P.M.)
de la noche in the evening, at night (P.M.)

*Mañana means "tomorrow"; la mañana means "morning."

Estudiante B

¡Por supuesto! Me gustaría mucho.
Lo siento, pero no puedo.
¡Ay! ¡Qué pena! Tengo que trabajar.
¡Genial! Nos vemos el sábado.
¡Qué buena idea! ¡Gracias!

¡Respuesta personal!

✏️ 2 Choose two events from step 1 and send a text or written message to make plans with another classmate. Your classmate will accept or decline with a written response. Switch roles.

204 doscientos cuatro • Tema 4 • Los pasatiempos

Differentiated Instruction

Spatial Learner

Have students draw a three-panel cartoon. In their cartoon, they should write a dialogue in which one character invites the other(s) to do something. There should be a response, and then a comment or conclusion. Ask students to post their cartoons or to present them to the class.

Heritage Speakers

Refer students to the *Exploración del lenguaje* at the top of p. 205. Ask students to identify additional Spanish words and expressions that are borrowed from English.

Exploración del lenguaje ‹ Spanish words borrowed from English

Languages often borrow words from one another. For example, "rodeo" and "patio" are Spanish words that have found their way into English. There are also many examples of English words that have entered Spanish. By recognizing these familiar words, you can increase your vocabulary in Spanish.

Try it out! Read the sentences and identify the "borrowed words." Don't forget to pronounce the words correctly in Spanish.

> Quiero hacer videos.
> ¿Quieres jugar al básquetbol conmigo?
> Practico el rugby y el ráquetbol.
> Juego al fútbol en el cámping.
> ¡Me encantan los sándwiches!

Radio taxi

Tel:
447 52 83
#65 Col. Centro

⏱ 24 horas a su servicio

12

Y tú, ¿qué dices?

🎤 ESCRIBIR, HABLAR

1. ¿A qué hora te gusta ir al cine?
2. ¿Estás más contento(a) cuando practicas un deporte o cuando ves la televisión?
3. ¿Qué deportes te gustan más?
4. ¿Este fin de semana tienes que trabajar o puedes pasar tiempo con amigos?

CULTURA ‹ México

La Noche de los Rábanos[1] es una de las muchas fiestas del mundo hispano. La noche del 23 de diciembre en el zócalo, en la plaza principal[2] de Oaxaca, México, hay mesas que presentan los rábanos con formas fantásticas. Los oaxaqueños y los visitantes caminan por la plaza para ver o comprar estas creaciones maravillosas.

Pre-AP® Integration: Definiciones de la creatividad ¿Conoces comunidades o regiones de los Estados Unidos famosas por sus artesanías[4] o productos?

🌐 **Mapa global interactivo** Explora la geografía de Oaxaca, México y describe lo que ves.

[1] radishes [2] town square [3] crafts

Rábanos esculpidos *(sculpted)*, Oaxaca, México

Capítulo 4B • doscientos cinco **205**

Enrich Your Teaching

Culture Note

A wide range of handicrafts is produced in Oaxaca, including black pottery, glass pottery, weavings, and brightly colored woodcarvings of small animals (**alebrijes**). Artisans bring their wares to the **zócalos** to sell. Artisans pass their knowledge from one generation to another.

21st Century Skills

Collaboration Have students work in small groups, divided into teams. Each team has to come up with five words in English borrowed from Spanish. Taking turns, a volunteer will go over to the opposite team, look at one of the words in their list, and mime it for his or her other team members to guess. Set a time limit for guessing, and assist students by verifying their loanword choices.

EXPLORACIÓN DEL LENGUAJE ‹

Standards: 4.1

Suggestions: Review *Try it out!* with students. For further practice, have them work with a partner to scan the glossary for additional borrowed words.

12

Standards: 1.1, 1.3

Suggestions: Encourage students to be as detailed as possible in their answers.

Answers will vary.

Extension: Have students create one additional question to ask their classmates. Then, as a class, ask volunteers to read their questions and select students to answer them.

CULTURA ‹

Standards: 2.1, 2.2, 4.2

Resources: Mapa global interactivo

Suggestions: Locate Oaxaca on the map. Ask students if they have seen foods carved into shapes. When is this done, and why? How does this practice in the United States differ from what is done with the *rábanos* in Oaxaca?

🌐 **Technology: Mapa global interactivo**, Actividad 1 Explore the geography of Oaxaca, México.

Additional Resources

📶 **Technology: Online Resources**
- Instant Check
- Guided, Core, Video, Audio
- *Para hispanohablantes*
- Teacher's Resource Materials: Audio Script
- Technology: Audio Cap. 4B
- Communication Activities: Audio Act. 6

Assessment

Pueba 4B-2 with Remediation (online only)
Quiz: Vocabulary Production
- Prueba 4B-2

Gramática

Standards: 4.1

Resources: Teacher's Resource Materials: Video Script; Technology: Video Cap. 4B

Suggestions: Emphasize that the second verb is always in the infinitive and that only the forms of *ir* change. Use the *GramActiva* Video to introduce the grammar or to reinforce your own presentation.

🔲 Technology: Interactive Whiteboard

Grammar Activities 4B Use the whiteboard activities in your Teacher Resources as you progress through the grammar practice with your class.

13

Standards: 1.2, 1.3

Resources: Teacher's Resource Materials: Audio Script; Technology: Audio Cap. 4B

Suggestions: Use the audio or read the script aloud. Have students first listen to the messages without taking notes.

🔊 Technology: Audio Script and Answers:

¡Hola! Soy Rosario. ¿Qué pasa? Tomás y yo vamos a patinar esta tarde. ¿Te gustaría ir con nosotros? Vamos a estar en el parque a las cuatro. Hasta luego. *(Rosario: 1. al parque; 2. patinar; 3. a las cuatro)*

¡Oye! ¿Cómo estás? Soy Pablo. ¿Puedes ir al gimnasio conmigo? No tengo que trabajar hoy. Muchos estudiantes van a jugar al vóleibol a las siete. Háblame por teléfono si puedes ir. *(Pablo: 1. al gimnasio; 2. jugar al vóleibol; 3. a las siete)*

14

Standards: 1.3

Recycle: Telling time

Answers:
1. Angélica va a ir de compras a las tres y media de la tarde.
2. Yo voy a nadar a las cuatro de la tarde.
3. Esteban y un amigo van a jugar al fútbol a las diez de la mañana.
4. Angélica y el Sr. Ríos van a ir de pesca a las siete de la mañana.
5. Los señores Ríos van a ir de compras (al centro comercial) a las siete y media de la noche.
6. Angélica, Esteban y yo vamos a ir al cine a las ocho de la noche.

206

Gramática

OBJECTIVES
▶ Listen to phone messages about invitations
▶ Write about and discuss plans
▶ Read an ad and extend an invitation by phone

Ir + *a* + infinitive

Just as you use "going" + an infinitive in English to say what you are going to do, in Spanish you use a form of the verb *ir* + *a* + **an infinitive** to express the same thing:

Voy a jugar al tenis hoy.
I'm going to play tennis today.

¿Tú **vas a jugar** al golf esta tarde?
Are you going to play golf this afternoon?

Mis amigas **van a ir** de cámping mañana.
My friends are going camping tomorrow.

Javier: **¿Van a jugar** conmigo, o no?
Ana: Sí, **vamos a jugar** contigo.

Más recursos ONLINE
▶ *GramActiva* video
▶ **Tutorials:** Future with *ir* + *a* + infinitive, *Vamos a* + infinitive
🔊 *Canción de hip hop:* ¿Qué vas a hacer?
✏️ *GramActiva* Activity

13

Escucha y escribe

🔊 ESCUCHAR, ESCRIBIR Rosario and Pablo have left messages on your answering machine telling you what they are going to do and inviting you to join them. On a sheet of paper, write their names and, under each one, the numbers 1–3. As you listen to each message, write down information to answer these three questions:

1. ¿Adónde quiere ir?   2. ¿Qué va a hacer?   3. ¿A qué hora va a ir?

14

Este fin de semana vamos a . . .

✏️ ESCRIBIR, HABLAR ¿Qué va a hacer la familia Ríos este fin de semana?

Modelo
Estela / 📖 / 8:00 🌙
Estela va a estudiar a las ocho de la noche.

1. Angélica / 🛍️ / 3:30 ☀️
2. Yo / 🏊 / 4:00 ☀️
3. Esteban y un amigo / ⚽ / 10:00 ☀️
4. Angélica y el Sr. Ríos / 🎣 / 7:00 ☀️
5. Los señores Ríos / 🏬 / 7:30 🌙
6. Angélica, Esteban y yo / 🎬 / 8:00 🌙

Differentiated Instruction

Challenge/Pre-AP®

Have students create a mini-journal in which they tell what they are going to do each day of the week after school. Have them include the phrases **de la mañana, de la tarde,** and **de la noche.** Suggest that they include details such as with whom they will do the activities, where they will go, and why they plan to do them.

Students with Learning Difficulties

You may want to provide a chart similar to the one in *Actividad* 15 to help students organize information for *Actividad* 13. Across the top, use the headings *Rosario* and *Pablo*. Down the side use the headings **¿Adónde?, ¿Qué?,** and **¿A qué hora?**

15 ¿Qué vas a hacer?

🎤 ESCRIBIR, HABLAR EN PAREJA

1 Make a chart like this one to describe five things you're going to do, when you're going to do them, and with whom. Use the following words to say when you're going to do these things: *esta tarde, esta noche, mañana, el jueves, el fin de semana.*

Modelo

¿Qué?	¿Cuándo?	¿Con quién?
tocar la guitarra	esta tarde	mis amigos

2 Ask your partner what his or her plans are and offer alternative activities. Develop a plan to spend time that you agree on.

▶ **Videomodelo**

A —¿Qué vas a hacer esta tarde?
B —Esta tarde mis amigos y yo vamos a tocar la guitarra.

▲ Mañana voy a tocar la guitarra.

16 El teléfono celular

📝 LEER, ESCRIBIR, HABLAR   Lee el anuncio para el teléfono celular y contesta las preguntas.

1. ¿Por qué es bueno tener un teléfono celular?
2. ¿Te gusta hablar por teléfono celular? ¿Con quién?
3. ¿Crees que es bueno o malo usar un teléfono celular en un restaurante? ¿Por qué?

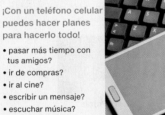

¿Te gustaría...   **¡Por supuesto!**

¡Con un teléfono celular puedes hacer planes para hacerlo todo!

• pasar más tiempo con tus amigos?
• ir de compras?
• ir al cine?
• escribir un mensaje?
• escuchar música?
• jugar a juegos?

17 ¿Quieres ir conmigo?

📝 ESCRIBIR EN PAREJA   Send your partner a text message and invite him or her to do something with you. Your partner can't go and should tell you why. Offer an alternative plan.

Modelo

A —Hola, Sara. Soy Rosa. ¿Quieres **jugar al tenis** conmigo **esta tarde**?
B —Lo siento, hoy no puedo. Voy a **estudiar para la clase de inglés.**
A —¡Ay! ¡Qué pena!

Capítulo 4B • doscientos siete **207**

15

Standards: 1.1, 1.3

Suggestions: Brainstorm a few activities to aid student recall.
Answers will vary.

16

Standards: 1.1, 1.2, 1.3

Suggestions: Form groups of students with varying abilities to interpret the ad. Discuss the questions as a class.

Answers:
1. ¡Con un teléfono celular puedes hacer planes para hacerlo todo!
2. Answers will vary.
3. Answers will vary.

17

Standards: 1.1

Suggestions: You may want students to prepare two conversations, so that they get a chance both to extend and decline an invitation. Each pair can choose one conversation to present aloud to the class. Encourage them to present it without a script.
Answers will vary.

Additional Resources

📶 **Technology: Online Resources**
• Instant Check
• Guided, Core, Video, Audio
• *Para hispanohablantes*
• Teacher's Resource Materials: Audio Script
• Technology: Audio Cap. 3A
• Communication Activities: Audio Act. 7
Print
• Guided WB pp. 143–144
• Core WB pp. 80–81

Assessment

Prueba 4B-3 with Remediation (online only)
Quiz: *Ir + a* + infinitive
• Prueba 4B-3

Enrich Your Teaching

Teacher-to-Teacher

Have small groups choose a Latin American country to research. They should find out about the foods, music, and customs associated with a particular *fiesta* in that country, then write an invitation to the *fiesta*. They should include what time, where, and what country they will be representing. You might want to write a model invitation, either on the board or as a handout. If possible, plan a day for your *fiestas,* complete with *comida, música, bailes ¡y más!*

Gramática

Resources: Teacher's Resource Materials: Video Script; Technology: Video Cap. 4B

Suggestions: Highlight the difference between a stem-changing verb, such as **jugar,** and a regular **-ar** verb, such as **hablar,** by using a different color chalk or pen for the stem-changes. Play the *GramActiva* Video as an introduction or to reinforce your own presentation of the verb **jugar.**

📱 Technology: Interactive Whiteboard

Grammar Activities 4B Use the whiteboard activities in your Teacher Resources as you progress through the grammar practice with your class.

18

Suggestions: Ask students if they recognize any of the athletes in the pictures. Point out the *También se dice...* to give students additional vocabulary.

Answers:
1. Sergio García juega al golf.
2. Carla Cortijo juega al básquetbol.
3. Pau Gasol juega al básquetbol.
4. David Villa juega al fútbol.
5. Hanley Ramírez juega al béisbol.
6. Garbiñe Muguruza juega al tenis.
7. Answers will vary.

Common Errors: With stem-changing verbs, students may overgeneralize and change all forms.

Extension: For homework, have students choose five sports. For each sport, ask them to write a sentence about one or more athletes who play it.

Project-Based Learning

Students can perform Step 5 at this point. Be sure they understand your corrections and suggestions. (For more information, see p. 170-b.)

Gramática

The verb *jugar*

Use the verb *jugar* to talk about playing a sport or a game. Even though *jugar* uses the same endings as the other *-ar* verbs, it has a different stem in some forms. For those forms, the *-u-* becomes *-ue-*. This kind of verb is called a "stem-changing verb." Here are the present-tense forms:

(yo)	**juego**	(nosotros) (nosotras)	**jugamos**
(tú)	**juegas**	(vosotros) (vosotras)	**jugáis**
Ud. (él) (ella)	**juega**	Uds. (ellos) (ellas)	**juegan**

Nota
Many Spanish speakers always use *jugar* a and the name of the sport or game:
• ¿Juegas al vóleibol?
Others do not use the a:
• ¿Juegas vóleibol?

Más recursos ONLINE
▶ *GramActiva* video
▶ Animated Verbs
✎ *GramActiva* Activity

18

¿A qué juegan?

✎ ESCRIBIR Escribe frases para decir qué deportes practican estas personas.

Modelo
Albert Pujols juega al béisbol.

Albert Pujols

También se dice . . .
el básquetbol = el baloncesto (muchos países)
el fútbol = el balompié (muchos países)
el vóleibol = el balonvolea (España)

1 Sergio García

2 Carla Cortijo

3 Pau Gasol

4 David Villa

5 Hanley Ramírez

6 Garbiñe Muguruza

7 Y tus amigos y tú, ¿a qué juegan Uds.?

208 doscientos ocho • Tema 4 • Los pasatiempos

Differentiated Instruction

Heritage Speakers

Have students prepare an oral presentation on their favorite sport or athlete. Students presenting a sport not covered in this chapter should provide a poster to support their presentation.

Students with Learning Difficulties

The advertisement in *Actividad* 20 might intimidate students because of all the unknown vocabulary. Help them review the ad for vocabulary they already know. Then read the ad with them, emphasizing key words and phrases that will help students understand the meaning.

19 Juego

DIBUJAR, ESCRIBIR, HABLAR EN GRUPO, GRAMACTIVA

1 On each of two index cards, draw a picture that represents a sport or game and write *muy bien, bien,* or *mal* to show how well you play that sport or game. Don't let your classmates see your cards.

2 Get together with five other students. Put all the cards face down in the center of your group. Choose a card and try to identify who drew it by asking the others how well they play what is pictured. Keep track of what you learn about your classmates.

Videomodelo

A —*Enrique, ¿juegas bien al tenis?*
B —*No, juego muy mal al tenis.*

3 Write six sentences about the sports and games the students in your group play.

Modelo
Óscar y Nacho juegan muy bien al fútbol. Teresa y yo jugamos bien al golf.

20 La ciudad deportiva

LEER, ESCRIBIR, HABLAR   Lee sobre el sueño *(dream)* de Iván Zamorano y contesta las preguntas.

1. ¿Cuál es el sueño de Iván Zamorano?

2. ¿Qué deportes juegan en la Ciudad Deportiva de Iván?

3. ¿Qué día empieza *(begins)* la inscripción para las escuelas? ¿A qué hora?

4. ¿A qué hora empiezan las actividades?

5. ¿Te gustaría ir a la Ciudad Deportiva de Iván Zamorano? ¿Por qué?

¹dream ²city ³children ⁴better ⁵place ⁶registration

Mi sueño¹

Quiero una ciudad² dedicada al deporte, a la familia y los niños.³ Quiero servicios de calidad internacional, con profesores de excelencia. En mi sueño, los niños y jóvenes juegan y practican deportes para ser mejores.⁴ Este sueño ya es realidad y quiero compartirlo contigo. Es el lugar⁵ para hacer deporte en familia.

Escuelas de Fútbol, Tenis, Hockey

Inicio de inscripción⁶: 23 de marzo, a las 8 horas
Inicio de actividades: 1 de abril, a las 14 horas

Avenida Pedro Hurtado 2650, Las Condes, Santiago, Chile
Teléfono: 212 2711

Capítulo 4B • doscientos nueve **209**

Enrich Your Teaching

Culture Note

Baseball was first introduced to Cuba over 100 years ago and its popularity spread to other Spanish-speaking countries of the Caribbean. The Dominican Republic has produced many baseball superstars. The government finances stadiums and local fields and pays the coaches' salaries.

21st Century Skills

Communication Have students create a proposal for their dream sports complex. They should describe the facilities available, the location of the complex, and which special training and activities are offered. Their complex can be devoted to one single sport or to several, to more traditional sports (like baseball), or less traditional ones (like underwater hockey).

19

Standards: 1.1, 1.3

Suggestions: Note the placement of **bien** and **muy mal.** To keep track of who plays what, have students take notes as each person speaks: **Ana: tenis/bien.** For part 3, encourage students to vary the subjects, as in the model, talking about what they play (**yo**), what another classmate plays (**él/ ella**), what other students play (**ellas/ellos**), and what they and others play (**nosotros**).

Answers will vary.

20

Standards: 1.2, 1.3, 3.2

Suggestions: Have students scan the ad for cognates. Read the ad aloud, and then ask a volunteer to reread it.

Answers:

1. Quiere una ciudad dedicada al deporte, a la familia y a los niños. Quiere servicios de calidad internacional, con profesores de excelencia.
2. fútbol, tenis y hockey
3. el 23 de marzo, a las ocho
4. a las dos de la tarde
5. Answers will vary.

Pre-AP® Integration

- **Learning Objective:** Interpretive: Print
- **Activity 20:** This activity helps students practice key interpretive skills. Remind students to practice strategies for effectively synthesizing information from authentic sources.

Additional Resources

📶 **Technology: Online Resources**
- Instant Check
- Guided, Core, Video, Audio
- *Para hispanohablantes*
- Teacher's Resource Materials: Audio Script
- Teachnology: Audio Cap. 4B
- Communication Activities: Audio Act. 8-9

Print
- Guided WB pp. 145–146
- Core WB p. 82

Assessment

Prueba 4B-4 with Remediation (online only)
Quiz: The verb *jugar*
- Prueba 4B-4

Pronunciación

Standards: 4.1

Resources: Teacher's Resource Materials: Audio Script; Technology: Audio Cap. 4B

Suggestions: Read the *Pronunciación* with students or use the audio. Model the two sounds of the letter *d*: exaggerating the *d* sound in **doce** and the *th* sound in **cansado.** Then have the class repeat. If possible, record the tongue twister as students say it. See if students can hear the difference between the two sounds.

El español en el mundo del trabajo

Standards: 5.1

Suggestions: Have students determine the meaning of the quotation in the reading and use it as a model to say how they feel about volunteer work. To help students answer the questions, brainstorm different volunteer opportunities on the board.

Answers will vary.

Extension: If possible, invite a health care worker to your class to talk about ways in which knowledge of Spanish is helpful in his or her job.

Active Classroom

Have students create a brochure for a favorite vacation spot. They should include artwork and text that describes the kinds of activities available for guests. You may wish to provide a model, or refer them to the brochure on p. 211.

Pronunciación · The vowels *a, e,* and *i*

In Spanish, the pronunciation of the letter *d* is determined by its location in a word. When d is at the beginning of a word, or when it comes after *l* or *n*, it sounds similar to the *d* in "dog." Listen, then say these words:

diccionario	doce	donde
domingo	desayuno	día
deportes	calendario	bandera

When *d* comes between vowels and after any consonant except *l* or *n*, it sounds similar to the *th* of "the." Listen, then say these words:

cansado	ocupado	puedes
idea	sábado	partido
tarde	ensalada	atrevido

Try it out! Here is a tongue twister to give you practice in pronouncing the *d*, but also to give you something to think about!

> **Porque puedo, puedes,**
> **porque puedes, puedo;**
> **Pero si no puedes,**
> **yo tampoco puedo.**

El español en el mundo del trabajo

There are many opportunities to use Spanish in the healthcare field—in hospitals, emergency rooms, and neighborhood clinics. This young woman volunteers in a California hospital. Since many of the patients come from Spanish-speaking homes, she is able to speak with them and their families in Spanish. *"Para mí, trabajar como voluntaria es una de mis actividades favoritas. Creo que mi trabajo es importante."*

• What opportunities are there in your community to do volunteer work where speaking Spanish is helpful?

210 doscientos diez • Tema 4 • Los pasatiempos

Differentiated Instruction

Heritage Speakers

Have students create a poster for a community organization that is looking for volunteers who speak Spanish.

Special Needs

Students may have difficulty hearing the difference between the two sounds of the letter *d* if they are looking at the words. Have them close their eyes as they listen. Some may have particular difficulty with the *th* sound. Consider writing a small *th* over the letter *d* in the relevant words on the board to help students get used to the sound.

Go **Online** to practice
PEARSON
realize™
AUDIO WRITING SPEAK/RECORD MAPA GLOBAL
PearsonSchool.com/Autentico

21

¡Vamos de cámping!

LEER, ESCRIBIR Tourism is an important industry in Spain. Many tourists prefer to go camping rather than stay in hotels. Read the following brochure about a campground and then answer the questions.

Conexiones ◂ Las matemáticas

1. ¿Qué distancia en millas¹ hay entre² Valencia y el Cámping Las Palmas?

2. ¿Qué distancia hay entre Alicante y el Cámping Las Palmas?

Para convertir kilómetros en millas, es necesario dividir el número de kilómetros por 1.6.

¹miles ²between

Cámping Las Palmas

Miramar
Teléfono: 962 41 42 73   Fax: 962 01 55 05

70 kilómetros al sur de Valencia
110 kilómetros al norte de Alicante

• Un cámping ideal
• Muchas actividades para todos
• Una buena opción para sus vacaciones

Ubicado³ junto a⁴ una bella playa. Ideal para toda la familia. Un sitio excelente para nadar.

³Located ⁴next to

🌐 **Mapa global interactivo** Compara las áreas costeras de España.

22

Y tú, ¿qué dices?

ESCRIBIR Write descriptions of simple situations. Use the questions as a guide.

1. ¿Con quién te gustaría ir a una fiesta? ¿Por qué?
2. ¿Qué prefieres, ir de pesca o ir a un baile?
3. ¿Qué vas a hacer mañana a las ocho de la noche?
4. ¿Qué vas a hacer este fin de semana?
5. ¿Te gustaría ver un partido de fútbol o ir a un concierto?

> **Para decir más . . .**
> 200 = doscientos

Capítulo 4B • doscientos once **211**

21

Standards: 1.2, 3.1

Resources: Mapa global interactivo

Suggestions: Before beginning, have students talk about the title and the photograph. Ask them to compare what they see to vacations and camping trips that they have been on or know about. Remind students that they will not know every word. Have them identify some cognates, such as *palmas* and *ideal.*

Answers:

1. Entre Valencia y el Camping Las Palmas hay 53.13 millas.
2. Entre Alicante y el Camping Las Palmas hay 68.75 millas.

🌐 **Technology: Mapa global interactivo**, Actividad 2 Compare the coastal areas of Spain

22

Standards: 1.1, 1.3

Suggestions: After students have written their answers, have them work with a partner to ask and answer the questions.

Answers will vary.

Extension: Have students create additional open-ended questions based on those in *Actividad* 22. For example, they can change **ir a una fiesta** to **jugar al tenis.** Encourage them to create original questions as well.

Project-Based Learning

Students can perform Step 6 at this point. Record their presentations for inclusion in their portfolios. (For more information, see p. 170-b.)

Teacher-to-Teacher

e-amigos: Have students write their *e-amigos* to ask three questions about leisure activities. Have them print out or e-mail you their questions and responses.

Enrich Your Teaching

Culture Note

Because Spain has a variety of landscapes, there are many different kinds of sporting activities available—from fishing, swimming, and parasailing to hiking, mountain climbing, cave exploring, and canoeing. In addition to all the activities, tourists enjoy the wonderful food, museums, architecture, and climate.

Teacher-to-Teacher

Choose a question from *Y tú, ¿qué dices?,* or create a similar one to ask students as they prepare to start class. If you present them with a question upon entering, communication can begin immediately.

Lectura

Standards: 1.2, 1.3, 5.2, 4.1

Suggestions

Pre-reading: Direct attention to the *Strategy*. Have students skim the two articles and write a list of cognates. Have them share their lists with the class and write them on the board. Encourage students to use other context clues, such as dates and numbers.

Reading: Have students read the article about Sergio García first. Ask them to make a list of words they do not understand. Then have them read the piece about Paola Espinosa. Did they find similar words, or were there additional unfamiliar words?

Post-reading: Ask students what they learned about Sergio García. What did they learn about Paola Espinosa? Discuss how these two athletes are alike. Then have students think about what makes each one unique.

Starter Activity

Have students identify these cognates in English:
objetivo profesional evidente universidad

(**Answers**: objective, professional, evident, university)

Pre-AP® Integration

- **Learning Objective:** Presentational Writing
- **Activity:** Have students write a brief persuasive paragraph describing their own favorite athlete. Remind them to supply supporting details that encourage their readers to view the athlete positively.
- **Pre-AP® Resource Materials:** Comprehensive guide to Pre-AP® writing development

Lectura

OBJECTIVES
▶ Read about and compare the lives of two famous athletes
▶ Use cognates to understand new words
▶ Learn more about an Hispanic athlete and role model

Strategy
Cognates Use the cognates in the text to help you infer the meaning of new words and understand key details about the athletes.

Sergio y Paola:
Dos deportistas dotados[1]

Lee dos artículos de una revista deportiva. Vas a conocer a[2] Sergio García y a Paola Espinosa, dos atletas famosos.

Sergio García es uno de los golfistas profesionales más populares del mundo.

Sergio juega para el Club de Campo del Mediterráneo en Borriol, Castellón, donde su padre Víctor es golfista profesional. Juega al golf desde la edad[3] de tres años y a los 12 años es campeón[4] del Club de Campo. Es el golfista más joven en competir en el campeonato PGA desde 1921 y gana[5] el segundo lugar.[6] Tiene el nombre "El niño." A los 15 años, juega en un torneo del circuito europeo de profesionales. Y a la edad de 17 años gana su primer torneo de profesionales.

Hoy Sergio García es uno de los 20 mejores golfistas del mundo.

Sergio García

Nombre: Sergio García

Fecha de nacimiento: 9/1/80

Lugar de nacimiento: Borriol, Castellón (España)

Club: Club de Campo del Mediterráneo

Su objetivo: Ser el mejor del mundo

Profesional: Desde abril del 99

Aficiones[7]: Real Madrid, tenis, fútbol, videojuego, carros rápidos

[1]gifted [2]You will meet [3]age [4]champion
[5]he wins [6]second place [7]Interests

Differentiated Instruction

Challenge

Have students choose an athlete in the school to interview. Suggest that they find out information similar to what they have read about Sergio and Paola. Tell them that they can conduct the interview in English, if the athlete is not a Spanish-speaking student, but that they should write a summary in Spanish to share with the class.

Heritage Speakers

Ask students to discuss athletes they are familiar with from a variety of sports. As they are talking, guide their discussion by asking: How old is this person? Where was he or she born? What are some of his or her biggest accomplishments or statistics? Do you think that he or she is a good role model? Why or why not?

Nombre: Paola Milagros Espinosa Sánchez

Fecha de nacimiento: 31/7/86

Su objetivo: Ser la clavadista[8] número uno del mundo

Lugar de nacimiento: La Paz, Baja California (México)

Aficiones: Nadar, practicar gimnasia, viajar, pasar tiempo con su familia

Paola Milagros Espinosa Sánchez

Paola Espinosa es la mejor[9] clavadista de saltos[10] en plataforma y en saltos sincronizados de México. Tiene el nombre de "la princesa mexicana del clavado" y es una heroína nacional.

De niña, le gusta nadar y hacer gimnasia. Compite[11] como clavadista desde la edad de 10 años. A los 18 años, participa en sus primeros Juegos Olímpicos. ¡Y a los 22 años gana la medalla de bronce en los Juegos Olímpicos de Beijing!

Paola dice que es necesario practicar todos los días. En Londres gana de nuevo una medalla olímpica, esta vez[12] de plata.

[8]diver [9]best [10]dives [11]competes [12]this time

¿Comprendes?

1. Copy this Venn diagram. Identify and list at least eight key details about Sergio and Paola in your diagram. Include information about Sergio in the left oval, Paola in the right oval, and any fact that applies to both in the middle oval.

   Sergio *Los dos* *Paola*

2. Which cognates helped you to infer the meaning of difficult sentences?

CULTURA ◄ Estados Unidos

Una jugadora profesional Rebecca Lobo es una ex jugadora profesional de básquetbol. Ganó[1] una medalla de oro en las Olimpiadas de 1996. Es una de las primeras jugadoras del WNBA. Rebecca escribió[2] un libro, *The Home Team*, sobre la lucha[3] contra el cáncer. Rebecca ayuda[4] a los estudiantes con pocos recursos[5] que quieren estudiar medicina. Ahora, Rebecca es comentarista y trabaja para el canal ESPN.

- Rebecca Lobo es una oradora motivacional[6]. ¿Qué mensaje crees que comunica a su público?

[1]won [2]wrote [3]struggle [4]helps [5]resources [6]motivational speaker

Capítulo 4B • doscientos trece 213

¿Comprendes?

Suggestions: Create and project a blank Venn diagram. Remind students to look at both the profiles and the paragraphs to find facts about the two athletes. When reviewing answers, ask students questions such as: *¿Quién juega en el Club de Campo del Mediterráneo?*

Answers: will vary but may include:

Sergio García:
from Spain
began playing golf when three years old
his father is a golfer
Los dos:
they both want to be the best
they both achieved success young
Paola Espinosa:
from Mexico
is called the "princess of the diving board"
likes to travel

CULTURA ◄

Suggestions: After reading the text, discuss the question with students. Encourage them to think about how Rebecca Lobo's struggles and accomplishments may affect her message. Ask students to name other celebrities or athletes who have overcome struggles. How do they compare with Rebecca Lobo?

Answers will vary.

Teacher-to-Teacher

Have students write a short autobiographical "snapshot." They can follow the format used in the boxes to the right of the photos. Encourage them to use vocabulary from this chapter.

For Further Reading

Student Resource: *Para hispanohablantes* Lectura 2

Additional Resources

Technology: Online Resources
- Guided, Writing, Reading
- Cultural Reading Activity
- *Para hispanohablantes*

Print
- Guided WB p. 147
- Literacy Skills WB

Enrich Your Teaching

Culture Note

In the 1950s, the "*Ticas*" of Costa Rica formed the first women's soccer team in Latin America. However, it wasn't until 1982 that the Federation of International Football Associates decided to make women's soccer official. By 1985, only one South American country had a team—Brazil. Today almost all South American countries have women's soccer teams. Despite a long struggle for acceptance, women's professional sports teams are gaining popularity.

Perspectivas del mundo hispano

Standards: 2.1, 4.2

Suggestions: Ask students what they do in their spare time. Tell them that in many Spanish-speaking countries, spare time is not necessarily free time. Many students use it to learn a foreign language or practice a sport in an athletic club. Have students read the text and point out similarities and differences between their experience and that of the students described. Direct attention to the photos. Of course many students in the United States also participate in these and similar activities. Mention that in general, high-school students in Spanish-speaking countries do not have jobs.

Have students think about how a schedule like the one described would affect their lives. What would change? Would they have to stop doing something? Ask if this schedule sounds enjoyable. Remember that many students today hold jobs out of necessity, and that many have very full schedules, much like the one described here.

Direct attention to the *Investigar* and *Comparación cultural* sections and have students discuss the questions.

Answers will vary.

Teacher-to-Teacher

Careers: *Tema* 4 has focused on leisure activities. Have students work in small groups to talk about a career in the field of recreation. Have them write a list of activities that they might implement as director of an after-school recreation center for middle school students. Ask groups to share their lists.

Online Cultural Reading

After doing the online activity, ask students to identify and list three cultural practices that differ from their own.

Additional Resources

📡 **Technology: Online Resources**
  • Cultural Reading Activity
  • *Para hispanohablantes*

Perspectivas del mundo hispano

¿Qué haces en tu tiempo libre?

In many Spanish-speaking countries, extracurricular activities traditionally play a much smaller role in school life than in the United States. Students usually participate in activities such as music and athletics at clubs and institutions outside of school.

Although some schools have teams, many students who are interested in sports attend clubs such as el Club Deportivo General San Martín. At these clubs teens practice and compete on teams. They also participate in individual sports such as tennis. The competition between clubs is sometimes more intense than the competition between schools.

Students with artistic talents often go to a private institute to take music, dance, or art lessons. They might attend el Instituto de Música Clásica or el Instituto de Danza Julio Bocca. Many students spend their time outside of classes studying a foreign language. They might learn English at la Cultura Inglesa or French at la Alianza Francesa.

In general, students do not hold jobs. They spend their time studying, being with family and friends, and participating in different activities.

¿Te gusta jugar al ajedrez?

Trabajando después de las clases

Online Cultural Reading

Go to Auténtico ONLINE to read and understand how a soccer team is organized.

Investigar What do you like to do in your free time? Do you play sports, or learn how to play an instrument? What about your friends? Survey your friends to answer these questions, then complete the statements explaining what you and your friends like to do after school.

Modelo
En mi tiempo libre, me gusta *ir a ver una película.*

1. En mi tiempo libre, me gusta _____.
2. Después de las clases voy a _____.
3. A mis amigos les gusta _____ en su tiempo libre.

Comparación cultural How do the practices in your community compare with what you have learned about young people's after-school activities in Spanish-speaking countries?

214 doscientos catorce • Tema 4 • Los pasatiempos

Differentiated Instruction

Challenge

Have students research schools in the United States where students can go if they have artistic talents; for example, the Juilliard School, music conservatories, etc. Have them find out more about the schools listed in the text. Ask them to compare the schools and make a short presentation to the class.

Special Needs

Students may participate in special activities or groups. If they wish, invite them to share their experiences with the class.

Presentación escrita

OBJECTIVES
▸ Write an invitation to a special event
▸ Organize information by using an invitation format

Go **Online** to practice

PEARSON realize™

PearsonSchool.com/Autentico

WRITING

Una invitación

Task Write an email to invite a friend to go to a special event with you.

1 Prewrite Think of an event to invite a friend to, such as a concert, game, or party. Write an invitation that includes information about the situation.

- the name of the event
- the day, time, and location
- who is going

2 Draft Use the information from Step 1 to write a first draft. Begin your invitation with *¡Hola . . . !* and close with *Tu amigo(a)* and your name.

3 Revise Check your note for spelling and grammar, then share with a partner. Your partner should check the following:

- Did you give all the necessary information?
- Is there anything to add or change?
- Are there any errors?

4 Publish Write a final copy of your invitation. You might give it to your friend or include it in your portfolio.

5 Evaluation The following rubric will be used to grade your invitation.

Strategy

Organizing information Thinking about the correct format and necessary information beforehand will help you create a better invitation.

Rubric	Score 1	Score 3	Score 5
Amount of information	You give very few or no details or examples about locations and activities.	You give only a few details or examples about locations and activities.	You consistently give many details and examples about locations, times, and activities.
Use of vocabulary expressions	You have very little variation of vocabulary usage with frequent incorrect usage.	You have limited usage of vocabulary; some usage errors.	You have extended use of a variety of vocabulary; few usage errors.
Accuracy of sentence structures	You have at least three sentences; many grammar errors.	You have at least three sentences; some grammar errors.	You have at least three sentences; very few grammar errors.

Capítulo 4B • doscientos quince **215**

Presentación escrita

Standards: 1.3

Suggestions: Review the assignment, the 5-step approach, and the rubric with the class. Make an invitation of your own as a model for students to use. Refer them to the *Strategy*, and have them write the information to be included in their invitations before beginning. You may wish to have them give you rough drafts.

In Spanish, review the 5-Ws: *Who, What, Where, When, Why,* and have volunteers suggest how these could be included in an invitation.

Encourage students to make their invitations appealing with artwork or calligraphy.

Pre-AP® Integration

Pre-AP® Resource Materials: Comprehensive guide to Pre-AP® writing skill development

Teacher-to-Teacher

Have students work in groups to create a singing telegram inviting a special friend to an event. The class can evaluate the telegrams in categories, such as most original, best singing, most humorous.

Digital Portfolio

Attach a copy of the grading rubric to the final copy of the invitation, and include both in students' portfolios.

Additional Resources

Technology: Online Resources
- Guided Presentation
- *Para hispanohablantes*

Assessment

Presentación escrita
- **Assessment Program:** Rubrics

Go over the descriptions of the different levels of performance. After assessing students, help individuals understand how their performance could be improved. (See Teacher's Resource Materials for suggestions on using rubrics in assessment.)

Enrich Your Teaching

21st Century Skills

Communication Have students review the proposed activities and decide as a group which one would be most appropriate to share with a real or imaginary exchange student from a Spanish-speaking country. Have them adjust the invitation for that person, including why it would be an interesting cultural event. Each person in the group should have a specific assignment in creating the new invitation.

Auténtico

Standards: 1.2

Resources: *Authentic Resources Wkbk*, Cap. 4B

Authentic Resources: Cap 4B Videoscript

AP Theme: *La vida contemporánea: El entretenimiento y la diversión*

Before You Watch

Discuss the *Strategy* with students. Have them look at chapter vocabulary and identify cognates that relate to the video and to the chapter theme. Have them look at the image, and describe the image in Spanish, identifying which of the words that they used are cognates. Then review the key vocabulary with the class. Again, have students comment on any new cognates that are useful to them in describing the theme and the image. Ask what they can anticipate about the video with these key words.

Technology: Watch the Video

Before starting the video, direct students' attention to the *Mientras ves* activity. Review with students the English equivalents for each word or phrase in the list.

Play the video once completely through, without pausing, and tell students to listen for the cognates they recognize in the video. Remind students that they will not understand every word, but that they should listen and watch for overall understanding. Replay the video, stopping as necessary for students to complete the listening activity and to check comprehension. Ask students what other cognates they noticed while viewing and how those words helped them to understand details of the video. Show the video a final time without pausing.

Auténtico

Partnered with **IDB**

Deporte, cultura e innovación

Before You Watch

Use the Strategy: Cognates

As you watch the video, *Deporte, cultura e innovación* listen and watch for cognates to help you understand key words and key details. Cognates are words that look like English and share a meaning. What words do you see or hear that are similar to English words?

Read this Key Vocabulary

éxito = success	**habilidades** = abilities
fomentan = encourages	**felicidad** = happiness
desarrollo = develop	**barreras** = barriers

▶ Watch the Video

What do teens need to be successful? What type of programs or opportunities should be provided to all teens?

Go to **PearsonSchool.com/Autentico** and watch the video *Deporte, cultura, e innovación* to see what a program in Uruguay believes that teens need.

Complete the Activities

Mientras ves As you watch the video, listen and watch for the cognates that are used, and use them to identify the key details of the video. Read the cognates below and indicate when you hear them. List any other cognates you hear.

honestidad
respeto
cooperación
lenguaje es universal
creativos y creadores

Differentiated Instruction

Challenge

Have students research to create an infographic of a popular sports team from a Spanish-speaking country, using vocabulary words from this and previous chapters to describe the sport, the team, and the players. Students can present their infographics to the class.

Heritage Speakers

Ask students to make a list of unfamiliar words from the resource, and use a dictionary to look up their meanings. Then have students write a few sentences on the chapter theme using these new words. Have students read their writing out loud to further practice pronunciation and usage.

Complete the Activities

Mientras ves

Standards: 1.2

Suggestions: Students may need to be reminded of the definition of cognates. Most cognates will appear as a list on screen after the activity is described in the video.

Answers:

honestidad
respeto
cooperación
lenguaje es universal
creativos y creadores
inclusión
diversidad
pasión

Después de ver

Standards: 1.2

Suggestions: Students may need to review the conjugation of –ar and –er verbs, as well as interrogative words in order to answer the question.

Answers:

1. Los adolescentes necesitan el deporte y la cultura.
2. Los adolescentes aprenden cooperación
3. Answers may vary.

For more Authentic resources: Assign the *Authentic Resources Workbook* activities for homework, so that students can play the video on their own and complete the workbook activities at their own pace.

Pre-AP® Integration

Standards: 1.2, 1.3

Resources: *Authentic Resources Workbook,* Cap. 4B; Authentic Resources: Cap 4B; Videoscript

Suggestions: Before completing the Pre-AP® activity, have students go to the workbook and complete the worksheets for these two additional resources.

Integration

Después de ver Review the video as needed and use key words and details to answer the following questions.

1. ¿Qué actividades necesitan los adolescentes?

2. ¿Qué aprenden los adolescentes de las actividades?

3. In the video several cognates are used to describe what teens can gain from different types of activities. Do you agree? Write a brief sentence that describes what you learn from your activities, using one or two cognates.

📖 **For more activities, go to the *Authentic Resources Workbook*.**

Los adolescentes

Expansión Find other authentic resources for this chapter in *Auténtico* online, then answer the questions.

📁 **4B Auténtico**

Integración de ideas In the authentic resources other pastimes and opportunities for young people in Spanish-speaking countries are described. Use the resources to write which of these activities you enjoy and what you think you learn from them.

Comparación cultural Compare activities for teens in Spanish-speaking cultures that you have learned about in these resources. Also compare them with your own activities.

Enrich Your Teaching

Culture Note

Soccer, known as *fútbol*, is considered the most popular sport in the world. Every four years an international tournament called the World Cup is held. Uruguay, Argentina and Spain are 3 of the seven countries that have won the tournament, showing that soccer is very special in Spanish-speaking culture around the world.

Perspectivas: Are the sports that you enjoy playing and watching representative of your community?

Using Authentic Resources

Have students create a list of additional vocabulary words from the resources, and use these words to write a short description of a pastime that they learned about from the resources.

Review Activities

Talking about leisure activities and describing how someone feels: Have students work in pairs to quiz each other. They should take turns being Student A and Student B. Student A can pantomime an activity as Student B says the word in Spanish.

Extending, accepting, and declining invitations; telling what time something happens: Student A will invite Student B to an activity and state what time it will take place. Student B will give an excuse why he or she cannot go based on how he or she feels.

Jugar: Have students write the six pronouns on separate note cards, shuffle the cards, and hold them up one at a time. Student pairs will take turns saying the appropriate form of *jugar*. To reinforce vocabulary, ask them to add a sport to create sentences, for example, Ellos juegan al *tenis*.

Digital Portfolio

Invite students to review the activities they completed in this chapter, including written reports, posters or other visuals, recordings of oral presentations, or other projects. Have them select one or two items they feel best demonstrate their achievements in Spanish. Include these items in students' portfolios. Have them include this with the Chapter Checklist and Self-Assessment Worksheet.

Pre-AP® Integration

- **Learning Objective:** Interpersonal speaking
- **Pre-AP® Resource Materials Activity Sheets, Tema 4:** Have students work in pairs, and choose from questions 1–10 to guide their conversation.

Additional Resources

Technology: Online Resources
- Instant Check
- Integrated Performance Assessment
- *Para hispanohablantes*
- Communication Activities

Print
- Core WB pp. 83–84

Teacher Resources
- Teacher's Resource Materials: Situation Cards, Clip Art
- Assessment Program: Chapter Checklist and Self-Assessment Worksheet

---

Repaso del capítulo

OBJECTIVES
▶ Review the vocabulary and grammar
▶ Demonstrate you can perform the tasks on p. 219

🔊 Vocabulario

to talk about leisure activities

el baile	dance
el concierto	concert
la fiesta	party
ir + a + infinitive	to be going to + *verb*
ir de cámping	to go camping
ir de pesca	to go fishing
jugar al básquetbol	to play basketball
jugar al béisbol	to play baseball
jugar al fútbol	to play soccer
jugar al fútbol americano	to play football
jugar al golf	to play golf
jugar al tenis	to play tennis
jugar al vóleibol	to play volleyball
el partido	game, match
(yo) sé	I know (how)
(tú) sabes	you know (how)

to describe how someone feels

cansado, -a	tired
contento, -a	happy
enfermo, -a	sick
mal	bad, badly
ocupado, -a	busy
triste	sad

to tell what time something happens

¿A qué hora?	(At) what time?
a la una	at one (o'clock)
a las ocho	at eight (o'clock)
de la mañana	in the morning
de la noche	in the evening, at night
de la tarde	in the afternoon
esta noche	this evening
esta tarde	this afternoon
este fin de semana	this weekend

to extend, accept, or decline invitations

conmigo	with me
contigo	with you
(yo) puedo	I can
(tú) puedes	you can
¡Ay! ¡Qué pena!	Oh! What a shame!
¡Genial!	Great!
lo siento	I'm sorry
¡Oye!	Hey!
¡Qué buena idea!	What a good / nice idea!
(yo) quiero	I want
(tú) quieres	you want
¿Te gustaría?	Would you like?
Me gustaría	I would like
Tengo que ____.	I have to ____.

other useful words and expressions

demasiado	too
entonces	then
un poco (de)	a little

Gramática

jugar (a) to play *(games, sports)*

juego	jugamos
juegas	jugáis
juega	juegan

For *Vocabulario adicional,* see pp. 472–473.

Differentiated Instruction

Students with Learning Difficulties

Have students review the *Repaso del capítulo* and create flashcards for any words that they do not know. Pair them with a student who is more confident with the vocabulary to practice. Before the test, provide students with a practice test, so they can become comfortable with the format.

Heritage Speakers

Have students write a few paragraphs telling about their perfect game or other sports event: Where is it going to be? Whom are they going to invite to play (or see the event) with them? What sport will they play or see? Encourage them to use as many vocabulary words from this chapter as they can.

Preparación para el examen

Más recursos PearsonSchool.com/Autentico

- Games
- Flashcards
- Instant check
- Tutorials
- *Gram*Activa videos
- Animated verbs

What you need to be able to do for the exam . . .	Here are practice tasks similar to those you will find on the exam . . .	For review go to your print or digital textbook . . .
Interpretive		
1 ESCUCHAR I can listen to and understand messages that give information about when and where to meet someone.	On your answering machine, you hear your friend asking if you can go somewhere with her this weekend. Based on her message, try to tell: a) where she is going; b) what she is going to do; and c) what time she wants to go.	**pp. 198–201** *Vocabulario en contexto* **p. 203** **Actividad 9** **p. 206** **Actividad 13**
Interpersonal		
2 HABLAR I can make excuses for not accepting an invitation.	You and a friend have planned a camping trip this weekend, but another friend now wants you to do something with him. With a partner, take turns rehearsing excuses for declining his invitation.	**p. 202** **Actividad 4** **p. 203** **Actividad 8** **p. 204** **Actividad 11** **p. 207** **Actividad 17**
Interpretive		
3 LEER I can read and understand short messages about accepting or declining invitations.	You find notes under your desk that were written to the person who was sitting there before you. Read them to see why people declined an invitation to a party: a) Me gustaría, pero no puedo. Tengo que estudiar para un examen. b) ¡Genial! ¡Una fiesta! Ay, pero no puedo. Voy de cámping. c) ¿A las siete? No puedo. Juego un partido de vóleibol a las siete y media. Lo siento.	**pp. 198–201** *Vocabulario en contexto* **p. 203** **Actividad 7** **pp. 212–213** *Lectura*
Presentational		
4 ESCRIBIR I can write a short note telling what I am going to do during the week.	As a counselor for an after-school program for children, you must write a note to the parents telling them at least three things their children are going to do during the week. (Hint: Start your note with *¡Hola! Esta semana . . .*)	**pp. 198–201** *Vocabulario en contexto* **p. 206** *ir + a + infinitive;* **Actividad 14** **p. 207** **Actividad 15** **p. 215** *Presentación escrita*
Cultures		
5 Comparar I can demonstrate an understanding of cultural differences regarding extra-curricular activities.	Think about what you and your friends typically do after school. Are your activities usually school-related? How would you compare what you do to what some Hispanic teens do in their after-school time?	**p. 214** *Perspectivas del mundo hispano*

Differentiated Assessment

Core Assessment
- Assessment Program: Examen del capítulo 4B
- Technology: Audio Cap. 4B
- ExamView: Chapter Test, Test Banks A and B

Challenge/Pre-AP®
- ExamView: Pre-AP® Test Bank
- Pre-AP® Resource Materials

Extra Support
- Alternate Assessment Program: Examen del capítulo 4B
- Technology: Audio Cap. 4B

Heritage Speakers
- Assessment Program: *Para hispanohablantes*: Examen del capítulo 4B
- ExamView: Heritage Learner Test Bank

Performance Tasks

Standards: 1.1, 1.2, 1.3, 4.2

Student Resource: *Para hispanohablantes*
Teacher Resources: Teacher's Resource Materials: Audio Script; Technology: Audio Cap. 4B

1. Escuchar

Suggestions: Use the audio or read the script.

Technology: Audio Script and Answers:
Hola, Toni, soy Susi. Yo voy al centro comercial después de las clases, a las cuatro de la tarde. ¿Te gustaría ir conmigo? Voy a comprar algo para un amigo.
   a. Susi is going to the mall.
   b. Susi is going to buy something for her friend.
   c. Susi is going at 4:00 in the afternoon.

2. Hablar

Suggestions: Remind students that their excuses should sound legitimate. Ask them to tell how they feel, and to mention another activity that is preventing them from attending.
Answers will vary.

3. Leer

Suggestions: Tell students to scan the readings for the key word that says why the person cannot go, and then have them read the entire passage.
Answers:
   a. The person has to study for a test.
   b. The person is going camping.
   c. The person is going to a volleyball game.

4. Escribir

Suggestions: Remind students that verbs will be in the third person since they are describing what students will do.
Answers will vary.

5. Comparar

Suggestions: Have students refer to *Perspectivas del mundo hispano* on p. 214.
Answers will vary.

Vocabulario adicional

Tema 1

Las actividades

coleccionar sellos / monedas to collect stamps / coins

jugar al ajedrez to play chess

patinar sobre hielo to ice-skate

practicar artes marciales *(f.)* to practice martial arts

tocar to play *(an instrument)*

    el bajo bass

    la batería drums

    el clarinete clarinet

    el oboe oboe

    el saxofón *pl.* **los saxofones** saxophone

    el sintetizador synthesizer

    el trombón *pl.* **los trombones** trombone

    la trompeta trumpet

    la tuba tuba

    el violín *pl.* **los violines** violin

Tema 2

Las clases

el alemán German

el álgebra *(f.)* algebra

el anuario yearbook

la banda band

la biología biology

el cálculo calculus

el drama drama

la fotografía photography

el francés French

la geografía geography

la geometría geometry

el latín Latin

la química chemistry

la trigonometría trigonometry

Las cosas para la clase

la grapadora stapler

las grapas staples

el sacapuntas *pl.* **los sacapuntas** pencil sharpener

el sujetapapeles *pl.* **los sujetapapeles** paper clip

las tijeras scissors

Tema 3

Las comidas

Las frutas

el aguacate avocado

la cereza cherry

la ciruela plum

el coco coconut

el durazno peach

la frambuesa raspberry

el limón *pl.* **los limones** lemon

el melón *pl.* **los melones** melon

la pera pear

la sandía watermelon

la toronja grapefruit

Las verduras

el apio celery

el brócoli broccoli

la calabaza pumpkin

el champiñón *pl.* **los champiñones** mushroom

la col cabbage

la coliflor cauliflower

los espárragos asparagus

las espinacas spinach

el pepino cucumber

La carne

la chuleta de cerdo pork chop

el cordero lamb

la ternera veal

Los condimentos

la mayonesa mayonnaise

la mostaza mustard

la salsa de tomate ketchup

Otro tipo de comidas

los fideos noodles

Tema 4

Los lugares y actividades

el banco bank

el club club

el equipo de . . . ___ team

la farmacia pharmacy

la oficina office

la práctica de . . . ___ practice

la reunión *pl.* **las reuniones de . . .** ___ meeting

el supermercado supermarket

Tema 5

Los animales

el conejillo de Indias guinea pig

el conejo rabbit

el gerbo gerbil

el hámster *pl.* **los hámsters** hamster

el hurón *pl.* **los hurones** ferret

el loro parrot

el pez *pl.* **los peces** fish

la serpiente snake

la tortuga turtle

Los miembros de la familia

el bisabuelo, la bisabuela great-grandfather, great-grandmother

el nieto, la nieta grandson, granddaughter

el sobrino, la sobrina nephew, niece

Las descripciones de personas

llevar anteojos to wear glasses
ser
    calvo, -a bald
    delgado, -a thin
    gordo, -a fat
tener
    la barba beard
    el bigote moustache
    las pecas freckles
    el pelo lacio straight hair
    el pelo rizado curly hair
    las trenzas braids

Tema 6

Las partes de la casa y cosas en la casa

el balcón *pl.* **los balcones** balcony
la estufa stove
el jardín *pl.* **los jardines** garden
el lavadero laundry room
la lavadora washing machine
el lavaplatos *pl.* **los lavaplatos** dishwasher
el microondas *pl.* **los microondas** microwave oven
los muebles furniture
el patio patio
el refrigerador refrigerator
la secadora clothes dryer
el sillón *pl.* **los sillones** armchair
el sofá sofa
el tocador dressing table

Los quehaceres

quitar
    la nieve con la pala to shovel snow
    los platos de la mesa to clear the table
rastrillar las hojas to rake leaves

Los colores

(azul) claro light (blue)
(azul) marino navy (blue)
(azul) oscuro dark (blue)

Tema 7

Las expresiones para las compras

ahorrar to save
el dinero en efectivo cash
gastar to spend
la(s) rebaja(s) sale(s)
regatear to bargain
se vende for sale

La ropa

la bata bathrobe
el chaleco vest
las pantimedias pantyhose
el paraguas *pl.* **los paraguas** umbrella
el pijama pajamas
la ropa interior underwear
el saco loose-fitting jacket
los tenis tennis shoes
las zapatillas slippers
los zapatos atléticos athletic shoes
los zapatos de tacón alto high-heeled shoes

Tema 8

Las expresiones para los viajes

el aeropuerto airport
la agencia de viajes travel agency
los cheques de viajero travelers' checks
el equipaje luggage
hacer una reservación to make a reservation

el lugar de interés place of interest
el pasaporte passport
volar *(o → ue)* to fly

Los animales del zoológico

el ave *(f.) pl.* **las aves** bird
el canguro kangaroo
la cebra zebra
el cocodrilo crocodile
el delfín *pl.* **los delfines** dolphin
el elefante elephant
la foca seal
el gorila gorilla
el hipopótamo hippopotamus
la jirafa giraffe
el león *pl.* **los leones** lion
el oso bear
el oso blanco polar bear
el pingüino penguin
el tigre tiger

Tema 9

Las expresiones para las computadoras

la búsqueda search
comenzar *(e → ie)* **la sesión** to log on
el disco duro hard disk
la impresora printer
imprimir to print
el marcapáginas *pl.* **los marcapáginas** bookmark
multimedia multimedia
la página inicial home page
la tecla de borrar delete key
la tecla de intro enter key

Adjectives describe nouns: *a red* car.

Adverbs usually describe verbs; they tell when, where, or how an action happens: *He read it **quickly***. Adverbs can also describe adjectives or other adverbs: ***very tall, quite well***.

Articles are words in Spanish that can tell you whether a noun is masculine, feminine, singular, or plural. In English, the articles are ***the***, ***a***, and ***an***.

Commands are verb forms that tell people to do something: ***Study!, Work!***

Comparatives compare people or things.

Conjugations are verb forms that add endings to the stem in order to tell who the subject is and what tense is being used: *escrib**o**, escrib**iste***.

Conjunctions join words or groups of words. The most common ones are ***and***, ***but***, and ***or***.

Direct objects are nouns or pronouns that receive the action of a verb: *I read the **book**. I read **it***.

Gender in Spanish tells you whether a noun, pronoun, or article is masculine or feminine.

Indirect objects are nouns or pronouns that tell you to whom / what or for whom / what something is done: *I gave **him** the book.*

Infinitives are the basic forms of verbs. In English, infinitives have the word "to" in front of them: ***to walk***.

Interrogatives are words that ask questions: ***What** is that?* ***Who** are you?*

Nouns name people, places, or things: ***students, Mexico City, books***.

Number tells you if a noun, pronoun, article, or verb is singular or plural.

Prepositions show relationship between their objects and another word in the sentence: *He is **in** the classroom.*

Present tense is used to talk about actions that always take place, or that are happening now: *I always **take** the bus; I **study** Spanish.*

Present progressive tense is used to emphasize that an action is happening *right now*: *I **am doing** my homework; he **is finishing** dinner.*

Preterite tense is used to talk about actions that were completed in the past: *I **took** the train yesterday; I **studied** for the test.*

Pronouns are words that take the place of nouns: ***She** is my friend.*

Subjects are the nouns or pronouns that perform the action in a sentence: ***John** sings.*

Superlatives describe which things have the most or least of a given quality: *She is the **best** student.*

Verbs show action or link the subject with a word or words in the predicate (what the subject does or is): *Ana **writes**; Ana **is** my sister.*

Nouns, Number, and Gender

Nouns refer to people, animals, places, things, and ideas. Nouns are singular or plural. In Spanish, nouns have gender, which means that they are either masculine or feminine.

Singular Nouns		Plural Nouns	
Masculine	**Feminine**	**Masculine**	**Feminine**
libro	carpeta	libros	carpetas
pupitre	casa	pupitres	casas
profesor	noche	profesores	noches
lápiz	ciudad	lápices	ciudades

Definite Articles

El, *la*, *los*, and *las* are definite articles and are the equivalent of "the" in English. *El* is used with masculine singular nouns; *los* with masculine plural nouns. *La* is used with feminine singular nouns; *las* with feminine plural nouns. When you use the words *a* or *de* before *el*, you form the contractions *al* and *del*: *Voy **al** centro; Es el libro **del** profesor*.

Masculine	
Singular	**Plural**
el libro	los libros
el pupitre	los pupitres
el profesor	los profesores
el lápiz	los lápices

Feminine	
Singular	**Plural**
la carpeta	las carpetas
la casa	las casas
la noche	las noches
la ciudad	las ciudades

Indefinite Articles

Un and *una* are indefinite articles and are the equivalent of "a" and "an" in English. *Un* is used with singular masculine nouns; *una* is used with singular feminine nouns. The plural indefinite articles are *unos* and *unas*.

Masculine	
Singular	**Plural**
un libro	unos libros
un escritorio	unos escritorios
un baile	unos bailes

Feminine	
Singular	**Plural**
una revista	unas revistas
una mochila	unas mochilas
una bandera	unas banderas

Pronouns

Subject pronouns tell who is doing the action. They replace nouns or names in a sentence. Subject pronouns are often used for emphasis or clarification: *Gregorio escucha música. **Él** escucha música.*

A *direct object* tells who or what receives the action of the verb. To avoid repeating a direct object noun, you can replace it with a *direct object pronoun*. Direct object pronouns have the same gender and number as the nouns they replace: *¿Cuándo compraste **el libro? Lo** compré ayer.*

An *indirect object* tells to whom or for whom an action is performed. *Indirect object pronouns* are used to replace an indirect object noun: ***Les** doy dinero. (I give money to them.)* Because *le* and *les* have more than one meaning, you can make the meaning clear, or show emphasis, by adding *a* + the corresponding name, noun, or pronoun: ***Les** doy el dinero a **ellos.***

After most prepositions, you use *mí* and *ti* for "me" and "you." The forms change with the preposition *con: conmigo, contigo.* For all other persons, you use subject pronouns after prepositions.

The Personal a

When the direct object is a person, a group of people, or a pet, use the word *a* before the object. This is called the "personal a": *Visité **a** mi abuela. Busco **a** mi perro, Capitán.*

Subject Pronouns		Direct Object Pronouns		Indirect Object Pronouns		Objects of Prepositions	
Singular	**Plural**	**Singular**	**Plural**	**Singular**	**Plural**	**Singular**	**Plural**
yo	nosotros, nosotras	me	nos	me	nos	(para) mí, conmigo	nosotros, nosotras
tú	vosotros, vosotras	te	os	te	os	(para) ti, contigo	vosotros, vosotras
usted (Ud.)	ustedes (Uds.)	lo, la	los, las	le	les	Ud.	Uds.
él, ella	ellos, ellas					él, ella	ellos, ellas

Adjectives

Words that describe people and things are called adjectives. In Spanish, most adjectives have both masculine and feminine forms, as well as singular and plural forms. Adjectives must agree with the noun they describe in both gender and number. When an adjective describes a group including both masculine and feminine nouns, use the masculine plural form.

Masculine		Feminine	
Singular	**Plural**	**Singular**	**Plural**
alto	altos	alta	altas
inteligente	inteligentes	inteligente	inteligentes
trabajador	trabajadores	trabajadora	trabajadoras
fácil	fáciles	fácil	fáciles

Shortened Forms of Adjectives

When placed before masculine singular nouns, some adjectives change into a shortened form.

One adjective, **grande**, changes to a shortened form before any singular noun: *una **gran** señora, un **gran** libro.*

bueno	buen chico
malo	mal día
primero	prímer trabajo
tercero	tercer plato
grande	gran señor

Possessive Adjectives

Possessive adjectives are used to tell what belongs to someone or to show relationships. Like other adjectives, possessive adjectives agree in number with the nouns that follow them.

Only *nuestro* and *vuestro* have different masculine and feminine endings. *Su* and *sus* can have many different meanings: *his, her, its, your,* or *their.*

Singular	Plural
mi	mis
tu	tus
su	sus
nuestro, -a	nuestros, -as
vuestro, -a	vuestros, -as
su	sus

Demonstrative Adjectives

Like other adjectives, demonstrative adjectives agree in gender and number with the nouns that follow them. Use *este, esta, estos, estas* ("this" / "these") before nouns that name people or things that are close to you. Use *ese, esa, esos, esas* ("that" / "those") before nouns that name people or things that are at some distance from you.

Singular	Plural	Singular	Plural
este libro	estos libros	ese niño	esos niños
esta casa	estas casas	esa manzana	esas manzanas

Interrogative Words

You use interrogative words to ask questions. When you ask a question with an interrogative word, you put the verb before the subject. All interrogative words have a written accent mark.

¿Adónde?	¿Cuándo?	¿Dónde?
¿Cómo?	¿Cuánto, -a?	¿Por qué?
¿Con quién?	¿Cuántos, -as?	¿Qué?
¿Cuál?	¿De dónde?	¿Quién?

Comparatives and Superlatives

Comparatives Use *más . . . que* or *menos . . . que* to compare people or things: *más interesante que . . . , menos alta que . . .*

When talking about number, use *de* instead of *que: Tengo **más de** cien monedas en mi colección.*

Superlatives Use this pattern to express the idea of "most" or "least."

el
la + noun + más / menos + adjective
los
las

Es la chica más seria de la clase.
Son los perritos más pequeños.

Several adjectives are irregular when used with comparatives and superlatives.

older	mayor
younger	menor
better	mejor
worse	peor

Affirmative and Negative Words

To make a sentence negative in Spanish, *no* usually goes in front of the verb or expression. To show that you do not like either of two choices, use *ni . . . ni.*

Alguno, alguna, algunos, algunas and *ninguno, ninguna* match the number and gender of the noun to which they refer. *Ningunos* and *ningunas* are rarely used. When *alguno* and *ninguno* come before a masculine singular noun, they change to *algún* and *ningún*.

Affirmative	Negative
algo	nada
alguien	nadie
algún	ningún
alguno, -a, -os, -as	ninguno, -a, -os, -as
siempre	nunca
también	tampoco

Adverbs

To form an adverb in Spanish, *-mente* is added to the feminine singular form of an adjective. This *-mente* ending is equivalent to the "-ly" ending in English. If the adjective has a written accent, such as *rápida, fácil*, and *práctica*, the accent appears in the same place in the adverb form.

general	→	generalmente
especial	→	especialmente
fácil	→	fácilmente
feliz	→	felizmente
rápida	→	rápidamente
práctica	→	prácticamente

Verbos

Regular Present and Preterite Tenses

Here are the conjugations for regular -*ar*, -*er*, and -*ir* verbs in the present and preterite tense.

Infinitive	Present		Preterite	
estudiar	estudio	estudiamos	estudié	estudiamos
	estudias	estudiáis	estudiaste	estudiasteis
	estudia	estudian	estudió	estudiaron
correr	corro	corremos	corrí	corrimos
	corres	corréis	corriste	corristeis
	corre	corren	corrió	corrieron
escribir	escribo	escribimos	escribí	escribimos
	escribes	escribís	escribiste	escribisteis
	escribe	escriben	escribió	escribieron

Present Progressive

When you want to emphasize that an action is happening *right now*, you use the present progressive tense.

estudiar	estoy	estudiando	estamos	estudiando
	estás	estudiando	estáis	estudiando
	está	estudiando	están	estudiando
correr	estoy	corriendo	estamos	corriendo
	estás	corriendo	estáis	corriendo
	está	corriendo	están	corriendo
escribir	estoy	escribiendo	estamos	escribiendo
	estás	escribiendo	estáis	escribiendo
	está	escribiendo	están	escribiendo

Affirmative **tú** Commands

When telling a friend, a family member, or a young person to do something, use an affirmative *tú* command. To give these commands for most verbs, use the same present-tense forms that are used for *Ud., él, ella.* Some verbs have an irregular affirmative *tú* command.

Regular	Irregular	
¡Estudia!	decir	di
¡Corre!	hacer	haz
¡Escribe!	ir	ve
	poner	pon
	salir	sal
	ser	sé
	tener	ten
	venir	ven

Stem-changing Verbs

Here is an alphabetical list of the stem-changing verbs. Next year, you will learn the preterite verb forms that are shown here in italic type.

Infinitive and Present Participle	Present		Preterite	
costar (o → ue) costando	cuesta	cuestan	costó	costaron
doler (o → ue) doliendo	duele	duelen	dolió	dolieron
dormir (o → ue) *durmiendo*	duermo duermes duerme	dormimos dormís duermen	dormí dormiste *durmió*	dormimos dormisteis *durmieron*
empezar (e → ie) empezando	empiezo empiezas empieza	empezamos empezáis empiezan	*empecé* empezaste empezó	empezamos empezasteis empezaron
jugar (u → ue) jugando	juego juegas jueg	jugamos jugáis juegan	jugué jugaste jugó	jugamos jugasteis jugaron
llover (o → ue) lloviendo	llueve		llovió	
nevar (e → ie) nevando	nieva		nevó	
pedir (e → i) *pidiendo*	pido pides pide	pedimos pedís piden	pedí pediste *pidió*	pedimos pedisteis *pidieron*
pensar (e → ie) pensando	pienso piensas piensa	pensamos pensáis piensan	pensé pensaste pensó	pensamos pensasteis pensaron
preferir (e → ie) *prefiriendo*	prefiero prefieres prefiere	preferimos preferís prefieren	preferí preferiste *prefirió*	preferimos preferisteis *prefirieron*
sentir (e → ie) *sintiendo*	*See* preferir			
servir (e → i) *sirviendo*	*See* pedir			

Spelling-changing Verbs

These verbs have spelling changes in different tenses. The spelling changes are indicated in black. Next year, you will learn the preterite verb forms that are shown here in italic type.

Infinitive and Present Participle	Present	Preterite	
buscar (c → qu) buscando	*See regular verbs*	**busqué** buscaste buscó	buscamos buscasteis buscaron
comunicarse (c → qu) *comunicándose*	*See reflexive verbs*	*See reflexive verbs and* **buscar**	
conocer (c → zc) conociendo	**conozco** conocemos **conoces** conocéis **conoce** conocen	*See regular verbs*	
creer (i → y) *creyendo*	*See regular verbs*	*creí creíste* ***creyó***	*creímos creísteis* ***creyeron***
empezar (z → c) empezando	*See stem-changing verbs*	**empecé** empezaste empezó	empezamos empezasteis empezaron
enviar (i → í) enviando	**envío** enviamos **envías** enviáis **envía** envían	*See regular verbs*	
esquiar (i → í) esquiando	*See* **enviar**	*See regular verbs*	
jugar (g → gu) jugando	*See stem-changing verbs*	**jugué** jugaste jugó	jugamos jugasteis jugaron
leer (i → y) leyendo	*See regular verbs*	*See* **creer**	
pagar (g → gu) pagando	*See regular verbs*	*See* **jugar**	
parecer (c → zc) pareciendo	*See* **conocer**	*See regular verbs*	
practicar (c → qu) practicando	*See regular verbs*	*See* **buscar**	
recoger (g → j) recogiendo	**recojo** recogemos **recoges** recogéis **recoge** recogen	*See regular verbs*	
sacar (c → qu) sacando	*See regular verbs*	*See* **buscar**	
tocar (c → qu) tocando	*See regular verbs*	*See* **buscar**	

Irregular Verbs

These verbs have irregular patterns. Next year, you will learn the preterite verb forms that are shown here in italic type.

Infinitive and Present Participle	Present		Preterite	
dar dando	doy das da	damos dais dan	di diste dio	dimos disteis dieron
decir *diciendo*	digo dices dice	decimos decís dicen	*dije* *dijiste* *dijo*	*dijimos* *dijisteis* *dijeron*
estar estando	estoy estás está	estamos estáis están	*estuve* *estuviste* *estuvo*	*estuvimos* *estuvisteis* *estuvieron*
hacer haciendo	hago haces hace	hacemos hacéis hacen	hice hiciste hizo	hicimos hicisteis hicieron
ir *yendo*	voy vas va	vamos vais van	fui fuiste fue	fuimos fuisteis fueron
poder *pudiendo*	puedo puedes puede	podemos podéis pueden	*pude* *pudiste* *pudo*	*pudimos* *pudisteis* *pudieron*
poner poniendo	pongo pones pone	ponemos ponéis ponen	*puse* *pusiste* *puso*	*pusimos* *pusisteis* *pusieron*
querer queriendo	quiero quieres quiere	queremos queréis quieren	*quise* *quisiste* *quiso*	*quisimos* *quisisteis* *quisieron*
saber sabiendo	sé sabes sabe	sabemos sabéis saben	*supe* *supiste* *supo*	*supimos* *supisteis* *supieron*
salir saliendo	salgo sales sale	salimos salís salen	salí saliste salió	salimos salisteis salieron
ser siendo	soy eres es	somos sois son	fui fuiste fue	fuimos fuisteis fueron
tener teniendo	tengo tienes tiene	tenemos tenéis tienen	*tuve* *tuviste* *tuvo*	*tuvimos* *tuvisteis* *tuvieron*

Irregular Verbs (continued)

Next year, you will learn the preterite verb forms that are shown here in italic type.

Infinitive and Present Participle	Present		Preterite	
traer *trayendo*	traigo traes trae	traemos traéis traen	*traje* *trajiste* *trajo*	*trajimos* *trajisteis* *trajeron*
venir *viniendo*	vengo vienes viene	venimos venís vienen	*vine* *viniste* *vino*	*vinimos* *vinisteis* *vinieron*
ver viendo	veo ves ve	vemos veis ven	vi viste vio	vimos visteis vieron

Reflexive Verbs

Next year, you will learn the preterite verb forms that are shown here in italic type.

Infinitive and Present Participle	Present	
comunicarse *comunicándose*	me comunico te comunicas *se comunica*	*nos comunicamos* *os comunicáis* *se comunican*
Affirmative Familiar *(tú)* Command	**Preterite**	
comunícate	me comuniqué te comunicaste *se comunicó*	*nos comunicamos* *os comunicasteis* *se comunicaron*

Expresiones útiles para conversar

The following are expressions that you can use when you find yourself in a specific situation and need help to begin, continue, or end a conversation.

Greeting Someone

Buenos días. Good morning.
Buenas tardes. Good afternoon.
Buenas noches. Good evening. Good night.

Making Introductions

Me llamo . . . My name is . . .
Soy . . . I'm . . .
¿Cómo te llamas? What's your name?
Éste es mi amigo *m.* **. . .** This is my friend . . .
Ésta es mi amiga *f.* **. . .** This is my friend . . .
Se llama. . . His / Her name is . . .
¡Mucho gusto! It's a pleasure!
Encantado, -a. Delighted.
Igualmente. Likewise.

Asking How Someone Is

¿Cómo estás? How are you?
¿Cómo andas? How's it going?
¿Cómo te sientes? How do you feel?
¿Qué tal? How's it going?
Estoy bien, gracias. I'm fine, thank you.
Muy bien. ¿Y tú? Very well. And you?
Regular. Okay. Alright.
Más o menos. More or less.
(Muy) mal. (Very) bad.
¡Horrible! Awful!
¡Excelente! Great!

Talking on the Phone

Aló. Hello.
Diga. Hello.
Bueno. Hello.
¿Quién habla? Who's calling?
Habla. . . It's [name of person calling].
¿Está. . . , por favor? Is . . . there, please?

¿De parte de quién? Who is calling?
¿Puedo dejar un recado? May I leave a message?
Un momento. Just a moment.
Llamo más tarde. I'll call later.
¿Cómo? No le oigo. What? I can't hear you.

Making Plans

¿Adónde vas? Where are you going?
Voy a. . . I'm going to . . .
¿Estás listo, -a? Are you ready?
Tengo prisa. I'm in a hurry.
¡Date prisa! Hurry up!
Sí, ahora voy. OK, I'm coming.
Todavía necesito. . . I still need . . .
¿Te gustaría. . . ? Would you like to . . . ?
Sí, me gustaría. . . Yes, I'd like to . . .
¡Claro que sí (no)! Of course (not)!
¿Quieres. . . ? Do you want to . . . ?
Quiero. . . I want to . . .
¿Qué quieres hacer hoy? What do you want to do today?
¿Qué haces después de las clases? What do you do after school (class)?
¿Qué estás haciendo? What are you doing?
Te invito. It's my treat.
¿Qué tal si. . . ? What about . . . ?
Primero. . . First . . .
Después. . . Later . . .
Luego. . . Then . . .

Making an Excuse

Estoy ocupado, -a. I'm busy.
Lo siento, pero no puedo. I'm sorry, but I can't.
¡Qué lástima! What a shame!
Ya tengo planes. I already have plans.
Tal vez otro día. Maybe another day.

Being Polite

Con mucho gusto. With great pleasure.
De nada. You're welcome.

Disculpe. Excuse me.
Lo siento. I'm sorry.
Muchísimas gracias. Thank you very much.
Te (Se) lo agradezco mucho. I appreciate it a lot.
Muy amable. That's very kind of you.
Perdón. Pardon me.
¿Puede Ud. repetirlo? Can you repeat that?
¿Puede Ud. hablar más despacio? Can you speak more slowly?

Keeping a Conversation Going

¿De veras? Really?
¿Verdad? Isn't that so? Right?
¿En serio? Seriously?
¡No lo puedo creer! I don't believe it!
¡No me digas! You don't say!
Y entonces, ¿qué? And then what?
¿Qué hiciste? What did you do?
¿Qué dijiste? What did you say?
¿Crees que. . . ? Do you think that . . .?
Me parece bien. It seems alright.
Perfecto. Perfect.
¡Qué buena idea! What a good idea!
¡Cómo no! Of course!
De acuerdo. Agreed.
Está bien. It's all right.

Giving a Description When You Don't Know the Name of Someone or Something

Se usa para. . . It's used to / for . . .
Es la palabra que significa. . . It's the word that means . . .
Es la persona que. . . It's the person who . . .

Ending a Conversation

Bueno, tengo que irme. Well, I have to go.
Chao. (Chau.) Bye.
Hasta pronto. See you soon.
Hasta mañana. See you tomorrow.

Vocabulario español-inglés

The *Vocabulario español–inglés* contains all active vocabulary from the text, including vocabulary presented in the grammar sections.

A dash (—) represents the main entry word. For example, **pasar la —** after **la aspiradora** means **pasar la aspiradora.**

The number following each entry indicates the chapter in which the word or expression is presented. The letter *P* following an entry refers to the *Para empezar* section.

The following abbreviations are used in this list: *adj.* (adjective), *dir. obj.* (direct object), *f.* (feminine), *fam.* (familiar), *ind. obj.* (indirect object), *inf.* (infinitive), *m.* (masculine), *pl.* (plural), *prep.* (preposition), *pron.* (pronoun), *sing.* (singular).

A

a to (prep.) (4A)

— **...le gusta(n)** he/she likes (5A)

— **...le encanta(n)** he/she loves (5A)

— **casa** (to) home (4A)

— **la derecha (de)** to the right (of) (6A)

— **la izquierda (de)** to the left (of) (6A)

— **la una de la tarde** at one (o'clock) in the afternoon (4B)

— **las ocho de la mañana** at eight (o'clock) in the morning (4B)

— **las ocho de la noche** at eight (o'clock) in the evening / at night (4B)

— **menudo** often (8B)

— **mí también** I do (like to) too (1A)

— **mí tampoco** I don't (like to) either (1A)

¿— **qué hora?** (At) what time? (4B)

— **veces** sometimes (1B)

— **ver** Let's see (2A)

el abrigo coat (7A)

abril April (P)

abrir to open (5A)

la abuela, el abuelo grandmother, grandfather (5A)

los abuelos grandparents (5A)

aburrido, -a boring (2A)

me aburre(n) it bores me (they bore me) (9A)

aburrir to bore (9A)

acabar de + *inf.* to have just ...(9A)

el actor actor (9A)

la actriz *pl.* **las actrices** actress (9A)

acuerdo:

Estoy de —. I agree. (3B)

No estoy de —. I don't agree. (3B)

¡Adiós! Good-bye! (P)

¿Adónde? (To) where? (4A)

agosto August (P)

el agua *f.* water (3A)

ahora now (5B)

al *(a + el),* **a la,** to the (4A)

al lado de next to (2B)

la alfombra rug (6A)

algo something (3B)

¿— **más?** Anything else? (5B)

allí there (2B)

el almacén *pl.* **los almacenes** department store (7B)

el almuerzo lunch (2A)

en el — for lunch (3A)

alto, -a tall (5B)

amarillo, -a yellow (6A)

el amigo male friend (1B)

la amiga female friend (1B)

anaranjado, -a orange (6A)

la anciana, el anciano older woman, older man (8B)

los ancianos older people (8B)

el anillo ring (7B)

el animal animal (8A)

anoche last night (7B)

los anteojos de sol sunglasses (7B)

antes de before (9A)

el año year (P)

el — pasado last year (7B)

¿Cuántos años tiene(n) ...? How old is/are ...? (5A)

Tiene(n) ... años. He/She is / They are ... (years old). (5A)

el apartamento apartment (6B)

aprender (a) to learn (to) (8A)

aquí here (2B)

el árbol tree (8A)

los aretes earrings (7B)

el armario closet (6A)

arreglar el cuarto to straighten up the room (6B)

el arroz rice (3B)

el arte:

la clase de — art class (2A)

artístico, -a artistic (1B)

asco:

¡Qué —! How awful! (3A)

la atracción *pl.* **las atracciones** attraction(s) (8A)

atrevido, -a daring (1B)

el autobús *pl.* **los autobuses** bus (8A)

el avión *pl.* **los aviones** airplane (8A)

¡Ay! ¡Qué pena! Oh! What a shame/pity! (4B)

ayer yesterday (7B)

ayudar to help (6B)

el azúcar sugar (5B)

azul blue (6A)

B

bailar to dance (1A)

el baile dance (4B)

bajar (información) to download (9B)

bajo, -a short (5B)

la bandera flag (2B)

el baño bathroom (6B)

el traje de — swimsuit (7A)

barato, -a inexpensive, cheap (7B)

el barco boat, ship (8A)

el barrio neighborhood (8B)

el básquetbol: jugar al — to play basketball (4B)

bastante enough, rather (6B)

beber to drink (3A)

las bebidas beverages (3B)

béisbol: jugar al — to play baseball (4B)

la biblioteca library (4A)

bien well (P)

el bistec steak (3B)

blanco, -a white (6A)

la blusa blouse (7A)

la boca mouth (P)

el boleto ticket (8A)

el bolígrafo pen (P)

la bolsa bag, sack (8B)

el bolso purse (7B)

bonito, -a pretty (6A)

las botas boots (7A)

el bote: pasear en — to go boating (8A)

la botella bottle (8B)

el brazo arm (P)

bucear to scuba dive, to snorkel (8A)

bueno (buen), -a good (1B)

Buenas noches. Good evening. (P)

Buenas tardes. Good afternoon. (P)

Buenos días. Good morning. (P)

buscar to look for (7A); to search (for) (9B)

C

el caballo: montar a — to ride horseback (8A)

la cabeza head (P)

cada día every day (3B)

la cadena chain (7B)

el café coffee (3A); café (4A)

la caja box (8B)

los calcetines socks (7A)

la calculadora calculator (2A)

la calle street, road (8B)

calor:

Hace —. It's hot. (P)

tener — to be warm (5B)

la cama bed (6A)

hacer la — to make the bed (6B)

la cámara camera (5A)

la — digital digital camera (9A)

el camarero, la camarera waiter, waitress (5B)

caminar to walk (3B)

la camisa shirt (7A)

la camiseta T-shirt (7A)

el campamento camp (8B)

el campo countryside (4A)

el canal (TV) channel (9A)

la canción pl. **las canciones** song (9B)

canoso: pelo — gray hair (5B)

cansado, -a tired (4B)

cantar to sing (1A)

cara a cara face-to-face (9B)

la carne meat (3B)

caro, -a expensive (7B)

la carpeta folder (P)

la — de argollas three-ring binder (2A)

la carta letter (9B)

el cartel poster (2B)

la cartera wallet (7B)

el cartón cardboard (8B)

la casa home, house (4A)

a — (to) home (4A)

en — at home (4A)

casi almost (9A)

castaño: pelo — brown (chestnut) hair (5B)

catorce fourteen (P)

la cebolla onion (3B)

celebrar to celebrate (5A)

la cena dinner (3B)

el centro:

el — comercial mall (4A)

el — de reciclaje recycling center (8B)

cerca (de) close (to), near (6B)

el cereal cereal (3A)

los cereales grains (3B)

cero zero (P)

la chaqueta jacket (7A)

la chica girl (1B)

el chico boy (1B)

cien one hundred (P)

las ciencias:

la clase de — naturales science class (2A)

la clase de — sociales social studies class (2A)

cinco five (P)

cincuenta fifty (P)

el cine movie theater (4A)

la ciudad city (8A)

la clase class (2A)

la sala de clases classroom (P)

¿Qué — de...? What kind of ...? (9A)

el coche car (6B)

la cocina kitchen (6B)

cocinar to cook (6B)

el collar necklace (7B)

el color pl. **los colores** (6A)

¿De qué — ...? What color ... ? (6A)

la comedia comedy (9A)

el comedor dining room (6B)

comer to eat (3A)

cómico, -a funny, comical (9A)

la comida food, meal (3A)

como like, as (8A)

¿cómo?:

¿— eres? What are you like? (1B)

¿— es? What is he/she like? (1B)

¿— está Ud.? How are you? *formal* (P)

¿— estás? How are you? *fam.* (P)

¿— lo pasaste? How was it (for you)? (8A)

¿— se dice ...? How do you say ...? (P)

¿— se escribe ...? How is ... spelled? (P)

¿— se llama? What's his/her name? (1B)

¿— te llamas? What is your name? (P)

¿— te queda(n)? How does it (do they) fit you? (7A)

la **cómoda** dresser (6A)

compartir to share (3A)

complicado, -a complicated (9B)

la **composición** *pl.* **las composiciones** composition (9B)

comprar to buy (7A)

comprar recuerdos to buy souvenirs (8A)

comprender to understand (3A)

la **computadora** computer (2B)

la **— portátil** laptop computer (9B)

usar la — to use the computer (1A)

comunicarse to communicate (9B)

(tú) te comunicas you communicate (9B)

(yo) me comunico I communicate (9B)

la **comunidad** community (8B)

con with (3A)

— mis/tus amigos with my/your friends (4A)

¿— quién? With whom? (4A)

el **concierto** concert (4B)

conmigo with me (4B)

conocer to know, to be acquainted with (9B)

contento, -a happy (4B)

contigo with you (4B)

la **corbata** tie (7B)

correr to run (1A)

cortar el césped to cut/to mow the lawn (6B)

las **cortinas** curtains (6A)

corto, -a short (5B)

los pantalones cortos shorts (7A)

la **cosa** thing (6A)

costar (o → ue) to cost (7A)

¿Cuánto cuesta(n) ... ? How much does (do) ... cost? (7A)

crear to create (9B)

creer to think (3B)

Creo que ... I think ... (3B)

Creo que no. I don't think so. (3B)

Creo que sí. I think so. (3B)

el **cuaderno** notebook (P)

el **cuadro** painting (6A)

¿Cuál? Which?, What? (3A)

¿— es la fecha? What is the date? (P)

¿Cuándo? When? (4A)

¿cuánto?: ¿— cuesta(n) ... ? How much does (do) ... cost? (7A)

¿cuántos, -as? how many? (P)

¿Cuántos años tiene(n) ...? How old is/are ...? (5A)

cuarenta forty (P)

el **cuarto** room (6B)

cuarto, -a fourth (2A)

y — (time) quarter past (P)

menos — (time) quarter to (P)

cuatro four (P)

cuatrocientos, -as four hundred (7A)

la **cuchara** spoon (5B)

el **cuchillo** knife (5B)

la **cuenta** bill (5B)

el **cumpleaños** birthday (5A)

¡Feliz —! Happy birthday! (5A)

el **curso: tomar un curso** to take a course (9B)

dar to give (6B)

— + movie or TV program to show (9A)

— de comer al perro to feed the dog (6B)

de of (2B); from (4A)

¿— dónde eres? Where are you from? (4A)

— la mañana/la tarde/la noche in the morning /afternoon / evening (4B)

— nada. You're welcome. (5B)

— plato principal as a main dish (5B)

— postre for dessert (5B)

¿— qué color ...? What color ...? (6A)

¿— veras? Really? (9A)

debajo de underneath (2B)

deber should, must (3B)

decidir to decide (8B)

décimo, -a tenth (2A)

decir to say, to tell (8B)

¿Cómo se dice ...? How do you say ...? (P)

dime tell me (8A)

¡No me digas! You don't say! (4A)

¿Qué quiere — ...? What does ... mean? (P)

Quiere — ... It means ... (P)

Se dice ... You say ... (P)

las **decoraciones** decorations (5A)

decorar to decorate (5A)

el **dedo** finger (P)

delante de in front of (2B)

delicioso, -a delicious (5B)

los **demás, las demás** others (8B)

demasiado too (4B)

el **dependiente, la dependienta** salesperson (7A)

deportista sports-minded (1B)

derecha: a la — (de) to the right (of) (6A)

el **desayuno** breakfast (3A)

en el — for breakfast (3A)

descansar to rest, to relax (8A)

los **descuentos: la tienda de —** discount store (7B)

desear to wish (5B)

¿Qué desean (Uds.)? What would you like? (5B)

desordenado, -a messy (1B)

el **despacho** office (home) (6B)

el **despertador** alarm clock (6A)

después afterwards (4A)

después (de) after (4A)

detrás de behind (2B)

el **día** day (P)

Buenos —s . Good morning. (P)

cada — every day (3B)

¿Qué — es hoy? What day is today? (P)

todos los —s every day (3A)

la **diapositiva** slide (9B)

dibujar to draw (1A)

el **diccionario** dictionary (2A)

diciembre December (P)

diecinueve nineteen (P)

dieciocho eighteen (P)

dieciséis sixteen (P)

diecisiete seventeen (P)

diez ten (P)

difícil difficult (2A)

digital: la cámara — digital camera (9B)

dime tell me (8A)

el **dinero** money (6B)

la **dirección electrónica** e-mail address (9B)

el **disco compacto** compact disc (6A)

grabar un disco compacto to burn a CD (9B)

divertido, -a amusing, fun (2A)

doce twelve (P)

el **documento** document (9B)

doler (o → ue) to hurt (9A)

domingo Sunday (P)

dónde:

¿—? Where? (2B)

¿De — eres? Where are you from? (4A)

dormir (o → ue) to sleep (6A)

el **dormitorio** bedroom (6A)

dos two (P)

los/las dos both (7A)

doscientos, -as two hundred (7A)

el **drama** drama (9A)

los **dulces** candy (5A)

durante during (8A)

durar to last (9A)

E

la **educación física: la clase de —** physical education class (2A)

el **ejercicio: hacer —** to exercise (3B)

el the *m. sing.* (1B)

él he (1B)

los **electrodomésticos: la tienda de —** household appliance store (7B)

electrónico, -a: la dirección — e-mail address (9B)

ella she (1B)

ellas they *f. pl.* (2A)

ellos they *m. pl.* (2A)

emocionante touching (9A)

empezar (e → ie) to begin, to start (9A)

en in, on (2B)

— + *vehicle* by, in, on (8A)

— casa at home (4A)

— la ... hora in the ... hour (class period) (2A)

— la Red online (7B)

¿— qué puedo servirle? How can I help you? (7A)

encantado, -a delighted (P)

encantar to please very much, to love (9A)

a él/ella le encanta(n) he/she loves (5A)

me/te encanta(n) ... I/you love ... (3A)

encima de on top of (2B)

enero January (P)

enfermo, -a sick (4B)

la **ensalada** salad (3A)

la — de frutas fruit salad (3A)

enseñar to teach (2A)

entonces then (4B)

entrar to enter (7A)

enviar (i → í) to send (9B)

el **equipo de sonido** sound (stereo) system (6A)

¿Eres...? Are you ...? (1B)

es is (P); (he/she/it) is (1B)

— el *(number)* **de** *(month)* it is the ... of ... *(in telling the date)* (P)

— el primero de *(month).* It is the first of ... (P)

— la una. It is one o'clock. (P)

— necesario. It's necessary. (8B)

— un(a) ... it's a ... (2B)

la **escalera** stairs, stairway (6B)

escribir:

¿Cómo se escribe ...? How is ... spelled? (P)

— cuentos to write stories (1A)

— por correo electrónico to write e-mail (9B)

Se escribe ... It's spelled ... (P)

el **escritorio** desk (2B)

escuchar música to listen to music (1A)

la **escuela primaria** primary school (8B)

ese, esa that (7A)

eso: por — that's why, therefore (9A)

esos, esas those (7A)

los **espaguetis** spaghetti (3B)

el **español: la clase de —** Spanish class (2A)

especialmente especially (9A)

el **espejo** mirror (6A)

la **esposa** wife (5A)

el **esposo** husband (5A)

esquiar (i → í) to ski (1A)

la **estación** *pl.* **las estaciones** season (P)

el **estadio** stadium (8A)

el estante shelf, bookshelf (6A)

estar to be (2B)

    ¿Cómo está Ud.? How are you? *formal* (P)

    ¿Cómo estás? How are you? *fam.* (P)

    — + *present participle to be* + *present participle* (6B)

    — en línea to be online (9B)

    Estoy de acuerdo. I agree. (3B)

    No estoy de acuerdo. I don't agree. (3B)

este, esta this (7A)

    esta noche this evening (4B)

    esta tarde this afternoon (4B)

    este fin de semana this weekend (4B)

el estómago stomach (P)

estos, estas these (7A)

Estoy de acuerdo. I agree. (3B)

el/la estudiante student (P)

    estudiar to study (2A)

    estudioso, -a studious (1B)

la experiencia experience (8B)

F

fácil easy (2A)

la falda skirt (7A)

faltar to be missing (9A)

la familia family (1B)

fantástico, -a fantastic (8A)

fascinante fascinating (9A)

favorito, -a favorite (2A)

febrero February (P)

la fecha: ¿Cuál es la —? What is the date? (P)

¡Feliz cumpleaños! Happy birthday! (5A)

feo, -a ugly (6A)

la fiesta party (4B)

el fin de semana:

    este — this weekend (4B)

    los fines de semana on weekends (4A)

la flor *pl.* **las flores** flower (5A)

la foto photo (5A)

las fresas strawberries (3A)

frío:

    Hace —. It's cold. (P)

    tener — to be cold (5B)

fue it was (8A)

    — un desastre. It was a disaster. (8A)

el fútbol: jugar al — to play soccer (4B)

el fútbol americano: jugar al — to play football (4B)

G

la galleta cookie (3A)

el garaje garage (6B)

el gato cat (5A)

    generalmente generally (4A)

    ¡Genial! Great! (4B)

la gente people (8B)

el gimnasio gym (4A)

el globo balloon (5A)

el golf: jugar al — to play golf (4B)

la gorra cap (7A)

    grabar un disco compacto to burn a CD (9B)

    gracias thank you (P)

    gracioso, -a funny (1B)

los gráficos computer graphics (9B)

    grande large (6A)

las grasas fats (3B)

    gris gray (6A)

los guantes gloves (7B)

    guapo, -a good-looking (5B)

los guisantes peas (3B)

gustar:

    a él/ella le gusta(n) he/she likes (5A)

    (A mí) me gusta … I like to … (1A)

    (A mí) me gusta más … I like to … better (I prefer to …) (1A)

    (A mí) me gusta mucho … I like to … a lot (1A)

    (A mí) no me gusta … I don't like to … (1A)

    (A mí) no me gusta nada … I don't like to … at all. (1A)

    Le gusta … He/She likes … (1B)

    Me gusta … I like … (3A)

    Me gustaría … I would like … (4B)

    Me gustó. I liked it. (8A)

    No le gusta … He/She doesn't like … (1B)

    ¿Qué te gusta hacer? What do you like to do? (1A)

    ¿Qué te gusta hacer más? What do you like better (prefer) to do? (1A)

    Te gusta … You like … (3A)

    ¿Te gusta …? Do you like to …? (1A)

    ¿Te gustaría …? Would you like … ? (4B)

    ¿Te gustó? Did you like it? (8A)

H

hablar to talk (2A)

    — por teléfono to talk on the phone (1A)

hacer to do (3B)

    hace + *time expression* ago (7B)

    Hace calor. It's hot. (P)

    Hace frío. It's cold. (P)

    Hace sol. It's sunny. (P)

    — ejercicio to exercise (3B)

    — la cama to make the bed (6B)

    — un video to videotape (5A)

    haz *(command)* do, make (6B)

    ¿Qué hiciste? What did you do? (8A)

    ¿Qué tiempo hace? What's the weather like? (P)

    (yo) hago I do (3B)

    (tú) haces you do (3B)

hambre: Tengo —. I'm hungry. (3B)

la **hamburguesa** hamburger (3A)

hasta:

— **luego.** See you later. (P)

— **mañana.** See you tomorrow. (P)

Hay There is, There are (P, 2B)

— **que** one must (8B)

el **helado** ice cream (3B)

el **hermano, la hermana** brother, sister (5A)

el **hermanastro, la hermanastra** stepbrother, stepsister (5A)

los **hermanos** brothers; brother(s) and sister(s) (5A)

el **hijo, la hija** son, daughter (5A)

los **hijos** children; sons (5A)

la **hoja de papel** sheet of paper (P)

¡Hola! Hello! (P)

el **hombre** man (5B)

la **hora:**

en la ... — in the ... hour (class period) (2A)

¿A qué hora? At what time? (4B)

el **horario** schedule (2A)

horrible horrible (3B)

el **horror: la película de —** horror movie (9A)

el **hospital** hospital (8B)

el **hotel** hotel (8A)

hoy today (P)

los **huevos** eggs (3A)

I

la **iglesia** church (4A)

igualmente likewise (P)

impaciente impatient (1B)

importante important (6A)

impresionante impressive (8A)

increíble incredible (8B)

infantil childish (9A)

la **información** information (9B)

el **informe** report (9B)

el **inglés: la clase de —** English class (2A)

inolvidable unforgettable (8B)

inteligente intelligent (1B)

interesante interesting (2A)

interesar to interest (9A)

me interesa(n) it interests me (they interest me) (9A)

el **invierno** winter (P)

ir to go (4A)

— **a** + *inf.* to be going to + *verb* (4B)

— **a la escuela** to go to school (1A)

— **de cámping** to go camping (4B)

— **de compras** to go shopping (4A)

— **de pesca** to go fishing (4B)

— **de vacaciones** to go on vacation (8A)

¡Vamos! Let's go! (7A)

izquierda: a la — (de) to the left (of) (6A)

J

el **jardín** *pl.* **los jardines** garden, yard (8B)

los **jeans** jeans (7A)

el **joven, la joven** young man, young woman (5B)

joven *adj.* young (5B)

la **joyería** jewelry store (7B)

las **judías verdes** green beans (3B)

jueves Thursday (P)

jugar (a) (u → ue) to play (games, sports) (4B)

— **al básquetbol** to play basketball (4B)

— **al béisbol** to play baseball (4B)

— **al fútbol** to play soccer (4B)

— **al fútbol americano** to play football (4B)

— **al golf** to play golf (4B)

— **al tenis** to play tennis (4B)

— **al vóleibol** to play volleyball (4B)

— **videojuegos** to play video games (1A)

el **jugo:**

— **de manzana** apple juice (3A)

— **de naranja** orange juice (3A)

el **juguete** toy (8B)

julio July (P)

junio June (P)

L

la **the** *f. sing.* (1B); **it, her** *f. dir. obj. pron.* (7B)

el **laboratorio** laboratory (9B)

lado: al — de next to, beside (2B)

el **lago** lake (8A)

la **lámpara** lamp (6A)

el **lápiz** *pl.* **los lápices** pencil (P)

largo, -a long (5B)

las the *f. pl.* (2B); **them** *f. dir. obj. pron.* (7B)

— **dos, los dos** both (7A)

la **lata** can (8B)

lavar to wash (6B)

— **el coche** to wash the car (6B)

— **la ropa** to wash the clothes (6B)

— **los platos** to wash the dishes (6B)

le (to/for) him, her, (*formal*) you *sing. ind. obj. pron.* (8B)

— **gusta ...** He/She likes ... (1B)

— **traigo ...** I will bring you ... (5B)

No — gusta ... He/She doesn't like ... (1B)

la **lección** *pl.* **las lecciones de piano** piano lesson (class) (4A)

la **leche** milk (3A)

la **lechuga** lettuce (3B)

el **lector DVD** DVD player (6A)

leer revistas to read magazines (1A)

lejos (de) far (from) (6B)

les (to/for) them, (*formal*) you *pl. ind. obj. pron.* (8B)

levantar pesas to lift weights (3B)

la librería bookstore (7B)

el libro book (P)

la limonada lemonade (3A)

limpiar el baño to clean the bathroom (6B)

limpio, -a clean (6B)

línea: estar en — to be online (9B)

llamar:

> **¿Cómo se llama?** What's his/her name? (1B)

> **¿Cómo te llamas?** What is your name? (P)

> **Me llamo ...** My name is ... (P)

el llavero key chain (7B)

llevar to wear (7A); to take, to carry, to bring (8B)

llover (o → ue): Llueve. It's raining. (P)

lo it, him *m. dir. obj. pron.* (7B)

> **— siento.** I'm sorry. (4B)

los the *m. pl.* (2B); them *m. dir. obj. pron* (7B)

> **— dos, las dos** both (7A)

> **— fines de semana** on weekends (4A)

> **— lunes, los martes ...** on Mondays, on Tuesdays ... (4A)

el lugar place (8A)

lunes Monday (P)

> **los lunes** on Mondays (4A)

la luz *pl.* **las luces** light (5A)

M

la madrastra stepmother (5A)

la madre (mamá) mother (5A)

mal bad, badly (4B)

malo, -a bad (3B)

la mano hand (P)

mantener: para — la salud to maintain one's health (3B)

la mantequilla butter (3B)

la manzana apple (3A)

> **el jugo de —** apple juice (3A)

---

mañana tomorrow (P)

la mañana:

> **a las ocho de la —** at eight (o'clock) in the morning (4B)

> **de la —** in the morning (4B)

el mar sea (8A)

marrón *pl.* **marrones** brown (6A)

martes Tuesday (P)

> **los martes** on Tuesdays (4A)

marzo March (P)

más:

> **¿Qué —?** What else? (8B)

> **— ... que** more ... than (2A)

> **— de** more than (9A)

> **— o menos** more or less (3A)

las matemáticas: la clase de — mathematics class (2A)

mayo May (P)

mayor older (5A)

me (to/for) me *ind. obj. pron.* (8B)

> **— aburre(n)** it/they bore(s) me (9A)

> **— falta(n) ...** I need ... (5B)

> **— gustaría** I would like (4B)

> **— gustó.** I liked it. (8A)

> **— interesa(n)** it/they interest(s) me (9A)

> **— llamo ...** My name is ... (P)

> **— queda(n) bien/mal.** It/They fit(s) me well/poorly. (7A)

> **— quedo en casa.** I stay at home. (4A)

> **¿— trae ...?** Will you bring me ...? (5B)

media, -o half (P)

> **y —** thirty, half-past (P)

mejor:

> **el/la —, los/las —es** the best (6A)

> **—(es) que** better than (6A)

menor younger (5A)

menos:

más o — more or less (3A)

> **— ... que** less/fewer ... than (6A)

> **— de** less/fewer than (9A)

el menú menu (5B)

> **menudo: a —** often (8B)

el mes month (P)

la mesa table (2B)

> **poner la —** to set the table (6B)

la mesita night table (6A)

la mezquita mosque (4A)

mi, mis my (2B, 5A)

mí:

> **a — también** I do (like to) too (1A)

> **a — tampoco** I don't (like to) either (1A)

> **para —** in my opinion, for me (6A)

miedo: tener — (de) to be scared (of), to be afraid (of) (9B)

miércoles Wednesday (P)

mil a thousand (7A)

mirar to look (at) (7B)

mismo, -a same (6A)

la mochila bookbag, backpack (2B)

el momento: un — a moment (6B)

el mono monkey (8A)

las montañas mountains (4A)

montar:

> **— a caballo** to ride horseback (8A)

> **— en bicicleta** to ride a bicycle (1A)

> **— en monopatín** to skateboard (1A)

el monumento monument (8A)

morado, -a purple (6A)

mucho a lot (2A)

> **— gusto** pleased to meet you (P)

muchos, -as many (3B)

la mujer woman (5B)

el museo museum (8A)

muy very (1B)

> **—bien** very well (P)

N

nada nothing (P)

  (A mí) no me gusta — ... I don't like to ... at all. (1A)

  De —. You're welcome. (5B)

nadar to swim (1A)

la naranja: el jugo de — orange juice (3A)

la nariz *pl.* **las narices** nose (P)

navegar en la Red to surf the Web (9B)

necesario: Es —. It's necessary. (8B)

necesitar:

  (yo) necesito I need (2A)

  (tú) necesitas you need (2A)

negro, –a black (6A)

  el pelo — black hair (5B)

nevar (e → ie) Nieva. It's snowing. (P)

ni ... ni neither ... nor, not ... or (1A)

el niño, la niña young boy, young girl (8B)

los niños children (8B)

  No estoy de acuerdo. I don't agree. (3B)

  ¡No me digas! You don't say! (4A)

  no soy I am not (1A)

noche:

  a las ocho de la — at eight (o'clock) in the evening, at night (4B)

  Buenas —s. Good evening. (P)

  de la — in the evening, at night (4B)

  esta — this evening (4B)

  nos (to/for) us *ind. obj. pron.* (8B)

  ¡— vemos! See you later! (P)

nosotros, -as we (2A)

novecientos, -as nine hundred (7A)

noveno, -a ninth (2A)

noventa ninety (P)

noviembre November (P)

el novio, la novia boyfriend, girlfriend (7B)

nuestro(s), -a(s) our (5A)

nueve nine (P)

nuevo, -a new (7A)

nunca never (3A)

O

o or (1A)

la obra de teatro play (8A)

ochenta eighty (P)

ocho eight (P)

ochocientos, -as eight hundred (7A)

octavo, -a eighth (2A)

octubre October (P)

ocupado, -a busy (4B)

el ojo eye (P)

once eleven (P)

ordenado, -a neat (1B)

os (to/for) you *pl. fam. ind. obj. pron.* (8B)

el otoño fall, autumn (P)

otro, -a other, another (5B)

  otra vez again (8B)

¡Oye! Hey! (4B)

P

paciente patient (1B)

el padrastro stepfather (5A)

el padre (papá) father (5A)

los padres parents (5A)

  pagar (por) to pay (for) (7B)

la página Web Web page (9B)

el país country (8A)

el pájaro bird (8A)

el pan bread (3A)

  el — tostado toast (3A)

la pantalla (computer) screen (2B)

los pantalones pants (7A)

  los — cortos shorts (7A)

las papas potatoes (3B)

  las — fritas French fries (3A)

el papel picado cut-paper decorations (5A)

la papelera wastepaper basket (2B)

para for (2A)

  — + *inf.* in order to + *inf.* (4A)

  — la salud for one's health (3B)

  — mantener la salud to maintain one's health (3B)

  — mí in my opinion, for me (6A)

  ¿ — qué sirve? What's it (used) for? (9B)

  — ti in your opinion, for you (6A)

la pared wall (6A)

el parque park (4A)

  el — de diversiones amusement park (8A)

  el — nacional national park (8A)

el partido game, match (4B)

pasar:

  ¿Cómo lo pasaste? How was it (for you)? (8A)

  — la aspiradora to vacuum (6B)

  — tiempo con amigos to spend time with friends (1A)

  ¿Qué pasa? What's happening? (P)

  ¿Qué te pasó? What happened to you? (8A)

  pasear en bote to go boating (8A)

el pastel cake (5A)

los pasteles pastries (3B)

  patinar to skate (1A)

  pedir (e → i) to order (5B); to ask for (9B)

la película film, movie (9A)

  la — de ciencia ficción science fiction movie (9A)

  la — de horror horror movie (9A)

  la — policíaca crime movie, mystery (9A)

  la — romántica romantic movie (9A)

  ver una — to see a movie (4A)

pelirrojo, -a red-haired (5B)

el pelo hair (5B)

   el — canoso gray hair (5B)

   el — castaño brown (chestnut) hair (5B)

   el — negro black hair (5B)

   el — rubio blond hair (5B)

pensar (e → ie) to plan, to think (7A)

peor:

   el/la —, los/las —es the worst (6A)

   —(es) que worse than (6A)

pequeño, -a small (6A)

Perdón. Excuse me. (7A)

perezoso, -a lazy (1B)

el perfume perfume (7B)

el periódico newspaper (8B)

pero but (1B)

el perrito caliente hot dog (3A)

el perro dog (5A)

la persona person (5A)

   pesas: levantar — to lift weights (3B)

el pescado fish (3B)

el pie foot (P)

la pierna leg (P)

la pimienta pepper (5B)

la piñata piñata (5A)

la piscina pool (4A)

el piso story, floor (6B)

   primer — second floor (6B)

   segundo — third floor (6B)

la pizza pizza (3A)

la planta baja ground floor (6B)

el plástico plastic (8B)

el plátano banana (3A)

el plato plate, dish (5B)

   de — principal as a main dish (5B)

   el — principal main dish (5B)

la playa beach (4A)

pobre poor (8B)

poco: un — (de) a little (4B)

poder (o → ue) to be able (6A)

   (yo) puedo I can (4B)

   (tú) puedes you can (4B)

policíaca: la película — crime movie, mystery (9A)

el pollo chicken (3B)

poner to put, to place (6B)

   pon (*command*) put, place (6B)

   — la mesa to set the table (6B)

   (yo) pongo I put (6B)

   (tú) pones you put (6B)

por:

   — eso that's why, therefore (9A)

   — favor please (P)

¿— qué? Why? (3B)

   — supuesto of course (3A)

porque because (3B)

la posesión *pl.* **las posesiones** possession (6A)

el postre dessert (5B)

   de — for dessert (5B)

practicar deportes to play sports (1A)

práctico, -a practical (2A)

el precio price (7A)

preferir (e → ie) to prefer (7A)

   (yo) prefiero I prefer (3B)

   (tú) prefieres you prefer (3B)

preparar to prepare (5A)

la presentación *pl.* **las presentaciones** presentation (9B)

la primavera spring (P)

primer (primero), -a first (2A)

   — piso second floor (6B)

el primo, la prima cousin (5A)

los primos cousins (5A)

el problema problem (8B)

el profesor, la profesora teacher (P)

el programa program, show (9A)

   el — de concursos game show (9A)

   el — de dibujos animados cartoon (9A)

   el — de entrevistas interview program (9A)

   el — de la vida real reality program (9A)

el — de noticias news program (9A)

el — deportivo sports program (9A)

el — educativo educational program (9A)

el — musical musical program (9A)

propio, -a own (6A)

el proyecto de construcción construction project (8B)

puedes: (tú) — you can (4B)

puedo: (yo) — I can (4B)

la puerta door (2B)

pues well (*to indicate pause*) (1A)

la pulsera bracelet (7B)

   el reloj — watch (7B)

el pupitre student desk (P)

Q

que who, that (5A)

qué:

   ¿Para — sirve? What's it (used) for? (9B)

   ¡— + adj.! How ...! (5B)

   ¡— asco! How awful! (3A)

   ¡— buena idea! What a good/nice idea! (4B)

   ¿— clase de ...? What kind of ... ? (9A)

   ¿— desean (Uds.)? What would you like? (5B)

   ¿— día es hoy? What day is today? (P)

   ¿— es esto? What is this? (2B)

   ¿— hiciste? What did you do? (8A)

   ¿— hora es? What time is it? (P)

   ¿— más? What else? (8B)

   ¿— pasa? What's happening? (P)

   ¡— pena! What a shame/pity! (4B)

   ¿— quiere decir ... ? What does ... mean? (P)

¿— tal? How are you? (P)

¿— te gusta hacer? What do you like to do? (1A)

¿— te gusta más? What do you like better (prefer) to do? (1A)

¿— te parece? What do you think (about it)? (9B)

¿— te pasó? What happened to you? (8A)

¿— tiempo hace? What's the weather like? (P)

quedar to fit (7A), to stay (4A)

¿Cómo me queda? How does it fit (me)? (7A)

Me / te queda bien. It fits me / you well. (7A)

Me quedo en casa. I stay home. (4A)

el quehacer (de la casa) (household) chore (6B)

querer (e → ie) to want (7A)

¿Qué quiere decir ...? What does ... mean? (P)

Quiere decir ... It means ... (P)

quisiera I would like (5B)

(yo) quiero I want (4B)

(tú) quieres you want (4B)

el queso cheese (3A)

¿Quién? Who? (2A)

quince fifteen (P)

quinientos, -as five hundred (7A)

quinto, -a fifth (2A)

quisiera I would like (5B)

quitar el polvo to dust (6B)

quizás maybe (7A)

rápidamente quickly (9B)

el ratón *pl.* **los ratones** (computer) mouse (2B)

razón: tener — to be correct (7A)

realista realistic (9A)

recibir to receive (6B)

reciclar to recycle (8B)

recoger (g → j) to collect, to gather (8B)

los recuerdos souvenirs (8A)

comprar recuerdos to buy souvenirs (8A)

la Red:

en la — online (7B)

navegar en la — to surf the Web (9B)

el refresco soft drink (3A)

el regalo gift, present (5A)

regresar to return (8A)

regular okay, so-so (P)

el reloj clock (2B)

el — pulsera watch (7B)

reservado, -a reserved, shy (1B)

el restaurante restaurant (4A)

rico, -a rich, tasty (5B)

el río river (8B)

rojo, -a red (6A)

romántico, -a: la película — romantic movie (9A)

romper to break (5A)

la ropa: la tienda de — clothing store (7B)

rosado, -a pink (6A)

rubio, -a blond (5B)

S

sábado Saturday (P)

saber to know (how) (9B)

(yo) sé I know (how to) (4B)

(tú) sabes you know (how to) (4B)

sabroso, -a tasty, flavorful (3B)

el sacapuntas pencil sharpener (2B)

sacar:

— fotos to take photos (5A)

— la basura to take out the trash (6B)

la sal salt (5B)

la sala living room (6B)

la sala de clases classroom (P)

la salchicha sausage (3A)

salir to leave, to go out (8A)

la salud:

para la — for one's health (3B)

para mantener la — to maintain one's health (3B)

el sándwich de jamón y queso ham and cheese sandwich (3A)

sé: (yo) — I know (how to) (1B)

sed: Tengo —. I'm thirsty. (3B)

según according to (1B)

— mi familia according to my family (1B)

segundo, -a second (2A)

— piso third floor (6B)

seis six (P)

seiscientos, -as six hundred (7A)

la semana week (P)

este fin de — this weekend (4B)

la — pasada last week (7B)

los fines de — on weekends (4A)

señor (Sr.) sir, Mr. (P)

señora (Sra.) madam, Mrs. (P)

señorita (Srta.) miss, Miss (P)

separar to separate (8B)

septiembre September (P)

séptimo, -a seventh (2A)

ser to be (3B)

¿Eres ...? Are you ...? (1B)

es he/she is (1B)

fue it was (8A)

no soy I am not (1B)

soy I am (1B)

serio, -a serious (1B)

la servilleta napkin (5B)

servir (e → i) to serve, to be useful (9B)

¿En qué puedo servirle? How can I help you? (7A)

¿Para qué sirve? What's it (used) for? (9B)

Sirve para ... It's used for ... (9B)

sesenta sixty (P)

setecientos, -as seven hundred (7A)

setenta seventy (P)

sexto, -a sixth (2A)

si if, whether (6B)

sí yes (1A)

siempre always (3A)

siento: lo — I'm sorry (4B)

siete seven (P)

la **silla** chair (2B)

simpático, -a nice, friendly (1B)

sin without (3A)

la **sinagoga** synagogue (4A)

el **sitio Web** Web site (9B)

sobre about (9A)

sociable sociable (1B)

el **software** software (7B)

el **sol:**

> **Hace —.** It's sunny. (P)

> **los anteojos de —** sunglasses (7B)

> **tomar el —** to sunbathe (8A)

sólo only (5A)

solo, -a alone (4A)

Son las ... It's ... (*time*) (P)

la **sopa de verduras** vegetable soup (3A)

el **sótano** basement (6B)

soy I am (1B)

su, sus his, her, your *formal*, their (5A)

sucio, -a dirty (6B)

la **sudadera** sweatshirt (7A)

sueño: tener — to be sleepy (5B)

el **suéter** sweater (7A)

supuesto: por — of course (3A)

T

tal: ¿Qué — ? How are you? (P)

talentoso, -a talented (1B)

también also, too (1A)

> **a mí —** I do (like to) too (1A)

tampoco: a mí — I don't (like to) either (1A)

tanto so much (7A)

tarde late (8A); afternoon (4B)

a la una de la — at one (o'clock) in the afternoon (4B)

Buenas —s. Good afternoon. (P)

de la tarde in the afternoon (4B)

esta — this afternoon (4B)

la **tarea** homework (2A)

la **tarjeta** card (9B)

la **taza** cup (5B)

te (to/for) you *sing. ind. obj. pron.* (8B)

> **¿— gusta ...?** Do you like to ... ? (1A)

> **¿— gustaría ...?** Would you like ...? (4B)

> **¿— gustó?** Did you like it? (8A)

el **té** tea (3A)

> **el — helado** iced tea (3A)

el **teatro** theater (8A)

el **teclado** (computer) keyboard (2B)

la **tecnología** technology/computers (2A)

> **la clase de —** technology/computer class (2A)

la **telenovela** soap opera (9A)

el **televisor** television set (6A)

el **templo** temple; Protestant church (4A)

temprano early (8A)

el **tenedor** fork (5B)

tener to have (5A)

> **(yo) tengo** I have (2A)

> **(tú) tienes** you have (2A)

> **¿Cuántos años tiene(n) ...?** How old is/are ... ? (5A)

> **— calor** to be warm (5B)

> **— frío** to be cold (5B)

> **— miedo (de)** to be scared (of), to be afraid (of) (9B)

> **— razón** to be correct (7A)

> **— sueño** to be sleepy (5B)

> **Tengo hambre.** I'm hungry. (3B)

Tengo que ... I have to ... (4B)

Tengo sed. I'm thirsty. (3B)

Tiene(n) ... años. He/She is/They are ... years old. (5A)

el **tenis: jugar al —** to play tennis (4B)

tercer (tercero), -a third (2A)

terminar to finish, to end (9A)

ti you *fam. after prep.*

> **¿Y a —?** And you? (1A)

> **para —** in your opinion, for you (6A)

el **tiempo:**

> **el — libre** free time (4A)

> **pasar — con amigos** to spend time with friends (1A)

> **¿Qué — hace?** What's the weather like? (P)

la **tienda** store (7A)

> **la — de descuentos** discount store (7B)

> **la — de electrodomésticos** household appliance store (7B)

> **la — de ropa** clothing store (7A)

Tiene(n) ... años. He/She is / They are ... (years old). (5A)

el **tío, la tía** uncle, aunt (5A)

los **tíos** uncles; aunt(s) and uncle(s) (5A)

> **tocar la guitarra** to play the guitar (1A)

el **tocino** bacon (3A)

todos, -as all (3B)

> **— los días** every day (3A)

tomar:

> **— el sol** to sunbathe (8A)

> **— un curso** to take a course (9B)

los **tomates** tomatoes (3B)

tonto, -a silly, stupid (9A)

trabajador, -a hardworking (1B)

trabajar to work (1A)

el **trabajo** work, job (4A)

> **el — voluntario** volunteer work (8B)

traer:

    Le traigo ... I will bring you ... (5B)

    ¿Me trae ...? Will you bring me ...? (5B)

el traje suit (7A)

    el — de baño swimsuit (7A)

trece thirteen (P)

treinta thirty (P)

treinta y uno thirty-one (P)

tremendo, -a tremendous (8A)

el tren train (8A)

tres three (P)

trescientos, as three hundred (7A)

triste sad (4B)

tu, tus your (2B, 5A)

tú you *fam.* (2A)

Ud. (usted) you *formal sing.* (2A)

Uds. (ustedes) you *formal pl.* (2A)

¡Uf! Ugh!, Yuck! (7B)

un, una a, an (1B)

    un poco (de) a little (4B)

la una: a la — at one o'clock (4B)

uno one (P)

unos, -as some (2B)

usado, -a used (8B)

usar la computadora to use the computer (1A)

usted (Ud.) you *formal sing.* (2A)

ustedes (Uds.) you *formal pl.* (2A)

las uvas grapes (3B)

V

las vacaciones: ir de — to go on vacation (8A)

¡Vamos! Let's go! (7A)

el vaso glass (5B)

veinte twenty (P)

veintiuno (veintiún) twenty-one (P)

vender to sell (7B)

venir to come (5B)

la ventana window (2B)

ver to see (8A)

    a — ... Let's see (2A)

    ¡Nos vemos! See you later! (P)

    — la tele to watch television (1A)

    — una película to see a movie (4A)

el verano summer (P)

veras: ¿De —? Right? (9A)

¿Verdad? Right? (3A)

verde green (6A)

el vestido dress (7A)

la vez, *pl.* **las veces** time (8B)

    a veces sometimes (1B)

    otra — again (8B)

vi I saw (8A)

viajar to travel (8A)

el viaje trip (8A)

el video video (5A)

los videojuegos: jugar — to play video games (1A)

el vidrio glass (8B)

viejo, -a old (5B)

viernes Friday (P)

violento, -a violent (9A)

visitar to visit (8A)

    — salones de chat to visit chat rooms (9B)

¿Viste? Did you see? (8A)

vivir to live (6B)

el vóleibol: jugar al — to play volleyball (4B)

el voluntario, la voluntaria volunteer (8B)

vosotros, -as you *pl.* (2A)

vuestro(s), -a(s) your (5A)

Y

y and (1A)

    ¿— a ti? And you? (1A)

    — cuarto quarter past (P)

    — media thirty, half-past (*in telling time*) (P)

    ¿— tú? And you? *fam.* (P)

    ¿— usted (Ud.)? And you? *formal* (P)

ya already (9A)

yo I (1B)

el yogur yogurt (3A)

Z

las zanahorias carrots (3B)

la zapatería shoe store (7B)

los zapatos shoes (7A)

el zoológico zoo (8A)

English-Spanish Vocabulary

The *English-Spanish Vocabulary* contains all active vocabulary from the text, including vocabulary presented in the grammar sections.

A dash (—) represents the main entry word. For example, **to play —** after **baseball** means **to play baseball.**

The number following each entry indicates the chapter in which the word or expression is presented. The letter *P* following an entry refers to the *Para empezar* section.

The following abbreviations are used in this list: *adj.* (adjective), *dir. obj.* (direct object), *f.* (feminine), *fam.*(familiar), *ind. obj.* (indirect object), *inf.* (infinitive), *m.* (masculine), *pl.* (plural), *prep.* (preposition), *pron.* (pronoun), *sing.* (singular).

A

a, an un, una (1B)

  a little un poco (de) (4B)

  a lot mucho, -a (2A)

  a thousand mil (7A)

able: to be — poder (o → ue) (6A)

about sobre (9A)

according to según (1B)

  — my family según mi familia (1B)

acquainted: to be — with conocer (9B)

actor el actor (9A)

actress la actriz *pl.* las actrices (9A)

address: e-mail — la dirección electrónica (9B)

afraid: to be — (of) tener miedo (de) (9B)

after después (de) (4A)

afternoon:

  at one (o'clock) in the afternoon a la una de la tarde (4B)

  Good —. Buenas tardes. (P)

  in the — de la tarde (4B)

  this — esta tarde (4B)

afterwards después (4A)

again otra vez (8B)

ago hace + *time expression* (7B)

agree:

  I —. Estoy de acuerdo. (3B)

  I don't —. No estoy de acuerdo. (3B)

airplane el avión *pl.* los aviones (8A)

alarm clock el despertador (6A)

all todos, -as (3B)

almost casi (9A)

alone solo, -a (4A)

already ya (9A)

also también (1A)

always siempre (3A)

am:

  I — (yo) soy (1B)

  I — not (yo) no soy (1B)

amusement park el parque de diversiones (8A)

amusing divertido, -a (2A)

and y (1A)

  ¿— you? ¿Y a ti? *fam.* (1A); ¿Y tú? *fam.* (P); ¿Y usted (Ud.)? *formal* (P)

animal el animal (8A)

another otro, -a (5B)

Anything else? ¿Algo más? (5B)

apartment el apartamento (6B)

apple la manzana (3A)

  — juice el jugo de manzana (3A)

April abril (P)

Are you ... ? ¿Eres ... ? (1B)

arm el brazo (P)

art class la clase de arte (2A)

artistic artístico, -a (1B)

as como (8A)

  — a main dish de plato principal (5B)

to ask for pedir (e → i) (9B)

at:

  — eight (o'clock) a las ocho (4B)

  — eight (o'clock) at night a las ocho de la noche (4B)

  — eight (o'clock) in the evening a las ocho de la noche (4B)

  — eight (o'clock) in the morning a las ocho de la mañana (4B)

  — home en casa (4A)

  — one (o'clock) a la una (4B)

  — one (o'clock) in the afternoon a la una de la tarde (4B)

  — what time? ¿A qué hora? (4B)

attraction(s) la atracción *pl.* las atracciones (8A)

August agosto (P)

aunt la tía (5A)

aunt(s) and uncle(s) los tíos (5A)

autumn el otoño (P)

B

backpack la mochila (2B)

bacon el tocino (3A)

bad malo, -a (3B); mal (4B)

badly mal (4B)

bag la bolsa (8B)

balloon el globo (5A)

banana el plátano (3A)

baseball: to play — jugar al béisbol (4B)

basement el sótano (6B)

basketball: to play — jugar al básquetbol (4B)

bathroom el baño (6B)

to be ser (3B); estar (2B)

> **He/She is / They are … years old.** Tiene(n) … años. (5A)

> **How old is/are … ?** ¿Cuántos años tiene(n) … ? (5A)

> **to —** + *present participle* estar + *present participle* (6B)

> **to — able** poder (o → ue) (6A)

> **to — acquainted with** conocer (9B)

> **to — afraid (of)** tener miedo (de) (9B)

> **to — cold** tener frío (5B)

> **to — correct** tener razón (7A)

> **to — going to** + *verb* ir a + *inf.* (4B)

> **to — online** estar en línea (9B)

> **to — scared (of)** tener miedo (de) (9B)

> **to — sleepy** tener sueño (5B)

> **to — useful** servir (e → i) (9B)

> **to — warm** tener calor (5B)

beach la playa (4A)

bear el oso (8A)

because porque (3B)

bed la cama (6A)

> **to make the —** hacer la cama (6B)

bedroom el dormitorio (6A)

beefsteak el bistec (3B)

before antes de (9A)

to begin empezar (e → ie) (9A)

behind detrás de (2B)

best: the — el/la mejor, los/las mejores (6A)

better than mejor(es) que (6A)

beverages las bebidas (3B)

bicycle: to ride a — montar en bicicleta (1A)

bill la cuenta (5B)

binder: three-ring — la carpeta de argollas (2A)

bird el pájaro (8A)

birthday el cumpleaños (5A)

> **Happy —!** ¡Feliz cumpleaños! (5A)

black negro (6A)

black hair el pelo negro (5B)

blond hair el pelo rubio (5B)

blouse la blusa (7A)

blue azul (6A)

boat el barco (8A)

boating: to go — pasear en bote (8A)

book el libro (P)

bookbag la mochila (2B)

bookshelf el estante (6A)

bookstore la librería (7B)

boots las botas (7A)

to bore aburrir (9A)

> **it/they —(s) me** me aburre(n) (9A)

boring aburrido, -a (2A)

both los dos, las dos (7A)

bottle la botella (8B)

box la caja (8B)

boy el chico (1B)

> **—friend** el novio (7B)

> **young —** el niño (8B)

bracelet la pulsera (7B)

bread el pan (3A)

to break romper (5A)

> **breakfast** el desayuno (3A)

> **for —** en el desayuno (3A)

to bring traer (5B); llevar (8B)

> **I will — you …** Le traigo … (5B)

> **Will you — me … ?** ¿Me trae … ? (5B)

brother el hermano (5A)

brothers; brother(s) and sister(s) los hermanos (5A)

brown marrón *pl.* marrones (6A)

> **— (chestnut) hair** el pelo castaño (5B)

to burn a CD grabar un disco compacto (9B)

> **bus** el autobús *pl.* los autobuses (8A)

> **busy** ocupado, -a (4B)

> **but** pero (1B)

> **butter** la mantequilla (3B)

to buy comprar (7A)

> **to — souvenirs** comprar recuerdos (8A)

> **by** + *vehicle* en + *vehicle* (8A)

C

café el café (4A)

cake el pastel (5A)

calculator la calculadora (2A)

camera la cámara (5A)

> **digital —** la cámara digital (9B)

camp el campamento (8B)

can la lata (8B)

can:

> **I —** (yo) puedo (4B)

> **you —** (tú) puedes (4B)

candy los dulces (5A)

cap la gorra (7A)

car el coche (6B)

card la tarjeta (9B)

cardboard el cartón (8B)

carrots las zanahorias (3B)

to carry llevar (8B)

> **cartoon** el programa de dibujos animados (9A)

> **cat** el gato (5A)

> **CD: to burn a CD** grabar un disco compacto (9B)

to celebrate celebrar (5A)

> **cereal** el cereal (3A)

> **chain** la cadena (7B)

> **chair** la silla (2B)

> **channel (TV)** el canal (9A)

> **cheap** barato, -a (7B)

> **cheese** el queso (3A)

> **chicken** el pollo (3B)

> **childish** infantil (9A)

> **children** los hijos (5A); los niños (8B)

> **chore: household —** el quehacer (de la casa) (6B)

> **church** la iglesia (4A)

> **Protestant —** el templo (4A)

> **city** la ciudad (8A)

> **class** la clase (2A)

> **classroom** la sala de clases (P)

> **clean** limpio, -a (6B)

to clean the bathroom limpiar el baño (6B)

> **clock** el reloj (2B)

> **close (to)** cerca (de) (6B)

> **closet** el armario (6A)

> **clothing store** la tienda de ropa (7A)

coat el abrigo (7A)

coffee el café (3A)

cold:

It's —. Hace frío. (P)

to be — tener frío (5B)

to collect recoger (g → j) (8B)

color:

What — ...? ¿De qué color ...? (6A)

—s los colores (6A)

to come venir (5B)

comedy la comedia (9A)

comical cómico, -a (9A)

to communicate comunicarse (9B)

I — (yo) me comunico (9B)

you — (tú) te comunicas (9B)

community la comunidad (8B)

compact disc el disco compacto (6A)

to burn a — grabar un disco compacto (9B)

complicated complicado, -a (9B)

composition la composición *pl.* las composiciones (9B)

computer la computadora (2B)

— graphics los gráficos (9B)

— keyboard el teclado (2B)

— mouse el ratón (2B)

— screen la pantalla (2B)

—s/technology la tecnología (2B)

laptop — la computadora portátil (9B)

to use the — usar la computadora (1A)

concert el concierto (4B)

construction project el proyecto de construcción (8B)

to cook cocinar (6B)

cookie la galleta (3A)

correct: to be — tener razón (7A)

to cost costar (o → ue) (7A)

How much does (do) ... — ? ¿Cuánto cuesta(n)? (7A)

country el país (8A)

countryside el campo (4A)

course: to take a course tomar un curso (9B)

cousin el primo, la prima (5A)

—s los primos (5A)

to create crear (9B)

crime movie la película policíaca (9A)

cup la taza (5B)

curtains las cortinas (6A)

to cut the lawn cortar el césped (6B)

cut-paper decorations el papel picado (5A)

D

dance el baile (4B)

to dance bailar (1A)

daring atrevido, -a (1B)

date: What is the —? ¿Cuál es la fecha? (P)

daughter la hija (5A)

day el día (P)

every — todos los días (3A); cada día (3B)

What — is today? ¿Qué día es hoy? (P)

December diciembre (P)

to decide decidir (8B)

to decorate decorar (5A)

decorations las decoraciones (5A)

delicious delicioso, -a (5B)

delighted encantado, -a (P)

department store el almacén *pl.* los almacenes (7B)

desk el pupitre (P); el escritorio (2B)

dessert el postre (5B)

for — de postre (5B)

dictionary el diccionario (2A)

Did you like it? ¿Te gustó? (8A)

difficult difícil (2A)

digital camera la cámara digital (9B)

dining room el comedor (6B)

dinner la cena (3B)

dirty sucio, -a (6B)

disaster: It was a — . Fue un desastre. (8A)

discount store la tienda de descuentos (7B)

dish el plato (5B)

as a main — de plato principal (5B)

main — el plato principal (5B)

to do hacer (3B)

— (command) haz (6B)

— you like to ...? ¿Te gusta ...? (1A)

I — (yo) hago (3B)

What did you —? ¿Qué hiciste? (8A)

you — (tú) haces (3B)

document el documento (9B)

dog el perro (5A)

to feed the — dar de comer al perro (6B)

door la puerta (2B)

to download bajar (información) (9B)

drama el drama (9A)

to draw dibujar (1A)

dress el vestido (7A)

dresser la cómoda (6A)

to drink beber (3A)

during durante (8A)

to dust quitar el polvo (6B)

DVD player el lector DVD (6A)

E

e-mail:

— address la dirección electrónica (9B)

to write an — message escribir por correo electrónico (9B)

early temprano (8A)

earrings los aretes (7B)

easy fácil (2A)

to eat comer (3A)

educational program el programa educativo (9A)

eggs los huevos (3A)

eight ocho (P)

eight hundred ochocientos, -as (7A)

eighteen dieciocho (P)

eighth octavo, -a (2A)

eighty ochenta (P)

either tampoco (1A)

    I don't (like to) — a mí tampoco (1A)

eleven once (P)

else:

Anything —? ¿Algo más? (5B)

    What —? ¿Qué más? (8B)

to end terminar (9A)

    English class la clase de inglés (2A)

enough bastante (6B)

to enter entrar (7A)

    especially especialmente (9A)

    evening:

        Good —. Buenas noches. (P)

        in the — de la noche (4B)

        this — esta noche (4B)

    every day cada día (3B); todos los días (3A)

    Excuse me. Perdón. (7A)

to exercise hacer ejercicio (3B)

    expensive caro, -a (7B)

    experience la experiencia (8B)

    eye el ojo (P)

F

face-to-face cara a cara (9B)

fall el otoño (P)

family la familia (1B)

fantastic fantástico, -a (8A)

far (from) lejos (de) (6B)

fascinating fascinante (9A)

fast rápidamente (9B)

father el padre (papá) (5A)

fats las grasas (3B)

favorite favorito, -a (2A)

February febrero (P)

to feed the dog dar de comer al perro (6B)

fewer:

    — ... than menos ... que (6A)

    — than ... menos de ... (9A)

fifteen quince (P)

fifth quinto, -a (2A)

fifty cincuenta (P)

film la película (9A)

finger el dedo (P)

to finish terminar (9A)

    first primer (primero), -a (2A)

    fish el pescado (3B)

    to go —ing ir de pesca (4B)

to fit:

    How does it (do they) fit me / you? ¿Cómo me / te queda(n)? (7A)

    It / They —(s) me well / poorly. Me queda(n) bien / mal. (7A)

five cinco (P)

five hundred quinientos, -as (7A)

flag la bandera (2B)

flavorful sabroso, -a (3B)

floor el piso (6B)

    ground — la planta baja (6B)

    second — el primer piso (6B)

    third — el segundo piso (6B)

flower la flor *pl.* las flores (5A)

folder la carpeta (P)

food la comida (3A)

foot el pie (P)

football: to play — jugar al fútbol americano (4B)

for para (2A)

    — breakfast en el desayuno (3A)

    — lunch en el almuerzo (3A)

    — me para mí (6A)

    — you para ti (6A)

fork el tenedor (5B)

forty cuarenta (P)

four cuatro (P)

four hundred cuatrocientos, -as (7A)

fourteen catorce (P)

fourth cuarto, -a (2A)

free time el tiempo libre (4A)

French fries las papas fritas (3A)

Friday viernes (P)

friendly simpático, -a (1B)

from de (4A)

    Where are you —? ¿De dónde eres? (4A)

fruit salad la ensalada de frutas (3A)

fun divertido, -a (2A)

funny gracioso, -a (1B); cómico, -a (9A)

G

game el partido (4B)

    — show el programa de concursos (9A)

garage el garaje (6B)

garden el jardín *pl.* los jardines (8B)

to gather recoger (g → j) (8B)

    generally generalmente (4A)

gift el regalo (5A)

girl la chica (1B)

    —friend la novia (7B)

    young — la niña (8B)

to give dar (6B)

    glass el vaso (5B); el vidrio (8B)

    gloves los guantes (7B)

to go ir (4A)

    Let's —! ¡Vamos! (7A)

        to be —ing to + *verb* ir a + *inf.* (4B)

        to — boating pasear en bote (8A)

        to — camping ir de cámping (4B)

        to — fishing ir de pesca (4B)

        to — on vacation ir de vacaciones (8A)

        to — shopping ir de compras (4A)

        to — to school ir a la escuela (1A)

        to — out salir (8A)

golf: to play — jugar al golf (4B)

good bueno (buen), -a (1B)

    — afternoon. Buenas tardes. (P)

    — evening. Buenas noches. (P)

    — morning. Buenos días. (P)

Good-bye! ¡Adiós! (P)

good-looking guapo, -a (5B)

grains los cereales (3B)

grandfather el abuelo (5A)

grandmother la abuela (5A)

grandparents los abuelos (5A)

grapes las uvas (3B)

graphics los gráficos (9B)

gray gris (6A)

   — **hair** el pelo canoso (5B)

Great! ¡Genial! (4B)

green verde (6A)

   — **beans** las judías verdes (3B)

ground floor la planta baja (6B)

guitar: to play the — tocar la guitarra (1A)

gym el gimnasio (4A)

H

hair el pelo (5B)

   black — el pelo negro (5B)

   blond — el pelo rubio (5B)

   brown (chestnut) — el pelo castaño (5B)

   gray — el pelo canoso (5B)

half media, -o (P)

   — **-past** y media (P)

ham and cheese sandwich el sándwich de jamón y queso (3A)

hamburger la hamburguesa (3A)

hand la mano (P)

happy contento, -a (4B)

   — **birthday!** ¡Feliz cumpleaños! (5A)

hardworking trabajador, -a (1B)

to have tener (5A)

   to — **just ...** acabar de + *inf.* (9A)

   I — **to ...** tengo que + *inf.* (4B)

he él (1B)

he/she is es (1B)

   He/She is / They are ... years old. Tiene(n) ... años. (5A)

head la cabeza (P)

health:

   for one's — para la salud (3B)

   to maintain one's — para mantener la salud (3B)

Hello! ¡Hola! (P)

to help ayudar (6B)

   How can I — **you?** ¿En qué puedo servirle? (7A)

her su, sus *possessive adj.* (5A); la *dir. obj. pron.* (7B); le *ind. obj. pron.* (8B)

here aquí (2B)

Hey! ¡Oye! (4B)

him lo *dir. obj. pron.* (7B); le *ind. obj. pron.* (8B)

his su, sus (5A)

home la casa (4A)

   at — en casa (4A)

   — **office** el despacho (6B)

   (to) — a casa (4A)

homework la tarea (2A)

horrible horrible (3B)

horror movie la película de horror (9A)

horseback: to ride — montar a caballo (8A)

hospital el hospital (8B)

hot:

   — **dog** el perrito caliente (3A)

   It's —. Hace calor. (P)

hotel el hotel (8A)

**hour: in the ... ** — en la ... hora (class period) (2A)

house la casa (4A)

household:

   — **chore** el quehacer (de la casa) (6B)

   — **appliance store** la tienda de electrodomésticos (7B)

how:

   — **+** *adj.*! ¡Qué + *adj.*! (5B)

   — **awful!** ¡Qué asco! (3A)

how? ¿cómo? (P)

   — **are you?** ¿Cómo está Ud.? *formal* (P); ¿Cómo estás? *fam.* (P); ¿Qué tal? *fam.* (P)

   — **can I help you?** ¿En qué puedo servirle? (7A)

   — **do you say ... ?** ¿Cómo se dice ...? (P)

   — **does it (do they) fit (you)?** ¿Cómo te queda(n)? (7A)

   — **is ... spelled?** ¿Cómo se escribe ...? (P)

   — **many?** ¿cuántos, -as? (P)

   — **much does (do) ... cost?** ¿Cuánto cuesta(n) ...? (7A)

   — **old is/are ... ?** ¿Cuántos años tiene(n) ...? (5A)

   — **was it (for you)?** ¿Cómo lo pasaste? (8A)

hundred: one — cien (P)

hungry: I'm —. Tengo hambre. (3B)

to hurt doler (o → ue) (9A)

husband el esposo (5A)

I

I yo (1B)

   — **am** soy (1B)

   — **am not** no soy (1B)

   — **do too** a mí también (1A)

   — **don't either** a mí tampoco (1A)

   — **don't think so.** Creo que no. (3B)

   — **stay at home.** Me quedo en casa. (4A)

   — **think ...** Creo que ... (3B)

   — **think so.** Creo que sí. (3B)

   — **will bring you ...** Le traigo ... (5B)

   — **would like ...** Me gustaría (4B); quisiera (5B)

   — **'m hungry.** Tengo hambre. (3B)

   — **'m sorry.** Lo siento. (4B)

   — **'m thirsty.** Tengo sed. (3B)

ice cream el helado (3B)

iced tea el té helado (3A)

if si (6B)

impatient impaciente (1B)

important importante (6A)

impressive impresionante (8A)

in en (P, 2B)

   — **front of** delante de (2B)

   — **my opinion** para mí (6A)

   — **order to** para + *inf.* (4A)

   — **the ... hour** en la ... hora (class period) (2A)

   — **your opinion** para ti (6A)

incredible increíble (8B)

inexpensive barato, -a (7B)

information la información (9B)

intelligent inteligente (1B)

to interest interesar (9A)

    it/they interest(s) me me interesa(n) (9A)

interesting interesante (2A)

interview program el programa de entrevistas (9A)

is es (P)

    he/she — es (1B)

it la, lo *dir. obj. pron.* (7B)

    — fits (they fit) me well/ poorly. Me queda(n) bien/ mal. (7A)

    — is ... Son las *(in telling time)* (P)

    — is one o'clock. Es la una. (P)

    — is the ... of ... Es el *(number)* de *(month) (in telling the date)* (P)

    — is the first of ... Es el primero de *(month).* (P)

    — was fue (8A)

    — was a disaster. Fue un desastre. (8A)

    —'s a ... es un/una ... (2B)

    —'s cold. Hace frío. (P)

    —'s hot. Hace calor. (P)

    —'s necessary. Es necesario. (8B)

    —'s raining. Llueve. (P)

    —'s snowing. Nieva. (P)

    —'s sunny. Hace sol. (P)

J

jacket la chaqueta (7A)

January enero (P)

jeans los jeans (7A)

jewelry store la joyería (7B)

job el trabajo (4A)

juice:

    apple — el jugo de manzana (3A)

    orange — el jugo de naranja (3A)

July julio (P)

June junio (P)

just: to have — (done something) acabar de + *inf.* (9A)

K

key chain el llavero (7B)

keyboard (computer) el teclado (2B)

kind: What — of ... ? ¿Qué clase de ...? (9A)

kitchen la cocina (6B)

knife el cuchillo (5B)

to know saber (4B, 9B); conocer (9B)

    I — (yo) conozco (9B)

    I — (how to) (yo) sé (4B)

    you — (tú) conoces (9B)

    you — (how to) (tú) sabes (4B)

L

laboratory el laboratorio (9B)

lake el lago (8A)

lamp la lámpara (6A)

laptop computer la computadora portátil (9B)

large grande (6A)

last:

    — night anoche (7B)

    — week la semana pasada (7B)

    — year el año pasado (7B)

to last durar (9A)

    late tarde (8A)

    later: See you — ¡Hasta luego!, ¡Nos vemos! (P)

    lazy perezoso, -a (1B)

to learn aprender (a) (8A)

to leave salir (8A)

    left: to the — (of) a la izquierda (de) (6A)

    leg la pierna (P)

    lemonade la limonada (3A)

    less:

    less ... than menos ... que (6A)

    less than menos de (9A)

    Let's go! ¡Vamos! (7A)

    Let's see A ver ... (2A)

letter la carta (9B)

lettuce la lechuga (3B)

library la biblioteca (4A)

to lift weights levantar pesas (3B)

    light la luz *pl.* las luces (5A)

    like como (8A)

to like:

    Did you — it? ¿Te gustó? (8A)

    Do you — to ...? ¿Te gusta ...? (1A)

    He/She doesn't — ... No le gusta ... (1B)

    He/She —s ... Le gusta ... (1B); A él/ella le gusta(n) ... (5A)

    I don't — to ... (A mí) no me gusta ... (1A)

    I don't — to ... at all. (A mí) no me gusta nada ... (1A)

    I — ... Me gusta ... (3A)

    I — to ... (A mí) me gusta ... (1A)

    I — to ... a lot (A mí) me gusta mucho ... (1A)

    I — to ... better (A mí) me gusta más ... (1A)

    I —d it. Me gustó. (8A)

    I would — Me gustaría (4B); quisiera (5B)

    What do you — better (prefer) to do? ¿Qué te gusta más? (1A)

    What do you — to do? ¿Qué te gusta hacer? (1A)

    What would you —? ¿Qué desean (Uds.)? (5B)

    Would you —? ¿Te gustaría? (4B)

    You — ... Te gusta ... (3A)

    likewise igualmente (P)

to listen to music escuchar música (1A)

    little: a — un poco (de) (4B)

to live vivir (6B)

    living room la sala (6B)

    long largo, -a (5B)

to look:

    to — (at) mirar (7B)

    to — for buscar (7A)

    lot: a — mucho, -a (2A)

to love encantar (9A)

    He/She —s ... A él/ella le encanta(n) ... (5A)

I/You — ... Me/Te encanta(n)... (3A)

lunch el almuerzo (2A)

for — en el almuerzo (3A)

M

madam (la) señora (Sra.) (P)

main dish el plato principal (5B)

as a — de plato principal (5B)

to maintain one's health para mantener la salud (3B)

make *(command)* haz (6B)

to make the bed hacer la cama (6B)

mall el centro comercial (4A)

man el hombre (5B)

older — el anciano (8B)

many muchos, -as (3B)

how — ¿cuántos, -as? (P)

March marzo (P)

match el partido (4B)

mathematics class la clase de matemáticas (2A)

May mayo (P)

maybe quizás (7A)

me me *ind. obj. pron* (8B)

for — para mí (6A), me (8B)

— too a mí también (1A)

to — me (8B)

with — conmigo (4B)

meal la comida (3A)

to mean:

It —s ... Quiere decir ... (P)

What does ... — ? ¿Qué quiere decir ... ? (P)

meat la carne (3B)

menu el menú (5B)

messy desordenado, -a (1B)

milk la leche (3A)

mirror el espejo (6A)

miss, Miss (la) señorita (Srta.) (P)

missing: to be — faltar (9A)

moment: a — un momento (6B)

Monday lunes (P)

on Mondays los lunes (4A)

money el dinero (6B)

monkey el mono (8A)

month el mes (P)

monument el monumento (8A)

more:

— ... than más ... que (2A)

— or less más o menos (3A)

— than más de (9A)

morning:

Good —. Buenos días. (P)

in the — de la mañana (4B)

mosque la mezquita (4A)

mother la madre (mamá) (5A)

mountains las montañas (4A)

mouse (computer) el ratón (2B)

mouth la boca (P)

movie la película (9A)

to see a — ver una película (4A)

— theater el cine (4A)

to mow the lawn cortar el césped (6B)

Mr. (el) señor (Sr.) (P)

Mrs. (la) señora (Sra.) (P)

much: so — tanto (7A)

museum el museo (8A)

music:

to listen to — escuchar música (1A)

—al program el programa musical (9A)

must deber (3B)

one — hay que (8B)

my mi (2B); mis (5A)

— name is ... Me llamo ... (P)

mystery la película policíaca (9A)

N

name:

My — is ... Me llamo ... (P)

What is your —? ¿Cómo te llamas? (P)

What's his/her —? ¿Cómo se llama? (1B)

napkin la servilleta (5B)

national park el parque nacional (8A)

near cerca (de) (6B)

neat ordenado, -a (1B)

necessary: It's —. Es necesario. (8B)

necklace el collar (7B)

to need

I — necesito (2A)

I — ... Me falta(n) ... (5B)

you — necesitas (2A)

neighborhood el barrio (8B)

neither ... nor ni ... ni (1A)

never nunca (3A)

new nuevo, -a (7A)

news program el programa de noticias (9A)

newspaper el periódico (8B)

next to al lado de (2B)

nice simpático, -a (1B)

night:

at — de la noche (4B)

last — anoche (7B)

night table la mesita (6A)

nine nueve (P)

nine hundred novecientos, -as (7A)

nineteen diecinueve (P)

ninety noventa (P)

ninth noveno, -a (2A)

nose la nariz *pl.* las narices (P)

not ... or ni ... ni (1A)

notebook el cuaderno (P)

nothing nada (P)

November noviembre (P)

now ahora (5B)

O

o'clock:

at eight — a las ocho (4B)

at one — a la una (4B)

It's one —. Es la una. (P)

It's ... — Son las ... (P)

October octubre (P)

of de (2B)

— course por supuesto (3A)

office (home) el despacho (6B)

often a menudo (8B)

Oh! What a shame/pity! ¡Ay! ¡Qué pena! (4B)

okay regular (P)

old viejo, -a (5B)

  He/She is / They are ... years —. Tiene(n) ... años. (5A)

  How — is/are ... ? ¿Cuántos años tiene(n) ... ? (5A)

  —er mayor (5A)

  —er man el anciano (8B)

  —er people los ancianos (8B)

  —er woman la anciana (8B)

on en (2B)

  — Mondays, on Tuesdays ... los lunes, los martes ... (4A)

  — top of encima de (2B)

  — weekends los fines de semana (4A)

one uno (un), -a (P)

  at — (o'clock) a la una (4B)

one hundred cien (P)

one must hay que (8B)

onion la cebolla (3B)

online en la Red (7B)

  to be — estar en línea (9B)

only sólo (5A)

to open abrir (5A)

  opinion:

    in my — para mí (6A)

    in your — para tí (6A)

or o (1A)

orange anaranjado, -a (6A)

  — juice el jugo de naranja (3A)

to order pedir (e → i) (5B)

  other otro, -a (5B)

  others los/las demás (8B)

  our nuestro(s), -a(s) (5A)

  own propio, -a (6A)

painting el cuadro (6A)

pants los pantalones (7A)

paper: sheet of — la hoja de papel (P)

---

parents los padres (5A)

park el parque (4A)

  amusement — el parque de diversiones (8A)

  national — el parque nacional (8A)

party la fiesta (4B)

pastries los pasteles (3B)

patient paciente (1B)

to pay (for) pagar (por) (7B)

peas los guisantes (3B)

pen el bolígrafo (P)

pencil el lápiz *pl.* los lápices (P)

  — sharpener el sacapuntas (2B)

people la gente (8B)

  older — los ancianos (8B)

pepper la pimienta (5B)

perfume el perfume (7B)

person la persona (5A)

phone: to talk on the — hablar por teléfono (1A)

photo la foto (5A)

  to take —s sacar fotos (5A)

physical education class la clase de educación física (2A)

piano lesson (class) la lección *pl.* las lecciones de piano (4A)

pink rosado, -a (6A)

piñata la piñata (5A)

pizza la pizza (3A)

place el lugar (8A)

to place poner (6B)

to plan pensar (e → ie) (7A)

  plastic el plástico (8B)

  plate el plato (5B)

  play la obra de teatro (8A)

to play jugar (a) (u → ue) (4B); tocar (1A)

  to — baseball jugar al béisbol (4B)

  to — basketball jugar al básquetbol (4B)

  to — football jugar al fútbol americano (4B)

  to — golf jugar al golf (4B)

  to — soccer jugar al fútbol (4B)

---

to — sports practicar deportes (1A)

to — tennis jugar al tenis (4B)

to — the guitar tocar la guitarra (1A)

to — video games jugar videojuegos (1A)

to — volleyball jugar al vóleibol (4B)

please por favor (P)

to please very much encantar (9A)

  pleased to meet you mucho gusto (P)

  pool la piscina (4A)

  poor pobre (8B)

  possession la posesión *pl.* las posesiones (6A)

  poster el cartel (2B)

  potatoes las papas (3B)

  practical práctico, -a (2A)

to prefer preferir (e → ie) (7A)

  I — (yo) prefiero (3B)

  I — to ... (a mí) me gusta más ... (1A)

  you — (tú) prefieres (3B)

to prepare preparar (5A)

  present el regalo (5A)

  presentation la presentación *pl.* las presentaciones (9B)

  pretty bonito, -a (6A)

  price el precio (7A)

  primary school la escuela primaria (8B)

  problem el problema (8B)

  program el programa (9A)

  purple morado, -a (6A)

  purse el bolso (7B)

to put poner (6B)

  I — (yo) pongo (6B)

  — (command) pon (6B)

  you — (tú) pones (6B)

Q

quarter past y cuarto (P)

quarter to menos cuarto

quickly rápidamente (9B)

R

rain: It's —ing. Llueve. (P)

rather bastante (6B)

to read magazines leer revistas (1A)

realistic realista (9A)

reality program el programa de la vida real (9A)

Really? ¿De veras? (9A)

to receive recibir (6B)

to recycle reciclar (8B)

recycling center el centro de reciclaje (8B)

red rojo, -a (6A)

—-haired pelirrojo, -a (5B)

to relax descansar (8A)

report el informe (9B)

reserved reservado, -a (1B)

to rest descansar (8A)

restaurant el restaurante (4A)

to return regresar (8A)

rice el arroz (3B)

rich rico, -a (5B)

to ride:

to — a bicycle montar en bicicleta (1A)

to — horseback montar a caballo (8A)

right: to the — (of) a la derecha (de) (6A)

Right? ¿Verdad? (3A)

ring el anillo (7B)

river el río (8B)

road la calle (8B)

romantic movie la película romántica (9A)

room el cuarto (6B)

to straighten up the — arreglar el cuarto (6B)

rug la alfombra (6A)

to run correr (1A)

S

sack la bolsa (8B)

sad triste (4B)

salad la ensalada (3A)

fruit — la ensalada de frutas (3A)

salesperson el dependiente, la dependienta (7A)

salt la sal (5B)

same mismo, -a (6A)

sandwich: ham and cheese — el sándwich de jamón y queso (3A)

Saturday sábado (P)

sausage la salchicha (3A)

to say decir (8B)

How do you —? ¿Cómo se dice? (P)

You — ... Se dice ... (P)

You don't —! ¡No me digas! (4A)

scared: to be — (of) tener miedo (de) (9B)

schedule el horario (2A)

science:

— class la clase de ciencias naturales (2A)

— fiction movie la película de ciencia ficción (9A)

screen: computer — la pantalla (2B)

to scuba dive bucear (8A)

sea el mar (8A)

to search (for) buscar (9B)

season la estación pl. las estaciones (P)

second segundo, -a (2A)

— floor el primer piso (6B)

to see ver (8A)

Let's — A ver ... (2A)

— you later! ¡Nos vemos!, Hasta luego. (P)

— you tomorrow. Hasta mañana. (P)

to — a movie ver una película (4A)

to sell vender (7B)

to send enviar (i → í) (9B)

to separate separar (8B)

September septiembre (P)

serious serio, -a (1B)

to serve servir (e → i) (9B)

to set the table poner la mesa (6B)

seven siete (P)

seven hundred setecientos, -as (7A)

seventeen diecisiete (P)

seventh séptimo, -a (2A)

seventy setenta (P)

to share compartir (3A)

she ella (1B)

sheet of paper la hoja de papel (P)

shelf el estante (6A)

ship el barco (8A)

shirt la camisa (7A)

T- — la camiseta (7A)

shoe store la zapatería (7B)

shoes los zapatos (7A)

short bajo, -a; corto, -a (5B)

shorts los pantalones cortos (7A)

should deber (3B)

show el programa (9A)

to show + movie or TV program dar (9A)

shy reservado, -a (1B)

sick enfermo, -a (4B)

silly tonto, -a (9A)

to sing cantar (1A)

sir (el) señor (Sr.) (P)

sister la hermana (5A)

site: Web — el sitio Web (9B)

six seis (P)

six hundred seiscientos, -as (7A)

sixteen dieciséis (P)

sixth sexto, -a (2A)

sixty sesenta (P)

to skate patinar (1A)

to skateboard montar en monopatín (1A)

to ski esquiar (i fi í) (1A)

skirt la falda (7A)

to sleep dormir (o → ue) (6A)

sleepy: to be — tener sueño (5B)

slide la diapositiva (9B)

small pequeño, -a (6A)

to snorkel bucear (8A)

snow: It's —ing. Nieva. (P)

so much tanto (7A)

so-so regular (P)

soap opera la telenovela (9A)

soccer: to play — jugar al fútbol (4B)

sociable sociable (1B)

social studies class la clase de ciencias sociales (2A)

socks los calcetines (7A)

soft drink el refresco (3A)

software el software (7B)

some unos, -as (2B)

something algo (3B)

sometimes a veces (1B)

son el hijo (5A)

   —s; —(s) and daughter(s) los hijos (5A)

song la canción *pl.* las canciones (9B)

sorry: I'm —. Lo siento. (4B)

sound (stereo) system el equipo de sonido (6A)

soup: vegetable — la sopa de verduras (3A)

souvenirs los recuerdos (8A)

   to buy — comprar recuerdos (8A)

spaghetti los espaguetis (3B)

Spanish class la clase de español (2A)

to spell:

   How is ... spelled? ¿Cómo se escribe ... ? (P)

   It's spelled ... Se escribe ... (P)

to spend time with friends pasar tiempo con amigos (1A)

   spoon la cuchara (5B)

   sports:

      to play — practicar deportes (1A)

      — -minded deportista (1B)

      — show el programa deportivo (9A)

spring la primavera (P)

stadium el estadio (8A)

stairs, stairway la escalera (6B)

to start empezar (e → ie) (9A)

to stay: I — at home. Me quedo en casa. (4A)

   stepbrother el hermanastro (5A)

   stepfather el padrastro (5A)

   stepmother la madrastra (5A)

stepsister la hermanastra (5A)

stereo system el equipo de sonido (6A)

stomach el estómago (P)

store la tienda (7A)

   book— la librería (7B)

   clothing — la tienda de ropa (7A)

   department — el almacén *pl.* los almacenes (7B)

   discount — la tienda de descuentos (7B)

   household appliance — la tienda de electrodomésticos (7B)

   jewelry — la joyería (7B)

   shoe — la zapatería (7B)

story el piso (6B)

stories: to write — escribir cuentos (1A)

to straighten up the room arreglar el cuarto (6B)

   strawberries las fresas (3A)

   street la calle (8B)

   student el/la estudiante (P)

   studious estudioso, -a (1B)

to study estudiar (2A)

   stupid tonto, -a (9A)

   sugar el azúcar (5B)

   suit el traje (7A)

   summer el verano (P)

to sunbathe tomar el sol (8A)

   Sunday domingo (P)

   sunglasses los anteojos de sol (7B)

   sunny: It's —. Hace sol. (P)

to surf the Web navegar en la Red (9B)

   sweater el suéter (7A)

   sweatshirt la sudadera (7A)

to swim nadar (1A)

   swimming pool la piscina (4A)

   swimsuit el traje de baño (7A)

   synagogue la sinagoga (4A)

T

   T-shirt la camiseta (7A)

   table la mesa (2B)

to set the — poner la mesa (6B)

   to take llevar (8B)

to — a course tomar un curso (9B)

   to — out the trash sacar la basura (6B)

   to — photos sacar fotos (5A)

talented talentoso, -a (1B)

to talk hablar (2A)

   to — on the phone hablar por teléfono (1A)

tall alto, -a (5B)

tasty sabroso, -a (3B); rico, -a (5B)

tea el té (3A)

   iced — el té helado (3A)

to teach enseñar (2A)

   teacher el profesor, la profesora (P)

   technology/computers la tecnología (2A)

   technology/computer class la clase de tecnología (2A)

   television: to watch — ver la tele (1A)

   television set el televisor (6A)

to tell decir (8B)

   — me dime (8A)

   temple el templo (4A)

   ten diez (P)

   tennis: to play — jugar al tenis (4B)

   tenth décimo, -a (2A)

   thank you gracias (P)

   that que (5A); ese, esa (7A)

   —'s why por eso (9A)

   the el, la (1B); los, las (2B)

   — best el/la mejor, los/las mejores (6A)

   — worst el/la peor, los/las peores (6A)

   theater el teatro (8A)

   movie — el cine (4A)

   their su, sus (5A)

   them las, los *dir. obj. pron.* (7B); les *ind. obj. pron.* (8B)

   then entonces (4B)

   there allí (2B)

   — is/are hay (P, 2B)

   therefore por eso (9A)

these estos, estas (7A)
they ellos, ellas (2A)
thing la cosa (6A)
to think creer (3B)
    pensar (e → ie) (7A)
    I don't — so. Creo que no. (3B)
    I — ... Creo que ... (3B)
    I — so. Creo que sí. (3B)
    What do you — (about it)? ¿Qué te parece? (9B)
third tercer (tercero), -a (2A)
third floor el segundo piso (6B)
thirsty: I'm —. Tengo sed. (3B)
thirteen trece (P)
thirty treinta (P); y media *(in telling time)* (P)
thirty-one treinta y uno (P)
this este, esta (7A)
    — afternoon esta tarde (4B)
    — evening esta noche (4B)
    — weekend este fin de semana (4B)
    What is — ? ¿Qué es esto? (2B)
those esos, esas (7A)
thousand: a — mil (7A)
three tres (P)
three hundred trescientos, -as (7A)
three-ring binder la carpeta de argollas (2A)
Thursday jueves (P)
ticket el boleto (8A)
tie la corbata (7B)
time la vez *pl.* las veces (8B)
    At what —? ¿A qué hora? (4B)
    free — el tiempo libre (4A)
    to spend — with friends pasar tiempo con amigos (1A)
    What — is it? ¿Qué hora es? (P)
tired cansado, -a (4B)
to a *(prep.)* (4A)
    in order — para + *inf.* (4A)
    — the a la, al (4A)
    — the left (of) a la izquierda (de) (6A)
    — the right (of) a la derecha (de) (6A)

toast el pan tostado (3A)
today hoy (P)
tomatoes los tomates (3B)
tomorrow mañana (P)
    See you —. Hasta mañana. (P)
too también (1A); demasiado (4B)
    I do (like to) — a mí también (1A)
    me — a mí también (1A)
top: on — of encima de (2B)
touching emocionante (9A)
toy el juguete (8B)
train el tren (8A)
to travel viajar (8A)
tree el árbol (8A)
tremendous tremendo, -a (8A)
trip el viaje (8A)
Tuesday martes (P)
    on —s los martes (4A)
TV channel el canal (9A)
twelve doce (P)
twenty veinte (P)
twenty-one veintiuno (veintiún) (P)
two dos (P)
two hundred doscientos, -as (7A)

U

Ugh! ¡Uf! (7B)
ugly feo, -a (6A)
uncle el tío (5A)
uncles; uncle(s) and aunt(s) los tíos (5A)
underneath debajo de (2B)
to understand comprender (3A)
unforgettable inolvidable (8B)
us: (to/for) — nos *ind. obj. pron.* (8B)
to use:
    to — the computer usar la computadora (1A)
    What's it — d for? ¿Para qué sirve? (9B)
used usado, -a (8B)
useful:
    to be — servir (9B)
    is — for sirve para (9B)

V

vacation: to go on — ir de vacaciones (8A)
to vacuum pasar la aspiradora (6B)
    vegetable soup la sopa de verduras (3A)
    very muy (1B)
    — well muy bien (P)
    video el video (5A)
    video games: to play — jugar videojuegos (1A)
to videotape hacer un video (5A)
    violent violento, -a (9A)
to visit visitar (8A)
to — chat rooms visitar salones de chat (9B)
    volleyball: to play — jugar al vóleibol (4B)
    volunteer el voluntario, la voluntaria (8B)
    — work el trabajo voluntario (8B)

W

waiter, waitress el camarero, la camarera (5B)
to walk caminar (3B)
    wall la pared (6A)
    wallet la cartera (7B)
to want querer (e → ie) (7A)
    I — (yo) quiero (4B)
    you — (tú) quieres (4B)
    warm: to be — tener calor (5B)
    was fue (8B)
to wash lavar (6B)
    to — the car lavar el coche (6B)
    to — the clothes lavar la ropa (6B)
    to — the dishes lavar los platos (6B)
    wastepaper basket la papelera (2B)
    watch el reloj pulsera (7B)
to watch television ver la tele (1A)
    water el agua (f.) (3A)
    we nosotros, -as (2A)
to wear llevar (7A)

weather: What's the — like?
¿Qué tiempo hace? (P)

Web:

to surf the — navegar en la
Red (9B)

— page la página Web (9B)

— site el sitio Web (9B)

Wednesday miércoles (P)

week la semana (P)

last — la semana pasada (7B)

weekend:

on —s los fines de semana (4A)

this — este fin de semana (4B)

welcome: You're —. De nada.
(5B)

well bien (P); pues ... *(to indicate
pause)* (1A)

very — muy bien (P)

what? ¿cuál? (3A)

— are you like? ¿Cómo eres?
(1B)

(At) — time? ¿A qué hora? (4B)

— color ... ? ¿De qué color ...
? (6A)

— day is today? ¿Qué día es
hoy? (P)

— did you do? ¿Qué hiciste?
(8A)

**— do you like better (prefer)
to do?** ¿Qué te gusta
hacer más? (1A)

— do you like to do? ¿Qué te
gusta hacer? (1A)

— do you think (about it)?
¿Qué te parece? (9B)

— does ... mean? ¿Qué
quiere decir ... ? (P)

— else? ¿Qué más? (8B)

— happened to you? ¿Qué te
pasó? (8A)

— is she/he like? ¿Cómo es?
(1B)

— is the date? ¿Cuál es la
fecha? (P)

— is this? ¿Qué es esto? (2B)

— is your name? ¿Cómo te
llamas? (P)

— kind of ... ? ¿Qué clase
de...? (9A)

— time is it? ¿Qué hora es? (P)

— would you like? ¿Qué
desean (Uds.)? (5B)

—'s happening? ¿Qué pasa?
(P)

—'s his/her name? ¿Cómo se
llama? (1B)

—'s it (used) for? ¿Para qué
sirve? (9B)

—'s the weather like? ¿Qué
tiempo hace? (P)

what!:

— a good/nice idea! ¡Qué
buena idea! (4B)

— a shame/pity! ¡Qué pena!
(4B)

When? ¿Cuándo? (4A)

Where? ¿Dónde? (2B)

— are you from? ¿De dónde
eres? (4A)

(To) —? ¿Adónde? (4A)

whether si (6B)

which? ¿cuál? (3A)

white blanco, -a (6A)

who que (5A)

Who? ¿Quién? (2A)

Why? ¿Por qué? (3B)

wife la esposa (5A)

Will you bring me ... ? ¿Me
trae ... ? (5B)

window la ventana (2B)

winter el invierno (P)

with con (3A)

— me conmigo (4B)

— my/your friends con mis/
tus amigos (4A)

— whom? ¿Con quién? (4A)

— you contigo (4B)

without sin (3A)

woman la mujer (5B)

older woman la anciana (8B)

work el trabajo (4A)

volunteer — el trabajo
voluntario (8B)

to work trabajar (1A)

worse than peor(es) que (6A)

worst: the — el/la peor, los/las
peores (6A)

Would you like ...? ¿Te
gustaría ...? (4B)

to write:

to — e-mail escribir por
correo electrónico (9B)

to — stories escribir cuentos
(1A)

yard el jardín *pl.* los jardines (8B)

year el año (P)

**He/She is / They are ... —s
old.** Tiene(n) ... años. (5A)

last — el año pasado (7B)

yellow amarillo, -a (6A)

yes sí (1A)

yesterday ayer (7B)

yogurt el yogur (3A)

you *fam. sing.* tú (2A); *formal
sing.* usted (Ud.) (2A); *fam. pl.*
vosotros, -as (2A); *formal pl.*
ustedes (Uds.) (2A); *fam. after
prep.* ti (1A); *sing. ind. obj.
pron.* te (8B); *pl. fam. ind. obj.
pron.* os (8B); *ind. obj. pron.*
le, les (8B)

And — ? ¿Y a ti? (1A)

for — para ti (6A)

to/for — *fam. pl.* os (8B)

to/for — *fam. sing.* te (8B)

with — contigo (4B)

— don't say! ¡No me digas!
(4A)

— say ... Se dice ... (P)

You're welcome De nada (5B)

young joven (5B)

— boy/girl el niño, la niña (8B)

— man el joven (5B)

— woman la joven (5B)

—er menor (5A)

your *fam.* tu (2B); *fam.* tus,
vuestro(s), -a(s) (5A); *formal*
su, sus (5A)

Yuck! ¡Uf! (7B)

zero cero (P)

zoo el zoológico (8A)

Grammar Index

Structures are most often presented first in A *primera vista*, where they are practiced lexically. They are then explained later in a *Gramática* section or a *Nota*. Light-face numbers refer to the pages where structures are initially presented or, after explanation, where student reminders occur. **Bold-face numbers** refer to pages where structures are explained or are otherwise highlighted.

Acknowledgments

Cover A Rogdy Espinoza Photography/Getty Images

Cover B Jeremy Woodhouse/Spaces Images/Corbis

Chapter FM i,iii,T1 & T3: RM Floral/Alamy Stock Photo; **ixB:** Steve Debenport/E+/Getty Images; **ixT:** Monkey Business/Fotolia; **viii:** Image Source Plus/Alamy Stock Photo; **xxiiC:** Noche/Fotolia; **xxiiiC:** Esancai/Fotolia; **xxiiiL:** Noche/Fotolia; **xxiiiR:** Dikobrazik/Fotolia; **xxiiL:** Noche/Fotolia; xxiiR: Noche/Fotolia; **xxii xxiii:** Colin D. Young/Alamy Stock Photo; **xxiv:** Steve Russell/Toronto Star/Getty Images; **xxivC:** Noche/Fotolia; **xxivL:** Noche/Fotolia; **xxivR:** Vector Icon/Fotolia; **xxixC:** Noche/Fotolia; **xxixL:** Noche/Fotolia; **xxixR:** Noche/Fotolia; **xxvBL:** Noche/Fotolia; **xxviiC:** Globe Turner/Shutterstock; **xxviii:** Noche/Fotolia; **xxviii xxix:** Rolf Schulten/ImageBroker/Alamy Stock Photo; **xxviiL:** Noche/Fotolia; **xxviiR:** Noche/Fotolia; **xxviL:** Noche/Fotolia; **xxviR:** Noche/Fotolia; **xxvi xxvii:** Buena Vista Images/The Image Bank/Getty Images; **xxx:** Backyard Productions/Alamy Stock Photo; **xxxiii:** Noche/Fotolia; **xxxii xxxiii:** Efrain Padro/Alamy Stock Photo; **xxxiL:** Noche/Fotolia; **xxxiR:** Stakes/Shutterstock; **xx xxi:** Ethan Welty/Aurora Photos/Alamy Stock Photo; **xxx xxxi:** Sean Pavone/Alamy Stock Photo

Para Empezar Level A 001: Philip Scalia/Alamy Stock Photo; **002C:** Moodboard_Images/Brand X Pictures/Getty Images; **002C:** Moodboard_ImagesCLOSED/Brand X Pictures/Getty Images; **002L:** Marc Romanelli/Blend Images/Alamy Stock Photo; **002R:** Simmi Simons/E+/Getty Images; **004BL:** Pearson Education, Inc.; **004BR:** Pearson Education, Inc.; **004TC:** Pearson Education, Inc.; **004TL:** Pearson Education, Inc.; **004TR:** Fredrick Kippe/Alamy Stock Photo; **006BC:** Andres Rodriguez/Alamy Stock Photo; **006BL:** DCPhoto/Alamy Stock Photo; **006BR:** Deposit Photos/Glow Images; **006TL:** Kablonk/Golden Pixels LLC/Alamy Stock Photo; **006TR:** Juice Images/Alamy Stock Photo; **007:** Jeff Morgan 06/Alamy Stock Photo; **008:** The Museum of Modern Art/Licensed by SCALA/Art Resource, NY; **009L:** Alan Bailey/Rubberball/Getty Images; **009R:** Pearson Education, Inc.; **010BC:** Pearson Education, Inc.; **010BL:** Pearson Education, Inc.; **010BR:** Pearson Education, Inc.; **010CL:** Maksym Yemelyanov/Alamy Stock Photo; **010CML:** Pearson Education, Inc.; **010CMR:** Pearson Education, Inc.; **010CR:** Pearson Education, Inc.; **010TL:** Ronnie Kaufman/Flame/Corbis; **010TR:** Sam Bloomberg Rissman/Blend Images/Getty Images; **011BC:** Pearson Education, Inc.; **011BCL:** Ajr Images/Fotolia; **011BCR:** Maksym Yemelyanov/Alamy Stock Photo; **011BL:** Pearson Education, Inc.; **011BR:** Pearson Education, Inc.; **011T:** Pearson Education, Inc.; **012BC:** Pearson Education, Inc.; **012BCL:** Pearson Education, Inc.; **012BL:** Pearson Education, Inc.; **012BR:** Pearson Education, Inc.; **012C:** Pearson Education, Inc.; **012T:** David Fischer/Ocean/Corbis; **013:** Mayan/Museo Nacional de Antropologia, Mexico City, Mexico/Bridgeman Images; **014:** Pearson Education, Inc; **014:** Pearson Education, Inc.; **015:** Pearson Education, Inc.; **016:** Pedro Armestre/AFP/Getty Images; **017:** f9photos/Shutterstock; **017:** F9photos/Shutterstock; **018:** George Glod/SuperStock; **018BL:** George Glod/SuperStock; **018BR:** George Glod/SuperStock; **018L:** George Glod/SuperStock; **018MC:** Barry Diomede/Alamy Stock Photo; **018ML:** Frank and Helena/Cultura RM/Alamy Stock Photo; **018MR:** LWA/Dann Tardif/Blend Images/Alamy Stock Photo; **018TC:** RosalreneBetancourt 9/Alamy Stock Photo; **018TL:** DreamPictures/Blend Images/Corbis; **018TR:** Radius Images/Alamy Stock Photo; **019:** George Glod/SuperStock; **019ML:** Megastocker/Fotolia; **019MR:** Javier Larrea/AGE Fotostock/Alamy Stock Photo; **019R:** Blend Images REB Images/Brand X Pictures/Getty Images; **020BL:** Anna Stowe/LOOP IMAGES/Corbis; **020BR:** John Elk III/Alamy Stock Photo; **020C:** NASA Visible Earth; **020TL:** Comstock/Stockbyte/Getty Images; **020TR:** Sharon Day/Shutterstock

Chapter 01A 003: Hisham Ibrahim/PhotoV/Alamy Stock Photo; **024:** ©2016 Estate of Pablo Picasso/Artists Rights Society (ARS), New York; **024B:** The Museum of Modern Art/Licensed by SCALA/Art Resource, NY; **024T:** Pearson Education, Inc.; **025:** Emile D'Edesse/Impact/HIP/The Image Works; **026:** Anthony Hatley/Alamy Stock Photo; **026:** Jacek Chabraszewski/Shutterstock; **026BC:** DragonImages/Fotolia; **026BL:** Michael Robinson Chavez/Los Angeles Times/Getty Images; **026BR:** Jeff Greenberg/Alamy Stock Photo; **026C:** Anthony Hatley/Alamy Stock Photo; **026CL:** Jacek Chabraszewski/Shutterstock; **026CR:** YanLev/Shutterstock; **026ML:** Ranplett/E+/Getty Images; **026MR:** Nikokvfrmoto/Fotolia; **026TL:** Pearson Education, Inc.; **026TR:** Pearson Education, Inc.; **027BC:** Hero Images/Getty Images; **027BL:** Jon Sparks/Alamy Stock Photo; **027BR:** Monkey Business/Fotolia; **027TC:** Denis Radovanovic/Shutterstock; **027TL:** Iryna Tiumentseva/Fotolia; **027TR:** Monkey Business/Fotolia; **028B:** KidStock/Blend Images/Alamy Stock Photo; **028C:** Ace Stock Limited/Alamy Stock Photo; **028MR:** RosalreneBetancourt 3/Alamy Stock Photo; **028T:** Blend Images/Corbis; **029L:** Solvin Zankl/Nature Picture Library/Alamy Stock Photo; **029R:** David Cayless/Alamy Stock Photo; **030:** Hero Images/Getty Images; **030BCL:** Jon Sparks/Alamy Stock Photo; **030BCR:** Jeff Greenberg/Alamy Stock Photo; **030BML:** Anthony Hatley/Alamy Stock Photo;

Shutterstock; **074BR:** David Hanlon/iStock/Getty Images; **074CL:** Image Source/Getty Images; **074MC:** Bikeriderlondon/Shutterstock; **074TC:** Ian Shaw/ Alamy Stock Photo; **074TL:** John R. Kreul/Independent Picture Service/Alamy Stock Photo; **074TR:** Marmaduke St. John/Alamy Stock Photo; **075:** Pearson Education; **075:** Pearson Education, Inc.; **076B:** ZUMA Press Inc/Alamy Stock Photo; **076C:** KidStock/Blend Images/Corbis; **076T:** Felix Mizioznikov/Shutterstock; **077L:** Ian Shaw/Alamy Stock Photo; **077R:** Kaveh Kazemi/Getty Images News/Getty Images; **079BC:** John R. Kreul/Independent Picture Service/Alamy Stock Photo; **079BL:** Ian Shaw/Alamy Stock Photo; **079BR:** Hurst Photo/Shutterstock; **079CL:** Marmaduke St. John/Alamy Stock Photo; **079CML:** David Hanlon/ iStock/Getty Images; **079CR:** Bikeriderlondon/ Shutterstock; **079TR:** Sila Tiptanatoranin/123RF; **080:** Keith Dannemiller/Corbis; **081:** Design Pics/Newscom; **083BCL:** Monkey Business Images/Shutterstock; **083BCR:** Andy Dean/Fotolia; **083BL:** Creatas/Getty Images; **083BR:** Rob Marmion/Shutterstock; **083TCL:** Holbox/Shutterstock; **083TCR:** Panos Pictures; **083TL:** Tetra Images/Getty Images; **083TR:** Bill Bachmann/ Alamy Stock Photo; **085BL:** David Hanlon/iStock/Getty Images; **085BR:** Hurst Photo/Shutterstock; **085ML:** Ian Shaw/Alamy Stock Photo; **085MR:** Ifong/Shutterstock; **085TC:** Andrea Danti/Shutterstock; **085TL:** Sila Tiptanatoranin/123RF; **085TR:** Marmaduke St. John/ Alamy Stock Photo; **086:** Rosemary Harris/Alamy Stock Photo; **089:** Jochem Wijnands/Horizons WWP/ AGE Fotostock; **090B:** Martin Shields/Alamy Stock Photo; **090T:** Jose Fuste Raga/Encyclopedia/Corbis; **091B:** Krista Rossow/National Geographic Creative/ Alamy Stock Photo; **091T:** Ron Niebrugge/Alamy Stock Photo; **092:** John Vizcaino/Reuters/Landov LLC; 094 **095:** Wavebreakmedia/Shutterstock;

Chapter 02B 098: SUN/Newscom; **099:** Frederic Soreau/Photononstop/Passage/Corbis; **100C:** Pearson Education, Inc.; **100L:** Pearson Education, Inc.; **100R:** Pearson Education, Inc.; **101:** Pearson Education; **101:** Pearson Education, Inc.; **102L:** Stockbroker/MBI/Alamy Stock Photo; **102R:** Bruna/Shutterstock; **103L:** Bill Bachmann/Alamy Stock Photo; **103R:** Bill Bachmann/ Alamy Stock Photo; **104BCR:** Pearson Education, Inc.; **104BR:** Pearson Education, Inc.; **104MCR:** Pearson Education, Inc.; **105:** Pearson Education; **105:** Pearson Education, Inc.; **106B:** Flashover/Alamy Stock Photo; **106T:** Pearson Education, Inc.; **107BC:** Ian Shaw/ Alamy Stock Photo; **107BL:** David Hanlon/iStock/Getty Images; **107BR:** John R. Kreul/Independent Picture Service/Alamy Stock Photo; **107C:** Bikeriderlondon/ Shutterstock; **107CL:** Marmaduke St. John/Alamy Stock Photo; **107CR:** Sila Tiptanatoranin/123RF; **107T:** Ifong/Shutterstock; **108T:** Pearson Education, Inc.; **111:** Spencer Grant/PhotoEdit, Inc.; **112:** Jan

Halaska/Science Source; **113B:** Rayman/Photodisc/ Getty Images; **113T:** Keith Dannemiller/Alamy Stock Photo; **114:** Michael S. Lewis/National Geographic Creative/Alamy Stock Photo; **115L:** Sean Sprague/ Panos Pictures; **115R:** Jon Spaull/Panos Pictures; **116:** Keith Dannemiller/Alamy Stock Photo; **119:** NBC Learn videos

Chapter 03A 122: Two Children Eating a Melon and Grapes, 1645 46 (oil on canvas), Murillo, Bartolome Esteban (1618 82)/Alte Pinakothek, Munich, Germany/ Bridgeman Images; **123:** Blend Images/SuperStock; **124:** Foodfolio/Alamy Stock Photo; **124B:** Foodfolio/ Alamy Stock Photo; **124TC:** Mara Zemgaliete/Fotolia; **124TCL:** Almaje/Shutterstock; **124TCR:** Michael Gray/Fotolia; **124TL:** Dionisvera/Fotolia; **124TR:** Pakhnyushchyy/Fotolia; **125BC:** Viktor/Fotolia; **125BL:** Joe Gough/Fotolia; **125BR:** BillionPhotos.com/ Shutterstock; **125CL:** Tarasyuk Igor/Shutterstock; **125CR:** Volff/Fotolia; **125R:** Tetra Images/Alamy Stock Photo; **125TC:** Springfield Gallery/Fotolia; **125TL:** Mr Prof/Fotolia; **125TR:** Komar Maria/Fotolia; **126:** Enigmatico/Shutterstock; **126BL:** Aastock/ Shutterstock; 126BR Radius Images / Alamy Stock Photo;**126T:** DR/Fotolia; **127C:** Maria Galan/AGE Fotostock/Alamy Stock Photo; **127L:** Juanmonino/E+/ Getty Images; **127R:** InkkStudios/iStockphoto/Getty Images; **128:** Dmitri Ma/Shutterstock; **129:** Michael Gray/Fotolia; **129BCL:** Discovod/Fotolia; **129BCR:** Joe Gough/Fotolia; **129BL:** Almaje/Shutterstock; **129BMC:** Kostrez/Fotolia; **129BML:** V.S.Anandhakrishna/ Shutterstock; **129BMR:** Foodfolio/Alamy Stock Photo; **129BR:** Tetra Images/Alamy Stock Photo; **129C:** Gmevi Photo/Fotolia; **129TCL:** Pakhnyushchyy/Fotolia; **129TCR:** BillionPhotos.com/Fotolia; **129TL:** Almaje/ Shutterstock; **129TMR:** Volff/Fotolia; **129TR:** Ifong/ Shutterstock; **130:** Mara Zemgaliete/Fotolia; **130BCL:** Gertrudda/Fotolia; **130BCR:** Tore2527/Shutterstock; **130BL:** Adrianciurea69/Fotolia; **130BMC:** Margouillat Photo/Shutterstock; **130BML:** NorGal/Shutterstock; **130BMR:** Kostrez/Fotolia; **130BR:** Yurakp/Fotolia; **130CL:** Viktor/Fotolia; **130CR:** Springfield Gallery/ Fotolia; **130MCL:** Komar Maria/Fotolia; **130MCR:** Igor Dutina/Shutterstock; **130T:** Dionisvera/Fotolia; **130TC:** Mr Prof/Fotolia; **130TL:** Eugenesergeev/Fotolia; **130TR:** Volff/Fotolia; **131:** Gertrudda/Fotolia; **131BC:** Joe Gough/Shutterstock; **131BL:** Alinamd/Fotolia; **131BR:** Kar Sol/Fotolia; **131MR:** Eric Isselee/123RF; **131TL:** Jeffrey B. Banke/Shutterstock; **131TR:** AS Food studio/ Shutterstock; **133:** Michael Gray/Fotolia; **133B:** Tracy Whiteside/Shutterstock; **133BCL:** Tracy Whiteside/ Shutterstock; **133C:** Gmevi Photo/Fotolia; **133TCL:** Eugenesergeev/Fotolia; **133TCR:** Almaje/Shutterstock; **133TL:** Discovod/Fotolia; **133TML:** Komar Maria/ Fotolia; **133TMR:** Ifong/Shutterstock; **134:** Slim Plantagenate/Alamy Stock Photo; **135BCL:** Mr Prof/

Fotolia; **135BCR:** Kostrez/Fotolia; **135BL:** Springfield Gallery/Fotolia; **135BML:** Dionisvera/Fotolia; **135BMR:** Joe Gough/Fotolia; **135BR:** Almaje/Shutterstock; **135T:** Max Lashcheuski/Shutterstock; **137:** Pearson Education, Inc.; **137B:** Cindy Miller Hopkins/Danita Delimont Photography/Newscom; **137C:** Pearson Education, Inc.; **138B:** Paulo Vilela/Shutterstock; **138C:** Paulo Vilela/Shutterstock; **138T:** MSPhotographic/Shutterstock; **139B:** Sepp Puchinger/ImageBroker/Alamy Stock Photo; **139TC:** BillionPhotos.com/Shutterstock; **139TCL:** Bogdandimages/Fotolia; **139TCR:** Photoniko/Fotolia; **139TL:** Dionisvera/Fotolia; **139TR:** Danny Smythe/Shutterstock; **140BL:** Nampix/Shutterstock; **140BR:** AGcuesta/Fotolia; **140T:** Family Business/Fotolia; **141B:** Pearson Education, Inc.; **141T:** Moodboard/SuperStock; 142 **143:** FomaA/Fotolia;

Chapter 03B 146: ©2016 Banco de México Diego Rivera Frida Kahlo Museums Trust, Mexico, D.F./Artists Rights Society (ARS), New York; **146B:** Rivera, Diego (1886 1957)/Palacio Nacional, Mexico City, Mexico/Bridgeman Images; **146T:** Pearson Education, Inc.; **147:** ImageBroker/SuperStock; **148BC:** Vaivirga/Fotolia; **148BCL:** Multiart/iStock/Getty Images; **148BCR:** Sergiy Kuzmin/Shutterstock; **148BL:** S_Photo/Shutterstock; **148BML:** Inna Astakhova/Fotolia; **148BMR:** Yodaswaj/Fotolia; **148BR:** Tetxu/Shutterstock; **148TCL:** Africa Studio/Shutterstock; **148TCR:** Baloncici/Shutterstock; **148TL:** Blend Images/Shutterstock; **148TR:** Gareth Boden/Pearson Education, Inc.; **149BC:** Sommai/Fotolia; **149BR:** Tatyana Vyc/Shutterstock; **149C:** SeDmi/Shutterstock; **149CR:** Giulia Fiori Photography/Moment Open/Getty Images; **149TC:** Utoimage/Fotolia; **149TL:** Markin/YAY Micro/AGE Fotostock; **149TR:** Eskaylim/Fotolia; **150BL:** Susanna Price/Dorling Kindersley/Getty Images; **150BR:** Pixtal/AGE Fotostock; **150TL:** Michael De Leon/Getty Images; **150TR:** Michael De Leon/Getty Images; **151C:** Aleksandar Mijatovic/Fotolia; **151L:** Massman/123RF; **151R:** Pilipphoto/Fotolia; **152:** Lee Torrens/Shutterstock; **153:** Vaivirga/Fotolia; **153BCL:** Eskaylim/Fotolia; **153BCR:** Viktor/Fotolia; **153BL:** Africa Studio/Shutterstock; **153BM:** Aleksandar Mijatovic/Fotolia; **153BML:** Viktor/Fotolia; **153BMR:** Discovod/Fotolia; **153BR:** Tarasyuk Igor/Shutterstock; **153C:** Bogdandimages/Fotolia; **153CL:** Valentyn Volkov/Shutterstock; **153CML:** Johnfoto18/Shutterstock; **153CMR:** Eskaylim/Fotolia; **153CR:** Africa Studio/Shutterstock; **153MC:** Ultimathule/Shutterstock; **153MCL:** Sommai/Fotolia; **153MCR:** Sergiy Kuzmin/Shutterstock; **153ML:** Inna Astakhova/Fotolia; **153MR:** Yodaswaj/Fotolia; **153R:** Tetxu/Shutterstock; **153TCL:** Vaivirga/Fotolia; **153TCR:** Viktor1/Shutterstock; **153TL:** Tetxu/Shutterstock; **153TMC:** Gitusik/Fotolia; **153TR:** Utoimage/Fotolia; **156:** JTB Photo/Superstock; **159BCL:** Inna Astakhova/Fotolia; **159BCR:** Joe Gough/

Fotolia; **159BL:** Giulia Fiori Photography/Moment Open/Getty Images; **159BR:** Baibaz/Fotolia; **159C:** Yodaswaj/Fotolia; **159CL:** Multiart/iStock/Getty Images; **159CR:** Tarasyuk Igor/Shutterstock; **159T:** Ultimathule/Shutterstock; **159TCL:** Africa Studio/Shutterstock; **159TCR:** Sergiy Kuzmin/Shutterstock; **159TL:** Tetxu/Shutterstock; **159TR:** Bogdandimages/Fotolia; **160BL:** Pearson Education, Inc.; **160BR:** Charles Rex Arbogast/AP Images; **160TR:** Luis Davilla/Photolibrary/Getty Images; **161:** Juice Images/Alamy Stock Photo; **162BR:** Pearson Education, Inc.; **162C:** Pearson Education, Inc.; **162L:** Pearson Education, Inc.; **162R:** Pearson Education, Inc.; **163B:** Carl Recine/ZUMApress/Newscom; **163T:** Matthew Pearce/Icon Sportswire 169//Newscom; **164:** Dorothy Alexander/Alamy Stock Photo; 166 **167:** Martin Turzak/Alamy Stock Photo

Chapter 04A 170: Museo Nacional del Prado/Art Resource, NY; **171:** Oliver Gerhard/ImageBroker/Alamy Stock Photo; **172:** Hola Images/Collage/Corbis; **172BC:** Yadid Levy/Robertharding/Alamy Stock Photo; **172BL:** RosalreneBetancourt 5/Alamy Stock Photo; **172BR:** Alex Segre/Alamy Stock Photo; **172ML:** Jerónimo Alba/AGE Fotostock; **172MR:** Peter Horree/Alamy Stock Photo; **172T:** Hola Images/Collage/Corbis; **172TC:** Ivan Vdovin/Alamy Stock Photo; **172TL:** Syda Productions/Shutterstock; **172TR:** Hero Images Inc./Alamy Stock Photo; **173:** Jeffrey Blackler/Alamy Stock Photo; **173BC:** Picturenet/Blend Images/Getty Images; **173BL:** David Noton Photography/Alamy Stock Photo; **173BR:** Ruzanna/Shutterstock; **173CR:** Randy Faris/Cardinal/Corbis; **173TL:** Sue Anderson/Alamy Stock Photo; **173TR:** Jeffrey Blackler/Alamy Stock Photo; **174B:** Thomas Cockrem/Alamy Stock Photo; **174C:** Clsdesign/Fotolia; **174T:** Terry Vine/Blend Images/Getty Images; **174TC:** Endless Travel/Alamy Stock Photo; **175L:** Chris Fredriksson/Alamy Stock Photo; **175R:** F Scholz/ARCO/AGE Fotostock; **176BCL:** Yadid Levy/Robertharding/Alamy Stock Photo; **176BCR:** Alex Segre/Alamy Stock Photo; **176BL:** Jeffrey Blackler/Alamy Stock Photo; **176BMR:** Sue Anderson/Alamy Stock Photo; **176BR:** RosalreneBetancourt 5/Alamy Stock Photo; **176CL:** Syda Productions/Shutterstock; **176CML:** Hero Images Inc./Alamy Stock Photo; **176CMR:** Ivan Vdovin/Alamy Stock Photo; **176ML:** Endless Travel/Alamy Stock Photo; **176MR:** Peter Horree/Alamy Stock Photo; **176TCL:** Jerónimo Alba/AGE Fotostock; **176TCR:** Alex Segre/Alamy Stock Photo; **176TL:** Jeffrey Blackler/Alamy Stock Photo; **176TMC:** David Noton Photography/Alamy Stock Photo; **176TR:** Ruzanna/Shutterstock; **177:** akg images/Joseph Martin/Newscom; **177:** Joseph Martin/Akg Images/Newscom; **179:** Jeff Greenberg/AGE Fotostock; **180:** Martin Bernetti/AFP/Getty Images; **181:** Jack Hollingsworth/Spirit/Corbis; **182:** Pearson

Photo; **225R:** Carlos Mora/Alamy Stock Photo; **226:** Jennifer Booher/Alamy Stock Photo; **227TC:** Jacek Chabraszewski/Shutterstock; **227BC:** Anthony Hatley/Alamy Stock Photo; **227BL:** YanLev/Shutterstock; **227BR:** Michael Robinson Chavez/Los Angeles Times/Getty Images; **227TL:** Contrastaddict/iStock/Getty Images; **227TR:** Jeff Greenberg 6 of 6/Alamy Stock Photo; **228:** Corbis Premium RF/Alamy Stock Photo; **228BL:** Corbis Premium RF/Alamy Stock Photo; **228BR:** Anthony Ricci/Shutterstock; **228ML:** Dinodia Photos/Alamy Stock Photo; **228MR:** Ekler/Shutterstock; **230:** Europa Press/Getty Images; **231B:** Francisco De Goya/Prado museum/Art Resource, NY; **231T:** Self Portrait, 1815 (oil on canvas), Goya y Lucientes, Francisco Jose de (1746 1828)/Real Academia de Bellas Artes de San Fernando, Madrid, Spain/Bridgeman Images; **232L:** DreamPictures/Blend Images/Getty Images; **232R:** Rolf Bruderer/Blend Images/Getty Images; **233:** Pearson Education, Inc.; **234:** Pearson Education, Inc.; **235:** Steve Shott/Dorling Kindersley, Ltd.; **236B:** Schalkwijk/Art Resource, NY; **236T:** Roy Morsch/age fotostock/Superstock; **237:** FR Images/Alamy Stock Photo; **238:** Corbis/SuperStock; **239:** Corbis/SuperStock; **240:** AGCuesta Images/Alamy Stock Photo; **241:** Robert Daly/Ojo Images/AGE Fotostock; 242 243: EFE;

Chapter 05B 246B: Erich Lessing/Art Resource, NY; **246T:** Pearson Education; **247:** Gary Latham/Alamy Stock Photo; **248BC:** Jules Selmes/Pearson Education, Inc.; **248BL:** Tim UR/Shutterstock; **248BR:** Jeff Greenberg 6 of 6/Alamy Stock Photo; **248ML:** Lapas77/Fotolia; **248MR:** Africa Studio/Shutterstock; **248TL:** Jodi Matthews/iStock/Getty Images; **248TR:** Stewart Cohen/Blend Images/Alamy Stock Photo; **249BC:** KidStock/Blend Images/AGE Fotostock; **249BCL:** Jenny Elia Pfeiffer/Corbis; **249BCR:** YAY Media AS/Alamy Stock Photo; **249BL:** MBI/Alamy Stock Photo; **249BR:** Pete Saloutos/Image Source/Corbis; **249T:** Ronnie Kaufman/Larry Hirshowitz/Blend Images/Getty Images; **250BL:** Joe Gough/Shutterstock; **250BR:** Paul Brighton/Fotolia; **250TL:** Caroline Mowry/Somos Images/Corbis; **250TR:** Blend Images/Corbis; **251L:** The Washington Post/Getty Images; **251R:** Hola Images/Alamy Stock Photo; **252BC:** Steve Hix/Somos Images/Corbis; **252BL:** RubberBall/Alamy Stock Photo; **252BR:** Dean Drobot/Shutterstock; **252TC:** David Clifford/Aurora Photos/Alamy Stock Photo; **252TL:** Daniel M Ernst/Shutterstock; **252TR:** Dave & Les Jacobs/Blend Images/AGE Fotostock; **253:** Odua Images/Shutterstock; **253BL:** Asia Images Group Pte Ltd/Alamy Stock Photo; **253BR:** Andres Rodriguez/Alamy Stock Photo; **253MC:** Zoonar/Robert Byron/ZOONAR GMBH LBRF/AGE Fotostock; **253ML:** Gelpi José Manuel/Panther Media/AGE Fotostock; **253TL:**

Dinodia Photos/Alamy Stock Photo; **253TR:** Marc Romanelli/Blend Images/Getty Images; **254B:** CSP_iloveotto/Fotosearch LBRF/AGE Fotostock; **254T:** Patrick Byrd/Alamy Stock Photo; **255:** Russell Gordon/Danita Delimont/Alamy Stock Photo; **259B:** ©Jimmy Dorantes/LatinFocus.com; **259T:** Universal Images Group/Getty Images; **261:** Hal Beral/VWPics/Alamy Stock Photo; **262:** Ian G Dagnall/Alamy Stock Photo; **263:** Antony Souter/Alamy Stock Photo; **263T:** Frank Vetere/Alamy Stock Photo; **264:** David R. Frazier/Danita Delimont Photography/Newscom; **266 267:** EFE

Chapter 06A 270: ©Salvador Dalí, Fundació Gala Salvador Dalí, Artists Rights Society (ARS), New York 2016; **270:** Peter Horree/Alamy Stock Photo; **271:** William Panzer/Alamy Stock Photo; **272BL:** Janis Christie/Photodisc/Getty Images; **272BR:** Siraphol/123RF; **272C:** Anna Oleksenko/123RF; **272CML:** Anankkml/Fotolia; **272CMR:** CSP_Fckncg/Fotosearch LBRF/AGE Fotostock; **272ML:** Lukas Kurka/Shutterstock; **272MR:** Dorling Kindersley, Ltd.; **272T:** West Coast Surfer/Moodboard/AGE Fotostock; **273:** Digerati/Fotolia; **274:** Antoniodiaz/ShutterStock; **275L:** Oscar Garces/Camara Lucida RM/AGE Fotostock; **275R:** Hector Vivas/LatinContent/Getty Images; **276:** Blend Images/Shutterstock; **279:** Mindy Small/Film Magic/Getty Images; **281BC:** Denis Rozhnovsky/Shutterstock; **281BL:** Jonathan Gelber/Getty Images; **281BR:** Cobalt88/Shutterstock; **281TL:** Photographee.eu/Fotolia; **281TR:** Joby Sessions/Tap Magazine/Future/Getty Images; **282:** Perry Correll/Shutterstock; **285BL:** Jonathan Gelber/Getty Images; **285BR:** Joby Sessions/Tap Magazine/Future/Getty Images; **285TL:** Cobalt88/Shutterstock; **285TR:** Denis Rozhnovsky/Shutterstock; **286B:** Juan Barreto/AFP/Getty Images; **286T:** GoGo Images Corporation/Alamy Stock Photo; **287:** Travis houston/Shutterstock; **288B:** Redsnapper/Alamy Stock Photo; **288T:** Pearson Education, Inc.; **289:** Redsnapper/Alamy Stock Photo; **289:** Tom Sibley/Terra/Corbis; **290:** Ray Laskowitz/Ray Laskowitz/SuperStock; **291:** B2M Productions/Getty Images; 292 293: EFE;

Chapter 06B 296: Pearson Education, Inc; **296:** Pearson Education, Inc.; **297:** Greg Balfour Evans/Alamy Stock Photo; **298B:** IP Galanternik D.U./E+/Getty Images; **298MC:** Iriana Shiyan/Shutterstock; **298MCL:** Iriana Shiyan/Shutterstock; **298MCR:** ShortPhotos/Shutterstock; **298ML:** Iriana Shiyan/Shutterstock; **298MR:** Mark Hemmings/Newscom; **298T:** Myrleen Cate/Alamy Stock Photo; **299BCL:** Mint Images/SuperStock; **299BCR:** Justin Horrocks/E+/Getty Images; **299BL:** Africa Studio/fotolia; **299BR:** GK Hart/Vikki Hart/Taxi/Getty Images; **299CL:** Stefano Cavoretto/Alamy Stock Photo; **299CML:** Cathy Yeulet/Hemera/Getty Images Plus/Getty Images; **299CMR:** Florian Kopp/Westend61 RM/AGE Fotostock; **299CR:**

Blend Images/SuperStock; **299MCL:** Jupiterimages/Exactostock 1555/SuperStock; **299MCR:** Monkey Business Images/Alloy/Corbis; **299ML:** John Birdsall/AGE Fotostock; **299MR:** Myrleen Pearson/Alamy Stock Photo; **299T:** Nathan Alliard/Photononstop/Corbis; **300B:** 2/Andersen Ross/Ocean/Corbis; **300T:** Radius Images/Alamy Stock Photo; **301L:** Stuart Pearce/AGE Fotostock/Alamy Stock Photo; **301R:** LatitudeStock/Alamy Stock Photo; **303B:** AGE Fotostock/SuperStock; **303BL:** Nathan Alliard/Photononstop/Corbis; **303BML:** Florian Kopp/Westend61 RM/AGE Fotostock; **303C:** 2/Andersen Ross/Ocean/Corbis; **303CBL:** Jack Hollingsworth/Exactostock 1598/Superstock; **303CBR:** Justin Horrocks/E+/Getty Images; **303CL:** Darren Hubley/Shutterstock; **303CML:** Worldwide_Stock/Fotolia; **303CMR:** Andy Dean/Shutterstock; **303CR:** Karlowac/Shutterstock; **303MC:** Cathy Yeulet/Hemera/Getty Images Plus/Getty Images; **303MCL:** rangizzz/Shutterstock; **303ML:** Mnoor/Shutterstock; **303MR:** Vladyslav Starozhylov/123RF; **303R:** John Birdsall/AGE Fotostock; **303T:** Aigars Reinholds/Shutterstock; **304BC:** Florian Kopp/Westend61 RM/AGE Fotostock; **304BL:** Fuse/Getty Images; **304BR:** Nathan Alliard/Photononstop/Corbis; **304MC:** Jupiterimages/Exactostock 1555/SuperStock; **304ML:** Jupiterimages/Stockbyte/Getty Images; **304MR:** Juice Images/Alamy Stock Photo; **304TR:** Blend Images/SuperStock; **306BC:** Mee Ting/Fotolia; **306BL:** Iriana Shiyan/Shutterstock; **306BR:** Steve Prezant/Masterfile/Corbis; **306MC:** Pearson Education, Inc.; **306ML:** Emirkoo/Fotolia; **306MR:** Figure8Photos/E+/Getty Images; **306TC:** Vladimir Rublev/123RF; **308L:** Ed Bock/Comet/Corbis; **308R:** Susan Chiang/E+/Getty Images; **309:** Juice Images/Alamy Stock Photo; **309BC:** John Birdsall/AGE Fotostock; **309BL:** Florian Kopp/Westend61 RM/AGE Fotostock; **309BR:** Jupiterimages/Exactostock 1555/SuperStock; **309MC:** Blend Images/SuperStock; **309ML:** Jack Hollingsworth/Exactostock 1598/Superstock; **309MR:** Justin Horrocks/E+/Getty Images; **310:** Jiawangkun/Shutterstock; **314B:** Mark Boulton/Alamy Stock Photo; **314T:** AGE Fotostock/SuperStock; **315:** Age Fotostock/SuperStock; **316 317:** EFE

Chapter 07A **320:** ©Successió Miró/Artists Rights Society (ARS), New York/ADAGP, Paris 2016; **320:** RMN Grand Palais/ARS/Art Resource, NY; **321:** John Mitchell/Alamy Stock Photo; **322BC:** Michael Kraus/Shutterstock; **322BCL:** Elnur/Shutterstock; **322BCR:** Ruslan Kudrin/Shutterstock; **322BL:** Andrey Armyagov/Shutterstock; **322BR:** Tarzhanova/Shutterstock; **322C:** Andres Rodriguez/Fotolia; **322MCL:** popovaphoto/Shutterstock; **322MCR:** ekler/Shutterstock; **322ML:** Theartofphoto/Shutterstock; **322MR:** Dean bertoncelj/Shutterstock; **322T:** Rob Marmion/Shutterstock; **323:** Corbis Super RF/Alamy Stock Photo; **324C:** Radius Images/Alamy Stock Photo; **324L:** Pixel Memoirs/Alamy Stock Photo; **324R:** Spoilergen/Fotolia; **324T:** Rob Marmion/Shutterstock; **325L:** Adisa/Shutterstock; **325R:** Liza1979/Shutterstock; **326B:** SW Productions/Photodisc/Getty Images; **326TC:** Ableimages/Alamy Stock Photo; **326TCL:** Amble Design/Shutterstock; **326TCR:** Lev Dolgachov/Alamy Stock Photo; **326TL:** Mint Images Limited/Alamy Stock Photo; **326TR:** Gregg Vignal/Alamy Stock Photo; **327B:** Mi Futuro y mi Tierra, 2003(coloured pencil on paper), Ortiz, Oscar (b.1964) (Contemporary Artist)/Private Collection/Bridgeman Images; **327MCL:** PHB.cz (Richard Semik)/Shutterstock; **327MCR:** John Rowley/AGE Fotostock; **327ML:** VStock/Alamy Stock Photo; **327MR:** Sharplaninac/Fotolia; **327T:** Kemter/iStock/Getty Images; **328B:** Glyn Thomas/Alamy Stock Photo; **328C:** Aroas/Fotolia; **328MC:** Andrea Biraghi/Fotolia; **328T:** Anton Ivanov/Shutterstock; **329BC:** Moodboard/Alamy Stock Photo; **329BL:** Wavebreak Media Ltd/Alamy Stock Photo; **329BR:** Catherine Ledner/Stockbyte/Getty Images; **329TC:** John Lund/Paula Zacharias/Blend Images/Alamy Stock Photo; **329TL:** Miroslava Lipa/Alamy Stock Photo; **329TR:** Johnny Greig/Alamy Stock Photo; **331B:** Steve Hamblin/Alamy Stock Photo; **331CL:** Karkas/Shutterstock; **331ML:** Miran Buric/Alamy Stock Photo; **331MR:** Nadezda/Shutterstock; **331T:** Lubos Chlubny/Fotolia; **333B:** Pearson Education, Inc.; **333MC:** Cristi180884/Fotolia; **333MCL:** Juliko77/Fotolia; **333MCR:** Kuarmungadd/Fotolia; **333ML:** Vividz Foto/Fotolia; **333MR:** Ilya Starikov/Alamy Stock Photo; **333T:** Africa Studio/Shutterstock; **334:** Miran Buric/Alamy Stock Photo; **334BCR:** Vipman/Shutterstock; **334BL:** Karkas/Shutterstock; **334BR:** Tarzhanova/Shutterstock; **334TCL:** Karkas/Shutterstock; **334TCR:** Maryna Kulchytska/Shutterstock; **334TL:** Tarzhanova/Shutterstock; **334TR:** Elenovsky/Shutterstock; **335B:** Cindy Miller Hopkins/Danita Delimont/Alamy Stock Photo; **335C:** Steve Bly/Alamy Stock Photo; **335T:** Rob Kim/WireImage/Getty Images; **336BL:** Dixon Hamby/Alamy Stock Photo; **336BR:** Matt Ragen/Shutterstock; **336T:** Alfredo Maiquez/Lonely Planet Images/Getty Images; **337BR:** Alejandro Bolivar/Epa/Corbis; **337TL:** Cindy Miller Hopkins/Danita Delimont/Alamy Stock Photo; **337TR:** Ken Welsh/Alamy Stock Photo; **338:** Donald Nausbaum/Robertharding/Alamy Stock Photo; **339:** Javier Larrea/AGE Fotostock; **340 341:** EFE;

Chapter 7B **344B:** Pearson Education; **344T:** Jtb Media Creation, Inc./Alamy Stock Photo; **345:** Chad Ehlers/Alamy Stock Photo; **346BC:** MadDog/Fotolia; **346BL:** Travelwide/Alamy Stock Photo; **346BR:** Cris Haigh/Alamy Stock Photo; **346CL:** Art_girl/Shutterstock; **346CR:** Zoonar/Kudrin Ruslan/AGE Fotostock; **346ML:** ICP/AGE Fotostock; **346MR:** Caimacanul/Fotolia; **346TL:** John Warner/

450TR: Holbox/Shutterstock; **451:** Nan/Alamy Stock Photo; **451C:** Steve Debenpor/Vetta/Getty Images; **451L:** Marc Chapeaux/AGF/AGE Fotostock; **451TR:** Hero Images Inc./Alamy Stock Photo; **452B:** Mandy Godbehear/Alamy Stock Photo; **452T:** Image Source/ Getty Images; **453L:** Andresr/E+/Getty Images; **453R:** Oleksiy Mark/Shutterstock; **454:** AGE Fotostock/ Alamy Stock Photo; **455B:** Melba Photo Agency/Alamy Stock Photo; **455C:** Ariel Skelley/Blend Images/Getty Images; **455T:** Jerónimo Alba/Alamy Stock Photo; **456B:** KidStock/Blend Images/Getty Images; **456MCL:** Pearson Education, Inc.; **456MCR:** Tupungato/ Shutterstock; **456ML:** Ian Dagnall Laptop Computing/ Alamy Stock Photo; **456MR:** Inxti/Shutterstock; **456T:** Pearson Education, Inc.; **460BCL:** ImageBroker/Alamy Stock Photo; **460BCR:** Jochen Tack/ImageBroker/ AGE Fotostock; **460BL:** Kali Nine LLC/iStock/Getty Images; **460BML:** YAY Media AS/Alamy Stock Photo; **460BMR:** Hero Images/Getty Images; **460BR:** Ronnie Kaufman/Larry/Blend Images/AGE Fotostock; **460T:** George S De Blonsky/Alamy Stock Photo; **461:** Hect/ Shutterstock; **463B:** Fancy Collection/SuperStock; **463L:** De Agostini Picture Library/De Agostini/ Getty Images; **463R:** KidStock/Blend Images/Alamy Stock Photo; **465:** Andrey Armyagov/Fotolia; **466L:** OJO Images Ltd/Alamy Stock Photo; **466R:** Pearson Education, Inc.; **467:** BFG Images/Getty Images; 468 **469:** Thomas R. Fletcher/Alamy Stock Photo

Para Empezar Level B **PE 2:** Anthony Hatley/Alamy Stock Photo; **PE 2:** BlueSkyImages/Fotolia; **PE 2:** Denis Radovanovic/Shutterstock; **PE 2:** DragonImages/ Fotolia; **PE 2:** Hero Images/Getty Images; **PE 2:** Jacek Chabraszewski/Shutterstock; **PE 2:** Jeff Greenberg/ Alamy Stock Photo; **PE 2:** KidStock/Blend Images/ Alamy Stock Photo; **PE 2:** Michael Robinson Chavez/ Los Angeles Times/Getty Images; **PE 2:** Monkey Business/Fotolia; **PE 2:** Nikokvfrmoto/Fotolia; **PE 2:** Ronnie Kaufman/Larry/Blend Images/AGE Fotostock; **PE 2:** RosalreneBetancourt 3/Alamy Stock Photo; **PE 2:** YanLev/Shutterstock; **PE 3:** Anne Ackermann/ Getty Images; **PE 3:** Antoniodiaz/Shutterstock; **PE 3:** B Christopher/Alamy Stock Photo; **PE 3:** Germanskydive110/Fotolia; **PE 3:** Klaus Vedfelt/Taxi/ Getty Images; **PE 3:** Photofusion/UIG/Universal Images Group/AGE Fotostock; **PE 3:** Randy Faris/Corbis; **PE 3:** Ranplett/E+/Getty Images; **PE 3:** RosalreneBetancourt 10/Alamy Stock Photo; **PE 3:** RosalreneBetancourt 3/Alamy Stock Photo; **PE 3:** Sophie Bluy/Pearson Education, Inc.; **PE 3:** Yeko Photo Studio/ Shutterstock; **PE 4:** Antoniodiaz/Shutterstock; **PE 6:** Anne Ackermann/Getty Images; **PE 6:** Antoniodiaz/ Shutterstock; **PE 6:** Germanskydive110/Fotolia; **PE 6:** Klaus Vedfelt/Taxi/Getty Images; **PE 6:** Photofusion/ UIG/Universal Images Group/AGE Fotostock; **PE 6:** Randy Faris/Corbis; **PE 7:** Jacek Chabraszewski/ Shutterstock; **PE 7:** Jeff Greenberg/Alamy Stock Photo; **PE 7:** Monkey Business/Fotolia; **PE 7:** Ranplett/ E+/Getty Images; **PE 7:** RosalreneBetancourt 3/Alamy Stock Photo; **PE 8:** Bikeriderlondon/Shutterstock; **PE 8:** David Hanlon/iStock/Getty Images; **PE 8:** Hurst Photo/Shutterstock; **PE 8:** Ian Shaw/Alamy Stock Photo; **PE 8:** Ifong/Shutterstock; **PE 8:** Image Source/Getty Images; **PE 8:** John R. Kreul/ Independent Picture Service/Alamy Stock Photo; **PE 8:** Marmaduke St. John/Alamy Stock Photo; **PE 8:** Sila Tiptanatoranin/123RF; **PE 9:** Pearson Education, Inc.

PE 10: Holbox/Shutterstock; **PE 12:** Denis Radovanovic/Shutterstock; **PE 12:** Hero Images/Getty Images; **PE 12:** KidStock/Blend Images/Alamy Stock Photo; **PE 12:** Michael Robinson Chavez/Los Angeles Times/Getty Images; **PE 12:** Nikokvfrmoto/Fotolia; **PE 12:** Ronnie Kaufman/Larry/Blend Images/AGE Fotostock; **PE 12:** RosalreneBetancourt 3/Alamy Stock Photo; **PE 12:** YanLev/Shutterstock; **PE 12:** Yeko Photo Studio/Shutterstock; **PE 13:** Pearson Education, Inc.; **PE 14:** BillionPhotos.com/Fotolia; **PE 14:** BillionPhotos. com/Shutterstock; **PE 14:** Bogdandimages/Fotolia; **PE 14:** Gmevi Photo/Fotolia; **PE 14:** Michael Gray/ Fotolia; **PE 14:** Tarasyuk Igor/Shutterstock; **PE 14:** Tetra Images/Alamy Stock Photo; **PE 14:** Viktor/ Fotolia; **PE 15:** Africa Studio/Shutterstock; **PE 15:** Baloncici/Shutterstock; **PE 15:** Multiart/iStock/Getty Images; **PE 15:** S_Photo/Shutterstock; **PE 15:** Sergiy Kuzmin/Shutterstock; **PE 15:** Sommai/Fotolia; **PE 15:** Tetxu/Shutterstock; **PE 15:** Utoimage/Fotolia; **PE 15:** Vaivirga/Fotolia; **PE 15:** Yodaswaj/Fotolia; **PE 16:** Giulia Fiori Photography/Moment Open/Getty Images; **PE 16:** Komar Maria/Fotolia; **PE 16:** Pearson Education, Inc.; **PE 17:** Bogdandimages/Fotolia; **PE 17:** Eskaylim/ Fotolia; **PE 17:** Ifong/Shutterstock; **PE 17:** Igor Dutina/Shutterstock; **PE 17:** Jacek Chabraszewski/ Shutterstock; **PE 17:** NorGal/Shutterstock; **PE 18:** Anne Ackermann/Getty Images; **PE 18:** Germanskydive110/Fotolia; **PE 18:** Klaus Vedfelt/ Taxi/Getty Images; **PE 18:** Ranplett/E+/Getty Images; **PE 18:** RosalreneBetancourt 10/Alamy Stock Photo; **PE 18:** RosalreneBetancourt 3/Alamy Stock Photo; **PE 19:** Africa Studio/Shutterstock; **PE 19:** Baloncici/ Shutterstock; **PE 19:** Giulia Fiori Photography/Moment Open/Getty Images; **PE 19:** S_Photo/Shutterstock; **PE 20:** Alex Segre/Alamy Stock Photo; **PE 20:** David Noton Photography/Alamy Stock Photo; **PE 20:** Hero Images Inc./Alamy Stock Photo; **PE 20:** Ivan Vdovin/ Alamy Stock Photo; **PE 20:** Jeffrey Blackler/Alamy Stock Photo; **PE 20:** Jerónimo Alba/AGE Fotostock; **PE 20:** Peter Horree/Alamy Stock Photo; **PE 20:** Picturenet/Blend Images/Getty Images; **PE 20:** Randy Faris/Cardinal/Corbis; **PE 20:** Robertharding/

Grateful acknowledgement is made to the following for copyrighted material:

ACTFL

World Readiness Standards for Language Learners by The American Council on the Teaching of Foreign Languages. Copyright ©ACTFL. Used by permission.

Fundación Puertorriqueña de Conservación

¡Tú puedes ser parte de la solución del problema de la basura en nuestra isla! ©Fundación Puertorriqueña de Conservación. Reprinted by permission.

Note: Every effort has been made to locate the copyright owner of material reproduced in this component. Omissions brought to our attention will be corrected in subsequent editions.